T0385036

Renault Clio
Owners Workshop Manual

Pete Gill

(6425 - 352)

Models covered

Hatchback

Petrol: 0.9 litre (898cc) turbo & 1.2 litre (1149cc) non-turbo
Turbo-diesel: 1.5 litre (1461cc)

Does NOT cover features specific to Convertible
Does NOT cover 1.2 litre turbo petrol models, Renaultsport models or EDC automated dual clutch transmission

© Haynes Publishing 2018

A book in the **Haynes Owners Workshop Manual Series**

ABCDE
FGHIJ
KLMNO
PQRST

ISBN **978 1 78521 425 7**

British Library Cataloguing in Publication Data
A catalogue record for this book is available from the British Library.

Printed in Malaysia

Haynes Publishing
Sparkford, Yeovil, Somerset BA22 7JJ, England

Haynes North America, Inc
859 Lawrence Drive, Newbury Park, California 91320, USA

Printed using NORBRITE BOOK 48.8gsm (CODE: 40N6533) from NORPAC; procurement system certified under Sustainable Forestry Initiative standard. Paper produced is certified to the SFI Certified Fiber Sourcing Standard (CERT - 0094271)

Contents

Contents

REPAIRS AND OVERHAUL

Engine and Associated Systems

Transmission

Brakes and suspension

Body equipment

Wiring diagrams

REFERENCE

Index

The new Clio IV continues as Renault's best-selling small car. The cars have passed the highest safety standards and have been awarded 5 stars in the Euro NCAP safety tests. All cars have a minimum of six airbags. Side curtain airbags are fitted to all models apart from the entry level cars. Anti-lock brakes (ABS) are standard throughout the range, with ESP (electronic stability program) and EBD (electronic brake assist) optional on all models. All models have 3-point seat belts have pretensioners, including the rear seatbelts.

Two petrol engines and one diesel engine are available in the Clio range covered by this manual. The petrol engines are in 0.9 and 1.2 litre sizes and the diesel engine is a 1.5 litre. The 0.9 litre is a 3-cylinder turbocharged engine. The 1.2 litre covered in this manual is a 4-cylinder normally aspirated engine (a 1.2 litre turbocharged 'TCe' - Turbo Control efficiency engine, is also available). All petrol engines use a fuel injection system with catalyst monitoring, and diesel engines use a common rail direct injection system. All the engines comply with the Euro VI emissions regulations.

The Clio is available as a 5 door Hatchback for the UK market. A wide range of fittings and interior trims are fitted depending on the model specification. Cruise control, climate control and keyless entry are available on all but the most basic models. TPMS (Tyre Pressure Monitoring System) and adaptive Xenon headlights are also available.

Fully-independent front suspension is fitted, with the components attached to a subframe assembly. The rear suspension is semi-independent, with torsion beam and trailing arms. Variable electric steering is standard throughout the range. A five- or six-speed manual gearbox and electronically-controlled four-speed automatic transmission (not covered in this manual) are available.

The Clio is conventional in design, and the DIY mechanic should find most servicing work straightforward. Most components are reasonable accessible. The only awkward component being the oil filter on the diesel models and the headlight bulbs.

Your Renault Clio Manual

The aim of this manual is to help you get the best value from your vehicle. It can do so in several ways. It can help you decide what work must be done (even should you choose to get it done by a garage), provide information on routine maintenance and servicing, and give a logical course of action and diagnosis when random faults occur. However, it is hoped that you will use the manual by tackling the work yourself. On simpler jobs, it may even be quicker than booking the car into a garage and going there twice, to leave and collect it. Perhaps most important, a lot of money can be saved by avoiding the costs a garage must charge to cover its labour and overheads.

The manual has drawings and descriptions to show the function of the various components, so that their layout can be understood. Then the tasks are described and photographed in a clear step-by-step sequence.

References to the 'left' or 'right' are in the sense of a person in the driver's seat, facing forward.

Acknowledgements

Thanks are due to Draper Tools Limited and AST tools, who provided some of the workshop tools, and to all those people at Sparkford who helped in the production of this manual.

We take great pride in the accuracy of information given in this manual, but vehicle manufacturers make alterations and design changes during the production run of a particular vehicle of which they do not inform us. No liability can be accepted by the authors or publishers for loss, damage or injury caused by any errors in, or omissions from, the information given.

Working on your car can be dangerous. This page shows just some of the potential risks and hazards, with the aim of creating a safety-conscious attitude.

General hazards

Scalding

• Don't remove the radiator or expansion tank cap while the engine is hot.

• Engine oil, transmission fluid or power steering fluid may also be dangerously hot if the engine has recently been running.

Burning

• Beware of burns from the exhaust system and from any part of the engine. Brake discs and drums can also be extremely hot immediately after use.

Crushing

• When working under or near a raised vehicle, always supplement the jack with axle stands, or use drive-on ramps.

Never venture under a car which is only supported by a jack.

• Take care if loosening or tightening high-torque nuts when the vehicle is on stands. Initial loosening and final tightening should be done with the wheels on the ground.

Fire

• Fuel is highly flammable; fuel vapour is explosive.

• Don't let fuel spill onto a hot engine.

• Do not smoke or allow naked lights (including pilot lights) anywhere near a vehicle being worked on. Also beware of creating sparks (electrically or by use of tools).

• Fuel vapour is heavier than air, so don't work on the fuel system with the vehicle over an inspection pit.

• Another cause of fire is an electrical overload or short-circuit. Take care when repairing or modifying the vehicle wiring.

• Keep a fire extinguisher handy, of a type suitable for use on fuel and electrical fires.

Electric shock

• Ignition HT and Xenon headlight voltages can be dangerous, especially to people with heart problems or a pacemaker. Don't work on or near these systems with the engine running or the ignition switched on.

• Mains voltage is also dangerous. Make sure that any mains-operated equipment is correctly earthed. Mains power points should be protected by a residual current device (RCD) circuit breaker.

Fume or gas intoxication

• Exhaust fumes are poisonous; they can contain carbon monoxide, which is rapidly fatal if inhaled. Never run the engine in a confined space such as a garage with the doors shut.

• Fuel vapour is also poisonous, as are the vapours from some cleaning solvents and paint thinners.

Poisonous or irritant substances

• Avoid skin contact with battery acid and with any fuel, fluid or lubricant, especially antifreeze, brake hydraulic fluid and Diesel fuel. Don't syphon them by mouth. If such a substance is swallowed or gets into the eyes, seek medical advice.

• Prolonged contact with used engine oil can cause skin cancer. Wear gloves or use a barrier cream if necessary. Change out of oil-soaked clothes and do not keep oily rags in your pocket.

• Air conditioning refrigerant forms a poisonous gas if exposed to a naked flame (including a cigarette). It can also cause skin burns on contact.

Asbestos

• Asbestos dust can cause cancer if inhaled or swallowed. Asbestos may be found in gaskets and in brake and clutch linings. When dealing with such components it is safest to assume that they contain asbestos.

Special hazards

Hydrofluoric acid

• This extremely corrosive acid is formed when certain types of synthetic rubber, found in some O-rings, oil seals, fuel hoses etc, are exposed to temperatures above 4000C. The rubber changes into a charred or sticky substance containing the acid. *Once formed, the acid remains dangerous for years. If it gets onto the skin, it may be necessary to amputate the limb concerned.*

• When dealing with a vehicle which has suffered a fire, or with components salvaged from such a vehicle, wear protective gloves and discard them after use.

The battery

• Batteries contain sulphuric acid, which attacks clothing, eyes and skin. Take care when topping-up or carrying the battery.

• The hydrogen gas given off by the battery is highly explosive. Never cause a spark or allow a naked light nearby. Be careful when connecting and disconnecting battery chargers or jump leads.

Air bags

• Air bags can cause injury if they go off accidentally. Take care when removing the steering wheel and trim panels. Special storage instructions may apply.

Diesel injection equipment

• Diesel injection pumps supply fuel at very high pressure. Take care when working on the fuel injectors and fuel pipes.

Warning: Never expose the hands, face or any other part of the body to injector spray; the fuel can penetrate the skin with potentially fatal results.

Remember...

DO

• Do use eye protection when using power tools, and when working under the vehicle.

• Do wear gloves or use barrier cream to protect your hands when necessary.

• Do get someone to check periodically that all is well when working alone on the vehicle.

• Do keep loose clothing and long hair well out of the way of moving mechanical parts.

• Do remove rings, wristwatch etc, before working on the vehicle – especially the electrical system.

• Do ensure that any lifting or jacking equipment has a safe working load rating adequate for the job.

DON'T

• Don't attempt to lift a heavy component which may be beyond your capability – get assistance.

• Don't rush to finish a job, or take unverified short cuts.

• Don't use ill-fitting tools which may slip and cause injury.

• Don't leave tools or parts lying around where someone can trip over them. Mop up oil and fuel spills at once.

• Don't allow children or pets to play in or near a vehicle being worked on.

The following pages are intended to help in dealing with common roadside emergencies and breakdowns. You will find more detailed fault finding information at the back of the manual, and repair information in the main chapters.

If your car won't start and the starter motor doesn't turn

☐ Open the bonnet and make sure that the battery terminals are clean and tight.

☐ Switch on the headlights and try to start the engine. If the headlights go very dim when you're trying to start, the battery is probably flat. Get out of trouble by jump starting (see next page) using a friend's car.

If your car won't start even though the starter motor turns as normal

☐ Is there fuel in the tank?

☐ Has the engine immobiliser been deactivated? This should happen automatically, on inserting the ignition key. However, if a replacement key has been obtained (other than from a Renault dealer) it may not contain the transponder chip necessary to deactivate the system.

☐ If it's a model with automatic transmission, the footbrake must be applied.

☐ Is there moisture on electrical components under the bonnet? Switch off the ignition, then wipe off any obvious dampness with a dry cloth. Spray a water-repellent aerosol product (WD-40 or equivalent) on ignition and fuel system electrical connectors like those shown in the photos.

A Check the condition and security of the battery connections

B Check that the wiring connectors are securely connected to the ignition coils on the 0.9 litre petrol engines. On 1.2 litre engines, check the security of the HT leads.

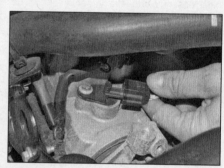

C Check the plugs and wiring of all the critical engine connectors. Work around the engine bay methodically (Checking camshaft sensor wiring connector - 0.9 litre petrol engine).

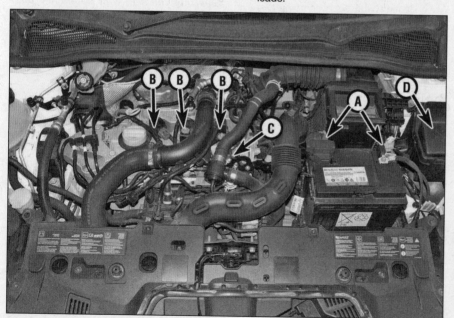

Check that electrical connections are secure (with the ignition switched off) and spray with water dispersant if you suspect a problem due to damp.

D With the ignition off, check the fuses in the main fusebox, and the fusebox adjacent to the battery.

Jump starting

When jump-starting a car using a booster battery, observe the following precautions:

✔ Before connecting the booster battery, make sure that the ignition is switched off.

Caution: Remove the key in case the central locking engages when the jump leads are connected

✔ Ensure that all electrical equipment (lights, heater, wipers, etc) is switched off.

✔ Take note of any special precautions printed on the battery case.

✔ Make sure that the booster battery is the same voltage as the discharged one in the vehicle.

✔ If the battery is being jump-started from the battery in another vehicle, the two vehicles MUST NOT TOUCH each other.

✔ Make sure that the transmission is in neutral (or P, in the case of automatic transmission).

HAYNES HiNT *Jump starting will get you out of trouble, but you must correct whatever made the battery go flat in the first place. There are three possibilities:*

1 The battery has been drained by repeated attempts to start, or by leaving the lights on.

2 The charging system is not working properly (alternator drivebelt slack or broken, alternator wiring fault or alternator itself faulty).

3 The battery itself is at fault (electrolyte low, or battery worn out).

1 Connect one end of the red jump lead to the positive (+) terminal of the flat battery

2 Connect the other end of the red lead to the positive (+) terminal of the booster battery.

3 Connect one end of the black jump lead to the negative (-) terminal of the booster battery

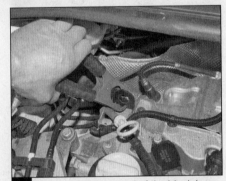

4 Connect the other end of the black jump lead to a bolt or bracket on the engine block, well away from the battery, on the vehicle to be started.

5 Make sure that the jump leads will not come into contact with the fan, drive-belts or other moving parts of the engine.

6 Start the engine using the booster battery and run it at idle speed. Switch on the lights, rear window demister and heater blower motor, then disconnect the jump leads in the reverse order of connection. Turn off the lights etc.

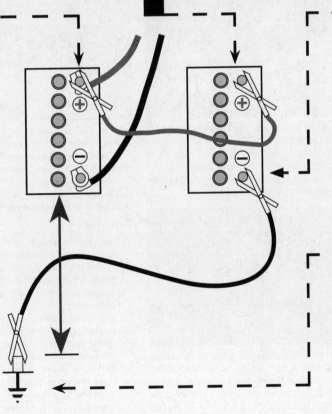

Wheel changing

Note: *Depending on model, there may not be a spare wheel fitted. On these models, there will be a container of sealant and an electric compressor to inflate the tyre. Follow the instructions included, with the items, under the luggage compartment carpet.*

⚠ **Warning: Do not change a wheel in a situation where you risk being hit by other traffic. On busy roads, try to stop in a lay-by or a gateway. Be wary of passing traffic while changing the wheel – it is easy to become distracted by the job in hand.**

Preparation

☐ When a puncture occurs, stop as soon as it is safe to do so.
☐ Park on firm level ground, if possible, and well out of the way of other traffic.
☐ Use hazard warning lights if necessary.

☐ If you have one, use a warning triangle to alert other drivers of your presence.
☐ Apply the handbrake and engage first or reverse gear (or P on models with automatic transmission).

☐ Chock the wheel diagonally opposite the one being removed – a couple of large stones will do for this.
☐ If the ground is soft, use a flat piece of wood to spread the load under the jack.

Changing the wheel

1 The spare wheel is located under the rear floor. To remove it, open the tailgate, lift up the carpet and remove the tool tray to reveal the spare wheel release mechanism.

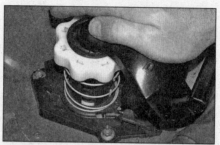

2 Unscrew the large white plastic locking ring and then push the handle towards the front of the vehicle.

3 Keep clear because the spare wheel will drop to the floor. Unhook the wheel from the cable. Place the spare wheel under the sill next to the jacking point as an emergency back up, should the vehicle slip off the jack.

4 Remove the cover (alloy wheels) or prise off the wheel trim (steel wheels) from the punctured wheel, using the tools provided.

5 Use the wheel brace to loosen each wheel bolt by half a turn. On models with alloy wheels, one of the wheel bolts may be of the locking type – use the 'key' tool (a special socket usually provided in the glovebox) with the wheel brace to undo this.

6 Locate the jack head below the jacking point nearest the wheel to be changed. The jacking points are directly below the arrow shape in the sill panel. Ensure that the slot in the jack head engages with the sill flange at the jacking point. Turn the jack handle clockwise until the wheel is raised clear of the ground.

Finally . . .

☐ Remove the wheel chocks and stow the jack and tools in the correct locations in the car.
☐ Check the tyre pressure on the wheel just fitted. If it is low, drive slowly to the nearest garage and inflate the tyre to the correct pressure.
☐ The space saver spare wheel is for temporary use only. Drive with extra care – limit yourself to a maximum of 50 mph (80 kph), and to the shortest possible journeys, while it is fitted.
☐ Have the wheel nuts tightened to the specified torque (see Chapter 10) at the earliest possible opportunity.
☐ Have the damaged tyre or wheel repaired as soon as possible, or another puncture will leave you stranded.

7 Remove the bolts and lift the punctured wheel clear. Place the wheel under the sill instead of the spare.

8 Fit the spare wheel, using the correct wheel bolts, and tighten moderately with the wheel brace. Lower the car to the ground, then finally tighten the wheel bolts in a diagonal sequence. **Note:** *Some spare wheels require shorter wheel bolts (see sticker on wheel).*

Identifying leaks

Puddles on the garage floor or drive, or obvious wetness under the bonnet or underneath the car, suggest a leak that needs investigating. It can sometimes be difficult to decide where the leak is coming from, especially if an engine undershield is fitted. Leaking oil or fluid can also be blown rearwards by the passage of air under the car, giving a false impression of where the problem lies.

 Warning: Most automotive oils and fluids are poisonous. Wash them off skin, and change out of contaminated clothing, without delay.

 The smell of a fluid leaking from the car may provide a clue to what's leaking. Some fluids are distinctively coloured. It may help to remove the engine undershield, clean the car carefully and to park it over some clean paper overnight as an aid to locating the source of the leak.
Remember that some leaks may only occur while the engine is running.

Sump oil

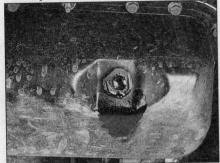

Engine oil may leak from the drain plug...

Oil from filter

...or from the base of the oil filter.

Gearbox oil

Gearbox oil can leak from the seals at the inboard ends of the driveshafts.

Antifreeze

Leaking antifreeze often leaves a crystalline deposit like this.

Brake fluid

A leak occurring at a wheel is almost certainly brake fluid.

Towing

When all else fails, you may find yourself having to get a tow home – or of course you may be helping somebody else. Long-distance recovery should only be done by a garage or breakdown service. For shorter distances, DIY towing using another car is easy enough, but observe the following points:

☐ Use a proper tow-rope – they are not expensive. The vehicle being towed must display an ON TOW sign in its rear window.

☐ Always turn the ignition key to the 'On' position when the vehicle is being towed, so that the steering lock is released, and the direction indicator and brake lights work.

☐ The towing eye is located with the jack and wheel brace in the luggage compartment **(see illustration)**.

☐ To fit the towing eye, prise out the cover on the right-hand side of the front bumper (or left-hand side of the rear bumper) and remove it. Screw the towing eye in as far as it will go. Tighten the towing eye with the wheel brace **(see illustrations)**.

☐ Before being towed, release the handbrake and select neutral on the transmission. **Note:** *Do not attempt to tow models with automatic transmission.*

☐ Note that greater-than-usual pedal pressure will be required to operate the brakes, since

the vacuum servo unit is only operational with the engine running.

☐ Greater-than-usual steering effort will also be required.

☐ The driver of the car being towed must keep the tow-rope taut at all times to avoid snatching.

☐ Make sure that both drivers know the route before setting off.

☐ Only drive at moderate speeds and keep the distance towed to a minimum. Drive smoothly and allow plenty of time for slowing down at junctions.

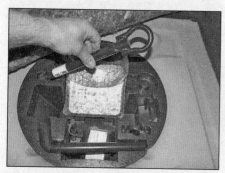

Location of towing eye

Remove the front cover...

...and screw in the towing eye

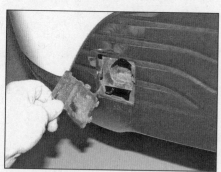

Remove the rear cover...

...and screw in the towing eye

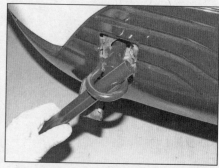

Tighten the towing eye with the wheel brace

Introduction

There are some very simple checks which need only take a few minutes to carry out, but which could save you a lot of inconvenience and expense.

These *Weekly checks* require no great skill or special tools, and the small amount of time they take to perform could prove to be very well spent, for example:

☐ Keeping an eye on tyre condition and pressures, will not only help to stop them wearing out prematurely, but could also save your life.

☐ Many breakdowns are caused by electrical problems. Battery-related faults are particularly common, and a quick check on a regular basis will often prevent the majority of these.

☐ If your car develops a brake fluid leak, the first time you might know about it is when your brakes don't work properly. Checking the level regularly will give advance warning of this kind of problem.

☐ If the oil or coolant levels run low, the cost of repairing any engine damage will be far greater than fixing the leak, for example.

Underbonnet check points

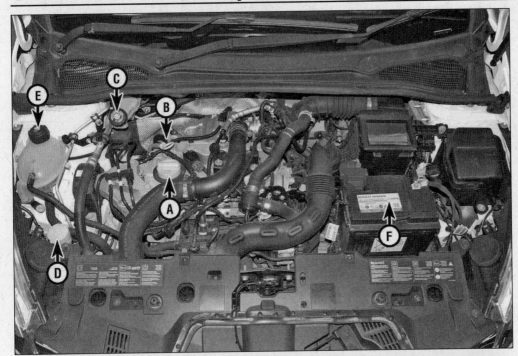

◀ 0.9 litre petrol engine

A *Engine oil filler cap*

B *Engine oil level dipstick*

C *Brake and clutch fluid reservoir*

D *Screen washer fluid reservoir*

E *Coolant reservoir (expansion tank)*

F *Battery*

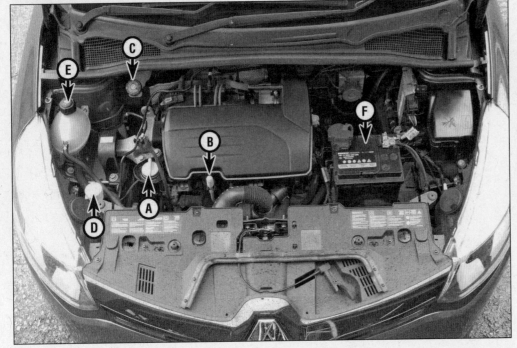

◀ 1.2 litre petrol engine

A *Engine oil filler cap*

B *Engine oil level dipstick*

C *Brake and clutch fluid reservoir*

D *Screen washer fluid reservoir*

E *Coolant reservoir (expansion tank)*

F *Battery*

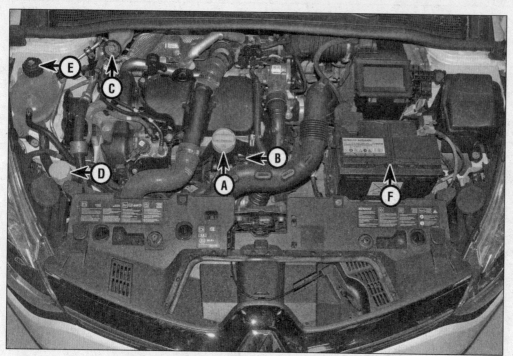

◀ 1.5 litre diesel engine

A Engine oil filler cap

B Engine oil level dipstick

C Brake and clutch fluid reservoir

D Screen washer fluid reservoir

E Coolant reservoir (expansion tank)

F Battery (under cover)

Engine oil level

Before you start

✔ Make sure that the car is on level ground.
✔ Check the oil level before the car is driven, or at least 5 minutes after the engine has been switched off.

HAYNES HiNT *If the oil is checked immediately after driving the vehicle, some of the oil will remain in the upper engine components, resulting in an inaccurate reading on the dipstick.*

The correct oil

Modern engines place great demands on their oil. It is very important that the correct oil for your car is used (see *Lubricants and fluids*).

Car care

● If you have to add oil frequently, you should check whether you have any oil leaks. Place some clean paper under the car overnight, and check for stains in the morning. If there are no leaks, then the engine may be burning oil.
● Always maintain the level between the upper and lower dipstick marks (see photos 5, 6 or 7 depending on engine). If the level is too low, severe engine damage may occur. Oil seal failure may result if the engine is overfilled by adding too much oil.

1 On 0.9 litre petrol models, the dipstick is located in a tube at the drivers side rear of the engine. Withdraw the oil level dipstick, from the dipstick tube.

2 On 1.2 litre petrol models, the dipstick is located in a tube at the front of the engine. Withdraw the oil level dipstick, from the dipstick tube.

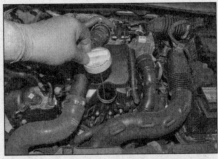
3 On 1.5 litre diesel models, the dipstick is located in the oil filler neck at the front of the engine (the dipstick is also the oil filler cap). Turn the filler cap and then withdraw the oil level cap/dipstick.

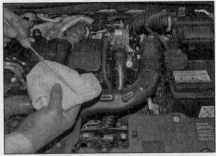
4 Using a clean rag or paper towel, wipe all the oil from the dipstick. Insert the clean dipstick into the tube as far as it will go, then withdraw it again.

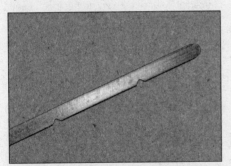
5 Note the oil level on the end of the dipstick, which should between the upper and lower mark on the 0.9 litre petrol engine …

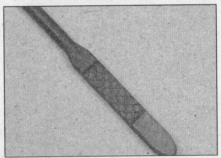
6 … or within the 'hatched' area on the 1.2 litre petrol engine dipstick …

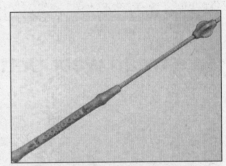
7 … and within the 'hatched' area on the 1.5 litre diesel engine dipstick. Approximately 1.0 to 1.5 litres of oil will raise the level from the lower to the upper mark.

8 Oil is added through the filler cap, unscrew the cap (0.9 litre petrol engine…

9 …and then top up the oil level (1.2 litre petrol engine…

10 …on 1.5 litre diesel engines the dipstick is also the oil filler cap. A funnel may help to reduce spillage. Add the oil slowly, checking the level on the dipstick often. Don't overfill.

Tyre condition and pressure

It is very important that tyres are in good condition, and at the correct pressure - having a tyre failure at any speed is highly dangerous. Tyre wear is influenced by driving style - harsh braking and acceleration, or fast cornering, will all produce more rapid tyre wear. As a general rule, the front tyres wear out faster than the rears. Interchanging the tyres from front to rear ("rotating" the tyres) may result in more even wear. However, if this is completely effective, you may have the expense of replacing all four tyres at once!

Remove any nails or stones embedded in the tread before they penetrate the tyre to cause deflation. If removal of a nail does reveal that the tyre has been punctured, refit the nail so that its point of penetration is marked. Then immediately change the wheel, and have the tyre repaired by a tyre dealer.

Regularly check the tyres for damage in the form of cuts or bulges, especially in the sidewalls. Periodically remove the wheels, and clean any dirt or mud from the inside and outside surfaces. Examine the wheel rims for signs of rusting, corrosion or other damage. Light alloy wheels are easily damaged by "kerbing" whilst parking; steel wheels may also become dented or buckled. A new wheel is very often the only way to overcome severe damage.

New tyres should be balanced when they are fitted, but it may become necessary to re-balance them as they wear, or if the balance weights fitted to the wheel rim should fall off. Unbalanced tyres will wear more quickly, as will the steering and suspension components. Wheel imbalance is normally signified by vibration, particularly at a certain speed (typically around 50 mph). If this vibration is felt only through the steering, then it is likely that just the front wheels need balancing. If, however, the vibration is felt through the whole car, the rear wheels could be out of balance. Wheel balancing should be carried out by a tyre dealer or garage.

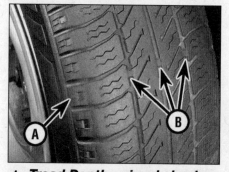

1 Tread Depth - visual check
The original tyres have tread wear safety bands (B), which will appear when the tread depth reaches approximately 1.6 mm. The band positions are indicated by a triangular mark on the tyre sidewall (A).

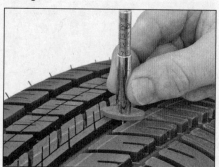

2 Tread Depth - manual check
Alternatively, tread wear can be monitored with a simple, inexpensive device known as a tread depth indicator gauge.

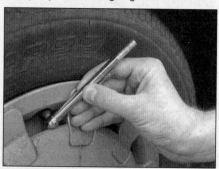

3 Tyre Pressure Check
Check the tyre pressures regularly with the tyres cold. Do not adjust the tyre pressures immediately after the vehicle has been used, or an inaccurate setting will result.

Tyre tread wear patterns

Shoulder Wear

Underinflation (wear on both sides)
Under-inflation will cause overheating of the tyre, because the tyre will flex too much, and the tread will not sit correctly on the road surface. This will cause a loss of grip and excessive wear, not to mention the danger of sudden tyre failure due to heat build-up.
Check and adjust pressures
Incorrect wheel camber (wear on one side)
Repair or renew suspension parts
Hard cornering
Reduce speed!

Centre Wear

Overinflation
Over-inflation will cause rapid wear of the centre part of the tyre tread, coupled with reduced grip, harsher ride, and the danger of shock damage occurring in the tyre casing.
Check and adjust pressures

If you sometimes have to inflate your car's tyres to the higher pressures specified for maximum load or sustained high speed, don't forget to reduce the pressures to normal afterwards.

Uneven Wear

Front tyres may wear unevenly as a result of wheel misalignment. Most tyre dealers and garages can check and adjust the wheel alignment (or "tracking") for a modest charge.
Incorrect camber or castor
Repair or renew suspension parts
Malfunctioning suspension
Repair or renew suspension parts
Unbalanced wheel
Balance tyres
Incorrect toe setting
Adjust front wheel alignment
Note: *The feathered edge of the tread which typifies toe wear is best checked by feel.*

Coolant level

Warning: Do not attempt to remove the expansion tank pressure cap when the engine is hot, as there is a very great risk of scalding. Do not leave open containers of coolant about, as it is poisonous.

Car care

● Adding coolant should not be necessary on a regular basis. If frequent topping-up is required, it is likely there is a leak. Check the radiator, all hoses and joint faces for signs of staining or wetness, and rectify as necessary.

● It is important that antifreeze is used in the cooling system all year round, not just during the winter months. Don't top-up with water alone, as the antifreeze will become too diluted.

1 The coolant level varies with the temperature of the engine. The see-through expansion tank (located on the drivers side inner wing panel) has MAX (full) and MIN (low) level markings on the front. When cold, the level should be between the two marks. When the engine is hot, the level may rise slightly above the MAX mark.

2 If topping-up is necessary, wait until the engine is cold, then remove the cap on the expansion tank.

3 Add a mixture of water and antifreeze to the expansion tank, until the coolant is up to the MAX mark. Use antifreeze of the same type as that which is already in the system. Refit the cap securely.

Brake and clutch fluid level

Warning:
• **Brake fluid can harm your eyes and damage painted surfaces, so use extreme caution when handling and pouring it.**
• **Do not use fluid that has been standing open for some time, as it absorbs moisture from the air, which can cause a dangerous loss of braking effectiveness.**

Safety first!

● If the reservoir requires repeated topping-up this is an indication of a fluid leak somewhere in the system, which should be investigated immediately.

● If a leak is suspected, the car should not be driven until the braking system has been checked. Never take any risks where brakes are concerned.

 • **Make sure that your car is on level ground.**

• **The fluid level in the reservoir will drop slightly as the brake pads and shoes wear down, but the fluid level must never be allowed to drop below the MIN mark.**

1 The MAXI and MINI marks are indicated on the side of the reservoir, which is located at the back of the engine compartment, on the driver's side. The fluid level must be kept between these two marks.

2 If topping-up is necessary, first wipe the area around the filler cap with a clean rag, then unscrew the cap. Take care not to lose the seal. When adding fluid, it's a good idea to inspect the reservoir. The fluid should be changed if it appears to be dark, or if dirt is visible.

3 Carefully add fluid, avoiding spilling it on surrounding paintwork. Use only the specified hydraulic fluid; mixing different types of fluid can cause damage to the system and/or a loss of braking effectiveness. After filling to the correct level, refit the cap securely. Wipe off any spilt fluid.

Screen washer fluid level

Note: *The underbonnet reservoir also serves the tailgate washer.*

● Screenwash additives not only keep the windscreen clean during bad weather, they also prevent the washer system freezing in cold weather – which is when you are likely to need it most. Don't top-up using plain water, as the screenwash will become diluted, and will freeze in cold weather.

 Warning: On no account use engine coolant antifreeze in the screen washer system – this may damage the paintwork.

1 The windscreen/tailgate washer fluid reservoir filler neck is located on the driver's side of the engine compartment, at the rear of the headlight unit. If topping-up is necessary, open the cap.

2 When topping-up the reservoir, a screenwash additive should be added in the quantities recommended on the bottle.

Wiper blades

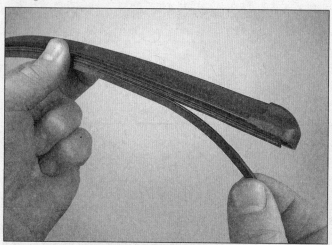

1 Check the condition of the wiper blades; if they are cracked or show any signs of deterioration, or if the glass swept area is smeared, renew them. For maximum clarity of vision, wiper blades should be renewed annually, as a matter of course.

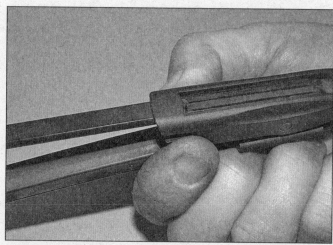

2 To remove a windscreen wiper blade, depress the locking clips.

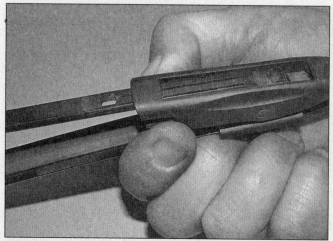

3 Slide the blade off the wiper arm, taking care not to allow the wiper arm to spring back and damage the windscreen.

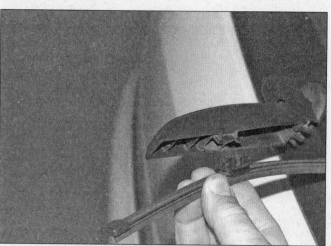

4 For the rear wiper, lift the wiper from the screen, then pull the wiper blade to unclip it from the wiper arm.

Battery

Caution: Before carrying out any work on the vehicle battery, read the precautions given in 'Safety first!' at the start of this manual. If the battery is to be disconnected, refer to Chapter 5A, Section 4 before proceeding.

✔ Make sure that the battery tray is in good condition, and that the clamp is tight. Corrosion on the tray, retaining clamp and the battery itself can be removed with a solution of water and baking soda. Thoroughly rinse all cleaned areas with water. Any metal parts damaged by corrosion should be covered with a zinc-based primer, and then painted.

✔ Periodically (approximately every three months), check the charge condition of the battery as described in Chapter 5A. The battery is of the maintenance-free type. Topping-up is not possible.

✔ If the battery is flat, and you need to jump start your vehicle, see *Roadside Repairs*.

HAYNES HINT *Battery corrosion can be kept to a minimum by applying a layer of petroleum jelly to the clamps and terminals after they are reconnected.*

1 The battery is located on the passenger side of the engine compartment. The exterior of the battery should be inspected periodically for damage such as a cracked case or cover.

3 If corrosion (white, fluffy deposits) is evident, remove the cables from the battery terminals, clean them with a small wire brush and then refit them. Automotive stores sell a tool for cleaning the battery post...

2 Check the tightness of the battery cable clamps to ensure good electrical connections. You should not be able to move them. Also check each cable for cracks and frayed conductors.

4 ...as well as the battery cable clamps.

Electrical systems

✔ Check all external lights and the horn. Refer to Chapter 12 for details if any of the circuits are found to be inoperative.

✔ Visually check all accessible wiring connectors, harnesses and retaining clips for security, and for signs of chafing or damage.

HAYNES HINT *If you need to check your brake lights and indicators unaided, back up to a wall or garage door and operate the lights. The reflected light should show if they are working properly.*

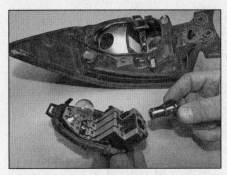

1 If a single indicator light, brake light or headlight has failed, it is likely that a bulb has blown and will need to be renewed. Refer to Chapter 12 for details. If both brake lights have failed, it is possible that the brake light switch operated by the brake pedal has failed. Refer to Chapter 9 for details.

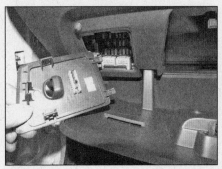

2 If more than one indicator light or headlight has failed, it is likely that either a fuse has blown, or that there is a fault in the circuit (see Chapter 12). The main fuses are mounted behind a panel inside the glovebox on the passenger side of the facia. Unclip the panel and release it from the facia.

3 To renew a blown fuse, remove it using the plastic tweezer tool provided (on the rear of the fuse box cover panel). Fit a new fuse of the same rating, available from car accessory shops. It is important that you find the reason that the fuse blew (see *Electrical fault finding* in Chapter 12).

Lubricants and fluids

Petrol engine . . . . Multigrade engine oil, SAE 5W-30 to 5W-40 to specification API SG, SH or better (ACEA A3/A5)

Diesel engine . . . . Multigrade engine oil SAE 5W-40 to 0W-40 (ACEA A3/B4)

Diesel engine (with particulate filter) . . . . Multigrade engine oil SAE 5W-30 or 5W-40 (to Renault specification RN0720)

Cooling system . . . . Glacerol RX-D*

Manual transmission . . . . Gear oil, SAE 75W-80 specification API GL-4

Automatic transmission . . . . Automatic transmission fluid (ATF)

Brake and clutch systems . . . . Hydraulic fluid to DOT 4

Do not mix types of coolant with each other, nor top-up with any other type of coolant. Alternative types of coolant may only be used once the system has been drained and completely flushed, as described in Chapter 1A, Section 27 or Chapter 1B, Section 27.

Tyre pressures

Note: *Pressures given here are a guide only, and apply to original-equipment tyres – the recommended pressures may vary if any other make or type of tyre is fitted; check with the car handbook, or the tyre manufacturer or supplier for the latest recommendations. A tyre pressure label is fitted, on the rear edge of the driver's door.*

Normal load (up to 2 people)	Front	Rear
165/65 R15 tyres	2.2 bar (32 psi)	2.0 bar (29 psi)
185/60 R15 tyres	2.2 bar (32psi)	2.0 bar (29 psi)
195/50 R16 tyres	2.4 bar (35psi)	2.2 bar (32 psi)

Chapter 1 Part A
Routine maintenance and servicing – petrol models

Contents

Degrees of difficulty

 Easy, suitable for novice with little experience

Fairly easy, suitable for beginner with some experience

Fairly difficult, suitable for competent DIY mechanic

Difficult, suitable for experienced DIY mechanic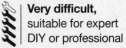

Very difficult, suitable for expert DIY or professional

Specifications

Lubricants and fluids. . . . .   Refer to *Weekly checks* on page 0•18

Capacities

Engine oil (including oil filter):
   0.9 litre engines . . . .   4.1 litres
   1.2 litre engines . . . .   4.0 litres
   Difference between MAX and MIN dipstick marks. . . . .   1.0 to 1.5 litres depending on engine
Cooling system. . . . .   5.0 litres
Manual transmission . . . .   3.4 litres
Fuel tank . . . .   45 litres

Cooling system

Antifreeze mixture:	Antifreeze	Water
Protection to –23°C	35%	65%
Protection to –40°C	50%	50%

Fuel system

Specified idle speed (non-adjustable) . . . .   750 ± 50 rpm
Idle mixture CO content (non-adjustable) . . . .   0.5% maximum (0.3% at 2500 rpm)

Ignition system

Location of No 1 cylinder . . . .   Flywheel end
Ignition timing. . . . .   Controlled by ECU – see Chapter 5B

Spark plugs: *	Type	Electrode gap
0.9 litre engines		0.8 mm
1.2 litre engine	NGK LZKAR7B	0.9 mm

* Spark plug recommendations are correct at time of writing. For further information consult the spark plug maker's catalogue.

Brakes

Front disc brakes:
   Pad thickness (including backing):
      New . . . .   17.4 mm
      Minimum thickness. . . . .   8.0 mm
Rear disc brakes:
   Pad thickness (including backing):
      New . . . .   15.8 mm
      Minimum thickness. . . . .   7.5 mm
Rear drum brakes:
   Shoe thickness (including backing):
      New . . . .   5.5 mm
      Minimum thickness. . . . .   2.4 mm

Torque wrench settings	Nm	lbf ft
Auxiliary belt tensioner:		
0.9 litre engines	62	46
1.2 litre engines	50	37
HT coils (0.9 litre engines)	10	8
Roadwheel bolts.	105	77
Spark plugs:		
0.9 litre engine	25	18
1.2 litre engine	25 to 30	18 to 22
Sump plug:		
0.9 litre engine	50	37
1.2 litre engine	20	15

1 Maintenance schedule – petrol models

1 The maintenance intervals in this manual are provided with the assumption that you, not the dealer, will be carrying out the work. These are the minimum maintenance intervals recommended by us for vehicles driven daily.

If you wish to keep your vehicle in peak condition at all times, you may wish to perform some of these procedures more often. We encourage frequent maintenance, because it enhances the efficiency, performance and resale value of your vehicle.
2 When the vehicle is new, it should be serviced by a dealer service department (or other workshop recognised by the vehicle manufacturer as providing the same standard

of service) in order to preserve the warranty. The vehicle manufacturer may reject warranty claims if you are unable to prove that servicing has been carried out as and when specified, using only original equipment parts or parts certified to be of equivalent quality.
3 If the vehicle is driven in dusty areas, used to tow a trailer, or driven frequently at slow speeds (idling in traffic) or on short journeys, more frequent intervals are recommended.

Every 250 miles or weekly
☐ Refer to *Weekly checks*.

Every 9000 miles
☐ Renew the engine oil and filter (Section 4)

Note: *Frequent oil and filter changes are good for the engine. We recommend changing the oil at the mileage specified here, or at least twice a year.*

Every 18 000 miles or 2 years, whichever comes first
In addition to all the items listed previously, carry out the following:
☐ Renew the pollen filter (Section 5)
☐ Check the handbrake (Section 6)
☐ Check the brake pads and discs (Section 7)
☐ Check the operation of the clutch (Section 8)
☐ Check the condition of the auxiliary drivebelt (Section 9)
☐ Check the condition of the seat belts (Section 10)
☐ Check the operation of all electrical systems (Section 11)
☐ Check the condition of the exhaust system and mountings (Section 12)
☐ Check the suspension and steering components (Section 13)
☐ Check all underbonnet components and hoses for fluid leaks (Section 14)
☐ Check the tightness of the roadwheel bolts (Section 15)
☐ Check the bodywork and underbody for damage and corrosion (Section 16)
☐ Check the front and rear shock absorbers (Section 17)

Every 36 000 miles or 4 years, whichever comes first
In addition to all the items listed previously, carry out the following:
☐ Renew the spark plugs and check the ignition system (Section 18)
☐ Renew the air filter element (Section 19)
☐ Check the rear brake shoes and drums (Section 20)
☐ Check the manual transmission oil level (Section 21)
☐ Check the front wheel alignment (Section 22)
☐ Check the operation of the air conditioning system (Section 23)
☐ Carry out a road test (Section 24)
☐ Renew the timing belt (1.2 litre engines) (Section 25)*
☐ Renew the brake fluid (Section 26)
☐ Renew the coolant (Section 27)

Note: **Although the normal interval for timing belt renewal is 72 000 miles, it is strongly recommended that the interval is reduced to 36 000 miles on vehicles which are subjected to intensive use, ie, mainly short journeys or a lot of stop-start driving. The actual belt renewal interval is therefore very much up to the individual owner, but bear in mind that severe engine damage may result if the belt breaks.*

Underbonnet view of a 0.9 litre petrol model

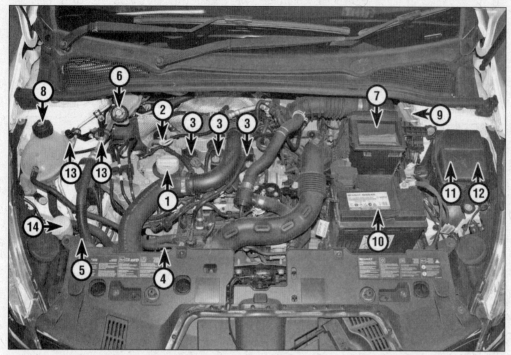

1 Engine oil filler cap
2 Engine oil level dipstick
3 Ignition leads and coil pack
4 Alternator
5 Evaporative emissions control solenoid
6 Brake master cylinder fluid reservoir
7 Air filter
8 Coolant expansion tank
9 Engine management ECU
10 Battery
11 Engine related fusebox
12 Switching and protection unit (fusebox)
13 AC service ports
14 Screen washer fluid reservoir

Front underbody view of a 0.9 litre petrol model

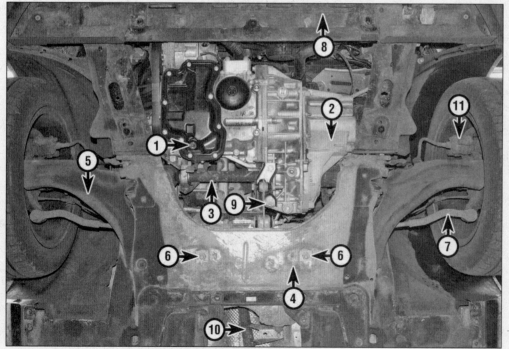

1 Engine oil drain plug
2 Manual transmission
3 Driveshafts
4 Front suspension subframe
5 Front suspension lower arms
6 Anti-roll bar mounting bolts
7 Track rod ends
8 Radiator support panel (subframe)
9 Engine steady bar (torque rod)
10 Exhaust mounting
11 Brake calipers

Underbonnet view of a 1.2 litre petrol model

1 Engine oil level dipstick
2 Engine oil filler cap
3 Throttle body
4 Inlet manifold
5 ABS brake modulator
6 Brake master cylinder fluid reservoir
7 Air filter housing
8 Coolant expansion tank
9 Screen washer fluid reservoir
10 Engine management ECU
11 Switching and protection unit (fusebox)
12 Battery
13 Relay plate (and fuses)
14 Air inlet duct

Front underbody view of a 1.2 litre petrol model

1 Engine oil drain plug
2 Manual transmission
3 Driveshafts
4 Front suspension subframe
5 Front suspension lower arms
6 Anti-roll bar mounting bolts
7 Track rod ends
8 Radiator support panel (subframe)
9 Engine steady bar (torque rod)
10 Catalytic converter
11 Brake calipers
12 Transmission drain plug

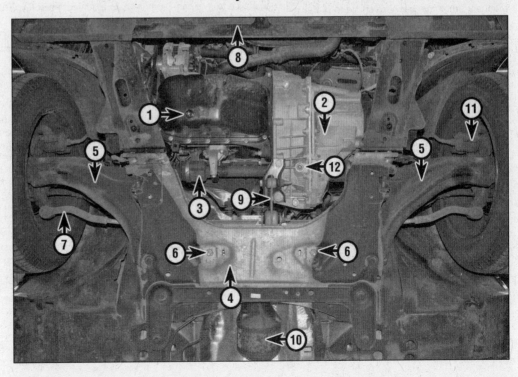

Rear underbody view of a 1.2 litre petrol model (0.9 litre similar)

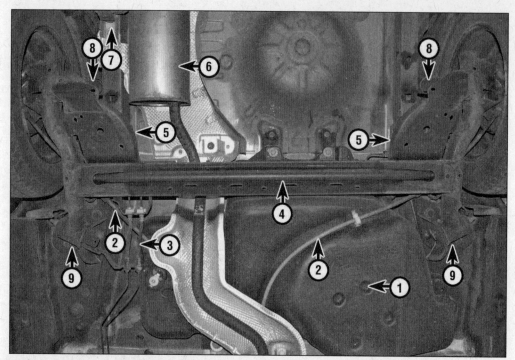

1 Fuel tank
2 Handbrake cables
3 Brake flexible hoses
4 Rear axle assembly
5 Rear coil springs
6 Exhaust rear silencer and tailpipe
7 Exhaust mounting
8 Shock absorbers
9 Rear axle mounting bush

Maintenance procedures

2 Introduction

1 This Chapter is designed to help the home mechanic maintain his/her vehicle for safety, economy, long life and peak performance.

2 The Chapter contains a master maintenance schedule, followed by Sections dealing specifically with each task in the schedule. Visual checks, adjustments, component renewal and other helpful items are included. Refer to the accompanying illustrations of the engine compartment and the underside of the vehicle for the locations of the various components.

3 Servicing your vehicle in accordance with the mileage/time maintenance schedule and the following Sections will provide a planned maintenance programme, which should result in a long and reliable service life. This is a comprehensive plan, so maintaining some items but not others at the specified service intervals will not produce the same results.

4 As you service your vehicle, you will discover that many of the procedures can – and should – be grouped together, because of the particular procedure being performed, or because of the proximity of two otherwise unrelated components to one another. For example, if the vehicle is raised for any reason, the exhaust can be inspected at the same time as the suspension and steering components.

5 The first step in this maintenance programme is to prepare yourself before the actual work begins. Read through all the Sections relevant to the work to be carried out, then make a list and gather all the parts and tools required. If a problem is encountered, seek advice from a parts specialist, or a dealer service department.

Warning lights and service indicator

6 All of the models covered in this manual have a sophisticated fault warning system fitted. The spanner symbol will illuminate, and on most models a message will be displayed pointing towards the possible fault. Serious faults will also bring on the STOP warning light. If only the spanner symbol is displayed it is generally safe to continue driving, although the fault should be investigated at the earliest opportunity. If the STOP message illuminates, stop as soon as it is safe to do so.

7 Most models in this manual are also fitted with Renault's 'oil control system' (OCS). The OCS monitors several parameters, in an attempt to calculate the time for an oil change based on time as well as distance covered. This calculation takes into account driving style, number of starts, time spent idling, average speed and coolant temperature. The information display shows the distance to the next service. When the service is due the spanner symbol will flash and 'Service vehicle' appears in the display.

8 To reset the display turn the ignition on and hold down one of the reset buttons (on the end of the windscreen wiper switch) for 10 seconds until the display stops flashing. If it is decided to change the oil (and filter) before the calculated service interval do not reset the display. This prevents the interval for other service parts from being exceeded.

3 Regular maintenance

1 If, from the time the vehicle is new, the routine maintenance schedule is followed closely, and frequent checks are made of fluid levels and high wear items, as suggested throughout this manual, the engine will be kept in relatively good running condition, and the need for additional work will be minimised.

2 It is possible that there will be times when the engine is running poorly due to the lack of regular maintenance. This is even more likely if a used vehicle, which has not received regular and frequent maintenance checks, is purchased. In such cases, additional work may need to be carried out, outside of the regular maintenance intervals.

3 If engine wear is suspected, a compression test (refer to Chapter 2B Section 2 or as applicable) will provide valuable information regarding the overall performance of the main internal components. Such a test can

be used as a basis to decide on the extent of the work to be carried out. If, for example, a compression test indicates serious internal engine wear, conventional maintenance as described in this Chapter will not greatly improve the performance of the engine, and may prove a waste of time and money, unless extensive overhaul work is carried out first.

4 The following series of operations are those most often required to improve the performance of a generally poor running engine:

Primary operations

a) *Clean, inspect and test the battery (refer to 'Weekly checks').*
b) *Check all the engine related fluids (refer to 'Weekly checks').*
c) *Check the condition of the auxiliary drivebelt (Section 9).*
d) *Check the condition of all hoses, and check for fluid leaks (Section 14).*
e) *Renew the spark plugs (Section 18).*
f) *Check the condition of the air filter, and renew if necessary (Section 19).*

5 If the above operations do not prove fully effective, carry out the following secondary operations:

Secondary operations

6 All items listed under *Primary operations*, plus the following:
a) *Check the charging system (Chapter 5A).*
b) *Check the ignition system (Chapter 5B).*
c) *Check the fuel system (refer to Chapter 4A).*

Every 9000 miles

4   Engine oil and filter renewal

Note: *Refer to Section 2 for information on setting the service indicator.*

1 Before starting this procedure, gather together all the necessary tools and materials **(see illustration)**. Also make sure that you have plenty of clean rags and newspapers handy to mop up any spills. Ideally, the engine oil should be warm, as it will drain better and more built up sludge will be removed with it. Take care, however, not to touch the exhaust or any other hot parts of the engine when working under the vehicle. To avoid any possibility of scalding, and to protect yourself from possible skin irritants and other harmful contaminants in used engine oils, it is advisable to wear rubber gloves when carrying out this work. Apply the handbrake, then jack up the front of the vehicle and support it on axle stands (see *Jacking and vehicle support*). Alternatively, raise the vehicle on a lift or drive it onto ramps. Whichever method is chosen, make sure that the car remains as level as possible (depending on the position of the drain plug), to enable the oil to drain fully. Remove the engine undertray where applicable.

2 Remove the oil filler cap from the camshaft cover, then position a container beneath the sump. Clean the drain plug and the area around it, then slacken it half a turn using a special drain plug key **(see illustrations)**.

3 Allow some time for the old oil to drain **(see illustration)**, noting that it may be necessary to reposition the container as the oil flow slows to a trickle.

4 After all the oil has drained, wipe off the drain plug with a clean rag and renew its sealing washer. Clean the area around the drain plug opening, then refit and tighten the plug securely **(see illustrations)**.

5 Move the container into position under the

4.1 Tools and materials necessary for the engine oil change and filter renewal

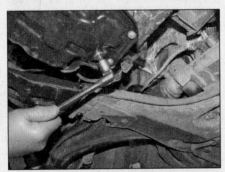

4.2a Slacken the sump plug (8mm square drive) – 0.9 litre engines

4.2b Slacken the sump plug (Hex drive) – 1.2 litre engines

4.3 Allow time for the oil to drain

4.4a Fit a new sealing washer...

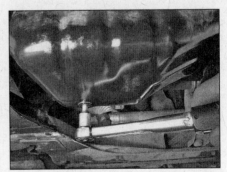

4.4b ...and tighten to the correct torque

4.5a Oil filter location – 0.9 litre engines

4.5b Oil filter location – 1.2 litre engine

4.6a Removing the oil filter on the 0.9 litre engine…

4.6b …and on the 1.2 litre engine

4.10a Fit new filter element…

4.10b …and tighten cover to the correct torque

oil filter. The oil filter is located inside the alloy part of the lower sump casing, on 0.9 litre engines, and on the rear of the cylinder block at the timing belt end on, 1.2 litre engines (see illustrations).

6 On 0.9 litre engines, the filter is of an element type, located under the filter cover in the sump casing. On 1.2 litre engines the filter is of screw-on canister type (see illustrations).

7 On 0.9 litre engines, using a ratchet/bar and socket, unscrew the plastic cover/cap from the sump a few turns and allow the oil to drain from the filter housing. When the oil

4.11 Oil the filter seal

has drained, unscrew the cover all the way and remove the filter element from inside the alloy sump casing. Discard the the filter and the O-ring from around the plastic cover.

8 On 1.2 litre engines, using an oil filter removal tool, slacken the filter initially. Loosely wrap some rags around the oil filter, then unscrew it and immediately position it with its open end uppermost to prevent further spillage of oil. Remove the oil filter from the engine compartment and empty the oil into the container.

9 Use a clean rag to remove all oil, dirt and sludge from the filter sealing area on the engine and inside the casing.

10 On 0.9 litre engines, fit the new filter element into the alloy sump casing, then fit new O-ring to the filter cover and screw it back into position(see illustrations), and tighten to the specified torque setting.

11 On 1.2 litre engines, check the old filter to make sure that the rubber sealing ring hasn't stuck to the engine. If it has, carefully remove it. Apply a light coating of clean oil to the sealing ring on the new filter (see illustration) then screw it into position on the engine. Tighten the filter firmly by hand only – do not use any tools. Wipe clean the exterior of the oil filter.

12 Remove the old oil and all tools from under the car and then lower the car to the ground.

13 Fill the engine with the specified quantity and grade of oil, as described in Weekly checks. Pour the oil in slowly, otherwise it may overflow. Check that the oil level is up to the maximum mark on the dipstick, then refit and tighten the oil filler cap.

14 Start the engine and run it for a few minutes, checking that there are no leaks around the oil filter seal and the sump drain plug. Note that when the engine is first started, the oil pressure warning light may briefly flicker while the new filter fills with oil. If the oil pressure warning light comes on (it may be accompanied by a warning message) and stays on, stop the engine immediately and check the oil level.

15 Switch off the engine and wait a few minutes for the oil to settle in the sump once more. With the new oil circulated and the filter now completely full, recheck the level on the dipstick and add more oil if necessary.

16 Apply the handbrake and then once again jack up the front of the vehicle and support it on axle stands (see Jacking and vehicle support). Check again for leaks around the sump drain plug and oil filter and then refit the engine undershield. Lower the vehicle to the ground and make a final check of the oil level, topping up as required.

17 Dispose of the used engine oil safely with reference to General repair procedures in the Reference section of this manual.

Every 18 000 miles or 2 years

5   Pollen filter renewal

1 The pollen filter is located in the left-hand side rear of the air distribution unit (see illustration).
2 The filter can be removed by working inside the passenger side footwell and reaching up behind the glovebox, to the rear of the heater housing.
3 Note the orientation of the filter, as it is withdrawn, unclip the plastic cover and then carefully extract the filter element by sliding it out from the housing (see illustration).
4 Fit the new element using a reversal of the removal procedure, but make sure that the air flow direction arrows on the filter, are in the same direction as noted on removal.

6   Handbrake check

1 The handbrake should be capable of holding the parked vehicle stationary, even on steep slopes, when applied with moderate force. The mechanism should be firm and positive in feel, with no trace of stiffness or sponginess from the cables, and should release immediately the handbrake lever is released. If the mechanism is faulty in any of these respects, it must be checked immediately as follows. Note: On models with rear drum brakes, if the handbrake is not functioning correctly or is incorrectly adjusted, the rear brake self-adjust mechanism will not function. This will lead to the brake pedal travel becoming excessive as the shoe linings wear.
2 Handbrake adjustment is made from inside the vehicle on the cable adjuster nut (see illustration).
3 Remove the rear section of the centre console, as described in Chapter 11 Section 27 to access the adjuster nut.
4 Jack up the rear of the vehicle and support it on axle stands (see Jacking and vehicle support).

Models with rear drum brakes

5 Remove both rear brake drums as described in Chapter 9 Section 11.
6 Check that the knurled adjuster wheel on the adjuster strut is free to rotate in both directions. If it is seized, the brake shoes and strut must be removed and overhauled as described in Chapter 9 Section 12.
7 If all is well, back off the adjuster wheel by five or six teeth so that the diameter of the brake shoes is slightly reduced.
8 Check that the handbrake cables slide freely by pulling on their front ends. Also check that the operating levers on the rear

brake trailing shoes return to their correct positions, with their stop-pegs in contact with the edge of the trailing shoe web.
9 With the aid of an assistant, tighten the adjuster nut on the handbrake lever operating rod so that the lever on each rear brake assembly starts to move as the handbrake is moved between the first and second notch (click) of its ratchet mechanism. This is the case when the stop-pegs are still in contact with the shoes when the handbrake is on the first notch of the ratchet, but no longer contact the shoes when the handbrake is on the second notch.
10 Refit the brake drums as described in Chapter 9 Section 11, then lower the vehicle to the ground.
11 With the vehicle standing on its wheels, repeatedly depress the footbrake to adjust the shoe-to-drum clearance. Whilst depressing the pedal, have an assistant listen to the rear drums to check that the adjuster strut mechanism is functioning; if this is so, a clicking sound will be heard from the adjuster strut as the pedal is depressed.
12 Lower the vehicle to the ground and refit the centre console.

Models with rear disc brakes

13 Check that the handbrake cables slide freely by pulling on their front ends, and check that the operating levers on the rear brake calipers move smoothly.
14 Move both of the caliper operating levers

as far rearwards as possible, then tighten the adjuster nut on the handbrake lever cable until all free play is removed from both cables. With the aid of an assistant, adjust the nut so that the operating lever on each rear brake caliper starts to move as the handbrake lever is moved between the first and second notch (click) of its ratchet mechanism.
15 Lower the vehicle to the ground and refit the centre console.

7   Brake pad and disc check

Note: Drum brake checks are in Section 20.
1 Firmly apply the handbrake, then jack up the front or rear of the vehicle (as applicable) and support it securely on axle stands (see Jacking and vehicle support). Remove the roadwheels.
2 For a quick check, the thickness of friction material remaining on each brake pad can be measured through the aperture in the caliper body (see Haynes Hint). If any pad's friction material is worn to the specified thickness or less, all four pads must be renewed as a set. Pad wear warning contacts are fitted to the inboard pads, but this should not be used as an excuse for omitting a visual check.
3 For a comprehensive check, the brake pads should be removed and cleaned. This will allow the operation of the caliper to be

5.1 The pollen filter location

5.3 Withdraw the filter

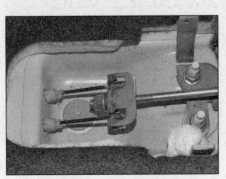

6.2 Handbrake cable adjusting nut

HAYNES HiNT

For a quick check, the thickness of friction material remaining on each brake pad can be measured through the aperture in the caliper body.

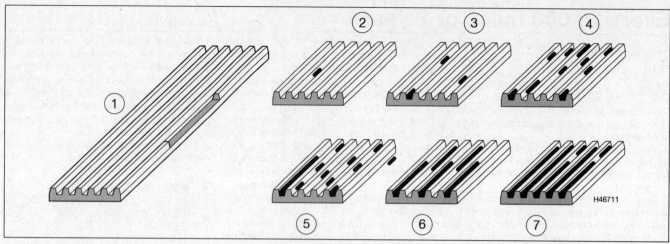

9.6 Check for drivebelt wear

1 *If sections are missing renew the belt*
2 *Small deposits in the grooves are not a concern*

3 *Small scattered deposits are not a concern*
4 *Deposits up to half of the rib height: renew the belt if noisy*

5 *Deposits up to half the rib height: renew the belt if noisy*
6 *Heavy deposits: renew the belt*
7 *Heavy deposits: renew the belt*

checked, and the brake disc itself to be fully examined for condition on both sides. Refer to Chapter 9 for further information.

8 Clutch check

1 Check that the clutch pedal moves smoothly and easily through its full travel, and that the clutch itself functions correctly, with no trace of slip or drag.
2 Check the brake fluid level. The brake fluid reservoir supplies the clutch hydraulic system. The level will drop slightly as the clutch and brake components wear.
3 A dramatic fall in the level should be investigated immediately as it could be a hydraulic leak in the clutch system, or the brake system.

9 Auxiliary drivebelt check and renewal

Note: *Renault recommend that the belt is*

always renewed if it is removed. A new tensioner must also be fitted and where the retaining bolt has a 'Torx' type head, this must be replaced with a standard hexagonal head bolt. The belt and tensioner should be renewed every 72 000 miles or 5 years regardless of condition.*

Checking

1 The auxiliary drivebelt is located on the right-hand side of the engine.
2 Due to their function and material makeup, drivebelts are prone to failure after a period of time and should therefore be inspected, and if necessary adjusted periodically.
3 A basic check for obvious faults can be made from the engine compartment or by removing the right-hand road wheel and plastic inner wing liner, so inspection can only be made from below.
4 If checking from underneath, jack up the front of the car, and support it on axle stands (see *Jacking and vehicle support*).
5 Remove the right-hand wheel and the wing liner.
6 With the engine stopped and the keys out of the ignition, inspect the full length of the drivebelt for cracks and separation of the belt plies **(see illustration)**. It will be necessary to

turn the engine (using a spanner or socket and bar on the crankshaft pulley bolt) in order to move the belt from the pulleys so that the belt can be inspected thoroughly. Twist the belt between the pulleys so that both sides can be viewed. Also, check for fraying and glazing which gives the belt a shiny appearance. Check the pulleys for nicks, cracks, distortion and corrosion.

Renewal

Automatic tensioner

Note: *Before removal of the belt, note the fitted position. On some models, the compressor pulley has six grooves, the belt has five. In this case the inner groove is left unused, so that the run of the belt is straight.*

7 After checking the belt (as described above), renew the belt by using a spanner on the outer nut on the tensioner, turn the tensioner clockwise to release the tension on the belt **(see illustrations)**, then lift the drivebelt from the pulleys, noting its fitted position.

9.7a Turning the spanner clockwise from under the vehicle (0.9 litre engine)...

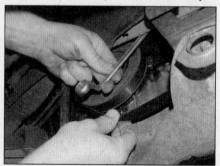

9.7b ...and on 1.2 litre engines

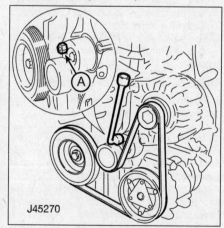

9.7c ...or from above, using hexagon (A) on the tensioner pulley

8 If the belt is removed it must be renewed.
9 Unbolt the tensioner unit and fit a new one **(see illustration)**. Tighten the single bolt to the specified torque.
10 Using the spanner on the outer nut on the tensioner, hold the tensioner clockwise, to allow the new belt to be fitted around the pulleys, making sure that it is correctly located in the grooves.
11 Fit a socket to the crankshaft pulley and rotate the engine several times to check the belt alignment.
12 Where applicable, refit the inner wing liner and roadwheel, then lower the vehicle to the ground.

Manual tensioner – 1.2 litre engines
Note: *A special belt tool is used by Renault technicians to tension the belt correctly.*
13 A protective cover may be fitted to the accessory belt tensioner. Remove this if fitted.
14 Using a ring spanner to hold the tensioner, loosen the locking Torx head bolt **(see illustration)**.
15 Push the tensioner upwards and remove the belt **(see illustration)**.
16 Unbolt and remove the tensioner – a new one will be required.
17 Fit the new tensioner and then fit the new accessory belt. If the special tool is available, adjust the belt to give a reading of 210 Hz on models with no air conditioning and a reading of 277Hz on models fitted with air conditioning.
18 If the specialist tool is not available, adjust the tensioner so that it is just possible to twist the belt through 90° in the middle of the longest belt run. If there are any concerns regarding the belt tension, have it checked by a Renault dealer, or garage with suitable equipment.
19 Run the engine for about 5 minutes, then recheck the tension.
20 Refit the wing liner and wheel. Lower the vehicle to the ground.

10 Seat belt check

1 Carefully examine the seat belt webbing for cuts, or any signs of serious fraying or deterioration. If the belt is of the retractable type, pull the belt all the way out of the inertia reel, and examine the full extent of the webbing.
2 Fasten and unfasten the belt, ensuring that the locking mechanism holds securely, and releases properly when intended. If the belt is of the retractable type, check also that the retracting mechanism operates correctly when the belt is released.
3 Check the security of all seat belt mountings and attachments which are accessible without removing any trim or other components.

9.7d Drivebelt routing – 0.9 litre engines with A/C

11 Electrical systems check

1 Check the operation of all electrical equipment, ie, lights, direction indicators, horn, etc. Refer to the appropriate Sections of Chapter 12 for details if any of the circuits are found to be inoperative.
2 Note that stop-light switch adjustment is described in Chapter 9 Section 19.
3 Visually check all accessible wiring connectors, harnesses and retaining clips for security, and for signs of chafing or damage. Rectify any faults found.

12 Exhaust system check

1 With the engine cold (at least an hour after the vehicle has been driven), check the complete exhaust system from the engine to the end of the tailpipe. Ideally, the inspection should be carried out with the vehicle on a hoist to permit unrestricted access, but if a hoist is not available, raise and support the vehicle safely on axle stands (see).
2 Check the exhaust pipes and connections for evidence of leaks, severe corrosion and damage. Make sure that all brackets and mountings are in good condition and tight. Leakage at any of the joints or in other parts

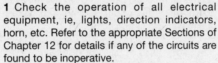

9.14 Loosen the tensioner

of the system will usually show up as a black sooty stain in the vicinity of the leak.
3 Rattles and other noises can often be traced to the exhaust system, especially the brackets and mountings. Try to move the pipes and silencers. If the components can come into contact with the body or suspension parts, secure the system with new mountings or if possible, separate the joints and twist the pipes as necessary to provide additional clearance.
4 Run the engine at idling speed. Have an assistant place a cloth or rag over the rear end of the exhaust pipe, and listen for any escape of exhaust gases that would indicate a leak.
5 On completion, lower the car to the ground.

13 Suspension and steering check

Front suspension and steering
1 Raise the front of the vehicle, and securely support it on axle stands (see *Jacking and vehicle support*).
2 Visually inspect the balljoint dust covers and the steering rack and pinion gaiters for splits, chafing or deterioration. Any wear of these components will cause loss of lubricant, together with dirt and water entry, resulting in rapid deterioration of the balljoints or steering gear.
3 Grasp the roadwheel at the 12 o'clock and

9.9 Unbolt the automatic tensioner – 0.9 litre engines

9.15 Remove the belt

13.3 Check for wear in the hub bearings by grasping the wheel and trying to rock it

6 o'clock positions, and try to rock it **(see illustration)**. Very slight free play may be felt, but if the movement is appreciable, further investigation is necessary to determine the source. Continue rocking the wheel while an assistant depresses the footbrake. If the movement is now eliminated or significantly reduced, it is likely that the hub bearings are at fault. If the free play is still evident with the footbrake depressed, then there is wear in the suspension joints or mountings.

4 Now grasp the wheel at the 9 o'clock and 3 o'clock positions, and try to rock it as before. Any movement felt now may again be caused by wear in the hub bearings or the steering track rod balljoints. If the outer balljoint is worn, the visual movement will be obvious. If the inner joint is suspect, it can be felt by placing a hand over the rack and pinion rubber gaiter and gripping the track rod. If the wheel is now rocked, movement will be felt at the inner joint if wear has taken place.

5 Using a large screwdriver or flat bar, check for wear in the suspension mounting bushes by levering between the relevant suspension component and its attachment point. Some movement is to be expected, as the mountings are made of rubber, but excessive wear should be obvious. Also check the condition of any visible rubber bushes, looking for splits, cracks or contamination of the rubber.

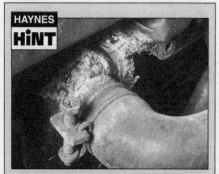

A leak in the cooling system will usually show up as white- or antifreeze-coloured deposits on the area adjoining the leak.

6 With the car standing on its wheels, have an assistant turn the steering wheel back-and-forth, about an eighth of a turn each way. There should be very little, if any, lost movement between the steering wheel and roadwheels. If this is not the case, closely observe the joints and mountings previously described. In addition, check the steering column universal joints for wear, and also check the rack and pinion steering gear itself.

Rear suspension

7 Chock the front wheels, then jack up the rear of the vehicle and support securely on axle stands (see *Jacking and vehicle support*).

8 Working as described previously for the front suspension, check the rear hub bearings, the suspension bushes and the shock absorber mountings for wear. Note: The handbrake will need to be in the released position before checking the rear wheel bearings.

14 Hose and fluid leak check

1 Visually inspect the engine joint faces, gaskets and seals for any signs of water or oil leaks. Pay particular attention to the areas around the valve cover, cylinder head, oil filter and sump joint faces. Bear in mind that, over a period of time, some very slight seepage from these areas is to be expected – what you are really looking for is any indication of a serious leak. Should a leak be found, renew the offending gasket or oil seal by referring to the appropriate Chapters in this manual.

2 Also check the security and condition of all the engine related pipes and hoses, and all hydraulic and braking system pipes and hoses. Ensure that all cable ties or securing clips are in place, and in good condition. Clips which are broken or missing can lead to chafing of the hoses, pipes or wiring, which could cause more serious problems in the future.

3 Carefully check the radiator hoses and heater hoses along their entire length. Renew any hose which is cracked, swollen or deteriorated. Cracks will show up better if the hose is squeezed. Pay close attention to the hose clips that secure the hoses to the cooling system components. Hose clips can pinch and puncture hoses, resulting in cooling system leaks. If the crimped type hose clips are used, it may be a good idea to use standard worm drive clips.

4 Inspect all the cooling system components (hoses, joint faces, etc) for leaks **(see Haynes Hint)**. Where any problems are found on system components, renew the component or gasket with reference to Chapter 3.

5 With the vehicle raised, inspect the fuel tank and filler neck for punctures, cracks

and other damage. The connection between the filler neck and tank is especially critical. Sometimes a rubber filler neck or connecting hose will leak due to loose retaining clamps or deteriorated rubber.

6 Carefully check all rubber hoses and metal fuel lines leading away from the fuel tank. Check for loose connections, deteriorated hoses, crimped lines, and other damage. Pay particular attention to the vent pipes and hoses, which often loop up around the filler neck and can become blocked or crimped. Follow the lines to the front of the vehicle, carefully inspecting them all the way. Renew damaged sections as necessary. Similarly, whilst the vehicle is raised, take the opportunity to inspect all underbody brake fluid pipes and hoses.

7 From within the engine compartment, check the security of all fuel, vacuum and brake hose attachments and pipe unions, and inspect all hoses for kinks, chafing and deterioration.

8 Check the condition of the automatic transmission fluid cooler pipes and hoses, where applicable.

15 Roadwheel bolt check

1 Remove the wheel trims, where applicable, then slacken the roadwheel bolts slightly.

2 Tighten the bolts to the specified torque, using a torque wrench.

16 Bodywork and underbody condition check

1 Once the car has been washed and all tar spots and other surface blemishes have been cleaned off, carefully check all paintwork, looking closely for chips or scratches. Pay particular attention to vulnerable areas such as the front panels (bonnet and spoiler), and around the wheel arches. Any damage to the paintwork must be rectified as soon as possible to comply with the terms of the manufacturer's anti-corrosion warranties; check with a Renault dealer for details.

2 If a chip or light scratch is found which is recent and still free from rust, it can be touched up using the appropriate touch up stick which can be obtained from Renault dealers. Any more serious damage, or rusted stone chips, can be repaired as described in Chapter 11 Section 4, but if damage or corrosion is so severe that a panel must be renewed, seek professional advice as soon as possible.

3 Always check that the door and ventilation opening drain holes and pipes are completely clear, so that water can drain out.

4 The wax-based underbody protective coating should be inspected annually, preferably just prior to Winter, when the

underbody should be washed down as thoroughly as possible without disturbing the protective coating (see Chapter 11, Section 2, regarding the use of steam cleaners). Any damage to the coating should be repaired using a wax-based sealer. If any of the body panels are disturbed for repair or renewal, do not forget to renew the coating and to inject wax into door panels, sills and box sections, to maintain the level of protection provided by the vehicle manufacturer.

17 Shock absorber check

1 Viewing over the roadwheels into the wheel arches, check for any signs of fluid leakage around the front and rear shock absorber bodies, or from the rubber gaiters around the piston rods. Should any fluid be noticed, the shock absorber is defective internally, and

should be renewed. **Note:** *Shock absorbers should always be renewed in pairs on the same axle.*
2 The efficiency of the shock absorber may be checked by bouncing the vehicle at each corner. Generally speaking, the body will return to its normal position and stop after being depressed. If it rises and returns on a rebound, the shock absorber is probably suspect. Also examine the shock absorber upper and lower mountings for any signs of wear.

Every 36 000 miles or 4 years

18 Spark plug renewal and ignition system check

⚠️ *Warning: High voltages are produced by the electronic ignition system. Extreme care must be taken when working on the system with the ignition switched on. Persons with surgically implanted cardiac pacemaker devices should keep well clear of the ignition circuits, components and test equipment.*

1 The correct functioning of the spark plugs is vital for the correct running and efficiency of the engine. It is essential that the plugs fitted are appropriate for the engine, the type being specified at the start of this Chapter. If the correct type of plug is used and the engine is in good condition, the spark plugs should not need attention between scheduled servicing intervals. Spark plug cleaning is rarely necessary, and should not be attempted unless specialised equipment is available, as damage can easily be caused to the firing ends.
2 To remove the plugs, first open the bonnet and (where fitted) unclip the engine upper cover. On 1.2 litre models remove the air filter housing as described in Section 19.
3 On 0.9 litre engines, remove the retaining bolt and withdraw the ignition HT coils from the top of the spark plugs, as described in Chapter 5B Section 3 **(see illustration)**.
4 On 1.2 litre engines, disengage the HT leads from the spark plugs **(see illustration)**. Do not pull on the lead, always grasp the plug boot to remove it.
5 It is advisable to remove any dirt from the spark plug recesses using a clean brush, a vacuum cleaner or compressed air before removing the plugs, to prevent the dirt dropping into the cylinders.
6 Unscrew the plugs using a spark plug spanner, box spanner or a deep socket and extension bar. Keep the socket in alignment with the spark plug, otherwise if it is forcibly moved to either side, the ceramic top of the spark plug may be broken off **(see**

illustrations). As each plug is removed, examine it as follows.
7 Examination of the spark plugs will give a good indication of the condition of the engine. If the insulator nose of the spark plug is clean and white, with no deposits, this is indicative of a weak mixture or too hot a plug (a hot plug transfers heat away from the electrode slowly, a cold plug transfers heat away quickly).
8 If the tip and insulator nose are covered with hard black-looking deposits, then this is indicative that the mixture is too rich. Should the plug be black and oily, then it is likely that the engine is fairly worn, as well as the mixture being too rich.
9 If the insulator nose is covered with light tan to greyish-brown deposits, then the mixture

is correct and it is likely that the engine is in good condition.
10 If the spark plug has not completed its service interval, it may be refitted, however, check that the condition of the plug and the gap is correct before refitting. If, due to engine condition, the spark plug is not serviceable, it should be renewed.
11 The spark plug gap is of considerable importance as, if it is too large or too small, the size of the spark and its efficiency will be seriously impaired. For best results, the spark plug gap should be as set out in the Specifications at the start of this Chapter. Note that a plus or minus 0.05mm tolerance is acceptable. Note that for vehicles fitted with iridium plugs the gap is not adjustable.

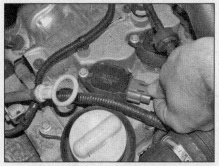

18.3 Unplug the electrical connector from the coil

18.4 Disconnecting the HT leads from the spark plugs – 1.2 engine

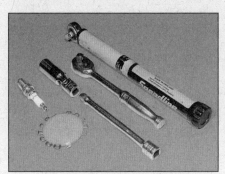

18.6a Tools required for spark plug removal, gap checking and refitting

18.6b Using a special spark plug deep socket to remove the spark plugs

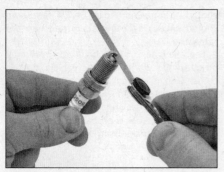

18.12a Measuring the spark plug gap with a feeler blade…

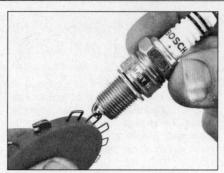

18.12b …and with a wire gauge

HAYNES HiNT

It is very often difficult to insert spark plugs into their holes without cross-threading them. To avoid this possibility, fit a short length of rubber hose over the end of the spark plug. The flexible hose acts as a universal joint to help align the plug with the plug hole. Should the plug begin to cross-thread, the hose will slip on the spark plug, preventing thread damage to the aluminium cylinder head.

12 The spark gap on non iridium plugs is adjustable, however this is not recommended. Measure the gap (see illustrations) and if it is outside the tolerances allowed it should always be replaced and not adjusted.
13 Before fitting the spark plugs, check that the threaded connector sleeves are tight (where applicable), and that the plug exterior surfaces and threads are clean. Apply a little anti-seize compound to the threads.
14 Insert each spark plug into the cylinder head and screw them in by hand, taking extra care to enter the plug threads correctly (see Haynes Hint).
15 Tighten the plugs to the specified torque using the spark plug socket and a torque wrench (see illustration).
16 The spark plug (HT) leads, where applicable, should be checked whenever new spark plugs are fitted. On the 1.2 litre unclip or open the lead holder and release the leads. Ensure that the leads are numbered before removing them, to avoid confusion when refitting. Check inside the end fitting for signs of corrosion, which will look like a white crusty powder. Push the end fitting back onto the spark plug, ensuring that it is a tight fit on the plug. Using a clean rag, wipe the entire length of the lead to remove any built-up dirt and grease. Once the lead is clean, check for burns, cracks and other damage. Do not bend the lead excessively, nor pull the lead lengthwise – the conductor inside might break. Disconnect the other end of the lead, and check for corrosion and a tight fit. If an ohmmeter is available, check the resistance of the lead. Check the remaining leads one at a time.

17 On 0.9 litre engines, refit the ignition HT coils with reference to Chapter 5B Section 3.
18 On models with the 1.2 litre engines, check that the HT leads are correctly located in their retaining clips or holder. Reconnect the HT leads to their respective spark plugs and refit the air filter housing.

19 Air filter element renewal

0.9 litre engines

1 Press the two retaining clips in (one at each side), and withdraw the air filter element and cover from the air cleaner houisng (see illustrations).
2 Lift the filter element from the air filter cage, noting its fitted position (see illustration).
3 Clean the inside of the main body and then insert the new filter element in the cage.
4 Refit the filter element and cage into the housing making sure the cover is located correctly – the bottom must locate securely, and the top must engage correctly to make a good seal.

1.2 litre engines

5 Using a screwdriver, unclip the air inlet hose from the bonnet slam panel (see illustrations).
6 Unclip the transmission breather pipe from the side of the upper housing (see illustration).
7 Disconnect the crankcase ventilation hose from the rear and then slacken the hose clip at the throttle body (see illustrations). Lift off the complete housing.

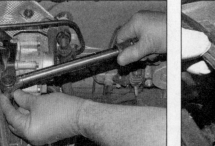

18.15 Use a torque wrench to tighten the spark plugs

19.1a Release the clips…

19.1b …and withdraw the cover and filter

19.2 Remove the filter from the cage

19.5a Release the securing clip...

19.5b ...and release the air inlet hose

19.6 Unclip the transmission breather hose

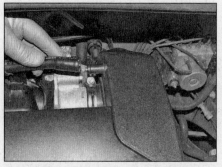

19.7a Disconnect the hose...

19.7b ...slacken the securing clip...

19.7c ...and remove the air cleaner housing

8 Invert the housing, slacken the screws and then remove the air filter element **(see illustrations)**.
9 Refitting is a reversal of removal.

4 The oil level should be up to the lower edge of the filler/level plug aperture **(see illustration)**.

5 If necessary, top-up using the specified type of lubricant until the transmission oil level is correct. Fill the transmission until oil starts

20 Rear brake shoe and drum check

1 Remove the rear brake drums, and check the brake shoes for signs of wear or contamination. At the same time, also inspect the wheel cylinders for signs of leakage, and the brake drum for signs of wear. Refer to the relevant Sections of Chapter 9 for further information.

21 Manual transmission oil level check

1 Either position the vehicle over an inspection pit, or jack up the front and rear of the vehicle and support it on axle stands (see *Jacking and vehicle support*). The vehicle must be level for the check to be accurate.
2 Remove the engine undertray from the bottom of the transmission.
3 Clean the area around the filler/level plug, which is located on the front facing side of the transmission, then unscrew and remove the plug **(see illustration)**.

19.8a Slacken the captive screws...

19.8b ...and lift out the air filter element

21.3 Remove the transmission oil filler/level plug

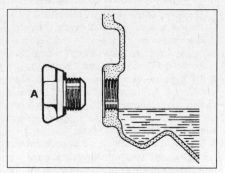

21.4 Manual transmission filler/level plug (A) – correct oil level shown

21.5 Topping-up the transmission fluid

to flow out and allow excess oil to drain **(see illustration)**.

6 Once the transmission oil level is correct, refit the filler/level plug and tighten it securely.

7 Refit the engine undertray cover or transmission bottom cover as applicable, then lower the vehicle to the ground. Note that frequent need for topping-up indicates a leak, possibly through an oil seal. The cause should be investigated and rectified.

22 Front wheel alignment check

1 Refer to the information given in Chapter 10 Section 20.

23 Air conditioning system check

1 The following maintenance checks will ensure that the air conditioner operates at peak efficiency:

a) *Check the auxiliary drivebelt (see Section 9).*

b) *Check the system hoses for damage or leaks.*

c) *Inspect the condenser fins for leaves, insects and other debris. Use a clean paint brush to clean the condenser. The condenser is mounted in front of the radiator.*

d) *Check that the drain tube from the evaporator housing is clear – the hose is located under the facia. Note that it is normal to have clear fluid (water) dripping from this while the system is in operation, to the extent that quite a large puddle can be left under the car when it is parked.*

2 It's a good idea to operate the system for about 30 minutes at least once a month, particularly during the winter. Long term non-use can cause hardening, and subsequent failure, of the seals.

3 The most common cause of poor cooling is simply a low system refrigerant charge. If a noticeable drop in cool air output occurs, the following quick check will help you determine if the refrigerant level is low:

a) *Turn the ignition on.*

b) *Turn the AC off.*

c) *Set the temperature control to minimum.*

d) *Set the blower motor to the maximum speed.*

e) *Select the air recirculation position.*

f) *Turn the air distribution control to the facia vent position.*

g) *Start the engine.*

4 Allow the system to operate for a minimum of 10 minutes and then check the cabin temperature – it should be below ambient temperature and the compressor should cycle on and off.

5 With the compressor engaged – the clutch will make an audible click, and the centre of the clutch will rotate – feel the inlet and outlet pipes at the compressor. One side should be cold, and one hot. If there's no perceptible difference between the two pipes, there's something wrong with the compressor or the system. It might be a low charge – it might be something else. Take the car to a dealer service department or an automotive air conditioning specialist.

24 Road test

Instruments and electrical equipment

1 Check the operation of all instruments and electrical equipment.

2 Make sure that all instruments read correctly, and switch on all electrical equipment in turn, to check that it functions properly.

Steering and suspension

3 Check for any abnormalities in the steering, suspension, handling or road 'feel'.

4 Drive the vehicle, and check that there are no unusual vibrations or noises.

5 Check that the steering feels positive, with no excessive 'sloppiness', or roughness, and check for any suspension noises when cornering and driving over bumps.

Drivetrain

6 Check the performance of the engine, clutch, transmission and driveshafts.

7 Listen for any unusual noises from the engine, clutch and transmission.

8 Make sure that the engine runs smoothly when idling, and that there is no hesitation when accelerating.

9 Check that, where applicable, the clutch action is smooth and progressive, that the drive is taken up smoothly, and that the pedal travel is not excessive. Also listen for any noises when the clutch pedal is depressed.

10 Check that all gears can be engaged smoothly without noise, and that the gear lever action is smooth and not abnormally vague or 'notchy'.

11 On automatic transmission models, make sure that all gearchanges occur smoothly, without snatching, and without an increase in engine speed between changes. Check that all of the gear positions can be selected with the vehicle at rest. If any problems are found, they should be referred to a Renault dealer.

12 Listen for a metallic clicking sound from the front of the vehicle, as the vehicle is driven slowly in a circle with the steering on full lock. Carry out this check in both directions. If a clicking noise is heard, this indicates wear in a driveshaft joint (see Chapter 8 Section 5).

Braking system

13 Make sure that the vehicle does not pull to one side when braking, and that the wheels do not lock when braking hard.

14 Check that there is no vibration through the steering when braking.

15 Check that the handbrake operates correctly, without excessive movement of the lever, and that it holds the vehicle stationary on a slope.

16 Test the operation of the brake servo unit as follows. Depress the footbrake four or five times to exhaust the vacuum, then start the engine. As the engine starts, there should be a noticeable 'give' in the brake pedal as vacuum builds-up. Allow the engine to run for at least two minutes, and then switch it off. If the brake pedal is now depressed again, it should be possible to detect a hiss from the servo as the pedal is depressed. After about four or five applications, no further hissing should be heard, and the pedal should feel considerably harder.

25 Timing belt renewal

1 Refer to Chapter 2B Section 7 (1.2 litre engines).

26 Brake fluid renewal

⚠️ *Warning: Brake hydraulic fluid can harm your eyes and damage painted surfaces, so use extreme caution when handling and pouring it. Do not use fluid that has been standing open for some time, as it absorbs moisture from the air. Excess moisture can cause a dangerous loss of braking effectiveness.*

1 The procedure is similar to that for the bleeding of the hydraulic system as described in Chapter 9 Section 5, except that the brake fluid reservoir should be emptied by siphoning, using a clean poultry baster or similar before starting, and allowance should be made for the old fluid to be expelled when bleeding a section of the circuit.

2 Working as described in Chapter 9 Section 5, open the first bleed screw in the sequence, and pump the brake pedal gently until nearly all the old fluid has been emptied from the master cylinder reservoir. Top up to the MAXI level with new fluid, and continue pumping until only the new fluid remains in the reservoir, and new fluid can be seen emerging from the bleed screw. Tighten the screw, and top the reservoir level up to the MAXI level line.

3 Work through all the remaining bleed screws in sequence until new fluid can be seen at all of them. Be careful to keep the master cylinder reservoir topped-up to above the MINI level at all times, or air may enter the system and greatly increase the length of the task.

4 When the operation is complete, check that all bleed screws are securely tightened, and that their dust caps are refitted. Wash off all traces of spilt fluid, and recheck the master cylinder reservoir fluid level.

5 Check the operation of the brakes before taking the car on the road.

27 Coolant renewal

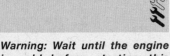

⚠️ *Warning: Wait until the engine is cold before starting this procedure. Do not allow antifreeze to come in contact with your skin, or with the painted surfaces of the vehicle. Rinse off spills immediately with plenty of water. Never leave antifreeze lying around in an open container, or in a puddle in the driveway or on the garage floor. Children and pets are attracted by its sweet smell, but antifreeze can be fatal if ingested.*

Cooling system draining

1 With the engine completely cold, remove the expansion tank filler cap. Turn the cap anti-clockwise, wait until any pressure remaining in the system is released, then unscrew it and lift it off.

2 Where applicable, remove the undertray, then position a container beneath the radiator bottom hose connection.

3 Loosen the hose clip, pull off the hose and allow the coolant to drain into the container **(see illustration)**.

4 To assist draining, open the cooling system bleed screw(s). See the cooling system layouts in Chapter 3, Section 1.

5 When the flow of coolant stops, reposition the container below the cylinder block drain plug where fitted. It is located either on the front left-hand side or rear right-hand side of the cylinder block. Remove the drain plug, and allow the coolant to drain into the container.

6 If the coolant has been drained for a reason other than renewal, then provided it is clean and less than two years old, it can be re-used.

7 Refit the radiator bottom hose and cylinder block drain plug on completion of draining.

Cooling system flushing

8 If coolant renewal has been neglected, or if the antifreeze mixture has become diluted, then in time, the cooling system may gradually lose efficiency, as the coolant passages become restricted due to rust, scale deposits, and other sediment. The cooling system efficiency can be restored by flushing the system clean.

9 The radiator should be flushed independently of the engine, to avoid unnecessary contamination.

Radiator flushing

10 Disconnect the top and bottom hoses and any other relevant hoses from the radiator, with reference to Chapter 3 Section 3.

11 Insert a garden hose into the radiator top inlet. Direct a flow of clean water through the radiator, and continue flushing until clean water emerges from the radiator bottom outlet.

12 If, after a reasonable period, the water still does not run clear, the radiator can be flushed with a good proprietary cleaning agent. It is important that the manufacturer's instructions are followed carefully. If the contamination is particularly bad, insert the hose in the radiator bottom outlet, and reverse flush the radiator.

Engine flushing

13 To flush the engine, first refit the cylinder block drain plug.

14 Remove the thermostat as described in Chapter 3 Section 5, then temporarily refit the top hose at its engine connection.

15 With the top and bottom hoses

27.3 Draining the coolant

disconnected from the radiator, insert a garden hose into the radiator top hose. Direct a clean flow of water through the engine, and continue flushing until clean water emerges from the radiator bottom hose.

16 On completion of flushing, refit the thermostat and reconnect the hoses with reference to Chapter 3 Section 5.

Cooling system filling

17 Before attempting to fill the cooling system, make sure that all hoses and clips are in good condition, and that the clips are tight. Note that an antifreeze mixture must be used all year round, to prevent corrosion of the engine components. Also check that the cylinder block drain plug is in place and tight.

18 Remove the expansion tank filler cap.

19 Open the cooling system bleed screws **(see illustrations)**.

27.19a Bleed screw in heater hose (0.9 litre engine)…

27.19b …and in coolant housing (0.9 litre engine)…

27.19c …also in small hose top right-hand side of radiator (0.9 litre engine)

27.19d Bleed screw in heater hose (1.2 litre engine)…

27.19e ...and in thermostat housing (1.2 litre engine)

20 Slowly fill the system until the coolant level reaches the MAXI mark on the expansion tank.

21 Close the bleed screw(s) when coolant free from air bubbles emerges.

22 Start the engine, and run it at a fast idle speed (do not exceed 1500 rpm) for approximately 4 minutes. Keep the level topped-up to the top of the expansion tank filler neck.

23 Refit and tighten the expansion tank filler cap.

24 Allow the engine to run at 2500 rpm for approximately 15 minutes, until the cooling fan cuts in and out.

25 Stop the engine and allow the engine to cool for at least 30 minutes.

26 Recheck the coolant level with reference to *Weekly checks*. Top-up the level if necessary and refit the expansion tank filler cap. Where applicable, refit the engine undertray.

Antifreeze mixture

27 The antifreeze should always be renewed at the specified intervals. This is necessary not only to maintain the antifreeze properties, but also to prevent corrosion which would otherwise occur as the corrosion inhibitors become progressively less effective.

28 Always use an ethylene-glycol based antifreeze which is suitable for use in mixed-metal cooling systems. The quantity of antifreeze and levels of protection are given in the Specifications.

29 Before adding antifreeze, the cooling system should be completely drained, preferably flushed, and all hoses checked for condition and security.

30 After filling with antifreeze, a label should be attached to the expansion tank, stating the type and concentration of antifreeze used, and the date installed. Any subsequent topping-up should be made with the same type and concentration of antifreeze.

Caution: Do not use engine antifreeze in the windscreen/tailgate washer system, as it will cause damage to the vehicle's paintwork. A screen wash additive should be added to the washer system in the quantities stated on the bottle.

Chapter 1 Part B
Routine maintenance and servicing – diesel models

Contents

Degrees of difficulty

Easy, suitable for novice with little experience 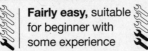 | **Fairly easy,** suitable for beginner with some experience 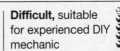 | **Fairly difficult,** suitable for competent DIY mechanic 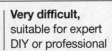 | **Difficult,** suitable for experienced DIY mechanic | **Very difficult,** suitable for expert DIY or professional

Specifications

Lubricants and fluids . . . . Refer to *Weekly checks* on page 0•18

Capacities
Engine oil:
  Including oil filter . . . . 4.5 litres
  Difference between MAX and MIN dipstick marks . . . . Approximately 1.0 litres
Cooling system . . . . 5.5 litres
Manual gearbox . . . . 3.4 litres
Fuel tank . . . . 45 litres

Cooling system

Antifreeze mixture:	Antifreeze	Water
#Protection to –23°C	35%	65%
#Protection to –40°C	50%	50%

Brakes
Front disc brakes:
  Pad thickness (including backing plate):
    New . . . . 17.4 mm
    Minimum thickness . . . . 8.0 mm
Rear disc brakes:
  Pad thickness (including backing plate):
    New . . . . 15.8 mm
    Minimum thickness . . . . 7.5 mm
Rear drum brakes:
  Shoe thickness (including backing plate):
    New . . . . 5.5 mm
    Minimum thickness . . . . 2.4 mm

Torque wrench settings

	Nm	lbf ft
Auxiliary belt tensioner	40	30
Roadwheel bolts	105	77
Sump plug	20	15

1 Maintenance schedule – diesel models

1 The maintenance intervals in this manual are provided with the assumption that you, not the dealer, will be carrying out the work. These are the minimum maintenance intervals recommended by us for vehicles driven daily.

If you wish to keep your vehicle in peak condition at all times, you may wish to perform some of these procedures more often. We encourage frequent maintenance, because it enhances the efficiency, performance and resale value of your vehicle.
2 When the vehicle is new, it should be serviced by a dealer service department (or other workshop recognised by the vehicle manufacturer as providing the same standard of service) in order to preserve the warranty.

The vehicle manufacturer may reject warranty claims if you are unable to prove that servicing has been carried out as and when specified, using only original equipment parts or parts certified to be of equivalent quality.
3 If the vehicle is driven in dusty areas, used to tow a trailer, or driven frequently at slow speeds (idling in traffic) or on short journeys, more frequent maintenance intervals are recommended.

Every 250 miles or weekly
☐ Refer to *Weekly checks*

Every 9000 miles
☐ Renew the engine oil and filter (Section 4)

Note: *Frequent oil and filter changes are good for the engine. We recommend changing the oil at the mileage specified here, or at least once a year.*

Every 18 000 miles or 2 years, whichever comes first
In addition to all the items listed previously, carry out the following:
☐ Renew the air filter element (Section 5)
☐ Renew the pollen filter (Section 6)
☐ Check the handbrake (Section 7)
☐ Check the brake pads and discs (Section 8)
☐ Check the operation of the clutch (Section 9)
☐ Check the condition of the auxiliary drivebelt (Section 10)
☐ Check the condition of the seat belts (Section 11)
☐ Check the operation of all electrical systems (Section 12)
☐ Check the condition of the exhaust system and mountings (Section 13)
☐ Check the suspension and steering components (Section 14)
☐ Check all underbonnet components and hoses for fluid leaks (Section 15)
☐ Check the tightness of the roadwheel bolts (Section 16)
☐ Check the bodywork and underbody for damage and corrosion (Section 17)
☐ Check the front and rear shock absorbers (Section 18)

Every 36 000 miles or 4 years, whichever comes first
In addition to all the items listed previously, carry out the following:
☐ Renew the fuel filter element (Section 19)
☐ Check the rear brake shoes and drums (Section 20)
☐ Check the manual transmission oil level (Section 21)
☐ Check the front wheel alignment (Section 22)
☐ Check the operation of the air conditioning system (Section 23)
☐ Carry out a road test (Section 24)
☐ Renew the timing belt (Section 25)*
☐ Renew the brake fluid (Section 26)
☐ Renew the coolant (Section 27)

Note: *Although the normal interval for timing belt renewal is 72 000 miles, it is strongly recommended that the interval is reduced to 36 000 miles on vehicles which are subjected to intensive use, ie, mainly short journeys or a lot of stop-start driving. The actual belt renewal interval is therefore very much up to the individual owner, but bear in mind that severe engine damage may result if the belt breaks.*

Underbonnet view

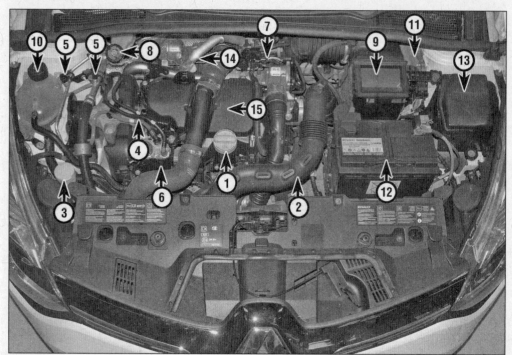

1 Engine oil filler cap/level dipstick
2 Air intake ducting
3 Screen washer fluid reservoir
4 Low pressure fuel lines
5 AC Service ports
6 High pressure fuel injection pump
7 EGR valve
8 Brake fluid reservoir
9 Air filter element
10 Coolant expansion tank
11 Electronic Control Unit (ECU)
12 Battery
13 Relay plate and fusebox
14 Turbocharger
15 Fuel injectors (under cover)

Front underbody view

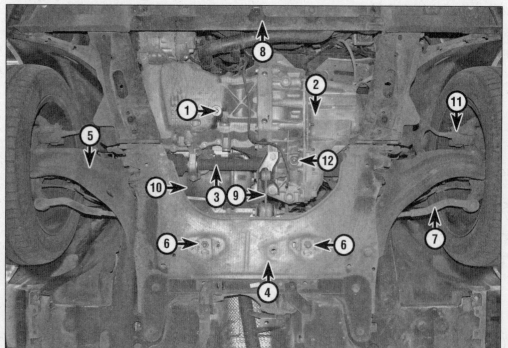

1 Engine oil drain plug
2 Manual transmission
3 Driveshafts
4 Front suspension subframe
5 Front suspension lower arms
6 Anti-roll bar mounting bolts
7 Track rod ends
8 Radiator support panel (subframe)
9 Engine steady bar (torque rod)
10 Catalytic converter
11 Brake calipers
12 Transmission drain plug

Rear underbody view

1 Fuel tank
2 Handbrake cables
3 Brake flexible hoses
4 Rear axle assembly
5 Rear coil springs
6 Exhaust rear silencer and tailpipe
7 Exhaust mounting
8 Shock absorbers
9 Rear axle mounting bushes

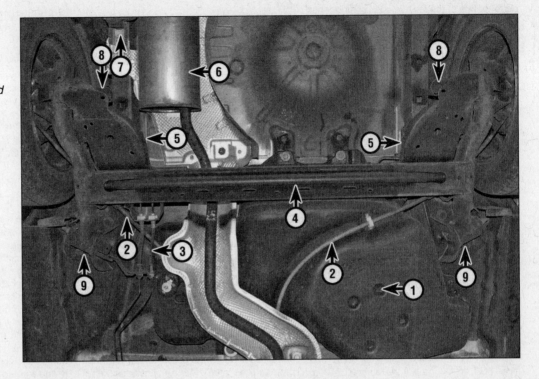

Maintenance procedures

2 Introduction

1 This Chapter is designed to help the home mechanic maintain his/her vehicle for safety, economy, long life and peak performance.

2 The Chapter contains a master maintenance schedule, followed by Sections dealing specifically with each task in the schedule. Visual checks, adjustments, component renewal and other helpful items are included. Refer to the accompanying illustrations of the engine compartment and the underside of the vehicle for the locations of the various components.

3 Servicing your vehicle in accordance with the mileage/time maintenance schedule and the following Sections will provide a planned maintenance programme, which should result in a long and reliable service life. This is a comprehensive plan, so maintaining some items but not others at the specified service intervals will not produce the same results.

4 As you service your vehicle, you will discover that many of the procedures can – and should – be grouped together, because of the particular procedure being performed, or because of the proximity of two otherwise unrelated components to one another. For example, if the vehicle is raised for any reason, the exhaust can be inspected at the

same time as the suspension and steering components.

5 The first step in this maintenance programme is to prepare yourself before the actual work begins. Read through all the Sections relevant to the work to be carried out, then make a list and gather all the parts and tools required. If a problem is encountered, seek advice from a parts specialist, or a dealer service department.

Warning lights and service indicator

6 All of the models covered in this manual have a sophisticated fault warning system fitted. The spanner symbol will illuminate, and on most models a message will be displayed pointing towards the possible fault. Serious faults will also bring on the STOP warning light. If only the spanner symbol is displayed it is generally safe to continue driving, although the fault should be investigated at the earliest opportunity. If the STOP message illuminates, stop as soon as it is safe to do so.

7 Most models in this manual are also fitted with Renault's 'oil control system' (OCS). The OCS monitors several parameters, in an attempt to calculate the time for an oil change based on time as well as distance covered. This calculation takes into account driving style, number of starts, time spent idling, average speed and coolant temperature. The information display shows the distance to

the next service. When the service is due the spanner symbol will flash and 'Service vehicle' appears in the display.

8 To reset the display turn the ignition on and hold down one of the reset buttons (on the end of the windscreen wiper switch) for 10 seconds until the display stops flashing. If it is decided to change the oil (and filter) before the calculated service interval do not reset the display. This prevents the interval for other service parts from being exceeded.

3 Regular maintenance

1 If, from the time the vehicle is new, the routine maintenance schedule is followed closely, and frequent checks are made of fluid levels and high wear items, as suggested throughout this manual, the engine will be kept in relatively good running condition, and the need for additional work will be minimised.

2 It is possible that there will be times when the engine is running poorly due to the lack of regular maintenance. This is even more likely if a used vehicle, which has not received regular and frequent maintenance checks, is purchased. In such cases, additional work may need to be carried out, outside of the regular maintenance intervals.

3 If engine wear is suspected, a compression

test (refer to Chapter 2C Section 2) will provide valuable information regarding the overall performance of the main internal components. Such a test can be used as a basis to decide on the extent of the work to be carried out. If, for example, a compression test indicates serious internal engine wear, conventional maintenance as described in this Chapter will not greatly improve the performance of the engine, and may prove a waste of time and money, unless extensive overhaul work is carried out first.

4 The following series of operations are those most often required to improve the performance of a generally poor running engine:

Primary operations

a) Clean, inspect and test the battery (refer to 'Weekly checks').
b) Check all the engine related fluids (refer to 'Weekly checks').
c) Check the condition of the auxiliary drivebelt (Section 10).
d) Check the condition of all hoses, and check for fluid leaks (Section 15).
e) Check the condition of the air filter, and renew if necessary (Section 5).
f) Check the fuel filter, and renew if necessary (Section 19).

5 If the above operations do not prove fully effective, carry out the following secondary operations:

Secondary operations

6 All items listed under Primary operations, plus the following:
a) Check the charging system (refer to Chapter 5A Section 5).
b) Check the preheating system (refer to Chapter 5C Section 1).
c) Check the fuel system (refer to Chapter 4A).

Every 9000 miles

4 Engine oil and filter renewal

Note: Refer to Section 2 for information on resetting the service indicator.

1 Before starting this procedure, gather together all the necessary tools and materials **(see illustration)**. Also make sure that you have plenty of clean rags and newspapers handy to mop-up any spills. Ideally, the engine oil should be warm, as it will drain better and more built up sludge will be removed with it. Take care, however, not to touch the exhaust or any other hot parts of the engine when working under the vehicle. To avoid any possibility of scalding, and to protect yourself from possible skin irritants and other harmful contaminants in used engine oils, it is advisable to wear rubber gloves when carrying out this work. Apply the handbrake, then jack up the front of the vehicle and support it on axle stands (see Jacking and vehicle support). Alternatively, raise the vehicle on a lift or drive it onto ramps. Whichever method is chosen, make sure that the car remains as level as possible, to enable the oil to drain fully. Remove the engine undertray where applicable.

2 Remove the oil filler cap, which also has the dipstick attached to it, then position a suitable container beneath the sump. Clean the drain plug and the area around it, then slacken it half a turn using the special drain plug key or socket **(see illustrations)**.

3 Allow some time for the old oil to drain, noting that it may be necessary to reposition the container as the oil flow slows to a trickle.

4 After all the oil has drained, wipe off the drain plug with a clean rag and renew its sealing washer **(see illustration)**. Clean the area around the drain plug opening, then refit and tighten the plug securely.

5 Move the container into position under the oil filter, located on the front of the cylinder block **(see illustration)**.

6 Using an oil filter removal tool, slacken the filter initially **(see illustrations)**. Access is difficult and the tool will have to be worked around the radiator hoses. Loosely wrap some rags around the oil filter, then unscrew it and immediately position it with its open end uppermost to prevent further spillage of oil. Remove the oil filter from the engine compartment and empty the oil into the container.

7 Use a clean rag to remove all oil, dirt and

4.1 Tools and materials necessary for the engine oil change and filter renewal

4.2a Remove the oil filler cap/dipstick

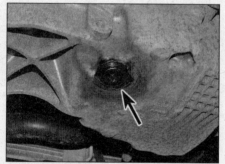

4.2b The engine oil drain plug

4.4 Always fit a new sealing washer

4.5 Oil filter location on the front of the engine

4.6a Slackening the oil filter with a removal tool

4.6b Remove the oil filter

4.8 Applying clean oil to the seal

4.10 Use a funnel to prevent spillage

sludge from the filter sealing area on the engine. Check the old filter to make sure that the rubber sealing ring hasn't stuck to the engine. If it has, carefully remove it.

8 Apply a light coating of clean oil to the sealing ring on the new filter, then screw it into position on the engine (see illustration). Tighten the filter firmly by hand only – do not use any tools. Wipe clean the exterior of the oil filter.

9 Remove the old oil and all tools from under the car and then lower the car to the ground.

10 Fill the engine with the specified quantity and grade of oil, as described in *Weekly checks*. Pour the oil in slowly, otherwise it may overflow from the top of the valve cover (see illustration). Check that the oil level is up to the maximum mark on the dipstick, then refit and tighten the oil filler cap.

11 Start the engine and run it for a few minutes, checking that there are no leaks around the oil filter seal and the sump drain plug. Note that when the engine is first started, there will be a delay of a few seconds before the oil pressure warning light goes out while the new filter fills with oil. Do not race the engine while the warning light is on.

12 Switch off the engine and wait a few minutes for the oil to settle in the sump once more. With the new oil circulated and the filter now completely full, recheck the level on the dipstick and add more oil if necessary.

13 Apply the handbrake and then once again jack up the front of the vehicle and support it on axle stands (see *Jacking and vehicle support*). Check again for leaks around the sump drain plug and oil filter and then refit the engine undershield. Lower the vehicle to the ground and make a final check of the oil level, topping up as required.

14 Dispose of the used engine oil safely with reference to General repair procedures in the Reference section of this manual.

Every 18 000 miles or 2 years

5 Air filter element renewal

1 Press the two retaining clips in (one at each side), and withdraw the air filter element and cover from the air cleaner houisng (see illustrations).

2 Lift the filter element from the air filter cage, noting its fitted position (see illustration).

3 Clean the inside of the main body and then insert the new filter element in the cage.

4 Refit the filter element and cage into the housing making sure the cover is located correctly – the bottom must locate securely, and the top must engage correctly to make a good seal.

6 Pollen filter renewal

1 The pollen filter is located in the left-hand side rear of the air distribution unit (see illustration).

2 The filter can be removed by working inside the passenger side footwell and reaching up behind the glovebox, to the rear of the heater housing.

5.1a Release the clips...

5.1b ...and withdraw the cover and filter

5.2 Remove the filter from the cage

6.1 Pollen filter location

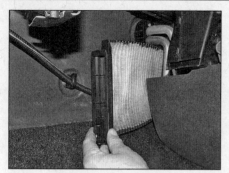

6.3 Withdraw the filter

3 Note the orientation of the filter, as it is withdrawn, unclip the plastic cover and then carefully extract the filter element by sliding it out from the housing **(see illustration)**.

4 Fit the new element using a reversal of the removal procedure, but make sure that the air flow direction arrows on the filter, are in the same direction as noted on removal.

7 Handbrake check

1 The handbrake should be capable of holding the parked vehicle stationary, even on steep slopes, when applied with moderate force. The mechanism should be firm and positive in feel, with no trace of stiffness or sponginess from the cables, and should release immediately the handbrake lever is released. If the mechanism is faulty in any of these respects, it must be checked immediately as follows. Note: On models with rear drum brakes, if the handbrake is not functioning correctly or is incorrectly adjusted, the rear brake self-adjust mechanism will not function. This will lead to the brake pedal travel becoming excessive as the shoe linings wear.

2 Handbrake adjustment is made from inside the vehicle on the cable adjuster nut **(see illustration)**.

3 Remove the rear section of the centre console, as described in Chapter 11 Section 27 to access the adjuster nut.

4 Jack up the rear of the vehicle and support it on axle stands (see *Jacking and vehicle support*).

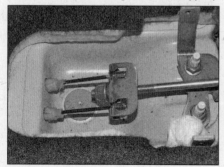

7.2 Handbrake cable adjusting nut

Models with rear drum brakes

5 Remove both rear brake drums as described in Chapter 9 Section 11.

6 Check that the knurled adjuster wheel on the adjuster strut is free to rotate in both directions. If it is seized, the brake shoes and strut must be removed and overhauled as described in Chapter 9 Section 12.

7 If all is well, back off the adjuster wheel by five or six teeth so that the diameter of the brake shoes is slightly reduced.

8 Check that the handbrake cables slide freely by pulling on their front ends. Also check that the operating levers on the rear brake trailing shoes return to their correct positions, with their stop-pegs in contact with the edge of the trailing shoe web.

9 With the aid of an assistant, tighten the adjuster nut on the handbrake lever operating rod so that the lever on each rear brake assembly starts to move as the handbrake is moved between the first and second notch (click) of its ratchet mechanism. This is the case when the stop-pegs are still in contact with the shoes when the handbrake is on the first notch of the ratchet, but no longer contact the shoes when the handbrake is on the second notch.

10 Refit the brake drums as described in Chapter 9 Section 11, then lower the vehicle to the ground.

11 With the vehicle standing on its wheels, repeatedly depress the footbrake to adjust the shoe-to-drum clearance. Whilst depressing the pedal, have an assistant listen to the rear drums to check that the adjuster strut mechanism is functioning; if this is so, a clicking sound will be heard from the adjuster strut as the pedal is depressed.

12 Lower the vehicle to the ground and refit the centre console.

Models with rear disc brakes

13 Check that the handbrake cables slide freely by pulling on their front ends, and check that the operating levers on the rear brake calipers move smoothly.

14 Move both of the caliper operating levers as far rearwards as possible, then tighten the adjuster nut on the handbrake lever cable until all free play is removed from both cables. With the aid of an assistant, adjust the nut so that the operating lever on each rear brake

For a quick check, the thickness of friction material remaining on each brake pad can be measured through the aperture in the caliper body.

caliper starts to move as the handbrake lever is moved between the first and second notch (click) of its ratchet mechanism.

15 Lower the vehicle to the ground and refit the centre console.

8 Brake pad and disc check

Note: *Drum brake checks are in Section 20.*
1 Firmly apply the handbrake, then jack up the front or rear of the vehicle (as applicable) and support it securely on axle stands (see *Jacking and vehicle support*). Remove the roadwheels.

2 For a quick check, the thickness of friction material remaining on each brake pad can be measured through the aperture in the caliper body (see Haynes Hint). If any pad's friction material is worn to the specified thickness or less, all four pads must be renewed as a set. Pad wear warning contacts are fitted to the inboard pads, but this should not be used as an excuse for omitting a visual check.

3 For a comprehensive check, the brake pads should be removed and cleaned. This will allow the operation of the caliper to be checked, and the brake disc itself to be fully examined for condition on both sides. Refer to Chapter 9 Section 8 for further information.

9 Clutch check

1 Check that the clutch pedal moves smoothly and easily through its full travel, and that the clutch itself functions correctly, with no trace of slip or drag.

2 Check the brake fluid level. The brake fluid reservoir supplies the clutch hydraulic system. The level will drop slightly as the clutch and brake components wear.

3 A dramatic fall in the level should be investigated immediately as it could be a hydraulic leak in the clutch system, or the brake system.

10 Auxiliary drivebelt check and renewal

Note: *Renault recommend that the belt is always renewed if it is removed. A new tensioner must also be fitted. The belt and tensioner should be renewed every 72 000 miles or 5 years regardless of condition.*

Checking

1 The auxiliary drivebelt is located on the right-hand side of the engine.

2 Due to their function and material makeup, drivebelts are prone to failure after a period of time and should therefore be inspected, and if necessary adjusted periodically.

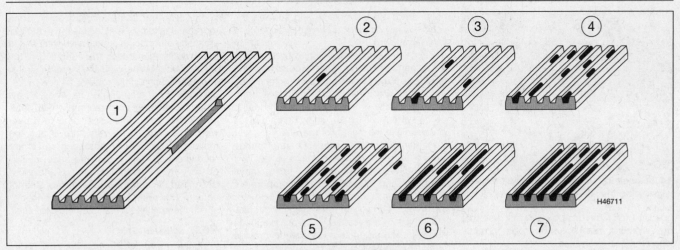

10.6 Check for drivebelt wear

1   If sections are missing renew the belt
2   Small deposits in the grooves are not a concern
3   Small scattered deposits are not a concern
4   Deposits up to half of the rib height: renew the belt if noisy
5   Deposits up to half the rib height: renew the belt if noisy
6   Heavy deposits: renew the belt
7   Heavy deposits: renew the belt

3 A basic check for obvious faults can be made from the engine compartment. However, because the belt runs very close to the right hand inner wing a through inspection can only be made from below.

4 Jack up the front of the car, and support it on axle stands (see *Jacking and vehicle support*). Remove the right-hand wheel and the wing liner.

5 Unbolt and remove the outer protective cover from the fuel filter. Lift up the fuel filter and move it aside – secure it to the inner wing if necessary. Unbolt and remove the inner protective cover.

6 With the engine stopped, inspect the full length of the drivebelt for cracks and separation of the belt plies **(see illustration)**. It will be necessary to turn the engine (using a spanner or socket and bar on the crankshaft pulley bolt) in order to move the belt from the pulleys so that the belt can be inspected thoroughly. Twist the belt between the pulleys so that both sides can be viewed. Also, check for fraying and glazing which gives the belt a shiny appearance. Check the pulleys for nicks, cracks, distortion and corrosion.

Renewal

Note: *Before removal of the belt, note the fitted position. On some models, the compressor pulley has six grooves, the belt has five. In this case the inner groove is left unused, so that the run of the belt is straight.*

Automatic tensioner

7 Using a spanner on the outer nut on the tensioner, turn the tensioner clockwise to release the tension on the belt **(see illustrations)**, then lift the drivebelt from the pulleys, noting its fitted position.

8 If the belt is removed it must be renewed.

9 Unbolt the tensioner unit and fit a new one. Tighten the single bolt to the specified torque.

10 Using the spanner on the outer nut on the tensioner, hold the tensioner clockwise, to allow the new belt to be fitted around the pulleys, making sure that it is correctly located in the grooves.

11 Fit a socket to the crankshaft pulley and rotate the engine several times to check the belt alignment.

12 Refit the fuel filter inner protector, filter and outer cover. Refit the wing liner and wheel. Lower the vehicle to the ground.

Manual tensioner

Note: *A special belt tool is used by Renault technicians to tension the belt correctly.*

13 Loosen the pivot bolt and the adjustment bolt on the tensioner. Push the tensioner upwards and nip up the aduster bolt. Remove the belt.

14 Unbolt the tensioner and fit a new one. Do not fully tighten the bolts at this stage. They should be just done up enough to allow the tensioner to rotate. Fit the new belt.

15 If the specialist tool is available, adjust the tension to give a reading of 254 ± 11 Hertz. If the reading is not within the tolerances given, then readjust the tension.

16 If the specialist tool is not available, adjust the tensioner so that it is just possible to twist the belt through 90° in the middle of the longest belt run. If there are any concerns regarding the belt tension, have it checked by a Renault dealer, or garage with suitable equipment.

17 Run the engine for about 5 minutes, then recheck the tension.

18 Refit the fuel filter inner protector, filter and outer cover. Refit the wing liner and wheel. Lower the vehicle to the ground.

11 Seat belt check

1 Carefully examine the seat belt webbing for cuts, or any signs of serious fraying or deterioration. If the belt is of the retractable type, pull the belt all the way out of the inertia reel, and examine the full extent of the webbing.

2 Fasten and unfasten the belt, ensuring that the locking mechanism holds securely, and releases properly when intended. If the

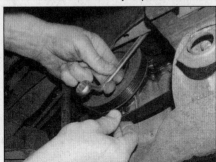

10.7a Turning the spanner clockwise from under the vehicle...

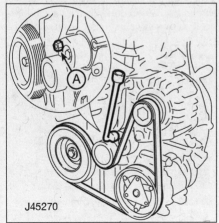

10.7b...or from above, using hexagon (A) on the tensioner pulley

14.3 Check for wear in the hub bearings by grasping the wheel and trying to rock it

belt is of the retractable type, check also that the retracting mechanism operates correctly when the belt is released.

3 Check the security of all seat belt mountings and attachments which are accessible without removing any trim or other components.

12 Electrical systems check

1 Check the operation of all electrical equipment, ie, lights, direction indicators, horn, etc. Refer to the appropriate Sections of Chapter 12 for details if any of the circuits are found to be inoperative.

2 Note that stop-light switch adjustment is described in Chapter 9 Section 19.

3 Visually check all accessible wiring connectors, harnesses and retaining clips for security, and for signs of chafing or damage. Rectify any faults found.

13 Exhaust system check

1 With the engine cold (at least an hour after the vehicle has been driven), check the complete exhaust system from the engine to the end of the tailpipe. Ideally, the inspection should be carried out with the vehicle on a hoist to permit unrestricted access, but if a

A leak in the cooling system will usually show up as white- or antifreeze-coloured deposits on the area adjoining the leak.

hoist is not available, raise and support the vehicle safely on axle stands (see *Jacking and vehicle support*).

2 Check the exhaust pipes and connections for evidence of leaks, severe corrosion and damage. Make sure that all brackets and mountings are in good condition and tight. Leakage at any of the joints or in other parts of the system will usually show up as a black sooty stain in the vicinity of the leak.

3 Rattles and other noises can often be traced to the exhaust system, especially the brackets and mountings. Try to move the pipes and silencers. If the components can come into contact with the body or suspension parts, secure the system with new mountings or if possible, separate the joints and twist the pipes as necessary to provide additional clearance.

4 Run the engine at idling speed. Have an assistant place a cloth or rag over the rear end of the exhaust pipe, and listen for any escape of exhaust gases that would indicate a leak.

5 On completion, lower the car to the ground.

14 Suspension and steering check

Front suspension and steering

1 Raise the front of the vehicle, and securely support it on axle stands (see *Jacking and vehicle support*).

2 Visually inspect the balljoint dust covers and the steering rack and pinion gaiters for splits, chafing or deterioration. Any wear of these components will cause loss of lubricant, together with dirt and water entry, resulting in rapid deterioration of the balljoints or steering gear.

3 Grasp the roadwheel at the 12 o'clock and 6 o'clock positions, and try to rock it **(see illustration)**. Very slight free play may be felt, but if the movement is appreciable, further investigation is necessary to determine the source. Continue rocking the wheel while an assistant depresses the footbrake. If the movement is now eliminated or significantly reduced, it is likely that the hub bearings are at fault. If the free play is still evident with the footbrake depressed, then there is wear in the suspension joints or mountings.

4 Now grasp the wheel at the 9 o'clock and 3 o'clock positions, and try to rock it as before. Any movement felt now may again be caused by wear in the hub bearings or the steering track rod balljoints. If the outer balljoint is worn, the visual movement will be obvious. If the inner joint is suspect, it can be felt by placing a hand over the rack and pinion rubber gaiter and gripping the track rod. If the wheel is now rocked, movement will be felt at the inner joint if wear has taken place.

5 Using a large screwdriver or flat bar, check for wear in the suspension mounting bushes by levering between the relevant suspension

component and its attachment point. Some movement is to be expected, as the mountings are made of rubber, but excessive wear should be obvious. Also check the condition of any visible rubber bushes, looking for splits, cracks or contamination of the rubber.

6 With the car standing on its wheels, have an assistant turn the steering wheel back-and-forth, about an eighth of a turn each way. There should be very little, if any, lost movement between the steering wheel and roadwheels. If this is not the case, closely observe the joints and mountings previously described. In addition, check the steering column universal joints for wear, and also check the rack and pinion steering gear itself.

Rear suspension

7 Chock the front wheels, then jack up the rear of the vehicle and support securely on axle stands (see *Jacking and vehicle support*).

8 Working as described previously for the front suspension, check the rear hub bearings, the suspension bushes and the shock absorber mountings for wear. Note: The handbrake will need to be in the released position before checking the rear wheel bearings.

15 Hose and fluid leak check

1 Visually inspect the engine joint faces, gaskets and seals for any signs of water or oil leaks. Pay particular attention to the areas around the valve cover, cylinder head, oil filter and sump joint faces. Bear in mind that, over a period of time, some very slight seepage from these areas is to be expected – what you are really looking for is any indication of a serious leak. Should a leak be found, renew the offending gasket or oil seal by referring to the appropriate Chapters in this manual.

2 Also check the security and condition of all the engine related pipes and hoses, and all hydraulic and braking system pipes and hoses. Ensure that all cable ties or securing clips are in place, and in good condition. Clips which are broken or missing can lead to chafing of the hoses, pipes or wiring, which could cause more serious problems in the future.

3 Carefully check the radiator hoses and heater hoses along their entire length. Renew any hose which is cracked, swollen or deteriorated. Cracks will show up better if the hose is squeezed. Pay close attention to the hose clips that secure the hoses to the cooling system components. Hose clips can pinch and puncture hoses, resulting in cooling system leaks. If the crimped type hose clips are used, it may be a good idea to renew them with standard worm drive clips.

4 Inspect all the cooling system components (hoses, joint faces, etc) for leaks **(see Haynes Hint)**. Where any problems are found on system components, renew the component or gasket with reference to Chapter 3.

5 With the vehicle raised, inspect the fuel tank and filler neck for punctures, cracks and other damage. The connection between the filler neck and tank is especially critical. Sometimes a rubber filler neck or connecting hose will leak due to loose retaining clamps or deteriorated rubber.

6 Carefully check all rubber hoses and metal fuel lines leading away from the fuel tank. Check for loose connections, deteriorated hoses, crimped lines, and other damage. Pay particular attention to the vent pipes and hoses, which often loop up around the filler neck and can become blocked or crimped. Follow the lines to the front of the vehicle, carefully inspecting them all the way. Renew damaged sections as necessary. Similarly, whilst the vehicle is raised, take the opportunity to inspect all underbody brake fluid pipes and hoses.

7 From within the engine compartment, check the security of all fuel, vacuum and brake hose attachments and pipe unions, and inspect all hoses for kinks, chafing and deterioration.

16 Roadwheel bolt check

1 Remove the wheel trims, where applicable, then slacken the roadwheel bolts slightly.
2 Tighten the bolts to the specified torque, using a torque wrench.

17 Bodywork and underbody condition check

1 Once the car has been washed and all tar spots and other surface blemishes have been cleaned off, carefully check all paintwork, looking closely for chips or scratches. Pay particular attention to vulnerable areas such as the front panels (bonnet and spoiler), and around the wheel arches. Any damage to the paintwork must be rectified as soon as possible to comply with the terms of the manufacturer's anti-corrosion warranties; check with a Renault dealer for details.
2 If a chip or light scratch is found which is recent and still free from rust, it can be touched up using the appropriate touch up stick which can be obtained from Renault dealers. Any more serious damage, or rusted stone chips, can be repaired as described in Chapter 11 Section 4, but if damage or corrosion is so severe that a panel must be renewed, seek professional advice as soon as possible.
3 Always check that the door and ventilation opening drain holes and pipes are completely clear, so that water can drain out.
4 The wax-based underbody protective coating should be inspected annually, preferably just prior to Winter, when the underbody should be washed down as thoroughly as possible without

disturbing the protective coating (see Chapter 11, Section 2, regarding the use of steam cleaners). Any damage to the coating should be repaired using a suitable wax-based sealer. If any of the body panels are disturbed for repair or renewal, do not forget to renew the coating and to inject wax into door panels, sills and box sections, to maintain the level of protection provided by the vehicle manufacturer.

18 Shock absorber check

1 Viewing over the roadwheels into the wheel arches, check for any signs of fluid leakage around the front and rear shock absorber bodies, or from the rubber gaiters around the piston rods. Should any fluid be noticed, the shock absorber is defective internally, and should be renewed. Note: Shock absorbers should always be renewed in pairs on the same axle.
2 The efficiency of the shock absorber may be checked by bouncing the vehicle at each corner. Generally speaking, the body will return to its normal position and stop after being depressed. If it rises and returns on a rebound, the shock absorber is probably suspect. Also examine the shock absorber upper and lower mountings for any signs of wear.

Every 36 000 miles or 4 years

19 Fuel filter renewal

1 Jack up the front of the car, and support it on axle stands (see *Jacking and vehicle support*).
2 Remove the right-hand wheel and the wing liner **(see illustration)**.
3 Undo the three securing nuts and remove the metal protective cover from the fuel filter **(see illustrations)**.
4 Have a suitable container ready to catch any fuel that spills from the filter.
5 Undo the drain plug from the bottom of the filter **(see illustration)**, fit a drain tube (piece of screen washer tube) to the drain plug to help catch the fuel in the container. Where applicable, disconnect the wiring connector for the water sensor on the base of the filter housing.
6 Lift the filter off its mounting and then, disconnect the wiring connector and fuel lines **(see illustrations)**, from the top of the filter assembly. Remove the filter from the vehicle. If the filter is not to be replaced immediately seal the open fuel lines.
7 Refitting is a reversal of removal, noting the following points:

19.2 Remove the liner

19.3a Undo the three securing nuts...

19.3b ...and remove the protective cover

19.5 Unscrew the drain plug at the base of the filter

19.6a Lift the filter off the mounting...

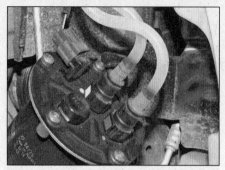

19.6b ...and disconnect the fuel lines and wiring connector

a) Starting the engine, will be considerably easier if the new filter is first filled with fresh diesel.
b) Make sure the wiring connectors are all secure.
c) Start the engine and check for leaks, from the fuel pipes, before refitting the inner wheel arch liner.

20 Rear brake shoe and drum check

1 Remove the rear brake drums, and check the brake shoes for signs of wear or contamination. At the same time, also inspect the wheel cylinders for signs of leakage, and the brake drum for signs of wear. Refer to the relevant Sections of Chapter 9 for further information.

21 Manual transmission oil level check

1 Either position the vehicle over an inspection pit, or jack up the front and rear of the vehicle and support it on axle stands (see Jacking and vehicle support). The vehicle must be level for the check to be accurate.
2 Remove the engine undertray from the bottom of the transmission.
3 Clean the area around the filler/level plug located on the front facing side of the

transmission, then unscrew and remove the plug (see illustration).
4 The oil level should be up to the lower edge of the filler/level plug aperture (see illustration).
5 If necessary, top-up using the specified type of lubricant until the transmission oil level is correct. Fill the transmission until oil starts to flow out and allow excess oil to drain (see illustration).
6 Once the transmission oil level is correct, refit the filler/level plug and tighten it securely.
7 Refit the engine undertray cover or transmission bottom cover as applicable, then lower the vehicle to the ground. Note that frequent need for topping-up indicates a leak, possibly through an oil seal. The cause should be investigated and rectified.

22 Front wheel alignment check

1 Refer to the information given in Chapter 10 Section 20.

23 Air conditioning system check

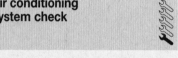

1 The following maintenance checks will ensure that the air conditioner operates at peak efficiency:

a) Check the auxiliary drivebelt (see Section 10).
b) Check the system hoses for damage or leaks.
c) Inspect the condenser fins for leaves, insects and other debris. Use a clean paint brush to clean the condenser. The condenser is mounted in front of the radiator.
d) Check that the drain tube from the evaporator housing is clear – the hose is located under the facia. Note that it is normal to have clear fluid (water) dripping from this while the system is in operation, to the extent that quite a large puddle can be left under the car when it is parked.
2 It's a good idea to operate the system for about 30 minutes at least once a month, particularly during the winter. Long term non-use can cause hardening, and subsequent failure, of the seals.
3 The most common cause of poor cooling is simply a low system refrigerant charge. If a noticeable drop in cool air output occurs, the following quick check will help you determine if the refrigerant level is low:
a) Turn the ignition on.
b) Turn the AC off.
c) Set the temperature control to minimum.
d) Set the blower motor to the maximum speed.
e) Select the air recirculation position.
f) Turn the air distribution control to the facia vent position.
g) Start the engine.
4 Allow the system to operate for a minimum of 10 minutes and then check the cabin temperature – it should be below ambient temperature and the compressor should cycle on and off.
5 With the compressor engaged – the clutch will make an audible click, and the centre of the clutch will rotate – feel the inlet and outlet pipes at the compressor. One side should be cold, and one hot. If there's no perceptible difference between the two pipes, there's something wrong with the compressor or the system. It might be a low charge – it might be something else. Take the car to a dealer service department or an automotive air conditioning specialist.

21.3 Remove the transmission oil filler/ level plug

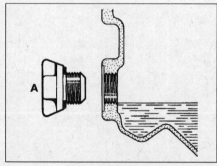

21.4 Manual transmission filler/level plug (A) – correct oil level shown

21.5 Topping-up the transmission fluid

24 Road test

Instruments and electrical equipment

1 Check the operation of all instruments and electrical equipment.
2 Make sure that all instruments read correctly, and switch on all electrical equipment in turn, to check that it functions properly.

Steering and suspension

3 Check for any abnormalities in the steering, suspension, handling or road 'feel'.
4 Drive the vehicle, and check that there are no unusual vibrations or noises.
5 Check that the steering feels positive, with no excessive 'sloppiness', or roughness, and check for any suspension noises when cornering and driving over bumps.

Drivetrain

6 Check the performance of the engine, clutch, transmission and driveshafts.
7 Listen for any unusual noises from the engine, clutch and transmission.
8 Make sure that the engine runs smoothly when idling, and that there is no hesitation when accelerating.
9 Check that the clutch action is smooth and progressive, that the drive is taken up smoothly, and that the pedal travel is not excessive. Also listen for any noises when the clutch pedal is depressed.
10 Check that all gears can be engaged smoothly without noise, and that the gear lever action is smooth and not abnormally vague or 'notchy'.
11 Listen for a metallic clicking sound from the front of the vehicle, as the vehicle is driven slowly in a circle with the steering on full lock. Carry out this check in both directions. If a clicking noise is heard, this indicates wear in a driveshaft joint (see Chapter 8 Section 5).

Braking system

12 Make sure that the vehicle does not pull to one side when braking, and that the wheels do not lock when braking hard.

13 Check that there is no vibration through the steering when braking.
14 Check that the handbrake operates correctly, without excessive movement of the lever, and that it holds the vehicle stationary on a slope.
15 Test the operation of the brake servo unit as follows. Depress the footbrake four or five times to exhaust the vacuum, then start the engine. As the engine starts, there should be a noticeable 'give' in the brake pedal as vacuum builds-up. Allow the engine to run for at least two minutes, and then switch it off. If the brake pedal is now depressed again, it should be possible to detect a hiss from the servo as the pedal is depressed. After about four or five applications, no further hissing should be heard, and the pedal should feel considerably harder.

25 Timing belt renewal

1 Refer to Chapter 2C Section 6.

26 Brake fluid renewal

⚠ *Warning: Brake hydraulic fluid can harm your eyes and damage painted surfaces, so use extreme caution when handling and pouring it. Do not use fluid that has been standing open for some time, as it absorbs moisture from the air. Excess moisture can cause a dangerous loss of braking effectiveness.*

1 The procedure is similar to that for the bleeding of the hydraulic system as described in Chapter 9 Section 5, except that the brake fluid reservoir should be emptied by siphoning, using a clean poultry baster or similar before starting, and allowance should be made for the old fluid to be expelled when bleeding a section of the circuit.
2 Working as described in Chapter 9 Section 5, open the first bleed screw in the sequence, and pump the brake pedal gently until nearly all the old fluid has been emptied from the master cylinder reservoir. Top up to the MAXI

level with new fluid, and continue pumping until only the new fluid remains in the reservoir, and new fluid can be seen emerging from the bleed screw. Tighten the screw, and top the reservoir level up to the MAXI level line.
3 Work through all the remaining bleed screws in sequence until new fluid can be seen at all of them. Be careful to keep the master cylinder reservoir topped-up to above the MINI level at all times, or air may enter the system and greatly increase the length of the task.
4 When the operation is complete, check that all bleed screws are securely tightened, and that their dust caps are refitted. Wash off all traces of spilt fluid, and recheck the master cylinder reservoir fluid level.
5 Check the operation of the brakes before taking the car on the road.

27 Coolant renewal

⚠ *Warning: Wait until the engine is cold before starting this procedure. Do not allow antifreeze to come in contact with your skin, or with the painted surfaces of the vehicle. Rinse off spills immediately with plenty of water. Never leave antifreeze lying around in an open container, or in a puddle in the driveway or on the garage floor. Children and pets are attracted by its sweet smell, but antifreeze can be fatal if ingested.*

Cooling system draining

1 With the engine completely cold, remove the expansion tank filler cap. Turn the cap anti-clockwise, wait until any pressure remaining in the system is released, then unscrew it and lift it off.
2 Remove the undertray, then position a suitable container beneath the radiator bottom hose connection.
3 Loosen the hose clip, pull off the hose and allow the coolant to drain into the container (see illustration).
4 To assist draining, open the cooling system bleed screw located on the thermostat housing (see illustrations).

27.3 Draining the coolant

27.4a Bleed screw in the heater hose…

27.4b …and thermostat housing

5 When the flow of coolant stops, reposition the container below the cylinder block drain plug located at the rear right-hand side of the cylinder block. Unscrew the plug and drain the coolant into the container.

6 Flush the system if necessary as described in the following paragraphs, then refit the drain plug and secure the bottom hose. Use a new hose clip if necessary. Refill the system as described later in this Section.

Cooling system flushing

7 If coolant renewal has been neglected, or if the antifreeze mixture has become diluted, then in time, the cooling system may gradually lose efficiency, as the coolant passages become restricted due to rust, scale deposits, and other sediment. The cooling system efficiency can be restored by flushing the system clean.

8 The radiator should be flushed independently of the engine, to avoid unnecessary contamination.

Radiator flushing

9 Disconnect the top and bottom hoses and any other relevant hoses from the radiator, with reference to Chapter 3 Section 3.

10 Insert a garden hose into the radiator top inlet. Direct a flow of clean water through the radiator, and continue flushing until clean water emerges from the radiator bottom outlet.

11 If after a reasonable period, the water still does not run clear, the radiator can be flushed with a good proprietary cleaning agent. It is important that the manufacturer's instructions are followed carefully. If the contamination is particularly bad, insert the hose in the radiator bottom outlet, and reverse flush the radiator.

Engine flushing

12 To flush the engine, remove the thermostat as described in Chapter 3 Section 5, and disconnect the bottom hose.

13 Insert a garden hose into the thermostat housing and direct a clean flow of water through the engine. Continue flushing until clean water emerges from the radiator bottom hose.

14 On completion, refit the thermostat and reconnect the bottom hose.

Cooling system filling

15 Before attempting to fill the cooling system, make sure that all hoses and clips are in good condition, and that the clips are tight. Note that an antifreeze mixture must be used all year round, to prevent corrosion of the engine components. Also check that the cylinder block drain plug is in place and tight.

16 Remove the expansion tank filler cap.

17 Open the cooling system bleed screw on the thermostat housing and on the heater hose below the windscreen cowl.

18 Slowly fill the system until the coolant level reaches the MAXI mark on the expansion tank. Close the bleed screws when coolant free from air bubbles emerges.

19 Start the engine, and run it at a fast idle speed (approx 2500 rpm) for approximately 4 minutes. Keep the level topped-up to the top of the expansion tank filler neck.

20 Refit and tighten the expansion tank filler cap.

21 Allow the engine to run at 2500 rpm for approximately 15 minutes until the cooling fan cuts in and out.

22 Stop the engine and allow the engine to cool for at least 30 minutes.

23 Recheck the coolant level with reference to *Weekly checks*. Top-up the level if necessary and refit the expansion tank filler cap.

Antifreeze mixture

24 The antifreeze should always be renewed at the specified intervals. This is necessary not only to maintain the antifreeze properties, but also to prevent corrosion which would otherwise occur as the corrosion inhibitors become progressively less effective.

25 Always use an ethylene-glycol based antifreeze which is suitable for use in mixed-metal cooling systems. The quantity of antifreeze and levels of protection are given in the Specifications.

26 Before adding antifreeze, the cooling system should be completely drained, preferably flushed, and all hoses checked for condition and security.

27 After filling with antifreeze, a label should be attached to the expansion tank, stating the type and concentration of antifreeze used, and the date installed. Any subsequent topping-up should be made with the same type and concentration of antifreeze.

Caution: Do not use engine antifreeze in the windscreen/tailgate washer system, as it will cause damage to the vehicle's paintwork. A screen wash additive should be added to the washer system in the quantities stated on the bottle.

Chapter 2 Part A
0.9 litre petrol engine in-car repair procedures

Contents

Degrees of difficulty

Easy, suitable for novice with little experience	**Fairly easy,** suitable for beginner with some experience	**Fairly difficult,** suitable for competent DIY mechanic	**Difficult,** suitable for experienced DIY mechanic	**Very difficult,** suitable for expert DIY or professional

Specifications

Engine (general)

Engine code	H4B
Capacity	898 cc
Bore	72.2 mm
Stroke	73.1 mm
Direction of crankshaft rotation	Clockwise (viewed from right-hand side of vehicle)
No. 1 cylinder location	At timing chain end of block
Firing order	1-3-2
Compression ratio	9.5-1

Valve clearances

Cold engine:	
Inlet	0.25 to 0.35 mm
Exhaust.	0.46 to 0.54 mm

Camshaft and followers

Drive	Chain
Number of bearings	4
Endfloat	0.206 to 0.236 mm
Camshaft lobe height:	
Inlet	44.322 to 44.522 mm
Exhaust.	43.664 to 43.864 mm
Camshaft bearing journal outer diameter:	
No 1 bearing.	27.934 to 28.000 mm
Nos 2 to 4 bearings	24.969 to 25.000 mm
Camshaft journal-to-bearing clearance:	
No 1 bearing.	0.045 to 0.086 mm
Nos 2 to 4 bearings	0.030 to 0.071 mm
Camshaft run-out:	
Standard.	0.02 mm
Limit	0.01 mm
Camshaft sprocket run-out	Less than 0.15 mm

Lubrication system

Oil pump type.	Gear-type, chain-driven off the crankshaft right-hand end
Minimum oil pressure at normal operating temperature (approx. 80°C):	
At Idle speed.	0.60 bars (minimum)
At 2000 rpm	2.70 bars (minimum)

Torque wrench settings

	Nm	lbf ft
Big-end bearing cap nuts:		
Stage 1	10	8
Stage 2	25	18
Stage 3	Angle-tighten a further 110°	
Camshaft bearing cap bolts	10	8
Camshaft sprocket retaining bolts (Variable valve timing):		
Inlet	78	58
Exhaust	78	58
Crankshaft pulley bolt:		
Stage 1	50	36
Stage 2	Angle-tighten 180°	
Cylinder head bolts:		
Stage 1	25	18
Stage 2	Angle-tighten 270°	
Cylinder head cover bolts	10	8
Cylinder head closing plate – transmission end	25	18
Engine-to-transmission fixing bolts	48	35
Flywheel:		
Stage 1	30	22
Stage 2	Angle-tighten 50°	
Left-hand transmission mounting:		
Through-bolt/stud nut	65	48
Through-bolt/stud-to-bracket	65	48
Mounting-to-bracket nuts	105	77
Mounting bracket-to-inner wing panel bolts	80	59
Mounting-to-transmission bolts	45	33
Main bearing cap bolts:		
Stage 1	25	18
Stage 2	32	23
Stage 3	Angle-tighten 62°	
Oil level sensor retaining bolt	8	6
Rear engine/transmission torque/link arm mounting:		
Mounting-to-front subframe bolt	110	81
Mounting bracket-to-transmission bolt	110	81
Right-hand engine mounting:		
Bracket bolts to engine	55	41
Mounting bolts to inner wing	55	41
Mounting bolt to engine bracket (horizontal)	125	92
Sump oil drain plug	35	26
Lower sump oil pan bolts	10	8
Upper sump pan bolts to transmission	48	35
Upper sump casing bolts to cylinder block	25	18
Timing chain cover bolts (see text):		
Lower bolts x 9 (6mm)	25	18
Upper bolts x 5 (8mm)	55	41
Smaller centre bolts x 3	10	8
Timing chain guide bolts	25	18
Timing chain tensioner bolts	10	8

1 General Information

Using this Chapter

1 This part of Chapter 2 is devoted to in-car repair procedures for the 0.9 litre petrol engine. Similar information covering the other engine types can be found in Parts B and C. All procedures concerning engine removal and refitting, and engine block/cylinder head overhaul can be found in Part D of this Chapter.
2 Note that, while it may be possible physically to overhaul items such as the piston/ connecting rod assemblies while the engine is in the car, such tasks are not normally carried out as separate operations. Usually, several additional procedures (not to mention the cleaning of components and of oil ways) have to be carried out. For this reason, all such tasks are classed as major overhaul procedures, and are described in Part D of this Chapter.
3 In Parts A, B and C, the assumption is made that the engine is installed in the car, with all ancillaries connected. If the engine has been removed for overhaul, the preliminary dismantling information, which precedes each operation, may be ignored.

Engine description

4 The engine is of the twelve-valve, in-line three-cylinder, double overhead camshaft (DOHC) type, mounted transversely at the front of the car with the transmission attached to the left-hand end.
5 The crankshaft runs in four main bearings. Thrust washers are fitted to No 3 main bearing (upper half) to control crankshaft end float.
6 The connecting rods rotate on horizontally split bearing shells at their big ends. The pistons are attached to the connecting rods by gudgeon pins, which are a press fit in the small end of the connecting rod. The aluminium-alloy pistons are fitted with three

piston rings – two compression rings and an oil control ring.

7 The cylinder block is made of aluminium alloy and the cylinder bores are an integral part of the block. On this type of engine the cylinder bores are sometimes referred to as having dry liners.

8 The inlet and exhaust valves are each closed by coil springs, and operate in guides pressed into the cylinder head; the valve seat inserts are also pressed into the cylinder head, and can be renewed separately if worn. The inlet camshaft has a variable valve sprocket to the end which is oil fed through a control solenoid valve.

9 The camshafts are driven by a timing chain, and operates the twelve valves via bucket-type followers. The followers are situated directly below the camshafts. Valve clearances are adjusted by replacing the relevant follower with a different thickness. The camshafts rotate directly in the cylinder head.

10 Lubrication is by means of an oil pump, which is chain driven off the right-hand end of the crankshaft. It draws oil through a strainer located in the sump, and then forces it through an oil filter into galleries in the cylinder block/crankcase. From there, the oil is distributed to the crankshaft (main bearings) and camshaft. The big-end bearings are supplied with oil via internal drillings in the crankshaft, while the camshaft bearings also receive a pressurised supply. The camshaft lobes and valves are lubricated by splash, as are all other engine components.

Repairs with engine in car

11 The following work can be carried out with the engine in the car:

a) *Compression pressure – testing.*
b) *Cylinder head cover – removal and refitting.*
c) *Timing chain cover – removal and refitting.*
d) *Timing chain – removal, inspection and refitting.*
e) *Timing chain tensioner, guides and sprockets – removal, inspection and refitting.*
f) *Camshaft and followers – removal, inspection and refitting.*
g) *Valve clearances – adjustment.*
h) *Cylinder head – removal and refitting.*
i) *Cylinder head and pistons – decarbonising.*
j) *Sump oil pan – removal and refitting.*
k) *Oil pump – removal, inspection and refitting.*
l) *Crankshaft oil seals – renewal.*
m) *Engine/transmission mountings – inspection and renewal.*
n) *Flywheel/driveplate – removal, inspection and refitting.*

2 Compression test – description and interpretation

1 When engine performance is down, or if misfiring occurs which cannot be attributed to the ignition or fuel systems, a compression test can provide diagnostic clues as to the engine's condition. If the test is performed regularly, it can give warning of trouble before any other symptoms become apparent.

2 The engine must be fully warmed-up to normal operating temperature, the battery must be fully charged, and the aid of an assistant will also be required.

3 Depressurise the fuel system by removing the fuel pump fuse from the fusebox – the fuses can usually be identified from the label inside the fusebox cover, or from the wiring diagrams at the end of this manual (see Chapter). With the fuse removed, start the engine, and allow it to run until it stalls. Try to start the engine at least twice more, to ensure that all residual pressure has been relieved.

4 Remove the spark plugs as described in Chapter 1A Section 18.

5 Fit a compression tester to the No 1 cylinder spark plug hole – the type of tester which screws into the plug thread is to be preferred.

6 Have the assistant hold the throttle wide open, and crank the engine on the starter motor; after two or three revolutions, the compression pressure should build-up to a maximum figure, and then stabilise. Record the highest reading obtained.

7 Repeat the test on the remaining cylinders, recording the pressure in each.

8 All cylinders should produce very similar pressures; any difference greater than that specified indicates the existence of a fault. Note that the compression should build-up quickly in a healthy engine; low compression on the first stroke, followed by gradually increasing pressure on successive strokes, indicates worn piston rings. A low compression reading on the first stroke, which does not build-up during successive strokes, indicates leaking valves or a blown head gasket (a cracked head could also be the cause). Deposits on the undersides of the valve heads can also cause low compression.

9 If the pressure in any cylinder is reduced to the specified minimum or less, carry out the following test to isolate the cause. Introduce a teaspoonful of clean oil into that cylinder through its spark plug hole and repeat the test.

10 If the addition of oil temporarily improves the compression pressure, this indicates that bore or piston wear is responsible for the pressure loss. No improvement suggests that leaking or burnt valves, or a blown head gasket, may be to blame.

11 A low reading from two adjacent cylinders is almost certainly due to the head gasket having blown between them; the presence of coolant in the engine oil will confirm this.

12 If one cylinder is about 20 percent lower than the others and the engine has a slightly rough idle; a worn camshaft lobe could be the cause.

13 If the compression reading is unusually high, the combustion chambers are probably coated with carbon deposits. If this is the case, the cylinder head should be removed and decarbonised.

14 On completion of the test, refit the spark plugs and fuel pump fuse.

3 Top dead centre (TDC) – locating

1 Disconnect the battery negative terminal (refer to Chapter 5A Section 4).

2 Apply the handbrake and ensure that the transmission is in neutral, then jack up the front of the car and support it on axle stands (see Chapter 13 Section 5). Remove the right-hand roadwheel.

3 From underneath the front of the car, undo the retaining screws and remove the wheel arch liner from underneath the wing to gain access to the crankshaft pulley.

4 Remover the cylinder head cover (as described in Section 4), then rotate the engine until the timing mark on the exhaust sprockets is uppermost and the lobes for the cams on No 1 cylinder are pointing outwards. This places cylinder No 1 at top dead centre on the compression stroke.

5 The precise position of TDC can also be determined with a dial gauge and extension bar through the spark plug hole. Once located this way it is recommended that permanent marks are made on the crank pulley and timing chain front cover.

4 Cylinder head cover – removal and refitting

Removal

1 Disconnect the battery negative terminal (see *Disconnecting the battery* in Chapter 5A Section 4).

2 Remove the injector rail and injectors, as described in Chapter 4A Section 13.

3 Remove the upper oxygen sensor, as described in Chapter 4C Section 2.

4 Undo the retaining screws and remove the heatshield from over the turbocharger **(see illustration)**.

4.4 Remove the heat shield

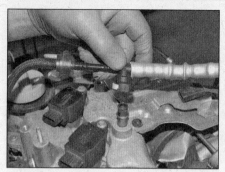

4.5a Unclip the breather pipe from the cover...

4.5b ...and the air intake hose

4.7 Remove the camshaft sensor

4.8 Undo the dipstick bracket bolt

4.9 Cover the inlet ports using duct tape

5 Disconnect the breather pipe from the cylinder head cover and the air intake hose, then move it to one side (see illustrations).
6 Disconnect the wiring connectors from the ignition coils, then undo the retaining bolts and remove them from the top of the cylinder head cover, with reference to Chapter 5B Section 3.
7 Disconnect the wiring connector from the camshaft sensor, undo the retaining bolt and remove it from the cylinder head cover (see illustration).
8 Undo the retaining bolt and disconnect the top of the dipstick tube from the cylinder head cover (see illustration).
9 Undo the retaining bolt and remove the vacuum capsule from the top of the cylinder head cover (see illustration).
10 Slacken and remove the cylinder head cover retaining bolts, then lift off the cylinder head cover, and recover the rubber seal,

which goes around the outer edge of the cover, and also around each of the spark plug holes. Note the position of the cylinder head bolts, as some of the bolts are of a different length.
11 Inspect the cover seals for signs of damage and deterioration, and renew as necessary. It is recommended that the cylinder head cover seal should always be renewed, if the cover is removed.

Refitting

12 Carefully clean the cylinder head and cover mating surfaces, and remove all traces of oil.
13 Apply a small amount of sealant to where the timing chain upper cover joins the cylinder head (see illustrations), and also at the transmission end of the cylinder head, where the closing plate is at the end of the inlet camshaft.

14 Fit the rubber seal to the cylinder head cover groove, ensuring that it is correctly located along its entire length, and around the four spark plug holes in the centre of the cover (see illustration).
15 Carefully lower the cylinder head cover onto the cylinder head, taking great care not to displace any of the rubber seal.
16 Make sure the cover is correctly seated, and then install the retaining bolts, making they are fitted in the correct place (due to length), as noted on removal. Working from the centre and spiraling outwards, tighten all the cover bolts to the specified torque.
17 Refit the vacuum capsule to the top of the cylinder head cover.
18 Refit the top of the dipstick tube to the cylinder head cover and tighten the retaining bolt.
19 Refit camshaft sensor and tighten the retaining bolt to the specified torque, then reconnect the wiring connector..
20 Refit the ignition coils, with reference to Chapter 5B Section 3.
21 Reconnect the breather pipe to the cylinder head cover and the air intake hose.
22 Refit the heatshield over the turbocharger and tighten the retaining screws.
23 Refit the upper oxygen sensor, with reference to Chapter 4C Section 2.
24 Refit the injector rail and injectors, with reference to Chapter 4A Section 13.
25 Reconnect the battery negative terminal. Run the engine and check for any oil leaks around the engine cylinder head cover.

4.13a Apply sealant to the joint ...

4.13b ... at both sides of the camshaft sprockets

4.14 Fit the new rubber gasket to the cylinder head cover

5.3 Using a homemade tool to hold the pulley

5.4 Remove the crankshaft pulley bolt

5.5a Remove the pulley using a puller ...

5.5b ... which can be made out of a piece of flat metal bar

5.6 Make sure the woodruff key (arrowed) is located securely

5.8 Align the slot in the pulley centre hub with the woodruff key

5 Crankshaft pulley – removal and refitting

Removal

1 Remove the auxiliary drivebelt as described in Chapter 1A Section 9.

2 If necessary, position No 1 cylinder at TDC on its compression stroke as described in Section 3.

3 To prevent crankshaft rotation while the pulley bolt is unscrewed, the pulley should be held by a suitable tool which locates in the slots in the pulley to prevent it from turning (see illustration). If this is not available, on manual transmission models, select top gear and have an assistant apply the brakes firmly.

4 Unscrew the pulley bolt, along with its washer (where applicable), and remove the pulley from the crankshaft (see illustration).

5 If the pulley is a tight fit on the end of the crankshaft, use a puller to withdraw the pulley from the end of the shaft. Refit the pulley bolt and screw it back into the end of the crankshaft, leaving it approx. 5mm out from the pulley face. Fit the puller (this can be a homemade puller, using a piece of flat bar and three bols/nuts) to the pulley and tighten the centre bolt to withdraw the pulley from the end of the crankshaft (see illustrations).

6 If the pulley Woodruff key is a loose fit in the end of the crankshaft (see illustration), remove it and store it with the pulley for safekeeping.

Refitting

7 Refit the Woodruff key (where removed).

8 Align the crankshaft pulley groove with the key (see illustration), then slide the sprocket onto the crankshaft and refit the retaining bolt

9 Lock the crankshaft by the method used on removal, and tighten the pulley retaining bolt to the specified torque settings. The head of the bolt/washer may have markings around its edge, dividing it into 60° segments. To carry out the final stage of the tightening procedure (angle tighten 180°), paint one of the marks on the bolt head, and also paint a mark on the pulley alongside the relevant mark. If there are no markings on the new bolt, make alignment marks at 180° apart (see illustration).

10 Refit the auxiliary drivebelt and adjust it as described in Chester 1A Section 9.

5.9 Make alignments marks at 180° on the pulley and bolt

6 Timing chain cover – removal and refitting

Removal

1 Disconnect the battery negative terminal (see Disconnecting the battery in Chapter 5A Section 4).

2 Firmly apply the handbrake, and then jack up the front of the vehicle and support it securely on axle stands (see Chapter 13 Section 5). Remove right-hand front road wheel.

3 Undo the fasteners and remove the plastic inner wheel arch liner, and undershields from beneath the right-hand front wing panel and the engine compartment.

4 Drain the engine oil, then clean and refit the engine oil drain plug using a new sealing washer, tightening it to the specified torque. If the engine is nearing its service interval when the oil and filter are due for renewal, it is recommended that the filter is also removed, and a new one fitted. After reassembly, the engine can then be refilled with fresh oil. Refer to Chapter 1A Section 4, for further information.

5 Remove the cylinder head cover as described in Section 4.

6 Remove the crankshaft pulley as described in Section 5.

7 Remove the alternator as described in Chapter 5A Section 7.

8 Undo the three retaining bolts and

6.8 Remove the coolant pump pulley

6.10 Remove the idler pulley

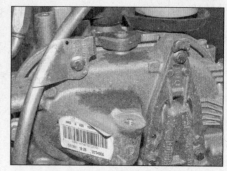

6.11a Undo the upper bolt...

6.11b ...and lower bolt, then remove tube

6.12a Remove the dephaser cover...

6.12b ...and dephaser valve

remove the coolant pump pulley **(see illustration)**.

9 Support the engine and remove the upper engine mount from the top of the timing chain cover, as described in Section 15.

10 Remove the plastic cap, then undo the retaining bolt and remove the idler pulley from the timing chain cover **(see illustration)**.

11 Undo the upper and lower mounting bolts and remove the dipstick tube from the timing chain cover **(see illustrations)**. Recover the O-ring seal from the bottom of the tube on removal and discard, as a new one will be required for refitting.

12 Undo the three retaining bolts and remove the dephaser cover from the top of the timing chain cover, also undo the bolt and withdraw the dephaser valve from the front of the timing chain cover **(see illustrations)**.

13 Working in the reverse of the tightening sequence **(see illustration 6.17)**, slacken and remove the timing chain cover retaining bolts. Note the correct fitted location of each bolt, as some of the bolts are different lengths. Also the six upper bolts are a larger diameter than the eight lower bolts **(see illustrations)**.

14 Also undo the three smaller bolts at the centre of the timing chain cover.

15 The timing chain cover has been fitted using a liquid gasket, and is bonded to the engine block/cylinder head. Taking care not to damage the timing chain cover work your way around the outside of the cover to release it from the engine. Also note that at the top of the timing chain cover there are two steel dowels, which can become very tight in the alloy cover.

Refitting

16 Prior to refitting the cover, it is recommended that the crankshaft oil seal should be renewed. Note the seals fitted position, and then carefully lever the old seal out of the cover using a large flat-bladed screwdriver **(see illustration)**. Fit the new seal to the cover, making sure its sealing lip is facing inwards. Drive the seal into position until it seats squarely in the position noted on removal, for further information see Section 13, of this Chapter.

17 Ensure that the timing chain cover and engine cylinder block/cylinder head mating surfaces are clean/dry and free from any silicone sealer. Clean the steel dowels on the cylinder block, and apply a small amount of oil to aid fitting.

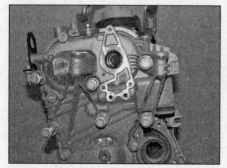

6.13a Timing chain cover upper retaining bolts...

6.13b ...and lower retaining bolts

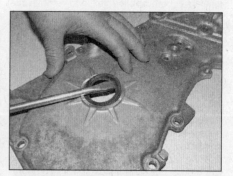

6.16 Note the fitted position, then remove the seal

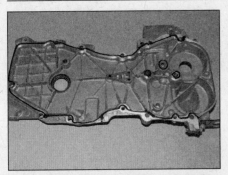

6.18a Apply a bead of sealant around the outside of the cover ...

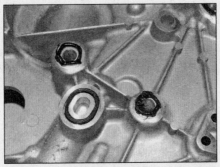

6.18b ... and around the centre mountings – also fit new seal

6.19 Apply sealant to the joints (arrowed) at both sides of the cylinder block

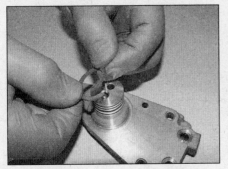

6.22a Fit new split seals/washers...

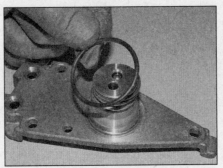

6.22b ...O-ring seal...

6.22c ...and small bolt recess seals

18 Apply a thin bead of suitable sealant (3mm to 4mm diameter) to the timing chain cover surface, not forgetting to apply sealant to the area around the two engine mounting bolt passages in the upper centre of the cover. Also make sure the new seal for the phaser valve, is fitted correctly in the timing chain cover (see illustrations).

19 Also apply a small amount of sealant to where the cylinder block joins the cylinder head, and where the cylinder block joins the upper sump housing (see illustration).

20 For this procedure the help of an assistant would be advisable; lower the timing chain cover into position taking care not to wipe the sealer off the face of the cover. With the assistant under the right-hand front wheel arch manoeuvre the cover into position over the end of the crankshaft, taking great care not to damage the oil seal lip.

21 Make sure the cover is correctly seated, and then install the retaining bolts. Working in sequence, tighten all the cover screws to the specified torque.

22 Fit new seals, to the dephaser cover and then refit to the timing chain cover, and the dephaser valve to the front of the timing chain cover (see illustrations).

23 Fit new O-ring seal to the bottom of the dipstick tube, then refit it to the timing chain cover and tighten the mounting bolts.

24 Refit the idler pulley to the timing chain cover, tighten the retaining bolt and refit the plastic cap.

25 Refit the coolant pump pulley and tighten the three retaining bolts.

26 Refit the engine mount to the top of the timing chain cover, with reference to Section 15.

27 Refit the alternator with reference to Chapter 5A Section 7.

28 Refit the crankshaft pulley as described in Section 5, of this Chapter.

29 Refit the cylinder head cover as described in Section 4, of this Chapter.

30 After reassembly, the engine can then be refilled with fresh oil. Refer to Chapter 1A Section 4 for further information.

31 Refit the plastic inner wheel arch liner and engine undershield.

32 Refit the front road wheel and lower the vehicle to the ground, then remove the jack from underneath the vehicle. Tighten the road wheel to the specified torque setting.

33 Reconnect the battery negative terminal. Run the engine and check for any oil leaks around the timing chain cover.

7 Timing chain, tensioner, guides and sprockets – removal, inspection and refitting

Removal

1 Position No 1 cylinder at TDC on its compression stroke, as described in Section 3.

2 Remove the cylinder head cover as described in Section 4.

3 Remove the timing chain cover as described in Section 6.

Note: The paint marks are used to align the timing marks on the crankshaft and camshaft sprockets when a new timing chain is fitted. When checking timing chain already fitted to engine, these timing marks will not be aligned, and may take numerous turns of the engine to get them back into line.

4 With No 1 cylinder set at TDC, the markings on the camshaft sprockets should be in line, as shown (see illustrations).

5 Whilst holding down the tensioner lever, push the tensioner plunger back into it body. With the plunger retracted, align the hole in the lever with the hole in the tensioner body and hold it in position by inserting a small-diameter rod through the plate hole and into the body of the tensioner (see illustrations).

6 Undo the two retaining bolts, and remove

7.4a Align the markings on the exhaust camshaft sprocket...

7.4b ...the inlet camshaft dephaser unit...

7.4c ...and the crankshaft sprocket

7.5a Push the tensioner lever down ...

7.5b ... and insert locking pin through tensioner

7.6 Remove the tensioner, keeping the locking pin in place

7.7 Rmove the tensioner guide

the tensioner from the end of the cylinder block. Keep the rod inserted into the tensioner to prevent the plunger from springing out **(see illustration)**.

7 Release the upper pivot point of the chain

7.8a Undo the mounting bolts...

tensioner guide, and remove it from the rear of the crankcase **(see illustration)**.

8 Unscrew the two mounting bolts, and remove the chain front guide from the crankcase **(see illustrations)**.

7.8b ...and remove the fixed chain guide

9 Disengage the timing chain from the crankshaft sprocket, and manoeuvre it out from the engine.

⚠ *Warning: Do not turn the crankshaft or camshafts while the timing chain is removed, otherwise piston and valve contact may occur causing damage.*

10 Slacken the exhaust camshaft sprocket retaining bolt, whilst retaining the camshafts with a large open-ended spanner fitted to the hexagonal section of each shaft. Remove the bolt along with its washer (where applicable), disengage the sprocket from the end of its camshaft **(see illustrations)**.

11 To remove the variable valve inlet sprocket from the inlet camshaft, carry out the same procedure as the exhaust sprocket in previous paragraph, using an open-ended spanner to prevent the camshaft from turning.

12 To remove the crankshaft sprocket from the end of the crankshaft, requires removing the oil pump chain and sprocket as a complete unit. See Section 12 for further information.

Inspection

13 Examine the teeth on the camshaft and crankshaft sprockets for any sign of wear or damage such as chipped, hooked or missing teeth. If there is any sign of wear or damage on either sprockets or timing chain then they should be renewed as a set.

14 Inspect the links of the timing chain for signs of wear or damage on the rollers. The extent of wear can be judged by checking the amount by which the chain can be bent

7.10a Using an open ended spanner to counter hold the camshaft ...

7.10b ... and remove the camshaft sprocket retaining bolt

sideways; a new chain will have very little sideways movement. If there is an excessive amount of side play in either timing chain, it must be renewed.

15 Note that it is a sensible precaution to renew the timing chain, regardless of apparent condition, if the engine has covered a high mileage, or if it has been noted that the chain has sounded noisy when the engine is running. Although not strictly necessary, it is always worth renewing the chain and sprockets as a matched set, since it is false economy to run a new chain on worn sprockets and viceversa. If there is any doubt about the condition of the timing chain and sprockets, seek the advice of a dealer service department, who will be able to advise you as to the best course of action.

16 Examine the chain guides for signs of wear or damage to their chain contact faces, renewing any which are badly marked.

17 Check the chain tensioner for signs of wear, and check that the plunger is free to slide freely in the tensioner body. The condition of the tensioner spring can only be judged in comparison to a new component. Renew the tensioner if it is worn or there is any doubt about the condition of its tensioning spring.

Refitting

18 Check the crankshaft is still positioned at TDC (the keyway will be in the 12 o'clock position, seen from the right-hand end of the engine).

19 Manoeuvre the exhaust camshaft sprocket into position, ensuring that the timing marks are facing the position noted on removal. Engage the sprocket with the chain and align the painted chain links with the alignment marks on the camshaft sprockets **(see illustrations 7.4a and 7.4b)**.

20 Tighten the exhaust camshaft bolt to the specified torque setting, whilst retaining the camshafts with a large open-ended spanner fitted to the hexagonal section of each shaft **(see illustration 7.10a)**.

21 Manoeuvre the chain into position, engaging it with the crankshaft sprocket so that its coloured link is aligned with the timing mark on the crankshaft sprocket **(see illustration 7.4c)**. Check that all the timing marks are correctly aligned with the chain links.

22 Fit the chain front fixed guide to the cylinder block, and tighten its retaining bolts to the specified torque.

23 Fit the chain rear tensioner guide to the upper pivot point and locate it in position **(see illustration 7.7)**.

24 Fit the chain tensioner to the cylinder block, and tighten its retaining bolts to the specified torque. Whilst holding the guide against the tensioner plunger, withdraw the rod, and check that the tensioner plunger is forced out against the guide to take up the slack in the chain **(see illustration)**.

25 Check that all the timing marks are still correctly aligned with the chain links. If all

7.24 Hold pressure against the tensioner and remove the locking pin

timing marks are aligned, fit the crankshaft pulley and turn the engine two complete turns, and check the timing marks on the sprockets are all re-aligned. **Note:** *The coloured links on the chain will not be re-aligned with the marks on the sprockets. The coloured links are just for the initial set up, and will take many turns before they will line up again, with the marks on the sprockets.*

26 Remove the crankshaft pulley and refit the timing chain cover as described in Section 6.

27 Refit the crankshaft pulley as described in Section 5 of this Chapter.

28 Refit the cylinder head cover as described in Section 4.

8 Valve clearances – checking and adjustment

Note: *This is not a routine operation. It should only be necessary at high mileage, after overhaul, or when investigating noise or power loss which may be attributable to the valve gear. Adjustment involves removing the camshaft and changing the cam followers (valve lifters) that are available in 31 different thicknesses (ranging from 2.96mm to 3.56mm, in steps of 0.02mm).*

Checking

1 The importance of having the valve clearances correctly adjusted cannot be overstressed, as they vitally affect the performance of the engine. The clearances are checked as follows.

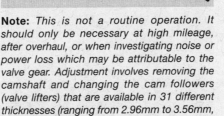
8.5 Check the clearances between the camshafts and the followers

2 Draw the outline of the engine on a piece of paper, numbering the cylinders 1 to 3, with No 1 cylinder at the timing chain end of the engine. Show the position of each valve, together with the specified valve clearance. Above each valve, draw two lines for noting the actual clearance and the amount of adjustment required.

3 Warm the engine up to normal operating temperature, then switch off. Remove the cylinder head cover as described in Section 4.

4 Position No 1 cylinder at TDC on its compression stroke, as described in Section 3.

5 With number 1 cylinder on the compression stroke, the lobes on the camshafts will be pointing upwards. Using feeler gauges, measure the clearance between the base of the cam and the follower **(see illustration)**, recording each clearance on the paper.

6 Rotate the crankshaft through half a turn (180º) clockwise until the lobes on number 3 cylinder are pointing up. No 3 cylinder is now at TDC on its compression stroke. Using feeler gauges, measure the clearance between the base of the cam and the follower, recording each clearance on the paper.

7 Rotate the crankshaft through a further half a turn (180º) clockwise until the lobes on number 2 cylinder are pointing up. No 2 cylinder is now at TDC on its compression stroke. Using feeler gauges, measure the clearance between the base of the cam and the follower, recording each clearance on the paper.

8 Calculate the difference between each measured clearance and the desired value, and record it on the piece of paper.

Adjustment

Note: *A micrometer or dial gauge and probe will be required for this operation.*

9 Where a valve clearance differs from the specified value, then the cam follower (valve lifter) for that valve must be substituted with a thinner or thicker one accordingly. The cam followers have the thickness stamped on the bottom face of the follower; e.g. 324 indicates the follower is 3.24 mm thick at the top centre of the follower **(see illustration)**.

10 If required use a micrometer or dial gauge to measure the true thickness of any follower removed, as it may have been reduced

8.9 Markings inside the follower for thickness

by wear. **Note:** *Followers are available in thicknesses between 3.00 mm and 3.50 mm, in steps of 0.02 mm.*

11 To access the cam followers (valve lifters), first remove the camshafts as described in Section 9. Remove and refit each follower separately, to avoid any confusion.

12 The size of follower required is calculated as follows. If the measured clearance is less than specified, subtract the measured clearance from the specified clearance, and deduct the result from the thickness of the existing follower. For example:

13 Sample calculation – clearance too small
14 Clearance measured (A) = 0.16 mm
15 Desired clearance (B) = 0.30 mm
16 Difference (B – A) = 0.14 mm
17 Cam follower thickness fitted = 3.50 mm
18 Cam follower thickness required = 3.50 – 0.14 = 3.36 mm

19 If the measured clearance is greater than specified, subtract the specified clearance from the measured clearance, and add the result to the thickness of the existing follower. For example:

20 Sample calculation – clearance too big
21 Clearance measured (A) = 0.40 mm
22 Desired clearance (B) = 0.30 mm
23 Difference (A – B) = 0.10 mm
24 Cam follower thickness fitted = 3.26 mm
25 Cam follower thickness required = 3.26 + 0.10 = 3.36 mm

26 Working on each separately, lift out the follower to be renewed, then oil the new one and carefully locate it in the cylinder head, on top of the valve.

27 Refit the camshafts with reference to Section 9.

28 It will be helpful for future adjustment if a record is kept of the thickness of cam followers (valve lifters) fitted at each position. The cam followers required could be purchased in advance once the clearances and the existing follower thicknesses are known.

29 Once all valve clearances have been adjusted, rotate the crankshaft through at least four complete turns in the correct direction of rotation, to settle all disturbed followers, then recheck the clearances as described above.

30 With all valve clearances correctly adjusted, refit the cylinder head cover as described in, and refit all components removed to gain access to the crankshaft pulley.

9 Camshafts and followers – removal, inspection and refitting

Removal

1 Position No 1 cylinder at TDC on its compression stroke, as described in Section 3.
2 Remove the cylinder head cover as described in Section 4.
3 Remove the timing chain, as described in Section 7.
4 Slacken the exhaust camshaft sprocket and inlet dephaser sprocket retaining bolts, whilst retaining the camshaft with a large open-ended spanner fitted to the hexagonal section on the shaft (see illustrations).

5 Remove the bolt along with its washer (where applicable), disengage the sprockets/dephaser unit from the end of its camshaft, and then release it from the timing chain.
6 Undo the retaining bolts and remove the closure plate from the transmission end of the inlet manifold.

⚠ **Warning: Do not turn the crankshaft or camshafts while the timing chain is removed, otherwise piston and valve contact may occur causing damage.**

7 Undo the camshaft bearing caps which have identification markings stamped into their top surface; the exhaust camshaft caps being marked 2, 3 and 4 and the inlet camshaft caps being marked A, B and C; the No 2 and A caps are fitted nearest the timing chain end of the engine. Note the markings on the caps for refitting. If the caps are not marked, suitable identification marks should be made prior to removal. Using white paint or suitable marker pen, mark each cap in some way to indicate its correct fitted orientation and position. This will avoid the possibility of installing the caps in the wrong positions and/ or the wrong way around on refitting.

8 Remove the three bolts and remove the camshaft bearing cap from the timing chain end of the cylinder head, then undo the two bolts and remove the camshaft bearing cap from the transmission end of the inlet camshaft (see illustrations).

9 Evenly and progressively slacken the twelve remaining camshaft bearing cap retaining bolts by one turn at a time, starting from the outside and working inwards to the centre caps, this will relieve the pressure of the valve springs on the bearing caps gradually and evenly (see illustration). Once the valve spring pressure has been relieved, the bolts can be fully unscrewed and the caps removed.

10 With the bearing caps removed the camshafts can be simply lifted off the top of the cylinder head, noting there fitted position. Note the position of the dowel on the sprocket end of the camshaft, and the position of the cam lobes, so that they can be refitted in the correct position for TDC on no.1 cylinder.

9.4a Undo the sprocket retaining bolts...

9.4b ...using an open ended spanner to counter hold the camshafts

9.8a Remove the bearing cap at the timing chain end...

9.8b ...and at the transmission end

9.9 Slacken the bolts starting from the outside working inwards

9.11 Remove the cam followers

9.14 Checking the cam lobe height with a micrometer

9.18 Lubricate the camshaft bearing surfaces

11 Obtain twelve small, clean plastic containers, and number them 1 to 12. Alternatively, divide a larger container into twelve compartments. Using a rubber sucker, withdraw each follower (valve lifter) in turn, and place it in its respective container **(see illustration)**. Do not interchange the cam followers, or the rate of wear will be increased.

Inspection

12 Inspect the cam bearing surfaces of the head and the bearing caps. Look for score marks and deep scratches. Check the camshaft lobes for heat discoloration (blue appearance), score marks, chipped areas or flat spots.
13 Camshaft run-out can be checked by supporting each end of the camshaft on V-blocks, and measuring any run-out at the centre of the shaft using a dial gauge. If the run-out exceeds the specified limit, a new camshaft will be required.
14 Measure the height of each lobe with a micrometer **(see illustration)**, and compare the results to the figures given in the Specifications. If damage is noted or wear is excessive, new camshaft(s) must be fitted.
15 The camshaft bearing oil clearance should now be checked.
16 Fit the bearing caps to the cylinder head, using the identification markings or the marks made on removal to ensure that they are correctly positioned. Tighten the retaining bolts starting from the centre camshaft bearing caps and working your way outwards, evenly and progressively tighten the camshaft bearing cap bolts by one turn at a time until the caps touch the cylinder head. Then go round again and tighten all the bolts to the specified torque setting. Work only as described, to impose the pressure of the valve springs gradually and evenly on the bearing caps. Measure the diameter of each bearing cap journal, and compare the measurements obtained with the results given in the Specifications at the start of this Chapter. If any journal is worn beyond the service limit, the cylinder head must be renewed. The camshaft bearing oil clearance can then be calculated by subtracting the camshaft bearing journal

diameter from the bearing cap journal diameter.
17 Check the cam follower and cylinder head bearing surfaces for signs of wear or damage.

Refitting

18 Liberally oil the cylinder head cam follower bores and the followers. Carefully refit the followers to the cylinder head; ensuring that each follower is refitted to its original bore. Some care will be required to enter the followers squarely into their bores. Liberally oil the camshaft bearing and lobe contact surfaces **(see illustration)**.
19 Refit the camshafts to their correct location in the cylinder head, in the position noted on removal.
20 Ensure that the bearing cap and head mating surfaces are completely clean, unmarked and free from oil.
21 Refit the bearing caps, using the identification markings or the marks made on removal to ensure that each is installed the correct way round and in its original location.
22 Tighten the retaining bolts starting from the centre camshaft bearing caps and working your way outwards, evenly and progressively tighten the camshaft bearing cap bolts by one turn at a time until the caps touch the cylinder head. Then go round again and tighten all the bolts to the specified torque setting. Work only as described, to impose the pressure of the valve springs gradually and evenly on the bearing caps.
23 Refit the camshaft sprockets and timing chain, as described in Section 7.
24 Check that the camshaft timing marks are still correctly aligned with the painted chain links and the crankshaft pulley is still set to TDC. If all timing marks are aligned, then turn the engine two complete turns, and check the timing marks on the sprockets are all re-aligned. **Note:** *The painted links on the chain will not be re-aligned with the marks on the sprockets. If required, see Section 7 for further information on setting the timing.*
25 If the cylinder head/camshafts have been overhauled, check and adjust the valve clearances as described in Section 8.
26 Refit the cylinder head cover as described in Section 4.

10 Cylinder head –
removal and refitting

Removal

1 Depressurise the fuel system as described in Chapter 4A Section 6.
2 Disconnect the battery negative lead as described in Chapter 5A Section 4.
3 Remove the timing chain as described in Section 7.
4 Remove the camshafts as described in Section 9.
5 Carry out the following operations as described in.
a) *Disconnect the exhaust system front pipe from the manifold.*
b) *Disconnect the fuel feed and return hoses from the fuel rail (plug all openings, to prevent loss of fuel and entry of dirt into the fuel system).*
c) *Disconnect the vacuum servo unit hose, coolant hose(s) and all the other relevant/ breather hoses from the manifold and associated valves.*
6 Slacken the retaining clip(s) and disconnect the coolant hose(s) from the cylinder head.
7 Starting from the outside and working inwards, progressively slacken the eight main cylinder head bolts by half a turn at a time, until all bolts can be unscrewed by hand.
8 Lift out the cylinder head bolts and recover the washers (where applicable), noting which way around they are fitted. Discard the bolts, as new ones will be required for refitting.
9 Lift the cylinder head away with the aid of an assistant, as it is a heavy assembly. Remove the gasket from the top of the block, noting the locating dowels fitted to the top of the cylinder block. If they are a loose fit in the block, remove the locating dowels, noting which way round they are fitted, and store them with the head for safekeeping.
10 If the cylinder head is to be dismantled for overhaul, then refer to.

Preparation for refitting

11 It is strongly recommended, that the bolts should be renewed as a complete set whenever they are disturbed. Clean out the

11.5 Using a flat ended scraper to prise the sump away

cylinder head bolts, using a syringe to draw out any oil that may have entered the bolt holes.

12 The mating faces of the cylinder head and cylinder block/crankcase must be perfectly clean before refitting the head. Use a hard plastic or wood scraper to remove all traces of gasket and carbon; also clean the piston crowns. Take particular care, as the surfaces are damaged easily. Also, make sure that the carbon is not allowed to enter the oil and water passages – this is particularly important for the lubrication system, as carbon could block the oil supply to any of the engine's components. Using adhesive tape and paper, seal the water, oil and bolt holes in the cylinder block/crankcase. To prevent carbon entering the gap between the pistons and bores, smear a little grease in the gap. After cleaning each piston, use a small brush to remove all traces of grease and carbon from the gap, and then wipe away the remainder with a clean rag. Clean all the pistons in the same way.

13 Check the mating surfaces of the cylinder block/crankcase and the cylinder head for nicks, deep scratches and other damage.

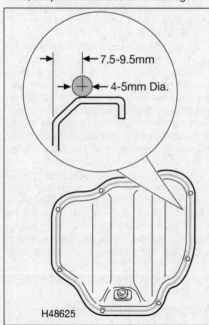

11.7 Apply a bead of sealant around the sump as shown

14 If warpage of the cylinder head gasket surface is suspected, use a straight-edge to check it for distortion. If necessary, refer to Chapter 2D Section 7.

Refitting

15 Wipe clean the mating surfaces of the cylinder head and cylinder block/crankcase. Check the locating dowels are in position at each end of the cylinder block/crankcase surface.

16 Fit a new gasket to the cylinder block/crankcase surface, aligning it with the locating dowels.

17 With the aid of an assistant, carefully refit the cylinder head assembly to the block, aligning it with the locating dowels.

18 Carefully enter each new bolt into its relevant hole (do not drop them in) and screw in, by hand only, until finger-tight.

19 Working progressively and starting from the centre and working outwards, tighten the cylinder head bolts to their Stage 1 torque setting, using a torque wrench and suitable socket. See specifications at the beginning of this Chapter.

20 Finally, go around again in the specified sequence and tighten the eight cylinder head bolts through the specified Stage 2 angle setting.

21 Reconnect the coolant hoses to the cylinder head and securely tighten the retaining clips.

22 Carry out the following operations:
a) Refit all disturbed wiring, hoses and control cable(s) to the inlet manifold and fuel system components.
b) Reconnect the exhaust system front pipe to the manifold, and reconnect the exhaust gas sensor wiring connector.
c) Refit the inlet manifold.

23 Refit the camshafts to the cylinder head as described in Section 9.

24 Fit the timing chains and sprockets as described in Section 7. **Note:** *If the cylinder head has been overhauled, check the valve clearances 'cold' prior to refitting the cylinder head cover (see Section 8).*

25 Start the engine and warm it up to normal operating temperature, check for any leaks from the engine, cooling circuit and fuel system.

11 Sump –
removal and refitting

Note: *The oil sump is made up of two parts; it has an upper alloy part and a lower steel oil pan. The following procedure is for the lower oil pan part. To remove the upper alloy part, the engine will need to be removed and the upper alloy sump then split from the cylinder block.*

Removal

1 Firmly apply the handbrake, and then jack up the front of the vehicle and support it securely on axle stands (see *Jacking and vehicle support*).

2 Slacken and remove the retaining bolts and remove the plastic undershield from beneath the engine.

3 Drain the engine oil, then clean and refit the engine oil drain plug, fit a new sealing washer on refitting. And then tighten it to the specified torque. If the engine is nearing its service interval when the oil and filter are due for renewal, it is recommended that the filter is also removed, and a new one fitted. Refer to for further information.

4 Progressively slacken and remove all of the steel oil pan retaining bolts.

5 The lower steel oil pan is sealed to the upper alloy sump casing with strong liquid gasket sealer, which is very difficult to remove, however methodical use of a spatula or thin knife will release the sump **(see illustration)**. Take care not to distort or damage the mating surfaces of the lower oil pan and upper alloy sump. Take adequate precautions to catch any oil remaining inside the sump housing, as the oil pan is removed.

Refitting

6 Clean all traces of sealant from the mating surfaces of the upper alloy part of the sump and steel oil pan, then use a clean rag to wipe out the oil pan and the sump interior.

7 Ensure that the lower oil pan and upper alloy casing mating surfaces are clean and dry. Apply a continuous bead of suitable sealant to the mating surface of the oil pan. Apply a 4mm to 5mm diameter bead of sealant to the oil pan, going around the inner edge of each bolt hole **(see illustration)**.

8 Offer up the sump, locating it in the correct position, and refit its retaining bolts. Tighten the bolts evenly and progressively to the specified torque and in the correct sequence **(see illustration)**.

9 Refit the engine undershield and securely tighten the retaining bolts.

10 After reassembly, the engine can then be refilled with fresh engine oil. Refer to Chapter, 1A Section 4 for further information.

11 Start the engine and warm it up to normal operating temperature, check for any leaks from the sump area.

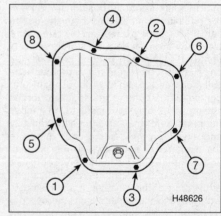

11.8 Tighten the bolts in the sequence shown

12.3 Remove the tensioner from the cylinder block

12.4a Undo the retaining bolts...

12.4b ...and remove the strainer

12 Oil pump, drive chain and sprockets – removal, inspection and refitting

Removal

1 Remove the timing chain as described in Section 7.

2 Remove the sump oil pan as described in Section 11.

3 Remove the chain tensioner from the pivot, noting the position of the spring located in the hole in the cylinder block **(see illustration)**.

4 Undo the retaining bolts and remove the oil pump strainer from the base of the oil pump **(see illustrations)**.Recover the sealing ring and discard, as a new one will be required for refitting.

5 Release the securing clip and release the oil pump electro valve from the alloy sump housing **(see illustrations)**.

6 Undo the retaining bolts and remove the oil pump from inside the alloy sump housing, releasing the oil ump sprocket as it is removed **(see illustrations)**.

7 The oil pump drive chain can now be removed, releasing the chain from the crankshaft sprocket.

Inspection

8 Clean the components and carefully examine the chain, sprockets, electro valve and pump for any signs of excessive wear. If evident, it is recommended that all the components are renewed as a set **(see illustration)**.

12.5a Release the securing clip...

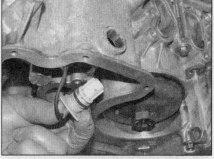

12.5b ...and remove the oil pump electro valve

9 Before refitting the oil pump, prime it by filling with clean engine oil whilst rotating the pump clockwise.

Refitting

10 Fit the oil pump back in place in the sump upper housing and tighten the retaining bolts.

11 Make sure the chain is located around the two sprocket correctly, and then refit them as a complete assembly to the oil pump drive shaft and crankshaft **(see illustration)**.

12.6a Undo the retaining bolts...

12.6b ...remove the oil pump...

12.6c ...and release the drive chain

12.8 Check the condition of all components

12.11 Make sure the chain is located around the sprocket correctly

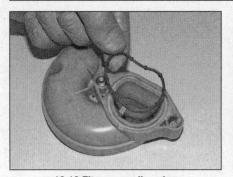

12.12 Fit new sealing ring

12.13 Make sure the tensioner spring (arrowed) is located correctly

13.2 Carefully prise out the oil seal

12 Fit a new sealing ring to the strainer **(see illustration)**, and then refit to the oil pump and tighten the retaining bolts.

13 Refit the chain tensioner to the pivot on the cylinder block, making sure the tensioner spring is located correctly in the cylinder block **(see illustration)**.

14 Refit the sump oil pan as described in Section 11.

15 Refit the timing chain cover as described in Section 6.

13 Crankshaft oil seals – renewal

Timing chain cover oil seal

1 Remove the crankshaft pulley as described in Section 5.

2 Carefully lever the oil seal out of position, using a large flat-bladed screwdriver, taking care not to damage the end of the crankshaft or timing cover **(see illustration)**.

3 Clean the seal housing, and polish off any burrs or raised edges, which may have caused the seal to fail in the first place.

4 Lubricate the lips of the new seal with a smear of clean oil and offer up the seal ensuring its sealing lip is facing inwards. Carefully ease the seal into position, taking care not to damage its sealing lip. Drive the seal into position until it seats flush with the face of the timing chain cover **(see illustrations)**. Take care not to damage the seal lips during fitting.

5 Wash off any traces of oil, then refit the crankshaft pulley as described in Section 5.

Flywheel oil seal

6 Remove the flywheel, as described in Section 14.

7 Note the fitted position of the old seal, then prise it out of the right-hand cover/housing using a screwdriver or suitable hooked instrument, taking care not to damage the surface of the crankshaft. Alternatively, the oil seal can be removed by drilling a hole in the seal, and then inserting a self-tapping screw. A pair of grips/pliers can then be used to pull out the oil seal **(see illustrations)**. **Note:** *Take care when drilling the hole, to not drill into anything other than the seal*.

8 Clean the seal housing, and polish off any burrs or raised edges, which may have caused the seal to fail in the first place **(see illustration)**.

9 Lubricate with clean oil the lips of the new seal and the crankshaft shoulder, then offer up the seal to the cylinder block/crankcase. Ease the sealing lip of the seal over the crankshaft shoulder by hand only, and press the seal

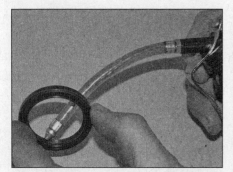

13.4a Lubricate the inner lip of the seal …

13.4b … press the seal into position …

13.4c … carefully fit the seal into the cover

13.7a Carefully drill a hole in the seal …

13.7b … insert a self tapping screw …

13.7c … and lever the seal out from the casing

13.8 Clean around the seal fitting surface area

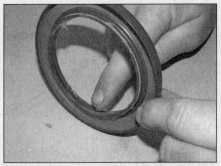

13.9a Using clean oil to lubricate the inner lip of the seal ...

13.9b ... press the seal into position ...

13.10a Apply some sealant around the outer edge of the seal ...

13.10b ... press the seal fully into position ...

13.10c ... then clean off the excess sealant from around the casing

evenly into its recess to make it square in the casing **(see illustrations)**.

10 With the seal still protruding out from the cylinder block, apply a coat of liquid gasket/sealant all the way around the outer edge of the seal. Carefully drive the seal into position until it seats flush with the face of the cylinder block, and then wipe off the excess liquid gasket/sealant from the casing **(see illustrations)**. Make sure the outer edge of the seal is sitting flush with the cylinder block casing.

11 Wash off any traces of oil or sealant, then refit the flywheel as described in Section.

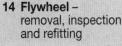

14 Flywheel –
removal, inspection and refitting

Note: *It is recommended that new flywheel bolts are used on refitting. Suitable thread-locking fluid will be required to coat the threads of the flywheel bolts.*

Removal

1 Remove the gearbox as described in Chapter 7 Section 7.
2 Remove the clutch as described in Chapter 6 Section 8.
3 Mark the flywheel in relation to the crankshaft.
4 The flywheel must now be held stationary whilst the bolts are loosened. To do this, locate a long bolt in one of the transmission mounting bolt holes, and either insert a wide-bladed screwdriver in the starter ring

gear, or use a piece of bent metal bar engaged with the ring gear. Alternatively, a suitable tool can be made up and bolted to the cylinder block **(see illustration 16.8)**. Do not insert a bar or tool into the engine speed (flywheel) sensor teeth on the flywheel.
5 Unscrew the mounting bolts and withdraw the flywheel from the crankshaft **(see illustrations)**. Be careful not to drop it – it is heavy.

Inspection

6 Examine the flywheel for scoring of the clutch face, and for wear or chipping of the ring gear teeth. If the clutch face is scored, it may be possible to have the flywheel machined, but renewal is preferable. If the ring gear is worn or damaged, it may be possible to renew it separately, but this job is best left

to a Renault dealer or engineering works. The temperature to which the new ring gear must be heated for installation is critical and, if not done accurately, the hardness of the teeth will be destroyed.

Refitting

7 Thoroughly clean the flywheel and crankshaft faces, then locate the flywheel on the crankshaft, making sure that any previously-made marks are aligned. Note that the flywheel bolts holes are offset, so the flywheel can only be fitted in one position.
8 Apply a few drops of locking fluid to the threads of the new flywheel bolts. Fit the bolts, and tighten them in a diagonal sequence to the specified torque in the two stages given in the Specifications. Prevent the flywheel from turning using

14.5a Unscrew the mounting bolts...

14.5b...and lift the flywheel from the crankshaft

14.8 Using a suitable tool to prevent the flywheel from turning when tightening the securing bolts

the method used during removal **(see illustration)**.

9 Refit the clutch with reference to Chapter 6 Section 8.

10 Refit the gearbox as described in Chapter 7 Section 7.

---

15 Engine/transmission mountings – inspection and renewal

Inspection

1 If improved access is required, firmly apply the handbrake, and then jack up the front of the vehicle and support it securely on axle stands (see Chapter 13 Section 5).

2 Check the mounting rubber to see if it is cracked, hardened or separated from the metal at any point; renew the mounting if any such damage or deterioration is evident.

3 Check that all the mounting's fasteners are securely tightened; use a torque wrench to check if possible.

4 Using a lever, check for wear in the mounting by carefully levering against it to check for free play. Where this is not possible, enlist the aid of an assistant to move the engine/transmission back-and-forth, or from side-to-side, while you watch the mounting. While some free play is to be expected even from new components, excessive wear should be obvious. If excessive free play is found, check first that the fasteners are correctly secured, and then renew any worn components as described below.

Renewal

Right-hand mounting

5 Place a jack beneath the engine, with a block of wood on the jack head. Raise the jack until it is supporting the weight of the engine **(see illustration)**.

6 Slacken and remove the two retaining bolts from the inner wing panel, remove the three retaining bolts from the engine mounting bracket, and then withdraw the complete mounting from the engine compartment **(see illustrations)**. Unclip the fuel pipes from the retaining clip on top of the mounting bracket.

7 Check carefully for signs of wear or damage on all components, and renew them where necessary.

8 On refitting, fit the engine mounting and bracket to the inner wing panel and engine, and then securely tighten its retaining bolts to the specified torque setting.

9 Clip the fuel pipes back into the retaining clip on top of the mounting.

10 With the engine mounting back in position, lower the jack and remove it from underneath the engine.

Left-hand mounting

11 Remove the battery, as described in Chapter 5A Section 4.

12 Place a jack and block of wood beneath the transmission, and raise the jack to take the weight of the transmission.

13 Slacken and remove the through-bolt/stud retaining nut from the centre of the mounting and the two outer nuts, then remove the mounting **(see illustrations)**.

14 If required, undo the retaining bolts from the transmission to remove the lower mounting bracket **(see illustrations)**.

15 Check carefully for signs of wear or damage on all components, and renew them where necessary.

16 On refitting, fit the upper and lower mounting brackets (where removed) and securely tighten the retaining bolts.

17 Align the left-hand rubber mounting with the bolt/stud on the lower mounting bracket and tighten its nut to the specified torque setting.

18 Refit the two outer retaining nuts, and tighten to the specified torque setting.

19 With the transmission mounting back in

15.5 Supporting the engine on a jack

15.6a Undo the two mounting bolts from the inner wing…

15.6b …and the three mounting bracket bolts…

15.6c …and remove the complete mounting bracket

15.13a Undo the retaining nuts…

15.13b …and withdraw the mounting

position, lower the jack and remove it from underneath the transmission.

20 Refit the battery, with reference to, Chapter 5A Section 4.

Rear lower mounting

21 If not already done, firmly apply the handbrake, and then jack up the front of the vehicle and support it securely on axle stands (see *Jacking and vehicle support*).

22 Slacken and remove the bolts securing the rear mounting bracket to the transmission, and then withdraw the bracket from transmission **(see illustration)**.

23 Slacken and remove the bolt securing the rear mounting link to the subframe, and then withdraw the mounting link from subframe **(see illustration)**.

24 Check carefully for signs of wear or damage on all components, and renew them where necessary.

25 On reassembly, fit the rear mounting to the subframe, and tighten the retaining bolt to the specified torque.

26 Refit the mounting bracket to the lower part of the transmission and tighten its retaining bolts to the specified torque.

27 With the transmission rear mounting link arm back in position, lower the vehicle to the ground.

15.14a Undo the retaining nuts…

15.14b …and withdraw the mounting

15.22 Remove the mounting bracket from the transmission

15.23 Remove the link arm from the subframe

Chapter 2 Part B
1.2 litre petrol engine in-car repair procedures

Contents

Degrees of difficulty

Easy, suitable for novice with little experience **Fairly easy,** suitable for beginner with some experience **Fairly difficult,** suitable for competent DIY mechanic **Difficult,** suitable for experienced DIY mechanic **Very difficult,** suitable for expert DIY or professional

Specifications

General

Type	Four cylinder, in-line, single overhead camshaft with 16 valves
Bore	69.0 mm
Stroke	76.8 mm
Capacity	1149 cc
Firing order	1-3-4-2 (No 1 cylinder at flywheel end)
Direction of crankshaft rotation	Clockwise viewed from pulley end
Compression ratio	9.8 : 1

Camshaft

Camshaft endfloat	0.08 to 0.178 mm

Valve clearances (cold)

Camshaft with groove:	
Inlet	0.25 to 0.32 mm
Exhaust	0.35 to 0.42 mm
Camshaft without groove:	
Inlet	0.10 to 0.17 mm
Exhaust	0.20 to 0.27 mm

Lubrication system

System pressure:	
At idle	1.5 bar
At 3000 rpm	3.9 bar
At 3000 rpm (maximum)	5.3 bar
Oil pump type	Twin gear

Torque wrench settings

	Nm	lbf ft
Air conditioning compressor	21	15
Alternator:		
Upper bolt	25	18
Lower bolt	50	37
Alternator mounting bracket	50	37
Camshaft:		
Stage 1 – tighten bearing cap No 5	9	7
Stage 2 – tighten all bolts	5	4
Stage 3 – fully-loosen bearing cap No 1, then tighten	7	5
Stage 4 – tighten bearing cap No 1	Angle-tighten a further 50° ± 6°	
Stage 5	Repeat Stages 3 and 4	
Camshaft sprocket bolt:		
Stage 1	30	22
Stage 2	Angle-tighten a further 45° ± 6°	
Clutch pressure plate	20	15
Connecting rod (big-end) cap:		
Stage 1	14	10
Stage 2	Angle-tighten a further 39° ± 6°	
Coolant outlet	9	7
Coolant temperature sensor	15	11
Crankshaft oil seal housing	9	7
Crankshaft pulley/sprocket bolt: *		
Stage 1	40	30
Stage 2	Angle-tighten a further 150° ± 6°	
Cylinder head bolts: *		
Stage 1	20	15
Stage 2	Angle-tighten a further 230° ± 6°	
Engine/transmission mountings (see Section 17):		
Left-hand mounting central nut	62	46
Left-hand mounting to body	21	15
Left-hand mounting to transmission	62	46
Rear mounting	62	46
Right-hand mounting central nut	105	77
Right-hand mounting to engine/body	62	46
Exhaust heat shield	15	11
Exhaust manifold	25	18
Flywheel bolts: *		
Stage 1	18	13
Stage 2	Angle-tighten a further 110° ± 6°	
Inlet manifold:		
Stage 1 – tighten all side bolts	Hand-tight	
Stage 2 – tighten side bolts 4 and 5	6	4
Stage 3 – side bolts 4 and 5	Slacken fully	
Stage 4 – tighten all side bolts	10	7
Stage 5 – tighten upper bolts	10	7
Knock sensor	20	15
Main bearing cap:		
Stage 1	20	15
Stage 2	Angle-tighten a further 76°	
Oil filter	20	15
Oil level sensor	38	28
Oil pump	9	7
Oil pump strainer	9	7
Roadwheel bolts	105	77
Rocker arm rail bolts:		
Stage 1	Tighten camshaft end bearing caps	
Stage 2	5	4
Stage 3	Slacken fully	
Stage 4	7	5
Stage 5	Angle-tighten a further 50° ± 6°	
Sump:		
Stage 1	8	6
Stage 2	10	7
To gearbox bellhousing	44	32
Timing belt lower and intermediate cover	10	7
Timing belt tensioner nut	24	18
Timing belt upper cover	33	24
Valve cover	10	7
Water pump	9	7

New bolt(s) must be fitted

1 General Information

1 This Part of Chapter 2 is devoted to in-car repair procedures for the 1.2 litre petrol engine. Similar information covering the other engine types can be found in Parts A and C. All procedures concerning engine removal and refitting, and engine block/cylinder head overhaul can be found in Part D of this Chapter.

2 Most of the operations included in this Part are based on the assumption that the engine is still installed in the car. Therefore, if this information is being used during a complete engine overhaul, with the engine already removed, many of the steps included here will not apply.

Engine description

3 The engine is of four cylinder, in-line, single overhead camshaft type, mounted transversely in the front of the car.

4 The cylinder bores are machined directly into the cast iron cylinder block. The crankshaft is supported within the cylinder block on five shell-type main bearings. Thrustwashers are fitted at the centre main bearing to control crankshaft endfloat.

5 The connecting rods are attached to the crankshaft by horizontally-split shell-type big-end bearings, and to the pistons by interference fit gudgeon pins. The aluminium alloy pistons are of the slipper type, and are fitted with three piston rings, comprising two compression rings and a scraper type oil control ring.

6 The overhead camshaft is driven by the crankshaft via a toothed rubber timing belt which also drives the water pump. The camshaft operates the valves via rocker arms located on a rocker shaft bolted to the top of the cylinder head. Each rocker arm operates two valves.

7 A semi-enclosed crankcase ventilation system is employed.

8 Lubrication is by pressure feed from a gear type oil pump, which is driven directly from the timing end of the crankshaft.

Operations with engine in place

9 The following operations can be carried out without having to remove the engine from the car.

a) Removal and refitting of the cylinder head.
b) Removal and refitting of the timing belt and sprockets.
c) Renewal of the camshaft oil seal.
d) Removal and refitting of the camshaft.
e) Removal and refitting of the sump.
f) Removal and refitting of the connecting rods and pistons*.
g) Removal and refitting of the oil pump.
h) Renewal of the crankshaft oil seals.
i) Renewal of the engine mountings.
j) Removal and refitting of the flywheel.

Note: *Although the operation marked with an asterisk can be carried out with the engine in the car after removal of the sump, it is better for the engine to be removed in the interests of cleanliness and improved access. For this reason, the procedure is described in Part D of this Chapter.

2 Compression test – description and interpretation

Note: A compression gauge will be required for this test.

1 A compression check will tell you what mechanical condition the top end (pistons, rings, valves, head gasket) of the engine is in. Specifically, it can tell you if the compression is down due to leakage caused by worn piston rings, defective valves and seats or a blown head gasket. **Note:** The engine must be at normal operating temperature, and the battery must be fully-charged, for this check.

2 Begin by cleaning the area around the spark plugs before you remove them (compressed air should be used, if available, otherwise a small brush or even a bicycle tyre pump will work). The idea is to prevent dirt from getting into the cylinders as the compression check is being done.

3 Remove all of the spark plugs from the engine (see Chapter 1A Section 18).

4 Disable the engine management system by removing the main engine protection fuse from the engine compartment fusebox.

5 Fit the compression gauge into the No 1 spark plug hole – the type of tester which screws into the plug thread is to be preferred **(see illustration).**

6 Have an assistant hold the accelerator pedal fully depressed, while at the same time cranking the engine over several times on the starter motor. Observe the compression gauge – the compression should build-up quickly in a healthy engine. Low compression on the first stroke, followed by gradually increasing pressure on successive strokes, indicates worn piston rings. A low compression reading on the first stroke,

2.5 Checking the compression

which does not build-up during successive strokes, indicates leaking valves or a blown head gasket (a cracked head could also be the cause). Deposits on the undersides of the valve heads can also cause low compression. Record the highest gauge reading obtained, then repeat the procedure for the remaining cylinders.

7 Add some engine oil (about three squirts from a plunger type oil can) to each cylinder, through the spark plug hole, and repeat the test.

8 If the compression increases after the oil is added, the piston rings are worn. If the compression does not increase significantly, the leakage is occurring at the valves or head gasket. Leakage past the valves may be caused by burned valve seats and/or faces, or warped, cracked or bent valves.

9 If two adjacent cylinders have equally low compression, there is a strong possibility that the head gasket between them is blown. The appearance of coolant in the combustion chambers or the crankcase would verify this condition.

10 Actual compression pressures for the engines covered by this manual are not specified by the manufacturer. However, bearing in mind the information given in the preceding paragraphs, the results obtained should give a good indication of engine condition and what course of action, if any, to take.

3 Top Dead Centre (TDC) for No 1 piston – locating

Note: Number one piston is at the flywheel end of the engine.

1 Top dead centre (TDC) is the highest point in the cylinder that each piston reaches as the crankshaft turns. Each piston reaches TDC at the end of the compression stroke, and again at the end of the exhaust stroke; however, for the purpose of timing the engine, TDC refers to the position of No 1 piston at the end of its compression stroke.

2 Apply the handbrake, then jack up the front right-hand side of the car and support it on axle stands. Remove the right-hand roadwheel.

3 Remove the plastic liners from within the right-hand wheel arch to give access to the crankshaft pulley bolt.

4 Remove the spark plugs as described in Chapter 1A Section 18.

5 Place a finger or inverted screwdriver handle over the No 1 spark plug hole in the cylinder head (nearest the flywheel). The spark plugs are deeply recessed at the bottom of metal tubes. Turn the engine in a clockwise direction, using a socket or spanner on the crankshaft pulley bolt, until pressure is felt in the No 1 cylinder. This indicates that No 1 piston is rising on its compression stroke.

3.6 A drill bit is used to lock the engine at top dead centre (TDC)

3.7 The camshaft sprocket correctly aligned

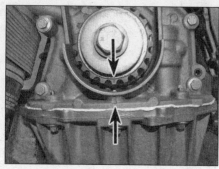

3.8 The crankshaft correctly aligned

6 A hole is provided at the gearbox end of the engine block to locate TDC. A special tool is available, but an 8 mm twist drill is perfectly adequate for the purpose. Rotate the engine in a clockwise direction until the drill bit or special tool slides into the hole provide at the rear of the flywheel **(see illustration)**. Note that access is awkward and more often than not the bore of the hole will be corroded. In necessary remove the starter motor to improve access (see Chapter 5A Section 9) and then clean the bore of the hole with a smaller diameter drill that has a been wrapped with emery cloth (or similar).

7 If pressure was felt as described in paragraph 5, then the engine is now at TDC with number one piston on the compression stroke. If this method proves inconclusive then remove the timing belt cover as described in Section 6. The timing mark on the camshaft pulley will be aligned correctly when the engine is at TDC on the compression stroke **(see illustration)**.

8 If the crankshaft pulley is now removed (see Section 5), the timing mark on the crankshaft sprocket should be aligned with the TDC mark at the bottom of the oil pump flange **(see illustration)**.

4 Valve clearances – adjustment

Note: *This operation is not part of the maintenance schedule. It should be*

undertaken if noise from the valve gear becomes evident, or if loss of performance gives cause to suspect that the clearances may be incorrect. A new valve cover gasket will be required.

1 Disconnect the battery negative lead, and position the lead away from the battery (Chapter 5A Section 4).

2 Remove the air filter housing and associated pipe work. On the non-turbo engine remove the inlet manifold. This is not necessary on the turbocharged engine.

3 On the turbocharged engine remove the intercooler pipe, exhaust manifold heat shield, the wiring connector to the oxygen sensor and the oil filler extension pipe **(see illustrations)**. Disconnect the crankcase breather pipe from the valve cover.

4 Remove the HT leads and ignition coil. Remove the spark plugs, with reference to Section, in order to make turning the engine easier. This however is not essential.

5 Unscrew the bolts **(see illustration)**. Remove the valve cover (metal or plastic depending on the model) and gasket. Discard the gasket, a new one must be used on refitting.

6 Draw the valve positions on a piece of paper, numbering them according to their cylinders, from the flywheel end of the engine (ie, 1E, 1I, 2E, 2I and so on). The inlet valves are on the inlet manifold side of the cylinder head, and the exhaust valves are on the exhaust manifold side. As the valve clearances are adjusted, cross them off.

7 Identify the camshaft fitted to the vehicle. There are two types fitted, one has a groove on the camshaft (between the cam lobes) on cylinder number two. The alternative camshaft has no groove.

8 There are two methods of adjusting the valve clearances; the degrees of crankshaft rotation method and the 'exhaust valve open' method. whichever method is chosen, access to the crankshaft pulley will be required. Jack up and support the front of the vehicle (see *Jacking and vehicle support*) and then remove the right-hand roadwheel and wing liner.

Exhaust valve method

9 Fit a socket and extension bar to the crankshaft pulley and turn the crankshaft in a clockwise direction until No 1 exhaust valve is completely open (ie, the valve spring is completely compressed). Note that each rocker arm operates two valves at the same time.

10 Insert a feeler blade of the correct thickness (see Section) between the No 3 cylinder inlet valve stems and the end of the rocker arms. It should be a firm sliding fit. If adjustment is necessary, loosen the locknut on the rocker arm using a ring spanner, and turn the adjustment screw with a screwdriver until the fit is correct **(see illustrations)**. Tighten the locknut and recheck the adjustment, then repeat the adjustment procedure on No 4 cylinder exhaust valves. Note that the clearances for the inlet and exhaust valves are different.

4.3a Disconnect the oxygen sensor wiring...

4.3b ...and unbolt the oil filler extension pipe

4.5 Removing the valve cover bolts

4.10a Check the clearance with a feeler gauge...

4.10b ...and adjust if necessary

4.12 A torque angle gauge, fitted to the crankshaft pulley

4.19a Applying a bead of sealant to the exhaust side bolt holes

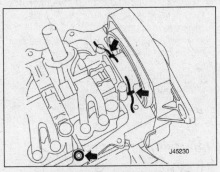
4.19b Apply sealant as shown to the right-hand bearing cap...

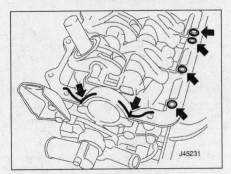
4.19c ...and the left-hand bearing cap

11 Turn the engine in a clockwise direction until No 3 exhaust valve is completely open, then adjust the valve clearances on No 4 inlet and No 2 exhaust valves. Continue to adjust the valve clearances in the following sequence.

Exhaust valves fully open	Inlet valves to adjust	Exhaust valves to adjust
1E	3I	4E
3E	4I	2E
4E	2I	1E
2E	1I	3E

Crankshaft degrees method

12 Fit the TDC locking pin (or 8 mm drill bit) and then fit a torque angle gauge to the crankshaft (see illustration).
13 Rotate the crankshaft 20° clockwise and adjust the clearances on exhaust valves 1 and 3.
14 Zero the gauge and then rotate the crankshaft 240° clockwise. Adjust the inlet valves on cylinders 1 and 3.
15 Zero the gauge and rotate the crankshaft 120° clockwise. Adjust the exhaust valves 2 and 4.
16 Zero the gauge and rotate the crankshaft 240° clockwise. Adjust the inlet valves 2 and 4.
17 Remove the socket or spanner from the crankshaft pulley bolt.

Both methods

18 Refit the spark plugs, with reference to Chapter 1A Section 18.
19 Apply beads of sealant to the camshaft end bearing caps and around the mounting bolt holes on the exhaust side (see illustrations).

20 New spark plug seals should be fitted to the cover before refitting. Refit the valve cover using a new gasket, and tighten the securing

4.20a Fit new spark plug tube seals to the valve cover...

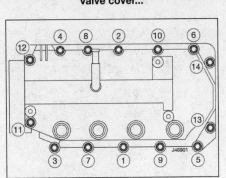
4.20c Tighten the bolts in the order shown (non-turbo engines). On some engines bolts 3 and 9 are not fitted

bolts to the specified torque (see illustrations).
21 Refitting of the remaining parts is a reversal of removal.

4.20b ...pushing them home with a suitable socket

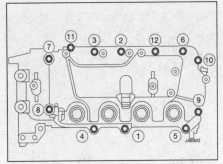
4.20d Tighten the bolts in the order shown (turbo engines)

5.6 Align the pulley correctly

5 Crankshaft pulley – removal and refitting

Removal

1 Apply the handbrake, then jack up the front of the car and support it securely on axle stands (see 'Jacking and support 13 '). Remove the right-hand front roadwheel.
2 Remove the plastic engine undershield and the wing liner from inside the wheel arch for access to the crankshaft pulley.
3 Remove the auxiliary drivebelt with reference to Chapter 1A Section 9.
4 The crankshaft must now be held stationary in order to loosen the crankshaft pulley bolt. Remove the access plate from the bell housing and either jam the flywheel ring gear

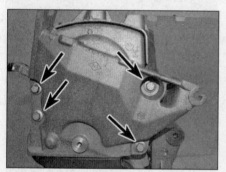

6.1 Remove the upper cover bolts

6.7a Remove the single bolt...

with a prybar, or preferably fit the correct flywheel locking tool (Renault Mot 582-01 or AST 4356).
5 With the crankshaft held securely in place, unscrew the pulley bolt and recover the washer, then remove the pulley from the crankshaft.

Refitting

6 Refitting is a reversal of removal, bearing in mind the following points.
a) Ensure that the locating pin (or slot) on the crankshaft sprocket engages with the corresponding hole in the pulley (see illustration).
b) Use a new bolt and tighten the pulley bolt to the specified torque, in the two stages given in the Specifications.
c) Fit and tension the auxiliary drivebelt as described in Chapter 1A Section 9.

6 Timing belt covers – removal and refitting

Upper timing belt cover

Removal

1 Support the engine and remove the upper engine mount as described in to Section 17. Prise free the wiring cable clip and then remove the cover (see illustration).

Refitting

2 Refitting is a reversal of removal.

6.4 Remove the bolts from the centre cover

6.7b ...and remove the cover from the engine

Centre cover

Removal

3 Support the engine and remove the upper engine mount as described in to Section 17.
4 Unscrew the two securing bolts and withdraw the centre plastic cover (see illustration).

Refitting

5 Refitting is a reversal of removal, but refit the upper timing belt cover and upper engine mount as described in Section 17.

Lower plastic cover

Removal

6 Remove the crankshaft pulley as described in Section 5.
7 Unscrew the securing bolt, and remove the lower plastic cover (see illustrations).

Refitting

8 Refitting is a reversal of removal, but refit the crankshaft pulley as described in Section 5.

7 Timing belt – removal, inspection, refitting and adjustment

Caution: If the timing belt breaks or slips in service, extensive engine damage may result. Renew the belt at the interval specified in Chapter 1A Section 25, or earlier if its condition is at all doubtful.

Removal

1 Disconnect the battery negative lead as described in Chapter 5A Section 4.
2 Jack up the front of the car, and support it on axle stands (see Jacking and vehicle support) and remove the right-hand wing liner.
3 Remove the crankshaft pulley as described in Section 5.
4 Temporarily refit the crankshaft pulley bolt, and turn the crankshaft to bring No 1 piston to TDC, as described in Section 3. Lock the engine in this position with the special tool (or an 8 mm drill bit) as described in Section 3.
5 Carefully, position a suitable jack and a large block of wood under the sump to support the engine. Raise the jack to take the weight of the engine (see illustration).

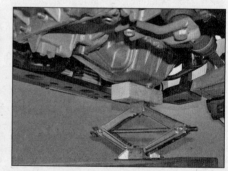

7.5 Support the engine with a suitable jack

6 Remove the right-hand upper engine mounting and the upper timing belt cover, with reference to Sections 6 and 17.

7 Remove the two plastic outer timing belt covers with reference to Section 6.

8 Check that the marks on the crankshaft and the camshaft pulley are aligned. Rotate the engine one revolution if the mark is not aligned on the camshaft.

9 Slacken the timing belt tensioner nut, and turn the tensioner pulley clockwise to relieve the belt tension **(see illustration)**. Slip the timing belt from the sprockets and pulleys. With the timing belt removed, do not turn the crankshaft or the camshaft until the belt has been refitted.

Inspection

10 Check the timing belt carefully for any signs of uneven wear, splitting or oil contamination and renew it if there is the slightest doubt about its condition. If the engine is undergoing an overhaul and has covered more than 36 000 miles since the original belt was fitted, it is advisable to renew the belt as a matter of course, regardless of its apparent condition. Note that Renault recommend that the belt and tensioner are always renewed if removed.

11 If signs of oil contamination are found, trace the source of the oil leak and rectify it, then wash down the engine timing belt area and all related components to remove all traces of oil.

Refitting and adjustment

12 Ensure that the timing marks on the camshaft sprocket and crankshaft sprocket are still aligned with the relevant mark on the valve cover and the oil pump flange.

13 The new tensioner is supplied with a locking pin, this should be left in place until the new belt is fiited. Fit the new tensioner to the engine, ensuring that the lugs on the rear are located correctly **(see illustration)**.

14 Fit the timing belt over the crankshaft and camshaft sprockets and around the water pump pulley, ensuring that the belt front run is taut, ie, all slack is on the tensioner pulley side of the belt, then fit the belt around the tensioner pulley and turn the pulley anti-clockwise. Where applicable, line up the two timing reference marks on the belt with the timing marks on the crankshaft and camshaft sprockets. Do not twist the belt sharply during refitting, and do make sure that the belt teeth are correctly seated centrally in the sprockets and that the timing marks remain in alignment **(see illustrations)**.

15 Locate a 6.0 mm Allen key in the tensioner eccentric hub and turn it anti-clockwise to bring the index pointer to the front of the timing window **(see illustration)**. Tighten the tensioner nut to the specified torque.

16 Remove the locking tool and temporarily refit the crankshaft pulley bolt, then turn the crankshaft clockwise through six complete revolutions, and align the timing marks again.

7.9 Slacken the timing belt tensioner nut and turn the tensioner pulley clockwise

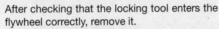

7.14a Align the timing reference marks on the belt with the timing marks on the crankshaft sprocket...

After checking that the locking tool enters the flywheel correctly, remove it.

17 Fit the Allen key, then loosen the tensioner nut and turn the eccentric hub until the index pointer is in the middle of the timing window **(see illustration)**. Tighten the tensioner nut to the specified torque.

18 At this point check that the tensioner does not contact the cylinder head. If the tensioner is in contact with the cylinder head, refit the timing pin and remove the belt. Remove the tensioner and reposition the roller pin on the tensioner.

7.13 Locate the lugs on the new tensioner correctly

7.14b ...and camshaft sprocket

19 Refit the two plastic outer timing belt covers.

20 Refit the upper timing belt cover, and the engine mounting bracket, with reference to Section 17.

21 Carefully lower the trolley jack and wooden block from under the sump.

22 Refit the crankshaft pulley as described in Section 5.

23 Refit the wing liner and roadwheel.

24 Reconnect the battery negative lead.

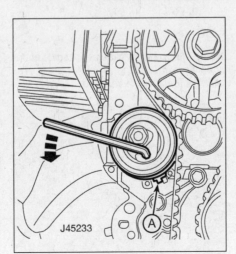

7.15 Adjust the tensioner so that the index pointer is at the front of the timing window (A)

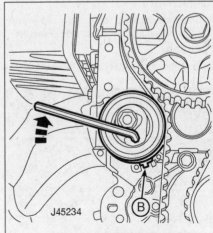

7.17 Align the pointer in the middle of the timing window (B) after turning the engine six complete turns

8.5 Ensure that the lug on the sprocket engages with the cut-out in the end of the camshaft

8.6a Tighten the sprocket bolt to the specified torque...

8.6b ...and the correct angle

8 Timing belt tensioner and sprockets – removal, inspection and refitting

Camshaft sprocket

Removal

1 Remove the timing belt as described in Section 7. Do not rotate the crankshaft or the camshaft until the timing belt has been refitted.

2 Slacken the camshaft sprocket retaining bolt and remove it, along with its washer. To prevent the camshaft from rotating, a tool can be fabricated from two lengths of steel strip (one long, the other short) and three nuts and bolts. One nut and bolt should form the pivot of a forked tool with the remaining two nuts and bolts at the tips of the forks to engage with the sprocket spokes (see illustration 8.6a). Alternatively, if the valve cover and rocker shaft are removed, the camshaft can be held stationary using a suitable spanner on the flats provided on the timing belt end of the camshaft. Do not allow the camshaft to rotate as the sprocket bolt is being loosened.

3 Withdraw the sprocket from the camshaft.

Inspection

4 Clean the sprocket thoroughly, and renew it if it shows signs of wear, damage or cracks.

Refitting

5 Refit the sprocket, ensuring that the lug on

the sprocket engages with the cut-out in the end of the camshaft (see illustration).

6 Prevent the sprocket from rotating by using the method employed on removal, then tighten the sprocket securing bolt to the specified torque setting (see illustrations). Do not allow the camshaft to turn as the bolt is tightened.

7 Fit and tension the timing belt as described in Section 7.

Crankshaft sprocket

8 With reference to Section 5 remove the crankshaft pulley and then remove the sprocket. Examine it for damage and wear.

Tensioner pulley

9 The tensioner must be renewed at the same time as the timing belt. Remove the timing belt as described in Section 7 and then unbolt the tensioner and renew it.

Water pump pulley

10 The water pump pulley is integral with the water pump, and cannot be removed separately.

9 Camshaft oil seal – renewal

Note: The oil seal is extremely fragile, and is supplied with a fitting protector/guide. The seal itself must not be touched.

1 Remove the camshaft sprocket as described in Section 8 (see illustration).

2 Note the fitted depth of the seal, then prise out the old oil seal using a small screwdriver, taking care not to damage the surface of the camshaft. Alternatively, the oil seal can be removed by drilling two small holes diagonally opposite each other and inserting self-tapping screws in them. A pair of grips can then be used to pull out the oil seal, by pulling on each side in turn.

3 If the camshaft is to be renewed it is far simpler to recover the seal after the bearing cap has been removed (see illustration).

4 Inspect the seal rubbing surface on the camshaft. If it is grooved or rough in the area where the old seal was fitted, the new seal should be fitted slightly less deeply, so that it rubs on an unworn part of the surface.

5 Renault technicians use a special tool (Mot. 1587) to fit the oil seal. The tool consists of a threaded rod, metal tube and nut. The rod is screwed into the end of the camshaft, and the protector/guide located on it. The metal tube is then fitted against the oil seal and the nut tightened to press the seal into the cylinder head/bearing cap. If the Renault tool cannot be obtained, a similar tool can be made out of threaded rod, metal tube, a washer and nut.

6 Press the oil seal squarely into position and drive it home with a suitable socket (see illustrations). Note that the Renault tool is designed to locate the seal at the original depth, however, if the camshaft sealing surface is excessively worn, position it less

9.1 Remove the camshaft sprocket to access the oil seal

9.3 The seal can easily be removed if the bearing cap is removed first

9.6a The new seal with protective guide in place

9.6b A suitable socket is used to fit the new oil seal

10.6a Remove the rocker shafts...

10.6b ...and recover the bearing caps

deeply so that it locates on the unworn surface.

7 After fitting the oil seal, remove the protector/guide and remove the tool.

8 Wipe away any excess oil, then refit the camshaft sprocket as described in Section 8.

10 Camshaft –
removal, inspection and refitting

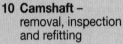

Note: *A new camshaft oil seal will be required on refitting.*

Removal

1 Jack up the front of the car, and support it on axle stands (see *Jacking and vehicle support*) and then remove the timing belt as described in Section 7.

2 Slacken the camshaft sprocket retaining bolt and remove it, along with its washer. Refer to paragraph 3 for details of a suitable tool to hold the sprocket. Remove the camshaft sprocket and the valve cover.

3 Using a suitable tool, lever out the camshaft plastic end cover from the left-hand end of the cylinder head. A new one will be required for refitting.

4 Using a marker pen, identify the camshaft bearing caps, the rocker arms and the two rocker shafts for position on the cylinder head. The inlet rocker shaft is the one at the front of the head.

5 Progressively unscrew the 10 bolts retaining the rocker shafts and camshaft bearing caps on the cylinder head.

6 Lift off the rocker shafts and arms, keeping all the components identified for position (**see illustrations**).

7 In order to measure the camshaft endfloat, the rocker arms must be removed from their shafts, then the shafts and camshaft bearing caps temporarily refitted. Tighten the bolts in their correct order to the specified torque and angle.

8 Using a dial gauge, measure the endfloat of the camshaft, and compare with that given in the Specifications.

9 Remove the rocker shafts and bearing caps again, then refit the arms to their correct shafts and retain them by temporarily inserting the end bolts.

10.10 Removing the camshaft

10 Carefully withdraw the camshaft from the cylinder head, taking care not to damage the bearing surfaces (**see illustration**).

Inspection

11 Keeping all the components in the correct order (**see illustration**) examine the camshaft bearing surfaces, and cam lobes for wear ridges and scoring. Renew the camshaft if any of these conditions are apparent.

12 Examine the condition of the bearing surfaces on the camshaft the bearing caps and in the cylinder head. If the surfaces are worn excessively, the cylinder head will need to be renewed.

13 Check the condition of the rocker shafts and the cam followers. Examine the roller bearing at the camshaft end and carefully check the lock nut and adjuster.

10.14 Lubricate the bearing surfaces

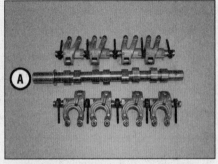

10.11 The camshaft, rocker shaft and followers in the correct order (A = Timing belt end of the engine)

Refitting

14 Lubricate the bearing surfaces in the cylinder head and bearing caps, then lower the camshaft onto the head (**see illustration**).

15 Apply 2.0 mm wide beads of sealant on the cylinder head (**see illustrations**) in the No 1 and No 5 bearing cap positions. Tighten bearing cap number 5 to 9 Nm.

16 Refit the remaining bearing caps in their correct positions.

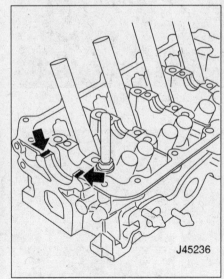

10.15a Apply beads of sealant on the cylinder head in the area of the No 1 bearing cap...

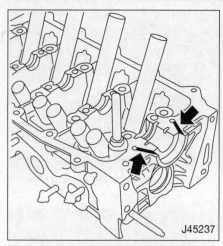

10.15b ...and No 5 bearing cap (caps numbered from the flywheel end of the engine)

17 Refit the rocker arms and shafts, insert the bolts, and tighten them in the correct order **(see illustration)** to the specified Stage 1 torque.
18 Loosen bolt 1 fully, then tighten it to the Stage 3 torque and Stage 4 angle **(see illustration)**.
19 Working on one bolt at a time and in the correct order, repeat the procedure on the remaining bearing cap/rocker shaft bolts.
20 Fit a new camshaft oil seal with reference to Section 9.
21 Refit the camshaft sprocket, making sure that the tab engages with the cut-out in the end of the camshaft. Hold the camshaft

10.18 Angle tighten the bolts

11.7 Remove the wiring loom

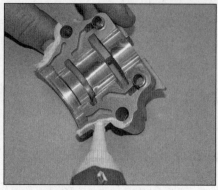

10.15c Applying sealant to the bearing cap

stationary using the method employed on removal, then insert the new bolt and tighten it to the specified torque and angle.
22 Carefully drive a new camshaft end cover into the left-hand end of the cylinder head. Renault technicians use tool Mot. 1605 to do this, however, a suitable metal tube may be used.
23 Adjust the valve clearances as described in Section 4.

11 Cylinder head – removal and refitting

Note: *A new cylinder head gasket, head bolts and a new valve cover gasket will be required on refitting.*

11.6 Remove the intercooler pipe from the inlet manifold

11.8 Recover the seal from the oil filler extension pipe

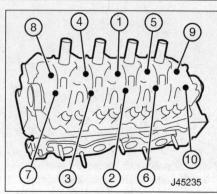

10.17 Tighten the bolts in the order shown

Removal

1 Apply the handbrake, then jack up the front of the vehicle and support securely on axle stands (see *Jacking and vehicle support*). Remove the front right-hand roadwheel and the engine compartment undertray.
2 Disconnect the battery negative lead as described in Chapter 5A Section 4.
3 Remove the right-hand wing liner.
4 Drain the cooling system as described in Chapter 1A Section 27.
5 Remove the auxiliary drivebelt and then remove the timing belt as described in Section 7. Make sure that the engine is adequately supported on a suitable jack.
6 Remove the air cleaner assembly and associated pipe work as described in Chapter 4A Section 2. On turbocharged engines remove the pipes from the intercooler **(see illustration)**.
7 Disconnect the wiring from the fuel injectors, throttle body and air temperature sensor **(see illustration)**.
8 Disconnect the fuel supply, observing the precautions given in Chapter 4A Section 1. Remove the oil filler extension taking care to recover the seal **(see illustration)**.
9 Remove the inlet manifold complete with the throttle body and fuel rail as described in Chapter 4A **(see illustration)**.
10 Disconnect the HT leads from the spark plugs. Remove the leads and the ignition coil.
11 Disconnect the charcoal canister pipe and the fuel vapour hoses from the solenoid purge valve.

11.9 Remove the inlet manifold

11.14 Remove the valve cover

11.16a Unplug the wiring from the knock sensor...

11.16b ...and the coolant temperature sensor

12 On turbocharged engines remove the coolant hoses, oil supply and oil return pipes from the turbocharger.

13 Unplug the wiring from the upstream oxygen sensor and remove the mounting from the rear of the cylinder head.

14 Unscrew the securing bolts, and withdraw the valve cover and gasket as described in Section 4 **(see illustration)**.

15 Loosen the clips and disconnect the hoses from the thermostat housing.

16 Unclip the wiring from the coolant temperature sensor and the knock sensor **(see illustrations)**.

17 Remove the bolts from the exhaust manifold flexible connection **(see illustration)**. Remove the manifold support bolt. On turbocharged engines remove the catalytic convertor as described in Chapter 4A Section 17. The cylinder head will be removed complete with the exhaust manifold.

18 Working in the reverse order of the tightening sequence **(see illustration 11.33)**, progressively unscrew (ie, slacken each bolt by one turn at a time) the cylinder head bolts. Withdraw the bolts.

19 Release the cylinder head from the cylinder block and locating dowels by rocking it. Do not prise between the mating faces of the cylinder head and block, as this may damage the gasket faces.

20 Carefully lift the cylinder head from the block and recover the cylinder head gasket.

21 Unbolt and remove the exhaust manifold.

22 If desired, the camshaft can be removed as described in Section 10, and the cylinder head can be dismantled as described in

Part D of this Chapter. If necessary, unbolt the thermostat housing and lifting eye from the left-hand end of the head. Remove and discard the housing gasket.

Refitting

23 The mating faces of the cylinder head and cylinder block/crankcase must be perfectly clean before refitting the head. Use a hard plastic or wood scraper to remove all traces of gasket and carbon. Also clean the piston crowns. Take particular care, as the soft aluminium alloy is damaged easily. Also, make sure that the carbon is not allowed to enter the oil and water passages – this is particularly important for the lubrication system, as carbon could block the oil supply to any of the engine components. Using adhesive tape and paper, seal the water, oil and bolt holes in the cylinder block/crankcase. To prevent carbon entering the gap between the pistons and bores, smear a little grease in the gap. After cleaning each piston, use a small brush to remove all traces of grease and carbon from the gap, then wipe away the remainder with a clean cloth. Clean all the pistons in the same way. Clean the head bolt hole threads in the cylinder block and remove all oil, if necessary using a syringe.

24 Check the mating surfaces of the cylinder block/crankcase and the cylinder head for nicks, deep scratches and other damage. If slight, they may be removed carefully with a file, but if excessive, machining may be the only alternative to renewal.

25 If warpage of the cylinder head gasket surface is suspected, use a straight-edge to

check it for distortion. Refer to Part D of this Chapter if necessary.

26 Wipe clean the mating surfaces of the cylinder head and cylinder block/crankcase. Check that the two locating dowels are in position at each end of the cylinder block/crankcase surface.

27 Check that No 1 piston is still positioned at TDC with the camshaft and crankshaft sprocket marks correctly aligned (see Section 3). Do not rotate the camshaft and crankshaft until the timing belt has been refitted.

28 Fit the new cylinder head gasket to the cylinder block, ensuring that it locates correctly over the dowels, with the TOP marking visible on the inlet manifold side of the engine **(see illustration)**. The notch in the edge of the gasket should be pointing towards the oil filter side of the engine.

29 As necessary, reassemble the cylinder head with reference to Part D of this Chapter, and refit the camshaft as described in Section 10. Where removed, refit the thermostat housing together with a new gasket. Also refit the lifting eye where removed.

30 Lower the cylinder head into position, locating it on the dowels.

31 Apply a light film of clean engine oil to the threads of the new cylinder head bolts, and to the undersides of the bolt heads.

32 Carefully fit the new cylinder head bolts, and screw them in, by hand only, until finger-tight.

33 Tighten the cylinder head bolts to the specified torque in sequence, and in the stages given in the Specifications at the beginning of this Chapter **(see illustration)**.

11.17 Remove the exhaust

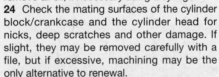

11.28 The cylinder head gasket TOP marking should be on the inlet manifold side of the engine

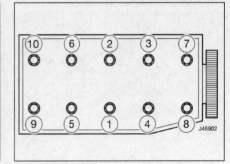

11.33 Cylinder head bolt tightening sequence

12.4 Oil level sensor wiring plug

12.5 Gearbox bellhousing cover plate securing bolts (1)

12.7 Remove the sump

12.9 Removing the oil pick-up pipe bolts

34 Reconnect the exhaust downpipe to the manifold with reference to Chapter 4A Section 17.

35 On turbocharged engines refit the catalytic converter.

36 Adjust the valve clearances. Apply beads of sealant to the camshaft end bearing caps and around the valve cover mounting bolt holes as shown in Section 4.

37 Refit the valve cover using a new gasket, and tighten the securing bolts to the specified torque.

38 Reconnect the hoses to the thermostat housing and tighten the clips.

39 Refit the inlet manifold, throttle body and fuel rail as described in Chapter 4A.

40 Reconnect the heater hoses to the water pump and to the support at the transmission end of the valve cover, and tighten the clips.

41 Reconnect the wiring to the temperature sensor, air sensor and throttle body.

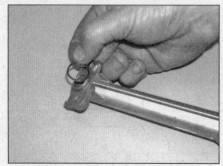

12.12 Fit a new O-ring to the oil pick-up pipe

42 Reconnect the charcoal canister pipe and the fuel vapour hoses to the solenoid purge valve.

43 Refit the crankcase breather hose.

44 Reconnect the HT leads to the spark plugs.

45 Reconnect the fuel supply.

46 Refit the air cleaner assembly with reference to Chapter 4A Section 2.

47 Reconnect the brake servo vacuum pipe to the inlet manifold.

48 Refit the timing belt as described in Section 7. A new belt and tensioner must be fitted.

49 Refill the cooling system as described in Chapter 1A Section 27.

50 Refit the engine compartment undertray and wing liner.

51 Refit the roadwheel and lower the vehicle to the ground, then reconnect the battery negative lead.

12 Sump and oil pick-up pipe – removal and refitting

Note: *A new sump gasket (or suitable sealant) and a new oil pick-up pipe O-ring will be required on refitting. On later engines, an aluminium sump is fitted instead of the previous steel type.*

Removal

1 Disconnect the battery negative lead as described in Chapter 5A Section 4.

2 Apply the handbrake, then jack up the front of the vehicle and support it on axle stands (see *Jacking and vehicle support*). Remove the engine compartment undertray.

3 Drain the engine oil, with reference to Chapter 1A Section 4 if necessary. Also pull out the oil level dipstick from its tube.

4 Disconnect the wiring from the oil level sensor (see illustration), then unscrew and remove the sensor from the sump. If necessary use a half-moon wrench.

5 Where fitted, unbolt the cover plate from the gearbox bellhousing (see illustration). On the later engines, unscrew the bolts securing the sump to the gearbox bellhousing.

6 Progressively unscrew the sump bolts in the reverse order to that shown (see illustration 12.14). Remove the sump securing bolts.

7 Release the sump from the crankcase (see illustration) then rotate it to the rear in order to release the oil pump strainer from the sump partition.

8 Lower the sump and withdraw it from under the vehicle. Where applicable, recover the gasket (note that the sump is sealed in production using sealant).

9 Unscrew the two bolts securing the oil pick-up pipe to the bottom of the oil pump. Remove the bolts, then withdraw the oil pick-up pipe and recover the O-ring (see illustration). Note that some engines do not have an O-ring or seal fitted.

Refitting

10 Clean all traces of sealant or gasket from the crankcase and sump mating faces, and wipe the mating faces dry.

11 Locate a new gasket on the sump, noting that the flat surface of the gasket should face the crankcase. Apply sealant evenly to the engine block on engines that do not have a traditional gasket.

12 Refit the oil pick-up pipe to the bottom of the oil pump together with a new O-ring (see illustration). Tighten the bolts securely.

13 Offer the sump onto the crankcase, rotating it as necessary over the oil pick-up pipe, and at the same time ensuring that the gasket remains in place. Insert the bolts and hand-tighten at this stage. On later engines, also hand-tighten the bolts securing the sump to the bellhousing, and make sure that the sump side face is in contact with the housing.

14 Tighten the sump-to-crankcase bolts in the order shown to the specified torque (see illustration).

15 On later engines, tighten the sump to bellhousing bolts to the specified torque.

16 Refit the gearbox bellhousing cover plate where applicable, and tighten the securing bolts.

17 Refit the oil level sensor to the sump and tighten securely, then reconnect the wiring.

18 Refit the oil level dipstick to its tube.

19 Refit the engine compartment undertray, then lower the vehicle to the ground.

20 Reconnect the battery negative lead.
21 Refill the engine with oil as described in Chapter 1A Section 4.

13 Oil pump – removal and refitting

Note: *New main oil gallery and oil pump pick-up tube O-rings will be required on refitting, and Rhodorseal 5661 sealant or a suitable alternative will be required.*

Removal

1 Remove the timing belt as described in Section 7.
2 Temporarily refit the right-hand engine mounting bracket/timing cover to the cylinder head, and tighten the securing bolts.
3 Working under the vehicle, withdraw the trolley jack and block of wood from under the sump
4 Remove the sump and oil pump pick-up pipe with reference to Section 12. On the turbocharged engine, clamp and then disconnect the oil cooler hoses.
5 Withdraw the crankshaft sprocket from the crankshaft and disconnect the wiring from the oil pressure switch.
6 Unscrew the securing bolts, and withdraw the oil pump from the cylinder block **(see illustration)**.
7 Recover the O-ring from the main oil gallery in the cylinder block **(see illustration)**.
8 Prise the crankshaft oil seal from the oil pump.

Refitting

9 Commence refitting by cleaning the mating faces of the oil pump and cylinder block.
10 Fit a new O-ring to the main oil gallery in the cylinder block.
11 Apply a 1.3 mm wide bead of Rhodorseal 5661 (available from a Renault dealer), or a suitable equivalent, to the cylinder block mating face of the oil pump **(see illustration)**. The bead must be on the inner side of the mounting bolt holes, and completely around the oil supply hole.
12 Slide the oil pump over the crankshaft, ensuring that the flats on the crankshaft engage with the cut-outs in the oil pump rotor, and that the positioning dowel engages with the hole in the oil pump **(see illustration)**. Wipe away any excess sealant.
13 Refit the oil pump securing bolts. Start at the bolt closest to the oil filter housing and work clockwise, tightening the bolts to the specified torque.
14 Fit a new crankshaft oil seal with reference to Section 15.
15 Refit the crankshaft sprocket, ensuring that the lug on the sprocket engages with the corresponding cut-out in the end of the crankshaft.
16 Refit the sump as described in Section 12.
17 Place the trolley jack and block of wood

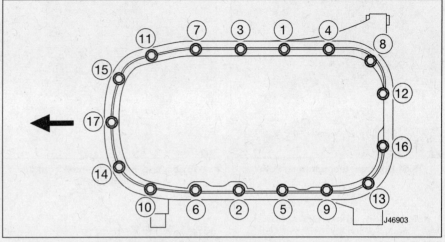

12.14 Tighten the sump bolts (in two stages) in the order shown. The arrow indicates the timing belt end of the engine

under the sump to support the engine, and then remove the right-hand engine mounting. Fit a new timing belt and tensioner and then refit the timing belt covers.
18 Refit the crankshaft pulley and the engine mounting. Refit the wing liner and wheel. Lower the vehicle to the ground.

14 Oil pump – dismantling, inspection and reassembly

1 No spare parts are available for the oil

pump, and no wear limit specifications are provided for the internal components. If wear or damage is suspected, a new pump assembly should be fitted.

15 Crankshaft oil seals – renewal

Timing belt end oil seal

Note: *The oil seal is very fragile. It should only be handled with the protective sleeve provided.*

13.6 Withdrawing the oil pump – viewed with engine removed and inverted

13.7 Recover the O-ring from the main oil gallery in the cylinder block

13.11 Apply a bead of sealant to the cylinder block mating face of the oil pump

13.12 Ensure that the flats on the crankshaft engage with the cut-outs in the oil pump rotor

16.5a Unscrew the mounting bolts...

16.5b ...and lift the flywheel from the crankshaft

16.8 Using a suitable tool to prevent the flywheel from turning when tightening the securing bolts

1 Remove the crankshaft sprocket, as described in Section 8.

2 Note the fitted depth of the seal, then prise out the old oil seal using a small screwdriver, taking care not to damage the surface on the crankshaft. Alternatively, the oil seal can be removed by drilling two small holes diagonally opposite each other and inserting self-tapping screws in them. A pair of grips can then be used to pull out the oil seal, by pulling on each side in turn.

3 Inspect the seal rubbing surface on the crankshaft. If it is grooved or rough in the area where the old seal was fitted, the new seal should be fitted slightly less deeply, so that it rubs on an unworn part of the surface.

4 Wipe clean the oil seal seating, then dip the new seal in fresh engine oil, and locate it over the crankshaft with its closed side facing outwards. Make sure that the oil seal lip is not damaged as it is located on the crankshaft.

5 Using a metal tube, drive the oil seal squarely into the bore to the depth noted before removal of the old seal (or less deeply if there is evidence of a wear groove on the crankshaft). A block of wood cut to pass over the end of the crankshaft may be used instead.

6 Refit the crankshaft sprocket as described in Section 8.

Flywheel end oil seal

7 Remove the flywheel as described in Section 16.

8 Proceed as described in paragraphs 2 to 5.

9 Refit the flywheel with reference to Section 16.

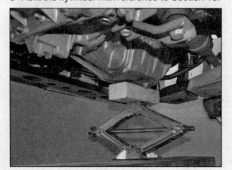

17.4 Support the engine with a suitable jack

16 Flywheel – removal, inspection and refitting

Note: *It is recommended that new flywheel bolts are used on refitting. Suitable thread-locking fluid will be required to coat the threads of the flywheel bolts.*

Removal

1 Remove the gearbox as described in Chapter 7 Section 7.

2 Remove the clutch as described in Chapter 6 Section 8.

3 Mark the flywheel in relation to the crankshaft.

4 The flywheel must now be held stationary whilst the bolts are loosened. To do this, locate a long bolt in one of the transmission mounting bolt holes, and either insert a wide-bladed screwdriver in the starter ring gear, or use a piece of bent metal bar engaged with the ring gear. Alternatively, a suitable tool can be made up and bolted to the cylinder block **(see illustration 16.8)**. Do not insert a bar or tool into the engine speed (flywheel) sensor teeth on the flywheel.

5 Unscrew the mounting bolts and withdraw the flywheel from the crankshaft **(see illustrations)**. Be careful not to drop it – it is heavy.

Inspection

6 Examine the flywheel for scoring of the clutch face, and for wear or chipping of the ring gear teeth. If the clutch face is scored, it may be possible to have the flywheel machined, but renewal is preferable. If the ring gear is worn or damaged, it may be possible to renew it separately, but this job is best left to a Renault dealer or engineering works. The temperature to which the new ring gear must be heated for installation is critical and, if not done accurately, the hardness of the teeth will be destroyed.

Refitting

7 Thoroughly clean the flywheel and crankshaft faces, then locate the flywheel on the crankshaft, making sure that any

previously-made marks are aligned. Note that the flywheel bolts holes are offset, so the flywheel can only be fitted in one position.

8 Apply a few drops of locking fluid to the threads of the new flywheel bolts. Fit the bolts, and tighten them in a diagonal sequence to the specified torque in the two stages given in the Specifications. Prevent the flywheel from turning using the method used during removal **(see illustration)**.

9 Refit the clutch with reference to Chapter 6 Section 8.

10 Refit the gearbox as described in Chapter 7 Section 7.

17 Engine/transmission mountings – inspection, removal and refitting

Inspection

1 Apply the handbrake, then jack up the front of the car and support it on axle stands (see *Jacking and vehicle support*). Where fitted, remove the engine compartment undertray.

2 Visually inspect the rubber pads on the two front and one rear engine/transmission mountings for signs of cracking and deterioration. Careful use of a lever will help to determine the condition of the rubber pads. If there is excessive movement in the mounting, or if the rubber has deteriorated, the mounting should be renewed.

3 Lower the vehicle to the ground.

Renewal

Right-hand front mounting

4 Support the right-hand end of the engine with a jack and block of wood beneath the sump **(see illustration)**.

5 Unclip the hose/pipes from the top of the engine mounting bracket, then undo the mounting bolts from the engine and inner wing panel and remove the complete mounting **(see illustration)**.

6 Fit the new mounting using a reversal of the removal procedure, but tighten the nuts/bolts to the specified torque wrench settings.

Left-hand front mounting

7 Remove the air inlet ducts from the left-hand side of the engine as applicable, for access to the engine/transmission left-hand mounting. Remove the battery as described in Chapter 5A Section 4.

8 Support the left-hand end of the transmission with a trolley jack and block of wood beneath the sump.

9 Unclip the battery vent pipe, and the wiring securing clips from the battery tray, then undo the three retaining bolts and remove the battery tray from the engine compartment **(see illustrations)**.

10 Unbolt the central nut from the mounting, and then at this point, the engine and gearbox can be lowered. However, if required undo all the mounting bolts and remove the mounting and bracket as a complete assembly **(see illustration)**.

11 Fit the new mounting using a reversal of the removal procedure, but tighten the nuts/bolts to the specified torque wrench setting.

Rear mounting

12 Apply the handbrake, then jack up the front of the vehicle and support it on axle stands (see *Jacking and vehicle support*). Note the rear mounting does not support the weight of the engine.

13 Unbolt the steady bar from the transmission **(see illustration)**.

14 Unbolt the mounting from the subframe and remove it from the vehicle.

15 Fit the new mounting using a reversal of the removal procedure, but tighten the nuts/bolts to the specified torque setting.

17.5 Unbolt the mounting from the engine and inner wing panel

17.9a Unclip the vent pipe...

17.9b ...the cable securing clips at the rear...

17.9c ...and the cable clip at the front...

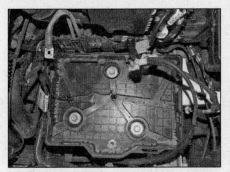
17.9d ...then undo the battery tray bolts

17.10 Transmission mounting and bracket

17.13 Rear lower mounting

Chapter 2 Part C
Diesel engine in-car repair procedures

Contents

Degrees of difficulty

Easy, suitable for novice with little experience 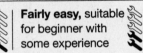 | **Fairly easy,** suitable for beginner with some experience | **Fairly difficult,** suitable for competent DIY mechanic | **Difficult,** suitable for experienced DIY mechanic | **Very difficult,** suitable for expert DIY or professional

Specifications

General

Type	Four cylinder, in-line, single overhead camshaft
Designation	K9K
Capacity	1461 cc
Bore	76.0 mm
Stroke	80.5 mm
Firing order	1-3-4-2 (No 1 cylinder at flywheel end)
Direction of crankshaft rotation	Clockwise viewed from timing belt end
Maximum distortion of cylinder head.	0.05 mm

Compression pressures

Engine warm – approximately 80°C:
Minimum pressure	18 bars
Maximum difference between cylinders.	4 bars

Camshaft

Drive	Toothed belt
Number of bearings	6
Camshaft endfloat	0.08 to 0.178 mm

Valve clearances (cold)

Inlet	0.13 – 0.20 mm (cold)
Exhaust	0.30 – 0.375 mm (cold)

Lubrication system

System pressure (at 80°C):
At idle	0.8 bar minimum
At 4000 rpm	3.4 bars minimum
Maximum	5.2 bars
Oil pump type.	Gear-type, chain-driven off the crankshaft right-hand end

Torque wrench settings

	Nm	lbf ft
Alternator	21	15
Big-end bearing caps: *		
Stage 1	25	18
Stage 2	Angle-tighten a further 110° ± 6°	
Brake vacuum pump	25	18
Camshaft bearing caps	10	7
Camshaft adjustable bolts	14	10
Camshaft hub: *		
Stage 1	30	22
Stage 2	Angle-tighten a further 86° ± 6°	
Clutch pressure plate:		
M6 bolts	14	10
M7 bolts	20	15
Crankshaft end plate	10	7
Crankshaft main bearing caps:		
Stage 1	25	18
Stage 2	Angle-tighten a further 47° ± 6°	
Crankshaft pulley bolt: *		
Stage 1	120	88
Stage 2	Angle-tighten a further 90° ± 15°	
Cylinder block TDC blanking plug	25	18
Cylinder head bolts: *		
Stage 1	25	18
Stage 2	Angle-tighten a further 270° ± 10°	
Cylinder head coolant outlet	10	7
Driveshaft support bracket	44	33
Engine right-hand cover	10	7
Engine/transmission mountings:		
Right-hand mounting to engine/body	62	46
Right-hand upper tie bar to the engine	115	85
Right-hand upper tie bar to the body	105	77
Left-hand mounting to transmission	62	46
Left-hand mounting to body	62	46
Left-hand mounting central nut/bolt	62	46
Rear mounting link to subframe	105	77
Rear mounting link to transmission	105	77
Exhaust gas recirculation valve	21	15
Exhaust manifold	26	19
Flywheel*		
Stage 1	20	15
Stage 2	Angle-tighten a further 36° ± 6°	
Glow plugs	15	11
High-pressure fuel pump	23	17
High-pressure fuel pump sprocket	70	52
High-pressure pipe	28	21
High-pressure rail	21	15
Injector flanges	27	20
Knock sensor	20	15
Multifunction support bracket lower bolt	25	18
Oil filter support	28	21
Oil level sensor	25	18
Oil pressure sensor	40	30
Oil pump	25	18
Roadwheel bolts	110	81
Sump to block bolts	14	10
Sump to transmission bolts	44	33
Timing belt tensioner	27	20
Turbocharger oil delivery pipe (on cylinder head)	25	18
Turbocharger oil delivery (banjo bolt)	14	10
Turbocharger oil return pipe	12	9
Turbocharger to exhaust manifold	26	19
Valve cover	11	8
Water pump	10	7
Water pump inlet pipe	25	18

* Use new nuts/bolts

1 General Information

How to use this Chapter

1 This Part of Chapter 2 is devoted to in-car repair procedures for the diesel engine. Similar information covering the petrol engine can be found in Part A or Part B. All procedures concerning engine removal and refitting, and engine block/cylinder head overhaul can be found in Part D of this Chapter.

2 Refer to *Vehicle identification numbers* in the Reference Section at the end of this manual for details of engine code locations.

3 Most of the operations included in this Part are based on the assumption that the engine is still installed in the car. Therefore, if this information is being used during a complete engine overhaul, with the engine already removed, many of the steps included here will not apply.

Engine description

4 The engine is of four cylinder, in-line, single overhead camshaft type, mounted transversely at the front of the vehicle.

5 The cylinder block is of cast iron with conventional dry liners bored directly into the cylinder block. The crankshaft is supported in five shell-type main bearings. Thrustwashers are fitted to No 3 main bearing to control crankshaft endfloat.

6 The connecting rods are attached to the crankshaft by 'cracked' horizontally split shell-type big-end bearings and to the pistons by gudgeon pins. The gudgeon pins are fully-floating and are retained by circlips. The aluminium alloy pistons are fitted with three piston rings, comprising two compression rings and a scraper-type oil control ring.

7 The single overhead camshaft is mounted directly in the cylinder head, and is driven by the crankshaft via a toothed timing belt.

8 The camshaft operates the valves via inverted bucket type tappets, which operate in bores machined directly in the cylinder head. The valve clearances are adjusted by changing the tappet buckets which are available in 25 different thicknesses. The inlet and exhaust valves are mounted vertically in the cylinder head and are each closed by a single valve spring.

9 The high-pressure fuel injection pump is driven by the timing belt and is described in further detail in Chapter 4B Section 11.

10 A semi-closed crankcase ventilation system is employed, and crankcase fumes are drawn from the cylinder block and passed via a hose to the inlet tract (see Chapter 4C Section 3 for further details).

11 Engine lubrication is by pressure feed from a gear type oil pump located beneath the crankshaft. Engine oil is fed through an externally-mounted oil filter to the main oil gallery feeding the crankshaft, auxiliary shaft (where fitted) and camshaft. Oil spray jets are fitted to the cylinder block to supply oil to the underside of the pistons. An oil cooler is mounted between the oil filter and the cylinder block.

Operations with engine in place

12 The following operations can be carried out without having to remove the engine from the vehicle:
a) *Removal and refitting of the cylinder head.*
b) *Removal and refitting of the timing belt and sprockets.*
c) *Renewal of the camshaft oil seals.*
d) *Removal and refitting of the camshaft.*
e) *Removal and refitting of the sump.*
f) *Removal and refitting of the connecting rods and pistons.* *
g) *Removal and refitting of the oil pump.*
h) *Renewal of the crankshaft oil seals.*
i) *Renewal of the engine mountings.*
j) *Removal and refitting of the flywheel.*

Note: * *Although the operation marked with an asterisk can be carried out with the engine in the car after removal of the sump, it is better for the engine to be removed in the interests of cleanliness and improved access. For this reason, the procedure is described in Chapter 2D Section 9.*

2 Compression and leakdown tests – description and interpretation

Compression test

Note: *A compression tester specifically designed for diesel engines must be used for this test.*

1 When engine performance is down, or if misfiring occurs which cannot be attributed to a fault in the fuel system, a compression test can provide diagnostic clues as to the engine's condition. If the test is performed regularly it can give warning of trouble before any other symptoms become apparent.

2 A compression tester is connected to an adaptor which screws into the glow plug hole. It is unlikely to be worthwhile buying such a tester for occasional use, but it may be possible to borrow or hire one – if not, have the test performed by a garage.

3 Unless specific instructions to the contrary are supplied with the tester, observe the following points:
a) *The battery must be in a good state of charge, the air filter must be clean and the engine should be at normal operating temperature.*
b) *All the glow plugs must be removed before starting the test and the wiring disconnected from the injectors.*

4 There is no need to hold the accelerator pedal down during the test.

5 The actual compression pressures measured are not so important as the balance between cylinders. Values are given in the specifications at the beginning of this Chapter.

6 The cause of poor compression is less easy to establish on a diesel engine than on a petrol one. The effect of introducing oil into the cylinders ('wet' testing) is not conclusive, because there is a risk that the oil will sit in the swirl chamber or in the recess on the piston crown instead of passing to the rings. However, the following can be used as a rough guide to diagnosis.

7 All cylinders should produce very similar pressures; any difference greater than that specified indicates the existence of a fault. Note that the compression should build-up quickly in a healthy engine; low compression on the first stroke, followed by gradually increasing pressure on successive strokes, indicates worn piston rings. A low compression reading on the first stroke, which does not build-up during successive strokes, indicates leaking valves or a blown head gasket (a cracked head could also be the cause).

8 A low reading from two adjacent cylinders is almost certainly due to the head gasket having blown between them.

Leakdown test

9 A leakdown test measures the rate at which compressed air fed into the cylinder is lost. It is an alternative to a compression test and in many ways it is better, since the escaping air provides easy identification of where pressure loss is occurring (piston rings, valves or head gasket).

10 The equipment needed for leakdown testing is unlikely to be available to the home mechanic. If poor compression is suspected, have the test performed by a suitably-equipped garage.

3 Engine assembly/ valve timing holes – general information and usage

Caution: Do not attempt to rotate the engine whilst the crankshaft and camshaft timing pins are in position. If the engine is to be left in this state for a long period of time, it is a good idea to place suitable warning notices inside the vehicle, and in the engine compartment. This will reduce the possibility of the engine being accidentally cranked on the starter motor, which would cause considerable damage.

Note: *Special timing tools are required for this work. These are available from Renault or specialist tool suppliers, such as AST tools or Draper tools.*

1 Top Dead Centre (TDC) is the highest point in the cylinder that each piston reaches as the crankshaft turns. Each piston reaches TDC at the end of the compression stroke and again at the end of the exhaust stroke; however, for the purpose of timing the engine, TDC refers to the position of No 1 piston at the end of its compression stroke. No 1 piston is at the flywheel end of the engine.

3.8a Disconnect the wiring plug from the camshaft sensor

3.8b Remove the upper timing belt cover

3.8c With the cover removed, note how the retaining clips fit together…

3.8d …and the position of the plastic screw

2 When No 1 piston is at TDC, the timing hole in the camshaft sprocket will be aligned with the hole in the cylinder head so that the timing pin can be inserted. Additionally, if the crankshaft timing pin is fully screwed into the cylinder block, it will just contact the timing flat on the crankshaft web.

3 Setting the TDC timing is necessary to ensure that the valve timing is maintained during operations that require removal and refitting of the timing belt. Note that the engine does not have a conventional diesel injection pump, however it is still necessary to align a mark on the pump sprocket the pump body. The mark should be one tooth to the right of vertical.

4 To set the engine at TDC, the right-hand engine mounting support and cover must be removed for access to the camshaft sprocket as described in Section of this Chapter. First

jack up the front of the car and support on axle stands (see Jacking and vehicle support)..

5 Remove the engine undertray and then remove the rear lower engine mounting. The engine will still be supported by the left and right-hand upper mountings. Remove the front right wheel and then remove the front section of the wheel arch liner.

6 To improve access further remove the windscreen wipers and both the upper and lower windscreen cowl panels as described in Chapter 11 Section 7. Whilst not essential this will allow the engine to be moved forward slightly (on a suitable jack) as well as up and down.

7 Remove the auxiliary drivebelt with reference to Chapter 1B Section 10.

8 Support the right-hand end of the engine with a jack and block of wood beneath the sump. Unbolt the right-hand engine mounting from

the engine and body (as described in Section of this Chapter) and unclip the upper timing cover. Note that the upper cover may be in one, or two pieces depending on the engine number. Where it is a single item release the lower clips and remove the plastic retaining screw (see illustrations). Access to the screw is limited, but it can if necessary be prized out from the expansion plug – a replacement will be required for refitting. Note that considerable dexterity will be required to remove the upper cover.

9 Where the upper cover is in two sections, unclip and remove the upper and then remove the plastic retaining screw. Unclip and remove the lower section of the upper cover.

10 Remove the lower timing cover by releasing the clips. It will be necessary to slightly raise and lower the engine to facilitate removal of the timing cover.

11 With the covers removed, unbolt and remove the engine mounting support bracket.

12 Unscrew and remove the plug from the TDC hole on the left-hand front of the cylinder block. This is directly below the starter motor (see illustration). If you are just checking the timing leave the starter motor in position, however if you are accessing the TDC timing hole for timing belt replacement, consider removing the starter motor (as described in Chapter 5A Section 9) as this gives easy access to the TDC timing hole, as well as making locking the crankshaft (for the removal of the crankshaft pulley) considerably easier.

13 The crankshaft must now be turned using a spanner on the crankshaft pulley bolt.

14 Turn the crankshaft clockwise until the timing hole in the camshaft sprocket is approaching the hole in the cylinder head – the hole will be in the eight o'clock position. The mark on the high pressure fuel pump should be in the ten o'clock position. If the pump timing mark is not in the correct position, rotate the crankshaft as required to obtain the correct position.

15 Insert and tighten the special TDC pin into the cylinder block timing hole (see illustration).

16 Slowly turn the crankshaft clockwise until its web contacts the timing pin. Now insert the remaining timing pin through the hole in the camshaft sprocket and into the cylinder head (see illustration). The engine is now

3.12 Remove the blanking plug

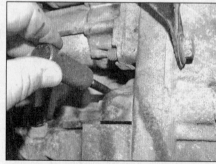

3.15 Fitting the crankshaft TDC pin

3.16 Fit the camshaft timing pin

positioned with No 1 piston at TDC on its compression stroke.

17 Check that the mark on the high-pressure injection pump sprocket is one tooth to the right of vertical **(see illustration)**. If the timing belt is to be replaced at this point mark the position of the fuel pump sprocket in relation the pump mounting.

18 On completion, remove the timing pins and refit all removed components.

4 Valve cover – removal and refitting

Removal

1 Jack up and support the front of the vehicle (see *Jacking and vehicle support*).

2 Remove the engine undershield and then support the right-hand end of the engine using a trolley jack with a block of wood on the jack head to spread the load on the engine sump.

3 Open the bonnet, disconnect the battery and (where fitted) remove the engine cover.

4 Whilst not strictly necessary access can be improved if the windscreen cowl panels are removed (Chapter 11 Section 7).

5 Raise the engine slightly and remove the right-hand engine mount (see Section 15). With the mount removed, unclip and remove the upper section of the timing belt cover as described in Section 3.

6 Undo the air intake securing bolt, then release the securing clips form each end of the air intake pipe and remove it from across the top of the engine **(see illustrations)**.

7 Unclip the wiring loom from the transmission end of the cover **(see illustration)**.

8 Release the two clips at the front, undo the two bolts at the rear of the cover, and then withdraw the soundproofing/protective cover from over the injectors **(see illustrations)**.

9 Disconnect the wiring plugs from the injectors, then unclip the wiring loom from the top of the valve cover **(see illustration)**, and move it to one side.

10 Where required, remove the bleed pipe from the injectors and then unclip the fuel return pipe. Note that Renault recommend

that this pipe is replaced if completely removed.

11 Disconnect the wiring plugs from the damper valve and the camshaft position sensor. To avoid damaging the sensor, unbolt and remove the camshaft position sensor **(see illustration)**.

12 Slacken and then remove the valve cover

3.17 The mark on the high-pressure pump sprocket must be one tooth to the right of vertical

4.6a Undo the retaining bolt…

4.6b …release the spring clips…

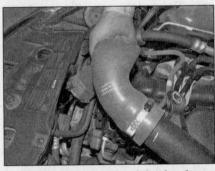
4.6c …and remove the air intake pipe

4.7 Disconnect the wiring plugs

4.8a Release the clips…

4.8b …undo the bolts…

4.8c …and remove the cover

4.9 Disconnect the wiring plugs from the fuel injectors

4.11 Remove the camshaft position sensor

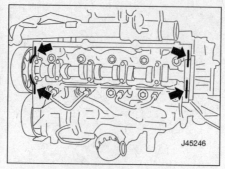

4.13 Apply 2.0 mm wide and 10mm long beads of sealant to the camshaft end bearing caps

bolts. Remove the cover and recover the gasket.

Refitting

13 Refitting is a reversal of removal, but bear in mind the following:
a) Clean the mounting surfaces.
b) Apply a 2 mm wide and 10 mm long bead of sealant at the points shown **(see illustration)**.
c) Tighten the bolts, starting at the centre, then working outwards in a spiraling direction.

5.6 Using a feeler blade to check the valve clearances

VALVES ROCKING ON CYLINDER	CHECK CLEARANCE ON CYLINDER
1	4
3	2
4	1
2	3

J45252

5.7 Valve clearance measurement

X Clearance
Y Tappet thickness

d) Fit new seals to the injectors and fit new high pressure supply pipes.
e) Fit a new gasket to the turbo outlet pipe.
f) Refit the remainder of the components in reverse order.

5 Valve clearances – checking and adjustment

Note: *This operation is not part of the maintenance schedule. It should be undertaken if noise from the valve gear becomes evident, or if loss of performance gives cause to suspect that the clearances may be incorrect. Adjustment involves removing the camshaft and changing the tappet buckets which are available in 25 different thicknesses.*

Checking

1 Remove the valve cover as described in Section 4 of this Chapter.
2 During the following procedure, the crankshaft must be turned using a spanner on the crankshaft pulley bolt. Improved access to the pulley bolt can be obtained by jacking up the front right-hand corner of the vehicle and removing the roadwheel and the lower wheel arch cover (secured by plastic clips).
3 If desired, to enable the crankshaft to be turned more easily, remove the glow plugs (Chapter 5C Section 2).

5.8 Using a dial gauge to measure the thickness of the removed tappet

4 Draw the valve positions on a piece of paper, numbering them 1 to 8 from the flywheel end of the engine. Identify them as inlet or exhaust (ie, 1E, 2I, 3E, 4I, 5E, 6I, 7E, 8I).
5 Turn the crankshaft until the valves of No 1 cylinder (flywheel end) are 'rocking'. The exhaust valve will be closing and the inlet valve will be opening. The piston of No 4 cylinder will be at the top of its compression stroke, with both valves fully closed. The clearances for both valves of No 4 cylinder may be checked at the same time.
6 Insert a feeler blade of the correct thickness (see Specifications) between the cam lobe and the top of the tappet bucket, and check that it is a firm sliding fit **(see illustration)**. If it is not, use the feeler blades to ascertain the exact clearance, and record this for use when calculating the thickness of the new tappet bucket required. Note that the inlet and exhaust valve clearances are different (see Section).
7 With No 4 cylinder valve clearances checked, turn the engine through half a turn so that No 3 valves are 'rocking', then check the valve clearances of No 2 cylinder in the same way. Similarly check the remaining valve clearances in the sequence shown **(see illustration)**.

Adjustment

Note: *A micrometer or dial gauge and probe will be required for this operation.*

8 Where a valve clearance differs from the specified value, the tappet bucket for that valve must be changed with a thinner or thicker one accordingly. On new tappets, the thickness is stamped on the bottom face of the tappet, however, the original tappets do have any thickness stamped on them. It is therefore prudent to use a micrometer or dial gauge to measure the true thickness of any tappet removed, as it may have been reduced by wear **(see illustration)**.
9 To access the tappet buckets, first remove the camshaft as described in Section 9. Remove and refit each bucket separately, to avoid confusion **(see illustration)**.
10 The size of tappet required is calculated as follows. If the measured clearance is less than specified, subtract the measured

5.9 Removing a tappet bucket

clearance from the specified clearance, and deduct the result from the thickness of the existing tappet. For example:

11 Sample calculation – clearance too small
12 Clearance measured (A) = 0.15 mm
13 Desired clearance (B) = 0.20 mm
14 Difference (B – A) = 0.05 mm
15 Tappet bucket thickness fitted = 3.70 mm
16 Tappet bucket thickness required = 3.70 – 0.05 = 3.65 mm
17 If the measured clearance is greater than specified, subtract the specified clearance from the measured clearance, and add the result to the thickness of the existing tappet. For example:
18 Sample calculation – clearance too big
19 Clearance measured (A) = 0.50 mm
20 Desired clearance (B) = 0.40 mm
21 Difference (A – B) = 0.10 mm
22 Tappet bucket thickness fitted = 3.45 mm
23 Tappet bucket thickness required = 3.45 + 0.10 = 3.55 mm
24 Working on each separately, lift out the bucket to be renewed, then oil the new one and carefully locate it in the cylinder head **(see illustration)**
25 Refit the camshaft with reference to Section 9.
26 Where removed, refit the glow plugs (Chapter 5C Section 2).
27 Remove the spanner from the crankshaft pulley bolt.
28 Wipe clean the contact surfaces on the valve cover and cylinder head, then apply four beads of sealant, 2.0 mm wide, to the camshaft end bearing caps (Nos 1 and 6) **(see illustration 4.14a)**.
29 Refit the valve cover and tighten the bolts to the specified torque in the order given **(see illustration 4.14b)**.
30 Refit the remaining components in reverse order to removal.

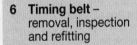

6 Timing belt –
removal, inspection and refitting

Caution: If the timing belt breaks in service, extensive engine damage will result. Renew the belt at the intervals specified in Chapter 1B Section 25, or earlier if its condition is at all doubtful.
Note: *The belt and tensioner must be replaced if removed.*

Removal

1 Disconnect the battery negative lead (refer to Chapter 5A Section 4). To improve access remove the upper and lower windscreen cowl panels (as described in Chapter 11 Section 7).
2 Jack up the front of the car and support on axle stands (see *Jacking and vehicle support*). Remove the front right wheel, engine/radiator undertray and wheel arch liner. Where fitted remove the engine cover.
3 Remove the auxiliary drivebelt with

5.24 Lubricate the tappet bucket before refitting it

reference to Chapter 1B Section 10, then unbolt and remove the drivebelt tensioner.
4 The crankshaft pulley must now be removed. There is a small gap beneath the starter motor into which a screwdriver or similar tool can be jammed into the starter ring gear teeth. Note however that access to both the ring gear and the TDC timing plug (below the starter motor) is considerably easier if the starter motor is removed first.
5 Using a long knuckle bar and socket remove the crankshaft pulley bolt. With the bolt removed, ease the pulley from the crankshaft. Mark the position of the keyway on the crankshaft sprocket, as it is difficult to see once the bolt is refitted **(see illustrations)**. Refit the bolt with a suitable spacer.
6 Remove the rear lower engine mounting. The engine will still be supported by the left and right-hand upper mountings. Support the

right-hand end of the engine with a jack. Place a block of wood on the head of the jack to spread the load on the sump.
7 Unbolt the right-hand engine mounting from the engine and body, then release and unclip the timing belt covers as described in Section 3 of this Chapter.
8 Unbolt and remove the engine mounting support bracket **(see illustration)**.
9 Unscrew and remove the blanking plug from the TDC hole on the left-hand front of the cylinder block **(see illustration 3.12)**.
10 The crankshaft must now be turned to the TDC position using a spanner on the crankshaft pulley bolt.
11 Turn the crankshaft clockwise until the timing hole in the camshaft sprocket is approaching the hole in the cylinder head. The hole will be approaching the nine o'clock position.
12 Insert and tighten the special TDC pin into the cylinder block timing hole **(see illustration 3.15)**.
13 Slowly turn the crankshaft clockwise until its web contacts the timing pin. Now insert the timing pin (or a suitable bolt) through the hole in the camshaft sprocket and into the cylinder head **(see illustration 3.16)**. The engine is now positioned with No 1 piston at TDC on its compression stroke.
14 Check that the mark on the high-pressure injection pump sprocket is one tooth to the right of vertical. It may be necessary to rotate the crankshaft again to align the mark on the pump sprocket **(see illustration)**.
15 Check that the keyway on the crankshaft

6.5a Unscrew and remove the crankshaft pulley bolt...

6.5b ...and remove the pulley

6.5c Refit the bolt and mark the position of the keyway

6.8 Remove the support bracket

6.14 Check that the position of the pump is correct. Note the alignment mark on the belt

6.16a Loosen the tensioner locknut...

6.16b ...then release the timing belt

6.25 Slacken the upper bolts and remove the lower

6.26 Align the timing marks on the belt with those on the camshaft and fuel injection pump sprockets

pulley is in the 12 O'clock position. For reference mark the position of all the sprockets in relation to the engine before removing the timing belt.

16 Loosen the tensioner bolt, then turn the tensioner clockwise to release the tension. If necessary, use a 6.0 mm Allen key in the eccentric hub plate to move the tensioner. Lock the tensioner in the relaxed position and remove the belt (see illustrations).

17 Do not turn the camshaft or the crankshaft whilst the timing belt is removed, as there is a risk of piston-to-valve contact. If it is necessary to turn the camshaft for any

reason, before doing so, turn the crankshaft anti-clockwise (viewed from the timing belt end of the engine) by a quarter turn to position all four pistons half-way down their bores. Leave the TDC pin tightened into the cylinder block.

18 Unbolt and remove the timing belt tensioner. Discard the tensioner – a new one must be fitted.

19 Clean the sprockets, water pump pulley and tensioner and wipe them dry, although do not apply excessive amounts of solvent to the water pump and tensioner pulleys otherwise the bearing lubricant may be contaminated. Also clean the rear timing belt cover, and the cylinder head and block.

Inspection

20 The belt and tensioner must be replaced once removed, however an examination of the

6.27b Pretensioning the timing belt

old belt may indicate other problems, such as worn or misaligned sprockets.

21 Check the waterpump for play and any signs of a coolant leak. Consider replacing the waterpump regardless of its condition as it is not uncommon for a waterpump to leak after timing belt replacement due to the change in loading on the waterpump bearing.

22 Thoroughly clean the nose of the crankshaft and the bore of the crankshaft sprocket, and also the contact surfaces of the sprocket and pulley.

Refitting

23 Check that the crankshaft, camshaft and high-pressure fuel injection pump sprockets are still positioned at TDC, and that the groove in the crankshaft nose is pointing upwards. If the pistons have been positioned half-way down their bores, turn the crankshaft clockwise until the web contacts the TDC tool.

24 Fit the new tensioner and check that the tensioner peg is correctly located in the groove in the cylinder head.

25 Slacken the 2 upper bolts (by one complete turn) on the camshaft sprocket and remove the lower bolt (see illustration). The sprocket should be free to rotate on the hub.

26 Align the timing marks on the belt with those on the camshaft and fuel injection pump sprockets (see illustration), ensuring that the running direction arrows on the belt are pointing clockwise (viewed from the timing belt end of the engine). Note that the belt should be marked with lines across its width to act as timing marks. Fit the timing belt over the crankshaft sprocket first, followed by the water pump pulley, fuel injection pump sprocket, camshaft sprocket, and tensioner. There should be 19 belt grooves between the timing marks on the camshaft and injection pump sprockets. And 51 belt grooves between the mark on the high pressure pump and the crankshaft sprocket – at the six o'clock position.

27 With the timing marks still aligned, use the 6.0 mm Allen key to pretension the belt by turning the tensioner anti-clockwise until the index pointer is positioned below the timing window (see illustrations). Hold the tensioner stationary and tighten the locknut to the specified torque. This torque is critical, since

J45242

6.27a Pretension the timing belt by positioning the tensioner pointer (1) as shown

if the nut were to come loose, considerable engine damage would result.

28 Refit the missing bolt from the camshaft sprocket and tighten all 3 bolts. Note that the bolts should not be tight against the adjustable slots in the sprocket.

29 Refit the crankshaft pulley, then insert the old bolt. After tightening the bolt, remove the timing pins from the cylinder block and camshaft sprocket.

30 Turn the crankshaft two complete turns in the normal direction of rotation, but just before the camshaft sprockets are aligned, refit and tighten the crankshaft timing pin. Slowly turn the crankshaft clockwise until its web is contacting the timing pin. Insert the timing pin through the hole in the camshaft sprocket and into the cylinder head. Slacken the 3 bolts in the camshaft sprocket.

31 Hold the tensioner with the Allen key, then loosen the locknut a maximum of one turn, and turn the tensioner clockwise until the index pointer is positioned in the middle of the timing window **(see illustration)**. Tighten the locknut to the specified torque and then tighten the camshaft sprocket bolts to the specified torque.

32 Remove the TDC timing pin and the camshaft sprocket timing pin. Rotate the engine two complete revolutions and refit the timing pins. Check that the pointer on the tensioner is at the mid point on the index marks. Repeat the tensioning procedure if this is incorrect.

33 Remove the camshaft timing pin and then remove the old crankshaft pulley bolt. Fit a new bolt and tighten it to the specified torque.

34 Remove the TDC timing pin from the engine block. Apply sealant to the threads, then refit the blanking plug to the cylinder block and tighten it to the specified torque.

35 Refit the engine mounting support bracket and tighten the bolts to the specified torque.

36 Refit the timing covers, using a new plastic screw if required.

37 Refit the right-hand engine mounting to the engine and body and tighten the bolts to the specified torque.

38 Fit a new auxiliary drivebelt and tensioner with reference to Chapter 1B Section 10.

39 Refit the engine undertray and wheel arch liner.

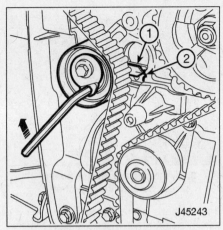

6.31 Position the pointer (1) to its final setting in the middle of the timing window (2)

40 Refit the front right wheel and lower the car to the ground. Tighten the wheel bolts to the specified torque.

41 Refit the windscreen cowl panels.

42 Reconnect the battery negative lead.

7 Timing belt sprockets, idler pulley and tensioner – removal and refitting

Note: *If the timing belt is removed, both the timing belt and the tensioner must be replaced.*

Crankshaft sprocket

Removal

1 Remove the timing belt as described in Section 6.

2 Slide the sprocket from the crankshaft, noting which way around it is fitted **(see illustration)**.

Refitting

3 Thoroughly clean the nose of the crankshaft and the bore of the crankshaft sprocket, and also the contact surfaces of the sprocket and pulley. This is necessary to prevent the possibility of the sprocket slipping in use.

4 Slide the sprocket onto the crankshaft the correct way around.

5 Refit the timing belt as described in Section 6.

Camshaft sprocket

Removal

6 Remove the timing belt as described in Section 6.

7 Hold the sprocket stationary using a suitable gear holding tool. Alternatively, an old timing belt can be wrapped around the sprocket and held firmly with a pair of grips. Unscrew and remove the central securing nut.

8 Release the sprocket from the camshaft, noting the integral spline on the sprocket and the corresponding cut-out in the end of the camshaft.

9 If the stud in the end of the camshaft comes loose it must be replaced.

Refitting

10 Refit the camshaft sprocket, making sure that the integral spline locates in the camshaft cut-out. Insert the bolt and tighten it to the specified torque and angle, holding the sprocket stationary as during removal **(see illustration)**.

11 Refit and tension the timing belt as described in Section 6.

Tensioner

Removal

12 Remove the timing belt as described in Section 6.

13 Unscrew the securing bolt, then withdraw the tensioner assembly from the engine **(see illustration)**.

Refitting

14 Refitting is a reversal of removal. Refit and tension the timing belt as described in Section 6.

High-pressure pump sprocket

Note: *A suitable puller will be required for this operation.*

Removal

15 Remove the timing belt and then remove the high pressure pump as described in Chapter 4B Section 10.

16 Clamp the pump firmly in a vice and then using a 32mm spanner to lock the pump, remove the sprocket retaining bolt.

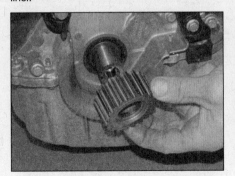

7.2 Removing the crankshaft sprocket

7.10 Angle-tightening the camshaft sprocket retaining bolt

7.13 Removing the timing belt tensioner

8.4a Screw the rod into the end of the camshaft...

8.4b ...locate the new oil seal and protector onto the camshaft...

8.4c ...then tighten the tool to press the seal into position

17 Use a puller to release the sprocket from the taper on the pump shaft. Recover the Woodruff key from the groove in the pump shaft.

Refitting

18 Refitting is a reversal of removal, bearing in mind the following points.
a) Ensure that the Woodruff key is correctly engaged with the pump shaft and sprocket.
b) Tighten the sprocket securing nut to the specified torque.
c) Refit and tension the timing belt as described in Section 6.

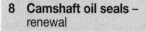

8 Camshaft oil seals – renewal

Timing belt end oil seal

1 Remove the camshaft sprocket as described in Section 7.
2 Note the fitted depth of the old oil seal. Using a small screwdriver, prise out the oil seal from the cylinder head taking care not to damage the sealing surface on the camshaft. Alternatively, the oil seal can be removed by drilling two small holes diagonally opposite each other and inserting self tapping screws in them. A pair of grips can then be used to pull out the oil seals, by pulling on each side in turn.

3 Inspect the seal rubbing surface on the camshaft. If it is grooved or rough in the area where the old seal was fitted, the new seal should be fitted slightly less deeply, so that it rubs on an unworn part of the surface.
4 Renault technicians use a tool (Mot. 1632) to fit the oil seal. The tool consists of a threaded rod, metal tube and nut, and a machined shoulder to locate the protector/ guide on. The rod is screwed into the end of the camshaft, and the protector/guide located on the shoulder. The metal tube is then fitted against the oil seal and the nut tightened to press the seal into the cylinder head/bearing cap **(see illustrations)**. If the Renault tool cannot be obtained, a similar tool can be made out of a threaded rod, metal tube, washer and nut.
5 Wipe clean the oil seal seating and the camshaft nose with a suitable solvent. Do not apply any lubricate to the housing, or the camshaft then press the oil seal squarely into position. Note that the Renault tool is designed to locate the seal at the original depth, however, if the camshaft sealing surface is excessively worn, position it less deeply so that it locates on the unworn surface.
6 After fitting the oil seal, remove the protector/guide and tool.

Flywheel end sealing

7 No oil seal is fitted to the flywheel end of the camshaft. The sealing is provided by a gasket between the cylinder head and the vacuum

pump housing, and on certain models by an O-ring fitted between the vacuum pump and the housing. The gasket and the O-ring, where applicable, can be renewed after unbolting the vacuum pump from the cylinder head (see Chapter 9 Section 22).

9 Camshaft and tappets – removal, inspection and refitting

Note: A new camshaft oil seal will be required, and suitable sealant will be required for the camshaft bearing caps and valve cover.

Removal

1 Removal of the camshaft will normally only be required for access to the tappet buckets (eg, for valve clearance adjustment) or during cylinder head overhaul. For cylinder head overhaul, remove the head as described in Section 10.
2 Remove the camshaft sprocket as described in Section 7.
3 Remove the valve cover as described in Section 4.
4 Remove the brake vacuum pump with reference to Chapter 9 Section 22. Note the position of the offset drive inside the pump which engages the slot in the end of the camshaft **(see illustrations)**.
5 Using a dial gauge, measure the camshaft endfloat, and compare with the value given in the Specifications. This will give an indication of the amount of wear present on the thrust surfaces.
6 If the original camshaft is to be refitted, it is advisable to measure the valve clearances at this stage as described in Section 5, so that any different thickness tappets required can be obtained before the camshaft is refitted.
7 Check the camshaft bearing caps for identification marks, and if none are present, make identifying marks so that they can be refitted in their original positions and the same way round. Number the caps from the flywheel end of the engine **(see illustration)**.
8 Progressively slacken the bearing cap bolts until the valve spring pressure is relieved. Remove the bolts and the bearing caps themselves.

9.4a Removing the brake vacuum pump and gasket

9.4b Offset drive in the pump which engages the slot in the end of the camshaft

9.7 The camshaft bearing caps are numbered from the flywheel end of the engine

9.9 Removing the camshaft from the cylinder head

9.10 Removing the tappets

9 Lift out the camshaft together with the oil seal **(see illustration)**.

10 Remove the tappets, keeping each identified for position **(see illustration)**. Place them in a compartment box, or on a sheet of card marked into eight sections, so that they may be refitted to their original locations. If any of the valve clearances measured in paragraph 9 is incorrect, use a micrometer to measure the thickness of the old tappet from its upper surface to the inner surface which contacts the valve stem. Refer to Section 5 and obtain new tappets of the correct thickness.

Inspection

11 Examine the camshaft bearing surfaces and cam lobes for wear ridges, pitting or scoring. Renew the camshaft if evident.

12 Renew the oil seal at the end of the camshaft as a matter of course. Lubricate the lips of the new seal before fitting, and store the camshaft so that its weight is not resting on the seal. Alternatively, the seal may be fitted after refitting the camshaft.

13 Examine the camshaft bearing surfaces in the cylinder head and bearing caps. Deep scoring or other damage means that the cylinder head must be renewed.

14 Inspect the tappet buckets for scoring, pitting and wear ridges. Renew as necessary.

Refitting

15 Oil the tappets (inside and out) and fit them to the bores from which they were removed; where applicable, fit the new tappets to their correct bores.

16 Oil the camshaft bearings. Place the camshaft without the oil seal onto the cylinder head.

17 Wipe clean the upper sealing edge of the cylinder head, then apply four beads of sealant, 7.0 mm wide, to the camshaft end bearing cap (Nos 1 and 6) contact areas as shown **(see illustrations)**.

18 Refit the camshaft bearing caps to their original locations, then insert the bearing cap bolts and progressively tighten them to the specified torque **(see illustrations)**.

19 If a new camshaft has been fitted, measure the endfloat using a dial gauge, and check that it is within the specified limits.

20 Fit the new oil seal with reference to Section 8.

21 Refit the brake vacuum pump with reference to Chapter 9 Section 22.

22 Wipe clean the contact surfaces on the valve cover and cylinder head and then refit the valve cover as described in Section 4.

23 Fit a new timing belt as described in Section 6.

24 Fit the remaining components in reverse order to removal.

10 Cylinder head – removal, inspection and refitting

Note: *A new cylinder head gasket must be fitted and all cylinder head bolts must be renewed. Sealant for the valve cover will also be required.*

Note: *The cylinder head can be removed*

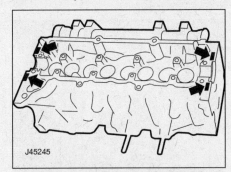

9.17a Apply 7.0 mm wide beads of sealant to the camshaft end bearing cap-to-cylinder head contact areas as shown

9.18a ...then refit the camshaft bearing caps

complete with the turbocharger, high pressure pump, fuel rail and injectors if necessary. This is a cost effective method if only the cylinder head gasket requires removal. An assistant will be require If this method Is adopted as the cylinder head Is a heavy Item. If the cylinder head requires machining for example it will be simpler to remove as many components as possible with the cylinder head in situ.

Removal

1 Before starting work, allow the engine to cool for as long as possible, to ensure the fuel pressure in the high-pressure lines, and the fuel temperature, are at a minimum (refer to Chapter 4B Section 1).

2 Disconnect the battery negative lead (Chapter 5A Section 4).

3 Jack up and support the front of the vehicle (see *Jacking and vehicle support*).

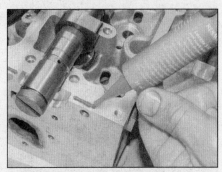

9.17b Apply the beads of sealant...

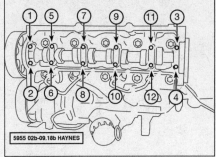

9.18b Tighten the bearing caps in the order shown

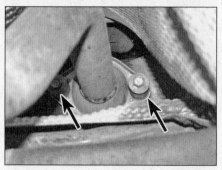
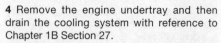

10.6 Disconnect the exhaust at the flexible mounting

10.11 Disconnect the breather pipe

10.13 Disconnect the wiring from the coolant temperature sensor

4 Remove the engine undertray and then drain the cooling system with reference to Chapter 1B Section 27.

5 With reference to Chapter 12 Section 19 and Chapter 11 Section 7 remove the wiper arms and the windscreen cowl panel.

6 Remove the catalytic convertor and (where fitted) the particulate filter at the manifold **(see illustration)** as described in Chapter 4B Section 18. Note, however, that the converter cannot be completely removed from the engine compartment, as the right-hand driveshaft is still in position; place or tie it to one side.

7 Unscrew the union nuts and remove the turbocharger oil return pipe from the cylinder block and turbocharger. To remove the turbocharger, unbolt the two support struts.

8 Unbolt and remove the rear engine mount – see Section 15.

9 Support the right-hand end of the sump on

a suitable jack. Protect the sump by spreading the load with a suitable block of wood.

10 Remove the right-hand engine mount, the timing belt (Section 6) and, if necessary, the camshaft sprocket (Section 7).

11 Remove the inter cooler inlet and outlet pipes and then disconnect the oil breather pipes from the engine and air filter housing **(see illustration)**.

12 Unclip and unbolt the sound proofing cover from the fuel rail and then unbolt and remove the pump high pressure pump protective cover – as described in Chapter 4B Section 10.

13 Disconnect the wiring from the following sensors:

a) *Air intake temperature (before turbocharger).*
b) *Air intake temperature (after turbocharger).*
c) *Air pressure (after turbocharger).*
d) *EGR valve control.*

e) *Air filter.*
f) *Coolant temperature sensor* **(see illustration)**.
g) *Camshaft position sensor*

14 At the rear of the high-pressure injection pump, disconnect the wiring from the fuel temperature sensor and the fuel pressure regulator **(see illustrations)**.

15 Disconnect the wiring from the four fuel injectors and glow plugs. If necessary, remove the glow plugs from the cylinder head.

16 Before removing the injectors, consider that Renault stipulate the high-pressure fuel lines must be renewed after removing them. If the removal of the cylinder head is just to renew the gasket, leave the injectors in position together with the fuel lines and high-pressure pump. If the cylinder head is to be stripped completely remove the fuel lines, fuel rail and fuel injectors as described in Chapter 4B.

17 Refer to Chapter 4B Section 1 and observe the precautions necessary when disconnecting the high-pressure fuel injection pipes. In particular, all disconnected pipes and components in the following paragraphs must be plugged to prevent entry of dust and dirt into the fuel system, and all removed high-pressure pipes must be renewed after removal.

18 Loosen the union nuts and disconnect the four high-pressure metal pipes between the fuel rail and injectors **(see illustration)**.

19 Loosen the union nut and disconnect the fuel supply pipe from the fuel rail.

20 Disconnect the wiring from the fuel pressure sensor on the fuel rail **(see illustration)**.

21 Release the clip securing the fuel return pipe and wiring, and release the wiring from the lifting eye.

22 Remove the hoses and coolant temperature sensor from the left-hand end of the cylinder head **(see illustration)**.

23 Unbolt and remove the timing belt tensioner from the cylinder head **(see illustration)**.

24 Remove the upper bolt from the alternator, slacken the lower bolt and move the alternator away from the cylinder head

25 Unbolt and remove the inner timing cover from the cylinder block and head **(see illustration)**.

10.14a Disconnect the fuel pressure regulator wiring plug...

10.14b ...or sensor wiring plug, depending on model

10.18 Removing the high-pressure pipes

10.20 Disconnect the wiring plug from the fuel pressure sensor

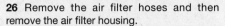

10.22 Remove the coolant hoses from the thermostat housing

10.23 Removing the timing belt tensioner

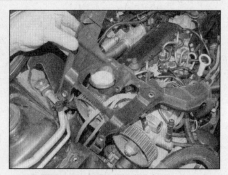

10.25 Remove the inner timing cover

26 Remove the air filter hoses and then remove the air filter housing.

27 Release the injector fuel return pipes from the clips on the valve cover.

28 Unscrew the bolts and remove the valve cover from the top of the cylinder head.

29 Disconnect the quick-release vacuum pipe from the brake vacuum pump on the left-hand end of the cylinder head (see illustration).

30 Unbolt the engine oil level dipstick tube from the cylinder head and remove it from the sump (see illustration).

31 The cylinder head assembly complete with high-pressure pump and ancillaries is very heavy. If they are to be left attached, it is advisable to use a hoist and suitable lifting tackle connected to the lifting eyes to lift the cylinder head. Alternatively, before loosening the cylinder head bolts, remove the turbocharger, manifolds, and high-pressure pump from the cylinder head with reference to the relevant Sections of Chapter 4B.

32 Before removing the cylinder head, turn the crankshaft anti-clockwise (viewed from the timing belt end of the engine) by a quarter turn to position all four pistons half-way down their bores. The TDC pin can remain in the cylinder block if necessary, however, remember that it is in position and do not turn the crankshaft further anti-clockwise.

33 Progressively slacken the cylinder head bolts in the reverse sequence to that shown (see illustration 10.43). With all the bolts loose, remove them (see illustration).

34 Lift the cylinder head upwards off the cylinder block. If it is stuck, tap it with a hammer and block of wood to release it. Do not try to turn the cylinder head (it is located by two dowels), nor attempt to prise it free using a screwdriver inserted between the block and head faces.

35 If necessary, remove the camshaft and tappets (Section 8).

Inspection

36 The mating faces of the cylinder head and block must be perfectly clean before refitting the head. Use a scraper to remove all traces of gasket and carbon, and also clean the tops of the pistons. Take particular care with the aluminium cylinder head, as the soft

metal is damaged easily. Also, make sure that debris is not allowed to enter the oil and water channels – this is particularly important for the oil circuit, as carbon could block the oil supply to the camshaft or crankshaft bearings. Using adhesive tape and paper, seal the water, oil and bolt holes in the cylinder block. Clean the piston crowns in the same way.

37 Check the block and head for nicks, deep scratches and other damage. If slight, they may be removed carefully with a file. Machining of the cylinder head or cylinder block is not recommended by the manufacturers.

38 If warpage of the cylinder head is suspected, use a straight-edge to check it for distortion. Refer to Chapter 2D Section 7 if necessary; if the warpage is more than the maximum, the cylinder head must be renewed, as regrinding is not allowed.

39 Clean out the cylinder head bolt holes in

10.29 Disconnect the quick-release vacuum pipe from the brake vacuum pump

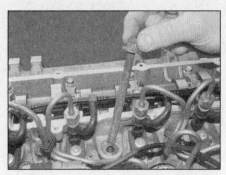

10.33 Remove the cylinder head bolts

the block using a pipe cleaner, or a rag and screwdriver. Make sure that all oil is removed, otherwise there is a possibility of the block being cracked by hydraulic pressure when the bolts are tightened. Examine the bolt threads in the cylinder block for damage, and if necessary, use the correct size tap to chase out the threads. The cylinder head bolts must be renewed each time they are removed, and must not be oiled before being fitted.

Refitting

40 Where removed, refit the tappets, camshaft and camshaft sprocket with reference to Section 9 and Section 7. Turn the camshaft so that the sprocket is at its TDC position.

41 Ensure that the cylinder head locating dowels are fitted to the cylinder block, then fit the new gasket the right way round on the cylinder block (see illustration).

10.30 Unbolt and remove the engine oil level dipstick tube

10.41 Locate the new gasket on the cylinder block

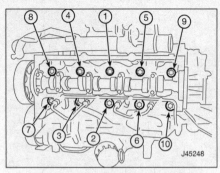

10.43 Cylinder head bolt tightening sequence

42 Carefully lower the cylinder head onto the dowels and gasket, then insert the new bolts and hand-tighten. Do not oil the threads or heads of the new bolts.

43 Tighten the bolts in sequence, and in the stages given in the Specifications **(see illustration)**.

44 Turn the crankshaft clockwise by a quarter turn until the internal web contacts the TDC timing pin.

45 Refit the turbocharger, manifolds and injection pump to the cylinder head with reference to the relevant Sections of Chapter 4B.

46 Refit the air filter support bracket and tighten securely.

47 Reconnect the vacuum pipe to the brake vacuum pump.

48 Reconnect the wiring to the fuel pressure sensor on the fuel rail.

49 Reconnect the fuel supply pipe to the fuel rail and tighten the union nut.

50 Refit the four fuel injectors as described in Chapter 4B Section 12.

51 Refit the four high-pressure pipes to the fuel rail and injectors and tighten the union nuts to the specified torque.

52 Wipe clean the contact surfaces on the valve cover and cylinder head, then apply four beads of sealant, 2.0 mm wide, to the camshaft end bearing caps (Nos 1 and 6) and refit the cover with reference to Section 3. Secure the fuel return pipes in the clips on the valve cover and reconnect the crankcase ventilation hose.

53 Refit the air filter assembly and tighten the mounting bolt, then reconnect the air hose.

54 Refit the inner timing cover and tighten the mounting bolts.

55 Refit the auxiliary drivebelt tensioner and tighten the mounting bolt.

56 Locate the timing belt tensioner roller on the cylinder head and hand-tighten the securing nut at this stage.

57 Refit the turbocharger oil return pipe and tighten the union nuts.

58 Refit the turbocharger and reconnect the exhaust downpipe and catalytic converter with reference to Chapter 4B Section 16, Section 18.

59 Refit the coolant temperature sensor and coolant hoses.

60 Secure the fuel return pipe and wiring with the clip.

61 Reconnect the wiring to the fuel temperature sensor and low-pressure flow adjuster on the rear of the high-pressure injection pump.

62 Reconnect the wiring to the air intake

temperature sensors, air pressure sensor, EGR valve and air filter.

63 Refit the timing belt as described in Section 6.

64 Reconnect the battery negative lead.

65 Prime and bleed the fuel system as described in Chapter 4B Section 6.

66 Refill and bleed the cooling system as described in Chapter 1B Section 27.

67 Start the engine and run it up to temperature, checking constantly for fuel, oil and coolant leaks.

11 Sump – removal and refitting

Removal

1 Disconnect the battery negative lead (Chapter 5A Section 4).

2 Jack up the front of the vehicle and support on axle stands (see *Jacking and vehicle support*). Remove the engine undertray and both front wheels.

3 Drain the engine oil referring to Chapter 1B Section 4, then refit and tighten the drain plug using a new washer.

4 Remove the bolts from the driveshaft intermediate bearing housing. This is possible with the driveshaft in place, but is considerably easier if the driveshaft is removed as described in Chapter 8 Section 2.

5 Unbolt and remove the rear engine mounting/tie bar.

6 Remove the lower bolt from the alternator/AC compressor mounting bracket.

7 Remove the drain hose (from the injector rail) from the transmission and the sump.

8 Disconnect the wiring plug from the oil level sensor and then remove the sensor **(see illustration)**.

9 Remove the 4 sump to transmission bolts and then remove the sump to block bolts.

10 If the sump can not be fully removed at this point (it will be fouling the oil pick up strainer) then (working through the gap between the sump and the block) slacken the oil pump mounting bolts sufficiently so that the sump can pass over the strainer.

11 Remove the sump and recover the gasket.

Refitting

12 Thoroughly clean the mating surfaces of the sump and cylinder block. Where removed, refit the baffle plate making sure that the tabs are correctly located in the cut-outs near the sump joint face **(see illustration)**.

13 Apply 2 drops 5 mm in diameter of Rhodorseal 5661 (or similar) sealant to the two points where the engine right-hand cover meets the cylinder block. Apply 12 mm long and 5 mm diameter beads of sealant to the angled areas on the right-hand cover and oil seal housing. Fit a new gasket on the sump. The gasket must be located over the baffle plate tabs **(see illustrations)**.

11.8 Remove the oil level sensor

11.12 Make sure the tabs are located in the cut-outs when refitting the baffle plate

11.13a Apply sealant where the right-hand cover meets the cylinder block...

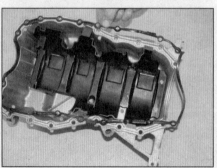

11.13b ...then locate a new gasket on the sump...

11.13c ...before refitting the sump

14 Partially fit the sump. If the oil pump mounting bolts were slackened then tighten them to the specified torque. Fit the sump and tighten the sump to transmission bolts followed by the sump to block bolts. Tighten the bolts to the specified torque in the sequence shown **(see illustration)**.
15 Refit the remainder of the components in reverse order to removal.
16 Refill the engine with oil and then disconnect the crankshaft sensor to stop the engine from starting. Crank the engine over on the starter motor for several seconds until the engine oil warning light extinguishes. Refit the crankshaft sensor, sart the engine and check for oil leaks.

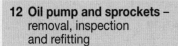

12 Oil pump and sprockets –
removal, inspection and refitting

Removal

1 Remove the sump as described in Section 11.
2 Unscrew the two mounting bolts and withdraw the oil pump, tilting it to disengage its sprocket from the drive chain. If the two locating dowels are displaced, refit them in their locations.
3 To remove the drive chain, first remove the crankshaft sprocket as described in Section 7, then unbolt the engine right-hand cover from the cylinder block. Prise out the oil seal with a screwdriver, and discard it as a new one must

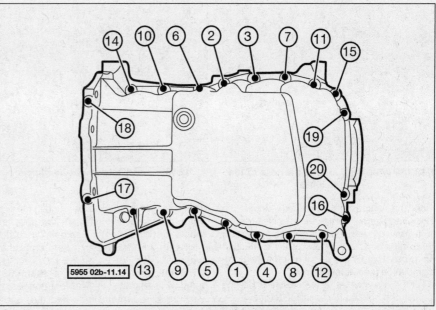

11.14 Sump bolt tightening sequence

be fitted on reassembly. If necessary, the new oil seal may be fitted with the right-hand cover on the bench **(see illustration)**.
4 Slide the oil pump drive sprocket and drive chain from the nose of the crankshaft **(see illustrations)**. Note that the drive sprocket is not keyed to the crankshaft, but relies on the pulley bolt being tightened correctly to clamp the sprocket. It is most important that the pulley bolt is correctly tightened otherwise there is the possibility of the oil pump not functioning properly.
5 Unhook the drive chain from the drive sprocket.

Inspection

6 Unscrew the retaining bolts and lift the pump cover over the driveshaft. Withdraw the idler gear and the drivegear/shaft. Mark the gears before removal, so that they can be refitted in their original position.
7 Extract the retaining clip and remove the oil pressure relief valve spring retainer, spring, spring seat and plunger.
8 Clean the components and carefully examine

the gears, pump body and relief valve plunger for any signs of scoring or wear. Renew the complete pump assembly if excessive wear is evident (no spare parts are available).
9 If the components appear serviceable, measure the clearance between the pump body and the gears using feeler gauges. Also measure the gear endfloat and check the flatness of the end cover. If the clearances exceed the specified tolerances, the pump must be renewed. There should be no discernible wear or distortion of the cover.
10 If the pump is satisfactory, reassemble the components in the reverse order of removal. Fill the pump with oil, then refit the cover and tighten the bolts securely.

Refitting

11 Wipe clean the oil pump and cylinder block mating surfaces and check that the two locating dowels are fitted in the cylinder block.
12 Engage the drive chain with the drive sprocket, then slide the sprocket onto the nose of the crankshaft.
13 Fit a new gasket to the right-hand cover.

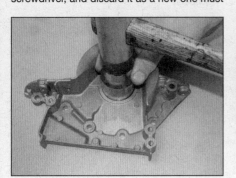

12.3 Fitting a new oil seal to the right-hand cover

12.4a Oil pump and mounting bolts

12.4b Removing the oil pump and drive chain

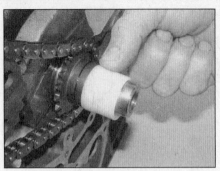

12.13a Wrap tape around the nose of the crankshaft...

12.13b ...and fit the right-hand cover

Refit the engine right-hand cover, insert the bolts and tighten them to the specified torque. If a new oil seal has already been fitted, wrap tape around the nose of the crankshaft to protect the oil seal, and remove it on completion **(see illustrations)**.
14 Fit a new gasket to the closure plate and tighten the bolts to the specified torque.
15 Tilt the oil pump and engage the sprocket with the drive chain, then position it on the dowels and insert the two mounting bolts. Tighten the bolts to the specified torque.
16 Refit the sump with reference to Section 11.

13 Crankshaft oil seals – renewal

Timing end cover oil seal

Note: *The new oil seal is extremely fragile and must only be handled by the protector. Do not touch the surface of the oil seal.*
1 Remove the crankshaft sprocket, as described in Section 7.
2 Note the fitted position of the old seal, then prise it out of the right-hand cover/housing using a screwdriver or suitable hooked instrument, taking care not to damage the surface of the crankshaft. Alternatively, the oil seal can be removed by drilling two small holes diagonally opposite each other and inserting self tapping screws in them. A pair of grips can then be used to pull out the oil seal, by pulling on each side in turn.
3 Inspect the seal rubbing surface on the

crankshaft. If it is grooved or rough in the area where the old seal was fitted, the new seal should be fitted slightly less deeply, so that it rubs on an unworn part of the crankshaft surface.
4 Renault technicians use a tool (Mot. 1586) to fit the oil seal. The tool consists of a threaded rod, metal tube and nut, and a machined shoulder to locate the protector/guide on. The rod is screwed into the end of the crankshaft, and the protector/guide located on the shoulder. The metal tube is then fitted against the oil seal and the nut tightened to press the seal into the right-hand cover. If the Renault tool cannot be obtained, a similar tool can be made out of a threaded rod, metal tube, washer and nut.
5 Using a suitable solvent clean the oil seal housing and the crankshaft nose. Do not apply any lubricant – the seal is designed to be fitted dry. Press the oil seal squarely into position. Note that the Renault tool is designed to locate the seal at the original depth, however, if the crankshaft sealing surface is excessively worn, position it less deeply so that it locates on the unworn surface.
6 After fitting the oil seal, remove the protector/guide and tool.
7 Refit the crankshaft sprocket as described in Section 7.

Flywheel end oil seal

8 Remove the transmission as described in Chapter 7 Section 7.
9 Remove the clutch assembly as described in Chapter 6 Section 8.

10 Remove the flywheel as described in Section 14.
11 Renew the oil seal as described in paragraphs 2 to 6 inclusive **(see illustration)**.
12 Refit the flywheel with reference to Section 14 and then refit (or replace) the clutch assembly. Refit the transmission.

14 Flywheel – removal, inspection and refitting

Note: *New flywheel bolts must be used on refitting.*

Removal

1 Remove the transmission as described in Chapter 7 Section 7.
2 Remove the clutch as described in Chapter 6 Section 8.
3 The flywheel must now be held stationary while the securing bolts are loosened. To do this, locate a long bolt in one of the engine-to-gearbox mounting bolt holes and insert a wide-bladed screwdriver or length of bent metal bar in the starter ring gear or use a suitable locking tool **(see illustration)**.
4 Unscrew the securing bolts and withdraw the flywheel from the crankshaft. Note that the flywheel bolt holes are offset so that the flywheel can only be fitted in one position. Discard the old bolts as new ones must be used on refitting.

Inspection

5 Examine the flywheel for scoring of the clutch face and for wear or chipping of the ring gear teeth. If the clutch face is scored, the flywheel may be machined until flat, but renewal is preferable.
6 If the ring gear teeth are worn or damaged, the flywheel must be renewed.

Refitting

7 Clean the flywheel and crankshaft faces.
8 Locate the flywheel on the crankshaft and insert the new bolts. Tighten the new bolts in a diagonal sequence to the specified torque. Hold the flywheel stationary as during removal **(see illustration)**. Do not oil the new bolt threads as they are supplied with locking compound.

13.11 Fitting a new oil seal to the flywheel end of the crankshaft

14.3 Hold the flywheel stationary using a screwdriver in the starter ring gear

14.8 Fit new flywheel bolts

9 Refit (or replace) the clutch as described in Chapter 6 Section 8.

10 Refit the manual transmission with reference to Chapter 7 Section 7.

15 Engine/transmission mountings – inspection, removal and refitting

Inspection

1 Apply the handbrake, then jack up the front of the car and support it on axle stands (see *Jacking and vehicle support*). Where fitted, remove the engine compartment undertray.

2 Visually inspect the rubber pads on the two front and one rear engine/transmission mountings for signs of cracking and deterioration. Careful use of a lever will help to determine the condition of the rubber pads. If there is excessive movement in the mounting, or if the rubber has deteriorated, the mounting should be renewed.

3 Lower the vehicle to the ground.

Renewal

Right-hand front mounting

4 Support the right-hand end of the engine with a jack and block of wood beneath the sump **(see illustration)**.

5 Unclip the hose/pipes from the top of the engine mounting bracket, then undo the mounting bolts from the engine and inner wing panel and remove the complete mounting **(see illustrations)**.

6 Fit the new mounting using a reversal of the removal procedure, but tighten the nuts/bolts to the specified torque wrench settings.

Left-hand front mounting

7 Remove the air inlet ducts from the left-hand side of the engine as applicable, for access to the engine/transmission left-hand mounting. Remove the battery as described in Chapter 5A Section 4.

8 Support the left-hand end of the transmission with a trolley jack and block of wood beneath the sump.

9 Unclip the battery vent pipe, and the wiring securing clips from the battery tray, then undo the three retaining bolts and remove

15.4 Support the engine with a suitable jack

15.5b ... then unbolt the mounting from the engine...

the battery tray from the engine compartment **(see illustrations)**.

10 Unbolt the central nut from the mounting, and then at this point, the engine and gearbox

15.5a Unclip the hoses/pipes...

15.5c ...and inner wing panel

can be lowered. However, if required undo all the mounting bolts and remove the mounting and bracket as a complete assembly **(see illustration)**.

15.9a Unclip the vent pipe...

15.9b ...the cable securing clips at the rear...

15.9c ...and the cable clip at the front...

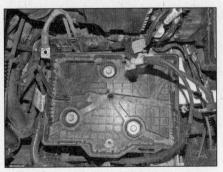

15.9d ...then undo the battery tray bolts

15.10 Transmission mounting and bracket

11 Fit the new mounting using a reversal of the removal procedure, but tighten the nuts/bolts to the specified torque wrench setting.

Rear mounting

12 Apply the handbrake, then jack up the front of the vehicle and support it on axle stands (see *Jacking and vehicle support*). Note the rear mounting does not support the weight of the engine.

13 Unbolt the steady bar from the transmission **(see illustration)**.

14 Unbolt the mounting from the subframe and remove it from the vehicle.

15 Fit the new mounting using a reversal of the removal procedure, but tighten the nuts/bolts to the specified torque setting.

16 Oil pressure switch –
removal and refitting

1 The oil pressure switch is a vital early warning of low oil pressure. The switch operates the oil warning light on the instrument panel – the light should come on with the ignition, and go out almost immediately when the engine starts.

2 If the light does not come on, there could be a fault on the instrument panel, the switch wiring, or the switch itself. If the light does not go out, low oil level, worn oil pump (or sump pick-up blocked), blocked oil filter, or worn main bearings could be to blame – or again, the switch may be faulty.

3 If the light comes on while driving, the best advice is to turn the engine off immediately,

15.13 Rear lower mounting

and not to drive the car until the problem has been investigated – ignoring the light could mean expensive engine damage.

Removal

4 The oil pressure switch is located on the front face of the engine, next to the oil filter.

5 Jack up the front of the car, and support it on axle stands (see *Jacking and vehicle support*) – to improve access, remove the oil filter, referring to Chapter 1B Section 4 if necessary.

6 Disconnect the wiring plug from the switch **(see illustration)**.

7 Unscrew the switch from the block, and remove it together with its sealing washer. There should only be a very slight loss of oil when this is done.

Inspection

8 Examine the switch for signs of cracking or splits. If the top part of the switch is loose, this is an early indication of impending failure.

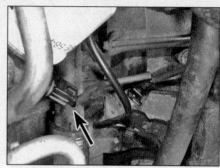

16.6 Disconnect the wiring plug from the oil pressure warning switch

9 Check that the wiring terminals at the switch are not loose, then trace the wire from the switch connector until it enters the main loom – any wiring defects will give rise to apparent oil pressure problems.

Refitting

10 Refitting is the reverse of the removal procedure, noting the following points:
a) *Clean the switch threads before fitting. Tighten the switch securely.*
b) *Reconnect the switch connector, making sure it clicks home properly. Ensure that the wiring is routed away from any hot or moving parts.*
c) *Lower the car to the ground, then check the engine oil level and top-up if necessary (see 'Weekly checks').*
d) *Check for signs of oil leaks once the engine has been restarted and warmed-up to normal operating temperature.*

Chapter 2 Part D
Engine removal and overhaul procedures

Contents

Degrees of difficulty

Easy, suitable for novice with little experience	Fairly easy, suitable for beginner with some experience	Fairly difficult, suitable for competent DIY mechanic	Difficult, suitable for experienced DIY mechanic	Very difficult, suitable for expert DIY or professional

Specifications

General
Engine codes:
0.9 litre petrol engine	H4B
1.2 litre petrol engine	D4F
Diesel engine	K9K

Valves
Valve spring free length:
0.9 litre petrol engine	N/A
1.2 litre petrol engine	40.20 mm
Diesel engine	43.31 mm

Cylinder head
Height:
0.9 litre petrol engine	N/A
1.2 litre petrol engine	99.0 mm
Diesel engine	127.0 mm
Maximum acceptable gasket face distortion	0.05 mm
Refinishing limit	No refinishing permitted
Valve depth in relation to head surface	0.00 ± 0.07 mm

Cylinder block
Bore diameter:
0.9 litre petrol engine:	
Class A	N/A
Class B	N/A
1.2 litre petrol engine:	
Class A	69.000 ± 0.015 mm
Class B	69.015 ± 0.015 mm
Diesel engine	N/A

Pistons and piston rings

Piston diameter:
  0.9 litre petrol engine:
    Class A . . . .   N/A
    Class B . . . .   N/A
  1.2 litre petrol engine (measured 9.0 mm from bottom of skirt):
    Class A . . . .   68.976 ± 0.006 mm
    Class B . . . .   68.984 ± 0.006 mm
  Diesel engine (measured 56.0 mm from crown) . . . .   75.94 ± 0.007 mm
Piston ring end gaps (installed):
  0.9 litre petrol engine . . . .   N/A
  1.2 litre petrol engine:
    Top compression . . . .   0.20 to 0.35 mm
    Second compression . . . .   0.35 to 0.50 mm
    Oil control . . . .   0.20 to 0.90 mm
  Diesel engine:
    Top compression . . . .   0.2 to 0.35 mm
    Second compression . . . .   0.7 to 0.9 mm
    Oil control (2 rails and expander) . . . .   0.25 to 0.5 mm
Ring gap spacing (all engines) . . . .   120°
Piston protrusion (diesel engine) . . . .   0.192 ± 0.093 mm

Crankshaft

Main bearing journal diameter:
  0.9 litre petrol engine . . . .   N/A
  1.2 litre petrol engines:
    Standard . . . .   44.000 mm ± 0.01 mm
    1st undersize . . . .   43.750 mm ± 0.01 mm
Crankpin (big-end) journal diameter:
  0.9 litre petrol engine . . . .   N/A
  1.2 litre petrol engines:
    Standard . . . .   40.000 +0 –0.016 mm
    1st undersize . . . .   39.750 mm +0 –0.016 mm
Crankshaft endfloat:
  0.9 litre petrol engine . . . .   N/A
  1.2 litre petrol engine . . . .   0.045 to 0.235 mm
  Diesel engines:
    New . . . .   0.045 to 0.252 mm
    Maximum . . . .   0.852 mm

Torque wrench settings

Refer to Parts A, B, or C of this Chapter.

---

1 General Information

How to use this Chapter

1 This Part of Chapter 2 is devoted to engine/transmission removal and refitting, to those repair procedures requiring the removal of the engine/transmission from the vehicle, and to the overhaul of engine components. It includes only the Specifications relevant to those procedures. Refer to Parts A, B or C for additional Specifications, and for all torque wrench settings.

General information

2 The information ranges from advice concerning preparation for an overhaul and the purchase of new parts, to detailed step-by-step procedures covering removal and installation of internal engine components and the inspection of parts.
3 The following Sections have been written

based on the assumption that the engine has been removed from the vehicle. For information concerning in-vehicle engine repair, as well as removal and installation of the external components necessary for the overhaul, see Parts A, B or C of this Chapter.
4 When overhauling the engine, it is essential to establish first exactly what parts are available. At the time of writing, very few under or oversized components are available for engine reconditioning (the exception being for the diesel engine). In many cases, it would appear that the easiest and most economically sensible course of action is to replace a worn or damaged engine with an exchange unit.

2 Engine overhaul – general information

1 It is not always easy to determine when, or if, an engine should be completely overhauled, as a number of factors must be considered.

2 High mileage is not necessarily an indication that an overhaul is needed, while low mileage does not preclude the need for an overhaul. Frequency of servicing is probably the most important consideration. An engine which has had regular and frequent oil and filter changes, as well as other required maintenance, will most likely give many thousands of miles of reliable service. Conversely, a neglected engine may require an overhaul very early in its life.
3 Excessive oil consumption is an indication that piston rings, valve stem oil seals and/or valves and valve guides are in need of attention. Make sure that oil leaks are not responsible before deciding that the rings and/or guides are bad. Perform a cylinder compression check to determine the extent of the work required.
4 Check the oil pressure with a gauge fitted in place of the oil pressure warning light switch and compare it with the value given in the Specifications. If it is extremely low, the main and big-end bearings and/or the oil pump are probably worn out.

5 Loss of power, rough running, knocking or metallic engine noises, excessive valve gear noise and high fuel consumption may also point to the need for an overhaul, especially if they are all present at the same time. If a complete tune-up does not remedy the situation, major mechanical work is the only solution.

6 An engine overhaul involves restoring all internal parts to the specification of a new engine. **Note:** *Always check first what parts are available before planning any overhaul operation – refer to Section 1.* Manufacturer main dealers, or a good engine reconditioning specialist/automotive parts supplier, may be able to suggest alternatives which will enable you to overcome the lack of parts.

7 During an overhaul, it is usual to renew the piston rings, and to rebore and/or hone the cylinder bores; where the rebore is done by an automotive machine shop, new oversize pistons and rings will also be installed – all these operations, of course, assume the availability of suitable parts. The main and big-end bearings are generally renewed and, if necessary, the crankshaft may be reground to restore the journals.

8 Generally, the valves are serviced as well during an overhaul, since they're usually in less than perfect condition at this point. While the engine is being overhauled, other components, such as the starter and alternator, can be renewed as well, or rebuilt, if the necessary parts can be found. The end result should be an as new engine that will give many trouble free miles. **Note:** *Critical cooling system components such as the hoses, drivebelt, thermostat and coolant pump MUST be renewed when an engine is overhauled.* The radiator should be checked carefully, to ensure that it isn't clogged or leaking (see Chapter 3 Section 3). Also, as a general rule, the oil pump should be renewed when an engine is rebuilt.

9 Before beginning the engine overhaul, read through the entire procedure to familiarise yourself with the scope and requirements of the job. Overhauling an engine isn't difficult, but it is time consuming. Plan on the vehicle being off the road for a minimum of two weeks, especially if parts must be taken to an automotive machine shop for repair or reconditioning. Check on availability of parts, and make sure that any necessary special tools and equipment are obtained in advance. Most work can be done with typical hand tools, although a number of precision measuring tools are required for inspecting parts to determine if they must be renewed. Often, an automotive machine shop will handle the inspection of parts, and will offer advice concerning reconditioning and renewal. **Note:** *Always wait until the engine has been completely dismantled, and all components, especially the cylinder block/crankcase, have been inspected, before deciding what service and repair operations must be performed by an automotive machine shop.* Since the block's

condition will be the major factor to consider when determining whether to overhaul the original engine or buy a rebuilt one, never purchase parts or have machine work done on other components until the cylinder block/ crankcase has been thoroughly inspected. As a general rule, time is the primary cost of an overhaul, so it doesn't pay to install worn or sub-standard parts.

10 As a final note, to ensure maximum life and minimum trouble from a rebuilt engine, everything must be assembled with care, in a spotlessly-clean environment.

3 Engine removal – methods and precautions

1 If you have decided that an engine must be removed for overhaul or major repair work, several preliminary steps should be taken.

2 Locating a suitable place to work is extremely important. Adequate work space, with storage space for the vehicle, will be needed. If a garage is not available, at the very least a flat, level, clean work surface is required.

3 Cleaning the engine compartment and engine before beginning the removal procedure will help keep tools clean and organised.

4 The engine can be removed complete with the transmission by lowering it from the engine compartment or if space permits by lifting it out of the engine compartment. Alternatively, the transmission can be removed first, then the engine lifted from the engine compartment. An engine hoist will be necessary; make sure the equipment is rated in excess of the combined weight of the engine and transmission. Safety is of primary importance, considering the potential hazards involved in removing the engine/transmission from the vehicle.

5 If this is the first time you have removed an engine, a helper should ideally be available. Advice and aid from someone more experienced would also be useful. There are many instances when one person cannot simultaneously perform all of the operations required when removing the engine/ transmission from the vehicle.

6 Plan the operation ahead of time. Arrange for, or obtain, all of the tools and equipment you'll need prior to beginning the job. Some of the equipment necessary to perform engine/ transmission removal and installation safely and with relative ease, and which may have to be hired or borrowed, includes (in addition to the engine hoist) a heavy duty trolley jack, a strong pair of axle stands, some wooden blocks, and an engine dolly (a low, wheeled platform capable of taking the weight of the engine/transmission, so that it can be moved easily when on the ground). A complete set of spanners and sockets (as described in the Reference section of this manual) will

obviously be needed, together with plenty of rags and cleaning solvent for mopping-up spilled oil, coolant and fuel. If the hoist is to be hired, make sure that you arrange for it in advance, and perform all of the operations possible without it beforehand. This will save you money and time.

7 Plan for the vehicle to be out of use for quite a while. A machine shop will be required to perform some of the work which the do-it-yourselfer can't accomplish without special equipment. These establishments often have a busy schedule, so it would be a good idea to consult them before removing the engine, to accurately estimate the amount of time required to rebuild or repair components that may need work.

8 Always be extremely careful when removing and installing the engine/transmission. Serious injury can result from careless actions. By planning ahead and taking your time, the job (although a major task) can be accomplished successfully.

4 Engine – removal and refitting

Note: *Read through the entire Section, as well as reading the advice in the preceding Section, before beginning this procedure. In this procedure, the engine and transmission are removed as a unit together with the subframe, lowered to the ground and removed from underneath, then separated outside the vehicle. However, if preferred, the transmission can be removed from the engine first (as described in Chapter 7 or) – this leaves the engine free to be either lifted out from above or lowered to the ground.*

Note: *On models fitted with air conditioning the system must be drained by a Renault dealer or an air conditioning specialist before removing the engine.*

Removal

1 Disconnect the battery negative lead, and position the lead away from the battery (as described in Chapter 5A Section 4).

2 Remove the air filter duct work and the air filter housing

3 Remove the battery as described in Chapter 5A Section 4.

4 Remove the windscreen wiper arms (Chapter 12 Section 19) and then remove the windscreen cowl panels (Chapter 11 Section 7).

5 Apply the handbrake, then jack up the front of the vehicle and support it on axle stands (see *Jacking and vehicle support*). Remove both front wheels and the engine undertray.

6 Remove the front bumper and the wing liners as described in Chapter 11 Section 6.

7 On turbocharged models remove the intercooler and its associated pipework, with reference to Chapter 4A Section 16 for 0.9 litre petrol engines or Chapter 4B Section 17 for diesel engines.

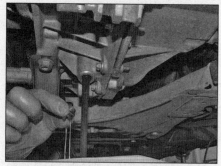

4.8 Draining the transmission

4.9 Remove the radiator bottom hose

4.10a Remove the bolts from the strut...

4.10b ...pull the outer joint free from the hub...

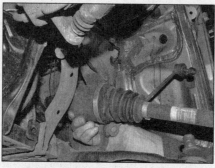

4.10c ...and remove the driveshaft

8 At this stage, the engine and transmission can be drained of oil **(see illustration)**.
9 Drain the cooling system as described in Chapter 1A Section 27 (petrol) or Chapter 1B Section 27 (diesel). To do this, the bottom hose must be disconnected from the radiator **(see illustration)** and then remove the radiator as described in Chapter 3 Section 3. On diesel models remove the side stiffener plate.

10 Remove the driveshafts as described in Chapter 8 Section 2 **(see illustrations)**.
11 Working in the engine bay, remove the cover from the fusebox (behind the left hand headlight). Trace the wiring loom and remove the connectors that lead to the engine sensors and actuators (see Chapter 12 Section 3. for further information on the engine compartment fusebox). Remove the maxi fuse and unclip the green and blue connectors from the battery mounted fusebox.
12 Unlock the connectors from the ECU and remove them. Remove the ECU to gain access to the wiring loom.
13 Remove the nuts and release the wiring loom from the inner wing. Remove the wiring from the support bracket and disconnect the earths from the left hand strut tower and inner wing **(see illustrations)**. The earth points may vary, depending on model.
14 On petrol engine models, disconnect the wiring from the purge valve. Also, disconnect the fuel supply hose and the carbon canister hose on the inlet manifold.
15 On manual transmission models, disconnect the clutch hydraulic hose at the transmission (Chapter 6 Section 4).
16 On diesel models, release the fuel lines from high-pressure pump.
17 On diesel models, remove the vacuum pipe from the brake vacuum pump.
18 With reference to Chapters 7 Section 4 and disconnect the gearchange mechanism **(see illustration)**.
19 On automatic models unplug the modular wiring connector and then unbolt it from the gearbox. Remove the coolant hoses from the oil cooler.
20 On the bulkhead at the rear of the engine, disconnect the hoses from the heater matrix stubs.
21 Unbolt the earth cable from the transmission **(see illustration)**.
22 Check that the front wheels are pointing straight-ahead, then secure the steering wheel in its central position with tape or string. This is important, as subsequent damage to the airbag clockspring may occur if the steering wheel is turned beyond its normal range.
23 On petrol models, disconnect the wiring from the oxygen sensor located upstream of the catalytic converter at the rear of the

4.13a Remove the earth connections from the strut tower...

4.13b ...and the inner wing – depending on model

4.18 The plastic gear cable support is easily damaged, so remove it

4.21 The gearbox earth

4.24 Remove the exhaust

4.25 Remove the rear engine steady bar

4.26 Preparing to remove the engine and gearbox

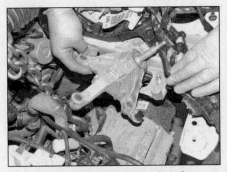

4.27 Remove the left-hand engine mounting bracket

4.28 Remove the right hand mounting

4.31 Separate the gearbox from the engine

engine compartment, and the second oxygen sensor located downstream of the converter beneath the car.

24 Working beneath the car unbolt the exhaust (or catalytic converter) from the downpipe **(see illustration)**.

25 Unbolt and remove the rear engine steady mounting **(see illustration)**.

26 Connect a hoist or engine lifting bar to the engine lifting eyes, and support the weight of the engine **(see illustration)**

27 Unscrew the retaining nuts from the left-hand engine/transmission mounting, and remove it along with the transmission mounting bracket **(see illustration)**.

28 Remove the right-hand engine mounting from the engine **(see illustration)**.

29 A final check should be made to ensure all hoses and electrical connectors have been released or removed.

30 Lower (or lift) the engine and gearbox from the vehicle.

31 Remove the manual or automatic transmission from the engine with reference to Chapter 7 Section 7 or **(see illustration)**.

Refitting

32 To reconnect the transmission and engine, reverse the operations used to separate them. Above all, do not use excessive force during these operations – if the two will not marry together easily, forcing them will only lead to damage. Do not tighten the bellhousing bolts to force the engine and transmission together. Ensure that the bellhousing and cylinder block

mating faces will butt together evenly without obstruction, before tightening the bolts fully. Reconnect any wiring on the engine/transmission assembly, routing it as noted on removal.

33 The remainder of the refitting procedure is the direct reverse of the removal procedure, noting the following points:

a) *Tighten all fasteners to the specified torque wrench settings, where applicable.*

b) *Ensure that all sections of the wiring harness follow their original routing; use new cable ties to secure the harness in position, keeping it away from sources of heat and abrasion.*

c) *Ensure that all hoses are correctly routed and are secured with the correct hose clips, where applicable. If the hose clips cannot be used again; proprietary worm-drive clips should be fitted in their place.*

d) *Refill the cooling system as described in Chapter 1A Section 27 or 1B Section 27.*

e) *Refill the engine with appropriate grade and quantity of oil, where necessary (Chapter 1A Section 4 or 1B Section 4).*

f) *Refill the transmission oil or fluid (see Chapter 1A Section 21 or 1B Section 21).*

g) *Where applicable, the refrigerant circuit must be recharged by a refrigeration specialist.*

h) *When the engine is started for the first time, check for coolant, lubricant and fuel leaks, etc. If the engine has been*

overhauled, read the notes in Section 18 before attempting to start it.

5 Engine overhaul – dismantling sequence

1 It is much easier to dismantle and work on the engine if it is mounted on a portable engine stand. These stands can often be hired from a tool hire shop. Before the engine is mounted on a stand, the flywheel/driveplate should be removed (Part A, B or C of this Chapter) so that the stand bolts can be tightened into the end of the cylinder block/crankcase.

2 If a stand is not available, it is possible to dismantle the engine with it mounted on blocks, on a sturdy workbench or on the floor. Be extra careful not to tip or drop the engine when working without a stand.

3 If you are going to obtain a reconditioned engine, all external components must be removed first, to be transferred to the new engine (just as they will if you are doing a complete engine overhaul yourself). **Note:** *When removing the external components from the engine, pay close attention to details that may be helpful or important during refitting. Note the fitted position of gaskets, seals, spacers, pins, washers, bolts and other small items. These external components include the following* **(see illustrations)**: See relevant chapters, for the information on engines being worked on.

5.3a Remove the combined alternator and compressor mounting – 1.2 litre petrol engine

5.3b Remove the inlet manifold

5.3c Unbolt the coolant pipe from the cylinder block...

5.3d ...and pull it from the coolant pump inlet

5.3e Remove the thermostat housing...

5.3f ...and the exhaust manifold

a) Alternator, air conditioning compressor and mounting bracket (Chapter 3 Section 15).
b) Coolant pipe.
c) Air conditioning compressor mounting brackets.
d) HT leads and spark plugs – petrol models (Chapters 1A Section 18 and Chapter 5B Section 3).
e) Fuel injection system components (Chapter 4A Section 13 or 4B Section 12).

5.3g Unbolt the oil cooler cover...

5.3h ...disconnect the hoses...

f) Brake vacuum pump – diesel models (Chapter 9 Section 22).
g) Thermostat and housing, coolant pipe and hoses (Chapter 3 Section 5).
h) Oil filler tube and dipstick.
i) All electrical switches and sensors.
j) Inlet and exhaust manifolds (Chapter 4A Section 14 or Chapter 4B Section 14).
k) Oil filter (Chapter 1A Section 4 or Chapter 1B Section 4) and oil cooler.
l) Engine/transmission mounting brackets (Chapter 2B Section 17).
m) Flywheel/driveplate (Chapter 2B Section 16, or Chapter 2C Section 14).

4 If you are obtaining a 'short' engine (which consists of the engine cylinder block/crankcase, crankshaft, pistons and connecting rods all assembled), then the cylinder head, sump, lower crankcase (where applicable), oil pump and timing belt will have to be removed also.

5 If you are planning a complete overhaul, the engine can be dismantled and the internal components removed in the following order.

a) Alternator and mounting bracket (Chapter 5A Section 7).
b) Inlet and exhaust manifolds (Chapter 4A Section 14 or Chapter 4B Section 14).
c) Timing belt and pulleys (Chapter 2B Section 7, or Chapter 2C Section 6).
d) Coolant pump (Chapter 3 Section 9).
e) Cylinder head (Chapter 2B Section 11, or Chapter 2C Section 10).
f) Air conditioning compressor mounting brackets.
g) Flywheel/driveplate (Chapter 2B Section 16, or Chapter 2C Section 14).

5.3i ...unscrew the special bolt...

5.3j ...and remove the oil cooler

6.2 The thermostat housing on the diesel engine

6.3 Engine rear lifting eye bolts

6.4a Remove the spring collets...

6.4b ...then lift off the cap...

6.4c ...valve spring...

6.4d ...and the spring seat

h) *Sump (Chapter 2B Section 12, or Chapter 2C Section 11).*
i) *Oil pump (Chapter 2B Section 13, or Chapter 2C Section 12).*
j) *Piston/connecting rod assemblies (Section 9).*
k) *Crankshaft (Section 10).*

6 Before beginning the dismantling and overhaul procedures, make sure that you have all of the correct tools necessary. Refer to the Reference section at the end of this manual for further information.

6 Cylinder head – dismantling

Note: *New and reconditioned cylinder heads are available from the manufacturers and from*

engine overhaul specialists. Due to the fact that some specialist tools are required for the dismantling and inspection procedures, and new components may not be readily available (refer to Section 1), it may be more practical and economical for the home mechanic to purchase a reconditioned head rather than to dismantle, inspect and recondition the original head.

1 Referring to Chapter 2B Section 10, (1.2 litre petrol) (1.6 litre petrol) or Chapter 2C Section 9 (1.5 litre diesel), remove the camshaft(s) and then remove the tappets.

2 On diesel engines, remove the brake vacuum pump (see Chapter 9 Section 22), thermostat housing **(see illustration)**, the fuel injectors, injection pump (if removed with the cylinder head) and glow plugs (Chapter 4B or Chapter 5C Section 2).

3 On all engines, if not already done so,

remove the inlet and exhaust manifolds, the engine lifting eyes **(see illustration)**, and coolant outlet elbow.

4 Using a valve spring compressor, compress each valve spring in turn until the split collets can be removed. Release the compressor and lift off the cap and spring. If, when the valve spring compressor is screwed down, the valve spring cap refuses to free and expose the split collets, gently tap the top of the tool, directly over the cap, with a light hammer. This will free the cap **(see illustrations)**.

5 Remove the valves from the combustion chambers. It is essential that the valves and associated components are kept in their correct order, unless they are so badly worn that they are to be renewed. If they are going to be kept and used again, place them in labelled polythene bags, or in a compartmented box **(see illustrations)**.

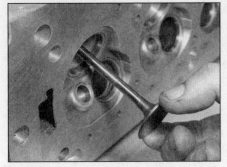

6.5a Withdrawing a valve from the cylinder head

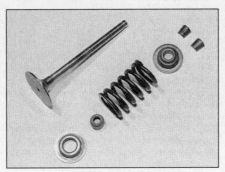

6.5b The valve components

6.5c Store the components in a labelled plastic bag

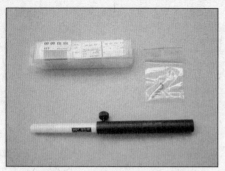

6.7a Renault special tool for measuring the height of the old valve oil seals in order to fit the new seals at the same height

6.7b Removing the oil seal from the top of the valve guide

6 On all petrol engines, the valve stem seals are integral with the valve spring lower seats, and may be difficult to remove.

7 On the diesel engine, before removing the valve stem oil seals, measure their fitted height above the cylinder head and record it. Renault technicians use a special tool which is adjusted according to the fitted height of the old seals; the tool is then used to tap the new seals to an identical height. Use a pair of pliers to pull the oil seals from the valve guides (see illustrations).

7 Cylinder head and valves – cleaning and inspection

1 Thorough cleaning of the cylinder head and valve components, followed by a detailed inspection, will enable you to decide how much valve service work must be carried out during the engine overhaul. **Note:** *If the engine has been severely overheated, it is best to assume that the cylinder head is warped, and to check carefully for signs of this.*

Cleaning

2 Scrape away all traces of old gasket material and sealing compound from the cylinder head. Take care not to damage the cylinder head surfaces.

3 Scrape away the carbon from the combustion chambers and ports, then wash the cylinder head thoroughly with paraffin or a suitable solvent.

7.6 Check the cylinder head for distortion with feeler blades

4 Scrape off any heavy carbon deposits that may have formed on the valves, then use a power-operated wire brush to remove deposits from the valve heads and stems.

Inspection and renovation

Note: *Be sure to perform all the following inspection procedures before concluding that the services of a machine shop or engine overhaul specialist are required. Make a list of all items that require attention.*

Cylinder head

5 Inspect the head very carefully for cracks, evidence of coolant leakage and other damage. If cracks are found, consult an automotive engineering specialist or manufacturer dealership, before purchasing a new head.

6 If warpage of the cylinder head gasket surface is suspected, use a straight-edge to check it for distortion (see illustration). If feeler blades are used, the degree of distortion can be assessed more accurately, and compared with the value specified. Check for distortion along the length and across the width of the head, and along both diagonals. If the head is warped, it may be possible to have it machined flat ('skimmed') at an engineering works – check with an engine specialist.

7 Examine the valve seats in each of the combustion chambers. If they are severely pitted, cracked or burned, then they will need to be renewed or recut by an engine overhaul specialist. If they are only slightly pitted, this can be removed by grinding in the valve heads

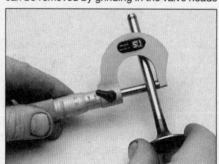

7.13 Measuring a valve stem using a micrometer

and seats with fine valve grinding compound, as described below. Note that on diesel engines the valve seats can only be recut to a limited depth, to avoid decreasing the compression ratio. Using a dial test indicator, check that valve depth below the cylinder head gasket surface is within the limits given in the Specifications.

8 If the valve guides are worn, indicated by a side-to-side motion of the valve, new guides must be fitted.

9 The renewal of valve guides is best carried out by an engine overhaul specialist, since if it is not done skilfully, there is a risk of damaging the cylinder head.

10 If the valve seats are to be recut, consult an automotive engineering specialist or manufacturer dealership.

11 Check the tappet bores in the cylinder head for wear. If excessive wear is evident, the cylinder head must be renewed.

Valves

12 Examine the head of each valve for pitting, burning, cracks and general wear, and check the valve stem for scoring and wear ridges. Rotate the valve, and check for any obvious indication that it is bent. Look for pits and excessive wear on the tip of each valve stem. Renew any valve that shows any such signs of wear or damage.

13 If the valve appears satisfactory at this stage, measure the valve stem diameter at several points, using a micrometer (see illustration). Any significant difference in the readings obtained indicates wear of the valve stem. Should any of these conditions be apparent, the valve(s) must be renewed.

14 If the valves are in satisfactory condition, they should be ground (lapped) into their respective seats, to ensure a smooth gas-tight seal. If the seat is only lightly pitted, or if it has been recut, fine grinding compound only should be used to produce the required finish. Coarse valve grinding compound should not be used unless a seat is badly burned or deeply pitted; if this is the case, the cylinder head and valves should be inspected by an expert, to decide whether seat recutting, or even the renewal of the valve or seat insert, is required.

15 Valve grinding is carried out as follows. Place the cylinder head upside down on a bench, with a block of wood at each end to give clearance for the valve stems.

16 Smear a trace of valve grinding compound on the seat face, and press a suction grinding tool onto the valve head. With a semi-rotary action, grind the valve head to its seat, lifting the valve occasionally to redistribute the grinding compound (see illustration). A light spring placed under the valve head will greatly ease this operation. If coarse grinding compound is being used, work only until a dull, matt even surface is produced on both the valve seat and the valve, then wipe off the used compound, and repeat the process with fine compound.

17 When a smooth unbroken ring of light grey matt finish is produced on both the valve and seat, the grinding operation is complete. Do not grind in the valves any further than absolutely necessary, or the seat will be prematurely sunk into the cylinder head.

18 When all the valves have been ground in, carefully wash off all traces of grinding compound, using paraffin or a suitable solvent, before reassembly of the cylinder head.

Valve components

19 Examine the valve springs for signs of damage and discoloration and also measure their free length using vernier calipers or a steel rule **(see illustration)** or by comparing the existing spring with a new component.

20 Stand each spring on a flat surface and check it for squareness. If any of the springs are damaged, distorted or have lost their tension, obtain a complete new set of springs.

Rocker arms (1.2 litre petrol engines)

21 Check the rocker arm contact surfaces for pits, wear, score marks or any indication that the surface hardening has worn through. Dismantle the rocker shaft and check the rocker arm and rocker shaft pivot and contact areas in the same way. Measure the internal diameter of each rocker and check their fit on the shaft. Clean out the oil spill holes in each rocker using a length of wire. Renew the rocker arm or the rocker shaft itself if any are suspect.

Valve stem oil seals

22 The valve stem oil seals should be renewed as a matter of course.

8 Cylinder head – reassembly

1 Regardless of whether or not the head was sent away for repair work, make sure that it is clean before beginning reassembly. Be sure to remove any metal particles and abrasive grit that may still be present from operations such as valve grinding or head resurfacing. Use compressed air, if available, to blow out all the oil holes and passages.

2 Lubricate the valve stems, then insert the

7.16 Grinding in a valve – lift the valve to distribute the paste evenly

valves into their original locations. If new valves are being fitted, insert them into the locations to which they have been ground **(see illustration)**.

3 On petrol engines, ease the valve stem oil seals/seats over the valve stems, then press them onto the valve guides, using a large socket on the seat area. On the diesel engine, press the new valve stem oil seals onto the guides to their previously-noted position, using the special guide to locate the seals over the valve stems **(see illustrations)**. Do not lubricate the oil seals before fitting them. Remove the guide after fitting the seal.

4 Working on each valve separately, locate the spring and cap over the valve stem. On the diesel engine, the springs are tapered and the smaller diameter taper must be positioned at the top.

5 Compress the valve spring and locate the

7.19 Checking the height of a valve spring

split collets in the recess in the valve stem. Release the compressor, then repeat the procedure on the remaining valves. Use a little grease to hold the collets in place **(see illustration)**.

6 With all the valves installed, place the cylinder head on the bench supported by blocks of wood. Place a block of wood on the valve stem and using pressure (and if necessary a suitable lever) settle the valve stem collets by slightly depressing the valve. *Caution: Do not attempt to settle the collets by using the traditional method of tapping on the valve stem with a hammer. This procedure carries the risk of inducing microfractures in the collets, leading to premature failure of the collet.*

7 Refit as necessary the manifolds, lifting eyes and coolant outlet elbow.

8 On diesel engines, refit the brake vacuum

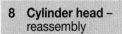

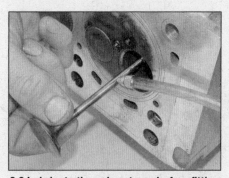
8.2 Lubricate the valve stems before fitting the valves

8.3a Fit the special guide onto the valve stem...

8.3b ...fit the oil seal...

8.3c ...and press it into the previously-noted position on the guide

8.5 Use a little grease to hold the collets in place

8.8 Locating a new seal on the thermostat housing – diesel engine

pump (see Chapter 9 Section 22), thermostat housing with a new seal **(see illustration)**, the fuel injectors, injection pump and glow plugs (Chapter 4B or 5C).
9 Referring to Chapter 2A Section 9, Chapter 2B Section 10 or Chapter 2C Section 9, refit the tappets and camshaft(s).

9 Piston/connecting rod assemblies – removal

Note: *Although this task is theoretically possible with the engine in the car, in practice, owners are advised to remove the engine first. The following paragraphs assume the engine is removed from the car.*
1 With the cylinder head, sump and oil pump removed, proceed as follows.

9.2 Big-end caps marked with a centre punch

9.4 Removing a big-end bearing upper shell

2 Rotate the crankshaft so that No 1 big-end cap (nearest the flywheel/driveplate position) is at the lowest point of its travel. If the big-end cap and rod are not already numbered, mark them with a centre punch **(see illustration)**. Mark both cap and rod to identify the cylinder they operate in.
3 Unscrew the big-end bearing cap nuts (1.6 litre petrol engines) or bolts (all other engines). Withdraw the cap, complete with shell bearing, from the connecting rod **(see illustration)**.
4 If only the bearing shells are being attended to, push the connecting rod up and off the crankpin and remove the upper bearing shell **(see illustration)**. Keep the bearing shells and cap together in their correct sequence if they are to be refitted.
5 Each piston has an arrow stamped on its crown, pointing towards the flywheel end of the engine.
6 Push the connecting rod up and remove the piston and rod from the top of the bore. Note that if there is a pronounced wear ridge at the top of the bore, there is a risk of damaging the piston rings as they foul the ridge. However, it is reasonable to assume that a rebore and new pistons will be required in any case if the ridge is so pronounced.
7 Repeat the procedure for the remaining piston/connecting rod assemblies. Ensure that the caps and rods are marked before removal, as described previously, and keep all components in order.
8 On diesel engines only, the gudgeon pins are a floating fit in the pistons, and can be

9.3 Removing a big-end bearing cap

10.3 Checking the crankshaft endfloat with a dial gauge

removed after releasing the circlips. On petrol engines, do not attempt to separate the pistons from the connecting rods; have an engine overhaul specialist carry out the work.

10 Crankshaft – removal

1 Remove the timing belt, crankshaft sprocket, oil pump (and drive sprocket on 1.6 litre petrol and diesel engines) Remove the flywheel/driveplate with reference to Chapters 2B Section 16, or 2C Section 14. The pistons/connecting rods must be free of the crankshaft journals, however it is not essential to remove them completely from the cylinder block.
2 Unbolt the crankshaft left-hand oil seal housing from the cylinder block.
3 Before the crankshaft is removed, check the endfloat using a dial gauge in contact with the end of the crankshaft **(see illustration)**. Push the crankshaft fully one way and then zero the gauge. Push the crankshaft fully the other way and check the endfloat. The result can be compared with the specified amount and will give an indication as to whether new thrustwashers are required.
4 If a dial gauge is not available, feeler gauges can be used. First push the crankshaft fully towards the flywheel/driveplate end of the engine, then slip the feeler gauge between the web of No 2 crankpin and the thrustwasher of the centre main bearing.
5 Identification numbers should already be cast onto the base of each main bearing cap, together with arrows pointing towards the flywheel/driveplate end of the engine. If not, number them 1 to 5 from the flywheel/driveplate end of the engine using a centre punch, as was done for the connecting rods and caps **(see illustration)**. Also mark the crankcase, so that the caps will be refitted the correct way round.
6 Unscrew the main bearing cap retaining bolts and withdraw the caps, complete with bearing shells **(see illustration)**. Tap the caps with a wooden or copper mallet if they are stuck.
7 Carefully lift the crankshaft from the crankcase **(see illustration)**.

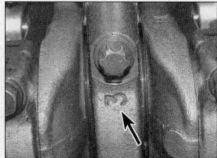

10.5 The main bearing caps are numbered for position

10.6 Removing a main bearing cap

10.7 Lifting the crankshaft from the crankcase

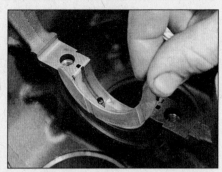

10.8 Removing the crankshaft thrustwashers – diesel engine

8 Remove the thrustwashers at each side of the centre main bearing where they are separate (diesel engine), then remove the bearing shell upper halves from the crankcase **(see illustration)**. Place each shell with its respective bearing cap, noting that the grooved shells are fitted on the crankcase and the plain shells in the caps.

11 Cylinder block/crankcase – cleaning and inspection

Cleaning

1 For complete cleaning, remove all external components and brackets, and all electrical switches/sensors. On the 1.6 litre petrol and diesel engines, the piston cooling oil jets are pressed into the cylinder block, and must be drilled in order to fit a removal tool; this work is best left to a specialist. If necessary, the core plugs can be removed. Drill a small hole in them, then insert a self-tapping screw and pull out the plugs using a pair of grips or a slide hammer.

2 Scrape all traces of gasket or sealant from the cylinder block, taking care not to damage the head and sump mating faces.

3 If the block is extremely dirty, it should be steam-cleaned.

4 After the block has been steam-cleaned, clean all oil holes and oil galleries one more time. Flush all internal passages with warm water until the water runs clear, dry the block thoroughly and wipe all machined surfaces with a light rust preventative oil. If you have access to compressed air, use it to speed up the drying process and to blow out all the oil holes and galleries.

5 If the block is not very dirty, you can do an adequate cleaning job with hot soapy water and a stiff brush. Take plenty of time and do a thorough job. Regardless of the cleaning method used, be sure to clean all oil holes and galleries very thoroughly, dry the block completely and coat all machined surfaces with light oil.

6 The threaded holes in the block must be clean to ensure accurate torque wrench readings during reassembly. Run the proper

size tap into each of the holes to remove rust, corrosion, thread sealant or sludge and to restore damaged threads. If possible, use compressed air to clear the holes of debris produced by this operation. Now is a good time to clean the threads on the head bolts and the main bearing cap bolts as well.

7 Refit the main bearing caps and tighten the bolts finger-tight.

8 After coating the mating surfaces of the new core plugs with suitable sealant, refit them in the cylinder block. Make sure that they are driven in straight and seated properly, or leakage could result. Special tools are available for this purpose, but a large socket, with an outside diameter that will just slip into the core plug, will work just as well.

9 If the engine is not going to be reassembled right away, cover it with a large plastic bag to keep it clean and prevent it rusting.

Inspection

10 Visually check the castings for cracks and corrosion. Look for stripped threads in the threaded holes. If there has been any history of internal coolant leakage, it may be worthwhile having an engine overhaul specialist check the cylinder block/crankcase for cracks with special equipment. If defects are found, have them repaired, if possible, or renew the assembly.

11 Check each cylinder bore for scuffing and scoring.

12 If in any doubt as the condition of the cylinder block have the block/bores inspected and measured by an engine reconditioning specialist. They will be able to advise on whether the block is serviceable, whether a rebore is necessary, and supply the appropriate new pistons and rings.

13 If the bores are in reasonably good condition and not excessively worn, then it may only be necessary to renew the piston rings.

14 If this is the case, the bores should be honed, to allow the new rings to bed-in correctly and provide the best possible seal. Consult an engine reconditioning specialist

15 The cylinder block/crankcase should now be completely clean and dry, with all components checked for wear or damage, and repaired or overhauled as necessary. Refit

as many ancillary components as possible, for safe-keeping. If reassembly is not to start immediately, cover the block with a large plastic bag to keep it clean, and protect the machined surfaces as described above to prevent rusting.

12 Piston/connecting rod assemblies – inspection

1 Before the inspection process can begin, the piston/connecting rod assemblies must be cleaned and the original piston rings removed from the pistons.

2 Carefully expand the old rings over the top of the pistons. The use of two or three old feeler blades will be helpful in preventing the rings dropping into empty grooves **(see illustration)**. Note that the oil control ring is in two sections.

3 Scrape away all traces of carbon from the top of the piston. A wire brush or a piece of fine emery cloth can be used once the majority of the deposits have been scraped away.

4 Remove the carbon from the ring grooves using a special groove cleaning tool. If a tool is not available, use an old ring. Break the ring in half to do this. Be very careful to remove only the carbon deposits; do not remove any metal, or scratch the sides of the ring grooves. Protect your fingers – piston rings are sharp.

5 Once the deposits have been removed, clean the piston/connecting rod assembly with paraffin or a suitable solvent and dry

12.2 Removing a piston ring with the aid of a feeler gauge

12.11a Use the piston to push the rings into the cylinder bores...

12.11b...then measure the ring end gaps

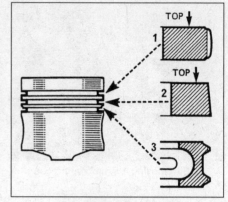

12.12 Piston ring profiles

1 Top compression ring
2 Lower compression ring
3 Oil control ring
Position the TOP markings as shown

thoroughly. Make sure the oil return holes in the ring grooves are clear.

6 If the pistons and cylinder bores are not damaged or worn excessively and if the cylinder block does not need to be rebored, the original pistons can be re-used. Normal piston wear appears as even vertical wear on the piston thrust surfaces and slight looseness of the top ring in its groove. New piston rings should always be used when the engine is reassembled.

7 Carefully inspect each piston for cracks around the skirt, at the gudgeon pin bosses and at the piston ring lands (between the piston ring grooves).

8 Look for scoring and scuffing on the sides of the skirt, holes in the piston crown and burned areas at the edge of the crown. If the skirt is scored or scuffed, the engine may have been suffering from overheating and/or abnormal combustion, which caused excessively high operating temperatures. The cooling and lubricating systems should be checked thoroughly. Scorch marks on the sides of the pistons show that blow-by has occurred and the rings are not sealing correctly. A hole in the piston crown is an indication that abnormal combustion (pre-ignition, knocking or detonation) has been occurring. If any of the above problems exist, the causes must be corrected, or the damage will occur again.

9 Corrosion of the piston, in the form of small pits, indicates that coolant is leaking into the combustion chamber and/or the crankcase. Again, the cause must be corrected, or the problem may persist in the rebuilt engine.

10 Check the fit of the gudgeon pin by twisting the piston and connecting rod in opposite directions. Any noticeable play indicates excessive wear, which must be corrected. The piston/connecting rod assemblies should be taken to a dealer or engine reconditioning specialist to have the pistons, gudgeon pins and rods checked, and new components fitted as required.

11 Before refitting the rings to the pistons, check their end gaps by inserting each of them in their cylinder bores. Use the piston to make sure that they are square **(see illustrations)**. Renault rings are supplied pre-gapped; no attempt should be made to adjust the gaps by filing.

12 Refit the piston rings as follows. Where the original rings are being refitted, use the marks or notes made on removal, to ensure that each ring is refitted to its original groove and the same way up. New rings generally have their top surfaces identified by markings (often an indication of size, such as STD, or the word TOP) – the rings must be fitted with such markings uppermost **(see illustration)**. **Note:** *Always follow the instructions printed on the ring package or box.*

13 The oil control ring (lowest one on the piston) is usually installed first. It is composed of three separate elements. Slip the spacer/ expander into the groove. Next, install the lower side rail. Place one end of the side rail into the groove between the spacer/ expander and the ring land, hold it firmly in place, and slide a finger around the piston while pushing the rail into the groove. Next,

install the upper side rail in the same manner **(see illustrations)**. After the three oil ring components have been installed, check that both the upper and lower side rails can be turned smoothly in the ring groove.

14 The second compression (middle) ring is installed next, followed by the top compression ring – ensure their marks are uppermost. Do not expand either ring any more than necessary to slide it over the top of the piston.

15 With all the rings in position, space the ring gaps (including the elements of the oil control ring) uniformly around the piston at 120° intervals **(see illustration)**. Repeat the procedure for the remaining pistons and rings.

12.13a Fit the oil control ring expander...

12.13b...followed by the ring

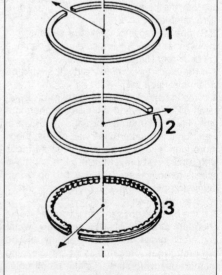

12.15 Position the piston ring end gaps 120° apart

1 Top compression ring
2 Lower compression ring
3 Oil control ring

13 Crankshaft – inspection

1 Clean the crankshaft and dry it with compressed air if available. Be sure to clean the oil holes with a pipe cleaner or similar probe.

 Warning: Wear eye protection when using compressed air.

2 Check the main and big-end bearing journals for uneven wear, scoring, pitting and cracking.

3 If the crankshaft has been reground, check for burrs around the crankshaft oil holes (the holes are usually chamfered, so burrs should not be a problem unless regrinding has been carried out carelessly). Remove any burrs with a fine file or scraper and thoroughly clean the oil holes as described previously.

4 Using a micrometer, measure the diameter of the main bearing and connecting rod journals and compare the results with the Specifications at the beginning of this Chapter **(see illustration)**. If in any doubt, take the crankshaft to an engine reconditioning specialist and have it measured.

5 By measuring the diameter at a number of points around each journal's circumference, you will be able to determine whether or not the journal is out of round. Take the measurement at each end of the journal, near the webs, to determine if the journal is tapered.

6 If the crankshaft journals are damaged, tapered, out of round, or worn beyond the limits specified in this Chapter, the crankshaft must be taken to an engine overhaul specialist, who will regrind it, and who can supply the necessary undersize bearing shells, where available. **Note:** *Renault state that regrinding the crankshaft on the diesel engine is not allowed.*

7 Check the oil seal journals at each end of the crankshaft for wear and damage. If either seal has worn an excessive groove in its journal, consult an engine overhaul specialist, who will be able to advise whether a repair is possible, or whether a new crankshaft is necessary.

14 Main and big-end bearings – inspection

1 Even though the main and big-end bearing shells should be renewed during the engine overhaul (where possible), the old shells should be retained for close examination, as they may reveal valuable information about the condition of the engine.

2 Bearing failure occurs because of lack of lubrication, the presence of dirt or other foreign particles, overloading the engine, and corrosion **(see illustration)**. Regardless of the

cause of bearing failure, it must be corrected before the engine is reassembled, to prevent it from happening again.

3 When examining the bearing shells, remove them from the cylinder block/crankcase and main bearing caps and from the connecting rods and the big-end bearing caps, then lay them out on a clean surface in the same general position as their location in the engine. This will enable you to match any bearing problems with the corresponding crankshaft journal. Do not touch any shell's bearing surface with your fingers while checking it, or the delicate surface may be scratched.

4 Dirt or other foreign matter gets into the engine in a variety of ways. It may be left in the engine during assembly, or it may pass through filters or the crankcase ventilation system. It may get into the oil, and from there into the bearings. Metal chips from machining operations and normal engine wear are often present. Abrasives are sometimes left in engine components after reconditioning, especially when parts are not thoroughly cleaned using the proper cleaning methods. Whatever the source, these foreign objects often end up embedded in the soft bearing material, and are easily recognised. Large particles will not embed in the material, and will score or gouge the shell and journal. The best prevention for this cause of bearing failure is to clean all parts thoroughly, and to keep everything spotlessly clean during engine assembly. Frequent and regular engine oil and filter changes are also recommended.

5 Lack of lubrication (or lubrication break down) has a number of inter-related causes. Excessive heat (which thins the oil), overloading (which squeezes the oil from the bearing face) and oil leakage (from excessive bearing clearances, worn oil pump or high engine speeds) all contribute to lubrication breakdown. Blocked oil passages, which usually are the result of misaligned oil holes in a bearing shell, will also starve a bearing of oil, and destroy it. When lack of lubrication is the cause of bearing failure, the bearing material is wiped or extruded from the shell's steel backing. Temperatures may increase to the point where the steel backing turns blue from overheating.

6 Driving habits can have a definite effect on bearing life. Full throttle, low speed operation (labouring the engine) puts very high loads on bearings, which tends to squeeze out the oil film. These loads cause the shells to flex, which produces fine cracks in the bearing face (fatigue failure). Eventually, the bearing material will loosen in pieces, and tear away from the steel backing. Short distance driving leads to corrosion of bearings, because insufficient engine heat is produced to drive off condensed water and corrosive gases. These products collect in the engine oil, forming acid and sludge. As the oil is carried to the engine bearings, the acid attacks and corrodes the bearing material.

7 Incorrect shell refitting during engine

13.4 Measuring a main bearing journal diameter using a micrometer

assembly will lead to bearing failure as well. Tight fitting shells leave insufficient bearing running clearance, and will result in oil starvation. Dirt or foreign particles trapped behind a bearing shell result in high spots on the bearing, which lead to failure. Do not touch any shell's bearing surface with your fingers during reassembly; there is a risk of scratching the delicate surface, or of depositing particles of dirt on it.

15 Engine overhaul – reassembly sequence

1 Before starting, ensure all new parts have been obtained and all necessary tools are available. Read through the entire procedure to familiarise yourself with the work involved and to ensure all items necessary for engine reassembly are at hand.

2 In addition to all normal tools and materials, obtain any necessary sealant and thread locking fluid.

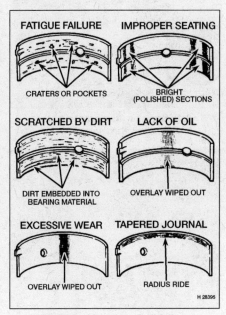

14.2 Typical bearing shell failures

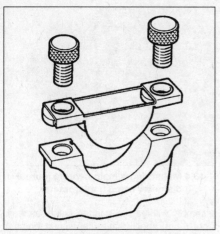

16.4a Tool for fitting main bearing shells –
1.6 litre petrol engines

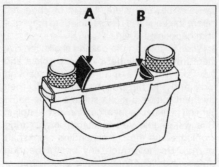

16.4b Press the bearing shell at (A) until it
contacts (B)

16 Crankshaft – refitting

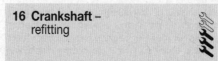

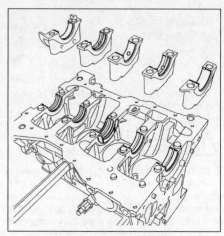

16.4c Bearing shell positions –
1.6 litre petrol engines

3 To save time and avoid problems, assembly can be carried out in the following order:
a) *Crankshaft.*
b) *Pistons/connecting rod assemblies.*
c) *Oil pump.*
d) *Sump.*
e) *Flywheel/driveplate.*
f) *Cylinder head.*
g) *Timing belt and sprockets.*
h) *Engine external components.*

4 At this stage, all engine components should be absolutely clean and dry, with all faults repaired. All components should be neatly arranged on a completely clean work surface or in individual containers.

1 Crankshaft refitting is the first major step in engine reassembly. It is assumed at this point that the cylinder block/crankcase and crankshaft have been cleaned, inspected and repaired or reconditioned as necessary. Position the engine upside down.

2 If temporarily refitted, remove the main bearing cap bolts, and lift out the caps. Lay the caps out in the proper order, to ensure correct installation.

3 If they are still in place, remove the old bearing shells from the block and the main bearing caps. Wipe the bearing recesses with a clean, lint free cloth. They must be kept spotlessly clean.

4 Clean the backs of the new main bearing shells. Fit the shells with an oil groove in each main bearing location in the block. Note on petrol engines the thrustwashers are integral with the No 3 (centre) upper main bearing shell. On diesel engines the thrustwasher halves are fitted either side of No 3 upper main bearing location. Fit the other shell from each bearing set in the corresponding main bearing cap. Make sure the tag where fitted on each bearing shell fits into the notch in the block or cap/lower crankcase. On engines where tags are not incorporated in the shells, it is recommended that the Renault tool Mot. 1493-01 is obtained. Note that the oil holes in the block must line up with the oil holes in the bearing shell. Where separate, fit the thrustwasher halves to No 3 main bearing position and retain with grease **(see illustrations)**. Do not hammer the shells into place, and do not nick or gouge the bearing faces.

5 Clean the bearing surfaces of the shells in the block, then apply a thin, uniform layer of clean molybdenum disulphide based grease, engine assembly lubricant, or clean engine oil to each surface **(see illustration)**. Coat the thrustwasher surfaces as well.

6 Lubricate the crankshaft oil seal journals with molybdenum disulphide based grease, engine assembly lubricant, or clean engine oil.

7 Make sure the crankshaft journals are clean, then lay the crankshaft back in place in the block **(see illustration)**.

8 Refit and tighten the main bearing caps as follows **(see illustrations)** :
a) *Clean the bearing surfaces of the shells in the caps, then lubricate them. Refit the caps in their respective positions, with the arrows pointing towards the flywheel/driveplate end of the engine.*
b) *Working on one cap at a time, from the centre main bearing outwards (and ensuring that each cap is tightened down squarely and evenly onto the block), tighten the main bearing cap bolts to the specified torque wrench setting.*

16.4d Smear a little grease on the
crankshaft thrustwashers...

16.4e ...and stick them to the centre main
bearing

16.5 Lubricate the main bearing shells
before fitting the crankshaft

16.7 Lay the crankshaft in position in the
crankcase

9 Rotate the crankshaft a number of times by hand, to check for any obvious binding.

10 Check the crankshaft endfloat (see Section 10). It should be correct if the crankshaft thrustwashers are not worn or damaged, or have been renewed.

11 Refit the crankshaft left-hand oil seal housing and install a new seal (Chapters 2B Section 15, or 2C Section 13).

12 Refit the flywheel/driveplate, oil pump (and drive sprocket on 1.6 litre petrol and diesel engines), crankshaft sprocket and timing belt (Chapters 2B Section 7, or 2C Section 14).

17 Piston/connecting rod assemblies – refitting

1 Clean the backs of the big-end bearing shells and the recesses in the connecting rods and big-end caps. If new shells are being fitted, ensure that all traces of the protective grease are cleaned off using paraffin. Wipe the shells and connecting rods dry with a lint-free cloth.

2 Press the big-end bearing shells into the connecting rods and caps in their correct positions. Note that tags are not incorporated in the shells and, to ensure correct fitting, it is recommended that the Renault tool Mot. 1492 is obtained **(see illustration)**.

3 Lubricate No 1 piston and piston rings and check that the ring gaps are still spaced at 120° intervals to each other. Also, lubricate the big-end bearing shell in the connecting rod **(see illustrations)**.

4 Fit a ring compressor to No 1 piston, then insert the piston and connecting rod into No 1 cylinder. The V arrow must point to the flywheel end of the engine. With No 1 crankpin at its lowest point, drive the piston

carefully into the cylinder with the wooden handle of a hammer, at the same time guiding the connecting rod onto the crankpin **(see illustration)**.

5 Liberally lubricate the crankpin journal and

16.8a Fitting No 5 main bearing cap – petrol engine

16.8b Tighten the main bearing cap bolts to the specified torque...

16.8c ...and angle

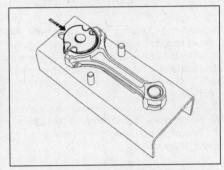

17.2 Using tool Mot. 1492 to fit the big-end shells

17.3a Lubricating the piston rings...

17.3b ...and big-end bearing shell in the connecting rod

17.4 Using the wooden handle of a hammer to drive the piston into the bore

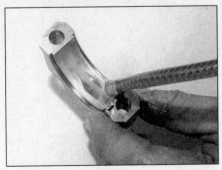

17.5a Lubricate the big-end cap bearing shell...

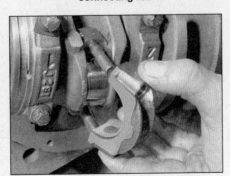

17.5b ...then refit the cap...

17.5c ...screw on the nuts...

17.5d ...and tighten them to the specified torque and angle

big-end cap bearing shells, then refit the correct cap and insert the nuts/bolts. Tighten them to the specified torque and angle **(see illustrations)**. Turn the crankshaft to make sure that it is free before moving on to the next assembly.

6 Repeat the above procedures on the remaining piston/connecting rod assemblies.

7 On completion, refit the oil pump, sump and cylinder head.

18 Engine – initial start-up after overhaul

1 With the engine refitted in the vehicle, double check the engine oil and coolant levels. Make a final check that everything has been reconnected, and that there are no tools or rags left in the engine compartment.

2 On petrol engined models, carry out the following:
a) *With the spark plugs removed and the engine management system disabled by removing the engine protection fuse from the engine compartment fusebox, crank the engine on the starter motor until the oil pressure light goes out.*
b) *Refit the spark plugs and the fuse.*
c) *Start the engine, noting that this may take a little longer than usual, due to the fuel system being empty.*

3 On diesel engine models, carry out the following:
a) *Prime the fuel system as described in Chapter 4B Section 6.*
b) *Fully depress the accelerator pedal, turn the ignition key to position M and wait for the preheating warning light to go out.*
c) *Start the engine. Additional cranking may be necessary to bleed the fuel system before the engine starts.*

4 Once started, keep the engine running at fast tickover. Check that the oil pressure light goes out. Do not be alarmed if there are some odd smells and smoke from parts getting hot and burning off oil deposits.

5 While the engine is idling, check for fuel, water and oil leaks.

6 Keep the engine idling until hot water is felt circulating through the top hose, indicating that the engine is at normal operating temperature, then switch it off.

7 After a few minutes, recheck the oil and water levels and top-up as necessary (see *Weekly checks*).

8 There is no requirement to retighten the cylinder head bolts.

9 If new pistons, rings or crankshaft bearings have been fitted, the engine must be run-in for the first 500 miles. Do not operate the engine at full throttle, nor allow it to labour in any gear during this period. It is recommended that the oil and filter be changed at the end of this period.

Chapter 3
Cooling, heating and air conditioning systems

Contents

Degrees of difficulty

Easy, suitable for novice with little experience	Fairly easy, suitable for beginner with some experience	Fairly difficult, suitable for competent DIY mechanic	Difficult, suitable for experienced DIY mechanic	Very difficult, suitable for expert DIY or professional

Specifications

General

Cooling system type . . . . Pressurised sealed system, with belt-driven pump, front mounted radiator and electric cooling fan

Cooling system pressure:
  Cap with yellow mark . . . . 1.4 bars
  Cap with brown valve . . . . 1.2 bars
Air conditioning refrigerant type R134a

Thermostat

Opening temperatures:
  Starts to open . . . . 89°C
  Fully open . . . . 99°C
Travel (closed to fully open) . . . . 7.5 mm
Type . . . . Wax

Coolant temperature sensor

Resistance:
  At –40°C . . . . 76 000 ± 7000 ohms
  At –10°C . . . . 12 500 ± 1130 ohms
  At 25°C . . . . 2252 ± 112 ohms
  At 50°C . . . . 810 ± 40 ohms
  At 80°C . . . . 280 ± 8 ohms
  At 110°C . . . . 115 ± 3 ohms
  At 120°C . . . . 88 ± 2 ohms

Thermo-plungers

Make . . . . Beru
Resistance (at 20°C) . . . . 0 to 1.2 ohms

Torque wrench settings

	Nm	lbf ft
Air conditioning:		
Compressor mounting bolts	21	15
Pressure relief valve	8	6
Condenser mounting bolts	8	6
Coolant pump bolts:		
0.9 litre petrol engine	N/A	
1.2 litre petrol engine	9	7
Diesel engine	11	8

1 General Information

1 The cooling system is of the pressurised type. The main components are a belt-driven pump, an aluminium cross flow radiator, an expansion bottle, an electric cooling fan, a thermostat, and the associated hoses (see illustrations).

2 The system functions as follows. When the engine is cold, coolant is pumped around the cylinder block and head passages. After cooling the cylinder bores, combustion surfaces and valve seats, the coolant passes through the heater and inlet manifold, and is returned to the water pump.

3 When the coolant reaches a predetermined temperature, the thermostat opens, and the hot coolant passes through the top hose to the radiator. As the coolant circulates through the radiator, it is cooled by the inrush of air when the car is in motion. The airflow is supplemented by the action of the electric cooling fan when necessary. Upon reaching the bottom of the radiator, the coolant returns

to the pump via the radiator bottom hose, and the cycle is repeated.

4 As the coolant warms up, it expands; the increased volume is accommodated in an expansion bottle. The bottle is 'hot': the coolant circulates through the bottle all the time that the engine is running.

5 The electric cooling fan is mounted behind the radiator and is controlled by the injection ECU, see Section 7 for details.

6 For details of the air conditioning system (when fitted) refer to Section 13.

⚠ Warning: Do not attempt to remove the expansion bottle filler cap, or to disturb any part of the cooling system, while the engine is hot, as there is a high risk of scalding. If the expansion bottle filler cap must be removed before the engine and radiator have fully cooled (even though this is not recommended), the pressure in the cooling system must first be relieved. Cover the cap with a thick layer of cloth to avoid scalding, and slowly unscrew the filler cap until a hissing sound is heard. When the hissing has stopped, indicating that the pressure has reduced, slowly unscrew the

filler cap until it can be removed; if more hissing sounds are heard, wait until they have stopped before unscrewing the cap completely. At all times, keep well away from the filler cap opening, and protect your hands.

⚠ Warning: Do not allow antifreeze to come into contact with your skin, or with the painted surfaces of the vehicle. Rinse off spills immediately, with plenty of water. Never leave antifreeze lying around in an open container, or in a puddle in the driveway or on the garage floor. Children and pets are attracted by its sweet smell, but antifreeze can be fatal if ingested.

⚠ Warning: If the engine is hot, the electric cooling fan may start rotating even if the engine is not running. Be careful to keep your hands, hair, and any loose clothing well clear when working in the engine compartment.

⚠ Warning: Refer to Section 13 for precautions to be observed when working on models equipped with air conditioning.

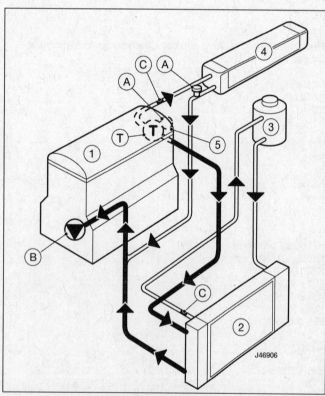

1.1a Petrol engine cooling system schematic – 1.2 litre petrol engine

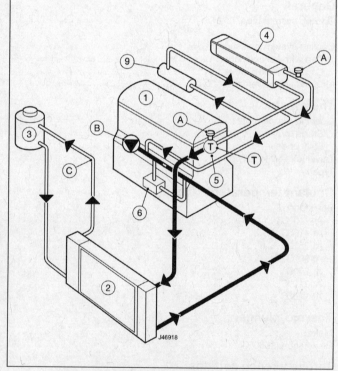

1.1b Diesel engine cooling system schematic

See illustration 1.1a for key

1 Cylinder block	6 Oil cooler	A Bleed screws
2 Radiator	7 Oil cooler –	B Water pump
3 Expansion bottle	automatic	C Choke
4 Heater matrix	gearbox only	T Thermostat
5 Thermostat	8 Turbocharger	
mounting	9 EGR	

2 Cooling system hoses – renewal

Note: *Refer to the warnings given in Section 1 of this Chapter before proceeding. Hoses should only be disconnected once the engine has cooled sufficiently to avoid scalding.*

1 The number, routing and pattern of hoses will vary according to model, but the same basic procedure applies. Before commencing work, make sure that the new hoses are to hand, along with new hose clips if needed. It is good practice to renew the hose clips at the same time as the hoses.

2 Drain the cooling system, as described in Chapter 1A or 1B, saving the coolant if it is fit for re-use. Squirt a little penetrating oil onto the hose clips if they are rusty.

3 Release the hose clips from the hose concerned. Three clip types are used: worm-drive (Jubilee), spring and quick-release. The worm-drive clip is released by turning its screw anti-clockwise. The spring clip is released by squeezing its tags together with pliers **(see illustration)**, at the same time working the clip away from the hose stub. The quick-release clips twist or press to release.

4 Unclip any wires, cables or other hoses which may be attached to the hose being removed. Make notes for reference when reassembling if necessary.

5 Release the hose from its stubs with a twisting motion. Be careful not to damage the stubs on delicate components such as

the radiator. If the hose is stuck fast, the best course is often to cut it off using a sharp knife, but again be careful not to damage the stubs.

6 Before fitting the new hose, smear the stubs with washing-up liquid or a suitable rubber lubricant to aid fitting. Do not use oil or grease, which may attack the rubber.

7 Fit the hose clips over the ends of the hose, then fit the hose over its stubs. Work the hose into position. When satisfied, locate and tighten the hose clips.

8 Refill the cooling system as described in Chapter 1A or 1B. Run the engine, and check that there are no leaks.

9 Recheck the tightness of the hose clips on any new hoses after a few hundred miles.

3 Radiator – removal, inspection, cleaning and refitting

Note: *If the radiator is to be removed for a period of more than 48 hours, precautions should be taken against internal corrosion. Either rinse the radiator with clean water and dry it thoroughly by blowing air through it, or fill it with coolant and plug the hose stubs.*

Removal

1 Jack up the front of the car, and support it on axle stands (see *Jacking and vehicle support*) and then remove the front bumper as described in Chapter 11, Section 6.

2 Unclip the upper air scoop from the front of the radiator/condenser **(see illustration)**.

3 Disconnect the wiring connector from the

2.3 Releasing a spring hose clip using self-locking grips

flap motor at the end of the lower air intake panel, then undo the two upper retaining nuts and remove the air intake assembly from the front of the vehicle **(see illustrations)**.

4 Remove the engine undertray and then drain the cooling system by disconnecting the radiator bottom hose. Save the coolant in a clean container, if it is fit for re-use.

5 On turbo engine models, remove the intercooler, as described in Chapter 4A Section 16, for petrol engine or Section, for diesel engines

6 Remove the cooling fan assembly, as described in Section 6.

7 Unclip the small plastic deflector from the top, then unclip the two parts of the air ducting from the front of the air-conditioning condenser **(see illustrations)**. Note, the outer cowling is removed upwards and the inner cowling downwards.

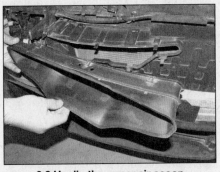

3.2 Unclip the upper air scoop

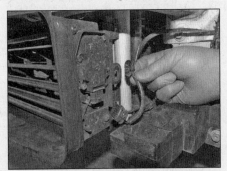

3.3a Disconnect the wiring connector…

3.3b …then undo the bolts and remove the lower air scoop

3.7a Unclip the deflector…

3.7b …and withdraw the outer cowling…

3.7c …then the inner cowling

3.8 Disconnect the upper coolant hose

3.9a Release the upper clip...

3.9b ...the lower clip...

3.9c ...then release the left-hand side of the condenser

3.10a Withdraw the radiator...

3.10b ...and check the lower mounting rubbers

8 Disconnect the upper hose from the top of the radiator **(see illustration)**.

9 Unclip the air-conditioning condenser from the front of the radiator **(see illustrations)** and move it forwards slightly, secure it to the front panel using cable ties (or similar). Take care not to damage the air-conditioning pipes or condenser as it is secured to the front panel.

10 The radiator can now be withdraw upwards from the lower crossmember **(see illustrations)**. Retrieve the rubber mountings from the lower crossmember and check them, make sure they are fitted securely on refitting.

Inspection and cleaning

11 If the radiator has been removed due to suspected blockage, reverse flush it as described in Chapter 1A or 1B. Clean dirt and debris from the radiator fins, using an airline (in which case, wear eye protection) or a soft

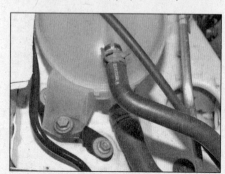

4.1 Undo the reservoir retaining bolt and hose clip (if required)

brush. Be careful, as the fins are sharp, and easily damaged.

12 If necessary, a radiator specialist can perform a 'flow test' on the radiator, to establish whether an internal blockage exists.

13 A leaking radiator must be referred to a specialist for permanent repair. Do not attempt to weld or solder a leaking radiator, as damage to the plastic components may result.

14 If the radiator is to be sent for repair or renewed, remove all hoses and the cooling fan switch (where fitted).

15 Inspect the condition of the mounting rubbers, and renew them if necessary.

Refitting

16 Refitting is a reversal of removal, bearing in mind the following points.
a) Take care not to damage the radiator fins during refitting.
b) Refit the front bumper, top crossmember and the bonnet catch with reference to Chapter 11.
c) On completion, refill the cooling system as described in Chapter 1A or 1B.

4   Expansion tank – removal and refitting

Removal

1 Undo the retaining bolt at the front of the reservoir **(see illustration)**, then pull the reservoir forwards to release it from the its locating pegs on the inner wing panel.

2 If the expansion bottle is being removed completely from the engine compartment, clamp the hoses with brake hose clamps and slide the spring clips off. Have a container ready to catch any spilt coolant and then remove the expansion bottle. Alternatively drain the cooling system as described in Chapter 1A or 1B.

Inspection

3 Clean the tank and inspect it for cracks and other damage. Renew it if necessary. Also inspect the cap; if there is evidence that coolant has been vented through the cap, renew it.

Refitting

4 Refit by reversing the removal operations. Refill and bleed the cooling system as described in Chapter 1A or 1B.

5   Thermostat – removal, testing and refitting

1 The thermostat is located in the cylinder head outlet elbow housing on the left-hand side of the engine, above the transmission bellhousing (see illustrations in Section 1 for location on 1.2 litre petrol and 1.5 litre diesel engines). On 0.9 litre engines, the thermostat is located at the front of the engine, and is part of the housing that is bolted to the cylinder block, below the inlet manifold. It may be necessary to remove the air inlet hoses or air filter housing to make easier access

5.4 Disconnect the coolant hoses

5.5 Remove the thermostat housing

5.6 Releasing the clip securing the hose to the thermostat cover

5.7a Undo the three retaining bolts...

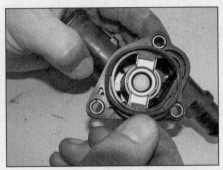

5.7b ...and fit a new sealing ring to the thermostat/cover assembly on the 1.2 litre petrol engine

5.11 Refit new seal – 0.9 litre engine

to the thermostat housing. See the relevant Chapters for information on the removal and refitting procedures.

Removal

Note: *A new thermostat sealing ring may be required on refitting. Check with your local Renault dealer for the availability of parts, as the thermostat may be part of the coolant housing.*

2 Partially drain the cooling system, as described in Chapter 1A or 1B, so that the coolant level is below the thermostat location.

0.9 litre engines

3 Remove the front bumper and upper crossmember, as described in Chapter 11 Section 6.

4 Working down the front of the engine, disconnect the coolant hoses from the coolant housing (see illustration).

5 Undo the mounting bolts and withdraw the thermostat housing from the front of the cylinder block (see illustration).

1.2 litre petrol and 1.5 litre diesel engines

6 Where necessary, loosen the clip and disconnect the hose from the thermostat cover (see illustration).

7 Unbolt the cover/thermostat assembly, noting that the thermostat may be integral with the cover. Recover the sealing ring from the housing (see illustrations).

8 On some of the 1.2 litre petrol engines, it is possible to remove the thermostat from the

housing. Rotate the locking clip, remove the spring and recover the thermostat.

Testing

9 To test whether the unit is serviceable, suspend it on a string in a saucepan of cold water, together with a thermometer. Heat the water, and note the temperature at which the thermostat begins to open. Continue heating the water until the thermostat is fully open, and then remove it from the water.

10 The temperature at which the thermostat should start to open is stamped on the unit. If the thermostat does not start to open at the specified temperature, does not fully open in boiling water, or does not fully close when removed from the water, then it must be discarded and a new one fitted.

6.3a Withdraw the securing pegs (one shown)...

Refitting

11 Refitting is a reversal of removal, bearing in mind the following points.
a) Where applicable renew the sealing ring *(see illustration).*
b) On completion, refill the cooling system as described in Chapter 1A or 1B.
c) On 0.9 litre engines, refit the bumper, as described in Chapter 11 Section 6.

6 Cooling fan assembly – removal and refitting

Removal

1 Jack up the front of the car, and support it on axle stands (see *Jacking and vehicle support*) and then remove the front bumper as described in Chapter 11, Section 6.

2 Remove the headlights, as described in Chapter 12 Section 10.

3 Release the three plastic locating pegs from the upper crossmember, wich secure the radiator and intercooler on turbo engines, then undo the two retaining bolts (one at each side) and move the upper crossmember to one side (see illustrations). If the crossmember needs to be removed completely, disconnect the wiring connector and bonnet release cable from the lock, then unclip them from the securing clips along the length of the crossmember.

4 Disconnect the wiring connectors from

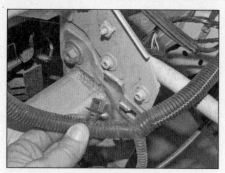

6.3b ...unclip the wiring loom...

6.3c ...then undo the bolt at each end and remove the crossmember

6.4a Disconnect the wiring connector from the fan...

6.4b ...and the fan relay

the cooling fan motor and the fan relay **(see illustrations)**.
5 Undo the retaining bolt and move the air intake pipe from the fan cowling **(see illustration)**. It may also be necessary,

(depending on model) to release the securing clip from the coolant hose across the bottom of the fan cowling.
6 Slide the cooling fan cowling assembly out from the rear of the radiator **(see illustration)**.

Take care not to damage the fins on the radiator, as the fan cowling is withdrawn.

Refitting
7 Refit by reversing the removal operations.

7 Cooling fan switch – general information

1 The operation of the fan is controlled by the fuel injection ECU and has a slow- and high-speed function This is controlled by information gathered from the coolant temperature sensor or when the air conditioning is selected on the instrument panel. See Section 15 at the end of this Chapter, for information on the removal and refitting procedures for the fan resistor/relay. **Note:** *If there is a fault on the slow-speed circuit, the fan will run at high-speed setting.*
a) *At slow speeds – if the coolant temperature is greater than 99°C the fan will operate. When the coolant temperature is lower than 96°C the fan stops operating.*
b) *At high speeds – if the coolant temperature is greater than 102°C the fan will operate. When the coolant temperature is lower than 99°C the fan stops operating.*
c) *The coolant temperature warning light will illuminate if the temperature is greater than 114°C. When the coolant temperature is lower than 111°C the light will go out.*

6.5 Unbolt the air intake pipe from the cowling

6.6 Withdraw the fan assembly out from the rear of the radiator

8 Coolant temperature sensor – testing, removal and refitting

1 The location of the temperature sensor varies according to model. It is located in the thermostat housing or the left-hand of the cylinder head, above the transmission bellhousing **(see illustrations)**.

Testing
Note: *The coolant temperature is also the primary sensor for the engine management system. Running the engine with the sensor disconnected will log a fault code and bring the warning light (MIL) on.*

8.1a Temperature sensor – diesel engine

8.1b Temperature sensor – 0.9 litre petrol engine

8.1c Temperature sensor – 1.2 litre petrol engine

8.9 Disconnecting the multiplug from the temperature sensor – 1.2 petrol engine

8.13a Release the retaining clip...

8.13b ...and withdraw the sensor from the housing – diesel engine

2 The temperature gauge is fed with a stabilised voltage from the instrument panel feed (via the ignition switch and a fuse). The gauge earth is controlled by the sender. The sender contains a thermistor – an electronic component whose electrical resistance decreases as its temperature rises. When the coolant is cold, the sender resistance is high, current flow through the gauge is reduced, and the gauge needle points towards the cold end of the scale. As the coolant temperature rises and the sender resistance falls, current flow increases, and the gauge needle moves towards the upper end of the scale. If the sender is faulty, it must be renewed.

3 The temperature warning light is fed with a voltage from the instrument panel. The light's earth is controlled by the sender. The sender is effectively a switch, which operates at a predetermined temperature to earth the light and complete the circuit.

4 If the gauge develops a fault, first check the other instruments; if they do not work at all, check the instrument panel electrical feed. If the readings are erratic, there may be a fault in the voltage stabiliser, which will necessitate renewal of the stabiliser (the stabiliser is integral with the instrument panel printed circuit board – see Chapter 12 Section 13). If the fault lies in the temperature gauge alone, check it as follows.

5 If the gauge needle remains at the 'cold' end of the scale when the engine is hot, disconnect the sender wiring plug, and earth the relevant wire to the cylinder head. If the needle then deflects when the ignition is

switched on, the sender unit is proved faulty, and should be renewed. If the needle still does not move, remove the instrument panel (Chapter 12) and check the continuity of the wire between the sender unit and the gauge, and the feed to the gauge unit. If continuity is shown, and the fault still exists, then the gauge is faulty, and the gauge unit should be renewed.

6 If the gauge needle remains at the 'hot' end of the scale when the engine is cold, disconnect the sender wire. If the needle then returns to the 'cold' end of the scale when the ignition is switched on, the sender unit is proved faulty, and should be renewed. If the needle still does not move, check the remainder of the circuit as described previously.

7 The same basic principles apply to testing the warning light. The light should illuminate when the relevant sender wire is earthed.

Removal and refitting

1.2 litre petrol engines

Note: *Suitable sealant will be required to coat the sender threads on refitting.*

8 Drain the cooling system as described in Chapter 1A. Alternatively, remove the expansion bottle cap to depressurise the system, and have the new sensor or a suitable bung to hand.

9 Disconnect the wiring connector and unscrew the temperature sensor from the transmission end of the cylinder head **(see illustration)**.

10 Apply a little sealant to the temperature

sensor threads, and screw it into the coolant housing. Reconnect the wiring connector to the sensor.

11 Top-up or refill the cooling system, with reference to *Weekly checks* or Chapter 1A.

Diesel engines

12 Drain the cooling system as described in Chapter 1B. Alternatively, remove the expansion bottle cap to depressurise the system, and have the new temperature sensor or a suitable bung to hand.

13 Disconnect the wiring connector, release the securing clip and withdraw the temperature sensor from the coolant housing **(see illustrations)**.

14 Refit the temperature sensor into the coolant housing making sure the seal is in position, then secure it in place with the retaining clip. Reconnect the wiring connector to the sensor.

15 Top-up or refill the cooling system, with reference to *Weekly checks* or Chapter 1B.

0.9 litre petrol engines

16 Drain the cooling system as described in Chapter 1B. Alternatively, remove the expansion bottle cap to depressurise the system, and have the new temperature sensor or a suitable bung to hand.

17 Disconnect the wiring connector, release the securing clip and withdraw the temperature sensor from the coolant housing **(see illustrations)**.

18 Refit the temperature sensor into the coolant housing making sure the seal is in position, then secure it in place with the

8.17a Disconnect the wiring connector...

8.17b ...release the retaining clip...

8.17c ...withdraw the sensor from the housing...

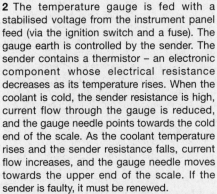

8.17d ...and recover the sealing ring

retaining clip. Reconnect the wiring connector to the sensor.
19 Top-up or refill the cooling system, with reference to *Weekly checks* or Chapter 1B.

9 Coolant pump – removal and refitting

Note: *If the coolant pump is leaking, or is noisy in operation, it must be renewed.*
1 Disconnect the battery negative lead, then drain the cooling system as described in Chapter 1A Section 27.
2 On 0.9 litre engines, slacken the three bolts that secure the coolant pump pulley in place, before removing the auxiliary belt **(see illustration)**. Do not remove them completely at this stage.

3 Remove the auxiliary drivebelt, as described in Chapter 1A Section 9, on petrol engines or Chapter 1B Section 10, on diesel engines.

0.9 litre petrol engine
Note: *A new gasket will be required on refitting.*
Removal
4 Unscrew the three retaining bolts, and remove the pulley from the coolant pump **(see illustration)**. If the bolts where not slackened previously, counterhold the pulley in order to unscrew the bolts. This is most easily achieved by wrapping an old drivebelt tightly around the pulley to act in a similar manner to a strap wrench.
5 Unscrew the retaining bolts, and withdraw the coolant pump from the cylinder block **(see illustrations)**. Have a container ready to catch any coolant spillage. Remove the gasket and discard, as a new one will be required for refitting.

Refitting
6 Commence refitting by thoroughly cleaning all traces of gasket/sealant from the mating faces of the pump and cylinder block.
7 Fit a new gasket to the cylinder block/coolant pump, then place it in position in the cylinder block, refit the bolts to their correct locations and tighten to the specified torque.
8 Refit the pump pulley and tighten to the specified torque. Counterhold the pulley using an old drivebelt as during removal.
9 Refit and tension the auxiliary drivebelt, as described in Chapter 1A Section 9.

10 Refill the cooling system as described in Chapter 1A Section 27.
11 Reconnect the battery negative terminal (refer to *Disconnecting the battery* in Chapter 5A Section 4).

1.2 litre petrol engine
Removal
12 Disconnect the battery negative lead.
13 Drain the cooling system as described in Chapter 1A Section 27.
14 Apply the handbrake, then jack up the front of the car and support securely on axle stands (see *Jacking and vehicle support*).
15 Remove the timing belt as described in Chapter 2B Section 7.
16 It is just about possible to remove the coolant pump with the alternator and AC compressor in place **(see illustration)**. Alternatively, remove the alternator (Chapter 5A Section 7), AC compressor and the mounting bracket. Do not disconnect the refrigerant lines from the compressor – unbolt it and secure it to the radiator support panel. Remove the compressor and alternator support bracket.
17 Disconnect the coolant pipe from the coolant pump **(see illustration)**.
18 Unbolt and remove the coolant pump from the cylinder block remove and discard the gasket **(see illustration)**. Tap it with a soft-faced mallet if it is stuck.

Refitting
19 Thoroughly clean all sealant from the mating faces of the coolant pump and the cylinder block.

9.2 Slacken the pulley bolts

9.4 Remove the coolant pump pulley

9.5a Remove the coolant pump...

9.5b ...and the gasket

9.16 The support bracket blocks access to the elbow mounting bolts

9.17 Remove the coolant pipe

9.18 Unbolt and remove the coolant pump

9.20 Fit a new seal to the coolant pipe

9.21a Fit a new gasket...

20 If the water elbow has been removed from the pump, a new gasket should be fitted. If the plastic pipe has been removed from the pump elbow, renew the O-ring – note that the plastic pipe is a push-fit in the elbow, and relies on the O-ring as the only form of sealing **(see illustration)**.

21 Fit a new gasket to the engine. Offer the pump into position on the cylinder block, ensuring that it engages with the locating dowels, then refit the bolts and tighten securely in the recommended order **(see illustrations)**.

22 Further refitting is a reversal of removal, bearing in mind the following points.

a) *Replacement pumps require holes tapping in the pump for the timing belt cover. Special self-tapping bolts are from available from Renault for this. Alternatively a tap can be used.*

b) *Refit and tension the timing belt as described in Chapter 2B Section 7.*

c) *On completion, refill the cooling system as described in Chapter 1A Section 27.*

Diesel engines

Note: *A new gasket will be required on refitting.*

Removal

23 Disconnect the battery negative lead, then drain the cooling system as described in Chapter 1B Section 27.

24 Remove the timing belt as described in Chapter 2C Section 6.

25 Undo the retaining bolts and remove the

9.21b ...offer up the pump...

rear timing belt cover from the cylinder block **(see illustration)**.

26 Unscrew the retaining bolts, then manoeuvre the coolant pump out of position **(see illustration)**. Recover the pump gasket and discard it; a new one must be used on refitting.

Refitting

27 Ensure that pump and cylinder block/housing mating faces are clean and dry, and that the locating dowels are correctly positioned.

28 Offer up the new gasket (dry) and fit the pump assembly, tightening its retaining bolts securely **(see illustration)**.

29 Refit the rear timing belt cover to the cylinder block and securely tighten the retaining bolts.

30 Refit the timing belt as described in Chapter 2C Section 6.

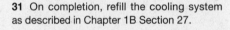
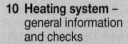

9.21c ...and bolt it in place in the order shown

31 On completion, refill the cooling system as described in Chapter 1B Section 27.

10 Heating system – general information and checks

General information

1 The heater and fresh air ventilation unit works on the principle of mixing hot and cold air in the proportions selected by means of the centre control knob. Coolant flows through the heater radiator all the time that the engine is running, regardless of the temperature selected.

2 Air distribution is selected by the left-hand control knob. Additional control is possible by opening, closing or redirecting individual

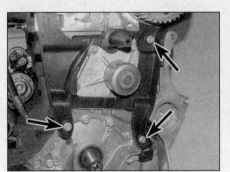

9.25 Unscrew the securing bolts

9.26 Undo the pump retaining bolts

9.28 Fitting a new gasket to the water pump

11.4 Remove the clutch pedal switch

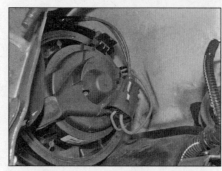

11.5 Disconnect the wiring connector

11.6a Depress the tab, then twist...

11.6b ...and withdraw the motor

vents in the facia panel. The right-hand knob is the recirculation control, which enables the outside air supply to be closed off, while the air inside the vehicle is recirculated. This can be useful to prevent unpleasant odours entering from outside the vehicle – for instance, when driving in heavy traffic – but should only be used briefly, as the recirculated air inside the vehicle will soon become stale and may cause light misting.

3 A four-speed blower is controlled by the centre knob.

11.9 Disconnect the wiring connector

11.10a Press down on the upper securing peg...

11.10b ...slide it to the left...

11.10c ...then withdraw it from the housing

4 For details of the air conditioning system fitted to some models, refer to Section 13.

Checks

5 Periodically check that all the controls operate as intended. Problems related to the temperature and air distribution controls may be due to cables being broken or disconnected (see Section 12).

6 If the blower does not operate at all, check the fuse and the blower multiplug before condemning the motor. If one or two speeds do not work, the fault is almost certainly in the heater blower resistor (see Section 11).

7 Check the condition and security of the coolant hoses which feed the heater radiator. The radiator-to-hose joints are at the bulkhead under the bonnet. If water leaks inside the car seem to be coming from the heater, establish whether the leak is of coolant (indicating a leaking heater radiator) or of rainwater (indicating a defective scuttle seal). Cooling system antifreeze has a distinctive sweet smell.

11 Heater components – removal and refitting

Blower assembly

Removal

1 Disconnect the battery negative lead as described in Chapter 5A Section 4.

2 Remove the drivers side lower trim panel and the centre console, right-hand side front trim panel, as described in Chapter 11.

3 Remove the steering column as described in Chapter 10 Section 15.This can be left connected at the lower end to the steering rack, carefully lower it down on to a block of wood (or similar), to prevent any damage to the column/motor.

4 Reaching up to the top of the clutch pedal, disconnect the wiring connector, then turn the switch anti-clockwise and remove it from the top of the clutch pedal mounting bracket (see illustration).

5 Reach up and disconnect the multiplug from the side of the blower assembly (see illustration).

6 Depress the locking tab at the top, then twist the motor to free it from the housing (see illustrations).

Refitting

7 Refitting is a reversal of removal, ensure the motor is firmly locked in place.

Heater blower resistor

Removal

8 Remove the glovebox as described in Chapter 11 Section 28.

9 Disconnect the multiplug wiring connector from the heater blower resistor (see illustration).

10 Press down on the upper securing peg, then slide the resistor to the left, and withdraw it from the heater housing (see illustrations).

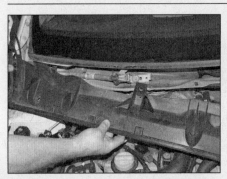

11.13 Remove the lower scuttle panel

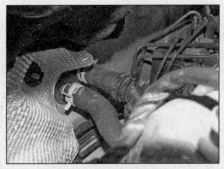

11.14 Disconnect the heater hoses

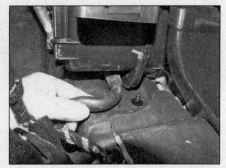

11.17 Disconnect the drain hose

Refitting

11 Refit by reversing the removal operations.

Air distribution unit

Removal

12 If the vehicle is fitted with air conditioning, have the system drained by a Renault dealer or an air conditioning specialist. Many specialists now offer a mobile service.

13 Working under the bonnet, disconnect the battery negative lead and to make access easier, remove the wiper arms, wiper cowl panels and the lower scuttle panel **(see illustration)**.

14 Remove the heater supply and return hoses, noting their locations **(see illustration)**. Fit brake hose type clamps to the hoses or plug the ends to avoid the loss of coolant. Otherwise drain the coolant, as described in Chapter 1A Section 27.

15 Disconnect the air-conditioning pipes from the expansion valve on the rear of the bulkhead, as described in Section 15 of this Chapter.

16 Working inside the car, remove the complete facia assembly and crossmember, as described in Chapter 11 Section 28. Note that the heater control cables can be left in place and removed on the bench.

17 If not already done so unplug the electrical connectors from the heater resister pack and the blower motor. Unclip the drain hose from the lower part of the heater houisng **(see illustration)**.

18 Remove the distribution unit from the

vehicle. Expect some coolant loss from the heater radiator as the distribution unit is removed.

Refitting

19 Refit by reversing the removal operations, but locate the unit correctly forr the drain hose and fit the retaining clip correctly. Top-up, or refill and bleed the cooling system as described in *Weekly checks* or Chapter 1A or 1B. Have the air conditioning system pressure-checked and then refilled by a specialist.

Heater matrix

Removal

20 Clamp the heater supply and return hoses under the bonnet. Remove the hoses **(see illustration 11.14)**, noting their locations. Otherwise drain the coolant, as described in Chapter 1A Section 27.

11.22 Move the electronic control unit to one side

21 Working inside the vehicle, remove the glovebox as described in Chapter 11 Section 28.

22 Undo the retaining screw and move the electronic control unit to one side **(see illustration)**.

23 Place absorbent material on the passenger floor. If the cooling system hasn't been drained and blown through, there will be considerable coolant loss as the heater matrix is removed.

24 Release the locking peg, and slide the securing clips from the pipe fitting, then pull the pipes to disengage them from the heater matrix **(see illustrations)** Recover the seals and discard, as new ones will be required for refitting.

25 Drill out the two plastic rivets and remove the cover from over the end of the heater matrix **(see illustrations)**.

26 Withdraw the heater matrix out from

11.24a Remove the securing clips...

11.24b ...pull the pipes from the matrix...

11.24c ...and discard the seals

11.25a Drill out the rivets...

11.25b ...and remove the end cover

11.26 Withdraw the matrix

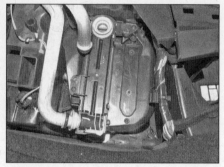

11.27 Secure matrix in position with two screws

the heater housing, holding the outer end upwards to prevent any more coolant spillage **(see illustration)**.

Refitting

27 Refit by reversing the removal operations, secure the matrix end cover in position with two retaining screws **(see illustration)** and fit new seals to the heater pipes,.Top-up the coolant and bleed the system as described in Chapter 1A Section 27 or Chapter 1B Section 27.

12 Heater controls – removal and refitting

Note: *On models with climate control, there are no heater control cables as all functions are controlled electronically. The procedure* *for the removal and refitting of the control panel is the same, ignoring the references to the heater cables.*

Control panel and bulb

Removal

1 Disconnect the battery negative lead, with reference to Chapter 5A Section 4.
2 Carefully unclip the facia centre trim panel, there are two retaining clips at the top and two at the bottom **(see illustrations)**.
3 Undo the four retaining screws, then release the locating clips at each end of the control panel and push the control panel forwards, in to the facia recess **(see illustrations)**.
4 Manouvre the control panel and out from the facia, If the reason for removing the panel is to renew the bulb, this can be done without further dismantling **(see illustration)**

5 To remove the panel completely, disconnect the multiplugs and the cables **(see illustration)**.

Refitting

6 Refit by reversing the removal operations. Check that the controls operate over their full range before securing the facia trim panel.

Control cables

Removal

7 Remove the control panel as described previously.
8 Remove the lower trim panel if access is required to the right-hand side of the air distribution unit. Remove the glovebox for access to the left-hand side. See Chapter 11 for the full procedure.
9 Remove the cables at the control panel if not already done so.

12.2a Carefully prise the trim panel...

12.2b ...and remove it from the facia

12.3a Remove the four screws...

12.3b ...and release the locating clips

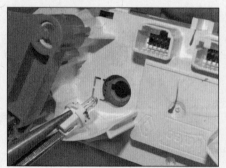

12.4 Long-nosed pliers can be used to release the bulbholder

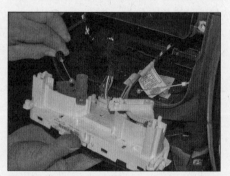

12.5 Disconnect the control cables – where fitted

12.10 Unclip the outer cable then release inner cable

10 At the other end, remove the outer cable from the retaining clip and then release the ball-end from the operating arm **(see illustration)**.

Refitting

11 Refitting is a reversal of removal. Connect the cables (where fitted) to the control levers making sure the clips are secure. Refit the control panel and check the operation of the controls.

13 Air conditioning system – general information

1 Air conditioning is available on most models. It enables the temperature of incoming air to be lowered; it also dehumidifies the air, which makes for rapid demisting and increased comfort **(see illustration)**.
2 The cooling side of the system works in the same way as a domestic refrigerator. Refrigerant gas is drawn into a belt-driven compressor, and passes into a condenser in front of the radiator, where it loses heat and becomes liquid. The liquid passes through an expansion valve to an evaporator, where it changes from liquid under high pressure to gas under low pressure. This change is accompanied by a drop in temperature, which cools the evaporator. The refrigerant returns to the compressor and the cycle begins again.
3 Air blown through the evaporator passes to the air distribution unit, where it is mixed with hot air blown through the heater matrix, to achieve the desired temperature in the passenger compartment.
4 Climate control is a refined version of air conditioning. The addition of a sunlight sensor and cabin temperature sensor allow precise control of the cabin temperature.
5 The heating side of the system works in the same way as on models without air conditioning.

⚠ *Warning: The refrigerant is potentially dangerous, and should only be handled by qualified persons. If it is splashed onto the skin, it can cause frostbite. It is not itself poisonous, but in the presence of a naked flame (including a cigarette) it forms a poisonous gas.*

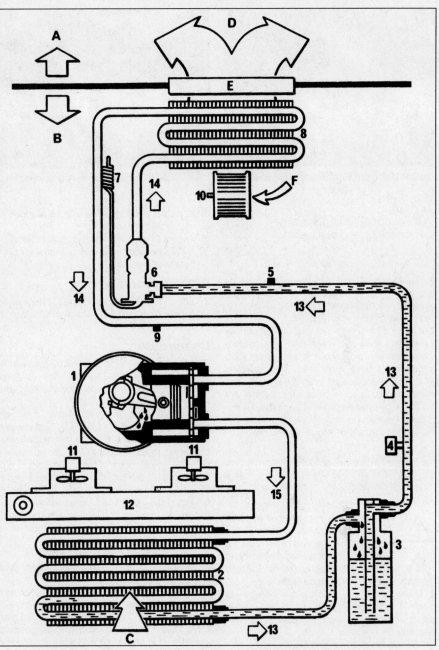

13.1 Schematic view of the air conditioning system

A Passenger compartment
B Engine compartment
C Outside air
D To air distribution unit
E Bulkhead
F Incoming air (fresh or recirculated)

1 Compressor
2 Condenser
3 Reservoir
4 Pressure switch
5 High-pressure bleed
6 Expansion valve
7 Thermostat
8 Evaporator

9 Low-pressure bleed
10 Blower
11 Cooling fans
12 Cooling system radiator
13 Liquid at high pressure
14 Gas at low pressure
15 Gas at high pressure

⚠ *Warning: Uncontrolled discharging of the refrigerant is dangerous, and damaging to the environment. It is also a criminal offence. It follows that any work on the air conditioning system which involves opening the refrigerant circuit must only be carried out after the system has been evacuated by a Renault dealer or an air conditioning specialist.*

15.6a Undo the refrigerant pipe retaining bolts...

15.6b ...and disconnect wiring connectors

15.7 Compressor mounting bolts – 0.9 litre petrol model shown

14 Air conditioning system – checking and maintenance

1 Routine maintenance is limited to checking the tension and condition of the auxiliary drivebelt, as described in Chapter 1A Section 9 or Chapter 1B Section 10.
2 It is recommended that a specialist service the system every two years. A service removes the refrigerant and vacuums the system for a minimum of twenty minutes. This removes all the moisture and oil from the system. The vacuum produced is monitored by the AC machine for a set length of time. If the system passes the vacuum test, it is then refilled with the correct amount of refrigerant and oil.

15 Air conditioning system – component removal and refitting

Warning: Do not attempt to open the refrigerant circuit. Refer to the Warnings at the end of Section 13.
Warning: It is a criminal offence to knowingly discharge refrigerant gas to the atmosphere.

1 There is nothing to stop the competent home mechanic from working on the air conditioning system, providing certain precautions are taken:
a) Always have the system evacuated by an air conditioning specialist with the necessary equipment.

b) Any parts dismantled should be plugged and sealed immediately.
c) Always fit new seals and gaskets. O-rings should be lubricated with compressor oil before fitting.

Compressor drivebelt

2 Refer to Auxiliary drivebelt check and renewal in Chapter 1A Section 9 or Chapter 1B Section 10.

Compressor

3 Have the AC system drained by a specialist and then jack up the front of the car, and support it on axle stands (see *Jacking and vehicle support*).
4 Remove the front bumper and on turbocharged models remove the intercooler. On all other models, remove the air deflector from next to the radiator. This provides easy access to pipework and mounting bolts.
5 Remove the auxiliary drivebelt as described in Chapter 1A Section 9 or Chapter 1B Section 10.
6 Unbolt the refrigerant pipes from the rear of the compressor, and disconnect the wiring connectors **(see illustrations)**. Seal the pipes immediately.
7 Undo the two mounting bolts and one retaining nut to remove the compressor **(see illustration)**.
8 Refitting is a reversal of removal, but fit new seals to the pipes and lubricate them with compressor oil. If a new compressor is being fitted then it must be filled with the correct grade and quantity of oil. Note that some compressors may be supplied already filled with oil.

Pressure sensor

Note: *The pressure sensor is located beside the condenser on the high-pressure pipe between the pressure relief valve and the dehydration canister. This can be removed without draining the system, as it is mounted on a 'schrader' valve. Note however that if there is any sound of escaping refrigerant as the sensor is unscrewed, stop immediately and have the system professionally evacuated.*
9 Jack up the front of the car, and support it on axle stands (see *Jacking and vehicle support*) and then remove the front bumper.
10 Disconnect the wiring connector from the sensor **(see illustration)**.
11 Slacken and remove the pressure sensor from the high-pressure pipe.
12 Refitting is a reversal of removal, but always renew the seal and lubricate it with P.A.G. SP10 oil.

Cooling fan relay/resistor

13 A two-speed cooling fan is fitted to models with air conditioning. The fan operates at low speed all the time that the air conditioning system is in use. If pressure rises in the refrigerant circuit or if the engine overheats, the fan operates at high speed.
14 The two fan speeds are obtained using a relay/resistor of 0.23 ohms. For low speed operation, the resistor is switched in series with the fan motor. For high speed operation, the resistor is bypassed.
15 Disconnect the wiring plugs, undo the retaining screw, then slide the resistor to the left, to disengage it from the cowling **(see**

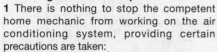

15.10 Location of pressure sensor

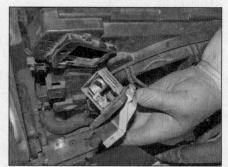

15.15a Undo the retaining screw...

15.15b ...then slide to the left and unclip the resistor from the cowling

15.22a Unbolt the upper pipe...

15.22b ...and lower pipe

15.23 Unclip the condenser from the radiator

illustrations). Refit by reversing the removal operations.

16 On most models, the resistor is located in the fan cowling to the left of the radiator. Its resistance can be checked without removing it, after disconnecting the multiplug.

Condenser/Dehydration canister

17 Have the AC system drained by a specialist and then jack up the front of the car, and support it on axle stands (see *Jacking and vehicle support*).

18 Remove the front bumper as described in Chapter 11, Section 6.

19 Unclip the upper air scoop from the front of the radiator/condenser (see illustration 3.2).

20 Disconnect the wiring connector from the flap motor at the end of the lower air intake panel, then undo the two upper retaining nuts and remove the air intake assembly from the front of the vehicle (see illustrations 3.3a and 3.3b).

21 Unclip the small plastic deflector from the top, then unclip the two parts of the air ducting from the front of the air-conditioning condenser (see illustrations 3.7a, 3.7b and 3.7c). Note, the outer cowling is removed upwards and the inner cowling downwards.

22 Unbolt the two refrigerant pipes from the right-hand side of the condenser (see illustrations). Seal the pipes immediately.

23 Unclip the air-conditioning condenser from the front of the radiator (see illustration) and move it forwards and out from the front of the vehicle.

24 Refitting is a reversal of removal, but renew all the seals. Have a specialist refill the system when all the work is completed.

Evaporator

25 The evaporater is incorporated in the air distribution unit. Remove the assembly as described in Section 11. At the time of writing the evaporator was only supplied with a complete air distribution assembly.

Expansion valve

26 Have the AC system drained by a specialist, and then remove the windscreen wipers, the windscreen cowl panels and the lower scuttle panel.

27 Unbolt and remove the soundproofing from the bulkhead.

28 Unbolt and remove the expansion valve connecting pipes, taking care not to damage them (see illustration). Seal the pipes immediately.

29 Remove the bolts from the expansion valve and remove it.

30 Refitting is a reversal of removal, but fit new seals (see illustration) and lubricate them before fitting.

Heating/ventilation control motors

Recirculation motor

31 Remove the glovebox as described in Chapter 11, Section 28.

32 The motor is mounted high on the air distribution assembly (see illustration).

33 Remove the wiring plug and then remove the three screws. Withdraw the motor.

34 Refitting is a reversal of removal.

Distribution motor

35 Remove the lower trim panel from below the steering wheel.

36 Remove the centre console and then remove the lower centre trim panel.

37 Remove the crossmember support strut from the right-hand side of the heater housing.

38 Unplug the wiring connector and remove the mounting screws. Remove the motor.

39 Refitting is a reversal of removal.

Mixer motor

40 Remove the glovebox, centre console and lower centre trim panel.

41 The mixer motor is located low on the air distribution assembly.

15.28a Pull back the soundproofing...

15.28b ...and unbolt the refrigerant pipes

15.30 Fit new seals

15.32 Location of heater flap motor

42 Unplug the wiring connector and then unbolt the motor. Remove the motor.

43 Refitting is a reversal of removal.

Cabin temperature sensor

44 The sensor is located above the rear mirror.

45 Lever the upper section towards the rear of the vehicle with a suitable plastic trim tool, and then unclip the lower section in the opposite direction.

46 Unclip the electrical connector and then unbolt the sensor.

47 Refitting is a reversal of removal.

Sunlight sensor

48 Lever up and free the auxiliary display panel from the centre of the facia.

49 Push up from below and release the sensor.

50 Refitting is a reversal of removal.

Exterior temperature sensor

51 The sensor is located in the driver's side door mirror. Remove the door mirror glass as described in Chapter 11, Section 17.

52 New sensors are supplied with 'flying' leads and require the use of a soldering iron, or crimp type connectors to fit them.

Chapter 4 Part A
Petrol engine fuel and exhaust systems

Contents

Degrees of difficulty

Easy, suitable for novice with little experience | **Fairly easy,** suitable for beginner with some experience | **Fairly difficult,** suitable for competent DIY mechanic | **Difficult,** suitable for experienced DIY mechanic | **Very difficult,** suitable for expert DIY or professional

Specifications

System type
All petrol models. . . . . Sequential multipoint injection

Recommended fuel
Minimum octane rating. . . . . 95 or 98 RON unleaded (if unavailable, 91 RON may be used). Leaded fuel or LRP must not be used

Fuel system data
Fuel pressure regulator control pressure . . . . 3.5 ± 0.06 bars
Fuel pump flow output (minimum) . . . . 80 to 100 litres/hour at 3.5 bars fuel pressure
Air temperature sensor resistance:
  At –10°C. . . . . 10 450 to 8625 ohms
  At 25°C. . . . . 2065 to 2040 ohms
  At 50°C. . . . . 815 to 805 ohms
Coolant temperature sensor resistance:
  At 25°C. . . . . 2360 to 2140 ohms
  At 50°C. . . . . 850 to 770 ohms
  At 80°C. . . . . 290 to 275 ohms
  At 110°C. . . . . 117 to 112 ohms
Injector resistance . . . . 14.5 ± 1.5 ohms at 20°C
TDC sensor resistance. . . . . 200 to 270 ohms
Fuel tank level sender unit resistance at height of float pin (approx):
  At 164 mm . . . . 3.5 ± 3.5 ohms
  At 143 mm . . . . 61 ± 7 ohms
  At 110 mm . . . . 110 ± 10 ohms
  At 81 mm . . . . 190 ± 16 ohms
  At 52 mm . . . . 280 ± 20 ohms
  At 47 mm . . . . 310 ± 10 ohms
Specified idle speed (non-adjustable) . . . . 750 ± 50 rpm
Idle mixture CO content (non-adjustable) . . . . 0.5% maximum at 2500 rpm

Torque wrench settings

	Nm	lbf ft
Exhaust manifold:		
0.9 litre engine	35	25
1.2 litre engine:		
Stage 1	10	7
Stage 2	25	18
Heat shield	15	11
Fuel rail:		
0.9 litre engine	10	7
1.2 litre engine	7	5
Fuel tank	21	15
Inlet manifold:		
Stage 1	6	4
Stage 2	10	7
Knock sensor	20	15
Motorised throttle valve (1.2 litre engine)	7	5
Oxygen sensor	45	33
Throttle body (0.9 litre engine)	10	7

1 General information and precautions

1 The fuel system consists of a fuel tank which is mounted under the rear of the vehicle with an electric fuel pump immersed in it, and a fuel feed line leading to the fuel rail on the engine. A further line from the fuel tank leads to the charcoal canister. In comparison to the fuel system on earlier models, there is no return line to the fuel tank. This is commonly referred to as a 'returnless system' **(see illustration)**.

The fuel pump supplies fuel to the fuel rail, which acts as a reservoir for the fuel injectors which inject fuel into the inlet tracts. The fuel pressure regulator is located either in the base of the fuel pump or the end of the fuel rail, depending on model. The Electronic Control Unit (ECU) is located on the left-hand side of the engine compartment, and the system includes various sensors, electrical components and related wiring.

2 Refer to Section 5 for further information on the operation of each fuel injection system, and to Section 17 for information on the exhaust system.

⚠️ **Warning:** *Many of the procedures in this Chapter require the removal of fuel lines and connections, which may result in some fuel spillage. Before carrying out any operation on the fuel system, refer to the precautions given in 'Safety first!' at the beginning of this manual, and follow them implicitly. Petrol is a highly dangerous and volatile liquid, and the precautions necessary when handling it cannot be overstressed* **Note:** *Residual pressure will remain in the fuel lines long after the vehicle was last used. When disconnecting any fuel line, first depressurise the fuel system as described in Section 6.*

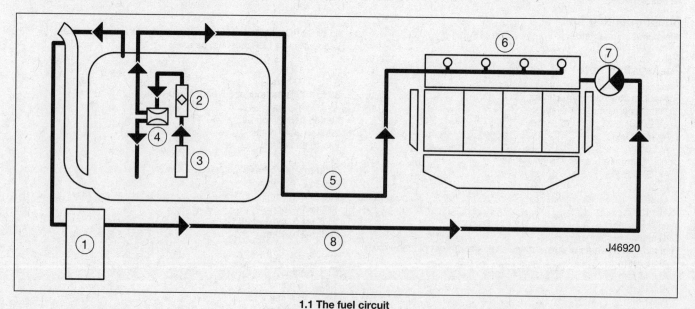

1.1 The fuel circuit

1 Fuel vapour canister	4 Pressure regulator	7 Vapour control solenoid
2 Filter	5 Supply pipe	8 Vapour line
3 Fuel pump	6 Fuel rail	

2.1a Release the securing clip...

2.1b ...then remove the inlet pipe

2.2 Unclip the breather pipe

2 Air cleaner assembly and inlet ducts – removal and refitting

1.2 litre engine

Removal

1 Remove the inlet pipe from the front panel by releasing the securing clip and pulling it free, (see illustrations).

2 Unclip the gearbox breather hose from the side of the housing (see illustration).

3 Release the crankcase breather hose and slacken the hose clip holding the housing to the throttle body (see illustrations).

4 Work the housing free from the mountings on the valve cover and inlet manifold, moving it to the right to free it from the throttle body (see illustrations).

Refitting

5 Refitting is a reversal of removal.

0.9 litre engine

Removal

6 Remove the inlet pipe from the front panel by releasing the securing clip and pulling it free, then disconnect it from the air cleaner housing (see illustrations).

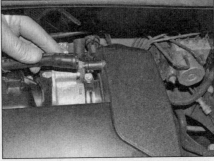

2.3a Disconnect the breather hose

2.3b Slacken the hose clip

2.4a Remove the air cleaner housing...

2.4b ...from the mounting points in the manifold

2.6a Release the pipe from the front panel...

2.6b ...and the air cleaner housing...

2.6c ...then remove the inlet pipe

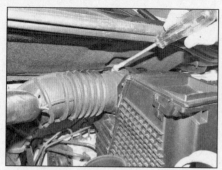

2.7 Slacken the hose clip and remove the outlet hose

2.8a Undo the mounting bolt...

2.8b ...and remove the air cleaner housing...

2.8c ...releasing it from the rubber grommet in the mounting bracket

7 Slacken the securing clip and disconnect the air outlet rubber hose from the rear of the air cleaner housing (see illustration).
8 Undo the mounting bolt and withdraw the air cleaner housing upwards, from the rubber grommet in the transmission mounting bracket (see illustrations).

Refitting

9 Refitting is a reversal of removal.

3 Accelerator pedal – removal and refitting

Removal

1 Remove the lower trim panel from under the steering column as described in Chapter 11, Section 28.

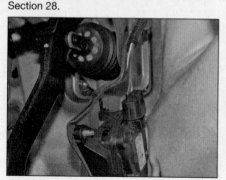

3.2 Disconnect the wiring connector

2 Disconnect the wiring plug from the top of the accelerator pedal (see illustration).
3 Remove the two bolts that secure the accelerator pedal in position, then pull it downwards to release the locating peg, from the mounting bracket (see illustration).
4 Withdraw the accelerator pedal.
5 Examine the pedal and pivot for signs of wear and renew as necessary.

Refitting

6 Refitting is a reversal of removal.

4 Unleaded petrol – general information and usage

1 All petrol models are designed to run on fuel with an octane rating of 95 or 98 RON, however, if unavailable, 91 octane fuel may

3.3 Undo the two bolts and remove pedal

be used. All models have a catalytic converter, and so must be run on unleaded fuel only. Under no circumstances should leaded fuel or LRP be used, as this will damage the converter.

5 Fuel injection systems – general information

1 All models are equipped with the sequential multipoint fuel injection/ignition system.
2 The system is of closed-loop type incorporating two oxygen (lambda) sensors, one located upstream and the other downstream of the catalytic converter. An evaporative emission control system is fitted.
3 The multipoint injection system uses one injector and one ignition coil for each cylinder, and the injectors are operated individually and sequentially at the beginning of the inlet stroke. The electronic control unit (ECU) is able to determine which cylinder is on its inlet stroke without the use of a camshaft position sensor, however if the unit is renewed, the car must be taken for a road test lasting at least 25 minutes to enable the ECU to reprogramme itself. The idle speed stepper motor must also be reset.
4 The system incorporates a closed-loop catalytic converter and an evaporative emission control system. The fuel injection side of the system operates as follows; refer to Chapter 5B for information on the ignition system.
5 The fuel pump is immersed in the fuel tank, and pumps fuel from the fuel tank to the fuel rail on the engine. Fuel supply pressure is controlled by a pressure regulator in the fuel pump. The regulator operates by allowing excess fuel to return to the tank. On 0.9 litre engines, there are three injectors (one per cylinder) and on 1.2 litre engines, there are four injectors (one per cylinder), these are located in the inlet manifold downstream of the throttle valve. All the injectors are fed from the fuel rail.
6 No models are fitted with an accelerator cable, as the throttle valve is motorised and has an integral potentiometer; the accelerator pedal also incorporates a potentiometer.
7 The electrical control system consists of the ECU, along with the following sensors:
a) Throttle potentiometer – informs the ECU of the throttle position, and the rate of throttle opening or closing.
b) Coolant temperature sensor – informs the ECU of engine temperature.
c) Inlet air temperature sensor – informs the ECU of the temperature of the air passing through the throttle body.
d) Oxygen (lambda) sensors – informs the ECU of the oxygen content of the exhaust gases and the efficiency of the catalytic converter (explained in greater detail in Part C of this Chapter).

e) *Idle speed regulation stepper motor (where fitted) – controls the idle speed.*
f) *Crankshaft speed/position (TDC) sensor – informs the ECU of engine speed and crankshaft position.*
g) *Air pressure sensor – turbo engine only.*
h) *Knock sensor – informs the ECU when pre-ignition ('pinking') is occurring (explained in greater detail in Chapter 5B).*
i) *Manifold absolute pressure (MAP) sensor – informs the ECU of the engine load by monitoring the pressure in the inlet manifold.*
j) *Fuel vapour recirculation valve – operates the fuel evaporative control system (explained in greater detail in Part C of this Chapter).*
k) *Vehicle speed sensor – informs the ECU of the vehicle speed.*
l) *Brake pedal switch – reduces the fuelling under braking.*

8 All the above information is analysed by the ECU and, based on this, the ECU determines the appropriate ignition and fuelling requirements for the engine. The ECU controls the fuel injector by varying its pulse width – the length of time the injector is held open – to provide a richer or weaker mixture, as appropriate. The mixture is constantly varied by the ECU, to provide the best setting for cranking, starting (with either a hot or cold engine), warm-up, idle, cruising and acceleration. On automatic transmission models, information from sensors on the transmission is sent to the ECU for processing to determine the most efficient settings for the engine.

9 The ECU also has full control over the engine idle speed, via a stepper motor which is fitted to the throttle body. The motor pushrod rests against a cam on the throttle spindle. When the throttle is closed (accelerator pedal released), the ECU uses the motor to vary the opening of the throttle valve and so control the idle speed.

10 The ECU also controls the exhaust and evaporative emission control systems, which are described in detail in Part C of this Chapter.

11 If there is an abnormality in any of the readings obtained from either the coolant temperature sensor, the inlet air temperature sensor or the oxygen sensor, the ECU enters its back-up mode. In this event, the ECU ignores the abnormal sensor signal, and assumes a pre-programmed value which will allow the engine to continue running (albeit at reduced efficiency). If the ECU enters this back-up mode, the warning light on the instrument panel will come on, and the relevant fault code will be stored in the ECU memory.

12 If the warning light comes on, the vehicle should be taken to a Renault dealer or competent garage at the earliest opportunity. A complete test of the engine management system can then be carried out, using a special electronic diagnostic test unit, which is plugged into the system's diagnostic connector (located beneath the ashtray on the centre console).

6 Fuel injection system – depressurisation

  Warning: Refer to the warning note in Section 1 before proceeding. The following procedure will merely relieve the pressure in the fuel system – remember that fuel will still be present in the system components, and take precautions accordingly before disconnecting any of them.
Note: *The fuel system referred to in this Section includes the tank mounted fuel pump, the fuel injectors, the pressure regulator, the fuel rail and the metal pipes and flexible hoses of the fuel lines between these components. All these contain fuel which will be under pressure while the engine is running, and/or while the ignition is switched on. The pressure will remain for some time after the ignition has been switched off, and it must be relieved when any of these components are disturbed for servicing work.*

Method 1
1 Disconnect the battery negative lead as described in Chapter 5A Section 4.
2 Place a suitable container beneath the connection or union to be disconnected, and have a large rag ready to soak up any escaping fuel not being caught by the container.
3 Slowly loosen the connection or union nut to avoid a sudden release of pressure, and position the rag around the connection, to catch any fuel spray which may be expelled. Once the pressure is released, disconnect the fuel line. Plug the pipe ends, to minimise fuel loss and prevent the entry of dirt into the fuel system.

Method 2
4 Lift up the rear seat, remove the cover and disconnect the fuel pump wiring plug (see section 8).
5 Start the engine and allow it to idle until it stops due to lack of fuel. Operate the starter motor a couple more times, to ensure that all fuel pressure has been relieved.
6 Switch off the ignition and refit the fuel wiring connector.

7 Fuel pipes and connections

1 Disconnect the cable from the negative battery terminal (see Chapter 5A Section 4) before proceeding.
2 The fuel supply pipe connects the fuel pump in the fuel tank to the fuel rail on the engine.

3 Whenever you're working under the vehicle, be sure to inspect all fuel and evaporative emission pipes for leaks, kinks, dents and other damage. Always replace a damaged fuel pipe immediately.
4 If you find signs of dirt in the pipes during disassembly, disconnect all pipes and blow them out with compressed air. Inspect the fuel strainer on the fuel pump pick-up unit for damage and deterioration.

Steel tubing
5 It is critical that the fuel pipes be replaced with pipes of equivalent type and specification.
6 Some steel fuel pipes have threaded fittings. When loosening these fittings, hold the stationary fitting with a spanner while turning the union nut.

Plastic tubing
⚠ **Warning: When removing or installing plastic fuel tubing, be careful not to bend or twist it too much, which can damage it. Also, plastic fuel tubing is NOT heat resistant, so keep it away from excessive heat.**
7 When replacing fuel system plastic tubing, use only original equipment replacement plastic tubing.

Flexible hoses
8 When replacing fuel system flexible hoses, use original equipment replacements, or hose to the same specification.
9 Don't route fuel hoses (or metal pipes) within 100 mm of the exhaust system or within 280 mm of the catalytic converter. Make sure that no rubber hoses are installed directly against the vehicle, particularly in places where there is any vibration. If allowed to touch some vibrating part of the vehicle, a hose can easily become chafed and it might start leaking. A good rule of thumb is to maintain a minimum of 8.0 mm clearance around a hose (or metal pipe) to prevent contact with the vehicle underbody.

Disconnecting Fuel pipe Fittings
10 Typical fuel pipe fittings:

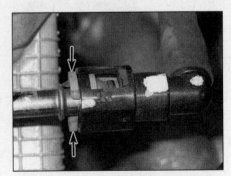

7.10a Two-tab type fitting; depress both tabs with your fingers, then pull the fuel pipe and the fitting apart

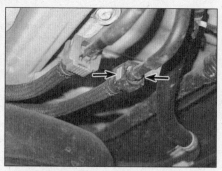

7.10b On this type of fitting, depress the two buttons on opposite sides of the fitting, then pull it off the fuel pipe

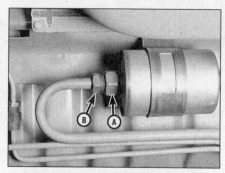

7.10c Threaded fuel pipe fitting; hold the stationary portion of the pipe or component (A) while loosening the union nut (B) with a flare-nut spanner

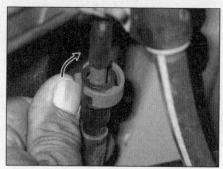

7.10d Plastic collar-type fitting; rotate the outer part of the fitting

7.10e Metal collar quick-connect fitting; pull the end of the retainer off the fuel pipe and disengage the other end from the female side of the fitting...

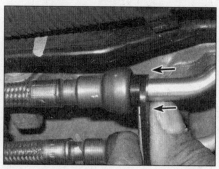

7.10f ...insert a fuel pipe separator tool into the female side of the fitting, push it into the fitting and pull the fuel pipe off the pipe

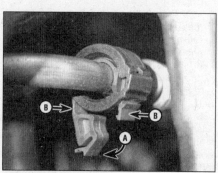

7.10g Some fittings are secured by lock tabs. Release the lock tab (A) and rotate it to the fully-opened position, squeeze the two smaller lock tabs (B)...

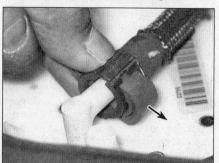

7.10h ...then push the retainer out and pull the fuel pipe off the pipe

7.10i Spring-lock coupling; remove the safety cover, install a coupling release tool and close the tool around the coupling...

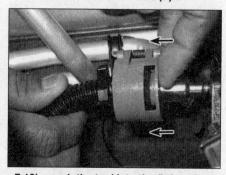

7.10j ...push the tool into the fitting, then pull the two pipes apart

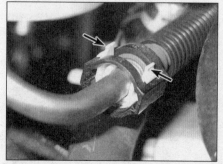

7.10k Hairpin clip type fitting: push the legs of the retainer clip together, then push the clip down all the way until it stops and pull the fuel pipe off the pipe

8.3 Prising the access cover from the rear floor

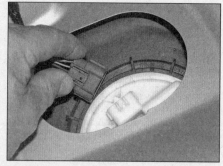

8.4 Disconnecting the wiring from the fuel pump

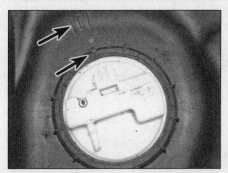

8.6a Alignment arrows on the pump cover, fuel tank and locking ring

8.6b Using a home-made removal tool to unscrew the locking ring from the fuel tank

8.6c Removing the locking ring

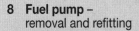

8 Fuel pump – removal and refitting

 Warning: *Refer to the warning note in Section 1 before proceeding.*

Removal

1 Disconnect the battery negative lead as described in Chapter 5A Section 4.

2 Remove the rear seat, or rear seat cushion as described in Chapter 11 Section 22, for access to the fuel pump cover.

3 Carefully prise the access cover from the floor to expose the fuel pump **(see illustration)**.

4 Disconnect the wiring connector from the fuel pump, and tape the connector to the vehicle body, to prevent it disappearing behind the tank **(see illustration)**.

5 To access the pump remove the fuel tank as described in Section 10.

6 Noting the alignment arrows on the pump cover, locking ring and fuel tank, unscrew the locking ring and remove it from the tank. This can be accomplished by using a screwdriver on the raised ribs of the locking ring – carefully tap the screwdriver to turn the ring anti-clockwise until it can be unscrewed by hand. Alternatively a removal tool can be fabricated out of metal bar and two bolts **(see illustrations)**.

7 Carefully lift the fuel pump assembly out of the fuel tank, taking great care not to damage the fuel level gauge sender arm, or to spill fuel in the interior of the vehicle. Remove the rubber sealing ring and check it for deterioration; if it is in good condition, it may be re-used, however if the pump is to remain out of the fuel tank for several hours, the locking ring should be refitted temporarily to prevent the sealing ring from distorting. If the sealing ring is unserviceable, obtain a new one **(see illustrations)**.

8 Note that the fuel pump/fuel gauge sender unit is only available as a complete assembly – no components are available separately.

8.7a Removing the fuel pump from the tank

Refitting

9 Ensure that the fuel pump pick-up filter is clean and free of debris. Fit the sealing ring to the top of the fuel tank.

10 Carefully manoeuvre the pump assembly into the fuel tank.

11 Align the arrow on the fuel pump cover with the arrow on the fuel tank (the arrow must point to the rear of the vehicle), then refit the locking ring. Securely tighten the locking ring until the arrow is pointing rearwards, then recheck that the pump cover and tank marks are all correctly aligned.

12 Reconnect the hose to the top of the fuel pump.

13 Reconnect the wiring connector.

14 Reconnect the battery and start the engine. Check the fuel pump and hose(s) for signs of leakage.

15 Refit the plastic access cover and the rear seat cushion.

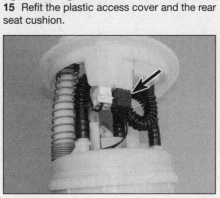

9.3 Disconnect the wiring from the cover

8.7b Removing the rubber sealing ring

9 Fuel gauge sender unit and pressure regulator – testing, removal and refitting

Testing

1 The fuel gauge sender unit is supplied as part of the fuel pump assembly, however it is possible to test its operation and remove it.

2 To test the sender unit, first remove the pump as described in Section 8.

3 Disconnect the wiring plug from the cover and connect an ohmmeter to the two terminals **(see illustration)**.

4 With the pump assembly upright on the bench, measure the resistance of the sender unit at the different heights given in the Specifications **(see illustration)**. The resistances are approximate but it should be clear if the sender unit is not operating correctly.

9.4 Testing the sender unit with an ohmmeter

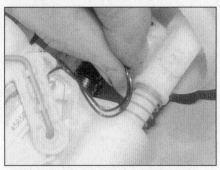

9.5a Remove the wiring from the clips...

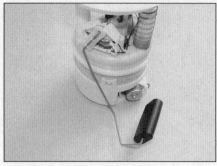

9.5b ...then unclip the unit from the main body

9.6a Release the clips and remove the base cover...

9.6b ...then pull out the spring clip to remove the pressure regulator

Removal

5 To remove the sender unit, first release the wiring from the clips, then unclip the unit from the main body (see illustrations).

6 To remove the fuel pressure regulator, unclip the base cover, then pull out the retaining spring clip and remove the regulator (see illustrations).

7 Use a screwdriver to prise off the gauze filter, then clean any sediment from the filter and cover.

Refitting

8 Refitting is a reversal of removal, but test the unit before refitting the pump assembly to the tank.

10 Fuel tank –
removal and refitting

⚠ Warning: Refer to the warning note in Section 1 before proceeding

Removal

1 Before removing the fuel tank, all fuel must be drained from it. Since a drain plug is not provided, it is preferable to carry out the removal operation when the tank is nearly empty.

2 Remove the rear seat, or rear seat cushion (Chapter 11 Section 22), for access to the fuel pump cover.

3 Using a screwdriver, carefully prise the plastic access cover from the floor to expose the fuel pump.

4 Disconnect the wiring connector from the fuel pump, and tape the connector to the vehicle body, to prevent it disappearing behind the tank.

5 Disconnect the battery negative lead as described in Chapter 5A Section 4.

6 Chock the front wheels, then jack up the rear of the vehicle and support on axle stands (see Jacking and vehicle support).

7 Lower the exhaust system from its mountings and let it rest on the rear axle. There is no need to remove it from the vehicle (see illustrations).

8 Remove the heat shield from above the exhaust (see illustration).

9 Remove both roadwheels, disconnect and remove the handbrake cables as described in Chapter 9 Section 15. Unbolt the rear flexible hose support bracket (see illustrations).

10 Unclip and remove the right-hand inner wing liner.

10.7a Remove the bolts...

10.7b ...and lower the exhaust system

10.8 Remove the rear heat shield

10.9a Remove the handbrake cables...

10.9b ...and the brake pipe support bracket

10.11 Remove the hose clip

10.13 Disconnect the fuel lines as the tank is lowered

10.15 Work the fuel tank past the exhaust to remove

11 Working in the wheel arch, remove the tank retaining bolt and the hose clip from the fuel filler pipe. Disconnect the overflow pipe **(see illustration)**.

12 Place a trolley jack with an interposed block of wood beneath the tank, then raise the jack until it is supporting the weight of the tank.

13 Unscrew and remove the mounting bolts, then slowly lower the fuel tank out of position, disconnecting any other relevant pipes as they become accessible **(see illustration)**.

14 Separate the filler neck from the fuel tank as it is lowered.

15 With the help of an assistant remove the tank from underneath the vehicle, working it around the exhaust as necessary **(see illustration)**.

16 If the tank is contaminated with sediment or water, remove the fuel pump/sender unit (Section 8), and swill the tank out with clean fuel. The tank is injection moulded from a synthetic material – if seriously damaged, it should be renewed. However, in certain cases, it may be possible to have small leaks or minor damage repaired. Seek the advice of a specialist before attempting to repair the fuel tank.

Refitting

17 Refitting is the reverse of the removal procedure, noting the following points:
a) *When lifting the tank back into position, take care to ensure that the hoses are not trapped between the tank and vehicle body.*
b) *Ensure that all pipes and hoses are correctly routed. Make sure the sealing rings are in position in the quick-release fittings prior to fitting and make sure they are securely clipped in position.*
c) *On completion, refill the tank with a small amount of fuel, and check for signs of leakage prior to taking the vehicle out on the road.*

11 Throttle body/housing – removal and refitting

⚠ *Warning: Refer to the warning note in Section 1 before proceeding*

Note: *It is not possible to repair the throttle body/housing – if faulty it must be renewed as a complete assembly.*

1 Disconnect the battery negative lead as described in Chapter 5A Section 4.

0.9 litre engines

2 Remove the air cleaner inlet ducting from between the front panel and the air cleaner housing, as described in Section 2.

3 Disconnect the electrical connector from the pressure sensor on the air intake pipe to the throttle housing **(see illustration)**.

4 Slacken the securing clip and disconnect the breather hose from the air intake pipe **(see illustration)**.

5 Undo the bolt securing the air intake pipe to the bottom of the throttle housing, then remove two retaining bolts and remove the air intake pipe from the throttle body **(see illustrations)**. Check the sealing ring and renew as required.

6 Unplug the electrical connector from the throttle housing **(see illustration)**.

11.3 Disconnect the wiring connector...

11.4 ...and the breather hose

11.5a Undo the retaining bolt...

11.5b ...then remove the air intake pipe

11.6 Remove the wiring plug

11.7 Undo the mounting bolts

11.11 Remove the wiring plug

11.12 Undo the mounting bolts

7 Slacken and remove the four mounting bolts, securing the throttle body to the inlet manifold **(see illustration)**.

8 Withdraw the throttle body and recover the gasket/sealing ring.

9 Refitting is a reversal of removal, but a new gasket should be fitted. After reconnecting the battery, turn the ignition on and wait for a minimum of 30 seconds. During this time, the ECU will adapt the throttle minimum and maximum operating range. Note that the idle speed may be initially unstable, until the ECU adapts the throttle body fully to the engine. This will be completed over several varying drive cycles.

1.2 litre engines

10 Remove the air cleaner housing, as described in Section 2.

11 Unplug the electrical connector from the throttle housing **(see illustration)**.

12 Slacken and remove the four mounting bolts, securing the throttle body to the inlet manifold **(see illustration)**.

13 Withdraw the throttle body and recover the gasket.

14 Refitting is a reversal of removal, but a new gasket should be fitted. After reconnecting the battery, turn the ignition on and wait for a minimum of 30 seconds. During this time, the ECU will adapt the throttle minimum and maximum operating range. Note that the idle speed may be initially unstable, until the ECU adapts the throttle body fully to the engine. This will be completed over several varying drive cycles.

12.2 Diagnostic socket location

---

12 Fuel injection system – testing and adjustment

Testing

1 If a fault appears in the fuel injection system, first ensure that all the system wiring connectors are securely connected and free of corrosion. Ensure that the fault is not due to poor maintenance; ie, check that the air cleaner filter element is clean, the spark plugs are in good condition and correctly gapped, the cylinder compression pressures are correct, the ignition timing is correct, and that the engine breather hoses are clear and undamaged, referring to the relevant part of other chapters for further information.

2 If these checks fail to reveal the cause of the problem, the vehicle should be taken to a Renault dealer or suitably-equipped garage for testing. A diagnostic connector (located at the front of the centre console) is incorporated in the engine management circuit, into which a special electronic diagnostic tester can be plugged **(see illustration)**. The tester will help locate the fault quickly and simply, alleviating the need to test all the system components individually, which is a time-consuming operation that carries a risk of damaging the ECU. The Renault Clip diagnostic tester is specific for Renault dealerships Several aftermarket tools are also available, but none have the depth of coverage of the official factory tool. The diagnostic tool can display fault codes and live data from many components. In the hands of a skilled technician, faults can be quickly traced and rectified. However, it must be remembered that the diagnostic tool is only the first stage in the repair process. The fault must be confirmed by individual testing of the component identified.

3 If the 'electronic incident' warning light illuminates on the instrument panel whilst driving, or remains illuminated longer than 3 seconds after switching on the ignition, then the ECU has detected a fault within the system. The warning light is more commonly known as a MIL (malfunction indicator lamp). If the vehicle has no driving faults, then it is

---

worth completing a few drive cycles to see if the lamp has been falsely triggered by a software glitch (or intermittent fault) before having a diagnostic check carried out.

4 Basic fault code readers are now available at a reasonable cost. These testers will only display the mandatory EOBD (European On Board Diagnostic) emissions related fault codes. Most of these simple code readers will not display manufacturer specific fault codes. Some individual components may be tested for resistance after removal using the information given in the Specifications, however other items (such as the idle speed stepper motor) cannot be checked and are not adjustable.

Adjustment

5 Experienced home mechanics with a considerable amount of skill and equipment (including a tachometer and an accurately calibrated exhaust gas analyser) may be able to check the exhaust CO level and the idle speed. However, if these are found to be in need of adjustment, the car must be taken to a suitably-equipped garage for further testing. Neither the mixture adjustment (exhaust gas CO level) nor the idle speed are adjustable, and should either be incorrect, a fault must be present in the fuel injection system.

13 Multipoint injection system components – removal and refitting

⚠️ **Warning: Refer to the warning note in Section 1 before proceeding**

Fuel rail and injectors

Note: *If a faulty injector is suspected, before condemning the injector, it is worth trying the effect of one of the proprietary injector cleaning treatments.*

1 Depressurise the fuel system as described in Section 6, then disconnect the battery negative lead as described in Chapter 5A Section 4.

0.9 litre engines

2 Unclip the vacuum hose from the side of the

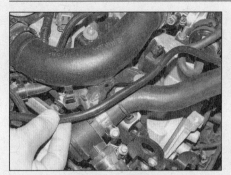

13.2a Unclip the vacuum hose…

13.2b …and undo the two mounting nuts

13.3a Release the securing clip from the turbo…

air intake pipe, then undo the two mounting nuts **(see illustrations)**.

3 Release the securing clips at each end of the air intake pipe, then remove it from across the top of the engine **(see illustrations)**.

4 Disconnect the vacuum pipe, slacken the securing clip and move the breather pipe to one side **(see illustrations)**.

5 Release the retaining clips and disconnect the vacuum pipe from the inlet manifold **(see illustration)**.

6 Release the retaining clips and remove the breather pipe from between the inlet manifold and cam cover **(see illustration)**.

7 Release the retaining clips and remove the air intake ducting from between the front panel and the air cleaner housing **(see illustration)**.

8 Disconnect the vacuum pipe from the pressure regulator **(see illustration)**.

13.3b …and intercooler…

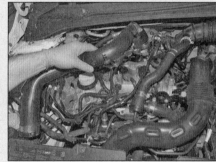

13.3c …then remove the air intake pipe

9 Disconnect the wiring connector from the MAP (manifold absolute pressure) sensor, and unclip the retaining clip from the fuel rail **(see illustration)**.

10 Undo the retaining bolts and remove the bracket from the lifting eye **(see illustration)**.

11 Release the retaining clips and disconnect

13.4a Disconnect the vacuum pipe…

13.4b …slacken the securing clip…

13.4c …and move the breather to one side

13.5 Disconnect the vacuum pipe

13.6 Remove the breather pipe

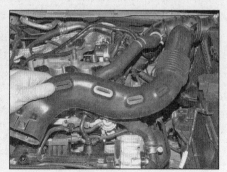

13.7 Remove the air intake ducting

13.8 Disconnect the vacuum pipe

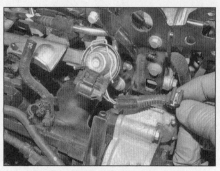

13.9 Disconnect the sensor wiring connector

13.10 Remove the bracket

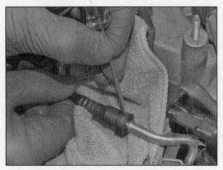

13.11a Release the securing clips…

13.11b …and disconnect the fuel pipes…

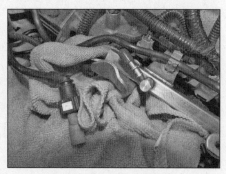

13.11c …then plug the ends

the fuel pipes from each end of the fuel rail **(see illustrations)**. Plug the ends to prevent dirt/moisture ingress.

12 Disconnect the wiring connectors from the top of the injectors and move the wiring to one side **(see illustration)**.

13 Unscrew the four bolts and gently free the fuel rail from the inlet manifold **(see illustration)**. The use of a lubricant may help free the injectors from the cylinder head, if required.

14 There may be fuel still in the rail, so be prepared to mop it up and then plug the end of the fuel rail.

15 To remove the fuel injectors from the fuel rail, release the spring clips from the fuel rail and pull the injectors free. Keep the injectors in the correct order **(see illustrations)**. Note the seal at the top of the injector may stay inside the fuel rail, remove it and refit it to the top of the injector before refitting.

16 With the injectors in the right order on the bench, check the resistance of each injector. They should all show a similar resistance, but any major variation will require further investigation. If any of the injectors are suspect they can be tested and ultrasonically cleaned by a garage with the correct specialist equipment.

13.12 Disconnect the injector wiring connectors

13.13 Remove the fuel rail complete with the injectors

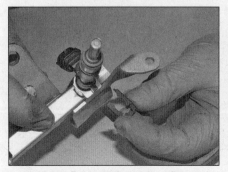

13.15a Remove the spring clip…

13.15b …and then the injector…

13.15c …recover the seal from the rail…

13.15d ...and fit it back to the top of the injector

13.23 Remove the fuel rail complete with the injectors

13.25a Remove the spring clip...

17 Refitting is a reversal of removal, noting the following points:

18 Renew the O-rings at the top and bottom of each injector (check on availability before removing the old O-rings), and ensure that the fuel rail is securely reconnected (the spring clip should click securely into position).

19 Refit the fuel rail assembly to the cylinder head, making sure the sealing rings remain correctly positioned, and tighten the retaining bolts to the specified torque.

20 On completion start the engine and check for fuel leaks.

1.2 litre engines

21 On all engines, remove the inlet manifold as described in Section 14.

22 Unplug the wiring connectors from each injector or alternatively disconnect the wiring multiplug. Disconnect the fuel supply.

23 Unscrew the two bolts and gently free the fuel rail from the inlet manifold. The use of a lubricant may help free the injectors from the cylinder head **(see illustration)**.

24 There may be fuel still in the rail, so be prepared to mop it up and then plug the end of the fuel rail.

25 To remove the fuel injectors from the fuel rail, release the spring clips from the fuel rail and pull the injectors free. Keep the injectors in the correct order **(see illustrations)**.

26 With the injectors in the right order on the bench, check the resistance of each injector. They should all show a similar resistance, but any major variation will require further investigation. If any of the injectors are

13.25b...and then the injector

suspect they can be tested and ultrasonically cleaned by a garage with the correct specialist equipment.

27 Refitting is a reversal of removal, but renew the O-rings at the top and bottom of each injector **(see illustration)** (check on availability before removing the old O-rings), and ensure that the fuel rail is securely reconnected (the spring clip should click securely into position).

28 Refit the fuel rail assembly to the cylinder head, making sure the sealing rings remain correctly positioned, and tighten the retaining bolts to the specified torque. Refit the inlet manifold.

29 On completion start the engine and check for fuel leaks.

Inlet air temperature sensor

30 On 0.9 litre turbo engine the sensor is mounted on the air inlet duct from the

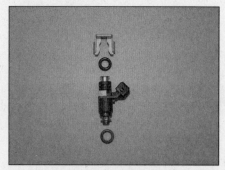

13.27 The injector components. Note that the lower seal is coloured green

intercooler to the throttle body. Disconnect the wiring connector and then undo the retaining screw and remove it from the air inlet duct **(see illustrations)**.

31 On the 1.2 litre engine the sensor is mounted at the front of the inlet manifold, close to the dipstick **(see illustration)**. Disconnect the wiring connector, then pull the sensor free from the manifold.

32 The air temperature sensor is easily checked with a meter. Its resistance will vary according to the air temperature. Check the resistance and compare it with the specification given at the beginning of this Chapter. Check that the resistance changes with a change in temperature. Placing it in a refrigerator for 20 minutes is a good method of checking that the resistance changes with the air temperature.

33 Refitting is a reversal of removal, but check the condition of the seal.

13.30a Disconnect the wiring connector...

13.30b ...then undo the retaining screw

13.31 Air temperature sensor

13.35a Knock sensor above starter motor – 0.9 litre engine

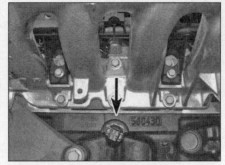

13.35b The knock sensor at the front of the engine – 1.2 litre engine

13.38 Location of MAP sensor – 0.9 litre engine

Coolant temperature sensor

34 The sensor is located on the thermostat housing or at the left-hand end of the cylinder head above the gearbox bellhousing. Refer to Chapter 3 Section 8, for removal and refitting details.

Knock sensor

35 The knock sensor is located on the front of the cylinder block **(see illustrations)**.
36 Refer to Chapter 5B Section 4 for the removal and refitting procedures.

Manifold absolute pressure sensor

37 The manifold absolute sensor is mounted on the top of the inlet manifold at the front on 0.9 litre engines, and at the rear drivers side of the manifold on 1.2 litre engines..
38 On 0.9 litre engines, disconnect the wiring connector, then undo the retaining screw and

remove the sensor from the manifold **(see illustration)**.
39 On 1.2 litre engines, disconnect the wiring connector and pull the sensor upwards to release it from the manifold.
40 Refitting is a reversal of removal.

Fuel system and fuel pump relays

41 The system does not have separate relays. All switching functions are controlled by the switching and control unit, located on the front left-hand side of the engine bay **(see illustration)** – next to the battery.

Camshaft sensor

42 The sensor is mounted at the transmission end of the camshaft cover **(see illustration)**.
43 Slacken the retaining clip and move the air intake hose to one side, to access the sensor **(see illustration)**.

44 Disconnect the wiring plug from the sensor, then undo the retaining bolt and remove the sensor from the camshaft cover.
45 Refitting is a reversal of removal. Ensure that the sensor retaining bolt is securely tightened.

Crankshaft TDC sensor

46 The sensor is mounted at the rear of the transmission bellhousing **(see illustration)**.
47 To remove the sensor, remove the air filter housing as described in Section 2, and if necessary remove the battery.
48 Disconnect the wiring plug from the sensor, then undo the retaining bolt and remove the sensor from the bell housing.
49 Refitting is a reversal of removal. Ensure that the sensor retaining bolt is securely tightened.

Electronic control unit (ECU)

Note: *The ECU is electronically-coded to match the engine immobiliser and certain other engine components. If the ECU is being removed in order to fit a new unit, it is highly recommended that the work be carried out by a Renault dealer.*
50 On all engines the ECU is located in the left-hand side of the engine compartment **(see illustration)** mounted next to the strut tower.
51 First disconnect the battery negative lead (refer to Chapter 5A Section 4).
52 On 0.9 litre engines, remove the air filter housing, as described in Section 2..

13.41 Relay/fuse box in engine compartment

13.42 The camshaft position sensor location

13.43 Move the air intake hose to one side

13.46 The crankshaft position sensor location

13.50 Location of ECU – 1.2 litre shown

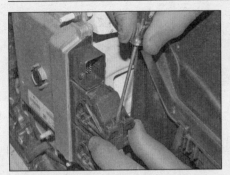

13.53a Release the locking clips...

13.53b ...and disconnect the wiring plugs

13.54 Undo the four mounting nuts

53 Release the locking clips and remove the three electrical connectors from the ECU **(see illustrations)**.

54 Remove the mounting nuts **(see illustration)**, and withdraw the control unit from the engine compartment.

55 Refitting is a reverse of the removal procedure ensuring that the wiring is securely reconnected. After the battery is reconnected the ECU must be adapted to the vehicle. To do this:

a) *Turn on the ignition and wait for a minimum of 30 seconds. The throttle body will operate and adapt the maximum and minimum position of the throttle plate.*

b) *Allow the vehicle to idle until the normal operating temperature is reached.*

c) *Drive the vehicle in third gear with an engine speed of between 3000 to 5000 rpm. Decelerate, without braking for at least 5 seconds.*

d) *Drive the vehicle in third gear with an engine speed of between 2000 to 4000 rpm and decelerate without braking for at least 5 seconds*

Note: *The ECU will continue to adapt to the engine for several drive cycles. During this time the idle speed and acceleration may be compromised.*

14 Manifolds – removal and refitting

Inlet manifold

0.9 litre engine

1 Depressurise the fuel system as described in Section 6, then disconnect the battery

negative lead as described in Chapter 5A Section 4.

2 Remove the fuel rail and injectors, as described in Section 13.

3 Remove the throttle body housing, as described in Section 11.

4 Undo the five retaining nuts and remove the manifold **(see illustration)**, and recover the gasket.

5 Refitting is a reversal of removal, but fit a new gasket and tighten the nuts, starting from the centre and working your way outwards. Tighten to the specified torque.

1.2 litre engine

6 Depressurise the fuel system as described in Section 6.

7 Disconnect the battery negative lead as described in Chapter 5A Section 4.

8 Remove the air cleaner assembly as described in Section 2.

9 Unbolt and remove the oil filler extension pipe. Seal the hole in the rocker cover with a rag or tape.

10 Disconnect the brake servo vacuum hose and the EVAP breather hose and the oil vapour hose from the rear of the cylinder head. Remove the HT leads, noting their positions (mark them if necessary) **(see illustrations)**.

11 Working around the top of the manifold, disconnect the electrical connectors from the MAP sensor, temperature sensor, fuel rail and throttle body **(see illustrations)**.

12 At the front of the manifold unclip the dipstick and then disconnect the fuel line **(see**

14.4 Undo the manifold retaining nuts

14.10a Disconnect the oil breather hose...

14.10b ... the brake servo hose...

14.10c ...and the evaporative emissions hose

14.10d Remove the HT leads

14.11a Unplug the MAP sensor...

14.11b ...and the air temperature sensor

14.12a Unclip the dipstick and remove it

14.12b Disconnect the fuel line (anticipate some fuel spillage)...

14.12c ...and then seal the fuel line and rail

ensure that the cylinder head and manifold mating surfaces are clean. Fit a new gasket and tighten the mounting bolts to the specified torque in two stages, in the order shown **(see illustration)**.

Exhaust manifold

0.9 litre engine

15 The exhaust manifold is part of the turbocharger **(see illustration)**, see Section 15, for the removal of the turbocharger.

1.2 litre engine

16 Disconnect the battery negative lead as described in Chapter 5A Section 4.
17 Whilst not strictly required, more working space can be gained by removing the windscreen wiper cowl panel and the lower scuttle panel, as described in Chapter 11, Section 7.
18 Apply the handbrake, then jack up the front of the vehicle and support it on axle stands (see *Jacking and vehicle support*). Remove the engine undertray.
19 Disconnect the exhaust front downpipe from the exhaust manifold on the front of the engine with reference to Section 17 and then remove the support strut from the manifold.
20 Unclip the oxygen sensor cable support and then disconnect the sensor wiring plug.
21 Unscrew the nuts and remove the heat shield from the exhaust manifold.
22 Progressively unscrew the bolts and remove the exhaust manifold from the cylinder head. Recover the gasket.

illustrations). Remove the main terminal from the starter motor and then release the wiring loom from the front of the manifold.
13 Remove the 3 upper mounting bolts and then remove the lower 8 manifold bolts

on the cylinder head in the reverse order to that shown **(see illustration 13.9)**. Remove the manifold and recover the gasket **(see illustrations)**.
14 Refitting is a reversal of removal but

14.13a Remove the manifold...

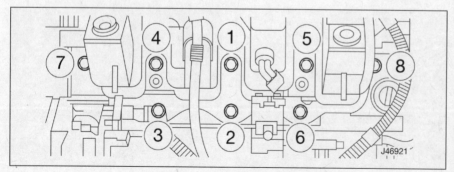

14.14 Tighten the bolts in the order shown

14.13b ...and recover the gaskets

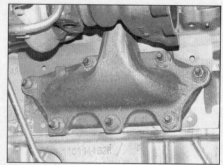

14.15 Exhaust manifold retaining nuts

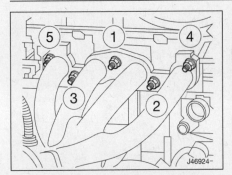

14.23 Tighten the bolts in two stages, in the order shown

15.3a Undo the two retaining nuts…

15.3b …then release the securing clip and remove the pipe

23 Refitting is a reversal of removal but use a new gasket and tighten the mounting bolts in the correct order **(see illustration)** to the specified torque. Ensure that the cylinder head and manifold mating surfaces are clean.

15 Turbocharger – removal and refitting

1 Disconnect the battery negative lead, and position the lead away from the battery (Chapter 5A Section 4) and then remove the engine cover.
2 Remove the air cleaner assembly, as described in Section 2.
3 Undo the two retaining nuts, then release the securing clip and remove the turbo outlet

pipe**(see illustrations)**, and move the pipe to one side.
4 Release the securing clip and remove the breather hose, then loosen the hose clip and remove the turbo inlet pipe **(see illustrations)**.
5 Remove the hose clips from the turbo cooling pipes and then pull the hoses from the pipes **(see illustration)**. Expect some coolant loss and then plug the pipes if necessary.
6 Disconnect the vacuum hose from the wastegate capsule.
7 Disconnect the wiring connector, remove the upper oxygen sensor, then undo the retaining bolts and remove the heat shield from over the turbocharger/manifold **(see illustration)**.
8 Jack up the front of the car, and support it on axle stands (see *Jacking and vehicle support*).

9 Remove the right-hand driveshaft as described in Chapter 8 Section 2, and then remove the catalytic converter as described in Section 17 of this Chapter. Recover the gasket.
10 Slacken the banjo bolt and remove the turbo oil supply from the top of the turbocharger **(see illustration)**. Collect and note the position of the sealing washers on the banjo bolts. Plug the pipes and turbo with a suitable seal.
11 Undo the two retaining bolts and disconnect the oil return pipe from under the turbocharger **(see illustrations)**. Collect and note the position of the sealing gasket, then pull the return pipe from the cylinder block. recover the sealing O-ring washer and discard, as a new one will be required on refitting.

15.4a Disconnect the breather hose…

15.4b …then slacken clip to disconnect air intake hose

15.5 Remove the coolant hoses

15.7 Remove the oxygen sensor and heatshield

15.10 Disconnect the oil supply pipe from the turbo

15.11a Undo the upper retaining bolts…

15.11b ...and pull return pipe from cylinder block

15.12 Remove the turbocharger

15.13a Fit new manifold gasket...

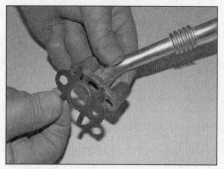

15.13b ...oil return pipe gasket...

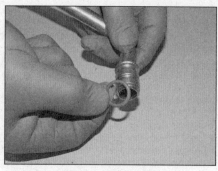

15.13c ...and seals

16 Intercooler –
removed and refitting

Removal

1 The intercooler is located behind the front bumper, to the right-hand side of the air conditioning condenser and radiator.

2 Remove the front bumper as described in Chapter 11 Section 6.

3 Remove the plastic air intake cowling from the front of the intercooler, this is removed in three separate pieces **(see illustrations)**.

4 Remove the headlight units, as described in Chapter 12 Section 10.

5 Release the three locating pegs, undo the two retaining bolts and remove the front crossmember from the top of the intercooler/radiator **(see illustrations)**. The bonnet release cable will still be attached, so just move the crossmember to one side.

6 Undo the retaining bolts and disconnect the air-conditioning pipe mounting brackets from the top and bottom of the intercooler **(see illustrations)**.

7 Loosen the clips and disconnect the air inlet and outlet ducts from the top and bottom of the intercooler **(see illustrations)**.

8 Release the intercooler from the side of the radiator, lift it upwards to release it from the lower rubber mounting, and then maneuver it downwards to remove **(see illustration)**.

12 Unbolt and remove the turbocharger **(see illustration)**. Withdraw it downwards and out from under the vehicle.

13 Refitting is a reversal of removal, but always renew all the seals and the gaskets **(see illustrations)**. Renault also recommend that the turbo oil supply pipes and fitting nuts are also renewed.

16.3a Remove the outer section...

16.3b ...middle section...

16.3c ...and inner section

16.5a Remove the locating pegs...

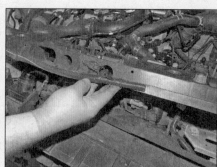

16.5b ...undo the bolts and remove the crossmember

16.6a Slacken and remove the lower…

16.6b …and upper pipe mounting brackets

16.7a Release the upper hose…

16.7b …and lower hose

16.8 Lower the intercooler out

16.9 Make sure rubber mounting is located in subframe

Refitting

9 Refitting is a reversal of removal, but tighten all nuts and bolts to the specified torque where given and make sure the rubber mounting is located correctly in the lower crossmember **(see illustration)**.

17 Exhaust system – general information, removal and refitting

General information

1 On new vehicles the exhaust system consists of just two sections; the front downpipe with catalytic converter and the remaining system consisting of a expansion box (not all models), silencer and tailpipe.

2 Each section however can be renewed separately. Renault have provided cutting points on the factory system to enable this. A special clamp is also available to join the old section to the new. **(see illustrations)**.

3 A flexible section (or joint) is incorporated into the exhaust or catalytic converter front section and the system is supported throughout on rubber mountings **(see illustration)**.

Removal

4 To remove a part of the system, first jack up the front or rear of the car, and support it on axle stands (see *Jacking and vehicle support*). Alternatively, position the car over an inspection pit, or on car ramps. Where fitted, remove the engine compartment undertray.

Front downpipe and catalytic converter

5 Trace the wiring back from the oxygen sensors and disconnect it at the wiring connectors. Free the wiring from any relevant retaining clips so the sensors are free to be removed with the front pipe.

6 Where applicable, unbolt the front pipe from the mounting bracket on the transmission.

7 Unscrew and remove the nuts/bolts securing the front pipe flange joint to the manifold, and recover the gasket.

8 If the original system is still in place, locate the cutting point and saw through the pipe with a hacksaw. If the system has been renewed previously, unscrew and remove the clamp and disconnect the front pipe and catalytic converter from the rear section. Withdraw the pipe from under the vehicle.

Intermediate pipe and resonator

9 Unscrew and remove the clamp bolts attaching the front pipe and catalytic converter to the rear section.

10 If the original rear section is fitted, it must be cut in half using either a hacksaw or pipe

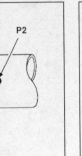

17.2a To cut the exhaust, mark a centre point (D) between the punch marks (P)

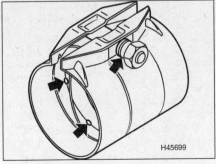

17.2b The special pipe clamp. Insert the exhaust pipe to the inner marks

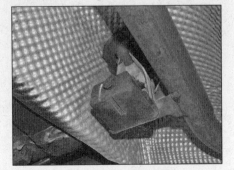

17.3 The exhaust mount

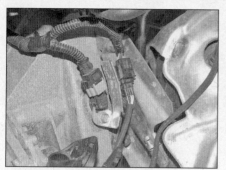

17.19 Disconnect the oxygen sensor wiring connector

17.20a Undo the mounting bolts...

17.20b ...and remove the support bracket

cutter. Locate the cutting area which is situated approximately midway between the rear silencer and intermediate mounting. The cutting point is marked with two circular punch marks on the side of the pipe. The punch marks are 80 mm apart and the exhaust section should be cut at the mid-point between the two punch marks.

11 With the intermediate pipe cut, withdraw the intermediate exhaust section from under the vehicle.

12 If the rear section is in two halves, unscrew the bolt and slide the clamp sleeve on to the rear section then release the rubber mountings and withdraw the intermediate section from under the vehicle.

Rear tailpipe and silencer

13 If the original rear section is fitted, follow the instructions given in paragraph 9.

14 If the rear section is in two halves, unscrew the bolt and slide the clamp sleeve

on to the intermediate section then release the rubber mountings and withdraw the tailpipe and silencer from under the vehicle.

Catalytic converter – 0.9 litre engine

15 On the 0.9 litre engine the converter is mounted high up, at the rear of the engine block.

16 Disconnect the battery negative lead, and position the lead away from the battery as described in Chapter 5A Section 4.

17 Jack up the front of the car, and support it on axle stands (see *Jacking and vehicle support*).

18 Remove engine undertray and then remove the the right-hand driveshaft as described in Chapter 8 Section 2.

19 Reaching down the rear of the engine, where the transmission is attached to the cylinder block, disconnect the lower oxygen sensor wiring connector, and then unclip the

wiring from the catalytic converter support bracket **(see illustration)**.

20 Remove the exhaust front pipe, and then undo the retaining bolts and remove the catalytic converter support bracket **(see illustrations)**.

21 Remove the driveshaft bearing support bracket **(see illustration)**.

22 Undo the retaining bolts and remove the support bracket from the end of the catalytic converter **(see illustration)**.

23 Working under the bonnet disconnect the wiring connector to the upper oxygen sensor and remove the turbocharger upper heat shield **(see illustration 15.7)**.

24 Undo the three retaining nuts and remove the converter from the turbocharger and lower it from the vehicle **(see illustrations)**.

25 Refitting is a reversal of removal, but new gaskets and new stud kit should be fitted **(see illustrations)**. The new kit has longer studs

17.21 Remove support bracket

17.22 Remove the end support bracket

17.24a Unbolt the catalytic converter...

17.24b...and remove it

17.25a New exhaust kit for catalytic converter

17.25b Fitting spacers on to the new studs

and spacers included, fit the spacers under the new securing nuts.

Heat shields

26 The heat shields are secured to the underbody by various nuts and bolts. Each shield can be removed separately but note that they overlap, making it necessary to loosen another section first. If a shield is being removed to gain access to a component located behind it, it may prove sufficient in some cases to remove the retaining nuts and/or bolts, and simply lower the shield, without disturbing the exhaust system. Otherwise remove the exhaust section as described earlier.

Refitting

27 Each section is refitted by reversing the removal sequence, noting the following points:

a) *Ensure that all traces of corrosion have been removed from the joints.*

b) *Inspect the rubber mountings for signs of damage or deterioration, and renew as necessary.*

c) *When reconnecting the intermediate pipe to the tailpipe, apply a smear of exhaust system jointing paste (Renault recommend the use of Sodicam) to the sleeve inner surface, to ensure a gas-tight seal. Make sure both inner ends of the cut pipe are positioned squarely against the stop of the clamp sleeve. Position the sleeve bolt vertically on the left-hand side of the pipe and securely tighten the nut until it is heard to click; the clamp bolt has a groove in it to ensure that the nut is correctly tightened (equivalent to a tightening torque of approximately 25 Nm/18 lbf ft).*

d) *Prior to tightening the exhaust system fasteners, ensure that all rubber mountings are correctly located, and that there is adequate clearance between the exhaust system and vehicle underbody.*

Chapter 4 Part B
Diesel engine fuel and exhaust systems

Contents

Degrees of difficulty

Easy, suitable for novice with little experience	**Fairly easy,** suitable for beginner with some experience	**Fairly difficult,** suitable for competent DIY mechanic	**Difficult,** suitable for experienced DIY mechanic	**Very difficult,** suitable for expert DIY or professional

Specifications

General

Type	Siemens
System type	Rear-mounted fuel tank, high-pressure pump with common-rail, direct injection
Firing order	1-3-4-2 (number 1 at flywheel end)
Idle speed	800 ± 50 rpm
Maximum no-load speed	4500 ± 150 rpm
Maximum under-load speed	5000 ± 150 rpm

High-pressure pump

Type	Delphi
Direction of rotation	Clockwise viewed from sprocket end

Injectors

Type	Delphi solenoid injector
Maximum pressure	1400 bars
Resistance	Not-measurable

Sensor resistances

Air temperature sensor:	
At -40° C	50 000 ± 6800 ohms
At 10° C	9500 ± 900 ohms
At 25° C	2051 ± 120 ohms
At 50° C	810 ± 47 ohms
At 80° C	310 ± 17 ohms
Coolant temperature sensor	282 ohms at 80°C
Crankshaft position sensor	680 ohms
Engine speed sensor	760 ohms
Fuel flow actuator (on pump)	5.3 ± 0.5 ohms
Fuel temperature sensor (on pump)	2.2 kohms
Turbocharger pressure sensor:	
Tracks A and B	9.0 kohms
Tracks A and C	4.0 kohms
Tracks B and C	5.0 kohms

Turbocharger

Type	Garrett
Boost pressure	1300 ± 2 mbars

Fuel tank

Fuel tank level sender unit resistance at height of float pin (approx):

At 164 mm	3.5 ± 3.5 ohms
At 143 mm	61 ± 7 ohms
At 110 mm	110 ± 10 ohms
At 81 mm	190 ± 16 ohms
At 52 mm	280 ± 20 ohms
At 47 mm	310 ± 10 ohms

Torque wrench settings

	Nm	lbf ft
Catalytic converter:		
Rear mounting	21	15
To side mounting strut	25	18
To turbocharger	26	19
Strut to engine	44	32
EGR valve	21	15
EGR valve heat shield	12	9
Engine lifting eye	21	15
Exhaust manifold	26	19
Exhaust pipe clamp	21	15
Flow actuator	6	4
Fuel gauge sender unit	65	48
Fuel injectors to cylinder head	28	21
Fuel tank	21	15
Fuel temperature sensor (on high-pressure pump)	15	11
High-pressure fuel rail	28	21
High-pressure pipe union nuts	24	18
High-pressure pump	21	15
High-pressure pump sprocket nut	55	41
High-pressure pump venturi	6	4
Turbocharger oil supply pipe:		
On cylinder head	23	17
On turbocharger	12	9
Turbocharger to exhaust manifold	26	19

1 General Information

1 The fuel system consists of a rear-mounted fuel tank, a fuel filter with integral water separator, a high-pressure pump with common rail injection system, electronic injectors and associated components.

2 The main components of the system are as follows:
a) Priming bulb on the low-pressure circuit.
b) Fuel filter.
c) High-pressure pump incorporating a low-pressure transfer pump.
d) Flow actuator attached to the pump.
e) Injector rail.
f) Pressure sensor located on the injector rail.
g) Four electronic solenoid injectors.
h) Fuel temperature sensor.
i) Coolant temperature sensor.
j) Upstream air temperature sensor.
k) Downstream air temperature sensor.
l) Cylinder reference sensor.
m) Engine speed sensor.
n) Turbocharging pressure sensor.
o) Accelerometer.
p) EGR solenoid valve.
q) Accelerator pedal potentiometer.
r) Atmospheric pressure sensor.
s) ECU.
t) Knock sensor.

3 The common rail injection system operates as follows. Fuel is drawn from the fuel tank to the high-pressure pump by a low-pressure transfer pump integrated in the high-pressure pump. Before reaching the high-pressure pump, the fuel passes through a fuel filter, where foreign matter and water are removed. As the fuel passes through the filter, it is heated by an electric heater. On reaching the high-pressure pump, the fuel is pressurised to a maximum of 1400 bars according to demand, and accumulates in the injection

1.5 Knock sensor

common rail. The pressure is accurately maintained in the fuel rail by a flow actuator located on the rear of the pump, the actuator being controlled by the engine management ECU. This arrangement keeps heat generation to a minimum, and improves engine output. The rail pressure is also maintained by the injectors themselves; short electrical pulses which are not long enough to open the injector allow fuel into the return (leak-off) circuit, and also the normal pulses which open the injectors cause a reduction in pressure. The ECU determines the exact timing and duration of the injection period according to engine operating conditions.

4 The four fuel injectors inject a homogeneous spray of fuel into the combustion chambers located in the cylinder head. The injectors operate sequentially according to the firing order of the cylinders, and each injector needle is lubricated by fuel, which accumulates in the spring chamber. Each injector has its own unique flow characteristics which are used by the system ECU to calculate the exact quantity of fuel to inject.

5 The knock sensor is mounted on the cylinder block to inform the ECU when the fuel injection timing needs to be retarded, in order to regain optimum engine efficiency **(see illustration)**.

TOOL TiP

The fuel system is very sensitive to contamination; even a small amount could be sufficient to cause extensive damage to fuel system components such as the high-pressure pump and electronic injectors. It is highly recommended that a set of fuel line plugs is obtained from a Renault dealership.

6 Provided that the specified maintenance is carried out, the fuel injection equipment will give long and trouble-free service. The main potential cause of damage to the high-pressure pump and injectors is dirt or water in the fuel **(see Tool tip)**.

7 Servicing of the high-pressure pump, injectors, and electronic equipment and sensors is very limited for the home mechanic, and any dismantling or adjustment other than that described in this Chapter must be entrusted to a Renault dealer or a diesel fuel injection specialist.

8 If a fault appears in the injection system, first ensure that all the system wiring connectors are securely connected and free of corrosion. Should the fault persist, a diagnostic connector (located at the front of the centre console) is incorporated in the engine management circuit, into which a special electronic diagnostic tester can be plugged **(see illustration)**. The vehicle should be taken to a Renault dealer or specialist who can test the system on a diagnostic tester. The tester will locate the fault quickly and simply, alleviating the need to test all the system components individually, which is a time-consuming operation that carries a risk of damaging the ECU. It is advisable to have any faulty components renewed by

the dealer as in many instances the tester is required to re-programme the ECU in the event of component or sensor renewal.

⚠️ *Warning: It is necessary to take certain precautions when working on the fuel system components, particularly the fuel injectors and high-pressure pump. Before carrying out any operations on the fuel system, refer to the precautions given in 'Safety first!' at the beginning of this manual, and to any additional warning notes at the start of the relevant Sections. Allow the engine to cool for 5 to 10 minutes to ensure the fuel pressure and temperature are at a minimum.*

2 Fuel pipe and connectors

1 Disconnect the cable from the negative battery terminal as described Chapter 5A Section 4 in before proceeding.
2 The fuel supply pipe connects the fuel pump in the fuel tank to the fuel filter on the engine.
3 Whenever you're working under the vehicle, be sure to inspect all fuel and evaporative emission pipes for leaks, kinks, dents and other damage. Always replace a damaged fuel pipe immediately.
4 If you find signs of dirt in the pipes during disassembly, disconnect all pipes and blow them out with compressed air. Inspect the fuel strainer on the fuel pump pick-up unit for damage and deterioration.

Steel tubing

5 It is critical that the fuel pipes be replaced with pipes of equivalent type and specification.
6 Some steel fuel pipes have threaded fittings. When loosening these fittings, hold the stationary fitting with a spanner while turning the union nut.

Plastic tubing

⚠️ *Warning: When removing or installing plastic fuel tubing, be careful not to bend or twist it too much, which can damage it. Also, plastic fuel tubing is NOT heat resistant, so keep it away from excessive heat.*

1.8 Diagnostic socket location

7 When replacing fuel system plastic tubing, use only original equipment replacement plastic tubing.

Flexible hoses

8 When replacing fuel system flexible hoses, use original equipment replacements, or hose to the same specification.
9 Don't route fuel hoses (or metal pipes) within 100 mm of the exhaust system or within 280 mm of the catalytic converter. Make sure that no rubber hoses are installed directly against the vehicle, particularly in places where there is any vibration. If allowed to touch some vibrating part of the vehicle, a hose can easily become chafed and it might start leaking. A good rule of thumb is to maintain a minimum of 8.0 mm clearance around a hose (or metal pipe) to prevent contact with the vehicle underbody.

Disconnecting fuel pipe fittings

10 Typical fuel pipe fittings (See Section 7, Chapter 4A).

3 Air cleaner assembly – removal and refitting

Removal

1 Remove the inlet pipe from the front panel by releasing the securing clip and pulling it free, then disconnect it from the air cleaner housing **(see illustrations)**. Release the wiring loom securing clip from the air inlet pipe, if required.

3.1a Release the pipe from the front panel...

3.1b ...and the air cleaner housing...

3.1c ...then remove the inlet pipe

3.2 Disconnect the wiring connector and slacken the hose clip

3.3a Undo the mounting bolt...

3.3b ...and remove the air cleaner housing...

3.3c ...releasing it from the rubber grommet in the mounting bracket

2 Disconnect the wiring connector from the air flow sensor, then slacken the securing clip, and disconnect the air outlet rubber hose from the rear of the air cleaner housing (see illustration).

3 Undo the mounting bolt on the inner wing panel and withdraw the air cleaner housing upwards, to release it from the rubber grommet in the transmission mounting bracket (see illustrations).

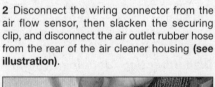

4.3 Remove the cover

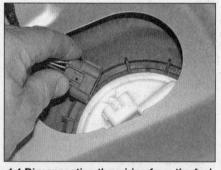

4.4 Disconnecting the wiring from the fuel gauge sender unit

4.6a Alignment arrows on the pump cover, fuel tank and locking ring

4.6b Using a home-made removal tool to unscrew the locking ring from the fuel tank

4.6c Removing the locking ring

Refitting

4 Refitting is a reversal of removal.

4 Fuel gauge sender unit – removal, testing and refitting

Warning: Refer to the warning note in Section 1 before proceeding.

Removal

1 Disconnect the battery negative lead as described in Chapter 5A Section 4.

2 Remove the rear seat, or rear seat cushion as described in Chapter 11 Section 22, for access to the fuel gauge sender unit cover.

3 Carefully prise the access cover from the floor to expose the fuel gauge sender unit (see illustration).

4 Disconnect the wiring connector, and tape it to the vehicle body, to prevent it disappearing behind the tank (see illustration).

5 The sender unit can only be accessed after the fuel tank has been removed. Remove the fuel tank as described in Section 5.

6 Noting the alignment arrows on the cover, locking ring and fuel tank, unscrew the locking ring and remove it from the tank. This can be accomplished by using a screwdriver on the raised ribs of the locking ring – carefully tap the screwdriver to turn the ring anti-clockwise until it can be unscrewed by hand. Alternatively a removal tool can be fabricated out of metal bar and two bolts (see illustrations).

7 Carefully lift the fuel gauge sender unit out of the fuel tank, taking great care not to damage the gauge sender arm, or to spill fuel in the interior of the vehicle. Remove the rubber sealing ring and check it for deterioration. If the pump is to remain out of the fuel tank for several hours, the locking ring should be refitted temporarily to prevent the fuel tank threads from distorting.

Testing

8 Note that the fuel gauge sender unit is only available as a complete assembly, however it is possible to test its operation and to remove it. To test the unit, disconnect the wiring plug from the cover and connect an ohmmeter to the two terminals.

9 With the assembly upright on the bench, measure the resistance of the sender unit at the different heights given in the Specifications. The resistances are approximate but it should be clear if the sender unit is not operating correctly.

10 To remove the sender unit, first release the wiring from the clips, then unclip and remove the cover from the main body.

11 Using a screwdriver, prise off the gauze filter from the bottom of the unit. Also recover the O-ring seal from the spring location column.

12 Carefully unclip the bottom section, then disconnect the wiring and slide out the sender unit and float.

Refitting

13 Ensure that the fuel gauge sender unit pick-up filter is clean and free of debris. Fit the new sealing ring to the top of the fuel tank.

14 Carefully manoeuvre the fuel gauge sender unit assembly into the fuel tank.

15 Align the arrow on the fuel gauge sender unit cover with the arrow on the fuel tank (the arrow must point to the rear of the vehicle), then refit the locking ring. Tighten the locking ring until the alignment marks on the unit and securing ring are aligned, then recheck that the fuel gauge sender unit cover and tank marks are all correctly aligned. **Note:** *If a suitable adapter is available tighten the locking ring to the specified torque.*

16 Refit the fuel tank.

17 Reconnect the wiring connector.

18 Reconnect the battery negative lead, and start the engine. Check the fuel gauge sender unit feed and return hoses for signs of leakage.

19 Refit the plastic access cover and the rear seat cushion.

5 Fuel tank – removal and refitting

 Warning: Refer to the warning note in Section 1 before proceeding.

Removal

1 Before removing the fuel tank, all fuel must be drained from it. Since a drain plug is not provided, it is preferable to carry out the

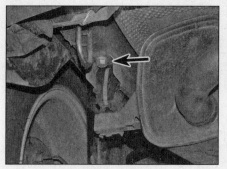
5.7a Remove the bolt...

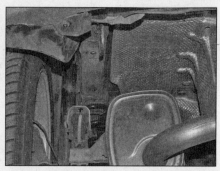
5.7b ...and lower the exhaust system

removal operation when the tank is nearly empty.

2 Remove the rear seat, or rear seat cushion (Chapter 11 Section 22), for access to the fuel pump cover.

3 Using a screwdriver, carefully prise the plastic access cover from the floor to expose the fuel pump.

4 Disconnect the wiring connector from the fuel pump, and tape the connector to the vehicle body, to prevent it disappearing behind the tank.

5 Disconnect the battery negative lead as described in Chapter 5A Section 4.

6 Chock the front wheels, then jack up the rear of the vehicle and support on axle stands (see *Jacking and vehicle support*).

7 Lower the exhaust system from its mountings and let it rest on the rear axle. There is no need to remove it from the vehicle **(see illustrations)**.

8 Remove the heat shield from above the exhaust **(see illustration)**.

9 Remove both roadwheels, disconnect and remove the handbrake cables as described in Chapter 9 Section 15. Unbolt the rear flexible hose support bracket **(see illustrations)**.

10 Unclip and remove the right-hand inner wing liner.

11 Working in the wheel arch, remove the tank retaining bolt and the hose clip from the fuel filler pipe **(see illustration)**. Disconnect the overflow pipe.

12 Place a trolley jack with an interposed block of wood beneath the tank, then raise the jack until it is supporting the weight of the tank.

13 Unscrew and remove the mounting bolts, then slowly lower the fuel tank out of position, disconnecting any other relevant pipes as they become accessible **(see illustration)**.

14 With the help of an assistant remove the tank from underneath the vehicle, working

5.8 Remove the rear heat shield

5.9a Remove the handbrake cables...

5.9b ...and the brake pipe support bracket

5.11 Remove the hose clip

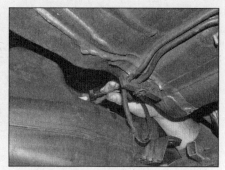
5.13 Disconnect the fuel lines as the tank is lowered

5.14 Work the fuel tank out and past the exhaust

6.5 The bleed valve is not designed to be opened, once closed

it around the exhaust as necessary **(see illustration)**. Separate the filler neck from the fuel tank as it is lowered.

15 If the tank is contaminated with sediment or water, remove the sender unit and swill the tank out with clean fuel. The tank is injection moulded from a synthetic material – if seriously damaged, it should be renewed. However, in certain cases, it may be possible to have small leaks or minor damage repaired. Seek the advice of a specialist before attempting to repair the fuel tank.

Refitting

16 Refitting is the reverse of the removal procedure, noting the following points:

a) When lifting the tank back into position, take care to ensure that the hoses are not trapped between the tank and vehicle body.

b) Ensure that all pipes and hoses are correctly routed. Make sure the sealing rings are in position in the quick-release fittings prior to fitting and make sure they are securely clipped in position.

c) On completion, refill the tank with a small amount of fuel, and check for signs of leakage prior to taking the vehicle out on the road.

---

6   Fuel system –
    priming and bleeding

 Warning: Refer to the precautions in Section 1 before proceeding. Do not attempt to bleed the

system by loosening any of the unions on the high-pressure circuit.
Note: *Priming of the fuel system after filter renewal will be improved if the filter is filled with clean diesel fuel before securing it to the filter head. To avoid spillages of fuel, keep the filter upright during refitting.*

1 After disconnecting part of the fuel supply system or running out of fuel, it is necessary to prime the system low-pressure circuit before restarting the engine.

2 All models are fitted with a hand operated priming bulb located next to the right-hand headlight.

3 Squeeze the priming bulb several times to purge the low-pressure circuit of air.

4 Attempt to start the engine normally, however, do not operate the starter motor for more than 5 seconds. If necessary, operate the starter motor in 4 to 5 second bursts followed by pauses of 8 to 10 seconds. As soon as the engine starts, let it run at fast idle speed until a regular idle speed is reached. If difficulty in purging the air from the system is experienced (engine may hunt), disconnect the blue high-pressure return pipe from the fuel filter and plug this hole, then place the end of the pipe in a container and continue to squeeze the priming bulb until the air is removed. Reconnect the return pipe and start the engine.

5 New low-pressure fuel lines are supplied with a bleed valve in the open position. The system can be bleed through these valves, however once closed **(see illustration)** they are not designed to be opened again (although it may be possible).

1 The engine management ECU uses the following inputs to calculate the recommended idle speed according to the varying load on the engine by peripheral electrical or mechanical components.

a) *Engine coolant temperature.*

b) *Battery voltage.*

c) *The gear selected.*

d) *Electrical consumers (heater fan, climate control system, thermoplungers, etc).*

2 At normal engine temperature with no electrical consumers switched on and neutral selected, the engine idle speed will be 850 rpm.

3 If the accelerator pedal potentiometer internal tracks are faulty, the ECU will override the idle speed to 1100 rpm, and the injection warning light will be illuminated on the instrument panel. If there is no output from the potentiometer, the idle speed will be 1300 rpm. In each case, if the brake pedal is depressed, the idle speed will revert to its normal level.

4 If there is an injector fault, the idle speed will be set to 1300 rpm and the warning light will be illuminated.

5 With Neutral, 1st or 2nd gear selected, the idle speed will be 850 rpm at an ambient temperature of more than 20°C; below this temperature the idle speed will increase accordingly. In 3rd, 4th or 5th gear, the idle speed will be 900 rpm.

6 Should the idle speed be incorrect, the car should be taken to a Renault dealer who will have the necessary diagnostic equipment to pin-point the faulty component responsible.

---

8   Accelerator pedal –
    removal and refitting

Removal

1 Remove the lower trim panel from under the steering column as described in Chapter 11, Section 28.

2 Disconnect the wiring plug from the top of the accelerator pedal **(see illustration)**.

3 Remove the two bolts that secure the accelerator pedal in position, then pull it downwards to release the locating peg, from the mounting bracket **(see illustration)**.

4 Withdraw the accelerator pedal.

5 Examine the pedal and pivot for signs of wear and renew as necessary.

Refitting

6 Refitting is a reversal of removal.

8.2 Disconnect the wiring connector

8.3 Undo the two bolts and remove pedal

9 Engine management ECU – removal and refitting

Note: *The engine management ECU is electronically-coded for the vehicle to which it is fitted, therefore new units are supplied without a code. If the ECU is being removed to enable a new unit to be fitted, the new unit must be programmed with the information from the old ECU by a Renault dealer.*

Removal

1 The ECU is located on the left-hand side of the engine compartment **(see illustration)** mounted next to the strut tower.
2 First disconnect the battery negative lead (refer to Chapter 5A Section 4).
3 Remove the air filter housing, as described in Section 3.
4 Release the locking clips and remove the three electrical connectors from the ECU **(see illustrations)**.
5 Remove the mounting nuts **(see illustration)**, and withdraw the control unit from the engine compartment.

Refitting

6 Refitting is a reverse of the removal procedure ensuring that the wiring is securely reconnected. After the battery is reconnected the ECU must be adapted to the vehicle. To do this:
a) *Turn on the ignition and wait for a minimum of 30 seconds. The throttle body will operate and adapt the maximum and minimum position of the throttle plate.*
b) *Allow the vehicle to idle until the normal operating temperature is reached.*
c) *Drive the vehicle in third gear with an engine speed of between 3000 to 5000 rpm. Decelerate, without braking for at least 5 seconds.*
d) *Drive the vehicle in third gear with an engine speed of between 2000 to 4000 rpm and decelerate without braking for at least 5 seconds*
Note: *The ECU will continue to adapt to the engine for several drive cycles. During this time the idle speed and acceleration may be compromised.*

9.1 Location of ECU

9.4a Release the locking clips...

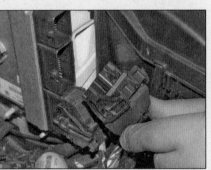

9.4b ...and disconnect the wiring plugs

9.5 Undo the four mounting nuts

10 High-pressure pump – removal and refitting

 Warning: Refer to the warning note in Section 1 before proceeding.
Caution: Before starting work, allow the engine to cool for 5 to 10 minutes, to ensure the fuel pressure and temperature are at a minimum.
Note: *The high-pressure pump is removed after first removing the timing belt as described in Chapter. However, if the special Renault locking tools Mot. 1525/1525-02/1606 are available, it is possible to remove the pump leaving the sprocket and timing belt supported independently. Using the latter method will prove quicker, as it will not be necessary to renew the timing belt, but note*

that this is not possible on the 106 bhp engine; the timing belt must be removed on these engines. All high-pressure pipes removed must be renewed as a matter of course.
Note: *Cleanliness is of critical importance when working on the fuel system of any modern diesel engine. The smallest speck of grit or dirt can cause extensive damage to the pump and injectors. Always clean thoroughly the pump and injector unions before dismantling. Immediately plug and seal all pipes and components. Components that are removed from the engine should immediately be placed in clean plastic bags.*

Removal

1 Disconnect the battery negative lead as described in Chapter 5A Section 4.
2 Remove the engine cover, then undo the mounting bolt, release the securing clips and remove the turbocharger supply pipe from the top of the engine **(see illustrations)**.

10.2a Undo the air intake pipe securing bolt...

10.2b ...release the securing clips...

10.2c ...and remove the air intake pipe

10.7 Undo the two mounting bolts from the dipstick tube

10.8a Remove the bolts...

10.8b ...release the clips...

10.8c ...and remove the cover

10.10a Release the fuel pipes from the top of the pump...

10.10b ...and remove the high-pressure pipe

3 Jack up the right-hand front of the car and support on axle stands. Remove the front right wheel, wheel arch liner and front bumper, as described in Chapter 11 Section 6.

4 Remove the auxiliary drivebelt with reference to Chapter 1B Section 10.

5 Support the right-hand end of the engine with a support bar across the engine compartment, with a hoist, or alternatively with a jack and block of wood beneath the sump.

6 Remove the timing belt, as described in Chapter 2C Section 6.

7 Undo the two retaining bolts and then move the dipstick tube forwards **(see illustration)**.

8 Undo the two retaining bolts at the rear of the cover, then release the two clips at the front and remove the protective cover **(see illustrations)**.

9 Loosen the alternator lower bolt and remove the top bolt. Tip the alternator away from the engine.

10 Place a clean rag over the alternator and then remove the fuel pipes from the pump **(see illustrations)**. Remove the high-pressure outlet pipe. Seal the pump and pipes immediately. Do not allow fuel to contaminate the alternator.

11 Unclip and remove the electrical connectors from the pump, the injectors and the glow plugs **(see illustrations)**.

12 Unbolt and remove the pump mounting bracket and then undo the pump mounting bolts. Check with Renault to make sure the sprocket can be removed from your type of fuel pump. Some new pumps, are supplied complete with a new sprocket already fitted. If required, place the pump in a vice and remove the sprocket, by using a strap wrench and a

ring spanner to do this. A puller will then be required to remove the sprocket from the pump

Refitting

Note: *The manufacturers stipulate that the high-pressure pipe must be renewed whenever it is removed.*

13 Refitting is a reversal of removal, but take care not to place the new high-pressure pipe under any stress. If fitting a new pump, it is highly recommended that the pump is primed with diesel on the bench before fitting.

14 New high-pressure pipes are supplied with a lubricant for the threads on the pipe. If no lubricant is supplied the pipes are self-lubricating and lubricant should not be applied.

15 Tighten all nuts and bolts to the specified torque and angle as applicable. When

10.11a Disconnect the wiring from the pump...

10.11b ...the injectors...

10.11c ...and the glow plugs

tightening the pipe union nuts onto the injectors, counter-hold the injectors with a further spanner. When angle-tightening the high-pressure pump sprocket nut, use an angle protractor. Prime and bleed the fuel system as described in Section 6.

11 High-pressure pump components – removal and refitting

Caution: Before starting work on the following components, allow the engine to cool for 5 to 10 minutes, to ensure the fuel pressure and temperature are at a minimum.

1 Disconnect the battery negative lead as described in Chapter 5A Section 4.

Flow actuator

2 Remove the engine top cover, turbocharger supply pipes and the protective pump cover (see Section 10).
3 Disconnect the wiring from the flow actuator (inner) and fuel temperature sensor (outer) located on the rear of the high-pressure pump.
4 Wrap some cloth rag over the fuel return pipe, then disconnect it by depressing the quick release fitting.
5 Wrap some cloth rag over the union nuts, then unscrew them and remove the high-pressure pipe for No 4 injector. **Note:** *The manufacturers stipulate that the pipe is renewed whenever removed.* Plug or tape over the fuel apertures.
6 Disconnect the wiring from the glow plugs and injectors for cylinders 3 and 4.
7 Unscrew the retaining bracket bolts and withdraw the flow actuator from the high-pressure pump. Do not pull on the wiring connector, but ease it out by hand only.
8 Only remove the new unit from its packaging just before fitting it, and do not lubricate it with used fuel or grease.
9 Carefully locate the actuator on the pump, making sure that the seal is not damaged. Insert the mounting bolts and tighten to the specified torque.
10 Reconnect all wiring, then fit the new high-pressure pipe and tighten the union nuts to the specified torque.
11 Refit the fuel return pipe and engine top cover.

Fuel temperature sensor

12 Remove the engine top cover.
13 Disconnect the wiring from the fuel temperature sensor located on the rear of the high-pressure pump. The sensor is nearest the outer edge of the pump.
14 Wrap some cloth rag over the sensor, then unscrew and remove it and recover the O-ring seal.
15 Lubricate the new O-ring seal with the lubricant supplied with the new sensor, then locate it on the sensor.

12.3 Thoroughly clean the around the injectors

16 Fit the sensor and seal to the pump and tighten to the specified torque.
17 Reconnect the wiring and refit the engine top cover.

Venturi

18 Remove the engine top cover.
19 Wrap some cloth rag over the fuel return pipe, then disconnect it by depressing the quick-release fitting.
20 Disconnect the injector leak-off pipe from the high-pressure pump.
21 Unscrew the bolts and remove the venturi from the pump. Recover the O-ring seal.
22 Lubricate the new O-ring seal with the lubricant supplied with the new venturi, then fit the unit to the pump and tighten to the specified torque.
23 Reconnect the leak-off pipe and return pipe.
24 Refit the engine top cover.

12 Fuel injectors – testing, removal and refitting

⚠ *Warning: Exercise extreme caution when working on the high-pressure fuel system. Do not attempt to test the fuel injectors or disconnect the high-pressure lines with the engine running. Never expose the hands or any part of the body to injector spray, as the high working pressure can*

12.5 Release the return pipes from the injectors

12.4 Disconnecting the fuel injector wiring

cause the fuel to penetrate the skin, with possibly fatal results. You are strongly advised to have any work which involves testing the injectors under pressure carried out by a dealer or fuel injection specialist. Refer to the precautions given in Section 1 of this Chapter before proceeding. After switching off the engine, allow the engine to cool for 5 to 10 minutes to allow the fuel pressure to drop before disconnecting any of the high-pressure fuel pipes.
Note: *Each new injector is supplied with a unique 16-digit code which specifies its flow characteristics. This code must be programmed into the engine management ECU with a special diagnostic tool, therefore this work should be entrusted to a Renault dealer or suitably-equipped garage.*

Testing

1 It is not possible to test the fuel injectors without specialist equipment, therefore, if they are thought to be faulty, consult a Renault dealer or diesel specialist.

Removal

Note: *Take care not to allow dirt into the injectors or fuel pipes during this procedure; clean around the area before commencing work. Note that all high-pressure pipes removed must be renewed as a matter of course. The injector flame shield washers must also be renewed.*

2 Disconnect the battery negative leadas described in Chapter 5A Section 4.
3 Remove the engine top cover, as described in Section 10. then thoroughly clean the area around the injectors **(see illustration)**.
4 Disconnect the fuel injector wiring connectors **(see illustration)**.
5 Using a screwdriver, release the securing clips and disconnect the fuel return pipes from the top of the injectors **(see illustration)**. Tape over or plug all fuel apertures to prevent entry of dust and dirt.
6 While holding the injector union with one spanner, unscrew the high-pressure pipe union nuts with a further spanner **(see illustration)**. Similarly, unscrew the union nuts from the fuel rail, then remove the pipes. Move the nuts and olives along the pipes

12.6 Unscrew the high-pressure pipe union nuts

when releasing the pipes from the rail and injectors.

7 Unscrew the bolt securing each injector clamp plate to the cylinder head. Lift off the clamp plates and remove the injectors then recover the flame shield washers between the injectors and the cylinder head. Take care not to drop the injectors or allow the needles at their tips to become damaged. The injectors are precision-made to fine limits and must not be handled roughly. In particular, do not mount them in a bench vice. It is recommended that the injectors are stored vertically at all times (see illustrations).

Refitting

8 Clean the cylinder head, taking care to prevent foreign matter entering the fuel apertures. The injectors can be cleaned with a lint-free cloth soaked in brake cleaning fluid or fresh diesel. Do not clean them with a wire brush or emery cloth.

9 Fit new sealing shims between the injectors and the cylinder head. Insert the injectors then fit the clamp plates. Tighten the clamp plate bolts to the specified torque.

10 Refit the leak-off pipes, then fit the new high-pressure fuel pipes together with the retaining clips. Before fitting the new pipes, lubricate the threads of the union nuts with oil from the sachet provided, and finger-tighten the nuts before tightening them to the specified torque. Use pliers to fit the retaining clips onto the fuel pipes.

11 Reconnect the fuel injector wiring.

12 Fit the new fuel return pipe to the high-pressure pump and fuel rail.

12.7a Unscrew the clamp securing bolt

13 Refit the engine oil level dipstick guide, the clip on the fuel rail, and the engine top cover.

14 Reconnect the battery negative lead.

15 Start the engine. If difficulty is experienced, bleed the fuel system as described in Section 6.

13 Injector rail (common rail) – removal and refitting

⚠️ *Warning: Refer to the warning note in Section 1 before proceeding. After switching off the engine, allow several minutes for the fuel pressure so subside before disconnecting any of the high-pressure fuel pipes.*

Note: *Take care not to allow dirt into the fuel pipes during this procedure; clean around the area before commencing work. Note that all high-pressure pipes removed must be renewed as a matter of course.*

Note: *Two types of fuel rail are fitted: spherical or linear. The removal procedure is the same for both types.*

Removal

1 Disconnect the battery negative lead as described in Chapter 5A Section 4.

2 Remove the engine top cover.

3 Disconnect the following wiring:

a) *Flow actuator on the rear of the high-pressure pump.*

b) *Fuel temperature sensor on the rear of the high-pressure pump.*

c) *Fuel injectors.*

d) *Heater (glow) plugs.*

4 Disconnect the fuel supply and return pipes from the high-pressure pump.

5 Disconnect the fuel leak-off return pipe from the high-pressure pump.

6 Unclip the wiring loom conduit from the high-pressure fuel rail.

7 Remove the engine oil level dipstick guide and tape over the hole.

8 Disconnect the wiring from the fuel pressure sensor on the fuel rail.

9 Release the clips from the two pairs of high-pressure injector pipes.

12.7b A suitable storage rack can be easily fabricated

10 While holding the injector central unions with one spanner, unscrew the high-pressure pipe union nuts with a further spanner. As a precaution against remaining pressure in the pipes, first wrap them loosely in cloth rag. Take care not to damage the leak-off stubs on the injectors. Similarly, unscrew the union nuts from the fuel rail, then remove the pipes. Move the nuts and olives along the pipes when releasing the pipes from the rail and injectors.

11 Tape over or plug all fuel apertures to prevent entry of dust and dirt into the fuel system.

12 Unbolt and remove the fuel rail. Note that the pressure sensor cannot be separated from the fuel rail; if the sensor fails, the complete rail must be renewed.

Refitting

13 Refitting is a reversal of removal, but take care not to place the new high-pressure pipe under any stress. Before fitting the new pipe, lubricate the threads of the union nuts with oil from the sachet provided, and finger-tighten the nuts before tightening them to the specified torque. When tightening the pipe union nuts onto the injectors, counter-hold the injectors with a further spanner.

14 Manifolds – removal and refitting

Removal

1 The inlet manifold is incorporated into the cylinder head and therefore cannot be removed separately. To remove the exhaust manifold, first apply the handbrake, then jack up the front of the vehicle and support it on axle stands (see *Jacking and vehicle support*).

2 Disconnect the exhaust downpipe from the exhaust manifold and support it to one side with reference to Section 18.

3 Remove the turbocharger as described in Section 16. If the reason of removing the manifold is simply to renew the gasket, the turbocharger can remain attached to the manifold.

4 Loosen the two clamps, then remove the EGR metal tube between the inlet and exhaust manifolds. The manufacturers recommend that the metal tube and clamps are renewed as a matter of course.

5 Unscrew the mounting bolts and remove the EGR unit from the inlet manifold.

6 Progressively unscrew the mounting nuts and remove the exhaust manifold from the studs on the cylinder head. Recover the metal gasket (see illustrations).

Refitting

7 Clean the surfaces of the cylinder head and exhaust manifold.

8 Locate a new gasket on the cylinder head studs.

14.6a Removing the exhaust manifold together with the turbocharger

14.6b Removing the exhaust manifold gasket

9 Refit the exhaust manifold and finger-tighten the retaining nuts. Tighten the nuts to the specified torque, working in a clockwise direction from the centre of the manifold.

10 Refit the EGR unit to the inlet manifold and tighten the mounting nuts to the specified torque.

11 Fit the new metal tube between the inlet and exhaust manifolds and secure with new clamps. Renault technicians use a special tool to tighten the clamps, however, it should be possible to tighten them using pliers and a screwdriver if care is taken.

12 Refit the turbocharger with reference to Section 16.

13 Refit the exhaust downpipe to the manifold with reference to Section 18.

14 Lower the vehicle to the ground.

15 Turbocharger – description

1 A turbocharger increases engine efficiency by raising the pressure in the inlet manifold above atmospheric pressure. Instead of the air simply being sucked into the cylinders, it is forced in. Additional fuel is supplied in proportion to the increased air intake.

2 Energy for the operation of the turbocharger comes from the exhaust gas. The gas flows through a specially-shaped housing (the turbine housing) and in so doing, spins the turbine wheel. The turbine wheel is attached to a shaft, at the end of which is another vaned wheel known as the compressor

wheel. The compressor wheel spins in its own housing and compresses the inducted air on the way to the inlet manifold.

3 Between the turbocharger and the inlet manifold on certain engine types, the compressed air passes through an intercooler. This is an air-to-air heat exchanger, mounted behind the front bumper, next to the air conditioning condenser and the coolant radiator. The purpose of the intercooler is to remove some of the heat gained in being compressed from the inducted air. Because cooler air is denser, removal of this heat further increases engine efficiency.

4 Boost pressure (the pressure in the inlet manifold) is limited by a wastegate, which diverts the exhaust gas away from the turbine wheel in response to a pressure-sensitive actuator. Turbocharging pressure is controlled by a pressure sensor located on the air cleaner outlet **(see illustration)**.

5 The turbo shaft is pressure-lubricated by an oil feed pipe from the main oil gallery. The shaft 'floats' on a cushion of oil. A drain pipe returns the oil to the sump.

Precautions

• The turbocharger operates at extremely high speeds and temperatures. Certain precautions must be observed to avoid premature failure of the turbo or injury to the operator.

• Do not race the engine immediately after start-up, especially if it is cold. Give the oil a few seconds to circulate.

• Always allow the engine to return to idle speed before switching it off – do not blip the

throttle and switch off, as this will leave the turbo spinning without lubrication.

• Allow the engine to idle for several minutes before switching off after a high speed run.

• Observe the recommended intervals for oil and filter changing, and use a reputable oil of the specified quality. Neglect of oil changing, or use of inferior oil, can cause carbon formation on the turbo shaft and subsequent failure.

> ⚠ *Warning: Do not operate the turbo with any parts exposed. Foreign objects falling onto the rotating vanes could cause excessive damage and (if ejected) personal injury.*

16 Turbocharger – removal and refitting

Note: *New oil supply pipe O-rings and copper washers must be used on refitting.*

Removal

1 Apply the handbrake, then jack up the front of the vehicle, and support securely on axle stands (see *Jacking and vehicle support*). Remove the right-hand front roadwheel.

2 Disconnect the battery negative lead as described in Chapter 5A Section 4.

3 Remove the engine top cover, then remove the air cleaner unit as described in Section 3.

4 At the rear of the engine, disconnect the wiring from the downstream air temperature sensor and EGR solenoid valve.

5 Disconnect the tube from the turbocharger pressure adjustment valve on the air duct.

6 Loosen the clips and disconnect the air ducts from between the EGR unit and turbocharger.

7 Unbolt and remove the engine lifting eye from the right-hand rear of the cylinder head.

8 Unscrew the bolt and remove the air inlet metal tube.

9 Unscrew the four nuts securing the catalytic converter to the turbocharger **(see illustration)**.

10 Working under the front of the car, unscrew the nuts and disconnect the intermediate pipe flexible flange from the catalytic converter. Also, unbolt the strut from the side of the catalytic converter and block **(see illustration)**.

15.4 Turbocharger pressure sensor

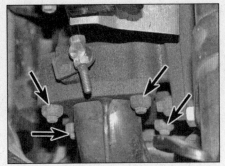

16.9 Nuts securing the catalytic converter to the turbocharger

16.10 Unbolt the strut from the side of the catalytic converter

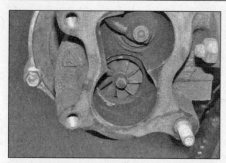

16.11 View of the turbocharger wastegate (upper) and vanes (lower) with the catalytic converter removed

16.13a Removing the oil supply pipe and copper sealing rings from the turbocharger

16.13b Removing the oil supply pipe from the cylinder head

16.14a Oil return pipe flange bolts on the bottom of the turbocharger

16.14b Removing the oil return pipe

14 Unscrew the bolts and detach the oil return pipe from the bottom of the turbocharger – if necessary, remove the pipe from the cylinder block **(see illustrations)**.

15 Unscrew the turbocharger upper and lower mounting nuts **(see illustrations)**, then remove the turbocharger together with the oil return pipe from the exhaust manifold. With the assembly on the bench, remove the oil return pipe. Do not attempt to separate the inlet and exhaust sections of the turbocharger.

Refitting

16 Refitting is a reversal of removal, but renew any damaged hose clamps, and use new turbocharger-to-exhaust manifold nuts which should be tightened to the specified torque. Fit new oil supply pipe O-rings and copper seals, then apply Loctite Frenetanch (or similar sealant) to the union threads before refitting the pipe and tightening the union nuts to the specified torque. Fit a new gasket to the top of the oil return pipe, and new O-ring seals to the grooves in the bottom of the pipe **(see illustrations)**. On completion, the following procedure must be observed before starting the engine in order to establish initial oil pressure in the turbocharger.

a) Disconnect the wiring from the fuel injectors.
b) Crank the engine on the starter motor until the instrument panel oil pressure warning light goes out (this may take several seconds).
c) Reconnect the wiring to the injectors, then start the engine using the normal procedure.

11 Unbolt the catalytic converter and lower it as far as possible **(see illustration)** or remove it completely.
12 In the engine compartment, unbolt the heat shield from the EGR solenoid valve.

13 Unscrew the union and disconnect the oil supply pipe from the turbocharger, collect the copper sealing rings, then unscrew the union nut and disconnect the pipe from the cylinder head **(see illustrations)**.

16.15a Turbocharger upper mounting nuts...

16.15b ...and lower mounting nut

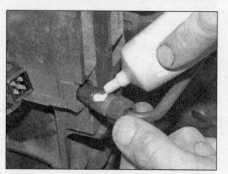

16.16a Applying sealant to the threads of the oil supply pipe union

16.16b Fit a new gasket to the top of the oil return pipe...

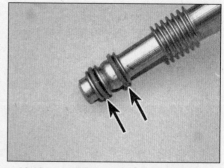

16.16c ...and fit new O-ring seals to the grooves in the bottom of the pipe

17.3a Remove the outer section...

17.3b ...middle section...

17.3c ...and inner section

d) Run the engine at idle speed, and check the turbocharger oil unions for leakage.
e) After the engine has been run, check the engine oil level, and top-up if necessary.

17 Intercooler – removal and refitting

Removal

1 The intercooler is located behind the front bumper, to the right-hand side of the air conditioning condenser and radiator.
2 Remove the front bumper as described in Chapter 11 Section 6.
3 Remove the plastic air intake cowling from the front of the intercooler, this is removed in three separate pieces (**see illustrations**).
4 Remove the headlight units, as described in Chapter 12 Section 10.
5 Release the three locating pegs, undo the two retaining bolts and remove the front crossmember from the top of the intercooler/radiator (**see illustrations**). The bonnet release cable will still be attached, so just move the crossmember to one side.
6 Undo the retaining bolts and disconnect the air-conditioning pipe mounting brackets from the top and bottom of the intercooler (**see illustrations**).
7 Loosen the clips and disconnect the air inlet and outlet ducts from the top and bottom of the intercooler (**see illustrations**).

8 Release the intercooler from the side of the radiator, lift it upwards to release it from the lower rubber mounting, and then maneuver it downwards to remove (**see illustration**).

17.5a Remove the locating pegs...

17.5b ...undo the bolts and remove the crossmember

Refitting

9 Refitting is a reversal of removal, but tighten all nuts and bolts to the specified torque where

17.6a Slacken and remove the lower...

17.6b ...and upper pipe mounting brackets

17.7a Release the upper hose...

17.7b ...and lower hose

17.8 Lower the intercooler out

17.9 Make sure rubber mounting is located in subframe

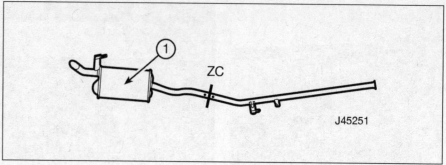

18.1 Factory-supplied exhaust system showing rear silencer (1) and cutting zone (ZC)

given and make sure the rubber mounting is located correctly in the lower crossmember **(see illustration)**.

18 Exhaust system –
general information and component renewal

General information

1 On new vehicles the exhaust system consists of just two sections; the catalytic converter (attached to the exhaust manifold), and the remaining system consisting of the intermediate pipe, tailpipe and silencer **(see illustration)**. The catalytic converter is attached to the intermediate pipe by a flexible flange joint.

18.9 Removing the catalytic converter

2 The rear section of the exhaust is located above the rear suspension; the intermediate pipe and tailpipe may be renewed separately by cutting the intermediate pipe with a hacksaw. The system is suspended through-out its entire length by rubber mountings.

Removal

3 To remove a part of the system, first jack up the front or rear of the car, and support it on axle stands (see *Jacking and vehicle support*). Alternatively, position the car over an inspection pit, or on car ramps. Where fitted, remove the engine compartment undertray.

Catalytic converter

4 Chock the rear wheels and firmly apply the handbrake, then jack up the front of the vehicle and support it on axle stands (see *Jacking and vehicle support*). Remove the right-hand front roadwheel.
5 Remove the engine undertray and top cover, then remove the air cleaner assembly as described in Section 3.
6 Working from above, unscrew the four nuts securing the catalytic converter to the exhaust manifold.
7 Remove the right-hand front driveshaft as described in Chapter 8 Section 2.
8 Working beneath the car, loosen the clamp, then unscrew the two mounting nuts and disconnect the exhaust intermediate pipe

flexible flange from the catalytic converter. Lower it as far as possible.
9 Unbolt the side strut from the catalytic converter, then unscrew and remove the rear mounting bolt from the rear strut. Withdraw the catalytic converter downwards from the engine compartment **(see illustration)**.

Diesel particulate filter

10 Some models are fitted with a diesel particulate filter **(see illustration)**. The filter is designed to remove particulates (soot) from the exhaust gas stream. When the filter reaches a preset level of saturation the engine management control unit will implement a 'regeneration' mode by altering the fueling so that the temperature of the filter is raised high enough to burn off the accumulated soot particles.
11 The saturation level of the filter is monitored by a pair of pressure sensors. When the pressure difference between the sensors reaches a certain level regeneration takes place. For this to happen the engine must be at normal operating temperature and the vehicle must driven at over 40 mph for a minimum of 60 miles. For most vehicles this will happen automatically, but for vehicles consistently used for short journeys regeneration may never take place.
12 When the filter is in danger of becoming blocked a warning light will appear on the

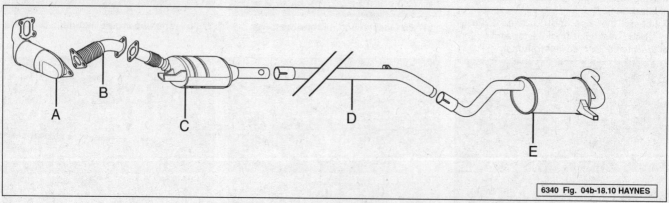

18.10 Diesel exhaust system (with a particulate filter)

A Catalytic converter
B Flexible pipe

C Particulate filter
D Intermediate pipe

E Rear silencer

instrument panel. It is important that the vehicle is then driven for at least 60 miles at an average speed of at least 40 mph. Failure to do this within a set time will illuminate the 'spanner' symbol on the instrument panel. The symbol will be accompanied with a 'Check antipollution' message. At this point the filter can only be regenerated with a forced regeneration using a diagnostic tool. Renault's Clip diagnostic tool can perform this function. Other diagnostic tools may also offer this function.

13 To remove the filter remove the pressure sensor pipe and the temperature sensor. Remove the intermediate pipe (as described below) and then remove the filter from the front flexible pipe. Support the filter and then remove the support bracket bolt. Remove the filter and dispose of the gasket – a new one must be fitted.

Intermediate pipe

14 Working beneath the car, loosen the clamp, then unscrew the two mounting nuts and disconnect the exhaust intermediate pipe flexible flange from the catalytic converter.

15 If the original rear section is fitted, it must be cut in half using either a hacksaw or pipe cutter. Locate the cutting area which is situated approximately midway between the rear silencer and intermediate mounting. The cutting point is marked with two circular punch marks on the side of the pipe. The punch marks are 9.0 mm apart and the exhaust sectionshould be cut at the mid-point between the two punch marks. **Note:** *Ensure that the exhaust pipe is cut squarely, or else it will be difficult to obtain a gas-tight seal when the exhaust is refitted.*

16 With the intermediate pipe cut, withdraw the intermediate exhaust section from under the vehicle.

17 If the rear section is in two halves, unscrew the bolt and slide the clamp sleeve on to the rear section then release the rubber mountings and withdraw the intermediate section from under the vehicle.

Rear tailpipe and silencer

18 If the original rear section is fitted, follow the instructions given in paragraph 11.

19 If the rear section is in two halves, unscrew the bolt and slide the clamp sleeve on to the intermediate section then release the rubber mountings and withdraw the tailpipe and silencer from under the vehicle.

Heat shield(s)

20 The heat shields are secured to the underbody by various nuts and bolts. Each shield can be removed separately but note that they overlap making it necessary to loosen another section first. If a shield is being removed to gain access to a component located behind it, it may prove sufficient in some cases to remove the retaining nuts and/or bolts and simply lower the shield without disturbing the exhaust system. Otherwise remove the exhaust section as described earlier.

Refitting

21 Each section is refitted by reversing the removal sequence, noting the following points:

a) Ensure that all traces of corrosion have been removed from the joints.

b) Inspect the rubber mountings for signs of damage or deterioration, and renew as necessary.

c) When reconnecting the intermediate pipe to the tailpipe, apply a smear of exhaust system jointing paste (Renault recommend the use of Sodicam) to the sleeve inner surface, to ensure a gas-tight seal. Make sure both inner ends of the cut pipe are positioned squarely against the stop of the clamp sleeve. Position the sleeve bolt vertically on the left-hand side of the pipe and securely tighten the nut until it is heard to click; the clamp bolt has a groove in it to ensure that the nut is correctly tightened (equivalent to a tightening torque of approximately 25 Nm/18 lbf ft).

d) On models fitted with a particulate filter refit the sensors and if a forced regeneration has been performed replace the filter flexible mountings.

e) Prior to tightening the exhaust system fasteners, ensure that all rubber mountings are correctly located, and that there is adequate clearance between the exhaust system and vehicle underbody.

Chapter 4 Part C
Emissions control systems

Contents

Degrees of difficulty

Easy, suitable for novice with little experience	Fairly easy, suitable for beginner with some experience	Fairly difficult, suitable for competent DIY mechanic	Difficult, suitable for experienced DIY mechanic	Very difficult, suitable for expert DIY or professional

Specifications

General

Oxygen (lambda) sensor voltage at 850°C (petrol engines):
   Rich mixture . . . .   > 625 mV
   Lean mixture . . . .   0 to 80 mV
Oxygen (lambda) sensor resistance at ambient temperature . . . .   3 to 15 ohms

Torque wrench setting

	Nm	lbf ft
Exhaust clamps (sleeves)	25	18
Oxygen (lambda) sensor	44	32
Particulate filter pressure sensor	21	15
Particulate filter temperature sensor	44	32

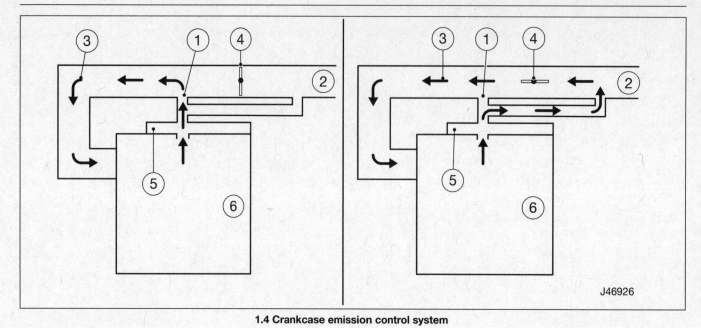

1.4 Crankcase emission control system

1 Calibrated choke	3 Inlet manifold	5 Vapour recovery plate
2 Air inlet	4 Throttle plate	6 Engine

1 General information and precautions

Petrol models

1 All petrol engines are designed to use unleaded petrol and also have various other features built into the fuel system to help minimise harmful emissions.

2 All models are equipped with a crankcase emissions control system, a catalytic converter and an evaporative emissions control system.

3 The emissions control systems function as follows.

Crankcase emissions control

4 To reduce the emission of unburned hydrocarbons from the crankcase into the atmosphere, the engine is sealed and the blow-by gases and oil vapour are drawn from inside the crankcase into the inlet manifold or throttle body to be burned by

1.7 The oxygen sensors on the 0.9 litre turbo petrol engine

the engine during normal combustion **(see illustration)**.

5 Under all conditions the gases are forced out of the crankcase by the (relatively) higher crankcase pressure.

6 The crankcase ventilation hoses and restrictors should be periodically cleaned to ensure correct operation of the system.

Exhaust emissions control

7 To minimise the amount of pollutants which escape into the atmosphere, all models are fitted with a catalytic converter in the exhaust system. The system is of the closed loop type, in which an oxygen (lambda) sensor **(see illustration)** in the exhaust system provides the fuel injection/ignition system ECU with constant feedback, enabling the ECU to adjust the mixture to provide the best possible conditions for the converter to operate. To comply with legislation all petrol vehicles also have an oxygen sensor fitted after the catalytic converter. This sensor monitors the efficiency of the converter.

8 The oxygen sensor has a heating element built-in that is controlled by the ECU through the sensor relay to bring the sensor's tip to an efficient operating temperature quickly. The sensor's tip is sensitive to oxygen and sends the ECU a varying voltage depending on the amount of oxygen in the exhaust gases; if the inlet air/fuel mixture is too rich, the exhaust gases are low in oxygen so the sensor sends a low voltage signal, the voltage rising as the mixture weakens and the amount of oxygen rises in the exhaust gases. Peak conversion efficiency of all major pollutants occurs if the inlet air/fuel mixture is maintained at the chemically correct ratio for the complete combustion of petrol of 14.7 parts (by weight) of air to 1 part of fuel (the 'stoichiometric'

ratio). The sensor output voltage alters in a large step at this point, the ECU using the signal change as a reference point and correcting the inlet air/fuel mixture accordingly by altering the fuel injector pulse width.

Evaporative emissions control

9 To minimise the escape into the atmosphere of unburned hydrocarbons, an evaporative emissions control system is also fitted to all models **(see illustration)**. The fuel tank filler cap is sealed and a charcoal canister is fitted. The canister collects the petrol vapours generated in the tank when the car is parked and stores them until they can be cleared from the canister (under the control of the fuel injection/ignition system ECU) via the purge valve into the inlet manifold to be burned by the engine during normal combustion.

10 To ensure that the engine runs correctly when it is cold and/or idling and to protect the catalytic converter from the effects of an over-rich mixture, the purge control valve is not opened by the ECU until the engine has warmed-up, and the engine is under load; the valve solenoid is then modulated on and off to allow the stored vapour to pass into the inlet manifold.

Diesel models

11 All diesel engine models are designed to meet strict emission requirements and are also equipped with a crankcase emissions control system. In addition to this, all models are fitted with an unregulated catalytic converter to reduce harmful exhaust emissions. To further reduce emissions, an exhaust gas recirculation (EGR) system is also fitted. Some models have a Diesel Particulate Filter (DPF) fitted (see Chapter 4B Section 18 for a full description of the particulate filter).

12 The emissions control systems function as follows.

Crankcase emissions control

13 To reduce the emission of unburned hydrocarbons from the crankcase into the atmosphere, the engine is sealed and the blow-by gases and oil vapour are drawn from inside the crankcase, through the cylinder head cover, then through a pressure sensitive recirculation valve into the turbocharger. From the turbocharger, the gases enter the inlet manifold to be burned by the engine during normal combustion **(see illustration)**.

14 There are no restrictors in the system hoses, since the minimal depression in the inlet manifold remains constant during all engine operating conditions.

Exhaust emissions control

15 To minimise the amount of pollutants which escape into the atmosphere, an unregulated catalytic converter is fitted in the exhaust system. The catalytic converter consists of a canister containing a fine mesh impregnated with a catalyst material, over which the exhaust gases pass. The catalyst speeds up the oxidation of harmful carbon monoxide, unburnt hydrocarbons and soot, effectively reducing the quantity of harmful products reaching the atmosphere. The catalytic converter operates remotely in the exhaust system, and there is no oxygen sensor as fitted to the petrol engines.

Exhaust gas recirculation system

16 The system is designed to recirculate small quantities of exhaust gas into the inlet tract, and therefore into the combustion process **(see illustration overleaf)**, reducing the level of oxides of nitrogen present in the final exhaust gas which is released into the atmosphere. The system is controlled by the engine management ECU which uses several sensors to determine when to switch the system on and off. The system is switched on if:

a) *The air temperature is greater than 15°C and the coolant temperature is greater than 70°C.*
b) *The air temperature is greater than 50°C and the coolant temperature is greater than 40°C.*
c) *The engine speed is between 850 and 1000 rpm.*
d) *The injected diesel fuel flow is between 2.0 and 5.0 mg/stroke.*
e) *The atmospheric pressure is between 980 and 1000 mbars.*

17 The system is switched off if the battery voltage is less than 9 volts, if the engine speed is less than 500 rpm, the mapping (engine speed/load) exceeds a given threshold, or the air conditioning compressor is activated.

18 The volume of exhaust gas recirculated is controlled by an electrically-operated exhaust gas recirculation (EGR) valve on the exhaust manifold, activated by the engine management ECU.

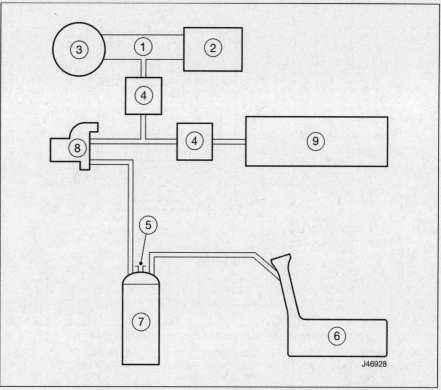

1.9 Evaporative emission control system – 1.2 litre petrol engine shown

1 Air filter outlet	4 Non-return valve	7 Charcoal canister
2 Air filter	5 Breather	8 Solenoid valve
3 Turbocharger	6 Fuel tank	9 Inlet manifold

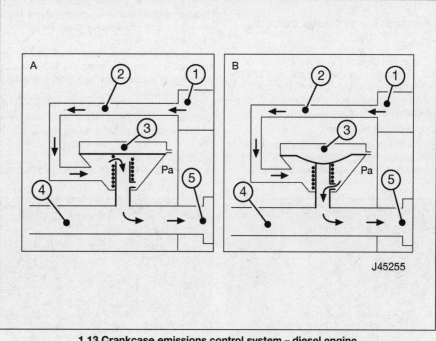

1.13 Crankcase emissions control system – diesel engine

A Low load conditions	1 Cylinder head cover	3 Pressure-sensitive recirculation valve
B Medium to high load conditions	2 Oil vapour rebreathing hose	4 Air inlet duct
Pa Atmospheric pressure		5 Turbocharger

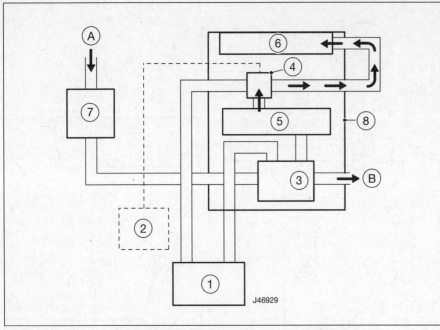

1.16 Exhaust gas recirculation system – diesel engine

A Air inlet
B Outlet to exhaust system
1 Intercooler
2 Engine management ECU
3 Turbocharger
4 Water-cooled EGR unit with solenoid valve
5 Exhaust manifold
6 Plenum
7 Air filter
8 Engine

2 Petrol engine emissions control systems – testing and component renewal

Crankcase emissions control

Testing

1 There is no specific test procedure for the crankcase emissions control system. If problems are suspected, check that the hoses are clean internally, and that the restrictors are not blocked or missing.

Component renewal

2 This is self-evident. Mark the various hoses before disconnecting them if there is any possibility of confusion on reassembly.

2.10a Downstream oxygen sensor located on the catalytic converter – 0.9 litre petrol engine

Exhaust emissions control

Testing

3 An exhaust gas analyser (CO meter) will be needed. The ignition system must be in good condition, the air cleaner element must be clean, and the engine must be in good mechanical condition.

4 Bring the engine to normal operating temperature, then connect the exhaust gas analyser in accordance with the equipment maker's instructions.

5 Run the engine at 2500 rpm for about 30 seconds, then allow it to idle and check the CO level (Chapter 4A Specifications 4A). If the CO level is within the specified limits, the system is operating correctly.

6 If the CO level is higher than specified, try

2.10b Removing the upper oxygen sensor – 0.9 litre petrol engine

the effect of disconnecting the oxygen sensor wiring. If the CO level rises when the sensor is disconnected, this suggests that the oxygen sensor is OK and that the catalytic converter is faulty. If disconnecting the sensor has no effect, this suggests a fault in the sensor.

7 If a digital voltmeter is available, the oxygen sensor output voltage can be measured. Voltage should alternate between the specified rich mixture and lean mixture values.

8 Renew the oxygen sensor if it is proved faulty.

Oxygen sensors renewal

9 To remove the upstream sensor on all engines, trace the wiring from the sensor located on the exhaust manifold to the connector and disconnect it. Unscrew the sensor from the manifold using a deep socket.

10 To remove the downstream sensor raise the front of the vehicle and support it on axle stands (see *Jacking and vehicle support*). Remove the engine compartment undertray, where fitted, then disconnect the sensor wiring. Unscrew the sensor from the exhaust downpipe and remove it **(see illustrations)**.

11 Clean the threads of the sensor (if it is to be refitted) and the threads in the exhaust pipe or manifold (as applicable).

12 Note that if the sensor wires are broken, the sensor must be renewed. No attempt should be made to repair them.

13 Apply high temperature anti-seize compound to the sensor threads. Screw the sensor in by hand, then tighten it to the specified torque.

14 Reconnect the sensor wiring, and where applicable refit the undertray and lower the vehicle to the ground.

Catalytic converter – renewal

15 The catalytic converter is renewed as part of the exhaust system. See Chapter 4A Section 17.

Evaporative emissions control

Testing

16 The operating principle of the system is that the solenoid valve is open only when the engine is warm with the throttle at least at the part throttle position.

17 Bring the engine to normal operating temperature, then switch it off. Connect a vacuum gauge (range 0 to 1000 mbars) into the hose between the canister and the solenoid valve. Connect a voltmeter to the solenoid valve terminals.

18 Start the engine and allow it to idle. There should be no vacuum shown on the gauge, and no voltage present at the solenoid.

19 If manifold vacuum is indicated although no voltage is present, the solenoid valve may be stuck open. Temporarily disconnect the hoses from the solenoid valve and blow through the outlets to dislodge any particles of carbon.

20 If voltage is present at idle, there is a fault in the wiring or the computer.

21 Depress the accelerator slightly. Voltage

should appear momentarily at the solenoid terminals, and manifold vacuum be indicated on the gauge.

22 If vacuum is not indicated even though voltage is present, either there is a leak in the hoses, or the valve is not opening.

23 If no voltage appears, there is a fault in the wiring or the computer.

Charcoal canister renewal

24 Apply the handbrake, then jack up the front of the vehicle and support it on axle stands (see *Jacking and vehicle support*). Remove the right-hand front wheel and inner wheel arch liner.

25 Disconnect the battery negative lead as described in Chapter 5A Section 4.

26 The canister is located behind the windscreen washer bottle, at the front right-hand side of the vehicle.

27 Note the location of the hoses, then disconnect the vapour inlet hose leading from the fuel tank, and the rebreathing hose leading to the inlet manifold. Prise free the release clip and withdraw the canister.

28 Dispose of the old canister safely, bearing in mind that it may contain liquid fuel and/or fuel vapour.

29 Fit the new canister using a reversal of the removal procedure. Make sure that the hoses are connected correctly.

Solenoid valve

30 The solenoid valve is located just above the charcoal canister, on the front right-hand side chassis leg **(see illustration)**.

31 Disconnect the wiring plug from the top of the solenoid valve **(see illustration)**.

32 Release the locking clip and disconnect the hoses from the top and bottom of the solenoid valve **(see illustrations)**, noting the fitted locations of the hoses.

33 Unclip the solenoid valve from the mounting bracket.

---

3 Diesel engine emissions control systems – testing and component renewal

---

Crankcase emissions control

Testing

1 If the system is thought to be faulty, firs check that the hoses are unobstructed. On high-mileage vehicles, particularly when regularly used for short journeys, a jellylike deposit may be evident inside the system hoses and oil separators. If excessive deposits are present, the relevant component(s) should be removed and cleaned.

2 Periodically inspect the system components for security and damage, and renew them as necessary.

Component renewal

3 This is self-evident. Mark the various hoses before disconnecting them if there is any possibility of confusion on reassembly.

2.30 The control valve for the evaporative emissions circuit

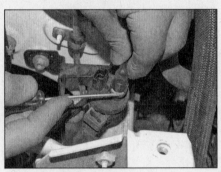
2.32a Release the locking clip...

Exhaust emissions control

Testing

4 The system can only be tested accurately using a suitable exhaust gas analyser (suitable for use with diesel engines).

Catalytic converter renewal

5 The catalytic converter is renewed as part of the exhaust system. Refer to Part B of this Chapter 4B Section 18.

Diesel particulate filter

6 The particulate filter is renewed as part of the exhaust system. Refer to Part B of this Chapter 4B Section 18.

Exhaust gas recirculation

Testing

7 Testing of the EGR system is best left to a

3.9 EGR solenoid valve

2.31 Disconnect the wiring connector

2.32b ...and disconnect the hoses

Renault dealer who will have the dedicated equipment necessary to carry out the test.

EGR valve unit

8 On models with coolant hoses fitted to the EGR valve, drain the cooling system, as described in Chapter 1B Section 27. The other option would be to clamp the coolant hoses to the EGR valve to prevent to much coolant spillage.

9 The EGR valve is mounted on the inlet manifold at the rear of the cylinder head **(see illustration)**.

10 Disconnect the battery negative lead (Chapter 5A Section 4).

11 Undo the mounting bolt, release the secuirng clips and remove the air intake hose from the intercooler to turbocharger **(see illustrations)**.

12 Slacken the retaining clip and disconnect

3.11a Undo the mounting bolt...

3.11b ...release the securing clips...

3.11c ...and remove the air intake hose

3.13 Unbolt and remove the pressure solenoid valve

3.14 Unplug the wiring connector

3.16a Unbolt...

3.16b ...and remove the EGR valve

3.17 Clean and inspect the valve seat

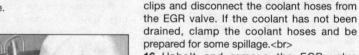

3.20 Disconnect the wastegate valve hose

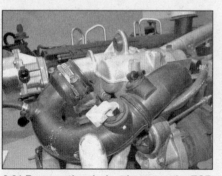

3.21 Remove the air duct between the EGR valve and turbocharger

3.23 Remove the inlet pipe

the air cleaner intake hose from the plastic intake ducting, undo the mounting bolts and remove the plastic air ducting from the turbocharger.

13 Undo the mounting nuts turbocharger pressure solenoid valve from the top of the engine (**see illustration**). The vacuum pipes can stay attached and the solenoid valve moved to one side.

14 Disconnect the wiring from the EGR solenoid valve (**see illustration**).

15 Where applicable, slacken the securing clips and disconnect the coolant hoses from the EGR valve. If the coolant has not been drained, clamp the coolant hoses and be prepared for some spillage.

16 Unbolt and remove the EGR valve (**see illustrations**). Recover the gasket.

17 Thoroughly clean and inspect the EGR valve. Ensure the valve seats correctly (**see illustration**).

18 Refitting is a reversal of removal, but a new gasket should be fitted.

EGR pipework

19 If required, the pipework between the valve housing and exhaust manifold can be removed for cleaning and inspection.

20 Disconnect the hose from the turbocharger pressure adjustment valve on the air duct (**see illustration**).

21 Loosen the clips and remove the air duct from between the EGR unit and turbocharger (**see illustration**).

22 Unbolt and remove the right-hand rear engine lifting eye.

23 Unscrew the bolt and remove the air inlet metallic tube (**see illustration**).

24 Where fitted, remove the heat shield from over the EGR solenoid valve.

25 Loosen both clamps and remove the EGR convoluted metal tube from the EGR valve and exhaust manifold (**see illustrations**).

26 Unscrew the mounting bolts and remove the EGR valve unit from its location on the

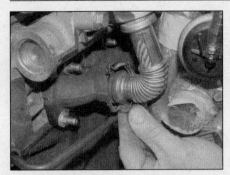

3.25a Release the clamps...

3.25b ...and remove the EGR convoluted metal tube

3.27 Use pincers to tighten the clamp

inlet manifold. Note that the solenoid valve is not available separately.

27 Refitting is a reversal of removal, but renew the air inlet duct O-rings. Check the condition of the convoluted metal tube retaining clamps and if necessary, renew them – if the special tool is not available, use a pair of pincers to tighten the clamps until the clip is engaged **(see illustration)**.

4 Catalytic converter – general information and precautions

1 The catalytic converter is a reliable and simple device which needs no maintenance in itself, but there are some facts of which an owner should be aware if the converter is to function properly for its full service life.

Petrol models

• DO NOT use leaded petrol or LRP in a car equipped with a catalytic converter – the lead will coat the precious metals, reducing their converting efficiency and will eventually destroy the converter.

• Always keep the ignition and fuel systems well maintained in accordance with the manufacturer's schedule.

• If the engine develops a misfire, do not drive the car at all (or at least as little as possible) until the fault is cured.

• DO NOT push or tow start the car – this will soak the catalytic converter in unburned fuel, causing it to overheat when the engine does start.

• DO NOT switch off the ignition at high engine speeds.

• DO NOT use fuel or engine oil additives – these may contain substances harmful to the catalytic converter.

• DO NOT continue to use the car if the engine burns oil to the extent of leaving a visible trail of blue smoke.

• Remember that the catalytic converter operates at very high temperatures. DO NOT park the car on dry undergrowth, over long grass or piles of dead leaves after a long run.

• Remember that the catalytic converter is FRAGILE – do not strike it with tools during servicing work or drop it.

• In some cases a sulphurous smell (like that of rotten eggs) may be noticed from the exhaust. This is common to many catalytic converter equipped cars and once the car has covered a few thousand miles the problem should disappear.

• The catalytic converter, used on a well maintained and well driven car, should last for between 50 000 and 100 000 miles – if the converter is no longer effective it must be renewed.

Diesel models

• DO NOT use fuel or engine oil additives – these may contain substances harmful to the catalytic converter.

• DO NOT continue to use the car if the engine burns oil to the extent of leaving a visible trail of blue smoke.

• Remember that the catalytic converter operates at very high temperatures. DO NOT park the car on dry undergrowth, over long grass or piles of dead leaves after a long run.

• Remember that the catalytic converter is FRAGILE – do not strike it with tools during servicing work or drop it.

Chapter 5 Part A
Starting and charging systems

Contents

Degrees of difficulty

Easy, suitable for novice with little experience	Fairly easy, suitable for beginner with some experience	Fairly difficult, suitable for competent DIY mechanic	Difficult, suitable for experienced DIY mechanic	Very difficult, suitable for expert DIY or professional

Specifications

Battery
Type	Lead-acid, 'maintenance-free'
Charge condition:	
Poor	12.5 volts
Normal	12.6 volts
Good	12.7 volts

Alternator
Type	Valeo or Bosch
Output	90, 120 or 150 amps
Regulated voltage	13.5 to 14.8 volts

Starter motor
Type	Valeo or Bosch

Torque wrench settings
	Nm	lbf ft
Alternator	25	18
Starter motor	44	32

1 General information and precautions

General information

1 The engine electrical system consists mainly of the charging and starting systems. Because of their engine-related functions, these components are covered separately from the body electrical devices such as the lights, instruments, etc (which are covered in Chapter 12). On petrol engine models, refer to Chapter 5B for information on the ignition system, and on diesel models, refer to Chapter 5C for information on the preheating system.

2 The electrical system is of the 12 volt negative earth type.

3 The battery is of the 'maintenance-free' (sealed for life) type, and is charged by the alternator, which is belt-driven from the crankshaft pulley.

4 The starter motor is of the pre-engaged type, incorporating an integral solenoid. On starting, the solenoid moves the drive pinion into engagement with the flywheel ring gear before the starter motor is energised. Once the engine has started, a one-way clutch prevents the motor armature being driven by the engine until the pinion disengages from the flywheel.

Precautions

5 It is necessary to take extra care when working on the electrical system, to avoid damage to semi-conductor devices (diodes and transistors), and to avoid the risk of personal injury. In addition to the precautions given in 'Safety first!' at the beginning of this manual, observe the following when working on the system:

6 Always remove rings, watches, etc, before working on the electrical system. Even with the battery disconnected, capacitive discharge could occur if a component's live terminal is earthed through a metal object. This could cause a shock or nasty burn.

7 Do not reverse the battery connections. Components such as the alternator, electronic control units, or any other components having semi-conductor circuitry could be irreparably damaged.

8 Never disconnect the battery terminals, the alternator, any electrical wiring or any test instruments with the engine running.

9 Do not allow the engine to turn the alternator when the alternator is not connected.

10 Never 'test' for alternator output by 'flashing' the output lead to earth.

11 Never use an ohmmeter of the type incorporating a hand-cranked generator for circuit or continuity testing.

12 Always ensure that the battery negative lead is disconnected when working on the electrical system.

13 If the engine is being started using jump leads and a slave battery, connect the batteries positive-to-positive and negative-to-negative (see Jump starting at the beginning of the manual). This also applies when connecting a battery charger.

14 Before using electric arc welding equipment on the car, disconnect the battery, alternator and components such as the electronic control units to protect them from the risk of damage.

15 The radio/cassette unit fitted may be equipped with a built-in security code to deter thieves. If the power source to the unit is cut, the anti-theft system will be activated. *Caution: If the audio unit in your vehicle is equipped with an anti-theft system, make sure you have the correct activation code before disconnecting the battery.*

2 Electrical fault finding – general information

1 Refer to Chapter 12 Section 2.

3 Battery – testing and charging

Testing

1 Topping-up and testing of the electrolyte in each cell is not possible. The condition of the battery can therefore only be tested using a battery condition indicator or a voltmeter.

2 All models are originally fitted with a maintenance-free battery, with a built-in charge condition indicator. The indicator is located in the top of the battery casing, and indicates the condition of the battery from its colour. If the indicator shows green, then the battery is in a good state of charge. If the indicator turns darker, eventually to black, then the battery requires charging, as described later in this Section. If the indicator shows clear/yellow, then the electrolyte level in the battery is too low to allow further use, and the battery should be renewed. Do not attempt to charge, load or jump start a battery when the indicator shows clear/yellow.

3 If testing the battery using a voltmeter, connect it to the terminals and compare the result with that given in the Specifications. The test is only accurate if the battery has not been subjected to any kind of charge for the previous six hours. If this is not the case, switch on the headlights for 30 seconds, then wait four to five minutes before testing the battery after switching off the headlights. All other electrical circuits must be switched off, so check that the doors and tailgate are fully shut when making the test.

4 If the voltage reading is less than 12.2 volts, then the battery is discharged, whilst a reading of 12.2 to 12.4 volts indicates a partially-discharged condition.

5 If the battery is to be charged, remove it from the vehicle (Section 4) and charge it as described later in this Section.

Charging

Note: *The following is intended as a guide only. Always follow the maker's recommendations (often printed on a label attached to the battery) before charging a battery.*

6 Charge the battery at a rate equivalent to 10% of the battery capacity (eg, for a 45 Ah battery charge at 4.5 A), and continue to charge the battery at this rate until no further rise in specific gravity is noted over a four hour period.

7 Alternatively, a trickle charger charging at the rate of 1.5 amps can safely be used overnight.

8 Specially rapid 'boost' charges which are claimed to restore the power of the battery in 1 to 2 hours are not recommended, as they can cause serious damage to the battery plates through overheating.

9 While charging the battery, note that the temperature of the electrolyte should never exceed 38°C.

10 Maintenance free batteries take considerably longer to fully recharge than a traditional type.

11 A constant voltage type charger is required, to be set, when connected, to 13.9 to 14.9 volts with a charger current below 25 amps. Using this method, the battery should be usable within three hours, giving a voltage reading of 12.5 volts, but this is for a partially-discharged battery and, as mentioned, full charging can take considerably longer.

12 If the battery is to be charged from a fully discharged state (condition reading less than 12.2 volts), have it recharged by your Renault dealer or invest in a modern 'intelligent' battery charger. Modern battery chargers can safely charge most if not all batteries safely regardless of the state of charge **(see illustration)**.

4 Battery – disconnecting, removal and refitting

Note: *Refer to the precautions given in 'Safety first!' and in Section 1 of this Chapter.*

Disconnecting

1 Lower the driver's window and then remove the key (or key card) from the vehicle. Before disconnecting the battery wait at least two minutes to allow time for the engine management system to shut down. If the the cooling fan is running wait until the fan stops.

2 Unclip and then remove the battery cover. The battery cover is in two sections.

3 Disconnect the battery negative (earth cable) and then move the cable to the side. Ensure the cable can not make contact with the battery negative cable.

Removal

4 Disconnect the negative (earth) terminal by unscrewing the retaining nut and removing the terminal clamp **(see illustration)**.

5 Undo the securing nut and disconnect the positive terminal lead(s). Where necessary, flip open or remove the red cover for access to the terminal **(see illustration)**.

3.12 A modern battery charger capable of charging all batteries regardless of the initial state of charge

4.4 Disconnect and remove the battery negative terminal

4.5 Open the cover for access to the positive battery terminal

6 Pull free the breather pipe from the upper end of the battery (see illustration).

7 Unscrew the clamp bolt, remove the clamp assembly, then lift the battery from its location (see illustration). Keep the battery in an upright position, to avoid spilling electrolyte on the bodywork.

8 If required, unclip the wiring loom from the sides of the battery tray, then undo the three retaining bolts and remove the battery tray (see illustrations).

Refitting and reconnecting

9 Refitting is a reversal of removal. Smear petroleum jelly on the terminals after reconnecting the leads to reduce corrosion. Always reconnect the positive lead first, and the negative lead last.

10 After reconnecting the battery proceed as follows:

a) Reach through the open window and turn on the side lights for a minute or so.

b) Turn the ignition on and rotate the steering wheel to the left (a quarter turn) and then to the right (a quarter turn). Return the wheel to the straight ahead position.

c) With the ignition switched on allow the throttle body to adjust itself. Wait 30 seconds until the ECU stores the relearned maximum and minimum positions.

d) Initialise the power windows by lowering them and closing them. Hold the switch in the fully closed position for 10 seconds.

e) Where a sunroof is fitted, start the engine and check that the sunroof opens and closes. Hold the switch in the fully closed position – a click-click will be heard. Hold this position for 5 seconds.

f) Reset the clock time. (Not required on vehicles fitted with a navigation system).

g) Reset the Audio unit – enter the security code and the station presets.

h) Where a tyre pressure monitoring system is fitted drive the vehicle for several minutes at a speed over 20 mph.

i) Warm up the engine by driving and then at between 3,000 and 3,500 rpm (whilst in third gear) decelerate for a minimum of 5 seconds. Repeat the procedure, but decelerate from an engine speed of 2,000 to 2,500 rpm (in third gear).

11 It will take several drive cycles for the engine management ECU to fully learn the optimum operating parameters. During this period the engine may suffer from reduced performance and/or economy.

5 Charging system – testing

Note: Refer to the warnings given in 'Safety first!' and in Section 1 of this Chapter before starting work.

1 If the ignition warning light fails to illuminate when the ignition is switched on, first check the alternator wiring connections for security.

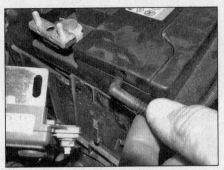
4.6 Pull free the breather pipe

If satisfactory, check that the warning light bulb has not blown, and that the bulbholder is secure in its location in the instrument panel (see Chapter 12). If the light still fails to illuminate, check the continuity of the warning light feed wire from the alternator to the bulbholder. If all is satisfactory, the alternator is at fault, and should be renewed or taken to an auto electrician for testing and repair.

2 If the ignition warning light illuminates when the engine is running, stop the engine and check that the drivebelt is correctly tensioned (see Chapter 1A or 1B) and that the alternator connections are secure. If all is so far satisfactory, have the alternator checked by an auto electrician for testing and repair.

3 If the alternator output is suspect even though the warning light functions correctly, the regulated voltage may be checked as follows.

4 Connect a voltmeter across the battery terminals and start the engine.

5 Increase the engine speed until the voltmeter reading remains steady; the reading should be between 13.2 and 14.8 volts.

6 Switch on as many electrical accessories (eg, the headlights, heated rear window and heater blower) as possible, and check that the alternator maintains the regulated voltage between 13.2 and 14.8 volts.

7 If the regulated voltage is not as stated, the fault may be due to worn brushes, weak brush springs, a faulty voltage regulator, a faulty diode, a severed phase winding, or worn or damaged slip-rings. The alternator should be renewed or taken to an auto-electrician for testing and repair.

4.8a Unclip the wiring loom...

4.7 Remove the battery retaining clamp bolt

6 Alternator – testing

1 If the alternator is thought to be suspect, it should be removed from the vehicle and taken to an auto electrician for testing. Most auto electricians will be able to supply and fit brushes at a reasonable cost. However, check on the cost of repairs before proceeding as it may prove more economical to obtain a new or exchange alternator.

7 Alternator – removal and refitting

Removal

1 Disconnect the battery negative lead (refer to Section 4).

2 On all models apply the handbrake, then jack up the front of the vehicle and support it on axle stands (see Jacking and vehicle support). Remove the roadwheels and the front bumper as described in Chapter 11, Section 6.

3 Remove the auxiliary drivebelt with reference to Chapter 1A or 1B.

4 On models with air conditioning, it may be necessary to remove the compressor mounting bolts and secure the compressor to the radiator crossmember. The AC system does not require draining for this operation.

4.8b ...then undo the mounting bolts

7.6 Disconnecting the wiring connectors

7.7 Removing the alternator mounting bolts

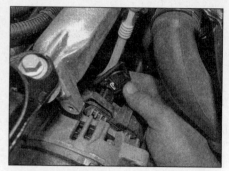

7.8 Disconnecting the wiring plug

Note. take care not to damage the air-conditioning pipes as the compressor is moved.

0.9 litre petrol engines

5 Remove the intercooler as described in Chapter 4A Section 16.

6 Remove the cover (where fitted) from the alternator main terminal, then unscrew the retaining nut and disconnect the main cable. Also disconnect the wiring plug from the rear of the alternator **(see illustration)**.

7 Remove the upper and the lower alternator mounting bolts and then withdraw the alternator through the front of the vehicle **(see illustration)**.

1.2 litre petrol engine

8 Remove the cover (where fitted) from the alternator main terminal, then unscrew the retaining nut and disconnect the main cable.

Also, disconnect the wiring plug from the rear of the alternator **(see illustration)**.

9 Unscrew and remove the alternator upper mounting bolt **(see illustration)** then support the alternator and unscrew the lower bolts.

10 Withdraw the alternator from the front of the engine **(see illustration)** or lower it. Where the inlet manifold has been removed the alternator can be removed upwards from the engine bay.

Diesel engine

11 Remove the intercooler, as described in Chapter 4B Section 17.

12 Unscrew the retaining nut and disconnect the alternator main cable. Disconnect the wiring plug from the rear of the alternator.

13 Remove the upper mounting bolt, loosen the lower bolt and remove it with the alternator.

Refitting

14 Refitting is a reversal of removal. Refer to the relevant part of Chapter 1A or 1B for details of fitting and tensioning the auxiliary drivebelt. Note that the alternator mounting holes are fitted with adjustable spacer (or spacers) which are clamped to the mounting bracket when the bolts are tightened. This makes the task of refitting the alternator difficult, and it is suggested that the spacers are tapped out slightly to provide additional clearance **(see illustrations)**.

8 Starting system – testing

Note: *Refer to the precautions given in 'Safety first!' and in Section 1 of this Chapter before starting work.*

1 If the starter motor fails to operate when the ignition key is turned to the appropriate position, the following may be the possible causes:

a) *The battery is faulty.*
b) *The electrical connections between the switch, solenoid, battery and starter motor are somewhere failing to pass the necessary current from the battery through the starter to earth.*
c) *The solenoid is faulty.*
d) *The starter motor is mechanically or electrically defective.*

2 To check the battery, switch on the headlights. If they dim after a few seconds, this indicates that the battery is discharged – recharge (see Section 3) or renew the battery. If the headlights glow brightly, operate the ignition switch and observe the lights. If they dim, then this indicates that current is reaching the starter motor, therefore the fault must lie in the starter motor. If the lights continue to glow brightly (and no clicking sound can be heard from the starter motor solenoid), this indicates that there is a fault in the circuit or solenoid – see the following paragraphs. If the starter motor turns slowly when operated, but the battery is in good condition, then this indicates that either the starter motor is faulty, or there is considerable resistance somewhere in the circuit.

7.9 Unscrew the upper alternator mounting bolt

7.10 Removing the alternator from the front of the vehicle

7.14a A nut, bolt and socket can be used to reposition the spacer...

7.14b ...or use the mounting bolt to reposition the spacer – diesel engine

9.4a Disconnect the wiring connectors...

9.4b ...undo the securing bolt/nut...

9.4c ...and move the wiring loom to one side

9.5a Remove the lower bolt...

9.5b ...the upper bolt...

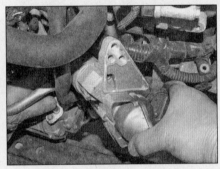

9.5c ...and withdraw the starter

3 If a fault in the circuit is suspected, disconnect the battery leads (including the earth connection to the body), the starter/solenoid wiring and the engine/transmission earth strap. Thoroughly clean the connections, and reconnect the leads and wiring, then use a voltmeter or test lamp to check that full battery voltage is available at the battery positive lead connection to the solenoid, and that the earth is sound. Smear petroleum jelly around the battery terminals to prevent corrosion – corroded connections are amongst the most frequent causes of electrical system faults.

4 If the battery and all connections are in good condition, check the circuit by disconnecting the wire from the solenoid blade terminal. Connect a voltmeter or test lamp between the wire end and a good earth (such as the battery negative terminal), and check that the wire is live when the ignition switch is turned to the 'start' position. If it is, then the circuit is sound – if not the circuit wiring can be checked as described in Chapter 12.

5 The solenoid contacts can be checked by connecting a voltmeter or test lamp between the battery positive feed connection on the starter side of the solenoid and earth. When the ignition switch is turned to the 'start' position, there should be a reading or lighted bulb, as applicable. If there is no reading or lighted bulb, the solenoid is faulty and should be renewed.

6 If the circuit and solenoid are proved sound, the fault must lie in the starter motor. In this

event, it may be possible to have the starter motor overhauled by a specialist, but check on the cost of spares before proceeding, as it may prove more economical to obtain a new or exchange motor.

9 Starter motor –
removal and refitting

Removal

Note: *On the petrol engines an alternative method is to remove the inlet manifold (see Chapter 4A, Section 14) and gain access to the alternator from above. Whilst this takes a little more time, it does mean that access is improved and there is no need to raise the vehicle.*

1 Before working on the starter motor, it will be necessary to disconnect the battery negative lead (refer to Section 4).

0.9 litre petrol engines

2 Apply the handbrake, then jack up the front of the vehicle and support it on axle stands (see *Jacking and vehicle support*). Remove the engine undertray.

3 Remove the air filter ducting with reference to Chapter 4A Section 2.

4 Disconnect the electrical connectors from the rear of the starter motor and then undo the retaining bolt and nut to release the wiring loom from above the starter motor **(see illustrations)**.

5 Slacken and remove the upper and lower

mounting bolts, then work the starter free from the locating dowel and withdraw the starter motor **(see illustrations)**.

1.2 litre petrol engine

6 It is possible to remove the starter either out through the front of the engine bay, or by lowering it out through the bottom.

7 The starter motor is located on the front of the cylinder block **(see illustration)**. Remove the air filter ducting and then remove the battery as described in Section 4.

8 Remove the bolts securing the cable support from above the gearbox bellhousing and move the cable support to the side **(see illustration)**.

9 Jack up the front of the car, and support it on axle stands (see *Jacking and vehicle support*).

9.7 Starter motor on the front of the engine

9.8 With the cable removed the bolt can be accessed

9.11 Unscrew the mounting bolts

10 Disconnect the wiring from the rear of the starter motor.
11 Loosen the bolts and tap or work the starter free from the locating dowel. Remove the bolts and withdraw the starter motor **(see illustration)**.

Diesel engine

12 Apply the handbrake. Jack up the front of the vehicle and support it on axle stands (see *Jacking and vehicle support*) and then remove the engine undertray.
13 Remove the air filter ducting with reference to Chapter 4B Section 3 and then remove the dipstick tube.
14 Disconnect the wiring from the rear of the starter motor.
15 Loosen the bolts and tap or work the starter free from the locating dowel. Remove the starter motor from below.

Refitting

16 Refitting is a reversal of removal, but where necessary position the starter motor on the location dowel. Finally, tighten the mounting bolts securely.

Chapter 5 Part B
Ignition system – petrol engines

Contents

Degrees of difficulty

Easy, suitable for novice with little experience | **Fairly easy,** suitable for beginner with some experience | **Fairly difficult,** suitable for competent DIY mechanic | **Difficult,** suitable for experienced DIY mechanic | **Very difficult,** suitable for expert DIY or professional

Specifications

General

Ignition system type:
- 0.9 litre engines . . . . Fully-electronic, computer-controlled, with three individual ignition coils, one on each spark plug
- 1.2 litre engines . . . . Fully-electronic, computer-controlled, with two dual output ignition coils serving cylinders 1 and 4, and 2 and 3

Firing order:
- 0.9 litre engines 1-3-2
- 1.2 litre engines 1-3-4-2
- Location of No 1 cylinder . . . . Flywheel end
- Ignition timing. . . . . Controlled by the ECU

Ignition HT coil resistances measured at ignition connector

0.9 litre engines . . . . N/A
1.2 litre engines:
- Primary resistance:
  - A to B . . . . 0.40 ± 0.02 ohms
  - C to D . . . . 0.40 ± 0.02 ohms
  - B to C . . . . 0.0 ± 0.02 ohms
- Secondary resistance:
  - Leads 1 and 4 . . . . 9.8 ± 0.5 kohms
  - Leads 2 and 3 . . . . 9.6 ± 0.5 kohms

Note: *The HT leads cannot be removed from the coils; therefore the secondary resistance includes the HT leads.*

Torque wrench settings

	Nm	lbf ft
Ignition coil (individual coils)	15	11
Ignition coil pack	10	7
Knock sensor	25	18
Spark plugs	See Chapter 1A	

1 Ignition system – general information and precautions

General information

1 The ignition system is integrated with the fuel injection system to form a combined engine management system under the control of one ECU (see Chapter 4A for further information). All engines are fitted with a distributorless ignition system.

2 On 0.9 litre engines the ignition system uses one coil for each cylinder, with each coil mounted on the relevant spark plug.

3 On 1.2 litre engines the ignition system consists simply of two ignition HT coils (combined into one unit), the crankshaft speed/position/TDC sensor and a knock sensor. Each coil supplies two cylinders (one coil supplies cylinders 1 and 4 and the other coil supplies cylinders 2 and 3). The ignition coils operate on the 'wasted spark' principle, ie, each spark plug sparks twice for every cycle of the engine, once on the compression stroke and once on the exhaust stroke.

4 The TDC sensor (see Chapter 4A, Section 13) is used to determine piston position as well as engine speed.

5 The power module for the ignition is integrated in the engine management ECU. The ECU uses the inputs from the sensors to calculate the required ignition advance setting and coil charging time – an integral amplifier circuit within the ECU switches the ignition coil primary (LT) circuit.

6 The knock sensor is mounted on the cylinder block to inform the ECU when the engine is 'pinking'. Its sensitivity to a particular frequency of vibration allows it to detect the impulses which are caused by the shock waves set up when the engine starts to 'pink' (pre-ignite). The knock sensor sends an electrical signal to the ECU which retards the ignition advance setting until the 'pinking' ceases – the ignition timing is then gradually returned to the 'normal' setting. This maintains the ignition timing as close to the knock threshold as possible – the most efficient setting for the engine under normal running conditions.

Precautions

7 The following precautions must be observed, to prevent damage to the ignition system components and to reduce risk of personal injury.

8 Ensure the ignition is switched off before disconnecting any of the ignition wiring.

9 Ensure that the ignition is switched off before connecting or disconnecting any ignition test equipment, such as a timing light.

10 Do not earth the coil primary or secondary circuits.

 Warning: Voltages produced by an electronic ignition system are considerably higher than those produced by conventional ignition systems. Extreme care must be taken when working on the system with the ignition switched on. Persons with surgically-implanted cardiac pacemaker devices should keep well clear of the ignition circuits, components and test equipment*

2 Ignition system – testing

1 The components of ignition systems are normally very reliable; most faults are far more likely to be due to loose or dirty connections, or to 'tracking' of HT voltage due to dirt, dampness or damaged insulation than to the failure of any of the system's components. Always check all wiring thoroughly before condemning an electrical component and work methodically to eliminate all other possibilities before deciding that a particular component is faulty.

2 The old practice of checking for a spark by holding the live end of a spark plug HT lead a short distance away from the engine is not recommended; not only is there a high risk of a powerful electric shock, but the HT coil or ECU may be damaged. However, if necessary each plug can be checked individually by removing it, then reconnecting the HT lead or coil (as applicable) and connecting the body of the spark plug to a suitable earthing point on the engine using a battery jumper lead. It is important to make a good earth connection if using this method. Never try to 'diagnose' misfires by pulling off one HT lead at a time.

Engine will not start

3 If the engine either will not turn over at all, or only turns very slowly, first check the battery and starter motor as described in Chapter 5A.

4 If the engine turns over at normal speed but will not start, the HT circuit of 1.2 litre engines can be checked by connecting a timing light to an HT lead (following the manufacturer's instructions) and turning the engine over on the starter motor. If the light flashes, voltage is reaching the spark plugs, so these should be removed and checked. If the light does

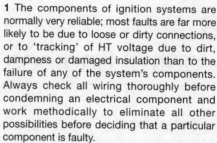
3.2a Unclip the vacuum pipe...

not flash, check the spark plug HT leads themselves with reference to Chapter 1A Section 18. **Note:** *On 0.9 litre engines, the coils are mounted on each individual spark plug, so it is not possible to use a conventional timing light to check the system.*

5 If there is still no spark, use an ohmmeter to check the resistances of the coils and compare with the information given in the Specifications. The tracks for 1.2 litre engines are as follows:
a) *Track number Allocation*
b) *1 Coil control for cylinders 3 and 2*
c) *2 + after ignition*
d) *3 + anti-interference condenser*
e) *4 Coil control for cylinders 1 and 4*

6 If these checks fail to reveal the cause of the problem, the vehicle should be taken to a Renault dealer for testing. A wiring block connector is incorporated in the engine management circuit, into which a special electronic diagnostic tester can be plugged. The tester will locate the fault quickly and simply, alleviating the need to test all the system components individually, which is a time-consuming operation that carries a high risk of damaging the ECU. If necessary, the system wiring and wiring connectors can be checked as described in Chapter 12, ensuring that the ECU wiring connector is first disconnected with the ignition switched off.

Engine misfires

7 An irregular misfire suggests either a loose connection or intermittent fault in the primary circuit, or an HT fault on the circuit between the coil and spark plugs.

8 With the ignition switched off, check carefully through the system ensuring that all connections are clean and securely fastened.

9 Check that the HT coil and the spark plug HT leads (where applicable) are clean and dry.

10 Regular misfiring of one spark plug may be due to a faulty spark plug, faulty injector, a faulty HT lead or loss of compression in the relevant cylinder. Regular misfiring of cylinders 1 and 4 only, or 2 and 3 only suggests a fault on the relevant coil. Regular misfiring of all the cylinders suggests a fuel supply fault, such as a clogged fuel filter or faulty fuel pump.

3 Ignition HT coils – removal, testing and refitting

Removal

1 Disconnect the battery negative lead as described in Chapter 5A Section 4. Where fitted, remove the engine cover.

0.9 litre engines

2 Unclip the vacuum pipe, undo the two retaining nuts, then release the securing clips at each end of the air intake pipe, and remove it from the top of the engine (see illustrations).

3 Cover the opening to the turbocharger (see

3.2b ...undo the two nuts...

3.2c ...release the clips...

3.2d ...and remove the air intake pipe

3.3 Using bottle cap to cover turbo inlet

3.4 Disconnect the wiring from each ignition coil

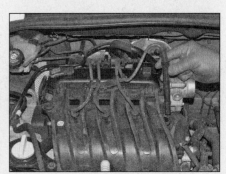
3.8 Remove the HT leads

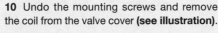
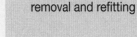

illustration), to make sure no debris enters the turbo.

4 Disconnect the wiring from each coil, taking care not to damage the connectors **(see illustration)**.

5 Undo the mounting screws and withdraw each coil off of its spark plug. Check the condition of the O-rings where the coils enter the valve cover, and if necessary renew them.

1.2 litre engine

6 Remove the air cleaner assembly, as described in Chapter 4A Section 2.

7 The ignition HT coils are located on the right-hand rear end of the valve cover.

8 Note their location, then disconnect the spark plug HT leads from the spark plugs **(see illustration)**. If necessary, identify each lead to ensure correct refitting.

9 Disconnect the wiring multiplug from the end of the coil pack.

10 Undo the mounting screws and remove the coil from the valve cover **(see illustration)**.

Testing

11 On 0.9 litre engines, testing of the ignition system should be carried out by a Renault dealer (or suitably-equipped garage) using specialised equipment connected to the engine management diagnostic socket.

12 On 1.2 litre engines, each coil can be tested as described in the previous Section, using an ohmmeter to check for the resistances given in the Specifications.

Refitting

13 Refitting is a reversal of removal, but tighten the mounting bolts to the specified torque, and ensure that the wiring connectors and spark plug HT leads (where applicable) are correctly and securely refitted.

4 Knock sensor – removal and refitting

Removal

1 The knock sensor is located on the front of the cylinder block, below the inlet manifold, and above the starter motor **(see illustrations)**.

2 On 0.9 litre engines, to remove the sensor, first disconnect the wiring, then unscrew the mounting bolt. Note the position of the sensor on the cylinder block, as the angle needs to be between 45 and 60 degrees upwards in relation to the horizontal line through the sensor, turning in an anti-clockwise direction..

3 On 1.2 litre engines, to remove the sensor, first disconnect the wiring, then unscrew the sensor from the cylinder block.

3.10 Remove the coil pack

4.1a Knock sensor location – 0.9 litre engine

4.1b Knock sensor location – 1.2 litre engine

Refitting

4 Refitting is a reversal of removal. Ensure that the sensor and its seating on the cylinder block or head are completely clean and tighten the sensor to the specified torque wrench setting. It is essential that these measures are scrupulously observed, as if the sensor is not correctly secured to a clean mating surface it may not be able to detect the impulses caused by pre-ignition. If this were to happen the correction of ignition timing would not take place, with the consequent risk of severe engine damage.

5 Ignition timing – checking and adjustment

1 With the type of ignition fitted, the ignition timing is constantly being monitored and adjusted by the engine management ECU and nominal checking values cannot be given. Therefore, it is not possible for the home mechanic to check the ignition timing. The only way in which the ignition timing can be checked is using special electronic test equipment, connected to the engine management system diagnostic connector (refer to Chapter 4A). No adjustment of the ignition timing is possible. Should the ignition timing be incorrect, then a fault must be present in the engine management system.

Chapter 5 Part C
Pre/post-heating system – diesel engines

Contents

Degrees of difficulty

Easy, suitable for novice with little experience	Fairly easy, suitable for beginner with some experience	Fairly difficult, suitable for competent DIY mechanic	Difficult, suitable for experienced DIY mechanic	Very difficult, suitable for expert DIY or professional

Specifications

Glow plugs
Resistance .... 0.6 ohms

Coolant temperature sensor
Resistance at:
-10° C .... 12 500 ± 7000 ohms
25° C .... 2252 ± 112 ohms
50° C .... 810 ± 40 ohms
80° C .... 280 ± 8 ohms
110° C .... 115 ± 3 ohms
120° C .... 88 ± 2 ohms

Fuel temperature sensor
Resistance at 25°C .... 2.2 kohms

Torque wrench setting	Nm	lbf ft
Glow plugs	15	11

1 Pre/post-heating system – description and testing

Description

1 The preheating/post-heating system consists of glow plugs screwed into the combustion chambers, a control unit mounted next to the battery on the left-hand side of the engine compartment, and a coolant temperature sensor located on the thermostat housing. The control unit is itself activated by the engine management ECU.

2 The glow plugs are supplied with current from the control unit in several phases, namely variable preheating, fixed preheating, starting heating, and variable post-heating.

3 The variable preheating phase occurs when the ignition is switched on, and during this phase the preheating warning light is illuminated on the instrument panel. The period of preheating depends on the temperature of the coolant and battery

voltage. The maximum period of 15 seconds occurs if the coolant temperature is low and the battery voltage is less than 9.3 volts. The period varies from 15 seconds to zero seconds according to the temperature of the coolant, and when the temperature reaches 80°C, no preheating occurs. With normal battery voltage the maximum period is 10 seconds.

4 The fixed preheating phase occurs straight after the variable phase finishes, after the warning light has extinguished, and lasts for up to 5 seconds. Normally, the driver will start the engine at some point during this phase.

5 During the period when the starter motor is in operation, the glow plugs are continuously supplied with current.

6 The variable post-heating phase occurs immediately after the engine has been started, and the period of post-heating depends on the temperature of the coolant. The maximum period of variable post-heating is 60 seconds, at which point the system is switched off. Variable post-heating will cease if the coolant temperature exceeds 80°C.

Testing

7 If the system malfunctions, testing is best carried out by a Renault dealer (or suitably-equipped garage) using dedicated test equipment, however, some preliminary checks may be made as follows.

8 Connect a voltmeter or 12 volt test lamp between the glow plug supply cable and earth (engine or vehicle metal). Make sure that the live connection is kept clear of the engine and bodywork. Have an assistant switch on the ignition and check that voltage is applied to the glow plugs. Note the time for which the warning light is lit and the total time for which voltage is applied before the system cuts out, and compare to the times given in the description above.

9 If there is no supply at all, the relay, control unit or associated wiring is at fault.

10 To locate a defective glow plug, disconnect the main supply cable and the interconnecting wire from the top of the glow plugs. Using an ohmmeter, check for continuity between each glow plug terminal

2.2a Undo the retaining bolt...

2.2b ...release the spring clips...

2.2c ...and remove the air intake pipe

and earth. The resistance of a glow plug in good condition is very low (less than 1 ohm), so if the test lamp does not light or the continuity tester shows a high resistance, the glow plug is defective.

11 If an ammeter is available, the current draw of each glow plug can be checked. After an initial surge of around 15 to 20 amps, each plug should draw around 10 amps. Any plug which draws much more or less than 10 amps is probably defective.

12 As a final check, the glow plugs can be removed and inspected as described in Section 2.

13 If the pre/post-heating system is faulty, first check the wiring to each individual component. If this does not locate the fault, ideally each component should be substituted with known good units until the fault is located. If this is not possible, take the vehicle

to a Renault dealer or diesel specialist who will have the diagnostic equipment necessary to pin point the fault quickly.

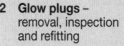

2 Glow plugs –
removal, inspection
and refitting

Caution: If the preheating system has just been energised, or if the engine has been running, the glow plugs may be very hot.

Removal

1 Open the bonnet, disconnect the battery and (where fitted) remove the engine cover.
2 Undo the air intake securing bolt, then release the securing clips form each end of the air intake pipe and remove it from across the top of the engine **(see illustrations)**.

3 Unclip the wiring loom from the transmission end of the cover **(see illustration)**.
4 Release the two clips at the front, undo the two bolts at the rear of the cover, and then withdraw the soundproofing/protective cover from over the injectors **(see illustrations)**.
5 Disconnect the wiring plugs from the glow plugs **(see illustration)**.
6 Clean the surrounding area, then unscrew and remove the glow plugs from the cylinder head.

Inspection

7 Inspect the glow plugs for physical damage. Burnt or eroded glow plug tips can be caused by a bad injector spray pattern. Have the injectors checked if this sort of damage is found.
8 If the glow plugs are in good physical condition, check them electrically using a 12 volt test lamp or continuity tester with reference to the previous Section.
9 The glow plugs can be energised by applying 12 volts to them to verify that they heat up evenly and in the required time. Observe the following precautions:
a) *Support the glow plug by clamping it carefully in a vice or self-locking pliers. Remember it will become red-hot.*
b) *Make sure that the power supply or test lead incorporates a fuse or overload trip to protect against damage from a short-circuit.*
c) *After testing, allow the glow plug to cool for several minutes before attempting to handle it.*

2.3 Disconnect the wiring plugs

2.4a Release the clips...

2.4b ...undo the bolts...

2.4c ...and remove the cover

2.5 Disconnecting the wiring from the glow plugs

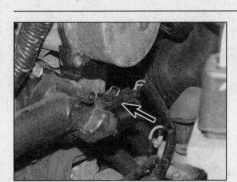

4.1 Location of temperature sensor

4.3a Release the retaining clip...

4.3b ...and withdraw the sensor from the housing

10 A glow plug in good condition will start to glow red at the tip after drawing current for 5 seconds or so. Any plug which takes much longer to start glowing, or which starts glowing in the middle instead of at the tip, is defective.

Refitting

11 Refit by reversing the removal operations. Apply a smear of copper based anti-seize compound to the plug threads and tighten the glow plugs to the specified torque. Do not overtighten, as this can damage the glow plug element.

3 Pre/post-heating system control unit – removal and refitting

Removal

1 The pre/post-heating control unit is located on the cooling fan cowling at the left-hand side of the engine compartment. Before proceeding, make sure that the ignition is switched off.
2 Disconnect the wiring from the control unit.
3 Unscrew the mounting nuts/bolts and remove the control unit from the cooling fan cowling.

Refitting

4 Refitting is a reversal of removal.

4 Coolant temperature sensor – removal, testing, and refitting

Note: *Also refer to Chapter 3, Section 8.*

Removal

1 The coolant temperature sensor is located on the thermostat housing on the left-hand end of the cylinder head **(see illustration)**.
2 Drain the cooling system as described in Chapter 1B. Alternatively, remove the expansion bottle cap to depressurise the system, and have the new temperature sensor or a suitable bung to hand.
3 Disconnect the wiring connector, release the securing clip and withdraw the temperature sensor from the coolant housing **(see illustrations)**.

Testing

Note: *A continuity tester or an ohmmeter will be required for testing.*
4 The sensor has two functions – the NTC (negative temperature coefficient) resistor informs the pre/post-heating control unit of the engine coolant temperature, and its switch interrupts the electrical supply to the EGR solenoid.
5 Connect a continuity tester or an ohmmeter to pins 1 and 4 of the sensor connector.

There should be infinite resistance at room temperature, showing that the contacts of the thermoswitch are open.
6 Next suspend the sensor in a container of water (using string) so that it is immersed but not touching the sides or the base of the container. Dip a thermometer into the water, apply heat and then check that the contacts of the thermoswitch remain open up to 20°C but close at temperatures above 30°C. With the contacts closed, the ohmmeter must show zero resistance.
7 Connect an ohmmeter across the switch terminals 2 and 3. Heat the water and check that the resistance of the thermistor (coolant temperature sensor) is in accordance with the figures given in the Specifications.
8 If the results obtained are not as specified, the switch is proved faulty and should be renewed.

Refitting

9 Refitting is the reverse of removal, but fit a new sealing ring.
10 Refit the temperature sensor into the coolant housing making sure the seal is in position, then secure it in place with the retaining clip. Reconnect the wiring connector to the sensor.
11 On completion, top-up or refill and bleed the cooling system, as necessary, as described in Chapter 1B Section 27.

Chapter 6
Clutch

Contents

Degrees of difficulty

Easy, suitable for novice with little experience	**Fairly easy,** suitable for beginner with some experience	**Fairly difficult,** suitable for competent DIY mechanic	**Difficult,** suitable for experienced DIY mechanic	**Very difficult,** suitable for expert DIY or professional

Specifications

General
Clutch type . . . . Single dry plate, diaphragm spring, hydraulically-operated release mechanism

Clutch friction disc
Friction material thickness (new) . . . . 7.0 mm (approximate)

Torque wrench settings

	Nm	lbf ft
Clutch pedal mounting bracket nuts	21	15
Clutch slave cylinder/release bearing	21	15
Pressure plate-to-flywheel bolts:		
Petrol engines	23	17
Diesel engines	15	11

1 General Information

1 The clutch consists of a friction disc, a pressure plate assembly, a release bearing and hydraulic slave cylinder; all of these components are contained in the large cast-aluminium alloy bellhousing, sandwiched between the engine and the transmission.

2 The hydraulic master cylinder is located in the pedal bracket on the bulkhead, and the clutch fluid reservoir is shared with the brake fluid reservoir on the top of the brake master cylinder. Inside the reservoir each circuit has its own compartment, so that in the event of fluid loss in the clutch circuit, the brake circuit remains fully operational.

3 The clutch friction disc is fitted between the engine flywheel and the clutch pressure plate, and is allowed to slide on the transmission input shaft splines.

4 The pressure plate assembly is bolted to the engine flywheel. When the engine is running, drive is transmitted from the crankshaft, via the flywheel, to the friction disc (these components being clamped securely together by the pressure plate assembly) and from the friction disc to the transmission input shaft.

5 To interrupt the drive, the spring pressure must be relaxed by the hydraulically-operated release mechanism. Depressing the clutch pedal operates the master cylinder which in turn operates the slave cylinder and presses the release bearing against the pressure plate spring fingers. This causes the springs to deform and releases the clamping force on the pressure plate. The slave cylinder and the release bearing are a combined assembly and cannot be renewed separately. This arrangement is often referred to as a concentric bearing.

6 When the pedal is released, the diaphragm spring forces the pressure plate into contact with the friction linings on the friction disc. The disc is now firmly sandwiched between the pressure plate and the flywheel, thus transmitting engine power to the transmission.

7 Wear of the friction material on the friction disc is automatically compensated for by the operation of the hydraulic system. As the friction material on the disc wears, the pressure plate moves towards the flywheel causing the clutch diaphragm spring inner fingers to move outwards. When the clutch pedal is released, excess fluid is expelled through the master cylinder into the fluid reservoir.

 Warning: Hydraulic fluid is poisonous; wash off immediately and thoroughly in the case of skin contact, and seek immediate medical advice if any fluid is swallowed or gets into the eyes. Certain types of hydraulic fluid are flammable, and may ignite when allowed into contact with hot components; when servicing any hydraulic system, it is safest to assume that the fluid is flammable, and to take precautions against the risk of fire as though it is petrol that is being handled. Hydraulic fluid is also an effective paint stripper, and will attack plastics; if any is spilt, it should be washed off immediately, using copious quantities of fresh water. Finally, it is hygroscopic (it absorbs moisture from the air) – old fluid may be contaminated and unfit for further use. When topping-up or renewing the fluid, always use the recommended type, and ensure that it comes from a freshly-opened sealed container.

2.5a Remove the rubber cap...

2.5b ...fit tube and release clip...

2.5c ...then pull the pipe out till it clicks into position

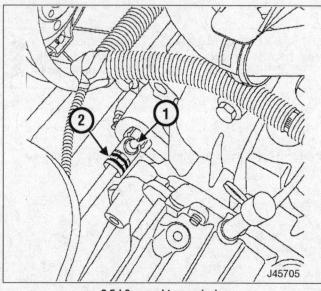

2.5d 6-speed transmission

1 Bleed nipple	2 Release clip

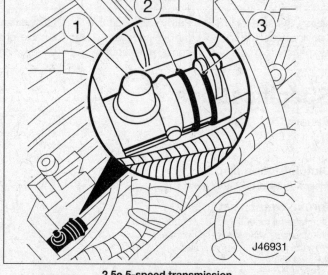

2.5e 5-speed transmission

1 Bleed nipple	2 Release clip	3 Locking clip

2 Clutch master cylinder – removal and refitting

Note: *Refer to the Warning in Section 1 before proceeding.*

Removal

1 Remove the air cleaner and inlet ducts as described in Chapter 4A or 4B, as applicable.

2.9 Prise the pushrod free from the clutch pedal

2 Remove the two clips that hold the bulkhead soundproofing in place. Move the soundproofing to the side to access the master cylinder supply pipe.

3 Fit a brake hose clamp over the section of flexible hose on the clutch master cylinder supply pipe.

4 Fit a length of transparent hose (screen washer hose is ideal for this) to the slave cylinder and place the end in a suitable container.

5 Depress the spring clip on the slave cylinder using a flat-bladed screwdriver on the 6-speed gearbox and remove the clip on 5-speed gearboxes. Pull the clutch fluid pipe outwards by one 'click' **(see illustrations)**.

6 Some models are fitted with a traditional bleed screw. Theses should be opened just sufficiently to allow the fluid to drain.

7 At this point, fluid will flow slowly into the container. Let the fluid flow until the reservoir is empty. Depress the clutch pedal a few times to empty the master cylinder and pipes.

8 Remove the driver's lower facia trim panel as described in Chapter 11, Section 28.

9 Disconnect the master cylinder pushrod from clutch pedal **(see illustration)**.

10 Place some absorbent cloth below the pipe connections on the master cylinder. Remove the clip from the supply pie and the outlet pipe. Mop-up any fluid spills and plug the pipes.

11 The master cylinder is a bayonet fit in the bulkhead. Turn the master cylinder a quarter turn clockwise to remove it. If this proves difficult a special tool (Emb 1596) is available for unlocking the master cylinder. Remove the master cylinder.

12 If the master cylinder is faulty it must be renewed – at the time of writing, repair kits were not available. Check, however, on parts availability from other sources before purchasing a new unit.

Refitting

13 Refitting is a reversal of removal, noting the following points:

a) *Check the condition of the pipe seals, and renew if necessary.*

b) *Ensure that all fluid hose connections are clean, and are securely made.*

c) *The master cylinder has a foolproof fitting – it will only fit one way*

d) *Fill and bleed the clutch system on*

completion, as described in Section 5.
Also check the operation of the brakes,
and if necessary, bleed the system as
described in Chapter 9 Section 5.

3 Clutch slave cylinder – removal and refitting

Note: *Refer to the Warning in Section 1 before proceeding.*

Removal

1 Remove the transmission as described in Chapter 7 Section 7.
2 Inside the bellhousing, unscrew and remove the two mounting bolts, then withdraw the slave cylinder and release bearing over the transmission input shaft **(see illustration)**.
3 The release bearing is part of the slave cylinder. No separate parts are available.

Refitting

4 Refitting is a reversal of removal, noting the following points:
a) Renew the slave cylinder-to-release bearing seal (normally supplied with the new bearing).
b) Tighten the release bearing mounting bolts to the specified torque
c) Refit the transmission as described in Chapter 7 Section 7.
d) On completion, bleed the clutch as described in Section 5.

4 Clutch hydraulic hoses – removal and refitting

Note: *Refer to the Warning in Section 1 before proceeding.*

Removal

1 Remove the battery and battery tray as described in Chapter 5A Section 4.
2 Remove the engine ECU as described in Chapter 4A or 4B, as applicable.
3 Remove the air cleaner and inlet ducts as described in Chapter 4A or 4B, as applicable.
4 Remove the plastic clips and move the soundproofing away from the bulkhead.
5 Empty the system of fluid as described in Section 2.
6 Unclip and remove the hose from the slave cylinder. Plug or tape over the slave cylinder connection to prevent further fluid loss **(see illustrations)**.
7 The pipe is in two sections. If required disconnect the pipe at the junction on the left-hand front inner wing. Plug the pipe at both ends.
8 Trace the pipe back to the bulkhead connections, releasing it from the mounting clips.
9 Place some absorbent cloth below the pipe connections on the master cylinder.

10 Pull out the clip from the master cylinder to release the pipe.
11 Remove the pipe from the vehicle.

Refitting

12 Refitting is a reversal of removal, but bleed the clutch system on completion as described in Section 5.

5 Clutch hydraulic system – bleeding

Note: *Refer to the Warning in Section 1 before proceeding.*

1 The correct operation of any hydraulic system is only possible after removing all air from the components and circuit; this is achieved by bleeding the system.
2 During the bleeding procedure, add only clean, unused hydraulic fluid of the recommended type; never re-use fluid that has already been bled from the system. Ensure that sufficient fluid is available before starting work.
3 If there is any possibility of incorrect fluid being already in the system, the hydraulic circuit must be flushed completely with uncontaminated, correct fluid.
4 If hydraulic fluid has been lost from the system, or air has entered because of a leak, ensure that the fault is cured before continuing further.
5 The bleed nipple is fitted to the slave cylinder at the front of the transmission bellhousing. Note that several versions are fitted (as described in Section 2).
6 Remove the battery and battery tray as described in Chapter 5A Section 4.
7 Unscrew the brake fluid reservoir cap, and top-up the fluid level to the MAXI mark. Keep an eye on the fluid level as bleeding progresses, and keep it topped-up above the MINI mark throughout.
8 Referring to Section 2, connect a piece of tube to the bleed nipple, and open the circuit as described – bleeding and filling the system is done by gravity.
9 If a new slave or master cylinder have been fitted they should be primed with clean fresh fluid on the bench.

3.2 Unscrew the two mounting bolts

10 If the system is known to be empty (or if new parts have been fitted), have an assistant hold the clutch pedal depressed until the flow of bubbles seen in the pipe ceases. Depress and release the clutch pedal a few times, to purge the air from the master cylinder and pipes. Top-up the fluid level as necessary.
11 When no more bubbles are seen in the fluid, release the clutch pedal, then press the slave cylinder pipe firmly back into place.
12 Top-up the fluid level to the MAXI mark, and refit the reservoir cap.
13 Check the operation of the clutch – any lack of response indicates the need for further bleeding.
14 If the clutch system was emptied, check the brakes for any sign of 'sponginess' in the pedal, which would mean the brakes also require bleeding, as described in Chapter 9 Section 5.
15 Discard any hydraulic fluid that has been bled from the system; it will not be fit for re-use.
16 Clutches that use a concentric release bearing system can often prove difficult to bleed. If the method described above fails to expel all the air from the system the circuit can be bled in reverse. A large syringe will be required for the task.
17 Remove adequate fluid from the master cylinder (an old battery hydrometer is ideal for this) and connect a large syringe to the hose. Ideally hold the syringe above the level of the master cylinder and fill it with brake fluid. There must be no air bubbles in the hose or syringe.

4.6a Plug the slave cylinder...

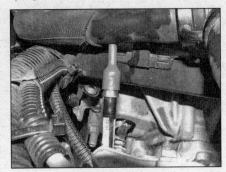

4.6b ...and the pipe

6.2 Model with two switches fitted

6.3 Remove the upper switch to access nut

6.5 Remove the pedal bracket nuts

18 Slowly force fluid back up through the system. Have an assistant depress the clutch pedal occasionally and monitor the level in the master cylinder constantly. Refit the clip in the slave cylinder and check the operation of the clutch. Repeat if necessary.

19 If the clutch is not operating correctly after repeated bleeding, the master cylinder or slave cylinder may be faulty.

6 Clutch pedal – removal and refitting

1 Remove the lower facia trim panel as described in Chapter 11, Section 28.
2 Unplug the wiring connector from the pedal switch – or switches, depending on model **(see illustration)**, and then remove the cable clip.
3 Where fitted, remove the upper switch from

the mounting bracket to access the upper mounting nut **(see illustration)**.
4 Prise free the master cylinder pushrod from the pedal **(see illustration 2.9)**.
5 Remove the pedal mounting nuts and withdraw the pedal assembly from the bulkhead **(see illustration)**.

7 Clutch pedal switches – removal and refitting

1 One or two cluch pedal switches are fitted. Key entry vehicles have one switch and key card vehicles two.
2 The signals from both switches may be used by the engine ECU to permit smoother gearchanging, and to enable other related control functions, such as idle speed control when the pedal is depressed.

7.5 Disconnect the wiring

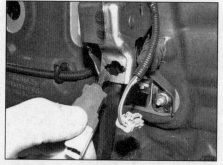

7.6 Twist and remove the switch from the pedal bracket

3 The end of pedal travel switch is used by the keyless card system, to signal that the clutch is fully depressed, to allow the engine to be started.

Removal

4 Remove the driver's lower facia trim panel as described in Chapter 11, Section 28.
5 Disconnect the wiring plugs from the relevant switch **(see illustration)**.
6 Twist the switch through a quarter-turn, and remove it from the pedal mounting bracket **(see illustration)**.

Refitting

7 Refitting is a reversal of removal, noting the following points:
a) *Before fitting the switch, the exposed length of the plunger should checked **(see illustration)**. If the correct dimension cannot be achieved the switch must be renewed. The switch will self-adjust when refitted.*
b) *Confirm the correct switch operation as follows. Firmly apply the handbrake, and make sure there is nothing in front of the car, as it could move forwards. Select a high gear, and try to start the engine without depressing the clutch – nothing should happen. With the clutch depressed, the engine should start.*

8 Clutch assembly – removal, inspection and refitting

⚠️ *Warning: Dust created by clutch wear and deposited on the clutch components may contain asbestos which is a health hazard. DO NOT blow it out with compressed air or inhale any of it. DO NOT use petrol or petroleum-based solvents to clean off the dust. Brake system cleaner or methylated spirit should be used to flush the dust into a suitable receptacle. After the clutch components are wiped clean with rags, dispose of the contaminated rags and cleaner in a sealed, marked container.*

Removal

1 Access to the clutch may be gained in

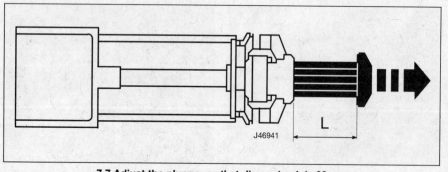

J46941

7.7 Adjust the plunger so that dimension L is 28mm

8.1 View of the clutch assembly with the gearbox removed

8.2 Mark the relationship of the pressure plate to the flywheel

8.3 Using a screwdriver in the ring gear teeth while unscrewing the clutch pressure plate bolts

one of two ways. Either the gearbox may be removed independently, as described in Chapter 7 Section 7, or the engine/gearbox unit may be removed as described in Chapter 2D Section 4, and the gearbox separated from the engine on the bench **(see illustration)**.

2 Having separated the gearbox from the engine, first use paint or a marker pen to mark the relationship of the clutch pressure plate to the flywheel **(see illustration)**.

3 Unscrew and remove the clutch pressure plate retaining bolts. Work in a diagonal sequence and slacken the bolts only a few turns at a time. Hold the flywheel stationary by positioning a screwdriver over the dowel on the cylinder block and engaging it with the starter ring gear **(see illustration)**. Alternatively use a locking tool or refit one of the gearbox mounting bolts.

4 Ease the pressure plate assembly off its locating dowels. Be prepared to catch the friction disc, which will drop out as the assembly is removed. Note which way round the disc is fitted.

Inspection

5 With the clutch assembly removed, clean off all traces of dust using a dry cloth. This is best done outside or in a well-ventilated area (refer to the warning at the beginning of this Section).

6 Examine the linings of the friction disc for wear or loose rivets, and the disc rim for distortion, cracks, broken torsion springs and worn splines **(see illustration)**. The surface

of the friction linings may be highly glazed, but as long as the friction material pattern can be clearly seen, this is satisfactory. If there is any sign of oil contamination, indicated by shiny black discoloration, the disc must be renewed and the source of the contamination traced and rectified. This will be a leaking crankshaft oil seal, gearbox input shaft oil seal, or both. The renewal procedure for the crankshaft oil seal is given in the relevant part of Chapter 2B. Renewal of the gearbox input shaft oil seal on 5-speed gearboxes should be entrusted to a Renault garage, as it involves dismantling the gearbox and the renewal of the clutch release bearing guide tube using a press. The seal can be renewed on 6-speed gearboxes after removal of the concentric slave cylinder. The disc friction must also be renewed if the linings have worn down to, or just above, the level of the rivet heads.

7 Check the machined faces of the flywheel and pressure plate. If either is grooved, or heavily scored, renewal is necessary. The pressure plate must also be renewed if any cracks are apparent, or if the diaphragm spring is damaged or its pressure suspect **(see illustrations)**.

8 Take the opportunity to check the condition of the release bearing, as described in Section 9.

9 It is good practice to renew the friction disc, pressure plate and release bearing at the same time.

Refitting

10 Before commencing the refitting procedure, lightly oil the splines of the input shaft or use a proprietary lubricant designed for the task. Do not use multipurpose grease. Distribute the lubricant by sliding the friction disc on and off the splines a few times. Remove the disc and wipe away any excess lubricant.

11 It is important that no oil or grease is allowed to come into contact with the friction material of the friction disc or the pressure plate and flywheel faces. It is advisable to refit the clutch assembly with clean hands, and to wipe the pressure plate and flywheel faces with a clean dry rag before assembly begins.

12 There are several different types of clutch alignment tool available to the home mechanic; the conventional type uses a spigot which centralises the disc with the hole in the end of the crankshaft, however, an alternative clamp-type tool centralises the disc onto the pressure plate before refitting them both to the flywheel.

Using a conventional alignment tool

13 Place the friction disc against the flywheel, with the side having the larger offset facing away from the flywheel, and hold the disc in position using the alignment tool **(see illustration)**.

14 Place the clutch pressure plate assembly over the dowels, and where applicable, align it with the previously-made mark. Refit the retaining bolts and tighten them finger-tight so

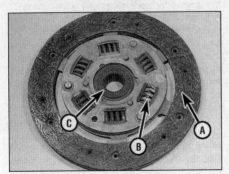

8.6 Inspect the friction linings (A), springs (B) and splines (C)

8.7a Check the machined face of the pressure plate...

8.7b ...and the diaphragm spring fingers for wear, especially at the tips

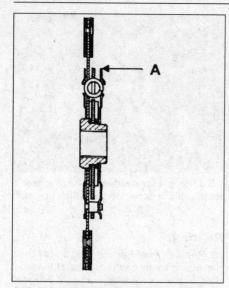

8.13 Clutch disc offset (A) faces away from flywheel

that the friction disc is gripped, but can still be moved.

15 The disc must now be centralised so that, when the engine and gearbox are reconnected, the splines of the gearbox input shaft will pass through the splines in the centre of the friction disc hub. If this is not done accurately, it will be impossible to refit the gearbox.

16 Centralisation can be carried out quite easily by inserting a round bar through the hole in the centre of the friction disc, so that the end of the bar rests in the hole in the end of the

8.20a Centralise the pressure plate on the disc...

8.21 Locate the assembly on the flywheel...

8.16 Using a clutch alignment tool to centralise the friction disc

crankshaft. Note that a plastic centralising tube is supplied with Renault clutch kits, making the use of a bar unnecessary. If a non-Renault clutch is being fitted, an alternative and more accurate method of centralisation is to use a commercially-available clutch alignment tool obtainable from most accessory shops (see illustration).

17 If a bar is being used, move it sideways or up-and-down until the friction disc is centralised. Centralisation can be judged by removing the bar and viewing the disc hub in relation to the bore in the end of the crankshaft. When the bore appears exactly in the centre of the disc hub, all is correct.

18 Once the disc is centralised, progressively tighten the pressure plate bolts in a diagonal sequence to the correct torque setting (see illustration). Remove the centralising tool.

19 The gearbox can now be refitted to the engine with reference to Chapter 7 Section 7.

8.20b ...fit the tool and tighten to clamp the disc to the pressure plate

8.22 ...then progressively tighten the bolts to the specified torque

8.18 Tightening the clutch pressure plate bolts

Using a clamp-type alignment tool

20 Position the pressure plate centrally on the friction disc, then insert the alignment tool and clamp the two items together with the tool (see illustrations). Check that the disc is correctly aligned with the pressure plate by viewing it from the flywheel side.

21 Position the plate and disc on the flywheel and insert the retaining bolts finger-tight (see illustration). Where applicable, align the previously-made marks on the plate and flywheel.

22 Progressively tighten the pressure plate bolts to the specified torque, then remove the tool (see illustration).

23 The gearbox can now be refitted to the engine with reference to Chapter 7 Section 7.

| 9 | Clutch release bearing – removal, inspection and refitting | |

Removal and refitting

1 For access to the clutch release bearing, the transmission must be removed as described in Chapter 7 Section 7.

2 The release bearing and the slave cylinder are a single combined (concentric) unit. The bearing is removed as described in Section 3.

Inspection

3 Note that it is often considered worthwhile to renew the release bearing as a matter of course regardless of its condition, considering the amount of work necessary to access it.

4 It should also be noted that the slave cylinder will have fully extended as the gearbox was removed. Worn clutch material may have entered the slave cylinder piston at this point. If the original slave cylinder is refitted this contamination may damage the piston seal, leading to the possibility of fluid loss and cylinder failure.

5 Check that the contact surface rotates smoothly and easily, with no sign of noise or roughness, and that the surface itself is smooth and unworn, with no signs of cracks, pitting or scoring. If there is any doubt about its condition, the bearing (and slave cylinder) must be renewed.

Chapter 7
Manual gearbox

Contents

Degrees of difficulty

Easy, suitable for novice with little experience	Fairly easy, suitable for beginner with some experience	Fairly difficult, suitable for competent DIY mechanic	Difficult, suitable for experienced DIY mechanic	Very difficult, suitable for expert DIY or professional

Specifications

General

Type . . . . Five or six forward speeds (all synchromesh) and reverse. Final drive differential integral with main gearbox

Lubrication

Type . . . . See *Lubricants and fluids* on page 0•18
Capacity:
  5-speed transmission. . . . . 3.4 litres
  6-speed transmission. . . . . 2.0 litres

Torque wrench settings

	Nm	lbf ft
Engine steady bar (5-speed gearbox)	105	77
Engine steady bar main support (6-speed gearbox)	180	133
Exhaust support bracket (6-speed gearbox)	21	15
Gear change assembly to transmission tunnel	21	15
Gearbox bellhousing to engine	45	33
Rear engine mounting to gearbox	See Chapter 2A, 2B or 2C	
Starter motor mounting bolt	45	33
Subframe front bolt	105	77
Subframe link arm bolts	21	15

1 General Information

1 Drive is transmitted from the crankshaft via the clutch to the input shaft, which rotates in sealed ball-bearings, and has a splined extension to accept the clutch friction disc. From the input shaft, drive is transmitted to the output shaft, which rotates in a roller bearing at its right-hand end, and a sealed ball-bearing at its left-hand end. From the output shaft, drive is transmitted to the differential crownwheel, which rotates with the differential case and planetary gears, thus driving the side gears and driveshafts. The rotation of the planetary gears on their shaft allows the inner roadwheel to rotate at a slower speed than the outer roadwheel when the car is cornering.

2 The input and output shafts are arranged side-by-side, parallel to the crankshaft and driveshafts, so that their gear pinion teeth are in constant mesh. In the neutral position, the output shaft gear pinions rotate freely, so that drive cannot be transmitted to the crownwheel. Synchromesh is provided on all forward speeds. Gear selection is via a floor-mounted lever and rod mechanism.

3 The gearbox selector rod causes the appropriate selector fork to move its respective synchro-sleeve along the shaft, in order to lock the gear pinion to the synchro-hub. Since the synchro-hubs are splined to the output shaft, this locks the pinion to the shaft so that drive can be transmitted. To ensure that gearchanges can be made quickly and quietly, a synchromesh system is fitted to all forward gears, consisting of baulk rings and spring-loaded fingers, as well as the gear pinions and synchro-hubs. The synchromesh cones are formed on the mating faces of the baulk rings and gear pinions.

2.3 Remove the oil filler plug on the front of the gearbox

2.4a Unscrew the drain plug...

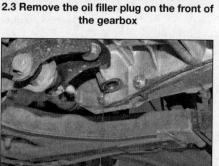

2.4b ...and allow the oil to drain

2.6 Refill the gearbox with fresh oil

2 Gearbox oil – draining and refilling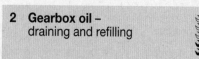

Note: *The filler plug is also used as the level plug.*

1 This operation is much quicker and more efficient if the car is first taken on a journey of sufficient length to warm the engine/gearbox up to operating temperature.

2 Park the car on level ground, switch off the ignition and apply the handbrake firmly. For improved access, jack up the car and support it securely on axle stands (see *Jacking and*

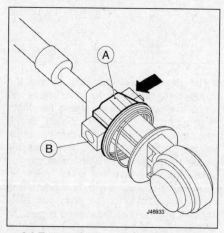

3.3 To unlock the cable compress the lock ring (A) and push the orange clip (B) upwards in the direction shown

vehicle support), or alternatively position the vehicle over an inspection pit or on car ramps. Note that, to ensure accuracy, the car must be level when checking the oil level. Remove the engine compartment undertray.

3 Remove all traces of dirt from around the drain and filler plugs, then unscrew the filler/level plug from the front face of the gearbox **(see illustration)**.

4 Position a suitable container under the gearbox, then unscrew the drain plug and allow the oil to drain completely into the container **(see illustrations)**. If the oil is hot, take precautions against scalding. Clean both the filler/level and the drain plugs, being especially careful to wipe any metallic particles off the magnetic inserts. The sealing washers should be renewed whenever they are disturbed.

5 When the oil has finished draining, clean the drain plug threads and those of the gearbox casing. Obtain a new sealing washer and refit the drain plug, tightening it securely.

6 Refilling the gearbox is an extremely awkward operation. Above all, allow plenty of time for the oil level to settle properly before checking it. Note that the car must be level when checking the oil level **(see illustration)**.

7 Refill the gearbox with the specified type of oil, then check the oil level as described in Chapter 1A or 1B. When the level is correct, refit the filler level plug with a new sealing washer and tighten securely.

8 Refit the plastic cover to the gearbox or the engine undertray (as applicable), then lower the vehicle to the ground.

3 Gearchange mechanism (6-speed gearbox) – adjustment

Note: *No adjustment is possible on the 5-speed gearboxes.*

1 First remove the battery (as described in Chapter 5A Section 4) and then remove the air filter housing and associated pipework to gain access to the linkage.

2 Working inside the vehicle remove the centre console (as described in Chapter 11 Section 27) and fit a 6 mm shim between the gear lever and the reverse stop. A suitable length of cord should be used to secure the gear lever tightly against the shim.

3 At the gearbox end, unlock the cable and remove any slack from the cable and then refit the locking clip. Adjustment is only possible on the cable fitted with the clip **(see illustration)**.

4 Check that all the gears can be selected and then refit the air filter housing, battery and centre console.

4 Gearchange mechanism – removal and refitting

Removal

1 Working inside the vehicle, remove the centre console as described in Chapter 11 Section 27.

2 Working under the bonnet remove the battery, air filter housing and the associated pipework. Prise free the inner cables from the gearbox and then remove the outer cable from the support by squeezing the clip together (5-speed gearboxes) or by pushing the locking clip backwards on the 6-speed gearbox **(see illustrations)**.

3 Chock the front wheels and then jack up and support the rear of the vehicle.

4 With the vehicle firmly supported, remove the rear exhaust rubber mounting and the centre exhaust mounting. Allow the exhaust system to rest on the rear axle and then lower the vehicle to the ground.

5 Firmly apply the handbrake, and then jack up the front of the vehicle and support it on

4.2a Prise the inner cable ball joint free...

4.2b ...release the securing clips...

4.2c ...and release the outer cables

4.9 Using a pair of grips to secure ball joint

axle stands (see *Jacking and vehicle support*). Remove the engine compartment undertray

6 Unbolt and remove the exhaust heat shield for access to the bottom of the gear lever.

7 Working inside the vehicle, remove the four bolts and then unclip the gear lever assembly from the transmission tunnel. From underneath the vehicle manoeuvre the assembly around the exhaust system and remove it from the vehicle..

8 No separate parts are available for the gear selector and lever assembly. If wear or damage is found the complete assembly must be renewed.

Refitting

9 Refitting is a reversal of removal, but lubricate all the pivot points with multipurpose grease and adjust the linkage on 6-speed gearboxes as described in Section 3 of this chapter. Make sure the gearchange ball joints are secure on the selector levers **(see illustration)**.

5   Oil seals –
       renewal

Driveshaft oil seals

Note: *The driveshaft oil seals must always be renewed when the driveshafts are removed.*

1 Apply the handbrake, then jack up the front of the car and support it on axle stands (see *Jacking and vehicle support*).

2 Remove the undertray and drain the gearbox oil as described in Section 2. Remove the appropriate roadwheel.

3 Referring to Chapter 8 Section 2, disconnect the driveshaft from the gearbox. Note that it is not necessary to remove the driveshaft completely, the shaft can be left attached to the hub assembly and slid off from the differential gear splines as the hub assembly is pulled outwards. **Note:** *Do not allow it to hang down under its own weight, as this could damage the constant velocity joints/ gaiters.*

4 Using a long lever and a block of wood to protect the gearbox, prise the old seal from the differential housing, taking care not to damage the housing. Wipe clean the oil seal seating in the casing **(see illustration)**.

5 The new seal may be of a slightly different design **(see illustration)**.

6 Oil the inner lip of the seal and then drive the seal into position using a suitable socket. The socket must only bear on the outer edge of the new seal **(see illustration)**.

7 Reconnect the driveshaft to the gearbox as described in Chapter 8 Section 2.

8 Refill the gearbox with oil as described in Section 2 and then refit the engine undertray.

9 Refit the roadwheel and lower the car to the ground. Tighten the wheel bolts to the specified torque.

Input shaft oil seal

Note: *It is not possible to remove the input shaft seal on the 5-speed gearbox. These gearboxes require dismantling to renew the seal, and this work should be left to a Renault dealer or specialist gearbox repairer.*

10 Remove the gearbox as described in

Section 7 and then remove the clutch release bearing as described in Chapter 6 Section 9.

11 Carefully drill a 2 mm hole in the oil seal and then fit a self-tapping screw. Pull on the screw with pliers to remove the oil seal.

12 Wrap insulation tape around the input shaft splines to protect the inner lip of the new seal and then press the seal into the housing with a suitable tube, socket or block of wood.

6   Reversing light switch –
       testing, removal and refitting

Testing

1 The reversing light circuit is controlled by a plunger type switch that is screwed into the left-hand end of the gearbox casing, just in front of the driveshaft inner joint **(see illustration)**. If a fault develops in the circuit,

5.4 Carefully remove the oil seal

5.5 The new seal may be of a different design

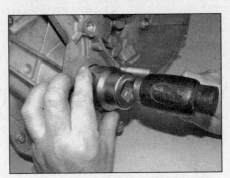

5.6 Drive the new seal into the housing with a suitable socket

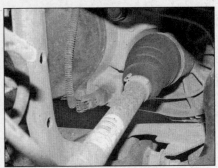

6.1 Reversing light switch on the bottom of the gearbox

7.7a Undo the front mounting bolts...

7.7b ...the side mounting bolts...

7.7c ...then remove the front lower cross member

first ensure that the circuit fuse has not blown.

2 To test the switch, disconnect the wiring connector, and use a multimeter (set to the resistance function) or a battery and bulb test circuit to check that there is continuity between the switch terminals only when reverse gear is selected. If this is not the case, and there are no obvious breaks or other damage to the wires, the switch is faulty, and must be renewed.

Removal

3 Firmly apply the handbrake, then jack up the front of the vehicle and support it on axle stands (see *Jacking and vehicle support*).
4 Remove the engine compartment undertray to access the switch from underneath or remove the left-hand front wheel to access the switch from inside the inner wheel arch..
5 Disconnect the wiring, then unscrew the

switch from the gearbox. Recover the sealing washer.

Refitting

6 Fit a new sealing washer to the switch, then screw it back into the gearbox casing and tighten it securely. Reconnect the wiring, and test the operation of the circuit. Where fitted, refit the engine compartment undertray, then lower the vehicle to the ground. If any oil was lost when the switch was removed, check the oil level as described in Chapter 1A or 1B.

7 Manual gearbox – removal and refitting

Note: *This Section describes the removal of the gearbox leaving the engine in position in the car. Alternatively, the engine and gearbox*

can be removed together, as described in Chapter 2D, then separated on the bench.

Removal

1 Apply the handbrake, then jack up the front of the vehicle and support it on axle stands (see *Jacking and vehicle support*). Remove the engine compartment undertray, both front roadwheels, both front wing inner liners and the front bumper as described in Chapter 11 Section 6.
2 Remove the battery and battery tray, as described in Chapter 5A Section 4.
3 On 0.9 litre petrol engines and 1.5 litre diesel engines, remove the air cleaner assembly, as described in Chapter 4A Section 2, or Chapter 4B Section 3.
4 Drain the gearbox oil as described in Section 2.
5 Disconnect the gearshift cables as described in Section 4.
6 Remove both driveshafts, as described in Chapter 8 Section 2, and on diesel engines remove the catalytic converter support bracket.
7 Using stout cord or cable ties secure the radiator to the bonnet slam panel and then remove the radiator lower support subframe **(see illustrations)**. Remove the link arms and the stiffener plate (6-speed gearbox only) from the left-hand chassis leg. On diesel engines, disconnect the coolant pump support and earth cable from the radiator support panel
8 Disconnect the reversing light switch and unbolt the gearbox earth cable from the bellhousing **(see illustration)**. On diesel engines the position of this cable is critical so mark its position precisely. Remove the wiring support bracket for the injectors on diesel engines.
9 Working underneath the vehicle, remove the rear engine steady bar mounting**(see illustration)**, as described in Chapter 2A Section 15.
10 Reaching down the back of the transmission, disconnect the wiring connectors from the crankshaft sensor and the lower oxygen sensor **(see illustrations)**. Unclip the wiring loom from the top of the transmission, and where applicable, remove the wiring support bracket from the top of the bellhousing.

7.8 Disconnect earth cable and reversing light switch

7.9 Unbolt and remove the steady bar

7.10a Disconnect the wiring connectors...

7.10b ...and unclip the wiring loom securing clips

7.11 Unclip the breather pipe

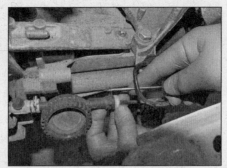
7.13a Release the securing clip...

7.13b ...disconnect the pipe and plug the ends

7.15a Remove the rubber mounting...

7.15b ...and mounting bracket

7.16 Remove the transmission stud

11 Unclip the breather pipe from the bracket on the end of the cylinder head **(see illustration)**.

12 Remove the starter motor as described in Chapter 5A Section 9.

13 Disconnect the clutch hydraulic pipe **(see illustrations)** and position it to one side with reference to Chapter 6 Section 4.

14 The engine and gearbox assembly must now be supported. A trolley jack with a suitable block of wood to spread the load can be used under the sump or alternatively an engine support bar across the engine compartment can be used.

15 With the engine supported, remove the transmission mounting and mounting bracket from the top of the transmission **(see illustrations)**.

16 Unscrew the gearbox-to-engine bolts but leave one upper bolt finger-tight until just before the gearbox is removed. At this point we attached a suitable rope to the top of the gearbox and over the support bar to help support the weight of the gearbox. If required, remove the two long studs **(see illustration)**, a Torx socket will be required, and then remove the final bolt. Pull back, and remove the gearbox, taking care to ensure that the weight of the gearbox is never held on the input shaft.

Refitting

17 Refitting is a reversal of removal, noting the following additional points.
a) *Make sure that all locating dowels are correctly positioned in the gearbox.*
b) *Lightly oil the splines of the input shaft or use a proprietary lubricant designed for the task. Do not use multipurpose grease.*
c) *Make sure that the locating dowel for the starter motor is correctly fitted.*
d) *Fit new driveshaft oil seals.*
e) *Refill the gearbox and check the gearbox oil level with reference to Chapter 1A Section 21 or Chapter 1B Section 21.*
f) *Tighten all nuts and bolts to the specified torque.*

8 Manual gearbox overhaul – general information

1 Overhauling a manual gearbox is a difficult and involved job for the DIY home mechanic. In addition to dismantling and reassembling many small parts, clearances must be precisely measured and, if necessary, changed by selecting shims and spacers. Gearbox internal components are also often difficult to obtain, and in many instances, extremely expensive. Because of this, if the gearbox develops a fault or becomes noisy, the best course of action is to have the unit overhauled by a specialist repairer, or to obtain an exchange reconditioned unit.

2 Nevertheless, it is not impossible for the more experienced mechanic to overhaul a gearbox, provided the special tools are available and the job is done in a deliberate step-by-step manner so that nothing is overlooked.

3 The tools necessary for an overhaul include internal and external circlip pliers, bearing pullers, a slide-hammer, a set of pin punches, a dial test indicator, and possibly a hydraulic press. In addition, a large, sturdy workbench and a vice will be required.

4 During dismantling of the gearbox, make careful notes of how each component is fitted, to make reassembly easier and more accurate.

5 Before dismantling the gearbox, it will help if you have some idea what area is malfunctioning. Certain problems can be closely related to specific areas in the gearbox, which can make component examination and renewal easier. Refer to the Fault finding 13 Section 9 Section at the end of this manual for more information.

Chapter 8
Driveshafts

Contents

Degrees of difficulty

| **Easy,** suitable for novice with little experience | | **Fairly easy,** suitable for beginner with some experience | | **Fairly difficult,** suitable for competent DIY mechanic | | **Difficult,** suitable for experienced DIY mechanic | | **Very difficult,** suitable for expert DIY or professional | |

Specifications

General
Driveshaft type	Solid steel shafts, splined to inner and outer constant velocity joints
Lubricant type/specification	Special grease supplied in sachets with gaiter kits – joints are otherwise pre-packed with grease and sealed

Torque wrench settings
	Nm	lbf ft
Anti-roll bar link arm upper nut	37	27
Brake caliper support bracket bolts	105	77
Driveshaft retaining nut (Enko self-locking nut with integral washer)*	280	207
Right-hand driveshaft bearing support bracket bolts	21	15
Roadwheel bolts	105	77
Strut lower mounting bolts	105	77
Track rod end balljoint retaining nut	37	27

*Use new nuts/bolts

1 General Information

1 Drive is transmitted from the differential to the front wheels by means of two conventional driveshafts.
2 Both driveshafts are fitted with a constant velocity (CV) joint at their outer ends, which are of the ball and cage type. Each joint has an outer member, which is splined at its outer end to accept the wheel hub and is threaded so that it can be fastened to the hub by a large nut. The complete assembly is protected by a rubber or thermoplastic flexible gaiter secured to the driveshaft and joint outer member.
3 The inboard end of the shaft is splined to engage with a tripod joint, containing needle roller bearings and cups. The tripod joint is free to slide within the yoke of the joint outer member, which is splined to engage with the differential sun gears. A thermoplastic or rubber flexible gaiter secured to the driveshaft and outer member protects the complete assembly. The right-hand driveshaft is supported at the centre with a bearing and carrier secured to the rear of the engine block.

2 Driveshaft – removal and refitting

Removal

1 Remove the wheel trim/hub cap (as applicable), then slacken the driveshaft nut with the vehicle resting on its wheels. Also slacken the wheel bolts.
2 Chock the rear wheels of the car, apply the handbrake, then jack up the front of the car and support it on axle stands (see *Jacking*

8•2 Driveshafts

2.3a Detach the ABS sensor wiring…

2.3b …and then unbolt the support bracket

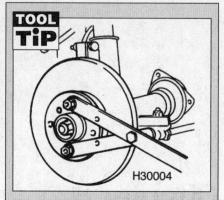

H30004

Using a fabricated tool to hold the front hub stationary whilst the driveshaft nut is slackened.

and vehicle support). Remove the front roadwheel.

3 Unclip the wiring for the ABS wheel sensor and the brake hose from the bracket on the bottom of the strut **(see illustrations)**.

4 Slacken and remove the driveshaft retaining nut. If the nut was not slackened with the wheels on the ground (see paragraph 1) a tool can be fabricated from two lengths of steel strip (one long, one short) and a nut and bolt with the nut and bolt forming the pivot of a forked tool **(see Tool Tip)**.

5 Unscrew the two bolts securing the brake caliper assembly to the swivel hub, and slide the caliper assembly off the disc. Using a piece of wire or string, tie the caliper to the front suspension coil spring to avoid placing any strain on the hydraulic brake hose **(see illustrations)**.

6 Slacken and remove the nut securing the

steering gear track rod end balljoint to the swivel hub. Release the balljoint tapered shank using a universal balljoint separator **(see illustrations)**.

7 Remove the anti-roll bar link arm from the suspension strut. Whilst not strictly necessary, this will make removing the driveshaft considerable easier.

8 Slacken and remove the two nuts from the bolts securing the swivel hub to the suspension strut, noting that the nuts are positioned on the rear side of the strut **(see illustration)**. Withdraw the upper bolt, but leave the lower bolt in position at this stage. Now proceed as described under the relevant sub-heading.

Left-hand driveshaft

9 Have a clean container ready to catch the transmission oil/fluid as the driveshaft is

removed, or alternatively drain the oil/fluid as described in Chapter 7 Section 2.

10 Using a soft-faced hammer, drive the shaft back through the swivel hub. If an ordinary hammer is used, place a small piece of wood over the end of the driveshaft in addition to the loosened driveshaft nut, this will protect the threads from damage.

11 It's likely that the splines will be very tight (corrosion may even be a factor, if the driveshaft has not been disturbed for some time), and considerable force may be needed to push the driveshaft out. Do not attempt to push the driveshaft all the way out, just free it off. In extreme cases, a suitable press may be

2.5a Remove the bolts…

2.5b …then remove the complete brake assembly…

2.5c …and secure it to the suspension strut

2.6a Use a Torx socket and spanner to remove the nut…

2.6b …and then use a balljoint separator to release the track rod end

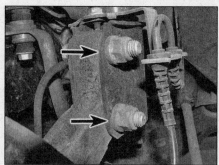

2.8 The nuts are fitted to the rear of the strut

2.11 Using an extractor to press the driveshaft out of the front hub

2.12a If required, lever the hub free from the strut...

2.12b ...and then pull the driveshaft from the hub

2.12c Support the driveshaft

2.13a Lever the inner joint free...

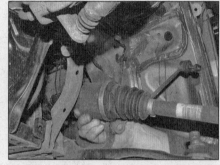

2.13b ...and then remove the complete shaft

required to release the driveshaft from the hub **(see illustration)**.

12 Remove the remaining lower bolt from the bottom of the suspension strut, remove the driveshaft nut and tip the hub assembly outwards to free the driveshaft **(see illustrations)**. Tie the driveshaft loosely to the strut with cord or a cable tie to avoid straining the inner joint.

13 On some models the driveshafts are held into the transmission by a spring circlip, which can take some effort to release. Use a pry bar with a block of wood behind to prise the inner joint out **(see illustrations)**. Take care not to damage the driveshaft boot or the securing clips. Be prepared for a small amount of oil/ fluid loss when the driveshaft releases (or a large amount, if the transmission was not drained).

14 Whilst the driveshaft is removed, plug the differential aperture with a clean, lint-free cloth to prevent dirt getting in.

Right-hand driveshaft

15 The same procedure should be used to remove the right-hand driveshaft, but the support bearing housing must also be removed.

16 Release the two bolts holding the bracket in place and then using a blunt drift drive the shaft from the gearbox **(see illustrations)**. The support bracket for the 1.6 litre petrol and diesel engines is of a different design, but it can be removed in a similar manner.

Refitting

17 All new driveshafts supplied by Renault are equipped with cardboard or plastic

protectors, to prevent damage to the gaiters. Even the slightest knock to the gaiter can puncture it, allowing the entry of water or dirt at a later date, which may lead to the premature failure of the joint. If the original driveshaft is being refitted, it is worthwhile making up some cardboard protectors as a precaution. They can be held in position with elastic bands. The protectors should be left on the driveshafts until the end of the refitting procedure.

18 Before refitting the driveshafts new differential oil seals should be fitted as described in Chapter 7 Section 5.

19 Ensure both the hub and driveshaft outer constant velocity joint splines are clean and dry.

20 Locate the new circlip in the groove on the inner end of the driveshaft, and turn the clip so its open side is facing downwards.

2.16a Remove the bolts...

2.16b ...and recover the bracket

21 Lubricate the driveshaft inner splines with transmission oil/fluid. Carefully refit the driveshaft into the transmission, taking care not to damage the oil seal. Turn the driveshaft until it engages the splines on the differential gears.

22 Push the driveshaft fully home. On models fitted with a circlip make sure the shaft engages fully. Try pulling the shaft out, to make sure the circlip is fully engaged.

23 Apply a little molybdenum disulphide grease to the driveshaft outer splines. Pull the hub outwards, and insert the outer end of the driveshaft. Turn the driveshaft to engage the splines in the hub.

24 Refit the retaining bracket to the support bearing on the right-hand driveshaft and tighten to the specified torque.

25 Slide the hub fully onto the driveshaft splines, and then insert the two suspension strut mounting bolts from the front side of the strut. Refit the washers and nuts to the rear of the bolts, and tighten them to the specified torque.

26 Refit the anti-roll bar link arm to the suspension strut.

27 Fit the new driveshaft Enko type retaining nut **(see illustration)**, tightening it by hand only at this stage.

28 Reconnect the steering track rod balljoint to the swivel hub, and tighten its retaining nut to the specified torque.

29 Clean the threads of the caliper bracket mounting bolts, and coat them with thread-locking compound (Renault recommends Loctite Frenbloc – available from your Renault dealer). Slide the caliper into position, making sure the pads pass either side of the disc, and tighten the caliper bracket bolts to the specified torque setting.

30 Using the method employed during removal to prevent the hub from rotating,

2.27 A new 'Enko type' driveshaft securing nut will be needed

tighten the new driveshaft retaining nut to the specified torque. Alternatively, lightly tighten the nut at this stage, and tighten it to the specified torque once the vehicle is resting on its wheels again.

31 Check that the hub rotates freely, then remove the protectors (where fitted) from the driveshaft, taking great care not to damage the flexible gaiters.

32 Refit the roadwheel. Lower the car to the ground and tighten the roadwheel bolts to the specified torque. If not already done, also tighten the driveshaft retaining nut to the specified torque.

33 Refill the gearbox with the specified type and amount of oil, and check the level using the information given in Chapter 7 Section 2.

3 Outer constant velocity joint gaiter – renewal

Note: *Check on the availability of a joint repair kit before removal. The type of retaining clip for the gaiter may vary; check the fitment of the clip is correct according to the type supplied with the kit.*

Note: *Plastic type gaiter clips are not suitable for thermoplastic gaiters. A metal clip must always be used with these gaiters.*

1 Remove the driveshaft as described in Section 2.

2 If required, mount the driveshaft in a vice.

3 Note the fitted locations of both of the outer joint gaiter retaining clips, then release the clips from the gaiter. Some types of factory fitted clips will require cutting with a hacksaw to remove them. Slide the gaiter back along the driveshaft **(see illustrations)**.

4 With the shaft secured in a suitable vice strike the inner section of the joint with brass drift or similar. It may take several hard blows to force the joint off the shaft. Recover the circlip from the end of the shaft **(see illustrations)**.

5 Scoop out all of the old grease, and then pack the joint with new grease (an 80g tube is supplied with Renault kits). Take care that the fresh grease does not become contaminated with dirt or grit as it is being applied **(see illustration)**.

6 Fit the inner clip and gaiter to the driveshaft, and with a soft-faced hammer drive the outer joint over the new circlip and onto the shaft **(see illustrations)**. The small diameter end of the gaiter must be located in the groove on the driveshaft.

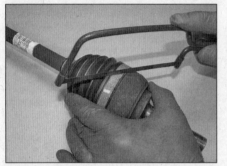
3.3a Cut free the retaining clips...

3.3b ...and slide back the gaiter

3.4a Drive off the outer joint...

3.4b ...recover the circlip...

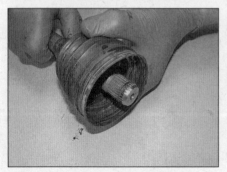
3.4c ...and slide off the old gaiter

3.5 Fill the joint with fresh grease

3.6a Fit the inner clip, the new outer gaiter...

3.6b ...and then fit a new circlip

3.6c Fit the outer joint and then slide the gaiter onto the outer joint

3.8 Crimping the large clip in place

7 Ensure that the gaiter is not twisted or distorted, and then insert a small screwdriver under the lip of the gaiter at the housing end to allow any trapped air to escape.
8 Remove the screwdriver, fit the new retaining clips and tighten them **(see illustration)**.
9 Check that the new gaiter is secure and then refit the driveshaft as described in Section 2.

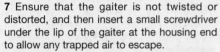

4 Driveshaft inner joint gaiter – renewal

1 Remove the driveshaft from the car, as described in Section 2.
2 If required, mount the driveshaft in a vice.
3 Note the fitted location of both of the inner joint gaiter retaining clips, then release the clips from the gaiter. Mark the driveshaft in relation to the joint housing, to ensure correct refitting and then slide the gaiter back along the driveshaft **(see illustrations)**.
4 Remove the inner joint housing from the tripod.
5 Extract the circlip retaining the tripod on the driveshaft **(see illustration)**. Some driveshafts may not have this circlip fitted; on these driveshafts, a simple peening of the splines retains the tripod. This can make removal difficult and a suitable puller may have to be employed to release the tripod.
6 Check that the inner end of the driveshaft is marked in relation to the splined tripod hub. If not, use dabs of paint on the driveshaft and one end of the tripod.

7 Using a soft-metal or wooden drift on the tripod centre hub (not on the outer rollers), tap off the tripod from the end of the driveshaft **(see illustrations)**.

8 Finally, slide off the inner gaiter **(see illustration)**.
9 If working on the right-hand driveshaft then this is an appropriate point to renew the

4.3a Cut through vthe large clip with a hacksaw...

4.3b ...prise free the smaller clip or drive it open

4.3c Make alignment marks between the shaft and the joint...

4.3d ...and then slide back the gaiter

4.5 Remove the circlip

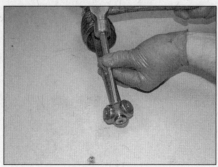

4.7a Use a drift to drive of the tripod...

4.7b ...or a suitable puller

4.8 Remove the gaiter

4.12a Note the previously made alignment marks

4.13a Where applicable, fit the new spring and cup...

4.16a Slide on the new clip...

4.11 Slide on the new gaiter

4.12b Fit a new circlip where necessary

4.13b ...and then pack the joint with fresh grease

4.16b ...and tighten

support bearing. Remove the retaining clip and using a suitable press extract the bearing taking care not to damage the machined surface on the shaft. It should be born in mind that if this bearing is worn than it is more than likely that the entire driveshaft is due for renewal.

10 Clean the driveshaft, and obtain a new joint retaining circlip. The gaiter retaining clips must also be renewed. Genuine Renault kits contain all these parts.

11 If necessary, tape the end of the shaft to prevent damage to the gaiter and then slide the new inner clip onto the shaft followed by the new gaiter (see illustration).

12 Refit the tripod on the driveshaft splines, if necessary using a soft-faced mallet and a suitable socket to drive it fully onto the splines. It must be fitted with the previously-made marks aligned (see illustrations). Secure it in position using a new circlip. Ensure that the circlip is fully engaged in its groove. On driveshafts with no circlip, peen the ends of the shaft splines with a suitable punch.

13 Scoop out all of the old grease from the joint housing. On left-hand side driveshafts, recover the spring and cup and then thoroughly clean all the components. Pack the joint and gaiter with new grease (a 100g tube is supplied with Renault kits). Guide the joint housing onto the tripod joint, making sure that the previously-made marks are aligned (see illustrations).

14 Slide the gaiter along the driveshaft, and locate it on the tripod joint housing. The small diameter end of the gaiter must be located in the groove on the driveshaft, while the larger end of the gaiter should also locate in a groove on the housing.

15 Ensure that the gaiter is not twisted or distorted, and then insert a small screwdriver under the lip of the gaiter at the housing end. This will allow trapped air to escape.

16 Remove the screwdriver, then fit the retaining clips and tighten them (see illustrations). Note that some driveshaft inner gaiters have a special low profile clip fitted to the transmission side of the joint. Compressing these clips is extremely difficult if the gaiter is made of a semi-rigid thermoplastic.

17 Check that the new gaiter is secure and then refit the driveshaft as described in Section 2.

5 Driveshaft overhaul – general information

1 If any of the checks described in Chapter 1A or 1B reveal wear in a driveshaft joint, first remove the roadwheel trim or centre cap (as appropriate) and check that the driveshaft retaining nut is still correctly tightened; if in doubt, use a torque wrench to check it. Refit the centre cap or trim, and repeat the check on the other driveshaft.

2 Road test the vehicle, and listen for a metallic clicking from the front as the vehicle is driven slowly in a circle on full lock. If a clicking or knocking noise can be heard, this may indicate wear in the outer constant velocity joint.

3 If vibration, consistent with roadspeed, is felt through the vehicle when accelerating, there is a possibility of wear in the inner constant velocity joints.

4 Constant velocity joints can be dismantled and inspected for wear. Motor factors may be able to supply the outer CV joint as a reconditioned separate assembly. The inner joint can only be renewed with a complete driveshaft.

Chapter 9
Braking system

Contents

Degrees of difficulty

| Easy, suitable for novice with little experience | Fairly easy, suitable for beginner with some experience | Fairly difficult, suitable for competent DIY mechanic | Difficult, suitable for experienced DIY mechanic | Very difficult, suitable for expert DIY or professional |

Specifications

General

System type . . . .   Servo-assisted hydraulic circuit, split diagonally with ABS anti-locking braking system
Front brakes . . . .   Disc, with single piston sliding caliper
Rear brakes . . . .   Self-adjusting drum or disc, according to model
Handbrake . . . .   Cable-operated, to rear wheels

Front brakes

Disc diameter . . . .   258.0 mm
Disc run-out . . . .   0.03 mm maximum
Disc thickness:
  New . . . .   22.0 mm
  Minimum. . . . .   19.8 mm
Piston diameter . . . .   48 mm
Brake pad thickness (friction material and backing plate):
  New . . . .   18.2 mm
  Minimum. . . . .   8.0 mm

Rear drum brakes

Drum internal diameter:
  New . . . .   203.20 mm
  Maximum diameter after machining. . . . .   204.40 mm
Brake shoe thickness:
  New . . . .   4.75 mm
  Minimum. . . . .   1.5 mm
Slave cylinder diameter . . . .   17.5 mm

Rear disc brakes

Disc diameter . . . .   240 mm
Disc thickness:
  New . . . .   8.0 mm
  Minimum. . . . .   7.0 mm
Disc run-out . . . .   0.07 mm maximum
Brake pad thickness (friction material and backing plate):
  New . . . .   15.8 mm
  Minimum. . . . .   7.5 mm

Torque wrench settings

	Nm	lbf ft
ABS system components:		
Modulator brake pipe union nuts	14	11
Wheel sensor retaining bolts	8 to 10	6 to 7
Brake caliper guide pin bolts*	32	26
Brake caliper bracket mounting bolts:		
Front	100	74
Rear	105	78
Brake disc retaining screw	20	15
Brake hose	17	13
Master cylinder brake pipe union nuts	15	11
Master cylinder reservoir bolt	9	7
Master cylinder-to-servo unit nuts	21	16
Oxygen sensor	45	34
Radiator cross member bolt	105	78
Rear hub nut	175	129
Rigid brake pipe	14	11
Roadwheel bolts	105	77
Subframe rear bolt	110	85
Vacuum servo unit mounting nuts	21	13

Use new bolts or nuts

1 General Information

1 ABS anti-lock braking system is fitted to all models as standard. The braking system is of the servo-assisted, dual circuit hydraulic type. All models are fitted with front disc brakes, but the rear brakes may be of drum or disc type, depending on model. Refer to Sections 20 and 21 for further information on ABS operation and components.

2 The front disc brakes are actuated by single piston sliding type calipers, which ensure that equal pressure is applied to each disc pad.

3 The rear drum brakes incorporate leading and trailing shoes, which are actuated by twin piston wheel cylinders (one cylinder per drum). As the brake shoe linings wear, footbrake operation automatically operates a self-adjuster mechanism, which effectively lengthens the strut between the shoes and reduces the lining-to-drum clearance.

4 On models with rear disc brakes, the brakes are actuated by single piston sliding calipers which incorporate a mechanical handbrake mechanism.

5 On all models, the handbrake provides an independent mechanical means of rear brake application.

Note: *When servicing any part of the braking system, work carefully and methodically; observe scrupulous cleanliness when overhauling any part of the hydraulic system. Always renew components (in axle sets, where applicable) if in doubt about their condition, and use only genuine Renault parts, or at least those of known good quality. Note the warnings given in 'Safety first!' and at relevant points in this Chapter, concerning the dangers of asbestos dust and hydraulic fluid.*

2 Brake pedal – removal and refitting

Removal

1 Disconnect the battery negative lead, and position the lead away from the battery as described in Chapter 5A Section 4.

2 Remove the drivers side facia end cover, lower panel and switches.

3 Disconnect the wiring plug for the accelerator pedal and the brake stop-light switch (see illustration).

4 Rotate and remove the special clevis pin locking the pedal to the servo pushrod (see illustration).

5 Remove the securing nuts and remove the pedal assembly complete with the accelerator pedal.

6 Inspect the pedal assembly for wear and correct operation. Pay particular attention to the condition of the collapsible pivot. If any faults are found, the pedal must be renewed as a complete assembly. No individual parts are available.

Refitting

7 Refitting is a reversal of removal, noting the following points:

a) *A new clevis pin must always be used.*
b) *Use new nuts.*
c) *Check the brake lights for correct operation on completion*

3 Vacuum servo unit – general information, testing, removal and refitting

General information

1 The vacuum servo unit can be removed from within the engine compartment. To do this, the brake master cylinder will have to be removed first as described in Section 7. The procedure for removal will vary according to the engine fitted, but all engines will require the removal of the brake pedal assembly and the scuttle cover panel.

Testing

2 To test the operation of the servo unit, depress the footbrake several times to exhaust the vacuum, then start the engine whilst keeping the pedal firmly depressed. As the engine starts, there should be a noticeable 'give' in the brake pedal as the vacuum builds-up. Allow the engine to run for at least two minutes, then switch it off. If the brake

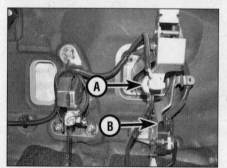

2.3 Disconnect the wiring plugs from the brake light switch (A) and the accelerator position switch (B)

2.4 Push the clip upward in the direction shown

pedal is now depressed it should feel normal, but further applications should result in the pedal feeling firmer, with the pedal stroke decreasing with each application.

3 If a vacuum pump is available, remove the check valve (Section 4) and then operate the pump until the vacuum reaches 500 mbar. The vacuum should not drop by more than 33 mbar within 15 seconds. If the vacuum drops more than this then the unit is faulty and must be replaced.

4 If the servo does not operate as described, inspect the servo check valve as described in Section 4. If the servo unit still fails to operate satisfactorily check that it is being supplied with a suitable vacuum from either the inlet manifold of the vacuum pump (depending on the model). Apart from external components, no spares are available, so a defective servo must be renewed.

Removal

Note: *A new master cylinder/servo O-ring seal will be required on refitting.*

5 Disconnect the battery negative lead as described in Chapter 5A Section 4.

6 Working under the bonnet, remove the engine cover (if fitted) and the windscreen cowl panels (Chapter 11 Section 7). On diesel engines remove the lifting eye and the EGR pipework.

7 Remove the air filter housing and the air intake ducting.

8 Remove the ignition coil on 1.2 litre petrol engines (Chapter 5B Section 3).

9 Disconnect the wiring connector, and then prise free the servo check valve and vacuum hose from the servo unit **(see illustration)**.

10 Remove the brake master cylinder as described in Section 7 of this Chapter.

11 Working inside the vehicle, remove the brake and clutch pedal assemblies as described in Section 2 of this Chapter and in Chapter 6 Section 6. Angle the servo pushrod downward to aid removal, and recover the gasket and spacer plate if fitted.

Refitting

12 Prior to refitting, check that the servo unit pushrod is correctly adjusted as follows: with the gasket removed, check the dimensions. If adjustment is necessary, dimension L can be altered by slackening the locknut **(see illustration)**.

13 Inspect the check valve sealing grommet for signs of damage or deterioration, and renew if necessary.

14 Fit a new O-ring seal to the rear of the master cylinder, and reposition the unit in the engine compartment.

15 Working inside the vehicle, refit the servo unit to the pedal assembly mounting plate. Ensure that the servo unit pushrod is correctly engaged with the brake pedal and tighten the four mounting nuts to their specified torque.

16 Fit a new clevis pin and secure it in position, and reconnect the wiring connectors to the brake, clutch and accelerator pedals.

3.9 Disconnect the wiring connector the free the servo check valve

17 Working inside the engine bay, reconnect the vacuum hose to the servo check valve, and refit the master cylinder.

18 Bleed both the clutch and brake systems and then reconnect the battery.

19 On completion, start the engine and check that there are no air leaks at the servo vacuum hose connection. Check the operation of the servo as described at the beginning of this Section.

4 Vacuum servo unit check valve – removal, testing and refitting

Removal

1 The check valve is mounted on the brake servo on all models **(see illustration 3.9)**. Vacuum is supplied to the servo through the check valve from either the inlet manifold (petrol engines) or from the vacuum pump (diesel engines) **(see illustrations)**.

2 Withdraw the valve from its rubber sealing grommet, using a pulling and twisting motion. Remove the grommet from the servo.

Testing

3 Examine the check valve for signs of damage, and renew if necessary. The valve may be tested by blowing through it in both directions. Air should flow through the valve in one direction only – when blown through from the servo unit end of the valve. Renew the valve if this is not the case.

4 Examine the rubber sealing grommet

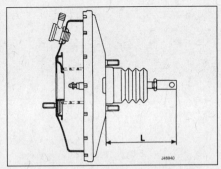
3.12 Dimension L should be 159.5 mm

and thermoplastic vacuum hose for signs of damage or deterioration, and renew as necessary.

Refitting

5 Fit the sealing grommet into position in the servo unit.

6 Ease the check valve into position, taking care not to displace or damage the grommet.

7 On completion, start the engine and check that there are no air leaks.

5 Hydraulic system – bleeding

⚠️ *Warning: Hydraulic fluid is poisonous; wash off immediately and thoroughly in the case of skin contact, and seek immediate medical advice if any fluid is swallowed or gets into the eyes. Certain types of hydraulic fluid are inflammable, and may ignite when allowed into contact with hot components; when servicing any hydraulic system, it is safest to assume that the fluid is inflammable, and to take precautions against the risk of fire as though it is petrol that is being handled. Finally, hydraulic fluid is hygroscopic (it absorbs moisture from the air) – old fluid may be contaminated and unfit for further use. When topping-up or renewing the fluid, always use the recommended type (see 'Lubricants and fluids'), and ensure that it comes from a freshly-opened, previously sealed container.*

4.1a The servo hose connector at the vacuum pump (diesel)...

4.1b ...or the inlet manifold (0.9 litre petrol)

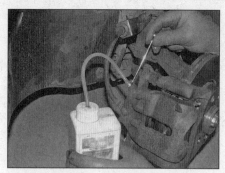

5.21 Bleeding a front brake caliper

Caution: Make sure the ignition switch is in the OFF position before disconnecting any braking system hydraulic union and do not switch it on until after the hydraulic system has been bled. Failure to do this could lead to air entering the ABS modulator. If air enters the modulator pump, it will prove very difficult (in some cases impossible) to bleed the unit.

General

1 The correct operation of any hydraulic system is only possible after removing all air from the components and circuit; this is achieved by bleeding the system.
2 During the bleeding procedure, add only clean, unused hydraulic fluid of the recommended type; never re-use fluid that has already been bled from the system. Ensure that sufficient fluid is available before starting work.
3 If there is any possibility of incorrect fluid being already in the system, the system must be flushed completely with uncontaminated, correct fluid, and new seals should be fitted to the various components.
4 If air has entered the hydraulic system because of a leak, ensure that the fault is cured before proceeding further.
5 Park the vehicle on level ground, switch off the engine and select first or reverse gear (or P on automatic transmission models). Chock the wheels and release the handbrake.
6 Check that all pipes and hoses are secure, unions tight and bleed screws closed. Clean any dirt from around the bleed screws.
7 Unscrew the master cylinder reservoir cap and top the master cylinder reservoir up to the MAX level line; refit the cap loosely. Remember to maintain the fluid level at least above the MIN level line throughout the procedure, or there is a risk of further air entering the system.
8 There are a number of one-man, do-it-yourself brake bleeding kits currently available from motor accessory shops. It is recommended that one of these kits is used whenever possible, as they greatly simplify the bleeding operation, and also reduce the risk of expelled air and fluid being drawn back into the system. If such a kit is not available, the basic (two-man)

method must be used, which is described in detail below.
9 If a kit is to be used, prepare the vehicle as described previously, and follow the kit manufacturer's instructions. The procedure may vary slightly according to the type of kit being used; general procedures are as outlined below in the relevant sub-section.
10 Whichever method is used, the same sequence must be followed (paragraphs 11 and 12) to ensure the removal of all air from the system.

Bleeding sequence

Note: *The engine must not be running when bleeding the brakes.*
11 If the system has been only partially disconnected, and the correct precautions were taken to minimise fluid loss, it should be necessary only to bleed that part of the system (ie, the primary or secondary circuit).
12 If the complete system is to be bled, then it should be done working in the following sequence:

a) Left-hand front brake.
b) Right-hand front brake.
c) Left-hand rear brake.
d) Right-hand rear brake.

Bleeding

Basic (two-man) method

13 Collect a clean glass jar, a length of plastic or rubber tubing which is a tight fit over the bleed screw, and a ring spanner to fit the screw. The help of an assistant will also be required.
14 Remove the dust cap from the first screw in the sequence. Fit the spanner and tube to the screw, place the other end of the tube in the jar, and pour in sufficient fluid to cover the end of the tube.
15 Ensure that the master cylinder reservoir fluid level is maintained at least above the MINI level line throughout the procedure.
16 Have the assistant fully depress the brake pedal several times to build-up pressure, then maintain it on the final stroke.
17 While pedal pressure is maintained, unscrew the bleed screw (approximately one turn) and allow the compressed fluid and air to flow into the jar. The assistant should maintain pedal pressure, following it down to the floor if necessary, and should not release it until instructed to do so. When the flow stops, tighten the bleed screw again. Have the assistant release the pedal slowly.
18 Repeat the steps given in paragraphs 16 and 17 until the fluid emerging from the bleed screw is free from air bubbles. Remember to recheck the fluid level in the master cylinder reservoir every five strokes or so. If the master cylinder has been drained and refilled, and air is being bled from the first screw in the sequence, allow approximately five seconds between strokes for the master cylinder passages to refill.

19 When no more air bubbles appear, tighten the bleed screw securely, remove the tube and spanner, and refit the dust cap. Do not overtighten the bleed screw.
20 Repeat the procedure on the remaining screws in the sequence until all air is removed from the system and the brake pedal feels firm.

Using a one-way valve kit

21 As their name implies, these kits consist of a length of tubing with a one-way valve fitted to prevent expelled air and fluid being drawn back into the system; some kits include a translucent container, which can be positioned so that the air bubbles can be more easily seen flowing from the end of the tube **(see illustration)**.
22 The kit is connected to the bleed screw, which is then opened. The user returns to the driver's seat and depresses the brake pedal with a smooth, steady stroke and slowly releases it; this is repeated until the expelled fluid is clear of air bubbles.
23 Note that these kits simplify work so much that it is easy to forget the master cylinder reservoir fluid level; ensure that this is maintained at least above the MINI level line at all times.

Using a pressure-bleeding kit

24 These kits are usually operated by the reservoir of pressurised air contained in the spare tyre, although it may be necessary to reduce the pressure in the tyre to lower than normal; refer to the instructions supplied with the kit.
25 By connecting a pressurised, fluid filled container to the master cylinder reservoir, bleeding can be carried out simply by opening each screw in turn (in the specified sequence) and allowing the fluid to flow out until no more air bubbles can be seen in the expelled fluid.
26 This method has the advantage that the large reservoir of fluid provides an additional safeguard against air being drawn into the system during bleeding.
27 Pressure bleeding is particularly effective when bleeding 'difficult' systems, or when bleeding the complete system at the time of routine fluid renewal.

All methods

28 When bleeding is complete and firm pedal feel is restored, wash off any spilt fluid, tighten the bleed screws securely and refit their dust caps.
29 Check the hydraulic fluid level, and top-up if necessary (see *Weekly checks*).
30 Discard any hydraulic fluid that has been bled from the system; it will not be fit for re-use.
31 Check the feel of the brake pedal. If it feels at all spongy, air must still be present in the system, and further bleeding is required. Failure to bleed satisfactorily after several repetitions of the bleeding procedure may be due to worn master cylinder seals.

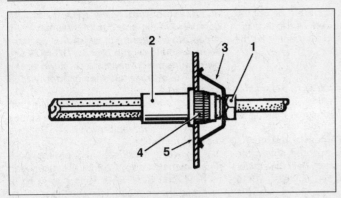

6.2a Hydraulic pipe connection to a flexible hose

6.2b Use a brake pipe spanner to unscrew a hydraulic union nut

1 Union nut
2 Flexible hose
3 Spring cable
  support
4 Splined end fitting
5 Bodywork

6 Hydraulic pipes and hoses – renewal

Note: *Before starting work, refer to the Warning at the beginning of Section 5 concerning the dangers of hydraulic fluid.*

1 If any pipe or hose is to be renewed, minimise fluid loss by removing the master cylinder reservoir cap and then tightening it down onto a piece of polythene (taking care not to damage the sender unit) to obtain an airtight seal. Alternatively, flexible hoses can be sealed, if required, using a proprietary brake hose clamp; metal brake pipe unions can be plugged (if care is taken not to allow dirt into the system) or capped immediately they are disconnected. Place a wad of rag under any union that is to be disconnected to catch any spilt fluid.

2 If a flexible hose is to be disconnected, unscrew the brake pipe union nut before removing the spring clip which secures the hose to its mounting bracket **(see illustrations)**.

3 To unscrew the union nuts, it is preferable to obtain a brake pipe spanner of the correct size (split ring); these are available from motor accessory shops. Failing this, a close fitting open ended spanner will be required, though if the nuts are tight or corroded, their flats may be rounded off if the spanner slips. In such a case, a self-locking wrench is often the only way to unscrew a stubborn union, but it follows that the pipe and the damaged nuts must be renewed on reassembly. Always clean a union and surrounding area before disconnecting it. If disconnecting a component with more than one union, make a careful note of the connections before disturbing any of them.

4 If a brake pipe is to be renewed, it can be obtained, cut to length and with the union nuts and end flares in place, from Renault dealers. All that is then necessary is to bend it to shape, following the line of the original, before fitting it to the car. Alternatively, most motor accessory shops can make up brake

pipes from kits, but this requires very careful measurement of the original to ensure that the new pipe is of the correct length. The safest answer is usually to take the original to the shop as a pattern.

5 On refitting, do not overtighten the union nuts. The specified torque wrench settings (where given) are not high, and it is not necessary to exercise brute force to obtain a sound joint.

6 Ensure that the pipes and hoses are correctly routed with no kinks, and that they are secured in the clips or brackets provided. In the case of flexible hoses, make sure that they cannot contact other components during movement of the steering and/or suspension assemblies.

7 After fitting, remove the polythene from the reservoir (or remove the plugs or clamps, as applicable), and bleed the hydraulic system as described in Section 5. Wash off any spilt fluid, and check carefully for fluid leaks.

7 Master cylinder – removal and refitting

Caution: Make sure the ignition switch is in the OFF position before disconnecting any braking system hydraulic union and do not switch it on until after the hydraulic system has been bled. Failure to do this could lead to air entering the ABS modulator. If air

enters the modulator pump, it will prove very difficult (in some cases impossible) to bleed the unit.
Note: *Before starting work, refer to the Warning at the beginning of Section 5 concerning the dangers of hydraulic fluid.*

Removal

1 Disconnect the battery negative lead as described in Chapter 5A Section 4.

2 Where fitted remove the engine cover and then remove the windscreen cowl panels as described in Chapter 11 Section 7.

3 Remove the master cylinder reservoir cap and siphon the hydraulic fluid from the reservoir. **Note:** *Do not siphon the fluid by mouth, as it is poisonous; use a syringe or an old antifreeze hydrometer.* Alternatively, open any convenient pair of bleed screws in the system (one in each hydraulic circuit) and gently pump the brake pedal to expel the fluid through plastic tubes connected to the screws (see Section 5).

4 Disconnected the sender unit wiring connector, from the top of the reservoir **(see illustration)**.

5 Once drained, remove the reservoir from the master cylinder by removing the bolt **(see illustration)** and then by pulling it upwards. Disconnect the supply pipe for the clutch master cylinder. Plug the pipe to minimise fluid loss.

6 Wipe clean the area around the brake pipe unions on the side of the master cylinder, and

7.4 Disconnect the wiring connector

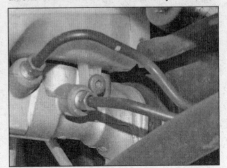

7.5 A single bolt secures the reservoir to the master cylinder

7.7 Remove the master cylinder mounting nuts

place absorbent rags beneath the pipe unions to catch any surplus fluid. Make a note of the correct fitted positions of the unions, then unscrew the union nuts and carefully withdraw the pipes. Plug or tape over the pipe ends and master cylinder orifices, to minimise the loss of brake fluid and to prevent the entry of dirt into the system. Wash off any spilt fluid immediately with cold water.

7 Slacken and remove the two nuts securing the master cylinder to the vacuum servo unit **(see illustration)**, then withdraw the master cylinder from the engine compartment. Remove the O-ring seal from the rear of the master cylinder, and discard it.

8 If the master cylinder is faulty, it must be renewed as a complete unit. The reservoir mounting bush seals should also be renewed if necessary. The O-ring seal fitted between the master cylinder and the vacuum servo

must be renewed as a matter of course whenever the unit is removed, as a leak at this point will allow atmospheric pressure into the servo unit.

Refitting

9 Remove all traces of dirt from the master cylinder and servo unit mating surfaces. Fit a new O-ring seal to the groove on the master cylinder body.

10 Fit the master cylinder to the servo, ensuring that the servo pushrod enters the master cylinder bore centrally. Refit the master cylinder mounting nuts, and tighten them to the specified torque.

11 Wipe clean the brake pipe unions, then refit them to the master cylinder ports. Tighten the union nuts to the specified torque.

12 Carefully align the reservoir with the mounting bush seals. Push the reservoir firmly into position.

13 On all models, refill the master cylinder reservoir with new fluid, and bleed the hydraulic system as described in Section 5.

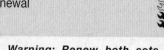

8 Front brake pads – renewal

⚠ *Warning: Renew both sets of front brake pads at the same time – never renew the pads on only one wheel, as uneven braking may result. Note that the dust created by wear of the pads may contain asbestos, which*

is a health hazard. Never blow it out with compressed air, and don't inhale any of it. An approved filtering mask should be worn when working on the brakes. DO NOT use petroleum based solvents to clean brake parts – use brake cleaner or methylated spirit only.

1 Apply the handbrake, then jack up the front of the vehicle and support it on axle stands (see *Jacking and vehicle support*). Remove the front roadwheels.

2 Follow the accompanying photos **(see illustrations 8.2a to 8.2n)** for the actual pad renewal procedure. Be sure to stay in order and read the caption under each illustration, and note the following points:

a) *New pads may have an adhesive foil on the backplates. Remove this foil prior to installation.*

b) *Thoroughly clean the caliper guide surfaces, and apply a little brake assembly (polycarbamide) grease.*

c) *Check the remaining friction material on the brake pads and compare it to the specifications. If there is any doubt about the remaining thickness or any apparent defect in the brake pads always replace them.*

d) *When pushing the caliper piston back to accommodate new pads, keep a close eye on the fluid level in the reservoir – note also the warning below.*

Note: *Pushing back the piston causes a reverse-flow of brake fluid, which has been known to 'flip' the master cylinder rubber seals, resulting in a total loss of braking. To*

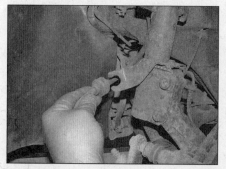

8.2a Release the flexible hose from the support bracket

8.2b Use a slim open-ended spanner to counter-hold the sliding pin...

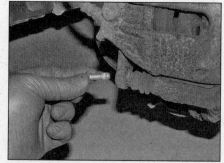

8.2c ...and remove the bolt

8.2d Rock the caliper slightly to clear the lip of the disc (if necessary) and then pivot the caliper upward to expose the brake pads.

8.2e Remove the outer brake pad...

8.2f ...the inner brake pad...

8.2g ...and then remove the lower anti-rattle shim...

8.2h ...followed by the upper shim

8.2i Slowly push the piston into the caliper

8.2j Wire brush the mounting surfaces and then fit the upper and lower anti-rattle shims

8.2k Apply a small amount of brake grease and fit the new brake pads...

8.2l ...and lower the caliper into position

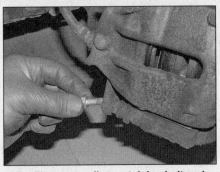

8.2m Fit a new caliper retaining bolt and...

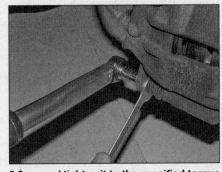

8.2n ...and tighten it to the specified torque

avoid this, best practise is to clamp the brake flexible hose and open the bleed screw – as the piston is pushed back, the fluid can be directed into a suitable container using a hose attached to the bleed screw. Close the screw just before the piston is pushed fully back, to ensure no air enters the system.

3 Refit the brake hose back into the clip on the front strut.

4 Check the fluid level – topping-up if necessary and then depress the brake pedal several times to bring the pads into firm contact with the brake disc.

5 Repeat the above procedure on the other front brake caliper.

6 Refit the roadwheels, then lower the vehicle to the ground and tighten the bolts to the specified torque.

Caution: If new pads have been fitted, full braking efficiency will not be obtained until the linings have bedded-in. Be prepared for longer stopping distances, and avoid harsh braking as far as possible for the first hundred miles or so after fitting new pads.

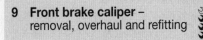

9 Front brake caliper –
removal, overhaul and refitting

Note: *Before starting work, refer to the Warnings at the beginning of Sections 5 and 8 concerning the dangers of hydraulic fluid and asbestos dust.*

Removal

1 Apply the handbrake, then jack up the front

of the vehicle and support it on axle stands (see *Jacking and vehicle support*). Remove the appropriate roadwheel.

2 Minimise fluid loss, either by removing the master cylinder reservoir cap and then tightening it down onto a piece of polythene to obtain an airtight seal (taking care not to damage the sender unit), or by using a brake hose clamp, a G-clamp or a similar tool with protected jaws to clamp the flexible hose.

3 Clean the area around the hose union, then loosen the brake hose union nut.

4 Slacken and remove the upper and lower caliper guide pin bolts, using a slim open-ended spanner to prevent the guide pin itself from rotating **(see illustration 8.2b)**. Discard the guide pin bolts; new bolts must be used on refitting. With the guide pin bolts removed, lift the caliper away from the brake disc, then unscrew the caliper from the end

of the brake hose. Note that the brake pads need not be disturbed, and can be left in position in the caliper mounting bracket.

Overhaul

Note: *Ensure that an appropriate caliper overhaul kit is obtained before starting work.*

5 With the caliper on the bench, wipe away all traces of dust and dirt, but avoid inhaling the dust, as it is injurious to health.

6 Using a small flat-bladed screwdriver, carefully prise the dust seal retaining clip out of the caliper bore.

7 Withdraw the partially-ejected piston from the caliper body and remove the dust seal. The piston can be withdrawn by hand, or if necessary forced out by applying compressed air to the union bolt hole.

Caution: The piston may be ejected with some force. Only low pressure should be

10.3 Measuring brake thickness with a micrometer

10.4 Measuring brake disc run-out with a dial gauge

10.6a Undo the carrier bolts...

required, such as is generated by a foot pump.

8 Extract the piston hydraulic seal using a blunt instrument such as a knitting needle or a crochet hook, taking care not to damage the caliper bore.

9 Withdraw the guide sleeves or pins from the caliper body or mounting bracket (as applicable) and remove the rubber gaiters.

10 Thoroughly clean all components using only methylated spirit, isopropyl alcohol or clean hydraulic fluid as a cleaning medium. Never use mineral based solvents, such as petrol or paraffin, which will attack the hydraulic system rubber components. Dry the components immediately, using compressed air or a clean, lint-ree cloth. Use compressed air to blow clear the fluid passages.

11 Check all components and renew any that are worn or damaged. Check particularly the cylinder bore and piston; if they are scratched, worn or corroded in any way, they must be renewed (note that this means the renewal of the complete body assembly). Similarly check the condition of the guide sleeves or pins and their bores; they should be undamaged and (when cleaned) a reasonably tight sliding fit in the body or mounting bracket bores. If there is any doubt about the condition of a component, renew it.

12 If the assembly is fit for further use, obtain the appropriate repair kit.

13 Renew all rubber seals, dust covers and caps disturbed on dismantling as a matter of course; these should never be re-used.

14 Before commencing reassembly, ensure that all components are absolutely clean and dry.

15 Dip the piston and the new piston (fluid) seal in clean hydraulic fluid. Smear clean fluid on the cylinder bore surface.

16 Fit the new piston (fluid) seal, using only the fingers to manipulate it into the cylinder bore groove. Fit the new dust seal to the piston. Refit the piston to the cylinder bore using a twisting motion, ensuring that the piston enters squarely into the bore. Press the piston fully into the bore, then press the dust seal into the caliper body.

17 Install the dust seal retaining clip, ensuring that it is correctly seated in the caliper groove.

18 Apply the grease supplied in the repair

kit, or a good quality high temperature brake grease or anti-seize compound to the guide sleeves or pins. Fit the sleeves or pins to the caliper body or mounting bracket. Fit the new rubber gaiters, ensuring that they are correctly located in the grooves on both the sleeve or pin, and body or mounting bracket (as applicable).

Refitting

19 Screw the caliper body fully onto the flexible hose union nut. Check that the brake pads are still correctly fitted in the caliper mounting bracket.

20 Position the caliper over the pads. Coat the threads of the new lower guide pin bolt with locking fluid, and fit the bolt. Apply locking fluid to the new upper guide pin bolt, press the caliper into position, and fit the bolt. Check that the anti-rattle springs are correctly located then tighten the guide pin bolts to the specified torque, starting with the lower bolt.

21 Tighten the brake hose union nut to the specified torque.

22 Remove the brake hose clamp or polythene, where fitted, and bleed the hydraulic system as described in Section 5. Providing the precautions described were taken to minimise brake fluid loss, it should only be necessary to bleed the relevant front brake.

23 Refit the roadwheel, then lower the vehicle to the ground and tighten the roadwheel bolts to the specified torque.

10 Front brake disc – inspection, removal and refitting

Note: *Before starting work, refer to the Warning at the beginning of Section 8 concerning the dangers of asbestos dust. If either disc requires renewal, both should be renewed at the same time, to ensure even and consistent braking. In principle, new pads should be fitted also.*

Inspection

1 Chock the rear wheels, firmly apply the handbrake, jack up the front of the vehicle and support on axle stands (see *Jacking and vehicle support*). Remove the appropriate front roadwheel.

2 Slowly rotate the brake disc so that the full area of both sides can be checked; remove the brake pads, as described in Section 8, if better access is required to the inboard surface. Light scoring is normal in the area swept by the brake pads, but if heavy scoring is found, the disc must be renewed.

3 It is normal to find a lip of rust and brake dust around the disc's perimeter; this can be scraped off if required. If, however, a lip has formed due to wear of the brake pad swept area, the disc thickness must be measured using a micrometer **(see illustration)**. Take measurements at several places around the disc at the inside and outside of the pad swept area; if the disc has worn at any point to the specified minimum thickness or less, it must be renewed.

4 If the disc is thought to be warped, it can be checked for run-out, ideally by using a dial gauge mounted on any convenient fixed point, while the disc is slowly rotated **(see illustration)**. In the absence of a dial gauge, use feeler blades to measure (at several points all around the disc) the clearance between the disc and a fixed point such as the caliper mounting bracket. If the measurements obtained are at the specified maximum or beyond, the disc is excessively warped, and must be renewed; however, it is worth checking first that the hub bearing is in good condition (Chapters 1A or 1B and 10). Also try the effect of removing the disc and turning it through 180° to reposition it on the hub; if run-out is still excessive, the disc must be renewed.

5 Check the disc for cracks (especially around the wheel bolt holes), and for any other wear or damage. Renew the disc if necessary.

Removal

Note: *Thread-locking fluid will be required to coat the threads of the brake caliper mounting bolts on refitting.*

6 Unscrew the two bolts securing the brake caliper and bracket to the swivel hub, and slide the caliper assembly off the disc. Using a piece of wire or string, tie the caliper to the front suspension coil spring, to avoid placing any strain on the hydraulic brake hose **(see illustrations)**.

7 If the same disc is to be refitted, use chalk

or paint to mark the relationship of the disc to the hub. Remove the two screws securing the brake disc to the hub **(see illustrations)**, and remove the disc. If it is tight, lightly tap its rear face with a hide or plastic mallet.

Refitting

8 Refitting is the reverse of the removal procedure, noting the following points:
a) *Ensure that the mating surfaces of the disc and hub are clean and flat.*
b) *If applicable, align the marks made on removal.*
c) *Securely tighten the disc retaining screws.*
d) *If a new disc has been fitted, use a suitable solvent to wipe any preservative coating from the disc before refitting the caliper.*
e) *Apply locking fluid to the threads of the brake caliper mounting bolts, and tighten them to the specified torque.*
f) *Refit the roadwheel, then lower the vehicle to the ground and tighten the roadwheel bolts to the specified torque. On completion, depress the brake pedal several times to bring the brake pads into contact with the disc.*

---

11 Rear brake drum –
removal, inspection
and refitting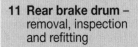

Note: *Before starting work, refer to the Warning at the beginning of Section 12 concerning the dangers of asbestos dust. If either drum requires renewal or refinishing, both should be dealt with at the same time, to ensure even and consistent braking. In principle, new shoes should be fitted also. A new hub nut will be required on refitting.*

Removal

1 Chock the front wheels, engage reverse gear (or P) and release the handbrake. Jack up the rear of the vehicle and support it on axle stands (see *Jacking and vehicle support*). Remove the appropriate rear wheel.
2 Using a hammer and large flat-bladed screwdriver, carefully tap and prise the cap out of the centre of the brake drum **(see illustration)**. Dispose of the dust cap – a new one must be used.
3 Using a socket and long bar, slacken and remove the rear hub nut **(see illustration)**.
4 It should now be possible to withdraw the brake drum and hub bearing assembly from the stub axle by hand. It may be difficult to remove the drum due to the tightness of the hub bearing on the stub axle, or due to the brake shoes binding on the inner circumference of the drum. If the bearing is tight, tap the periphery of the drum using a hide or plastic mallet, or use a universal puller secured to the drum with the wheel bolts to pull it off. If the brake shoes are binding, proceed as follows.
5 First ensure that the handbrake is fully off. From inside the vehicle, slacken the handbrake cable as described in Section 15.

10.6b ...remove the caliper complete with the brake pads...

10.7a If required use an impact driver to...

6 Insert a screwdriver through one of the wheel bolt holes in the brake drum, so that it contacts the handbrake operating lever on the trailing brake shoe. Push the lever until the stop-peg slips behind the brake shoe web, allowing the brake shoes to retract fully. Withdraw the brake drum off the stub axle.

Inspection

7 Working carefully, remove all traces of brake dust from the drum, but avoid inhaling the dust, as it is injurious to health.
8 Scrub clean the outside of the drum, and check it for obvious signs of wear or damage such as cracks around the roadwheel bolt holes; renew the drum if necessary.
9 Examine carefully the inside of the drum. Light scoring of the friction surface is normal,

10.6c ...and securely tie it to the coil spring

10.7b ...remove the disc retaining screws

but if heavy scoring is found, the drum must be renewed. It is usual to find a lip on the drum's inboard edge which consists of a mixture of rust and brake dust; this should be scraped away to leave a smooth surface which can be polished with fine (120 to 150 grade) emery paper. If the lip is due to the friction surface being recessed by wear, then the drum must be refinished (within the specified limits) or renewed.
10 If the drum is thought to be excessively worn or oval, its internal diameter must be measured at several points using an internal micrometer. Take measurements in pairs, the second at right-angles to the first, and compare the two to check for signs of ovality. Minor ovality can be corrected by machining; otherwise, renew the drum.

11.2 A blunt cold chisel can be used to remove the dust cap

11.3 Remove the hub nut

Refitting

Note: *New brake drums must always be fitted in pairs. Always fit new brake linings when replacing the brake drums.*

11 If a new brake drums are to be installed, use a suitable solvent to remove any preservative coating that may have been applied to its interior.

12 Ensure that the handbrake lever stop-peg is correctly repositioned against the edge of the brake shoe web **(see illustration)**. Apply a smear of gear oil to the stub axle, and slide on the brake drum, being careful not to get oil onto the brake shoes or the friction surface of the drum. Whilst not specified by Renault it is recommended that a new hub nut is fitted and tightened to the specified torque. Tap the new hub cap into place in the centre of the brake drum.

13 Depress the footbrake several times to operate the self-adjusting mechanism.

14 Repeat the above procedure on the remaining rear brake assembly (where necessary), then adjust the handbrake as described in Chapter 1A or 1B.

15 On completion, refit the roadwheel(s), lower the vehicle to the ground and tighten the wheel bolts to the specified torque.

---

12 Rear brake shoes –
inspection and renewal

⚠️ *Warning: Brake shoes must be renewed on both rear wheels at the same time – never renew the shoes*

11.12 Check that the handbrake lever stop-peg is correctly positioned against the trailing shoe edge

on only one wheel, as uneven braking may result. Also, the dust created by wear of the shoes may contain asbestos, which is a health hazard. Never blow it out with compressed air, and do not inhale any of it. An approved filtering mask should be worn when working on the brakes. DO NOT use petroleum based solvents to clean brake parts – use brake cleaner or methylated spirit only.

Inspection

1 Remove the brake drum as described in Section 11.

2 Working carefully, remove all traces of brake dust from the brake drum, backplate and shoes.

3 Measure the thickness of each brake shoe (friction material and shoe) at several points; if either shoe is worn at any point to the specified minimum thickness or less, all four shoes must

be renewed as a set. Also, the shoes should be renewed if any are fouled with oil or grease; there is no satisfactory way of degreasing friction material once contaminated.

4 If any of the brake shoes are worn unevenly, or fouled with oil or grease, trace and rectify the cause before reassembly.

Renewal

Note: *High temperature brake grease or anti-seize compound will be required to apply to the shoe contact surfaces on the brake backplate on refitting.*

5 Make a note of the correct fitted positions of the springs and adjuster strut, to use as a guide on reassembly.

6 Carefully unhook the lower return spring, and remove it from the brake shoes.

7 Using a pair of pliers, remove the leading shoe retainer spring clip by depressing it and sliding it free. With the clip removed, lift off the shoe from the lower pivot **(see illustrations)**.

8 Remove the trailing shoe retainer spring clip and pin as described above, then detach the handbrake cable and remove the shoes from the vehicle **(see illustrations)**. Do not depress the brake pedal until the brakes are reassembled; wrap a strong elastic band around the wheel cylinder to retain the pistons.

9 Make a note of the shoe assembly complete with springs for refitting. All return springs should be renewed, regardless of their apparent condition; spring kits are available from Renault dealers.

10 Withdraw the forked end from the adjuster strut. Carefully examine the assembly for signs of wear or damage, paying particular attention to the threads and the knurled adjuster wheel, and renew if necessary. Note that left-hand and right-hand struts are not interchangeable; the left-hand fork has a right-hand thread, and the right-hand fork has a left-hand thread.

11 Remove the elastic band fitted to the wheel cylinder. Peel back the rubber protective caps, and check the wheel cylinder for fluid leaks or other damage. Check that both cylinder pistons are free to move easily. Refer to Section 13, if necessary, for information on wheel cylinder renewal.

12 Prior to installation, clean the backplate and apply a thin smear of high temperature brake grease or anti-seize compound to all

12.7a Remove the leading shoe hold down clip...

12.7b ...and unhook the shoe

12.8a Remove the trailing shoe retaining clip...

12.8b ...and unhook the handbrake cable

12.12 Lubricate the shoe contact points on the backplate

those surfaces of the backplate which bear on the shoes **(see illustration)**, particularly the wheel cylinder pistons and lower pivot point. Do not allow the lubricant to foul the friction material.

13 Pre-assemble the shoes and springs on the bench, as noted on removal, and then fit them as a complete unit **(see illustration)**.

14 First connect the handbrake cable to the handbrake lever on the brake shoe, then engage the upper end of the shoes with the wheel cylinder pistons **(see illustration)**, then secure the shoe in position with the retainer pin, spring and spring cup.

15 Make sure the lower part of the brake shoes are located correctly with the lower return spring, then tap the shoes to centralise them on the backplate.

16 Using a screwdriver, turn the strut adjuster wheel until the brake drum will just pass over the brake shoes.

17 Slide the drum into position over the linings, but do not refit the hub nut yet.

18 Repeat the above procedure on the remaining rear brake.

Caution: Do not press the brake pedal with the drums removed, as this will cause the wheel cylinder pistons to be forced out.

19 Once both sets of rear shoes have been renewed, adjust the lining-to-drum clearance by repeatedly depressing the brake pedal. Whilst depressing the pedal, have an assistant listen to the rear drums to check that the adjuster strut is functioning correctly; if this is so, a clicking sound will be emitted by the strut as the pedal is depressed.

20 Remove both the rear drums, and check that the handbrake lever stop-pegs are still correctly located against the edges of the trailing shoes, and that each lever operates smoothly. If all is well, with the aid of an assistant, adjust the handbrake cable so that the handbrake lever on each rear brake assembly starts to move as the handbrake is moved between the first and second notch (click) of its ratchet mechanism, ie, so that the stop-pegs are still in contact with the shoes when the handbrake is on the first notch of the ratchet, but no longer contact the shoes when the handbrake is on the second notch. Once the handbrake adjustment is correct, hold the adjuster nut and securely tighten the locknut. Where necessary, refit the exhaust system heat shield to the vehicle underbody.

21 Refit the brake drums as described in Section 11.

22 On completion, check the hydraulic fluid level as described in *Weekly checks*.

23 If new shoes have been fitted, full braking efficiency will not be obtained until the linings have bedded-in. Be prepared for longer stopping distances, and avoid harsh braking as far as possible for the first hundred miles or so after fitting new shoes.

12.13 The shoes correctly assembled for refitting

13 Rear wheel cylinder – removal and refitting

Note: *Before starting work, refer to the Warnings at the beginning of Section 5 concerning the dangers of hydraulic fluid, and at the beginning of Section 12 concerning the dangers of asbestos dust.*

Removal

1 Remove the brake drum as described in Section 12.

2 Using pliers, carefully unhook the brake shoe upper return spring and remove it from the brake shoes. Pull the upper ends of the shoes away from the wheel cylinder to disengage them from the pistons.

3 Minimise fluid loss, either by removing the master cylinder reservoir cap and then tightening it down onto a piece of polythene to obtain an airtight seal (taking care not to damage the sender unit), or by using a brake hose clamp, a G-clamp or a similar tool with protected jaws to clamp the flexible hose at the nearest convenient point to the wheel cylinder.

4 Wipe away all traces of dirt around the brake pipe union at the rear of the wheel cylinder, and unscrew the union nut. Carefully ease the pipe out of the wheel cylinder, and plug or tape over its end to prevent dirt entry. Wipe off any spilt fluid immediately.

5 Unscrew the two wheel cylinder retaining bolts from the rear of the backplate **(see**

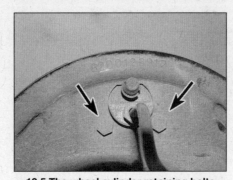

13.5 The wheel cylinder retaining bolts

12.14 The self-adjusting mechanism correctly assembled

illustration). Remove the cylinder, taking care not to allow hydraulic fluid to contaminate the brake shoe linings.

6 It is not possible to overhaul the cylinder, since no components are available separately. If faulty, the complete wheel cylinder assembly must be renewed.

Refitting

7 Ensure the backplate and wheel cylinder mating surfaces are clean, then spread the brake shoes and manoeuvre the wheel cylinder into position.

8 Engage the brake pipe, and screw in the union nut two or three turns to ensure that the thread has started.

9 Insert the two wheel cylinder retaining bolts, and tighten them securely. Now fully tighten the brake pipe union nut.

10 Remove the clamp from the brake hose, or the polythene from the master cylinder reservoir (as applicable).

11 Ensure that the brake shoes are correctly located in the cylinder pistons. Carefully refit the brake shoe upper return spring, using a screwdriver to stretch the spring into position.

12 Refit the brake drum as described in Section 12.

13 Bleed the brake hydraulic system as described in Section 5. Providing the correct precautions were taken to minimise loss of fluid, it should only be necessary to bleed the relevant rear brake.

14 Handbrake lever – removal and refitting

Removal

1 Chock the front wheels, engage reverse gear and release the handbrake. Jack up the rear of the vehicle and support it on axle stands (see *Jacking and vehicle support*).

2 Working from inside the vehicle, remove the centre console as described in Chapter 11 Section 27.

3 Disconnect the handbrake warning light switch **(see illustration)**.

4 Unscrew the handbrake cable adjuster

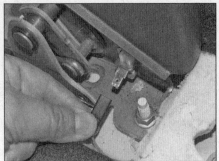

14.3 Disconnect the wiring connector

14.4 Slacken the adjuster nut to disconnect cables

14.5 The handbrake mounting nuts

locknut enough to remove the cables, from the equaliser plate (see illustration).

5 Working inside the vehicle, unscrew the nuts securing the lever to the floor, and remove the assembly from the vehicle (see illustration).

Refitting

6 Refitting is a reversal of removal. Adjust the handbrake as described in Chapter 1A or 1B.

15 Handbrake cables – removal and refitting

Removal

1 The handbrake cable consists of two sections, a right- and left-hand section, which are linked to the lever assembly by an equaliser plate. Each section can be removed individually as follows:

2 Working inside the vehicle remove the centre console as described in Chapter 11 Section 27, loosen the adjuster nut as described in Section 14 and unhook the cables (see illustrations).

3 Chock the front wheels, engage reverse gear and release the handbrake. Jack up the rear of the vehicle and support it on axle stands (see Jacking and vehicle support).

4 Remove both rear roadwheels and brake drums as described in Section 11. Lever the operating arm forward and unhook the cable from the brake shoes. Unclip the outer cable from the brake backplate.

5 On models with rear disc brakes, disengage the inner cable from the caliper handbrake lever. Tap the outer cable out of its mounting bracket on the caliper.

6 Working from underneath the vehicle, undo the clips securing the cables to the vehicle underbody and remove the cables. Note: It may be necessary to remove some heatshields from under the vehicle to access the cables.

Refitting

7 Refitting is a reversal of removal, but the self-adjusting mechanism on vehicles with drum brakes may need resetting. Adjust the handbrake as described in Chapter 1A or 1B.

16 Rear brake pads – inspection and renewal

⚠ Warning: Renew both sets of rear brake pads at the same time – never renew the pads on only one wheel, as uneven braking may result. Note that the dust created by wear of the pads may contain asbestos, which is a health hazard. Never blow it out with compressed air, and don't inhale any of it. An approved filtering mask should be worn when working on the brakes. DO NOT use petroleum based solvents to clean brake parts – use brake cleaner or methylated spirit only.

Inspection

1 Chock the front wheels, engage reverse

gear (or P) and release the handbrake. Jack up the rear of the car and support it on axle stands (see Jacking and vehicle support). Remove the rear wheels.

2 The pad thicknesses can be viewed without removing them from the caliper. Unlike some, the rear pads do not feature wear grooves. Wear rates for rear pads are generally far lower than for front pads, but if the friction material remaining is low, remember that this may also adversely affect the operation of the handbrake.

3 If either pad is worn at any point to the specified minimum thickness or less, all four pads must be renewed. Also, the pads should be renewed if any are fouled with oil or grease – there is no satisfactory way of degreasing friction material once contaminated. If any of the brake pads are worn unevenly, or fouled with oil or grease, trace and rectify the cause before reassembly. New brake pads and spring kits are available from Renault dealers.

Renewal

4 Unscrew the caliper guide pin bolts, using a second spanner on the pin outer hex fitting to prevent the pin turning (see illustration). Note: To just access the pads, only the lower pin need be unscrewed – the caliper can then be swung upwards. However, fitting new pads involves 'screwing' the caliper piston back into the caliper, which is more easily achieved with the caliper removed from its mounting bracket, which means removing both guide pin bolts.

5 Remove the caliper from the mounting

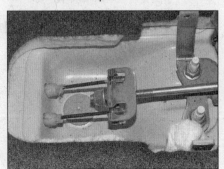

15.2a Unhook the cables from the equaliser plate...

15.2b ...and remove them from underneath the vehicle

16.4 Unscrew the guide pin bolts using two spanners

bracket, and suspend it under the wheel arch so that the fluid hose is not strained **(see illustration)**.

6 Unclip the inner and outer pads from the caliper mounting bracket, and remove them **(see illustration)**.

7 Carefully clean the pad locations in the caliper body/mounting bracket. Brush the dust and dirt from the caliper and piston, but do not inhale it, as it may be a health hazard.

8 Prior to fitting the pads, check that the guide sleeves are free to slide easily in the caliper body, and check that the rubber guide sleeve gaiters are undamaged. Inspect the dust seal around the piston for damage, and the piston for evidence of fluid leaks, corrosion or damage. If attention to any of these components is necessary, refer to Section 17. Also inspect the brake disc as described in Section 18.

9 If new brake pads are to be fitted, it will be necessary to retract the piston fully into the caliper bore by rotating it in a clockwise direction. This can be achieved using sturdy circlip pliers, noting that as well as being turned, the piston has to be pressed in very firmly. Special tools are available to achieve this with less effort **(see illustrations)**.

Caution: Pushing back the piston causes a reverse-flow of brake fluid, which has been known to 'flip' the master cylinder rubber seals, resulting in a total loss of braking. To avoid this, clamp the caliper flexible hose and open the bleed screw – as the piston is pushed back, the fluid can be directed into a suitable container using a hose attached to the bleed screw. Close the screw just before the piston is pushed fully back, to ensure no air enters the system.

10 If the recommended method of opening a bleed screw before pushing back the piston is not used, the fluid level in the reservoir will rise, and possibly overflow. Make sure that there is sufficient space in the brake fluid reservoir to accept the displaced fluid and, if necessary, siphon some off first. Any brake fluid spilt on paintwork should be washed off with clean water without delay – brake fluid is also a highly-effective paint-stripper.

11 Genuine Renault pads have a self-adhesive, anti-squeal coating applied to the pad backplates. Peel off the protective cover before fitting. If other makes of pads are being fitted, apply a little copper brake grease to the backs of the pads (none should be applied to the friction material) before fitting **(see illustrations)**.

12 Install the pads in the caliper mounting bracket, ensuring that the friction material of each pad is against the brake disc.

13 Lower the caliper over the pads. If the caliper will not fit properly, the piston has not been pushed back far enough (see paragraph 9). If removed, clip the brake hose back onto the suspension strut.

14 Refit the guide pin bolts, and tighten to the specified torque, preventing the bolt from

16.5 Lift the caliper off

16.9a Suitable pliers can be used to retract the piston...

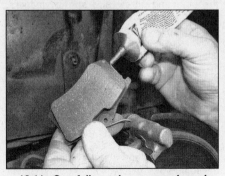

16.11a Carefully apply a copper-based lubricant to the pad edge...

turning using another spanner on the pin's outer hex fitting.

15 Depress the brake pedal several times to bring the pads into firm contact with the brake disc.

16 Repeat the above procedure on the other front brake caliper.

17 Refit the roadwheels, then lower the car to the ground and tighten the bolts to the specified torque.

18 Check the hydraulic fluid level as described in *Weekly checks*.

19 Check the handbrake cable adjustment as described in Chapter 1A or 1B.

20 If new pads have been fitted, full braking efficiency will not be obtained until the linings have bedded-in. Be prepared for longer stopping distances, and avoid harsh braking as far as possible for the first hundred miles or so after fitting new pads.

16.6 Remove the pads from the mounting bracket

16.9b ...but it will be easier with the correct tool

17 Rear brake caliper – removal, overhaul and refitting

Note: *Before starting work, refer to the Warnings at the beginning of Section 5 concerning the dangers of hydraulic fluid, and at the beginning of Section 12 concerning the dangers of asbestos dust.*

Removal

1 Chock the front wheels, engage reverse gear and release the handbrake. Jack up the rear of the car and support it on axle stands (see *Jacking and vehicle support*). Remove the relevant rear wheel.

2 Free the handbrake inner cable from the caliper handbrake operating lever, then unclip

16.11b ...and the pad back

17.2a Release the handbrake cable end fitting from the lever…

17.2b …then unclip the cable outer from its bracket

the outer cable from its bracket on the caliper body **(see illustrations)**.

3 Minimise fluid loss, either by removing the master cylinder reservoir cap and then tightening it down onto a piece of polythene to obtain an airtight seal (taking care not to damage the sender unit), or by using a brake hose clamp, a G-clamp or a similar tool with protected jaws to clamp the flexible hose at the nearest convenient point to the brake caliper.

4 Wipe away all traces of dirt around the brake pipe union on top of the caliper, and unscrew the union nut. Carefully ease the pipe out of position, and plug or tape over its end to prevent dirt entry. Wipe off any spilt fluid immediately.

5 Unscrew the caliper guide pin bolts, using a second spanner on the pin outer hex fitting to prevent the pin turning. Lift the caliper off the pads, and remove it.

Overhaul

Note: *Ensure the correct caliper overhaul kit is obtained before starting work.*

6 With the caliper on the bench, wipe away all traces of dust and dirt, but avoid inhaling the dust, as it is injurious to health.

7 Using a small screwdriver, carefully prise out the dust seal from the caliper bore, taking care not to damage the piston.

8 Remove the piston from the caliper bore by rotating it in an anti-clockwise direction. This can be achieved by using a square-section bar, such as the shaft of a screwdriver, which locates snugly in the caliper piston slots. Once the piston turns freely but does not come out any further, the piston can be withdrawn by hand, or if necessary pushed out by applying compressed air to the union bolt hole.

Caution: The piston may be ejected with some force – only low pressure should be required, such as is generated by a foot pump.

9 Using a blunt instrument such as a knitting needle or a crochet hook, extract the piston hydraulic seal, taking care not to damage the caliper bore.

10 Withdraw the guide sleeves from the caliper body, and remove the guide sleeve gaiters.

11 Inspect the caliper components as described in Section 9 for the front calipers. Renew as necessary, noting that the inside of the caliper piston must not be dismantled. If necessary, the handbrake mechanism can be overhauled as described in the following paragraphs. If it is not wished to overhaul the handbrake mechanism, proceed to paragraph 16.

12 Release the handbrake dust cover retaining clip, and peel the cover away from the rear of the caliper. Make a note of the correct fitted positions of the relative components to use as a guide on reassembly. Remove the circlip from the base of the operating lever shaft, then compress the adjusting screw spring washers, and withdraw the operating lever and dust cover from the caliper body. With the lever withdrawn, remove the return spring, plunger cam, adjusting screw, spring washers and thrustwasher from the rear of the caliper body. Using a pin punch, carefully tap the adjusting screw bush out of the caliper body and remove the O-ring.

13 Clean all the handbrake components in methylated spirit, and examine them for wear. If there is any sign of wear or damage, the complete handbrake mechanism assembly should be renewed.

14 Ensure that all components are clean and dry. Install the O-ring, then press the adjusting screw bush into position until its outer edge is flush with the rear of the caliper body; if necessary, tap the bush into position using a tubular drift. Fit the thrustwasher, then install the adjusting screw and spring washers, ensuring that the washers are correctly positioned. Locate the plunger cam in the end of the adjusting screw, and position the return spring in the caliper housing.

15 Fit the new dust cover to the operating lever, then compress the adjusting screw spring washers and insert the lever shaft through the caliper body, ensuring that it is correctly engaged with the return spring and plunger cam. Secure the operating lever in position with the circlip, then release the spring washers and check the operation of the handbrake mechanism. Apply a smear of high melting-point grease to the operating lever shaft and adjusting screw. Slide the dust

cover over the caliper body, and secure it in position with a cable tie.

16 Soak the piston and the new piston (fluid) seal in clean hydraulic fluid. Smear clean fluid on the cylinder bore surface.

17 Fit the new piston (fluid) seal, using only the fingers to manipulate it into the cylinder bore groove, and refit the piston assembly. Turn the piston in a clockwise direction, using the method employed on dismantling, until it is fully retracted into the caliper bore.

18 Fit the dust seal to the caliper, ensuring that it is correctly located in the caliper and also the groove on the piston.

19 Apply the grease supplied in the repair kit, or a good-quality high temperature brake grease or anti-seize compound to the guide sleeves. Fit the guide sleeves to the caliper body, and fit the new gaiters, ensuring that the gaiters are correctly located in the grooves on both the guide sleeve and caliper body.

Refitting

20 Position the caliper over the brake disc. Refit the two caliper guide pin bolts and tighten to the specified torque.

21 Wipe clean the brake pipe union. Refit the pipe to the caliper, and tighten its union nut securely.

22 Remove the clamp from the brake hose, or the polythene from the master cylinder reservoir (as applicable).

23 Clip the handbrake outer cable into position, then reconnect the inner cable to the caliper operating lever.

24 Bleed the hydraulic system as described in Section 5. Note that, providing the precautions described were taken to minimise brake fluid loss, it should only be necessary to bleed the relevant rear brake.

25 Repeatedly apply the brake pedal to bring the pads into contact with the disc. Check and if necessary adjust the handbrake cable as described in Chapter 1A or 1B.

26 Refit the roadwheel, lower the car to the ground and tighten the wheel bolts to the specified torque. On completion, check the hydraulic fluid level as described in *Weekly checks*.

18 Rear brake disc – inspection, removal and refitting

Inspection

1 Chock the front wheels, engage reverse gear and release the handbrake. Jack up the rear of the car and support it on axle stands (see *Jacking and vehicle support*). Remove the appropriate rear roadwheel.

2 Inspect the disc as described in Section 10.

Removal

3 Remove the brake pads as described in Section 16.

4 Remove the two caliper mounting

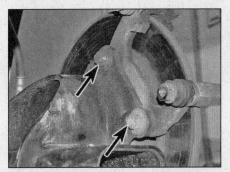
18.4a Unscrew the mounting bolts...

18.4b ...and lift off the caliper-mounting bracket

18.5 Use a blunt cold chisel to remove the dust cap

18.6 Unscrew and remove the rear hub nut

18.7 Withdraw the disc from the stub axle

18.9 Clean and inspect the ABS magnetic ring

bracket bolts, and lift the bracket off (see illustrations).
5 Using a hammer and a suitable punch (or a large flat-bladed screwdriver), carefully tap and prise the cap out of the centre of the brake disc (see illustration).
6 Using a socket and long bar, slacken and remove the rear hub nut – this will be very tight, so ensure that the car is well-supported, and that only good-quality, close-fitting tools are used (see illustration).
7 It should now be possible to withdraw the brake disc and hub bearing assembly from the stub axle by hand (see illustration). If the disc is tight, tap the periphery of the disc using a hide or plastic mallet.

Refitting

8 If new discs are being fitted, use a suitable solvent to wipe any preservative coating from its surface. Note that new discs (or at least

genuine Renault ones) are supplied with new rear wheel bearings prefitted – the bearings can, however, be renewed separately as described in Chapter 10 Section 9.
9 Before refitting the disc, carefully clean the ABS magnetic ring on the back, surrounding the hub bearing (see illustration).
10 Whilst not specified by Renault, it is recommended that a new hub nut is fitted. Fit the new rear hub nut and tighten it to the specified torque (see illustration). Tap the cap back into position in the centre of the disc (if the cap is in poor condition, a new one should be fitted).
11 Apply a few drops of locking fluid to the threads of the caliper mounting bracket bolts (see illustration). Offer up the bracket and refit the bolts, tightening them to the specified torque.
12 Refit the brake pads as described in Section 16.

13 Check the handbrake cable adjustment as described in Section 5 in Chapter 1A or 1B.
14 Refit the roadwheels and lower the car to the ground. Tighten the roadwheel bolts to the specified torque.

19 Stop-light switch – removal, refitting and adjustment

Removal

1 The stop-light switch is located on the pedal bracket beneath the facia.
2 To remove the switch, first remove the right-hand facia lower panel as described in Chapter 11 Section 28.
3 Disconnect the wiring plug and then rotate the switch a quarter turn anti-clockwise to remove it (see illustration).

18.10 Tighten the hub nut to the correct torque figure

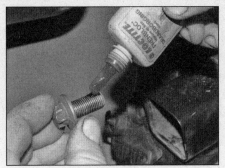
18.11 Apply thread-locking fluid to the caliper mounting bracket

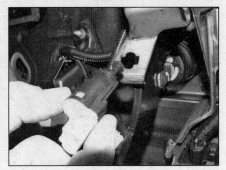
19.3 Rotate anti-clockwise and remove the stop-light switch

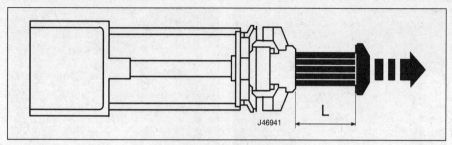

19.4 Adjust the plunger so that dimension L is 28 mm

Refitting and adjustment

4 Refitting is a reversal of removal. Before fitting the switch, the exposed length of the plunger should checked (see illustration). If the correct dimension cannot be achieved the switch must be renewed. The switch will self-adjust when refitted.

5 Depress the brake pedal and the switch will adjust – a ticking noise should be heard as the ratchet operates. Next depress the pedal by hand and then insert a 2mm feeler gauge between the pedal and the switch. Slowly release the pedal until the feeler gauge is held in position and then depress the pedal and remove the feeler gauge. Setting is now complete.

6 Re-connect the wiring plug and then refit the lower facia panel. Check the operation of the stop-lights.

20 Anti-lock braking system (ABS) – general information

1 The purpose of the system is to prevent the wheel(s) locking during heavy braking. This is achieved by automatic release of the brake on the relevant wheel, followed by reapplication of the brake.

2 The main components of the system are four wheel sensors (one per wheel), and a modulator block which contains the ABS computer, the hydraulic solenoid valves and accumulators, and an electrically-driven return pump.

3 The solenoids are controlled by the computer, which receives signals from the wheel sensors. The sensors detect the speed of rotation of a magnetic sensor incorporated within the wheel bearing. This type of sensor is known as an active sensor, because unlike earlier ABS systems that relied on a reluctor ring and a passive sensor it can detect a stationary vehicle. By comparing the speed signals from the four wheels, the computer can determine when a wheel is decelerating at an abnormal rate, and can therefore predict when a wheel is about to lock. During normal operation, the system functions in the same way as a non-ABS braking system does.

4 If the computer senses that a wheel is about to lock, the ABS system enters the 'pressure-maintain' phase. The computer operates the relevant solenoid valve in the modulator block; this isolates the brake on the wheel in question from the master cylinder, effectively sealing in the hydraulic pressure.

5 If the speed of rotation of the wheel continues to decrease at an abnormal rate, the ABS system then enters the 'pressure-decrease' phase. The return pump operates and pumps the hydraulic fluid back into the master cylinder, releasing pressure on the brake. When the speed of rotation of the wheel returns to an acceptable rate, the pump stops and the solenoid valve opens, allowing hydraulic pressure to return and reapply the brake. This cycle can be carried out at up to 10 times a second.

6 The action of the solenoid valves and return pump creates pulses in the hydraulic circuit. When the ABS system is functioning, these pulses can be felt through the brake pedal.

7 The solenoid valves connected to the front calipers operate independently, but the valve connected to the rear brakes operates both simultaneously. Since the braking circuit is split diagonally, a separate mechanical plunger valve in the modulator block divides the rear solenoid valve hydraulic outlet into two separate circuits.

8 The operation of the ABS system is entirely dependent on electrical signals. To prevent the system responding to any inaccurate signals, a built-in safety circuit monitors all signals received by the computer. If an inaccurate signal or low battery voltage is detected, the ABS system is automatically shut down, and the warning lamp on the instrument panel is illuminated to inform the driver that the ABS system is not operational. Normal braking is unaffected.

9 If a fault does develop in the ABS system, the vehicle must be taken to a Renault dealer (or suitably equipped garage) for fault diagnosis and repair. Check first, however, that the problem is not due to loose or damaged wiring connections, or badly routed wiring picking up spurious signals from the ignition system.

⚠ Warning: If the ABS fuse is removed, be careful during road tests not to brake hard as the Electronic Braking Distributor Function is no longer activated.

21 Anti-lock braking system (ABS) components – removal and refitting

Caution: Disconnect the battery before removing any braking system hydraulic unions and do not reconnect the battery until after the hydraulic system has been bled. Failure to do this could lead to air entering the modulator. If air enters the modulator pump, it will prove very difficult (in some cases impossible) to bleed the unit.

Modulator

Note: Before starting work, refer to the Warning at the beginning of Section 5 concerning the dangers of hydraulic fluid.

Removal

1 Disconnect the battery negative lead as described in Chapter 5A Section 4.

2 On 0.9 litre petrol and 1.5 litre diesel engines, remove the air cleaner assembly, as described in Chapter 4A Section 2, or Chapter 4B Section 3.

3 Release the locking clip and disconnect the large block connector (see illustrations), from the modulator.

4 Release any earth leads and wiring loom retaining clips from the mounting bracket.

5 Remove the master cylinder reservoir filler cap. Place a piece of polythene over the filler neck, and securely refit the cap (taking care not to damage the sender unit). This will minimise brake fluid loss during subsequent operations. On all models, be prepared for

21.3a Press down the locking clip...

21.3b ...and release the connector lever

some fluid spillage. As a precaution, place absorbent rags beneath the modulator brake pipe unions.

6 Wipe clean the area around the modulator brake pipe unions. Make a note of how the pipes are arranged **(see illustration)**, to use as a reference on refitting; the pipes may be colour-coded, and the modulator unions marked to aid refitting. Unscrew the union nuts and carefully withdraw the pipes. Plug or tape over the pipe ends and valve orifices, to minimise the loss of brake fluid and to prevent the entry of dirt into the system. Wash off any spilt fluid immediately with cold water.

7 To remove the modulator from the support bracket, undo the securing nuts **(see illustration)**.
Caution: Do not attempt to dismantle the modulator assembly. If faulty the unit must be replaced.

Refitting

8 Refitting is the reverse of the removal procedure, noting the following points:

a) *Tighten the modulator mounting nuts securely.*

b) *Refit the brake pipes to the correct unions, and tighten the union nuts to the specified torque.*

c) *Ensure the wiring is correctly routed, and the connectors firmly pressed into position.*

d) *Before reconnecting the battery, bleed the complete braking system as described in Section 6. Ensure the system is bled in the correct order, to prevent air entering the return pump.*

e) *If the modulator and electronic control unit are renewed they will need calibrating using suitable diagnostic equipment.*

ABS computer

9 The computer is part of the modulator assembly and can be removed. Remove the four bolts and separate the computer from the modulator. New bolts must be used when refitting the computer.

10 At the time of writing, no individual parts were available. The complete assembly must be renewed and calibrated using suitable diagnostic equipment.

Wheel sensors

11 Wheel speed sensors are fitted to all wheels. The front wheels have a magnetic signal generator integral to the wheel bearings and a pick-up. The rear wheels have a magnetic ring fitted to the brake disc (or brake drum) and a pick-up mounted on the stub axle **(see illustrations)**. They are of the 'active' type of sensor providing the ABS computer with a digital signal. There main advantage over earlier ABS systems that used an analogue signal is their ability to detect very low road speeds and a stationary vehicle. Resistance test must not be conducted on

21.6 Note location of pipes – 0.9 litre petrol model shown

21.11a The ABS sensor for the rear brake…

22.4 Undo the two retaining bolts – one out of view

these sensors, they can only be checked with dedicated diagnostic equipment or an oscilloscope. However, because this type of sensor requires a voltage supply to operate correctly it is possible to check for a supply voltage to the sensor with a digital multimeter.
12 The sensor is replaced by disconnecting the wiring and unbolting the sensor.

Yaw sensor

13 Vehicles fitted with ESP (electronic stabilty program) also have a yaw speed and lateral acceleration sensor fitted to the transmission tunnel forward of the gear lever. Disconnect the battery and remove the centre console as described in Chapter 11 Section 27.
14 Disconnect the wiring and unbolt the sensor. Refitting is straightforward but diagnostic equipment will be required to check the correct operation of the sensor.

21.7 The ABS modulator and integral ECU

21.11b …and the magnetic signal ring fitted to the drum brake

22 Vacuum pump (diesel engines) – removal, refitting and testing

Note: *The vacuum pump is bolted to the transmission end of the cylinder head; a new gasket will be required before refitting.*

Removal

1 Where fitted remove the engine cover from the top of the engine.
2 To improve access to the vacuum pump, remove the air filter housing, as described in Chapter 4B Section 3.
3 Release the retaining clip and disconnect the vacuum hose from the pump.
4 Slacken and remove the two mounting bolts securing the pump to the end of the cylinder head **(see illustration)**, then remove the pump. Recover the pump gasket and discard it; a new one should be used on refitting.

Refitting

5 Ensure that the pump and cylinder head mating surfaces are clean and dry and fit the new gasket to the head **(see illustration)**.
6 Manoeuvre the pump into position, then refit the pump mounting bolts and tighten them securely.

Testing

7 The operation of the braking system vacuum pump can be checked using a vacuum gauge.
8 Disconnect the vacuum pipe from the

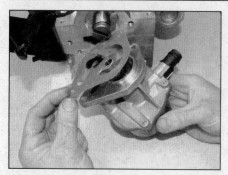

22.5 Fit a new gasket to the vacuum pump

pump, and connect the gauge to the pump union using a length of hose.

9 Start the engine and allow it to idle, then measure the vacuum created by the pump. As a guide, after one minute, a minimum of approximately 500 mm Hg should be recorded. If the vacuum registered is significantly less than this, it is likely that the pump is faulty. However, seek the advice of a Renault dealer before condemning the pump.

Chapter 10
Suspension and steering

Contents

Degrees of difficulty

Easy, suitable for novice with little experience	Fairly easy, suitable for beginner with some experience	Fairly difficult, suitable for competent DIY mechanic	Difficult, suitable for experienced DIY mechanic	Very difficult, suitable for expert DIY or professional

Specifications

Front suspension
Type . . . . Independent, MacPherson struts, with coil springs and integral shock absorbers. Anti-roll bar fitted to all models
Hub bearing endfloat . . . . 0 to 0.05 mm
Front ride height – difference between sides must not exceed . . . . 5.0 mm

Rear suspension
Type . . . . Independent, incorporating trailing arms with telescopic dampers and separate coil springs
Hub bearing endfloat . . . . 0 to 0.05 mm
Ride height – difference between sides must not exceed . . . . 5.0 mm

Steering
Type . . . . Electric power-assisted steering, rack-and-pinion

Wheel alignment and steering angles
Front wheel toe setting (vehicle unladen) . . . . 0° 00' ± 10' (0.0 mm ± 1.0 mm)
Front wheel camber (not adjustable) . . . . 0.0 ± 1
Front wheel castor (not adjustable) . . . . 4° 30' ± 1°
Rear wheel camber setting (vehicle unladen) . . . . – 1° 10' ± 25'
Rear wheel toe setting (vehicle unladen) . . . . – 0° 30' ± 30' toe-in

Tyres
Tyre size (depending on model)

Diameter	Profile	Rating
15"	185/60	84H
15"	185/60	88H
15"	185/65	88V
15"	175/65	88H
16"	195/50	88V
17"	215/45	87W
Pressures	See end of *Weekly checks* on page 0•18	

Roadwheels
Type . . . . Pressed-steel or aluminium alloy (depending on model)
Size . . . . 5.5J x 15, 6J x 16 or 7.5J X 17 (depending on model)
Maximum run-out at rim . . . . 1.2 mm

Torque wrench settings

	Nm	lbf ft
Front suspension		
Anti-roll bar mounting clamp bolts.............................	21	15
Anti-roll link arm	44	32
Engine tie-bar bolt	65	48
Subframe:		
Front bolt	105	77
Rear bolt	110	86
Lower arm balljoint clamp bolt..............................	70	55
Lower arm pivot bolts:		
Rear	105	77
Front	70	55
Radiator support panel......................................	105	77
Side stiffener	21	15
Strut-to-inner wing bolts	21	15
Strut-to-swivel hub bolts	105	77
Strut upper mounting nut....................................	62	46
Rear suspension		
Hub nut*	175	129
Rear trailing arm mounting bracket-to-chassis securing bolts	62	46
Rear trailing arm-to-mounting bracket securing bolt (pivot bolt)......	105	77
Shock absorber lower mounting bolt..........................	105	77
Shock absorber upper mounting nut	21	15
Stub axle/backplate mounting bolts	55	41
Steering		
Steering column mounting bolts	21	15
Steering gear mounting bolts................................	105	77
Steering wheel bolt*	45	33
Track rod end balljoint adjustment locknut	53	39
Track rod end balljoint-to-swivel hub retaining nut	35	26
Track rod-to-steering rack axial balljoint	80	59
Universal joint pinch-bolt	25	18
Roadwheels		
Wheel bolts..	105	77

Replace the nuts/bolts

1 General Information

1 The independent front suspension is of the MacPherson strut type, incorporating coil springs and integral telescopic shock absorbers. The MacPherson struts are located by transverse lower suspension arms, which utilise rubber inner mounting bushes and incorporate a balljoint at the outer ends.

2.3 Undo the mounting bracket bolts and slide the brake caliper off the disc

The front swivel hubs, which carry the wheel bearings, brake calipers and the hub/disc assemblies, are bolted to the MacPherson struts and connected to the lower arms via the balljoints. A front anti-roll bar is fitted to all models. The anti-roll bar is rubber mounted onto the subframe, and connects to the front shock absorbers via a link arm.

2 The rear suspension incorporates a beam axle, trailing arms, coil springs and separate telescopic dampers. The front ends of the trailing arms are attached to the vehicle underbody by rubber bushes, and the rear ends are located by the shock absorbers, which are bolted to the underbody at their upper ends. The coil springs are mounted separately from the shock absorbers and act directly between the axle and the under- body.

3 The steering column is connected by a universal joint to an intermediate shaft, which has a second universal joint at its lower end. The lower universal joint is attached to the steering gear pinion by means of an eccentric clamp bolt.

4 The steering gear is mounted onto the front subframe. It is connected by two track rods and balljoints to steering arms projecting rearwards from the swivel hubs. The track rod ends are threaded to enable wheel alignment adjustment.

5 All models have electric power steering (EPS), provided by a motor attached to the steering column and fitted under the facia. At the time of writing, no individual parts were available.

2 Front swivel hub assembly – removal and refitting

Removal

1 Chock the rear wheels, firmly apply the handbrake, then jack up the front of the vehicle and support it on axle stands (see *Jacking and vehicle support*). Remove the appropriate front roadwheel.

2 Refit at least two roadwheel bolts to the front hub, and tighten them securely. Remove and discard the driveshaft nut; a new one should be used on refitting.

3 If the hub bearings are to be disturbed, remove the brake disc as described in Chapter 9 Section 10. If not, unscrew the two bolts securing the brake caliper assembly to the swivel hub, and slide the caliper assembly off the disc **(see illustration)**.

2.4 Secure the caliper to the coil spring

2.5 Refit the nut to avoid damaging the track rod end threads when using a balljoint separator

2.6 Note the fitted direction of the lower strut bolts

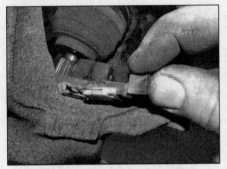

2.7a Unclip the ABS sensor wiring…

2.7b …and remove the ball joint bolt

2.8 Removing the swivel hub

4 Using a piece of wire or string, tie the caliper to the front suspension coil spring to avoid straining the brake hose **(see illustration)**.

5 Remove the nut securing the track rod end balljoint to the swivel hub. Release the balljoint tapered shank using a universal balljoint separator **(see illustration)**.

6 Remove the two nuts from the bolts securing the swivel hub to the suspension strut, noting that the nuts are positioned on the rear side of the strut **(see illustration)**. Withdraw the bolts and support the swivel hub assembly.

7 Unclip the ABS sensor and then remove the nut and clamp bolt securing the lower suspension arm to the swivel hub **(see illustrations)**. Carefully lever the balljoint out of the swivel hub, taking care not to damage the balljoint or driveshaft gaiters. Note the plastic protector plate which may be fitted to the balljoint shank.

8 Release the driveshaft joint from the hub, and remove the swivel hub assembly from the vehicle **(see illustration)**.

Refitting

9 Ensure that the driveshaft joint and hub splines are clean and dry.

10 Engage the joint splines with the hub, and slide the hub fully onto the driveshaft. Insert the two swivel hub-to-suspension strut mounting bolts from the front side of the strut, then refit the nuts to the bolts and tighten them to the specified torque.

11 Fit the new driveshaft nut, tightening it by hand only at this stage.

12 Ensure that the plastic protector is still fitted to the lower arm balljoint and then locate the balljoint shank in the swivel hub. Refit the balljoint clamp bolt, and tighten its retaining nut to the specified torque.

13 Reconnect the track rod end balljoint to the swivel hub, and tighten its retaining nut to the specified torque.

14 Refit the ABS sensor to the hub.

15 Refit the brake disc (if removed), aligning the marks made on removal, and securely tighten its retaining screws. Slide the brake caliper assembly into position over the brake disc. Apply a few drops of locking fluid to the caliper bolt threads. Refit the bolts and tighten them to the specified torque (Chapter 9).

16 Insert and tighten two wheel bolts. Tighten the driveshaft nut to the specified torque (Chapter 8), using the method employed during removal to prevent the hub from rotating.

17 Check that the hub rotates freely, then refit the roadwheel and lower the vehicle to the ground. Tighten the roadwheel bolts to the specified torque.

---

3 Front hub bearings –
checking, removal and refitting

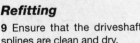

Note: *The bearing is a sealed, pre-adjusted and pre-lubricated, double-row roller type, and is intended to last the car's entire service life without maintenance or attention. Do not attempt to remove the bearing unless* absolutely necessary, as it will be damaged during the removal operation. Never overtighten the driveshaft nut in an attempt to 'adjust' the bearing.

Note: *A press will be required to dismantle and rebuild the assembly; if such a tool is not available, a large bench vice and spacers (such as large sockets) will serve as an adequate substitute. The bearing's inner races are an interference fit on the hub; if the inner race remains on the hub when it is pressed out of the hub carrier, a knife-edged bearing puller will be required to remove it.*

Checking

1 Wear in the front hub bearings can be checked by measuring the amount of side play (endfloat) present. To do this, a dial gauge should be fixed so that its probe is in contact with the disc face of the hub. The play should be as specified. If it is greater than this, the bearings are worn excessively, and should be renewed.

Removal

Note: *A new bearing circlip will be required on refitting.*

2 Remove the swivel hub assembly as described in Section 2.

3 Support the swivel hub securely on blocks or in a vice. Using a tubular spacer which bears only on the inner end of the hub flange, press the hub flange out of the bearing. If the bearing outboard inner race remains on the hub, remove it using a bearing puller **(see illustrations)**.

3.3a Drive the flange from the hub...

3.3b ...and use a knife edge puller to remove the inner race

3.4 Release the circlip fitted to retain the bearing in the hub assembly

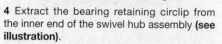
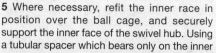

3.5 Remove the bearing

3.6 The bearing kit

3.7 Make sure the signal ring is not damaged

4 Extract the bearing retaining circlip from the inner end of the swivel hub assembly (see illustration).

5 Where necessary, refit the inner race in position over the ball cage, and securely support the inner face of the swivel hub. Using a tubular spacer which bears only on the inner race, press the complete bearing assembly out of the swivel hub (see illustration).

6 Thoroughly clean the hub and swivel hub, removing all traces of dirt and grease. Polish away any burrs or raised edges which might hinder reassembly. Check for cracks or any other signs of wear or damage, and renew the components if necessary. As noted above, the bearing and its circlip must be renewed whenever they are disturbed. A bearing kit, which consists of the bearing, circlip and hub nut is available from Renault dealers (see illustration).

Refitting

7 On reassembly, check that the new bearing is packed safely, as the magnetic signal ring is part of the bearing assembly (see illustration). Apply a light film of oil to the bearing outer race and to the hub flange shaft.

8 Securely support the swivel hub, and locate the bearing in the hub with the magnetic end of the bearing pointing inboard. Press the bearing into position, ensuring that it enters the hub squarely, using a tubular spacer which bears only on the outer race (see illustrations).

9 Once the bearing is correctly seated, secure it with the new circlip (see illustration).

10 Locate the bearing inner race over the end of the hub flange. Press the bearing onto the

3.8a Fit the bearing with the signal ring side in first

3.8b Using a flat bar to press the bearing into the hub...

3.8c ...then a socket to press it all the way in

3.9 Fit new circlip to secure bearing

3.10 Refitting the hub flange

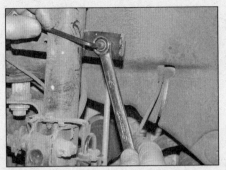

4.2a Using Allen key to hold ball joint, undo nut…

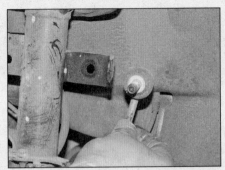

4.2b …and remove the anti-roll bar link arm

4.3a Unclip the brake hose…

4.3b …and the ABS wiring

4.4 Remove the two bolts/nuts, noting their fitted position

4.5 Remove the three upper mounting bolts

hub, using a tubular spacer which bears only on the inner race, until it seats against the hub flange (see illustration). Check that the hub flange rotates freely. Wipe off any excess oil or grease.

11 Refit the swivel hub assembly as described in Section 2.

4 Front strut – removal and refitting

Removal

1 Chock the rear wheels, firmly apply the handbrake, then jack up the front of the vehicle and support it on axle stands (see *Jacking and vehicle support*). Remove the appropriate roadwheel.

2 Remove the anti-roll bar link arm from the strut (see illustrations). Use an Allen key to prevent the ball joint from turning, when removing the securing nut.

3 Unclip the brake pipe hose and ABS wiring from the strut assembly (see illustrations).

4 Remove the two nuts from the bolts securing the swivel hub to the bottom of the suspension strut (see illustration), noting that the nuts are positioned on the rear side of the strut. Withdraw the bolts, and support the swivel hub assembly.

5 From within the engine compartment remove the windscreen cowl panel (as described in Chapter 11 Section 7), then remove the three suspension strut upper mounting bolts (see illustration). As the last

bolt is removed reached under the wing and support the strut and coil assembly. Note, before removing the upper mounting bolts, draw around the bolts/washers to aid refitting, as the bolt holes are larger than the bolts.

6 Lower the assembly from under the wing, releasing the strut from the swivel hub whilst taking care not to dislodge the driveshaft from the gearbox or damage the outer driveshaft gaiter.

Refitting

7 Manoeuvre the strut assembly into position, taking care not to damage the driveshaft gaiter.

8 Insert the two swivel hub-to-suspension strut mounting bolts from the front side of the strut. Refit the nuts to the rear of the bolts, and tighten them to the specified torque.

9 Refit the upper mounting bolts and tighten it to the specified torque.

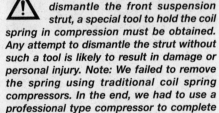

5.2 Using spring compressors, compress the suspension strut coil spring

10 Refit the anti-roll bar drop link and then refit the windscreen cowl panels and wiper arms.

11 Refit the roadwheel, lower the vehicle to the ground and tighten the roadwheel bolts to the specified torque.

12 When completed, take to the vehicle to a specialist to have the suspension settings and wheel alignment checked.

5 Front strut – dismantling, inspection and reassembly

⚠️ *Warning: Before attempting to dismantle the front suspension strut, a special tool to hold the coil spring in compression must be obtained. Any attempt to dismantle the strut without such a tool is likely to result in damage or personal injury. Note: We failed to remove the spring using traditional coil spring compressors. In the end, we had to use a professional type compressor to complete the job.*

Dismantling

1 With the strut removed from the vehicle as described in Section 4, clean away all external dirt. Mount the strut upright in a vice.

2 Fit the spring compressor, and compress the coil spring until all tension is relieved from the upper mounting plate. Ensure that the compressor tool is securely located on the spring according to the tool manufacturer's instructions (see illustration).

5.3 Slacken and remove the nut from the top of the strut

5.4 Remove the bearing, upper spring seat and coil spring

5.11 Refit the rubber dust cover to the strut piston

3 Slacken and remove the retaining nut from the top of the strut **(see illustration)**.
4 Remove the upper mounting plate, the bearing and the upper spring seat **(see illustration)**.
5 Carefully remove the coil spring, complete with the spring compressor, and store in a safe place for refitting. (It may be safer to release the spring compressor from the spring.)
6 Slide the rubber bump stop/dust cover off the strut piston.

Inspection

7 With the strut assembly now completely dismantled, examine all the components for wear, damage or deformation, and check the upper bearing for smoothness of operation. Renew any of the components as necessary.
8 Examine the strut for signs of fluid leakage. Check the strut piston for signs of pitting along its entire length, and check the strut body for signs of damage. Test the operation of the strut, while holding it in an upright position, by moving the piston through a full stroke and then through short strokes of 50 to 100 mm. In both cases, the resistance felt should be smooth and continuous. If the resistance is jerky or uneven, or if there is any visible sign of wear or damage, renewal is necessary.
9 If any doubt exists about the condition of the coil spring, gradually release the spring compressor (if not already done), and check the spring for distortion and signs of cracking. Since no minimum free length is specified by Renault, the only way to check the tension of the spring is to compare it to a new component. Renew the spring if it is damaged or distorted, or if there is any doubt as to its condition.
10 Inspect all other components for signs of damage or deterioration, and renew any that are suspect.

Reassembly

Note: *Apply grease between the ends of the spring and its stops.*
11 Ensure that all components are clean and dry. Slide the bump stop/dust cover into position over the strut piston **(see illustration)**.
12 Refit the compressed coil spring, followed by the upper spring seat. Ensure that both ends of the spring are correctly located in the spring seats.
13 Refit the strut bearing and upper mounting plate.
14 Slide the retaining collar (where fitted) onto the strut piston, and secure it in position with the retaining nut. Slowly and carefully release the spring compressor, watching to make sure that both ends of the spring remain correctly located in the spring seats.
15 Refit the strut to the vehicle as described in Section 4.

6 Front anti-roll bar – removal and refitting

Note: *Complete removal of the anti-roll bar requires removal of the front subframe assembly. Individual components can be removed with the subframe in place.*

Removal

1 Chock the rear wheels, apply the handbrake and then jack up the front of the vehicle and support it on axle stands (see *Jacking and vehicle support*). Remove both front roadwheels.
2 Working inside the vehicle position the wheels in the straight-ahead position, remove the key to lock the steering and then remove the steering column lower universal joint securing bolt **(see illustration)**. Note that on vehicles with a key card it is not possible to lock the wheels in the straight-ahead position.
3 Remove both front inner wheel arch liners, and then detach the track rod end, anti roll bar link arm and lower control arm balljoint **(see illustrations)**.
4 Strap the radiator to the front crossmember and remove the bumper lower bolts. Remove the bolts securing the side supports of the front crossmember.

6.2 Remove the steering column lower securing bolt

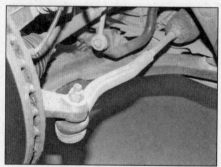

6.3a Disconnect the track rod end...

6.3b ...the anti-roll bar link arm...

6.3c ...and lower control arm ball joint

5 Disconnect the ABS sensors from both front wheels and remove the engine under tray. If Xenon headlights are fitted disconnect the wiring to the position sensor on the anti-roll bar.
6 Remove the rear engine steady bar and disconnect the wiring to the post catalytic converter oxygen sensor.
7 Place a suitable jack below the subframe and then unbolt the subframe mounting bolts. Carefully lower the jack so that the Oxygen sensor (petrol models) can be disconnected and the loom freed from the subframe. Fully lower the jack and subframe and then manoeuvre the subframe from underneath the vehicle.
8 Remove the anti-roll bar clamps from the subframe. If Xenon headlights are fitted, mark precisely the position of the clamp on the anti roll-bar before removal.
9 Inspect the anti-roll bar for damage and distortion.

Refitting

10 Refitting is a reversal of removal, noting the following points:
a) *Tighten all fixings to the correct torque.*
b) *Place a 10 mm shim between the subframe and the radiator crossmember to ensure correct alignment.*
c) *A new special bolt must be fitted to the steering column universal joint.*
d) *Vehicles with Xenon headlights must have the load position sensor checked with suitable diagnostic equipment.*

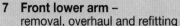

7   Front lower arm –
    removal, overhaul and refitting

Removal

1 Chock the rear wheels, apply the handbrake, jack up the front of the vehicle and support it on axle stands. (see *Jacking and vehicle support*). Remove the appropriate front roadwheel.
2 Using a strap or cable ties secure the radiator to the bonnet slam panel and then remove the front bumper lower bolts.
3 Remove the plastic wheel arch liners and then remove the engine undertray.
4 Remove the side stiffener lower bolts and the radiator support bolts **(see illustration)**. Remove the radiator support and then support the rear subframe with a suitable jack.
5 Remove the nut and clamp bolt securing the lower suspension arm balljoint to the swivel hub. Carefully lever the balljoint out of the swivel hub, taking care not to damage the balljoint or driveshaft gaiters. We used a long lever, chain and support block on the subframe. Remove the plastic protector plate which may be fitted to the balljoint shank **(see illustrations)**.
6 Remove the two pivot nuts and bolts, and remove the lower suspension arm from the vehicle.

7.4 Remove the radiator support panel bolts

7.5a Remove the lower suspension arm pinch-bolt...

7.5b ...lever the shank free...

7.5c ...and recover the plastic spacer

Overhaul

7 Clean the lower arm and the area around the arm mountings, then check for cracks, distortion or any other signs of damage. Check that the lower arm balljoint moves freely, without any sign of roughness, and that the balljoint gaiter is free from cracks and splits. Examine the shank of the pivot bolts for signs of wear or scoring. Renew worn components as necessary.
8 Inspect the lower arm pivot bushes. If they are worn, cracked, split or perished, the arm must be replaced – at the time of writing the flexible mountings were not available from Renault. The ball joint is available and can be replaced as described in the next Section 8.

Refitting

9 Offer up the lower suspension arm, and insert the two pivot bolts from the rear of the suspension arm. Refit the nuts, but tighten them by hand only at this stage.
10 Locate the balljoint shank in the swivel hub. Fit a new balljoint clamp bolt, and tighten its new retaining nut to the specified torque.
11 Before the inner pivot bolts can be fully tightened the lower arm must be positioned correctly **(see illustration)**. This is best achieved by carefully raising the lower arm with a jack placed under the outer balljoint. Extreme care must be taken as lifting the arm to the correct position may start to lift the vehicle from the axle stands. Tighten the bolts to the correct torque.

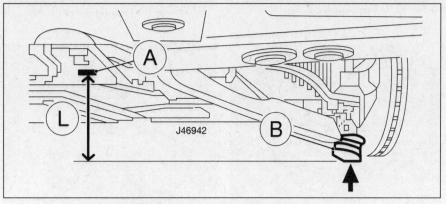

7.11 Adjust the arm so that dimension L = 6 mm

A Rear subframe bolt   *B Lower arm balljoint*

7.12 Place a 10mm shim between the subframe and the radiator support panel

12 Refit the radiator support panel, using a 10 mm shim to correctly locate it **(see illustration)** and then fit the side stiffener.
13 Refit the remaining components in the reverse order of removal.

8 Front lower arm balljoint – removal and refitting

1 At the time of writing, only the balljoint was available from Renault. Note however if the balljoint is worn the mounting bushes may also be worn. If both the balljoint and bushes are worn it will make economic sense to renew the complete arm.

Removal

2 Remove the arm from the vehicle as described in Section 7.

9.4 Extract the circlip

9.5b ...taking care not to damage the ABS signal ring

3 Remove the circlip from the balljoint and then with the arm supported drive out the balljoint with a hammer. If the balljoint can not be driven out, then it will need pressing out using a hydraulic press.

Refitting

4 The replacement balljoint must be pressed into position – do not attempt to drive it home with a hammer. Place the arm in a press and using a length of pipe (or large deep reach socket) that will fit over the balljoint press the new balljoint into position. It may also be possible to press the balljoint into the arm using a large vise.
5 Remove the arm from the press and fit the new circlip (supplied as part of the kit).
6 Refit the lower arm as described in Section 7.

9 Rear hub bearings – checking, removal and refitting

Note: *The bearing is a sealed, pre-adjusted and pre-lubricated, double-row tapered-roller type, and is intended to last the car's entire service life without maintenance or attention. Never overtighten the hub nut in an attempt to 'adjust' the bearings.*

Checking

1 Chock the front wheels and engage reverse gear (or P on automatic models). Jack up the rear of the vehicle and support it on axle stands (see *Jacking and vehicle support*).

9.5a Press the bearing out of the hub...

9.7 New wheel bearing, kit

Remove the appropriate rear roadwheel, and fully release the handbrake.
2 Wear in the rear hub bearings can be checked by measuring the amount of side play (endfloat) present. To do this, a dial test indicator should be fixed so that its probe is in contact with the hub outer face. The play should be as specified. If it is greater than this, the bearings are worn excessively and should be renewed.

Removal

3 Remove the rear brake disc or drum, as described in Chapter 9.
4 Using circlip pliers, extract the bearing retaining circlip from the centre of the brake disc or drum **(see illustration)**.
5 Securely support the disc or drum hub, then press the bearing out of the hub, using a length of threaded rod and a couple of large sockets **(see illustrations)**. The ABS magnetic signal ring is fitted to the inside of the hub, take care not to damage this as the bearing is being removed.
6 Thoroughly clean the hub, removing all traces of dirt and grease. Polish away any burrs or raised edges which might hinder reassembly. Check the hub for cracks or any other signs of damage, and renew if necessary. The bearing and its circlip must be renewed whenever they are disturbed. A bearing kit is available from Renault dealers.

Refitting

7 On reassembly, check the bearing kit, with new circlip and retaining nut **(see illustration)**. Apply a light film of gear oil to the bearing outer race and stub axle.
8 The new bearing can be draw into the hub with a length of threaded bar and suitable old sockets. The socket must bear on the edge of the outer race only **(see illustration)**.
9 Ensure that the bearing is correctly seated against the hub shoulder, and secure it in position with the new circlip. Ensure that the circlip is correctly seated in its groove.
10 Refit the brake disc or drum as described in Chapter 9.

9.8 A suitable set-up for fitting the new bearing

10.2a Raise the shock absorber slightly...

10.2b ...loosen and then remove the bolt

10.3 Slacken and remove the retaining nut

10 Rear shock absorber – removal, testing and refitting

Removal

1 Chock the front wheels and engage reverse gear (or P). Jack up the rear of the vehicle and support it on axle stands (see *Jacking and vehicle support*). Remove the appropriate rear roadwheel.
2 Using a jack, raise the trailing arm slightly until the shock absorber is slightly compressed. Remove the lower mounting bolt **(see illustrations)**.
3 Working inside the luggage compartment, unclip the luggage compartment side trim panels, as described in Chapter 11 Section 26. Slacken and remove the upper mounting nut **(see illustration)**, and remove the shock absorber from the vehicle.

Testing

4 Mount the shock absorber in a vice, and test as described in Section 5 for the front suspension strut. Also check the rubber mounting bushes for damage and deterioration. Renew the shock absorber complete if any damage or wear is evident; the mounting bushes are not available separately. Inspect the mounting bolts for signs of wear or damage, and renew as necessary.

Refitting

5 Prior to refitting the shock absorber, mount it upright in the vice, and operate it fully through several strokes in order to prime it. (This is necessary even if a new unit is being fitted, as it may have been stored horizontally, and so need priming.) Apply a smear of multipurpose grease to the shock absorber mounting bolts.
6 Offer up the shock absorber, then refit its upper mounting securing nut, tightening it by hand only at this stage.
7 Refit the lower shock absorber mounting bolt, again tightening it by hand only. Lower and remove the jack from under the trailing arm.
8 Refit the roadwheel, lower the vehicle to the ground and tighten the roadwheel bolts to the specified torque.
9 Rock the vehicle to settle the shock absorber mounting bushes in position, then tighten both the upper and lower mountings to the specified torque.

11 Rear coil spring – removal and refitting

Note: *The rear springs should be renewed in pairs, and it is advisable to renew the spring damping rubbers at the same time.*

Removal

1 Chock the front wheels and engage reverse gear. Jack up the rear of the vehicle and support it on axle stands. Remove the appropriate roadwheel.

2 Raise the relevant trailing arm slightly using a jack and then unclip the wheel sensor wiring loom from the trailing arm.
3 Unscrew and remove the bolt securing the lower end of the shock absorber to the trailing arm **(see illustration)**.
4 Carefully lower the jack supporting the trailing arm, and remove the coil spring and its damping rubbers from between the axle and underbody. Lever the trailing arm down slightly if necessary to remove the spring **(see illustration)**.

Refitting

5 Refitting is a reversal of removal, remembering the following points.
6 Ensure that the spring locates correctly on the damping rubbers, between the trailing arm and the underbody. The spring has a coloured paint mark **(see illustration)**, which must be facing towards the rear of the vehicle.
7 Tighten the lower shock absorber bolt as described in Section 10.
8 If the coil spring is being renewed, repeat the procedure on the other side of the vehicle.

12 Rear axle/trailing arm bushes – removal, overhaul and refitting

Removal

1 Chock the front wheels and engage reverse gear (or P on automatic models). Jack up the rear of the vehicle and support it on axle

11.3 Undo the lower mounting bolt

11.4 Lever the trailing arm downwards and remove the coil spring

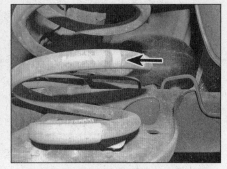
11.6 Coloured paint mark, facing towards the rear of the vehicle

12.3 Unbolt and remove the ABS wheel speed sensors

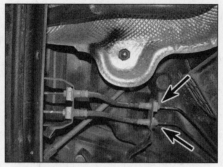

12.6 Disconnect the brake pipe connections from the axle crossmember

12.13 When refitting, use locking fluid on the threads of the bolts

stands (see *Jacking and vehicle support*). Remove both rear roadwheels.

2 If a new rear axle is to be installed, remove the brake disc or drums as described in Chapter 9.

3 Remove the rear wheel sensors and unclip the wiring from the rear axle **(see illustration)**.

4 To minimise the loss of brake fluid, secure a plastic bag or latex glove under the master cylinder reservoir cap.

5 Use a brake hose clamp, a G-clamp or a similar tool with protected jaws to clamp the brake flexible hose at the nearest convenient point.

6 Disconnect the rear brake pipes at the flexible hose unions which are clipped to the axle crossmember **(see illustration)**. Remove the retaining clips, free the flexible hoses from the crossmember, and plug or tape over the union ends to prevent dirt entry. Wash off any spilt fluid immediately.

7 Disconnect the handbrake cables from the rear brakes as described in Chapter 9.

8 Slacken, but do not remove the nuts securing the front ends of the trailing arms to the vehicle underbody.

9 Remove the rear coil springs as described in Section 11.

10 Support the weight of the rear axle on a trolley jack.

11 The help of an assistant at this point will ease this task to ensure that the axle beam does not slip off the jack. Remove the six securing nuts (three each side) from the axle mountings to the vehicle body. Withdraw the axle from underneath the vehicle.

12 If necessary, the trailing arm bushes can be renewed, referring to the later paragraphs.

13 If a new axle is being fitted, remove the brake pipes from the original and fit them to the new axle. Also transfer the brake backplates and stub axles assemblies. Use locking fluid on the threads of the retaining bolts **(see illustration)**.

Refitting

14 Place the rear axle on a trolley jack, and lift it into position underneath the vehicle. Insert the trailing arm mounting bolts from under the vehicle, ensuring that the mounting plate is correctly fitted. Refit the nuts and tighten them to the specified torque.

15 Refit the coil springs as described in Section 11.

16 Refit the brake hoses to the brackets on the crossmember, and secure them in position with the retaining clips. Reconnect the brake pipes to the hoses, and securely tighten the union nuts.

17 Feed the handbrake cables along the trailing arms, ensuring they are correctly located.

18 Refit the handbrake cables as described in Chapter 9.

19 Refit the ABS wheel sensors and bleed the brake hydraulic system on completion. Refer to the relevant Sections of Chapter 9.

20 Refit the roadwheels, lower the vehicle to the ground and tighten the wheel bolts to the specified torque.

21 Check the rear underbody height as described in Section 13.

Trailing arm bush renewal

22 Examine all the axle components for wear

and damage. If the trailing arm bushes require renewal, proceed as described below.

23 Make a note of the position of the bush in the trailing arm before removal, as the new bush will need to be fitted in the same position.

24 A special Renault tool is required to remove the bush **(see illustration)**. With the correct tool it is possibly to remove the bush with the axle still in the vehicle.

25 Removal of the bush may be made easier if the bush housing in the trailing arm is heated using a heat gun, or similar. Do not use a naked flame, due to the close proximity of the fuel tank (if renewing the bushes while the axle is still on the vehicle).

26 Draw the bush from the trailing arm using the tool described in paragraph 24.

27 Refit the new bush using the special tool used on removal. Draw the new bush back into the trailing arm, ensuring that it is fitted in the correct position in the trailing arm.

28 With the new bush in position, refit the axle mounting bolt. Using a jack placed under the trailing arm, correctly adjust the position of the trailing arm before tightening the bolt to the correct torque **(see illustration)**.

13 Vehicle ride height –
general information and checking

General information

1 The vehicle ride height measurements are used to ensure accuracy when checking the

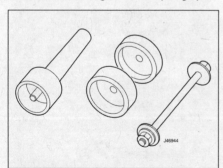

12.24 Renault tooling for removing and refitting the trailing arm bushes

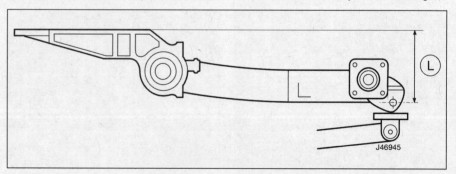

12.28 Adjust the jack so that dimension L = 150 mm (measured from the centre of the shock mounting to the lower sill)

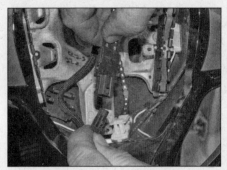
14.3a Disconnect the wiring connectors...

14.3b ...inside the steering wheel recess

14.4 Slacken the steering wheel retaining bolt

front suspension and steering angles (see Section 20). This is because the angles will vary slightly according to the ride height of the vehicle. A visual inspection should draw your attention to any major discrepancies in the vehicle ride height.

Checking

2 To check the ride height, position the unladen vehicle on a level surface, with the tyres correctly inflated and the fuel tank full. Check that all the tyres are also the correct size and profile. A check should also be made to ensure there are no major mechanical faults. A broken road spring, for example, will severely affect the ride height.
3 To check the front ride height, measure and record the distance from the front subframe rear mounting bolt head to the ground. Measure both sides and compare the figures. Expect a figure of 175 mm plus or minus 30 mm, depending on wheel size and equipment level.
4 To check the rear ride height, measure and record the distance from the trailing arm pivot bolt to the ground. Measure both sides. Expect a figure of 207 mm plus or minus 30 mm, depending on wheel size and equipment level.
5 The difference between the heights across each axle should not exceed 10 mm.
6 Note that no adjustment of the ride height is possible.
7 If further checks are required, take your vehicle to your local dealer who will have the specialised equipment to do this.

14 Steering wheel – removal and refitting

Note: *A new steering wheel retaining bolt will be required on refitting.*

Removal

1 Set the front wheels in the straight-ahead position.
2 Remove the airbag (referring to the warnings) as described in Chapter 12 Section 28.
3 Disconnect the wiring connectors inside the steering wheel recess **(see illustrations)**.
4 Slacken but do not remove the steering wheel retaining bolt **(see illustration)**. **Note:**

14.5 Withdrawing the wiring through the steering wheel as it is removed

The steering wheel splines are designed so that they can only be fitted in one position.
5 Lift the steering wheel off the column splines, carefully feeding the wiring through the steering wheel as it is removed **(see illustration)**. If it is tight tap the steering wheel, using the palm of the hand, or rock it from side-to-side whilst pulling upwards to release it from the shaft splines. Once the steering wheel is free, remove the securing bolt and lift off the steering wheel. Note : Do not turn the airbag contact ring assembly or the steering column shaft whilst the steering wheel is removed.

Refitting

6 Refitting is a reversal of removal, bearing in mind the following points.
a) *Make sure the steering wheel splines are aligned correctly with the steering column shaft.*

15.6 Disconnect the wiring to the transponder

14.6 Fit a new bolt to the steering wheel

b) *Tighten the new retaining bolt (see illustration) to the specified torque.*
c) *Check that all the wiring plugs are connected securely.*
d) *Refit the airbag as described in Chapter 12 Section 28 (referring to the warnings).*

15 Steering column/motor – removal, checking and refitting

Note: *The electric power steering motor can only be purchased as a complete unit complete with the steering column shaft.*
Note: *A new steering wheel bolt and universal joint bolt will be required on refitting. For more information on removal of individual components, check in the relevant Chapters.*

Removal

1 Disconnect the battery negative lead as described in Chapter 5A Section 4.
2 Set the wheels in the straight-ahead position.
3 Remove the steering wheel as described in Section 14.
4 Remove the upper and lower facia trim panels as described in Chapter 11 Section 28.
5 Remove the column switch assembly as described in Chapter 12 Section 7.
6 On vehicles with a key, disconnect and remove the transponder ring from the switch **(see illustration)**. On vehicles with a key card, disconnect the wiring and remove the column lock, noting that the securing bolt has a left-hand thread.

15.7 Remove the lower universal clamp bolt

15.9 Support the assembly on a suitable block of wood

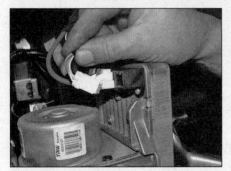

15.10 Disconnect the wiring to the motor

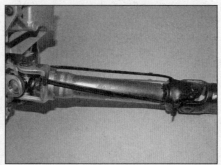

15.11 Use cable ties to lock the column sections together

7 Lift the carpet and remove the universal joint bolt cover and bolt **(see illustration)**.

8 Make sure the steering column height adjuster is in the locked position and then place a suitable block of wood on the floor below the motor assembly.

9 Remove the steering column mounting bolts and lower the assembly onto the block of wood. Take care as it is very heavy **(see illustration)**.

10 With the column supported on the block, disconnect the wiring connectors and then remove it from the vehicle **(see illustration)**.

11 Do not separate the column assembly. Secure the sections with suitable cable ties **(see illustration)**.

Checking

12 Check the steering shaft for signs of free play in the column bushes, and check the universal joints for signs of damage or roughness in the joint bearings. If damage or wear is found on the steering shaft universal joints or shaft bushes, the column must be renewed as an assembly.

Refitting

13 Making sure the steering column height adjuster is still in the locked position, manoeuvre the steering column assembly into position. Engage the universal joint with the steering gear pinion shaft.

14 Support the motor and column on the block of wood and reconnect the wiring to the motor

15 Refit the steering column mounting bolts.

16 Fit a new lower universal joint pinch-bolt and tighten it to the correct torque.

17 Tighten the steering column mounting bolts to their specified torque and refit the transponder ring or electric column switch.

18 Refit the upper and lower facia trim panels as described in Chapter 11 Section 28.

19 Refit the steering wheel as described in Section 14, and reconnect the battery negative terminal.

16 Steering gear rubber gaiter – renewal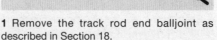

1 Remove the track rod end balljoint as described in Section 18.

2 Mark the correct fitted position of the gaiter on the track rod **(see illustration)**. Release the securing clips and slide the gaiter off the

16.2 Remove the securing clips from the gaiter

steering gear housing and track rod end.

3 Thoroughly clean the track rod and the steering gear housing, using fine abrasive paper to polish off any corrosion, burrs or sharp edges which might damage the sealing lips of the new gaiter on installation.

4 Recover the grease from inside the old gaiter. If it is uncontaminated with dirt or grit, apply it to the track rod inner balljoint. If the old grease is contaminated, or it is suspected that some has been lost, apply some new molybdenum disulphide grease.

5 Grease the inside of the new gaiter. Carefully slide the gaiter onto the track rod, and locate it on the steering gear housing. Align the outer edge of the gaiter with the mark made on the track rod prior to removal, then secure it in position with new retaining clips.

6 Refit the track rod balljoint as described in Section 18.

17 Steering gear assembly – removal, inspection and refitting

Note: *A balljoint separator tool will be required for this operation.*

Removal

1 Chock the rear wheels, apply the handbrake and then jack up the front of the vehicle and support it on axle stands (see *Jacking and vehicle support*). Remove both front roadwheels.

2 Working inside the vehicle, position the wheels in the straight-ahead position, remove the key to lock the steering and then remove the steering column lower universal joint. Note that on vehicles with a key card it is not possible to lock the wheels in the straight-ahead position.

3 Remove both front inner wing liners and then detach the track rod end, anti-roll bar link arm and control arm balljoint **(see illustrations 6.3a, 6.3b and 6.3c)**.

4 Strap the radiator to the front crossmember and remove the bumper lower bolts. Remove the bolts securing the side supports of the front crossmember.

5 Disconnect the ABS sensors from both front wheels and remove the engine under tray. If Xenon headlights are fitted, disconnect the wiring to the position sensor on the anti-roll bar.

6 Remove the rear engine steady bar and disconnect the wiring to the post catalytic converter oxygen sensor.

7 Place a suitable jack below the subframe and then unbolt the subframe mounting bolts. Carefully lower the jack and manoeuvre the subframe from underneath the vehicle.

8 With the subframe assembly removed from the vehicle, remove the heat shield. Tilt the anti-roll bar up and remove the steering gear mounting bolts.

9 Inspect the steering gear for damage and distortion.

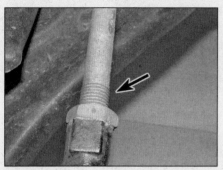

18.2 Count or measure the threads

18.4a Remove the locknut...

18.4b ...and use a balljoint separator to break the taper

Refitting

10 Refitting is a reversal of removal, noting the following points:

a) Tighten all fixings to the correct torque.

b) Place a 10 mm shim between the subframe and the radiator crossmember to ensure correct alignment.

c) A new special bolt must be fitted to the steering column universal joint.

d) Vehicles with Xenon headlights must have the load position sensor checked with suitable diagnostic equipment.

18 Track rod end balljoint – removal and refitting

Note: A balljoint separator tool will be required for this operation.

Removal

1 Apply the handbrake, then jack up the front of the vehicle and support it on axle stands (see Jacking and vehicle support). Remove the appropriate front roadwheel.

2 If the balljoint is to be re-used, precisely measure the exposed threads of the track rod **(see illustration)**.

3 Holding the balljoint, unscrew its locknut.

4 Remove the nut securing the track rod balljoint to the swivel hub. Release the balljoint tapered shank using a universal balljoint separator. If the balljoint is to be re-used, protect the threaded end of the shank by screwing the nut back on a few turns before using the separator **(see illustrations)**.

5 Unscrew the balljoint from the track rod end.

6 Carefully clean the balljoint and the threads. Renew the balljoint if its movement is sloppy or if it is too stiff; if it is excessively worn, or if it is damaged in any way. Carefully check the shank taper and threads. If the balljoint gaiter is damaged, the complete balljoint must be renewed; it is not possible to obtain the gaiter separately.

Refitting

7 Fit the new track rod end until it contacts the lock nut on the track rod.

8 Refit the balljoint shank to the swivel hub,

and tighten the retaining nut to the specified torque. If difficulty is experienced due to the balljoint shank rotating, jam it by exerting pressure on the underside of the balljoint, using a tyre lever or a jack.

9 With the track rod end fitted, hold it steady on the flat section provided and tighten the locknut. Check the measurement of the exposed threads as previously noted. Unlock and adjust the position of the track rod end if necessary to achieve the correct setting point.

10 Refit the roadwheel, lower the vehicle to the ground and tighten the roadwheel bolts to the specified torque.

11 Have a garage or tyre shop check the front wheel alignment with optical equipment.

19 Track rod and inner balljoint – removal and refitting

Note: In order to safely remove the track rod without the risk of damaging the steering rack, a special track rod wrench (Renault number Dir.1305-01) and rack retaining clamp (Renault number Dir.1741) will be required. The special wrench engages with the track rod inner balljoint housing allowing the track rod to be easily slackened/tightened, and the retaining clamp secures the rack to the steering gear housing to prevent any stress being exerted

on the steering gear pinion assembly **(see illustration)**. Note that without access to the special tools, track rod removal will be difficult, especially without causing damage.

Removal

1 Remove the track rod end balljoint as described in Section 18.

2 Cut the retaining clips, and slide the steering gear gaiter off the track rod. It is recommended that the gaiter is renewed, regardless of its apparent condition.

3 In the absence of the special tools, using a pair of grips, unscrew the track rod inner balljoint from the steering rack end. Prevent the steering rack from turning by holding the balljoint lockwasher/steering rack with a second pair of grips.

Caution: Take care not to mark the surfaces of the rack and balljoint.

4 Remove the track rod assembly from the steering rack. Discard the lockwasher assembly; a new one must be used on refitting.

5 Examine the inner balljoint for signs of slackness or tight spots. Check that the track rod itself is straight and free from damage. If necessary, renew the track rod.

Refitting

6 Prior to refitting the track rod remove all traces of locking compound from the rack and track rod threads.

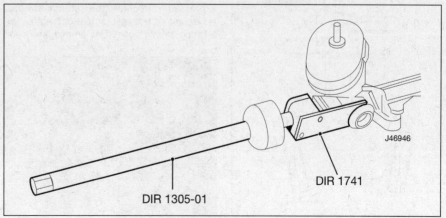

19.0 The special tools correctly positioned

DIR 1305-01

DIR 1741

J46946

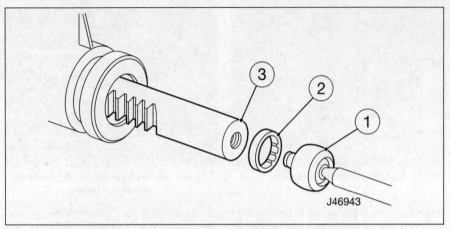

19.7 A new washer must be fitted to the track rod

1 Track rod   *2 Washer*   *3 Steering gear*

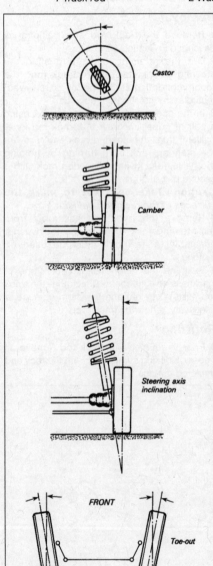

20.1 Wheel alignment and steering angles

7 Fit a new washer to the track rod **(see illustration)**.

8 Apply a coat of locking compound (Renault recommends the use of Loctite Frenbloc – available from your Renault dealer) to the threads of the track rod then fit the track rod to the end of the steering rack. Using the method employed on removal, tighten the track rod inner balljoint to the specified torque, taking great care not to marks either the rack or the balljoint.

9 Slide the new gaiter onto the track rod end, and locate it on the steering gear housing. Turn the steering from lock-to-lock to check that the gaiter is correctly positioned, then secure it with new retaining clips.

10 Refit the track rod end balljoint as described in Section 18.

20 Wheel alignment and steering angles – general information

General information

1 A car's steering and suspension geometry is defined in four basic settings **(see illustration)**. For this purpose, all angles are expressed in degrees (toe settings are also expressed as a measurement of length). The steering axis is defined as an imaginary line

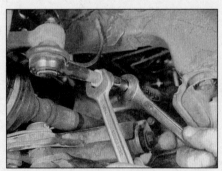

20.9 Adjusting the front wheel toe setting

drawn through the axis of the suspension strut, extended where necessary to contact the ground.

2 Camber is the angle between each roadwheel and a vertical line drawn through its centre and tyre contact patch, when viewed from the front or rear of the car. Positive camber is when the roadwheels are tilted outwards from the vertical at the top; negative camber is when they are tilted inwards.

3 Camber is not adjustable. Values are given for reference only. Checking is possible using a camber checking gauge, but if the figure obtained is significantly different from that specified, the vehicle must be taken for careful checking by a professional. Wrong camber settings can only be caused by wear or damage to the body or suspension components.

4 Castor is the angle between the steering axis and a vertical line drawn through each roadwheel's centre and tyre contact patch, when viewed from the side of the car. Positive castor is when the steering axis is tilted so that it contacts the ground ahead of the vertical; negative castor is when it contacts the ground behind the vertical.

5 Castor is not adjustable. As with camber, values are given for reference only; deviation can only be due to wear or damage.

6 Steering axis inclination/SAI – also known as kingpin inclination/KPI – is the angle between the steering axis and a vertical line drawn through each roadwheel's centre and tyre contact patch, when viewed from the front or rear of the car.

7 SAI/KPI is not adjustable, and is given for reference only.

8 Toe is the amount by which the roadwheels point outwards or inwards, viewed from above. Toe-in is when the roadwheels point inwards, towards each other at the front, while toe-out is when they splay outwards from each other at the front. The value for toe can be expressed as an angle (taking the centre line of the car as zero), or as a measurement of length (taking measurements between the inside rims of the wheels at hub height).

9 The front wheel toe setting is adjusted by screwing the balljoints in or out of their track rods to alter the effective length of the track rod assemblies **(see illustration)**.

10 Rear wheel toe setting is not adjustable, and is given for reference only. While it can be checked, if the figure obtained is significantly different from that specified, the vehicle must be taken for careful checking by a professional, as the fault can only be caused by wear or damage to the body or suspension components.

11 Due to the special measuring equipment necessary to check the wheel alignment, and the skill required to use it properly, the checking and adjustment of these settings is best left to a Renault dealer or similar expert. Most tyre fitting shops now possess sophisticated checking equipment.

Chapter 11
Bodywork and fittings

Contents

Degrees of difficulty

| Easy, suitable for novice with little experience | Fairly easy, suitable for beginner with some experience | Fairly difficult, suitable for competent DIY mechanic | Difficult, suitable for experienced DIY mechanic | Very difficult, suitable for expert DIY or professional |

Specifications

Torque wrench settings	Nm	lbf ft
Seat belt and seat belt height adjuster mountings.	21	16
Seat mounting bolts*	35	26

*Use new nuts/bolts

1 General Information

1 The bodyshell and floorpan are manufactured from pressed steel, and form an integral part of the vehicle's structure (monocoque), without the need for a separate chassis.
2 Various areas of the structure are strengthened to provide for suspension, steering and engine mounting points, and load distribution.
3 All models are fitted with front wings manufactured from a polymer compound, which can withstand an impact of up to 10 mph without sustaining permanent damage.
4 Corrosion protection is applied to all new vehicles. Various anti-corrosion preparations are used, including galvanising, zinc phosphatisation, and PVC underseal. An 'anti-gravel' undercoat is applied to the front section of the bonnet, to prevent corrosion and paint chipping caused by stones and other road debris hitting the front of the vehicle. Protective wax is injected into the box sections and other hollow cavities.
5 Extensive use is made of plastic for peripheral components, such as the radiator grille, bumpers and wheel trims, and for much of the interior trim. Plastic wheel arch liners are fitted to protect the metal body panels against corrosion due to a build-up of road dirt.
6 Interior fittings are to a high standard on all models, and a wide range of optional equipment is available throughout the range.

2 Maintenance – bodywork and underframe

1 The general condition of a vehicle's bodywork is the one thing that significantly affects its value. Maintenance is easy, but needs to be regular. Neglect, particularly after minor damage, can lead quickly to further deterioration and costly repair bills. It is important also to keep watch on those parts of the vehicle not immediately visible, for instance the underside, inside all the wheel arches, and the lower part of the engine compartment.
2 The basic maintenance routine for the bodywork is washing – preferably with a lot of water, from a hose. This will remove all the loose solids which may have stuck to the vehicle. It is important to flush these off in such a way as to prevent grit from scratching the finish. The wheel arches and underframe need washing in the same way, to remove any accumulated mud which will retain moisture and tend to encourage rust. Paradoxically enough, the best time to clean the underframe and wheel arches is in wet weather, when the mud is thoroughly wet and soft. In very wet weather, the underframe is usually cleaned of large accumulations automatically, and this is a good time for inspection.
3 Periodically, except on vehicles with a wax based underbody protective coating, it is a

good idea to have the whole of the underframe of the vehicle steam cleaned, engine compartment included, so that a thorough inspection can be carried out to see what minor repairs and renovations are necessary. Steam cleaning is available at many garages, and is necessary for the removal of the accumulation of oily grime, which sometimes is allowed to become thick in certain areas. If steam cleaning facilities are not available, there are one or two excellent grease solvents available, which can be brush applied; the dirt can then be simply hosed off. Note that these methods should not be used on vehicles with wax based underbody protective coating, or the coating will be removed. Such vehicles should be inspected annually, preferably just prior to Winter, when the underbody should be washed down, and any damage to the wax coating repaired. Ideally, a completely fresh coat should be applied. It would also be worth considering the use of such wax based protection for injection into door panels, sills, box sections, etc, as an additional safeguard against rust damage, where such protection is not provided by the vehicle manufacturer.

4 After washing paintwork, wipe off with a chamois leather to give an unspotted clear finish. A coat of clear protective wax polish will give added protection against chemical pollutants in the air. If the paintwork sheen has dulled or oxidised, use a cleaner/polisher combination to restore the brilliance of the shine. This requires a little effort, but such dulling is usually caused because regular washing has been neglected. Care needs to be taken with metallic paintwork, as special non-abrasive cleaner/polisher is required to avoid damage to the finish. Always check that the door and ventilator opening drain holes and pipes are completely clear, so that water can be drained out. Brightwork should be treated in the same way as paintwork. Windscreens and windows can be kept clear of the smeary film which often appears, by the use of proprietary glass cleaner. Never use any form of wax or other body or chromium polish on glass.

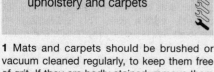

3 Maintenance –
upholstery and carpets

1 Mats and carpets should be brushed or vacuum cleaned regularly, to keep them free of grit. If they are badly stained, remove them from the vehicle for scrubbing or sponging, and make quite sure they are dry before refitting. Seats and interior trim panels can be kept clean by wiping with a damp cloth. If they do become stained (which can be more apparent on light coloured upholstery), use a little liquid detergent and a soft nail brush to scour the grime out of the grain of the material. Do not forget to keep the headlining clean in the same way as the upholstery. When using liquid cleaners inside the vehicle,

do not over wet the surfaces being cleaned. Excessive damp could get into the seams and padded interior, causing stains, offensive odours or even rot. If the inside of the vehicle gets wet accidentally, it is worthwhile taking some trouble to dry it out properly, particularly where carpets are involved. Do not leave oil or electric heaters inside the vehicle for this purpose.

4 Minor body damage –
repair

Minor scratches

1 If the scratch is very superficial, and does not penetrate to the metal of the bodywork, repair is very simple. Lightly rub the area of the scratch with a paintwork renovator, or a very fine cutting paste, to remove loose paint from the scratch, and to clear the surrounding bodywork of wax polish. Rinse the area with clean water.

2 Apply touch-up paint to the scratch using a fine paint brush; continue to apply fine layers of paint until the surface of the paint in the scratch is level with the surrounding paintwork. Allow the new paint at least two weeks to harden, then blend it into the surrounding paintwork by rubbing the scratch area with a paintwork renovator or a very fine cutting paste. Finally, apply wax polish.

3 Where the scratch has penetrated right through to the metal of the bodywork, causing the metal to rust, a different repair technique is required. Remove any loose rust from the bottom of the scratch with a penknife, then apply rust-inhibiting paint, to prevent the formation of rust in the future. Using a rubber or nylon applicator, fill the scratch with bodystopper paste. If required, this paste can be mixed with cellulose thinners, to provide a very thin paste which is ideal for filling narrow scratches. Before the stopper paste in the scratch hardens, wrap a piece of smooth cotton rag around the top of a finger. Dip the finger in cellulose thinners, and quickly sweep it across the surface of the stopper paste in the scratch; this will ensure that the surface of the stopper paste is slightly hollowed. The scratch can now be painted over as described earlier in this Section.

Dents

4 When deep denting of the vehicle's bodywork has taken place, the first task is to pull the dent out, until the affected bodywork almost attains its original shape. There is little point in trying to restore the original shape completely, as the metal in the damaged area will have stretched on impact, and cannot be reshaped fully to its original contour. It is better to bring the level of the dent up to a point which is about 3 mm below the level of the surrounding bodywork. In cases where the dent is very shallow anyway, it is not worth

trying to pull it out at all. If the underside of the dent is accessible, it can be hammered out gently from behind, using a mallet with a wooden or plastic head. Whilst doing this, hold a block of wood firmly against the outside of the panel, to absorb the impact from the hammer blows and thus prevent a large area of the bodywork from being 'belled-out'.

5 Should the dent be in a section of the bodywork which has a double skin, or some other factor making it inaccessible from behind, a different technique is called for. Drill several small holes through the metal inside the area – particularly in the deeper section. Then screw long self tapping screws into the holes, just sufficiently for them to gain a good purchase in the metal. Now the dent can be pulled out by pulling on the protruding heads of the screws with a pair of pliers.

6 The next stage of the repair is the removal of the paint from the damaged area, and from an inch or so of the surrounding 'sound' bodywork. This is accomplished most easily by using a wire brush or abrasive pad on a power drill, although it can be done just as effectively by hand, using sheets of abrasive paper. To complete the preparation for filling, score the surface of the bare metal with a screwdriver or the tang of a file, or alternatively, drill small holes in the affected area. This will provide a really good 'key' for the filler paste.

7 To complete the repair, see the Section on filling and respraying.

Rust holes or gashes

8 Remove all paint from the affected area, and from an inch or so of the surrounding 'sound' bodywork, using an abrasive pad or a wire brush on a power drill. If these are not available, a few sheets of abrasive paper will do the job most effectively. With the paint removed, you will be able to judge the severity of the corrosion, and therefore decide whether to renew the whole panel (if this is possible) or to repair the affected area. New body panels are not as expensive as most people think, and it is often quicker and more satisfactory to fit a new panel than to attempt to repair large areas of corrosion.

9 Remove all fittings from the affected area, except those which will act as a guide to the original shape of the damaged bodywork (eg, headlamp shells, etc). Then, using tin snips or a hacksaw blade, remove all loose metal and any other metal badly affected by corrosion. Hammer the edges of the hole inwards, in order to create a slight depression for the filler paste.

10 Wire brush the affected area to remove the powdery rust from the surface of the remaining metal. Paint the affected area with rust-inhibiting paint; if the back of the rusted area is accessible, treat this also.

11 Before filling can take place, it will be necessary to block the hole in some way. This can be achieved by the use of aluminium or plastic mesh, or aluminium tape.

12 Aluminium or plastic mesh, or glass fibre matting is probably the best material to use for a large hole. Cut a piece to the approximate size and shape of the hole to be filled, then position it in the hole so that its edges are below the level of the surrounding bodywork. It can be retained in position by several blobs of filler paste around its periphery.

13 Aluminium tape should be used for small or very narrow holes. Pull a piece off the roll, trim it to the approximate size and shape required, then pull off the backing paper (if used) and stick the tape over the hole; it can be overlapped if the thickness of one piece is insufficient. Burnish down the edges of the tape with the handle of a screwdriver or similar, to ensure that the tape is securely attached to the metal underneath.

Filling and respraying

14 Before using this Section, see the Sections on dent, deep scratch, rust holes and gash repairs.

15 Many types of bodyfiller are available, but generally speaking, those proprietary kits which contain a tin of filler paste and a tube of resin hardener are best for this type of repair. A wide, flexible plastic or nylon applicator will be found invaluable for imparting a smooth and well contoured finish to the surface of the filler.

16 Mix up a little filler on a clean piece of card or board – measure the hardener carefully (follow the maker's instructions on the pack), otherwise the filler will set too rapidly or too slowly. Using the applicator, apply the filler paste to the prepared area; draw the applicator across the surface of the filler to achieve the correct contour and to level the surface. As soon as a contour that approximates to the correct one is achieved, stop working the paste – if you carry on too long, the paste will become sticky and begin to 'pick-up' on the applicator. Continue to add thin layers of filler paste at 20 minute intervals, until the level of the filler is just proud of the surrounding bodywork.

17 Once the filler has hardened, the excess can be removed using a metal plane or file. From then on, progressively finer grades of abrasive paper should be used, starting with a 40 grade production paper, and finishing with a 400 grade wet-and-dry paper. Always wrap the abrasive paper around a flat rubber, cork, or wooden block – otherwise the surface of the filler will not be completely flat. During the smoothing of the filler surface, the wet-and-dry paper should be periodically rinsed in water. This will ensure that a very smooth finish is imparted to the filler at the final stage.

18 At this stage, the 'dent' should be surrounded by a ring of bare metal, which in turn should be encircled by the finely 'feathered' edge of the good paintwork. Rinse the repair area with clean water, until all of the dust produced by the rubbing down operation has gone.

19 Spray the whole area with a light coat of – this will show up any imperfections in the surface of the filler. Repair these imperfections with fresh filler paste or bodystopper, and once more smooth the surface with abrasive paper. If bodystopper is used, it can be mixed with cellulose thinners, to form a really thin paste which is ideal for filling small holes. Repeat this spray and repair procedure until you are satisfied that the surface of the filler, and the feathered edge of the paintwork, are perfect. Clean the repair area with clean water, and allow to dry fully.

20 The repair area is now ready for final spraying. Paint spraying must be carried out in a warm, dry, windless and dust-free atmosphere. This condition can be created artificially if you have access to a large indoor working area, but if you are forced to work in the open, you will have to pick your day very carefully. If you are working indoors, dousing the floor in the work area with water will help to settle the dust which would otherwise be in the atmosphere. If the repair area is confined to one body panel, mask off the surrounding panels; this will help to minimise the effects of a slight mis-match in paint colours. Bodywork fittings (eg, chrome strips, door handles etc) will also need to be masked off. Use genuine masking tape, and several thicknesses of newspaper, for the masking operations.

21 Before commencing to spray, agitate the aerosol can thoroughly, then spray a test area (an old tin, or similar) until the technique is mastered. Cover the repair area with a thick coat of primer; the thickness should be built up using several thin layers of paint, rather than one thick one. Using 400 grade wet-and-dry paper, rub down the surface of the primer until it is really smooth. While doing this, the work area should be thoroughly doused with water, and the wet-and-dry paper periodically rinsed in water. Allow to dry before spraying on more paint.

22 Spray on the top coat, again building up the thickness by using several thin layers of paint. Start spraying at the top of the repair area, and then, using a side-to-side motion, work downwards until the whole repair area and about 2 inches of the surrounding original paintwork is covered. Remove all masking material 10 to 15 minutes after spraying on the final coat of paint.

23 Allow the new paint at least two weeks to harden, then, using a paintwork renovator or a very fine cutting paste, blend the edges of the paint into the existing paintwork. Finally, apply wax polish.

Plastic components

24 With the use of more and more plastic body components by the vehicle manufacturers (eg, bumpers, spoilers, wings and in some cases major body panels), rectification of more serious damage to such items has become a matter of either entrusting repair work to a specialist in this field, or renewing complete components. Repair of such damage by the DIY owner is not really feasible, owing to the cost of the equipment and materials required for effecting such repairs. The basic technique involves making a groove along the line of the crack in the plastic, using a rotary burr in a power drill. The damaged part is then welded back together, using a hot air gun to heat up and fuse a plastic filler rod into the groove. Any excess plastic is then removed, and the area rubbed down to a smooth finish. It is important that a filler rod of the correct plastic is used, as body components can be made of a variety of different types (eg, polycarbonate, ABS, polypropylene).

25 Damage of a less serious nature (abrasions, minor cracks etc) can be repaired by the DIY owner using a two-part epoxy filler repair. Once mixed in equal, this is used in similar fashion to the bodywork filler used on metal panels. The filler is usually cured in twenty to thirty minutes, ready for sanding and painting.

26 If the owner is renewing a complete component himself, or if he has repaired it with epoxy filler, he will be left with the problem of finding a suitable paint for finishing which is compatible with the type of plastic used. At one time, the use of a universal paint was not possible, owing to the complex range of plastics encountered in body component applications. Standard paints, generally speaking, will not bond to plastic or rubber satisfactorily, but suitable paints to match any plastic or rubber finish, can be obtained from dealers. However, it is now possible to obtain a plastic body parts finishing kit which consists of a pre-primer treatment, a primer and coloured top coat. Full instructions are normally supplied with a kit, but basically, the method of use is to first apply the pre-primer to the component concerned, and allow it to dry for up to 30 minutes. Then the primer is applied, and left to dry for about an hour before finally applying the special coloured top coat. The result is a correctly coloured component, where the paint will flex with the plastic or rubber, a property that standard paint does not normally posses.

5 Major body damage – repair

1 Where serious damage has occurred, or large areas need renewal due to neglect, it means that complete new panels will need welding in, and this is best left to professionals. If the damage is due to impact, it will also be necessary to check completely the alignment of the bodyshell, and this can only be carried out accurately by a Renault dealer using special jigs. If the body is left misaligned, it is primarily dangerous, as the car will not handle properly, and secondly, uneven stresses will be imposed on the steering, suspension and possibly transmission, causing abnormal wear, or complete failure, particularly to such items as the tyres.

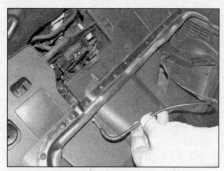

6.1 Release the bonnet cable

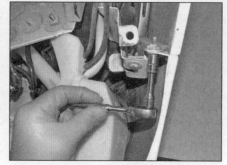

6.6 Undo the retaining bolts

6 Bumpers – removal and refitting

Front bumper

Removal

1 Open the bonnet and disconnect the bonnet release cable from the bonnet lock (see illustration). The release lever can stay attached to the top of the front bumper.
2 Jack up the front of the car and support it securely on axle stands (see *Jacking and vehicle support*). Remove both front wheels.
3 Undo the fasteners and remove the engine undershield and the front section of the inner wheel arch liners.
4 Working under the lower edge of the bumper, undo the two retaining screws at the centre, and one at each end of the lower panel.
5 Undo the two retaining screws from the lower part of the bumper, that secure the radiator ducting to the lower panel.
6 Remove the front section of the inner wheel arch liner, then slacken and remove the bolts that secure the bumper to the front wing panel (see illustration).
7 Reaching up behind the left-hand side of the bumper, disconnect the electrical connector for the front fog lights/daytime running lights.
8 Working along the upper edge of the bumper, undo the six retaining screws and unclip the top of the bumper panel from the bonnet slam panel.
9 Have an assistant support one end of the bumper, and then unclip the outer ends of the bumper from the front wings.

Refitting

10 Refitting is a reversal of removal, making sure the ends of the bumper locate correctly with the wing panels.

Rear bumper

Removal

11 Open the tailgate and remove the rear lights as described in Chapter 12, Section 10.
12 Unclip the plastic trim from the top edge of the bumper, at the lower part of the rear light aperture, then undo the retaining screw (see illustrations). Carry out the same procedure on the other side of the bumper.
13 To improve access, chock the front wheels, then jack up the rear of the car and support it securely on axle stands (see *Jacking and vehicle support*).
14 Working under the rear wheel arches, undo the two upper retaining screws, that secures the bumper to the rear wing panel and inner wheel arch liner, at each side of the vehicle (see illustration).
15 Working along the lower edge of the bumper cover, undo the five retaining screws, two at each end and one at the centre (see illustrations).
16 Working at the upper inner corners of the tailgate aperture, unclip the tailgate bump stops (see illustration).
17 Carefully unclip the outer edges of the bumper from the rear wing panel (see illustration).
18 With the help of an assistant to

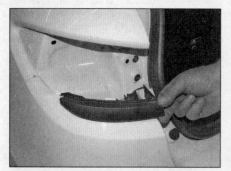

6.12a Unclip the plastic trim...

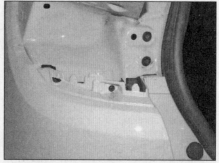

6.12b ...and remove the upper retaining screw

6.14 Remove the two retaining screws

6.15a Remove the two left hand side screws...

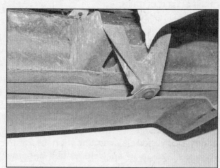

6.15b ...the one at the centre...

6.15c ...and the two right hand side screws

support the bumper, disconnect the wiring connector(s) from the left-hand side, as the bumper is removed.

Refitting

19 Refitting is a reversal of removal, but make sure the bumper side locates correctly with the rear wing panels.

---

7 Windscreen cowl panels – removal and refitting

Removal

1 Remove the windscreen wiper arms, as described in Chapter 12 Section 19.
2 Remove the weather seal from along the windscreen lower cowl panel **(see illustration)**.
3 Release the centre pin, then remove the securing clips **(see illustrations)**. There are two securing clips fitted at each side, on the top of the panel.
4 Unclip the small plastic trim panels from each side of the lower part of the windscreen **(see illustration)**.
5 Unclip the panel from the lower part of the windscreen, and then remove it from the rear of the engine compartment **(see illustration)**.
6 At this point it is possible to remove the lower section by removing the six retaining bolts. Remove the two pieces of foam (one at each side) from the top of the wing panels. Remove the two bolts at each end and then two central bolts **(see illustrations)**. This procedure is essential for access to the top

6.16 Uncip the tailgate bump stops

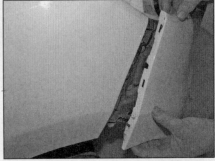
6.17 Carefully work the bumper free

7.2 Remove the weather seal

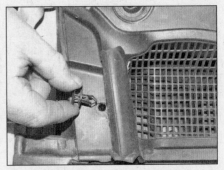
7.3a Release the securing clips...

of the suspension strut mountings and brake servo/master cylinder.

Refitting

7 Refitting is a reversal of removal, bearing in mind the following points.

8 Ensure that the weatherseal is correctly located along the trim panel, and that the panel securing clips are correctly fitted.
9 Refit the windscreen wiper arms with reference to Chapter 12 Section 19.

7.3b ...from each side of the cowling

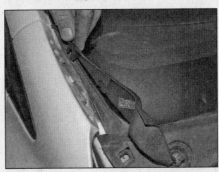
7.4 Unclip the plastic trim panel

7.5 Remove the panel

7.6a Remove the pieces of foam from the ends...

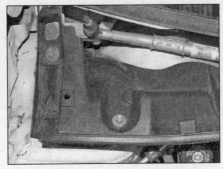
7.6b ...undo the bolts (one side shown)...

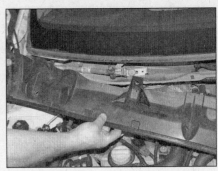
7.6c ...and then lift out the lower panel

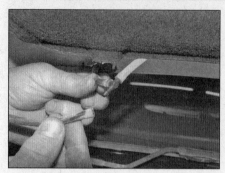

8.2 Disconnect the washer hose from the T-piece

8.3a Release the securing clip...

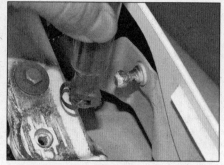

8.3b ...and pull the strut from the ball-joint – lower one shown, upper is the same

8.5a Remove the two bolts from the left...

8.5b ...and right-hand side hinges

Hinges

10 The bonnet hinges are bolted to the inner wing panel, and can only be removed after the front wing support panel has been removed. To access the support panel, remove the front wing, front bumper, wing liner and then partly remove the bonnet slam panel. Carefully mark the position of the support panel with a marker pen. This is critical since the position of the support panel determines the alignment of the front wing.

11 Remove the four mounting bolts and then cut free the expanding insert from the inner wing. With a sharp knife carefully cut through the sealant and remove the panel. To aid refitting, carefully mark the position of the hinge and the unbolt, and remove the bonnet hinge.

12 Refitting is a reversal of removal, but a suitable sealant and new expanding insert will be required.

8 Bonnet and hinges – removal and refitting

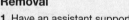

Bonnet

Removal

1 Have an assistant support the bonnet in the open position.

2 Disconnect the windscreen washer hose from the plastic T-piece at the right-hand side of the bonnet, under the edge of the soundproofing **(see illustration)**.

3 Release the securing clip and disconnect the hydraulic strut from the ball-joint on the left-hand side of the bonnet **(see illustrations)**.

4 If the original bonnet is to be refitted, mark the position of the hinges on the bonnet to aid alignment on refitting (a line can be drawn around the hinge using a suitable pen).

5 Remove the bolts securing the bonnet to the hinges (two bolts at each side) **(see illustrations)**, then carefully withdraw the bonnet from the car.

Refitting

6 Refitting is a reversal of removal, bearing in mind the following points.

7 Where applicable, align the hinges with the marks made on the bonnet before removal.

8 Close the bonnet (carefully, in case it fouls the surrounding bodywork), and check the alignment with the surrounding body panels.

9 If necessary, the alignment of the bonnet can be adjusted by altering the position of the bonnet on the hinges, using the elongated holes provided. The alignment of the front of the bonnet can also be adjusted by altering the position of the bonnet lock assembly, using the elongated bolt holes provided.

9 Bonnet lock components – removal and refitting

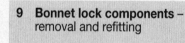

Lock assembly

Removal

1 Open the bonnet, and then push back the locking catch and release the inner cable from the lock assembly and unclip the outer cable from the mounting bracket. If required the locking catch lever, can be removed by carefully releasing it out from the upper panel **(see illustrations)**.

9.1a Release the inner cable...

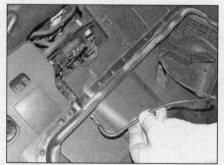

9.1b ...the outer cable...

9.1c ...then unclip the lever

9.3 Disconnect the wring connector

9.4a Remove the bolts....

9.4b ...and lift out the lock

2 Remove the front bumper, as described in Section 6.
3 At the front of the lock assembly on the front cross panel, disconnect the wiring connector from the lock assembly **(see illustration)**.
4 Note and mark the position of the lock on the panel to aid correct alignment when refitting. Unscrew the two securing bolts, then lift the lock assembly from the panel **(see illustrations)**.
5 Using pliers, release the outer cable from the lock assembly **(see illustration)**.
6 Disconnect the end of the inner release cable from the lock operating lever, and withdraw the lock assembly **(see illustration)**.

Refitting

7 Refitting is a reversal of removal, but align the assembly with the marks made on the panel before removal.
8 Make sure that the outer and inner cables are located correctly before closing the bonnet.
9 On completion, if necessary adjust the alignment of the bonnet with the surrounding body panels by altering the position of the lock/striker assembly, using the elongated bolt holes provided.

Lock striker

10 Open the bonnet (the lock striker is bolted to the bonnet).
11 Note and mark the position of the lock striker on the bonnet to aid correct alignment when refitting.
12 Unscrew the two securing nuts from the lock striker mounting bracket.
13 Unclip the bonnet safety catch pull and remove the lock striker from the bonnet.

Refitting

14 Refitting is a reversal of removal, but align the assembly with the marks made on the panel before removal.
15 On completion, if necessary adjust the alignment of the bonnet with the surrounding body panels by altering the position of the lock/striker assembly, using the elongated bolt holes provided.

Lock release cable/lever

Removal

16 Working inside the vehicle, carefully prise

9.5 Release the outer cable

the bonnet release lever off the bonnet cable release mechanism **(see illustration)**.
17 Remove the left-hand side front door step/sill panel, as described in Section 26.
18 Undo the retaining screw and unclip the assembly from the body **(see illustration)**.
19 To gain access to the cable through the engine compartment, remove the battery, as described in Chapter 5A Section 4.
20 Also, on 0.9 litre petrol engines and 1.5 litre diesel engines, remove the air cleaner assembly, as described in Chapter 4A Section 2, or Chapter 4B Section 3.
21 Remove the front bumper and the left-hand wheel arch liner. Using pliers, unclip the cable from the bonnet catch as described previously.
22 Remove the grommet from the bulkhead and remove the cable from any retaining clips along it length.

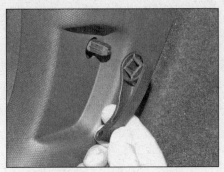
9.16 Remove the release lever

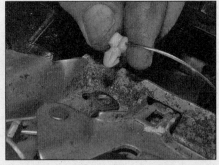
9.6 Unclip the inner cable

Refitting

23 Refitting is a reversal of removal, but ensure that the bulkhead grommet is securely located in the bulkhead. Route the cable as noted during removal.

10 Doors and check straps –
removal, refitting and adjustment

Doors

1 An assistant will be required since the doors are very heavy and the paintwork could easily be damaged.To remove a door, open it fully, and support it under its lower edge on blocks covered with pads of rag.
2 As the wiring to the doors will require disconnecting, it is best to disconnect the

9.18 Remove the screw at the base of the mechanism

10.3 Slide the locking section upwards to release the connector

10.4 Slide the locking section forwards to release the connector

10.5 Unbolt the check strap from the pillar

10.7a Undo the lower hinge…

10.7b …and upper hinge retaining nuts

Door check straps

11 Remove the door trim panel, as described in Section 26.

12 Undo the retaining bolt and disconnect the check strap from the A-pillar for the front doors, B-pillar for the rear doors (**see illustration 10.5**).
Caution: Make sure that the door does not open too far forward with the check strap disconnected, as it could damage the door and wing panel.

13 Undo the two mounting nuts and withdraw the check strap from inside the door frame (**see illustration**).

14 Refitting is a reversal of removal.

battery negative lead as described in Chapter 5A Section 4.

3 For the front doors, open the front door and disconnect the wiring connector by sliding the securing clip upwards, then pull the connector from its socket (**see illustration**).

4 For the rear doors, with the rear door closed and the front door open, slide the securing clip forwards, then pull the connector from its socket (**see illustration**).

5 Undo the retaining bolt and disconnect the check strap from the A-pillar for the front doors, B-pillar for the rear doors (**see illustration**).
Caution: Make sure that the door does not open too far forward with the check strap disconnected, as it could damage the door and wing panel.

6 Carefully mark the exact position of the door in relationship to the hinge. It is also

worth taking measurements of the gap between the door and wing before removal of the door.

7 Have an assistant support the door, then undo the mounting nuts that hold the door to the hinges (**see illustrations**).

8 Refitting is a reversal of removal.

Adjustment

9 The door hinges are all fully-adjustable. The vertical position of the front door can be adjusted by accessing the door-mounted hinge bolts. To alter the fore-and-aft position of the door, the front wing must be removed to access the hinge mounting bolts.

10 The vertical position of the rear door can be adjusted via the door-mounted hinge bolts. The fore-and-aft position of the door is altered by adjusting the hinge mounting bolts on the B-pillar (**see illustration**).

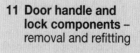

11 Door handle and lock components – removal and refitting

Door interior handle

Removal

1 Unclip the plastic cover and undo the retaining screw from inside the interior handle assembly (**see illustration**).

2 Withdraw the handle assembly from the door panel, then unclip the operating cable from the rear of the door handle (**see illustrations**).

Refitting

3 Refitting is a reversal of removal.

10.10 Hinge bolts on B-pillar

10.13 Undo the two mounting nuts

11.1 Remove the retaining screw

11.2a Unclip the door handle…

11.2b …and unclip the operating cable

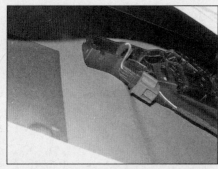

11.5 Disconnect the wiring connector

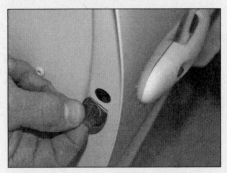

11.6a Remove the blanking grommet…

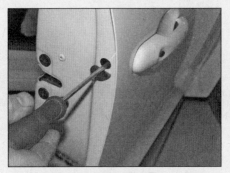

11.6b …and slacken the Torx screw

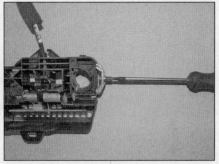

11.7a The locking collar (removed to show the principle of operation)…

Front door exterior handle

Removal

4 Remove the door inner trim panel as described in Section 26.

5 On models with Keyless entry, reach up inside the door panel, and disconnect the wiring connector from the rear of the door handle **(see illustration)**.

6 Remove the blanking grommet from the rear end of the door, and then insert a Torx screwdriver through the opening. Use the screwdriver to slacken the securing screw that locks the key barrel/push button into position **(see illustrations)**.

7 When the torx screw is fully slackened, the key barrel/push button can be withdrawn from the door handle **(see illustrations)**. **Note:** *It may necessary to pull the door handle out slightly, to help release the key barrel/push button.*

8 Slide the door handle to the rear of the door to release it from the door panel, then where applicable, as the handle is removed, withdraw the wiring connector out from the door panel **(see illustrations)**.

Refitting

9 Refitting is a reversal of removal; refit the door inner trim panel as described in Section 26.

Rear door exterior handle

Removal

10 Open the door and remove the inner trim panel from the rear of the door frame. With the

trim removed undo the two retaining screws from the rear of the door exterior handle **(see illustration)**.

11 Working on the outside of the door, lift up

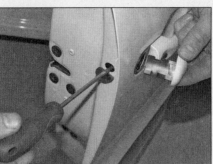
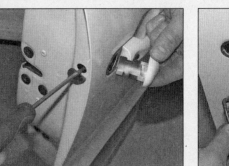

11.7b …allows the barrel to be removed

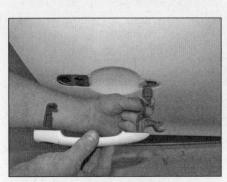

11.8b …and remove, withdrawing the wiring connector

the outer seal and remove the lower retaining screw **(see illustration)**.

12 Carefully prise the door handle from the door frame, then unclip the outer cable from

11.8a Slide the handle to the rear…

11.10 Unclip the trim and undo the two screws

11.11 Lift up the seal and undo the screw

11.12a Unclip the outer cable...

11.12b ...and then the inner cable

11.15 Remove the rear window guide

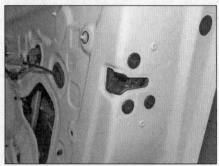

11.16 Remove the three Torx head screws

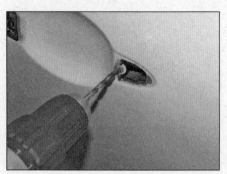

11.18 Drill out the rivet

the trim panel and the inner cable from the operating mechanism **(see illustrations)**.

Refitting

13 Refitting is a reversal of removal.

11.19 Unclip the door handle seal

11.20a Withdraw the lock assembly...

11.20b ...and disconnect the wiring and cables

11.21 If required, release the cable from the handle inner assembly

Front door lock

Removal

14 Remove the door inner trim panel as described in Section 26.

15 Undo the two retaining screws and withdraw the rear window channel guide from inside the door aperture **(see illustration)**.
16 Unscrew the three lock securing screws from the rear edge of the door **(see illustration)**.
17 Remove the key barrel and door handle, as described previously in this section (see paragraphs 4 to 8).
18 Drill out the blind rivet, that secures the inner mounting bracket to the door panel **(see illustration)**. If required, protect the door with masking tape, to prevent any scratches to the paintwork.
19 Unclip the seal from the outside of the door panel **(see illustration)**.
20 Working inside the door aperture, lower the lock assembly and door handle inner mounting bracket, then disconnect the wiring and cables **(see illustrations)**.
21 The door handle release cable can be disconnected from the lock assembly when the lock assembly is removed **(see illustration)**.

Refitting

22 A suitable rivet will be required to secure the exterior handle inner section **(see illustration)**. Refitting is then a reversal of removal, refitting the door inner trim panel as described in Section 26.

Rear door lock

Removal

23 Remove the door inner trim panel, as described in Section 26.

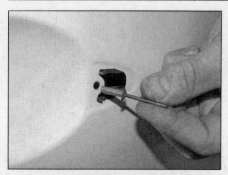

11.22 Use correct rivet to secure the handle mounting bracket

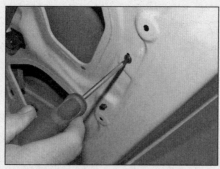

11.25a Undo the retaining screws...

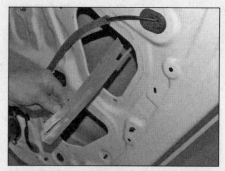

11.25b ...and remove the window guide channel

11.26 Undo the three screws

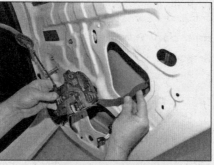

11.27a Lower the lock assembly...

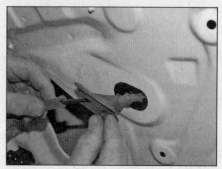

11.27b ...withdraw the operating cables...

24 Remove the exterior handle, as described previously in this section (see paragraphs 10 to 13).

25 Undo the retaining screws and withdraw the rear window channel guide from inside the door aperture **(see illustrations)**.

26 Unscrew the three lock securing screws from the rear edge of the door **(see illustration)**.

27 Working inside the door aperture, lower the lock assembly and operating cables, then release the locking clip and disconnect the wiring connector from the lock assembly **(see illustrations)**.

Refitting

28 Refitting is a reversal of removal, refitting the door inner trim panel as described in Section 26.

Lock striker

Removal

29 The lock striker is screwed onto the door pillar on the body **(see illustration)**.

30 Before removing the striker, mark its position, so that it can be refitted in exactly the same place.

31 To remove the striker, simply unscrew the securing screws using a Torx bit.

Refitting

32 Refitting is a reversal of removal, but if necessary adjust the position of the striker to achieve satisfactory closing of the door.

Central locking components

33 Refer to Section 15.

12 Door window glass and regulators – removal and refitting

Front door window

Removal

1 Remove the door inner trim panel, as described in Section 26.

2 Lower the window glass, temporarily reconnect the battery negative lead (if disconnected), and reconnect the wiring plug to the electric window operating switch to enable the window to be lowered.

3 Carefully prise the weatherseal from the inner lower edge of the window aperture **(see illustration)**.

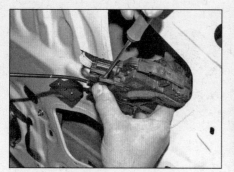

11.27c ...release the locking clip...

11.27d ...and disconnect the wiring connector

11.29 Door lock striker fitted to pillar

12.3 Remove the inner weather seal

12.4 Remove the mounting bolts from the door glass

12.6 Remove the door glass

4 Remove the two retaining bolts from the rear of the regulator window mounting bracket **(see illustration)**. The window glass may need to be raised or lowered to access these bolts, see paragraph 2.

5 Carefully disengage the regulator from the holes in the glass.

6 Carefully push the glass upwards, tilting the front edge forwards, and manipulate the glass out from the outside of the door frame **(see illustration)**.

Refitting

7 Refitting is a reversal of removal, bearing in mind the following points.

8 Ensure the bolts are secured correctly, do not over-tighten.

9 Before refitting the door inner trim panel, reconnect the battery and the electric window's operating switch and check the operation of the window mechanism.

10 Refit the door inner trim panel as described in Section 26.

Rear door window

Removal

11 Remove the door inner trim panel, as described in Section 26.

12 Carefully remove the inner weather shield from the door panel **(see illustration)**.

13 Carefully prise the inner weatherseals from the lower edge of the window aperture **(see illustration)**.

14 Temporarily refit the window winder handle or the window switch if electric rear windows are fitted. Raise the window until the screws securing the window glass to the regulator bracket is accessible **(see illustrations)**.

15 Carefully disengage the regulator from the holes in the glass.

16 Carefully push the glass upwards, tilting the front edge forwards, and manipulate the glass out from the outside of the door frame **(see illustration)**.

Refitting

17 Refitting is a reversal of removal, bearing in mind the following points.

18 When refitting the rubber seal, the use of a suitable lubricant will make fitting easier.

19 Ensure the screws are secured correctly, do not over-tighten.

20 Make sure that the weatherseals are correctly located on the lower edge of the window aperture.

21 Before refitting the door inner trim panel, temporarily refit the window winder handle, or switch and check the operation of the regulator mechanism.

22 Refit the door inner trim panel, as described in Section 26.

Front door regulator

Removal

23 Remove the door inner trim panel, as described in Section 26.

24 Remove the front door window glass as described earlier in this Section (or slide the glass up to the top of the window frame and tape in position) **(see illustration)**.

25 Disconnect the wiring plug connector from the window motor **(see illustration)**.

26 Remove the mounting nuts that hold the regulator and motor in position, then carefully manipulate the window regulator assembly

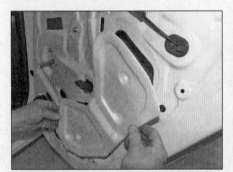

12.12 Remove the weather shield

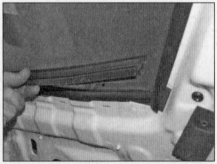

12.13 Remove the weather seal

12.14a Remove the grommet...

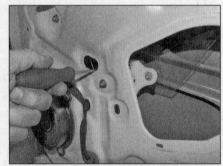

12.14b ...and undo the retaining screws

12.16 Remove the door glass

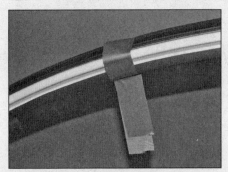

12.24 Tape the window in the closed position

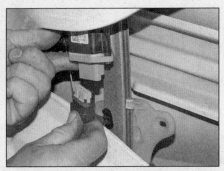

12.25 Disconnect the wiring connector

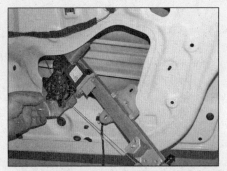

12.26 Work the regulator assembly out through the aperture

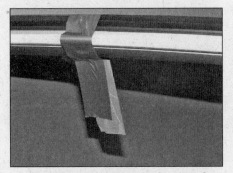

12.29 Tape the window in the closed position

12.31a Undo the four securing nuts…

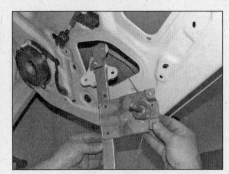

12.31b …and remove the regulator assembly

out through the lower aperture in the door **(see illustration)**.

Refitting

27 Refitting is a reversal of removal, reconnect the electrical switch and check the operation of the window before refitting the door inner trim panel as described in Section 25.

Rear door regulator

Removal

28 Remove the door inner trim panel, as described in Section 26.

29 Remove the rear door window glass as described earlier in this Section (or slide the glass up to the top of the window frame and tape in position) **(see illustration)**.

30 On models fitted with electric windows, disconnect the wiring plug from the electric window motor.

31 Remove the four securing nuts and then carefully manipulate the regulator assembly out through the door aperture **(see illustrations)**.

Refitting

32 Refitting is a reversal of removal, bearing in mind the following points.

33 Before refitting the door inner trim panel, check the operation of the window mechanism. Reconnect the battery and the electric windows operating switch, or refit the window winder handle, as applicable, and operate the window through its full range.

34 Refit the door inner trim panel as described in Section 26.

Electric window components

35 The motors are an integral part of the window regulator assemblies, and cannot be renewed independently.

36 Removal and refitting of the regulator assemblies are described in this Section. Refer to Section 16 for the switches.

13 Tailgate, hinges and support struts – removal and refitting

Tailgate

Removal

1 Disconnect the battery negative (earth) lead, and position it away from the terminal (see Chapter 5A Section 3).

13.3a Disconnect the wiring connectors…

2 Open the tailgate, and remove the trim panels as described in Section 26 of this Chapter.

3 Disconnect the wiring from the heated rear window, tailgate wiper motor, and central locking motor. Release the wiring loom from any securing clips **(see illustrations)**.

4 Remove the high level stop-light from the top of the tailgate, as described in Chapter 12 Section 10.

5 Release the wiring loom and hose grommets from the edge of the tailgate **(see illustration)**. Tie string to the wiring loom and hose, and pull them through the edge of the tailgate. Leave the string in position in the tailgate, to aid refitting.

6 Have an assistant support the tailgate. Disconnect the support struts from the tailgate by prising out the retaining clips using a screwdriver **(see illustrations)**.

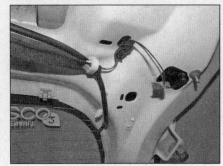

13.3b …from inside the tailgate

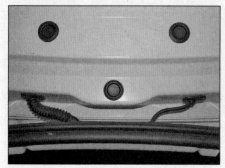

13.5 Release the wiring grommets from the tailgate

13.6a Release the securing clip...

13.6b ...and disconnect the strut from the ball joint

13.8 The tailgate hinge bolts

13.12 Tailgate lock striker

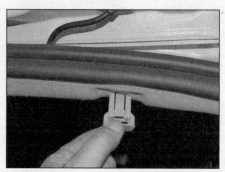

13.14 Release the securing clips

7 If the original tailgate is to be refitted, mark the positions of the securing bolts on the tailgate.

8 Unscrew the bolts **(see illustration)** and carefully withdraw the tailgate from the vehicle.

Refitting

9 Refitting is a reversal of removal, but where applicable, fit the tailgate securing nuts in their original positions, as noted before removal.

10 Do not fully-tighten the tailgate securing nuts until the top of the tailgate is aligned correctly with the roof panel and the rear body pillars.

11 On completion, if adjustment of the tailgate lower edge alignment is required, adjust the tailgate lock striker on the lower body panel.

12 Alter the position of the lock striker **(see illustration)** on the body (by means of

the elongated screw holes) to give correct alignment of the lower edge of the tailgate with the surrounding body panels.

13 Using the string left in the tailgate on removal, pull the wiring loom and hose back up through the tailgate.

Hinges

14 To remove the hinges from the roof panel, prise the plastic clips from the rear of the headlining **(see illustration)**, pull the rubber seal from along the upper edge of the tailgate aperture and carefully pull down the rear of the headlining for access to the tailgate hinge securing nuts.

Support struts

Removal

15 Open the tailgate, and have an assistant support it in the fully-open position.

16 Disconnect the support strut from the tailgate by prising out the securing clip using a small screwdriver **(see illustrations 13.6a and 13.6b)**.

17 Repeat the procedure for the clip securing the lower part of the strut to the body **(see illustrations)**, and withdraw the strut from the vehicle.

Refitting

18 Refitting is a reversal of removal.

14 Tailgate lock components – removal and refitting

Lock assembly

Removal

1 Open the tailgate and then disconnect the battery negative (earth) lead as described in Chapter 5A Section 4.

2 Remove the tailgate trim as described in Section 26.

3 Remove the two bolts and remove the lock assembly from the tailgate **(see illustration)**.

4 Disconnect the wiring connector from the lock mechanism **(see illustration)**.

5 In the event of an electrical failure of the lock assembly it is possible to open the tailgate from inside the vehicle **(see illustration)**. Working from inside the vehicle, drop down the rear seats to access the luggage compartment, then slide a

13.17a Release the securing clip...

13.17b ...and disconnect the strut from the ball joint

14.3 Remove the lock bolts

14.4 Disconnect the electrical connector

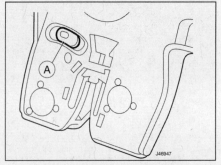

14.5 Slide the catch at point A with a screwdriver to release the tailgate lock

screwdriver between the lower edge of the door and the rear panel, to release the catch on the lock.

Refitting

6 Refitting is a reversal of removal.

Lock striker

Removal

7 The lock striker is attached to the tailgate slam panel.

8 Remove the rear trim from the rear body panel as described in Section 26.

9 The striker plate is adjustable so mark its position before removing the retaining bolts **(see illustration 13.13)**.

Refitting

10 Refitting is a reversal of removal, but if necessary adjust the position of the striker plate.

15 Central locking components – general information

1 The central locking is operated by radio frequency and is controlled by the UCH (Unite Centrale Habitacle). It is located under the left-hand side of the facia (as seen from the driver's seat) above the bonnet release lever. If there is a fault with this unit, it will require checking with a fault code reader. It is not possible to swap units from vehicle to vehicle without swapping other components as well. A new UCH is supplied as an blank unit and will require programming with a suitable diagnostic tool. At the time of writing only the Renault factory diagnostic tool can perform this function.

2 The door lock motors and switches are an

integral part of the door lock assembly. See Section 11 for removal and refitting of the door locking components and Section 14 for the removal and refitting of the tailgate locking components.

16 Electric window components – removal and refitting

Switches

Removal

1 Disconnect the battery negative (earth) lead, and position it away from the terminal (Chapter 5A Section 4).

Front doors

2 The switch assembly is a tight fit in the door trim panel, if required, remove the door trim panel, as described in Section 26.

3 Use a plastic trim tool and prise up the complete switch panel. if the panel is still fitted to the vehicle, disconnect the wiring plug as the switch panel is removed and then release the switch from the trim panel **(see illustrations)**.

4 The switches can the be removed from the switch panel, by releasing the securing clips and then withdrawing the switches from the panel **(see illustrations)**

Rear doors

5 Remove the blanking plug and undo the securing screw in the door grab handle, then carefully lift and pull back

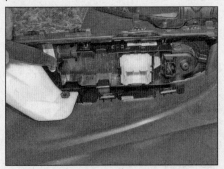

16.3a Release the switch panel at the rear...

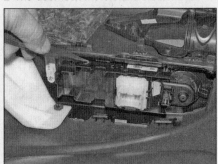

16.3b ...and at the side (sown with trim panel removed)...

16.3c ...then unhook the switch panel at the front from the trim panel

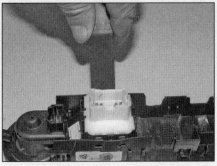

16.4a Release the secuirng clips...

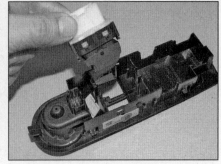

16.4b ...and remove the window switches

16.5a Remove the blanking plug...

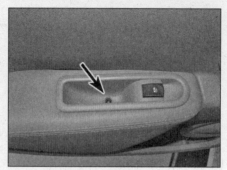

16.5b ...and the screw

16.5c Carefully remove the handle and switch

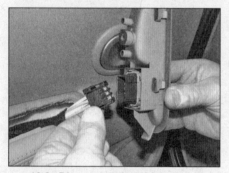

16.6a Disconnect the wiring plug...

16.6b ...and remove the switch

the handle to release it from the door (see illustrations).

6 Disconnect the wiring plug and withdraw the switch from the handle (see illustrations).

Refitting

7 Refitting is a reversal of removal.

Operating motors

8 The motors are an integral part of the window regulator assemblies, and cannot be renewed independently. Removal and refitting of the regulator assemblies are described in Section 12.

17 Mirrors – removal, refitting and glass renewal

Note: *The outside temperature sensor (where fitted) is located in the driver's side mirror.*

Door mirror

Removal

1 On models fitted with electric mirrors, disconnect the battery negative (earth) lead as described in Chapter 5A Section 4.

2 Remove the door trim panel as described in Section 26.

3 Disconnect the wiring connector, then release the rubber grommet from the door panel (see illustrations).

4 Support the mirror and then undo the securing nut on the inside of the door. Release the mirror from the door panel, withdrawing the wiring as it is removed (see illustrations).

Refitting

5 Refitting is a reversal of removal.

Glass renewal

6 Using a flat-bladed tool, carefully prise behind the top edge of the mirror glass (see illustration).

7 Support the glass, lever the tool forwards and the mirror glass will unclip from the mirror

17.3a Disconnect the wiring connector...

17.3b ...and remove the rubber grommet

17.4a Undo the retaining nut...

17.4b ...then withdraw the mirror and wiring

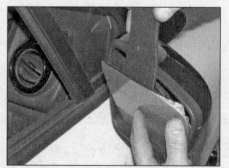

17.6 A broad-bladed plastic tool is used to release the mirror glass

17.8 Disconnect the wiring plug

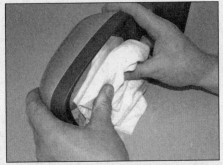

17.9 Protect the glass and push it firmly

17.11 Remove the outer shell cover

assembly. Take care not to drop the mirror glass as the clip is released.

8 Where applicable, disconnect the wiring connectors from the rear of the mirror glass **(see illustration)**.

9 To refit the glass, press the glass into position until it engages securely **(see illustration)**, taking care not to damage the glass.

Shell renewal

10 First remove the mirror glass, as described previously in this section, see paragraphs 7 to 10.

11 Release the retaining clips from inside the mirror housing, and remove the outer shell **(see illustration)**. It may be necessary to fold the mirror inwards, to release the outer shell from the pivot area.

Electric mirror switch

12 The switch assembly is a tight fit in the door trim panel, if required, remove the door trim panel, as described in Section 26.

13 Use a plastic trim tool and prise up the complete switch panel. if the panel is still fitted to the vehicle, disconnect the wiring plug as the switch panel is removed and then release the switch from the trim panel **(see illustrations 16.2a, 16.2b and 16.2c)**.

14 The switches can the be removed from the switch panel, by releasing the securing clips and then withdrawing the switches from the panel **(see illustrations)**.

Electric mirror motor

15 The motor is not available separately from the mirror. If it is faulty, the complete mirror assembly must be renewed.

Interior mirror

16 We found that the removal of the interior mirror may cause the windscreen to break, it is recommended that this procedure must therefore be entrusted to a Renault dealer, a windscreen specialist, or other competent professional.

17 The mounting bracket is fixed to the windscreen using a special adhesive, and should not be disturbed unless absolutely necessary. Note that there is a risk of cracking the windscreen glass if an attempt is made to remove the securely-bonded mounting bracket.

18 Windscreen and tailgate window glass – general information

1 The windscreen and the tailgate window glass are bonded in position using a special adhesive. Special tools, adhesives and expertise are required for successful removal and refitting of glass fixed by this method. Such work must therefore be entrusted to a Renault dealer, a windscreen specialist, or other competent professional.

19 Rear quarter window components – removal and refitting

1 The fixed rear quarter window glass is bonded in position using a special adhesive. Special tools, adhesives and expertise are required for successful removal and refitting of glass fixed by this method. Such work must therefore be entrusted to a Renault dealer, a windscreen specialist, or other competent professional.

20 Sunroof components – removal and refitting

1 This type of sunroof is a complex piece of equipment, consisting of a large number of components. It is strongly recommended

that the sunroof mechanism is not disturbed unless absolutely necessary. If the sunroof mechanism is faulty, or requires overhaul, consult a Renault dealer for advice.

2 The sunroof has an anti-trap function that may require resetting, especially after the battery has been disconnected for any length of time. To do this, proceed as follows:

3 Start the vehicle and turn the switch to the fully-closed position. This should trigger the anti-trap function and the roof will move back and forwards. Wait 10 seconds.

4 If the sunroof is now closed, press and hold the switch until the clicking noise of the motor can be heard. Release the switch and then promptly press the switch again – keep pressing until the roof opens and closes fully. Expect a 5 second delay between use of the switch and movement of the roof.

5 If the sunroof is open, press and hold the switch. The roof will close in stages. Keep pressing the switch until the clicking noise of the motor can be heard. Release and promptly press the switch again. Keep pressing until the roof opens and closes completely. Expect a 5 second delay between use of the switch and movement of the roof.

6 Release the switch and wait at least 10 seconds before checking the operation of the sunroof.

7 It is possible to over-ride the anti-trap function by pressing the switch just after the anti-trap function has been triggered. This feature enables the sunroof to be closed in the event of a malfunction of the system or in the case of damage to the sliding rails.

17.14a Release the clips at each side...

17.14b ...then unclip the mirror switch from the panel

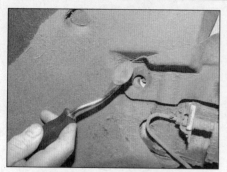

21.2 Release the plastic clips

21.3 Removing the front section of the liner

Rear door

11 Open the door, and remove the adhesive strip from the front edge of the door to expose the securing bolt.

12 Working outside the door, push the rubbing strip towards the front of the door and remove it.

13 Refitting is a reversal of removal.

Badges

Removal

14 The various badges may be secured with adhesives. To remove them, either soften the adhesive using a hot air gun or hairdryer (taking care to avoid damage to the paintwork), or separate the badge from the body by 'sawing' through the adhesive using a length of nylon cord. **Note:** *Some badges are located by pegs in plastic grommets, these will need to be carefully prised from the bodywork.*

Refitting

15 Clean off all traces of adhesive using white spirit, then wash the area with warm soapy water to remove all traces of spirit, and allow to dry. Ensure that the surface to which the new badge is to be fastened is completely clean, and free from grease and dirt.

16 A hot air gun can be used to warm the adhesive if necessary.

21 Body exterior fittings – removal and refitting

Wheel arch liners

Front liners

1 Jack up the front of the car, and support it on axle stands (see *Jacking and vehicle support*). Remove the appropriate roadwheel.

2 The front liner is in two parts, so can be removed independently of each other. The liners are secured by a combination of plastic clips, and screws or bolts. Remove the screws or bolts and plastic clips **(see illustration)**.

3 Work the liner free from the front edge first and then remove the rear section **(see illustration)**.

4 Refitting is a reversal of removal.

Rear liners

5 Jack up the rear of the car, and support it on axle stands (see see *Jacking and vehicle support*). Remove the appropriate roadwheel.

6 Remove the assorted bolts and clips and remove the liner.

7 Refitting is a reversal of removal.

Rubbing strips

Note: *Take care not to damage the paintwork when removing the rubbing strips.*

Front door

8 Open the door, and remove the plastic cover from the rear edge of the door to expose the securing bolt. Remove the side repeater and disconnect the wiring plug as described in Chapter 12 Section 10.

9 Working outside the door, slide the strip towards the rear of the door and remove it.

10 Refitting is a reversal of removal.

22 Seats – removal and refitting

Front seat

⚠️ *Warning: Warning: Disconnect the battery negative lead (see 'Disconnecting the battery' in Chapter 5A Section 4), then wait for five minutes before proceeding. If this waiting period is not observed, there is danger of the side airbags and seat belt tensioners being activated.*

Note: *On some models, there is a storage tray fitted under the front passenger seat. This is riveted into place and can only be removed after the front seat has been removed.*

Removal

1 Reaching down the side of the seat release the locking clip and disconnect the seat belt from the side of the seat frame **(see illustration)**.

2 Working under the front of the seat, release the locking clip and disconnect the wiring plug connector from under the seat **(see illustrations)**. Release the cable retaining clips from under the seat frame to free the wiring from the seat.

3 Slide the seat fully forward and remove the now exposed rear mounting bolts **(see illustration)**.

4 Slide the seat fully backwards and remove

22.1 Unclip the seat belt from the seat

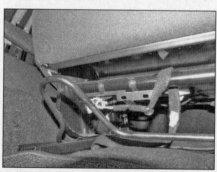

22.2a Working under the front of the seat...

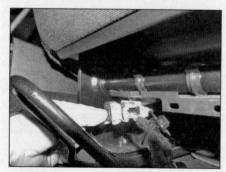

22.2b ...disconnect the wiring connector

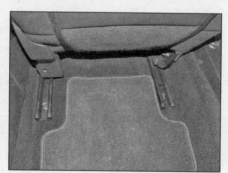

22.3 Remove the rear mounting bolts

22.4 Remove the front mounting bolts

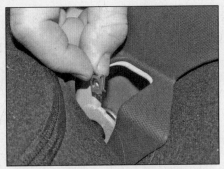

22.11a Remove the retaining clip…

22.11b …push back the locking bracket…

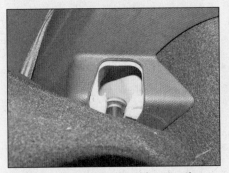

22.11c …to open up the side mounting…

22.11d …then remove the seat pivot

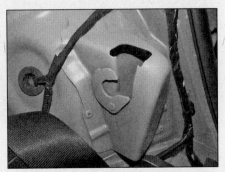

22.11e Seat locking bracket with trims removed

the now exposed front mounting bolts **(see illustration)**.

5 With the help of an assistant, remove the seat from the vehicle. Take care when removing the seat, that the seat runners do not catch the paintwork as the seat is removed. It may help to remove the headrest from the seat, before removal.

Refitting

6 Refitting is a reversal of removal, but fit new bolts and tighten to the correct torque.

Rear seat cushion

Removal

7 Lift up the front part of the seat cushion slightly, then pull the seat cushions upwards at the rear and tilt it forwards. Pull the check straps to the side to unhook them from the securing lugs in the floor panel.

Refitting

8 Refitting is a reversal of removal.

Rear seat back

Removal

9 Lift up and remove the seat cushions, as described previously and also remove the parcel shelf.
10 Release the securing catches at the top of the seat backs and fold them forwards.
11 Working at each end of the rear seat, remove the retaining clip, then using a screwdriver, push back the side mounting locking bracket and remove the seat back **(see illustrations)**.

Refitting

12 Refitting is a reversal of removal.

23 Seat belt components – removal and refitting

⚠️ **Warning: If the vehicle has been in an accident, all the deployed components of the seat belts must be renewed. This will include the seat belt, stalks, mounting bolts and the SRS control unit. Also note that the new control unit will require programming with a suitable diagnostic tool.**

Front belt

Removal

1 Disconnect the battery negative lead, and

23.3 Peel back the door seals

position the lead away from the battery (see Chapter 5A Section 4).
2 Reach down the outside of the seat, release the locking clip and disconnect the seat belt from the side of the seat frame **(see illustration 22.1)**.
3 Slide the front seat forwards as far as it will go, then peel back the door aperture rubber seals at each side of the B-pillar **(see illustration)**.
4 Unclip the lower part of the B-pillar trim from the pillar **(see illustrations)**.
5 Undo the mounting bolt and disconnect the seat belt guide plate from the B-pillar **(see illustrations)**.
6 Slide a small screwdriver behind the upper mounting trim cover to release the retaining clips (one at each side), then slide the trim cover upwards, to remove it from over the upper seat belt anchorage bolt **(see illustrations)**.

23.4a Prise the cover free…

23.4b ...to release the securing clips

23.5a Undo the retaining bolt...

23.5b ...and remove the guide bracket

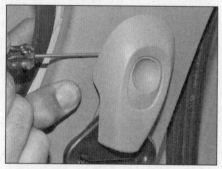

23.6a Slide a small screwdriver behind cover...

23.6b ...to release the retaining clips (cover removed to show clips)...

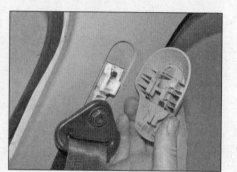

23.6c ...then slide the cover upwards to remove

7 Unscrew the mounting bolt, and withdraw the seat belt upper anchor bracket from the B-pillar **(see illustration)**.
8 Unclip the upper part of the B-pillar trim from the pillar **(see illustrations)**.

9 Release the locking clip, then disconnect the wiring connector from the top of the inertia reel assembly **(see illustration)**.
10 Unscrew the mounting bolt, and withdraw

the inertia reel assembly from the door pillar and out from the car.
11 If required, the upper mounting bracket can be removed from the B-pillar by removing the two mounting bolts **(see illustration)**.

Refitting

12 Refitting is a reversal of removal. Tighten the seat belt mounting bolts to the specified torque.

Rear inertia reel belts

Removal

13 Disconnect the battery negative lead, and position the lead away from the battery (see Chapter 5A Section 4).
14 Remove the rear seat cushion and rear seat back, with reference to Section 22.
15 Unclip the trim panel from the front edge

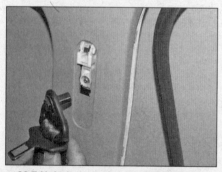

23.7 Unbolt the upper seat belt anchor

23.8a Release the lower part of the trim from the pillar...

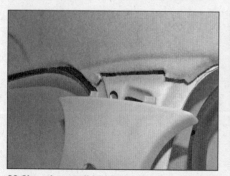

23.8b ...then pull it downwards to release it from the roof panel

23.9 Disconnect the wiring connector

23.11 Upper mounting bracket

23.15 Unclip the front trim panel

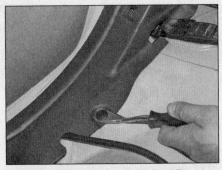

23.16a Release the retaining clip...

23.16b ...and lift trim to access bolt

of the of the luggage compartment side trim panel **(see illustration)**.
16 Release the retaining clip, then lift up the edge of the sill trim panel and undo the seat belt lower anchorage bolt **(see illustrations)**.
17 Undo the two retaining screws, then unclip the trim panel from along the top of the of the luggage compartment side trim panel **(see illustrations)**. If removing the right-hand side trim panel, disconnect the wiring connector from the luggage compartment light, as the trim panel is removed.
18 Release the retaining clips, then remove the luggage compartment side trim panel **(see illustrations)**.
19 Unclip the upper part of the C-pillar trim panel from the pillar **(see illustration)**, withdraw the seat belt through the trim panel as it is removed.

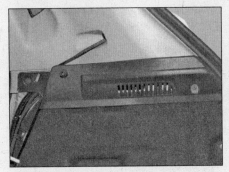

23.17a Undo the two retaining screws...

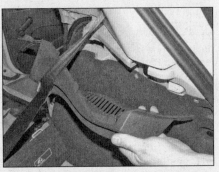

23.17b ...and unclip the upper trim panel

20 Undo the two retaining bolts and remove the seat belt guide from the rear panel **(see illustration)**.
21 Disconnect the wiring plug (where fitted)

and then unbolt the inertia reel from the rear panel **(see illustrations)**.
22 Undo the retaining bolt and remove the centre seat belt, upper anchorage

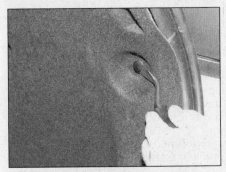

23.18a Release the retaining clips...

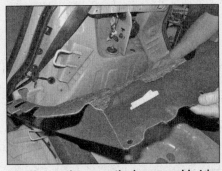

23.18b ...and remove the luggage side trim panel

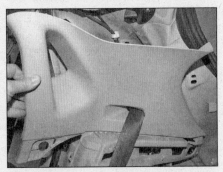

23.19 Unclip the upper trim panel

23.20 Undo the seat belt guide retaining bolts

23.21a Right-hand side Inertia reel seat belt...

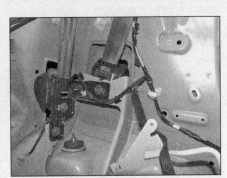

23.21b ...and left-hand side with centre inertia reel seat belt

23.22 Undo the centre belt upper mounting bot

bracket from the roof panel **(see illustration)**.
23 If required, the magnetic seat belt buckle holder can be unclipped from the headlining **(see illustration)**.

Refitting

24 Refitting is a reversal of removal. Tighten the seat belt mountings to the specified torque.

---

24 Seat belt pretensioner system – general information and component renewal

---

General information

1 The seat belt pretensioners are an integral part of the SRS (supplementary restraint system). They operate in conjunction with the deployment of the multiple airbags fitted to the Clio.
2 Seat belt pretensioners are fitted to remove any slack from the front seat belts in the event of a frontal impact. The system is designed to reduce the chances of injury to the driver and front seat passenger in the event of an accident due to the seat belts being slack.
3 The system consists of two special seat belt tensioner/stalk assemblies mounted directly on the front seats, and inertia reels with their own pretensioning system. On most models, the rear side seat belts also have pyrotechnic inertia reels, but not the seat belt stalk pretensioners.
4 Each tensioner/stalk assembly consist of a special buckle attached to a cable. The end of the cable is attached to a piston inside the tensioner cylinder.
5 The electronic control unit is mounted under the centre console, and incorporates a deceleration sensor and a trigger unit. Side impact sensors are also fitted. If the control unit senses a deceleration greater than a predetermined limit, the control unit sends signals to the ignition modules in the seat belt tensioner units and airbags. The seat belt tensioner electronic control unit is integrated with the airbag electronic control unit.
6 When a tensioner ignition module is triggered, a small capsule is energised, which rapidly releases gas into the tensioner

cylinder. As the gas is released, the piston is forced along the cylinder, pulling the cable (approximately 70 mm) and hence the seat belt stalk, which in turn removes any slack from the seat belt, pulling the belt tight against the wearer. The system works in conjuction with the inertia reels. These are also triggered to clamp or rapidly wind in any loose seatbelt webbing. Note that at this point the anti-submarine airbags fitted to front of the seat cushions will most likely also deploy.
7 Once a seat belt tensioner has been triggered, it must be renewed.

⚠ *Warning: Do not expose the pretensioner system to excessive heat.*

8 • If any work is to be carried out under the vehicle (eg, exhaust renewal) in the vicinity of the pretensioner system components which involves impacts or hammering, disconnect the battery negative lead and position the lead away from the battery (see Chapter 5A Section 4). Wait for at least five minutes before proceeding.
9 • When installing any electrical accessories (such as loudspeakers or alarm systems) which emit a magnetic field, the components must not be fitted near the pretensioner control unit.
10 • If an attempt has been made to steal the vehicle, if the vehicle has been stolen or if the vehicle has been involved in an impact which did not trigger the SRS system, the system should be tested using the Renault Clip diagnostic tool or any other suitable SRS system diagnostic tool.

Pretensioner system

Note: *Renault recommend that the Clip diagnostic tool is used to test the operation of the system before reactivation.*

De-activation

11 To de-activate the pretensioner system, in order to make the system safe, proceed as follows.
a) *Switch off the ignition.*
b) *Disconnect the battery negative lead.*
c) *Wait for a minimum of 5 minutes before carrying out any further work.*
d) *Working under each front seat in turn, separate the two halves of the seat belt pretensioner wiring connector.*

23.23 Unclip the magnetic belt buckle holder

Re-activation

12 To re-activate the pretensioner system after carrying out work, proceed as follows.
a) *Reconnect the pretensioner wiring connectors under the seats.*
b) *Reconnect the battery negative lead.*
c) *Switch the ignition on. Check that all the warning lights on the instrument panel are working correctly.*
d) *Renault recommend that the operation of the system is checked using the Renault diagnostic tool.*

Pretensioner assembly

Removal

13 De-activate the pretensioner system as described previously in this Section.
14 Remove the seat (see Section 22).
15 On models with seat height adjustment, remove the cover from the handle then remove the two securing bolts. Remove the handle.
16 Remove the screw from the seat side trim and then lever the trim free.
17 Discconect the wiring and then undo the securing bolt from the pretensioner assembly. Unclip the tensioner assembly and remove it from the seat frame.

⚠ *Warning: Do not expose the pretensioner assembly to shocks or excessive heat.*

Note: *Before discarding a pretensioner assembly which has not been triggered, the assembly must be rendered safe using the appropriate Renault special equipment.*

Refitting

18 Refitting is a reversal of removal.

Electronic control unit

19 The pretensioner system is part of the integrated SRS system and shares the same control unit as the airbag system. If the control unit is to be removed, follow the procedure for the removal and refitting of the airbag control unit as described in Chapter 12.

---

25 Interior trim – general information

Interior trim panels

1 The interior trim panels are all secured using either screws or various types of plastic fasteners.
2 Before removing a panel, study it carefully, noting how it is secured. Often, other panels or ancillary components (such as seat belt mountings, grab handles, etc) must be removed before a particular panel can be withdrawn.
3 Once any such components have been removed, check that there are no other panels overlapping the one to be removed. Usually, the sequence to be followed will become obvious on close inspection.
4 Remove all obvious fasteners, such as

screws, which may have plastic covers fitted. If the panel cannot be freed, it is probably secured by hidden clips or fasteners on the rear of the panel. Such fasteners are usually situated around the edge of the panel, and can be prised up to release them. Note that plastic clips can break quite easily, so it is advisable to have a few new clips of the correct type available for refitting. Generally, the best way of releasing such clips is to use a forked tool **(see illustration)**. If this is not available, an old, broad-bladed screwdriver with the edges rounded off and wrapped in insulating tape will serve as a good substitute.

5 The following Section and the accompanying illustrations describe removal and refitting of all the major trim panels. Note that the type and number of fasteners used often varies during the production run of a particular model, so differences may be found to the procedures provided.

6 When removing a panel, never use excessive force, or the panel may be damaged. Always check carefully that all fasteners have been removed or released before attempting to withdraw a panel.

7 When refitting, secure the fasteners by pressing them firmly into place. Ensure that all disturbed components are correctly secured, to prevent rattles. If adhesives were found at any point during removal, use white spirit to remove the old adhesive, then wash off the white spirit using soapy water. Use a trim adhesive (a Renault dealer should be able to recommend a proprietary product) on reassembly.

25.4 Forked tool for releasing plastic trim clips

Carpets

8 The carpet is not bonded and rests on the floor, it is held in position by the sill trim panels and other surrounding panels and components.

9 Carpet removal and refitting is reasonably straightforward, but very time consuming, due to the fact that many of the adjoining trim panels must be removed first. It will also be necessary to remove components such as the seats and their mountings, the centre console, etc.

Headlining

10 The headlining is bonded to the rear section of the roof, and is also held in place by the grab handles, sunvisors, sunroof trim, door pillar trim panels, rear quarter trim panels, weatherseals, etc. When all the fittings have been removed or prised clear, it can

then be withdrawn out through the tailgate aperture.

11 Note that headlining removal requires considerable skill and patience if it is to be carried out without damage, and is therefore best entrusted to an expert.

26 Interior trim panels – removal and refitting

Front door inner trim panel

Removal

1 Make sure the ignition is off before disconnecting any electrical connectors.

2 Open the door, then unclip the plastic trim cover and remove the screw securing the inner door lever. Unclip the door lever from the trim panel, and then disconnect the operating cable **(see illustrations)**.

3 Unclip the plastic trim cover, and then remove the screw securing the inner door trim panel under the grab handle **(see illustration)**.

4 Undo the retaining screws from the front, the rear edge and the bottom of the door trim panel **(see illustrations)**.

5 Working your way around the outside of the door, carefully release the securing clips around the edge of the trim panel, preferably using a forked tool.

6 Pull the trim panel from the door, and lift upwards off the inner weatherstrip. Support the panel and then disconnect the wiring plug

26.2a Unclip cover and remove screw...

26.2b ...then release cable to remove door lever

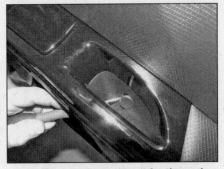
26.3 Remove the screw under the grab handle

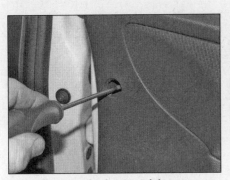
26.4a Remove the front retaining screw...

26.4b ...the rear retaining screw...

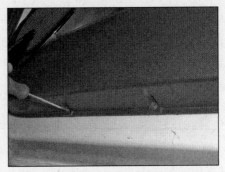
26.4c ...and the lower retaining screws

26.6a Unclip the door trim panel...

26.6b ...and disconnect the wiring connectors

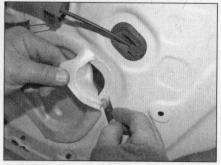

26.7 Remove the door membrane

connectors on the back of the switch panel **(see illustrations)**.

7 At this point, the door membrane can be removed. Use of a blunt scraper (or knife blade) and carefully remove the membrane **(see illustration)**. If the membrane is damaged during removal a new one is available from Renault.

Refitting

8 Refitting is a reversal of removal, bearing in mind the following points.

9 When refitting the membrane to the door, ensure that is fully bonded to the door panel.

10 Make sure all the wiring connectors are fitted correctly, before switching the ignition on or reconnecting battery.

Rear door inner trim panel

Removal

11 Remove the blanking plug and undo the

securing screw, then carefully lift and pull the grab handle backwards to release it from the door panel **(see illustrations)**. On models with rear electric windows disconnect the wiring plug as the handle is removed.

12 On models fitted with manual window winders, note the position of the window winder handle with the window fully open, then using a special tool or screwdriver to release the securing clip, pull the handle firmly to release it from the window regulator **(see illustrations)**.

13 Open the door, then unclip the plastic trim cover and remove the screw securing the inner door lever. Unclip the door lever from the trim panel, and then disconnect the operating cable **(see illustrations 26.2a and 26.2b)**.

14 Unclip the plastic trim cover from the top of the door, then undo the retaining screw and remove the screw securing top of the inner door trim panel **(see illustrations)**.

15 Carefully release the securing clips around the edge of the trim panel, preferably using a forked tool. Pull the trim panel from the door, and lift upwards off the inner weather strip.

16 Remove the door membrane, by using a blunt scraper (or knife blade) to remove the membrane **(see illustration 26.6)**.

Refitting

17 Refitting is a reversal of removal.

Footwell side/sill trim panels

Removal

18 Depending on panel being worked on, remove the front/rear seat, as described in Section 22.

19 Carefully pull off the lower part of the door seals, taking care not to damage the seal.

20 For the front left-hand sill trim to be removed, the bonnet release lever will have to be unclipped first, see Section 9.

26.11a Remove the screw...

26.11b ...and then lift out the grab handle.

26.12a Release the securing clip...

26.12b ...and remove the winder handle

26.14a Unclip the trim cover...

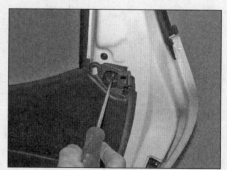

26.14b ...and remove the upper retaining screw

21 Unclip the panel at the rear by moving it towards the vehicle interior and then pull it upwards.

22 With the rear of the panel released, pull the panel in and backwards to free it from the footwell.

Refitting

23 Refitting is a reversal of removal. Ensure that the securing clips are correctly engaged, and tighten the seat belt mounting bolts to the specified torque.

A-pillar trim panel

Removal

24 Carefully pull the door seal away from the front windscreen pillar where it touches the trim panel, taking care not to damage the seal.

25 Carefully pull back the top of the panel from the pillar to release the securing clips. Withdraw the panel, lifting it upwards from the facia panel **(see illustration)**.

Refitting

26 Refitting is a reversal of removal.

B-pillar trim panel

27 The B-pillar trim panels are removed during the removal of the front seat belts, see description in Section 23, for further information.

C-pillar and rear quarter trim panels

28 The C-pillar and rear quarter trim panels are removed during the removal of the rear seat belts, see description in Section 23, for further information.

Luggage area rear trim panel

Removal

29 Partially free the tailgate seal from along the tailgate aperture, then remove the plastic clips from inside the trim panel **(see illustration)**.

30 Unbolt and remove the luggage securing clips from each corner of the panel **(see illustration)**.

31 Work the panel free, by pulling it upwards to release the securing clips **(see illustration)**.

Refitting

32 Refitting is a reversal of removal, but make sure the locating pegs are correctly positioned.

Tailgate trim panel

Removal

33 Open the tailgate and unclip the small trim panels that cover the lights in the tailgate **(see illustration)**.

34 Undo the two retaining screws from inside the grab handles and the two from the sides of the trim panel **(see illustrations)**.

35 Pull the trim panel outwards at the lock edge of the trim panel, then slide it downwards to release the retaining clips by the rear screen **(see illustration)**.

26.25 Removing the A-pillar trim panel

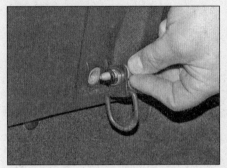
26.30 Unbolt the luggage securing clips

Refitting

36 Refitting is a reversal of removal. If required, retrieve the retaining clips from the tailgate panel and refit them to the tailgate trim panel before refitting **(see illustration)**.

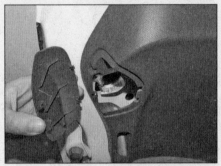
26.33 Unclip the small trim panels

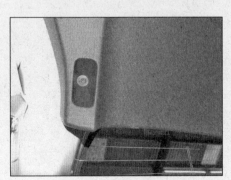
26.34b ...from the trim panel

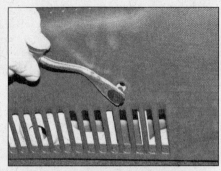
26.29 Remove the inner clips

26.31 Unclip the rear panel

Front seat trim panels

Removal

37 Remove the complete seat assembly as described in Section 22.

26.34a Undo the retaining screws...

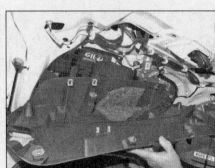
26.35 Removing the tailgate trim panel

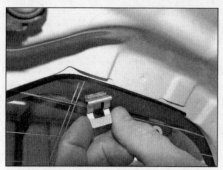

26.36 Retrieve clip and refit back to trim panel

26.38a Unclip cover, undo screws...

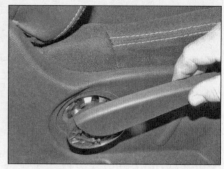

26.38b ...and remove seat handle

26.39a Undo the retaining screw...

26.39b ...and remove the seat trim panel

27 Centre console –
removal and refitting

Removal

Rear section

1 Unclip the trim panel from below the handbrake lever (see illustration).
2 Move the seats as far forwards as possible and then remove the two screws (one at each side) from the rear of the console (see illustration).
3 Slide the rear section of the centre console backwards to withdraw the front locating pegs, then lift it over the handbrake lever, disconnecting the wiring from the switches, as it is removed (see illustrations).

Front section

4 To remove the front section of the centre console, first unclip the gear lever gaiter trim from the top of the console (see illustration).
5 Unclip the trim panels from the left and right-hand side front of the centre console (see illustrations).
6 Unclip the trim from the rear of the gear lever housing (see illustration).
7 Remove the stop/start switch trim panel from below the heater control panel. Unclip the panel and disconnect the wiring connector from the switch as it is removed (see illustrations).
8 Pull the gear knob upwards to release it

38 Remove the cover from the height adjustment handle, undo the screws and remove the handle (see illustrations).
39 Remove the single screw from the rear of the panel, then unclip the panel and remove it (see illustrations).

Refitting

40 Refitting is a reversal of removal.

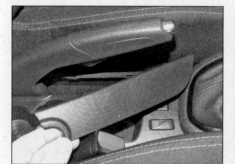

27.1 Remove the small trim piece from below the handbrake

27.2 Remove the screws

27.3a Slide the console backward...

27.3b ...then remove the centre console...

27.3c ...and disconnect the wiring connectors

27.4 Unclip the gear lever gaiter

27.5a Unclip the left-hand side...

27.5b ...and right-hand side trim panels

27.6 Unclip the plastic trim

27.7a Unclip the trim panel...

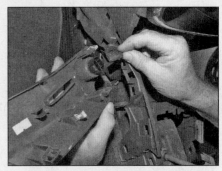

27.7b ...and disconnect the wiring connector

from the gear lever, if the gaiter has come away from the gear knob, then withdraw the gaiter and trim panel from over the gear lever **(see illustrations)**.

9 Undo the retaining screws from the front and the rear of the front console **(see illustrations)**.
10 Withdraw the front console from over the

gear lever, disconnecting the diagnostic plug from the front of the console, as it is removed **(see illustrations)**.

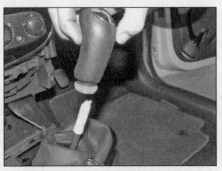

27.8a Pull the gear knob upwards to release it...

27.8b ...then withdraw the gaiter

27.9a Undo the screw from the rear...

27.9b ...and the two screws at each side at the front

27.10a Withdraw the console...

27.10b ...and unclip the diagnostic plug

27.11a Retrieve the rubber ring...

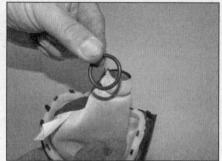

27.11b ...fit it back to the gaiter...

27.11c ...then fit gaiter to gear knob

Refitting

11 Refitting is a reversal of removal. If the gaiter is not attached to the gear knob, retrieve the rubber ring from around the gear lever and fit it back to the gaiter, and then back to the base of the gear knob before refitting **(see illustrations)**.

 ## 28 Facia panels and components – removal and refitting

⚠️ *Warning: Before carrying out any work on the facia panel, disconnect the battery negative lead, and position the lead away from the battery (also see 'Disconnecting the battery' in Chapter 5A Section 4). Read and follow the precautions given in Chapter 12 on airbags.*

Steering column shrouds

Removal

1 Release the steering column height lever and lower the steering column as far as it will go. Remove the steering wheel (Chapter 10 Section 14) and driver's airbag (Chapter 12 Section 28).

2 Unclip the upper plastic part of the shroud from the top of the steering column, then unclip the inner cover from the lower shroud **(see illustrations)**. Note the inner part of the upper shroud can stay in position on the facia.

3 Working under the steering column, remove the securing screws and withdraw the lower shroud from the steering column by sliding it upwards to release it from the locating guide, next to the steering column height lever **(see illustrations)**.

Refitting

4 Refitting is a reversal of removal.

Glovebox

Removal

5 Remove the facia end panel and remove the three retaining screws from the end of the glovebox **(see illustrations)**.

6 Open the glovebox lid and remove the upper screw inside the glovebox, then unhook and withdraw the glovebox from the locating slots in the facia **(see illustrations)**.

Refitting

7 Refitting is a reversal of removal.

Complete facia assembly

Note: *This is an involved procedure, which is likely to take some time. It is advisable to make*

28.2a Unclip the outer part of the upper shroud...

28.2b ...and also the inner part

28.3a Undo the retaining screws...

28.3b ...then slide the shroud upwards...

28.3c ...to release it from the plastic guide

28.5a Unclip the end panel...

28.5b ...and remove the retaining screws

28.6a Remove the upper screw...

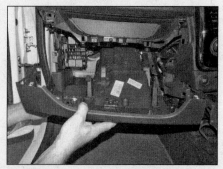

28.6b ...and remove the glovebox

28.6c Note the position of the locating pegs on the rear of the glovebox

28.12 Remove the screw from behind the instrument panel

28.17 Remove the end panel and disconnect the wiring connector

careful notes as the procedure progresses, to ensure correct refitting of all components, and correct routing of all wiring, etc. Specific details of fixings and components may vary from model to model, but the following will serve as a guide. Provided plenty of time is allowed, removal of the facia assembly should not present any problems.

Removal

8 Disconnect the battery negative lead as described in Chapter 5A Section 4.

9 Remove the steering wheel as described in Chapter 10 Section 14.

10 Remove the lower facia trim panel and steering column shrouds as described previously in this Section.

11 Disconnect and remove the column switches as described in Chapter 12 Section 7.

12 Remove and then disconnect the instrument panel as described in Chapter 12 Section 13. Remove the screw from behind the panel **(see illustration)**.

13 Remove the centre console as described in Section 27 of this Chapter and then remove the glovebox as described in paragraphs 5 and 6 in this Section.

14 Remove the key card reader from the lower part of the centre facia panel, a described in Chapter 12 Section 7.

15 Remove the audio unit, as described in Chapter 12 Section 23.

16 Remove the heater control panel, as described in Chapter 3 Section 12.

17 Unclip the end panel from the right-hand side of the facia, then disconnect the wiring connector from the passenger airbag inhibitor switch in the panel **(see illustration)**.

18 Undo the three retaining screws from

the right-hand side of the panel, then remove the drivers side lower facia panel. Disconnect the wiring connectors from the switches in the panel, as it is removed **(see illustrations)**.

19 Remove the A-pillar trim panels as described in Section 26 of this Chapter.

20 Reaching up behind the passenger side of the facia, undo the retaining bolts to release the airbag from the crossmember, then release the locking clip and disconnect the passenger airbag wiring connector **(see illustration)**.

21 Unclip the trim panel from above the glovebox aperture and remove the facia retaining screw **(see illustrations)**.

22 Working your way along the facia, remove the remaining screws from the facia **(see illustrations)**.

23 Where fitted, unclip the tweeter speakers

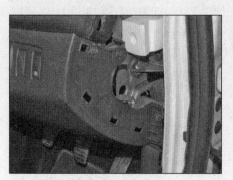

28.18a Undo the three screws...

28.18b ...and remove the lower trim panel

28.20 Passenger side airbag

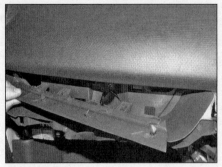

28.21a Unclip the trim panel...

28.21b ...and undo the retaining screw

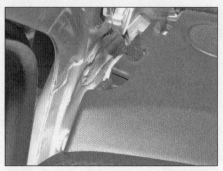

28.22a Remove the screws from the upper corners...

28.22b ...the four from the centre...

28.22c ...one to the left of the centre console...

28.22d ...and one to the right of the centre console

from the top of the facia and disconnect the wiring connector as they are removed **(see illustration)**.

24 Working above the card reader location, (where fitted) unclip and disconnect the door

28.23 Unclip and remove speaker – where fitted

28.30 Remove the support bracket

open/starting aerial sensor, and remove it from the facia **(see illustration)**.

25 Check around the facia to see if there is anything still connected, then make a note of the routing of the wiring and (with the help of

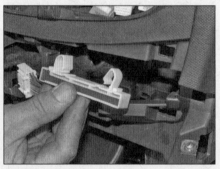

28.24 Unclip the door open/starting aerial from the facia

28.31a Remove the blanking grommet...

an assistant) remove the facia panel out of the vehicle via the passenger door. As the panel is removed, unclip the heater ducts and check for any wiring that is still connected.

26 If required, the steel crossmember can now be removed. With this removed the heater box can be easily be accessed.

27 Remove both front doors as described in Section 10. Also remove the steering column and the power steering motor as described in Chapter 10 Section 15.

28 Working around the crossmember, unclip and remove the multiple wiring clips. Feed the supply cables from the doors back through the A-pillar. Carefully work out which cables and connectors can be left on the crossmember and which ones need removal. Mark the position and take notes of the cables and their locations. Pay particular attention to the various earths.

29 Disconnect and remove the UCH (Unite Centrale Habitacle – commonly referred to as the 'body computer') from the left-hand side of the vehicle.

30 Undo the retaining bolts and remove the central support bracket from the crossmeber **(see illustration)**.

31 Remove the blanking plugs from the A-pillars to access the crossmember bolts **(see illustrations)**. These bolts are used to adjust the position of the crossmember therefore, before removing the bolts, measure the distance between the crossmember and the inner edge of the A-pillar. This will assist locating the crossmember when it is refitted.

32 Remove the crossmember side bolts **(see**

illustration) and with the help of an assistant remove the crossmember from the vehicle.

33 Refitting is a reversal of removal, noting the following points:

34 With the crossmember removed check the wiring for any damage. Also check the various plugs and connectors for any damage.

35 Position the crossmember according to the measurements taken on removal. This is critical to the alignment of all the other components.

36 Make sure all cable clips are refitted and check for any possibility of wires chafing and rubbing against the metalwork.

28.31b ...and remove the adjustable bolt

28.32 Remove the bolts. The central peg will support the crossmember

Chapter 12
Body electrical system

Contents

Degrees of difficulty

Easy, suitable for novice with little experience	**Fairly easy,** suitable for beginner with some experience	**Fairly difficult,** suitable for competent DIY mechanic	**Difficult,** suitable for experienced DIY mechanic	**Very difficult,** suitable for expert DIY or professional

Specifications

General

System type	12 volt, negative earth

Bulbs

Exterior lights	Wattage	Type
Direction indicator (orange-coloured)	21	PY21
Direction indicator side repeater	5	WY5
Foglight:		
Front	55	H11
Rear	21	P21
Headlight: *		
Halogen bulbs:		
Main beam	55	H1
Dipped beam	55	H7
Xenon bulbs:		
Main beam	55	H7
Dipped beam	37	D2S
Number plate light**	5	W5W
Reversing light	21	P21
Sidelight	5	W5W
Stop/tail light	21/5	P21/5

Interior lights	Wattage	Type
Courtesy lights:		
Wedge	5	W5W
Festoon	5	C5W
Glovebox illumination light	5	C5W
Luggage compartment light	5	C5W

Note: *As the headlights have plastic lenses, anti-UV type bulbs are used (the headlight may be damaged if any other type is used). Do not touch the glass of the bulbs, hold it by the base only.

Note: **Some models have festoon type bulbs.

Torque wrench setting	Nm	lbf ft
Passenger airbag securing bolts	8	6

1 General information and precautions

⚠️ *Warning: Before carrying out any work on the electrical system, read through the precautions given in 'Safety first!' at the beginning of this manual, and in Chapter 5A.*

1 The electrical system is of 12 volt negative earth type. Power for the lights and all electrical accessories is supplied by a lead-acid type battery, which is charged by the alternator.

2 This Chapter covers repair and service procedures for the various electrical components not associated with engine. Information on the battery, alternator and starter motor can be found in Chapter 5A.

3 It should be noted that, prior to working on any component in the electrical system, the battery negative terminal should first be disconnected, to prevent the possibility of electrical short-circuits and/or fires.

2 Electrical fault finding – general information

Note: *Refer to the precautions given in 'Safety first!' and at the beginning of Chapter 5A before starting work. The following tests relate to testing of the main electrical circuits, and should not be used to test delicate electronic circuits (such as anti-lock braking systems), particularly where an electronic control unit is used.*

General

1 A typical electrical circuit consists of an electrical component, any switches, relays, motors, fuses, fusible links or circuit breakers related to that component, and the wiring and connectors which link the component to both the battery and the chassis. To help to pinpoint a problem in an electrical circuit, wiring diagrams are included at the end of this Chapter.

2 Before attempting to diagnose an electrical fault, first study the appropriate wiring diagram, to obtain a more complete understanding of the components included in the particular circuit concerned. The possible sources of a fault can be narrowed down by noting whether other components related to the circuit are operating properly. If several components or circuits fail at one time, the problem is likely to be related to a shared fuse or earth connection.

3 Electrical problems usually stem from simple causes, such as loose or corroded connections, a faulty earth connection, a blown fuse, a melted fusible link, or a faulty relay (refer to Section 4 for details of testing relays). Visually inspect the condition of all fuses, wires and connections in a problem circuit before testing the components. Use the wiring diagrams to determine which terminal connections will need to be checked, in order to pinpoint the trouble-spot.

4 The basic tools required for electrical fault finding include a circuit tester or voltmeter (a 12 volt bulb with a set of test leads can also be used for certain tests); a self-powered test light (sometimes known as a continuity tester); an ohmmeter (to measure resistance); a battery and set of test leads; and a jumper wire, preferably with a circuit breaker or fuse incorporated, which can be used to bypass suspect wires or electrical components. Before attempting to locate a problem with test instruments, use the wiring diagram to determine where to make the connections.

5 To find the source of an intermittent wiring fault (usually due to a poor or dirty connection, or damaged wiring insulation), a 'wiggle' test can be performed on the wiring. This involves wiggling the wiring by hand, to see if the fault occurs as the wiring is moved. It should be possible to narrow down the source of the fault to a particular Section of wiring. This method of testing can be used in conjunction with any of the tests described in the following sub-Sections.

6 Apart from problems due to poor connections, two basic types of fault can occur in an electrical circuit – open-circuit, or short-circuit.

7 Open-circuit faults are caused by a break somewhere in the circuit, which prevents current from flowing. An open-circuit fault will prevent a component from working, but will not cause the relevant circuit fuse to blow.

8 Short-circuit faults are caused by a 'short' somewhere in the circuit, which allows the current flowing in the circuit to 'escape' along an alternative route, usually to earth.

Short-circuit faults are normally caused by a breakdown in wiring insulation, which allows a feed wire to touch either another wire, or an earthed component such as the bodyshell. A short-circuit fault will normally cause the relevant circuit fuse to blow.

Finding an open-circuit

9 To check for an open-circuit, connect one lead of a circuit tester or voltmeter to either the negative battery terminal or a known good earth.

10 Connect the other lead to a connector in the circuit being tested, preferably nearest to the battery or fuse.

11 Switch on the circuit, bearing in mind that some circuits are live only when the ignition switch is moved to a particular position.

12 If voltage is present (indicated either by the tester bulb lighting or a voltmeter reading, as applicable), this means that the section of the circuit between the relevant connector and the battery is problem-free.

13 Continue to check the remainder of the circuit in the same fashion.

14 When a point is reached at which no voltage is present, the problem must lie between that point and the previous test point with voltage. Most problems can be traced to a broken, corroded or loose connection.

Finding a short-circuit

15 To check for a short-circuit, first disconnect the load(s) from the circuit (loads are the components which draw current from a circuit, such as bulbs, motors, heating elements, etc).

16 Remove the relevant fuse from the circuit, and connect a circuit tester or voltmeter to the fuse connections.

17 Switch on the circuit, bearing in mind that some circuits are live only when the ignition switch is moved to a particular position.

18 If voltage is present (indicated either by the tester bulb lighting or a voltmeter reading, as applicable), this means that there is a short-circuit.

19 If no voltage is present, but the fuse still blows with the load(s) connected, this indicates an internal fault in the load(s).

Finding an earth fault

20 The battery negative terminal is connected to 'earth' – the metal of the engine/transmission unit and the car body – and most systems are wired so that they only receive a positive feed, the current returning via the metal of the car body. This means that the component mounting and the body form part of that circuit. Loose or corroded mountings can therefore cause a range of electrical faults, ranging from total failure of a circuit, to a puzzling partial fault. In particular, lights may shine dimly (especially when another circuit sharing the same earth point is in operation), motors (eg, wiper motors or the radiator cooling fan motor) may run slowly, and the operation of one circuit may have an apparently unrelated effect on another. Note that on many vehicles, earth

2.20a The earth (ground) connection to the transmission

2.20b Earth connections behind facia next to the fusebox

3.3a Release the securing clip...

3.3b ...and withdraw the fusebox

3.5 Unclip the fusebox cover

straps are used between certain components, such as the engine/transmission and the body, usually where there is no metal-to-metal contact between components, due to flexible rubber mountings, etc **(see illustrations)**.

21 To check whether a component is properly earthed, disconnect the battery, and connect one lead of an ohmmeter to a known good earth point. Connect the other lead to the wire or earth connection being tested. The resistance reading should be zero; if not, check the connection as follows.

22 If an earth connection is thought to be faulty, dismantle the connection, and clean back to bare metal both the bodyshell and the wire terminal or the component earth connection mating surface. Be careful to remove all traces of dirt and corrosion, then use a knife to trim away any paint, so that a clean metal-to-metal joint is made.

On reassembly, tighten the joint fasteners securely; if a wire terminal is being refitted, use serrated washers between the terminal and the bodyshell, to ensure a clean and secure connection. When the connection is remade, prevent the onset of corrosion in the future by applying a coat of petroleum jelly or silicone-based grease, or by spraying on (at regular intervals) a proprietary ignition sealer.

3 Fusebox – removal and refitting

Removal

Interior fusebox

1 Disconnect the battery negative lead as described in Chapter 5A Section 4.

2 Remove the glovebox, as described in Chapter 11 Section 28.

3 Release the securing clip and slide the fusebox from the facia crossmember bracket **(see illustrations)**.

4 Make a note of the connections, then disconnect the connectors from the rear of the fusebox to remove the fusebox completely from under the facia.

Engine compartment fusebox

5 Open the bonnet and unclip the cover from the top of the relay/fusebox **(see illustration)**.

6 Remove the plastic side panel, then release the locking clip and disconnect the wiring block connector **(see illustrations)**.

7 Release the securing clip and withdraw the relay section **(see illustrations)**.

8 Undo the retaining nut and disconnect the positive cable, then release the securing clip and withdraw the fuse block **(see illustrations)**.

3.6a Remove the side panel...

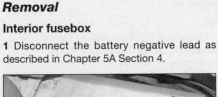

3.6b ...and disconnect the wiring block connector

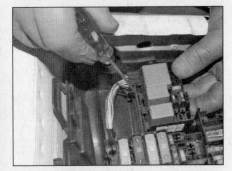

3.7a Release the securing clip...

3.7b ...and withdraw the relay block

3.8a Disconnect the positive cable...

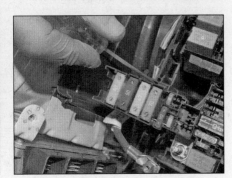

3.8b ...release the securing clip...

3.8c ...and withdraw the fuse block

3.9 Remove the last fuse/relay block

9 Release the securing clip and withdraw the last relay/fuse block (see illustration).

Refitting

10 Refitting is a reversal of removal.

4 Fuses and relays –
testing and renewal

Fuses

1 Fuses are designed to break a circuit when a predetermined current is reached, in order to protect components and wiring which could be damaged by excessive current flow. Any excessive current flow will be due to a fault in the circuit, usually a short-circuit (see Section 2).
2 The main fuses are located in the fusebox, behind a cover inside the glovebox.
3 For access to the fuses, open the glovebox and unclip the cover (see illustration).
4 A blown fuse can be recognised from its melted or broken wire.
5 To remove a fuse, first ensure that the relevant circuit is switched off.
6 Using the plastic tool provided on the inside of the fusebox cover, pull the fuse from its location (see illustrations).
7 Unusually spare fuses are not provided. We would recommend the purchase of an assortment of spare fuses.
8 Before renewing a blown fuse, trace and rectify the cause, and always use a fuse of the correct rating. Never substitute a fuse of a higher rating, or make temporary repairs using wire or metal foil; more serious damage, or even fire, could result.
9 Note that the fuses are colour-coded as follows. Refer to the wiring diagrams for details of the fuse ratings and the circuits protected.

Colour	Rating
Orange	5A
Red	10A
Blue	15A
Yellow	20A
Clear or white	25A
Green	30A

Relays

10 A relay is an electrically-operated switch, which is used for the following reasons.
a) A relay can switch a heavy current remotely from the circuit in which the current is flowing, therefore allowing the use of lighter gauge wiring and switch contacts.
b) A relay can receive more than one control input, unlike a mechanical switch.
c) A relay can have a 'timer' function – for example, the intermittent wiper relay.
11 Relays are located inside the vehicle, under the facia on the left-hand side. Remove the glovebox for access to them.
12 Other relays are located in the engine compartment switching and protection module located behind the left-hand headlight in the engine compartment.
13 Note that the UCH now performs many of the switching functions traditionally operated by mechanical relays.
14 If a circuit controlled by a relay develops a fault, and the relay is suspect, operate the circuit. If the relay is functioning, it should be possible to hear the relay click as it is energised. If this is the case, the fault lies with the components or wiring in the system. If the relay is not being energised, then either the relay is not receiving a switching voltage, or the relay itself is faulty (do not overlook the relay socket terminals when tracing faults). Testing is by the substitution of a known good unit, but be careful; while some relays are identical in appearance and in operation, others look similar, but perform different functions.

5 Electrical connectors

1 Most electrical connections on these vehicles are made with multiwire plastic connectors. The mating halves of many connectors are secured with locking clips molded into the plastic connector shells. The mating halves of some large connectors, such as some of those under the instrument panel, are held together by a bolt through the center of the connector.
2 To separate a connector with locking clips, use a small screwdriver to pry the clips apart carefully, then separate the connector halves. Pull only on the shell, never pull on the wiring harness, as you may damage the individual wires and terminals inside the connectors. Look at the connector closely before trying to separate the halves. Often the locking clips are engaged in a way that is not immediately clear. Additionally, many connectors have more than one set of clips.
3 Each pair of connector terminals has a male half and a female half. When you look at the end view of a connector in a diagram, be sure to understand whether the view shows the harness side or the component side of the connector. Connector halves are mirror images of each other, and a terminal shown on the right side end-view of one half will be on the left side end-view of the other half.

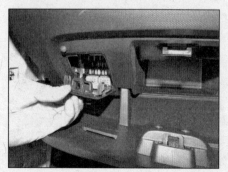

4.3 Fusebox location

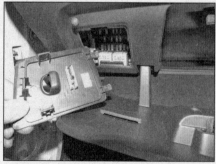

4.6a The fuse puller on inside of cover

4.6b Removing a fuse with the tool provided

5.5a Most electrical connectors have a single release tab that you depress to release the connector

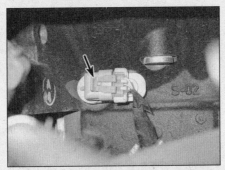

5.5b Some electrical connectors have a retaining tab which must be pried up to free the connector

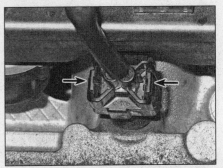

5.5c Some connectors have two release tabs that you must squeeze to release the connector

5.5d Some connectors use wire retainers that you squeeze to release the connector

5.5e Critical connectors often employ a sliding lock (1) that you must pull out before you can depress the release tab (2)

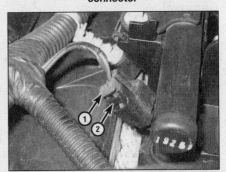

5.5f Here's another sliding-lock style connector, with the lock (1) and the release tab (2) on the side of the connector

4 It is often necessary to take circuit voltage measurements with a connector connected. Whenever possible, carefully insert a small straight pin (not your meter probe) into the rear of the connector shell to contact the terminal inside, then clip your meter lead to the pin. This kind of connection is called "backprobing." When inserting a test probe into a terminal, be careful not to distort the terminal opening. Doing so can lead to a poor connection and corrosion at that terminal later. Using the small straight pin instead of a meter probe results in less chance of deforming the terminal connector. "T" pins are a good choice as temporary meter connections. They allow for a larger surface area to attach the meter leads too.

5 Typical electrical connectors:

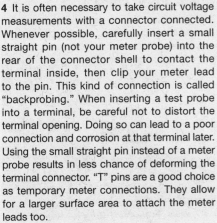
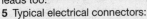

5.5g On some connectors the lock (1) must be pulled out to the side and removed before you can lift the release tab (2)

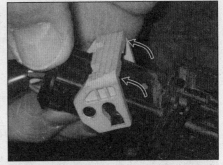

5.5h Some critical connectors, like the multi-pin connectors at the Electronic Control Module employ pivoting locks that must be flipped open

6 UCH (body systems controller) – general information, removal and refitting

General information

1 The UCH (Unite Centrale Habitacle) is located under the left-hand side of the facia panel, next to the fusebox. The UCH is more commonly know as the body control computer. It performs many of the tasks traditionally performed by separate components and relays.

2 The UCH is programmed to each individual vehicle. The unit cannot be simply swapped from vehicle to vehicle. It is normal practise (assuming the diagnostic tool can communicate with the UCH) for the software programmed onto the existing UCH to be downloaded to the diagnostic tool and then uploaded to the new UCH. New units are always supplied with no software loaded.

3 For models covered in this manual, there are two types of UCH fitted, depending on the type of key system fitted. Amongst other systems, the UCH controls:

a) Indicators and hazard warning lights.
b) Front and rear wipers.
c) Door and window controls.
d) Door locking when driving (unlocking on impact).
e) Door opening indicator light.
f) Central door locking indicator light.
g) Timed courtesy lighting.
h) Radio frequency remote control.
i) One touch windows.
j) Engine immobiliser.
k) Positive after ignition supply/starter control.
l) Passenger compartment horn (alarm).
m) Alarm connections.
n) Heated rear screen timing.
o) Daytime running lights.
p) Light controls.
q) Light sensors.
r) Headlight washer controls.
s) Rain sensors.
t) Screen washer pump.
u) Tailgate locking.

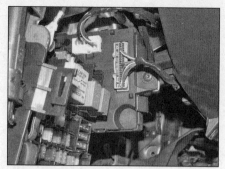

6.7 Location of UCH – control unit

Removal

4 Disconnect the battery negative lead as described in Chapter 5A Section 4.
5 Remove the passenger glovebox as described in Chapter 11 Section 28.
6 Release the securing clip and move the fusebox to one side, as described in Section 4.
7 Undo the retaining screw, disconnect the electrical connectors and withdraw the control unit from the support bracket **(see illustration)**.

Refitting

8 Refitting is a reversal of removal, bearing in mind the following points.
9 Make sure that the UCH is located correctly in the mounting bracket behind the facia panel.
10 Ensure that the wiring is secure and routed correctly.
11 The new UCH must be programmed.

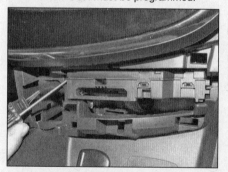

7.2a Release the retaining clips...

7.9 Remove the stop/start switch

---

7 Switches –
removal and refitting

Card reader

1 Unclip the trim panel from over the card reader and below the heater control panel **(see illustration)**. Disconnect the wiring connector from the stop/start switch, as the panel is removed.
2 Release the retaining clips and withdraw the key card reader from the facia **(see illustrations)**. Disconnect the wiring connector from the unit as it is removed.
3 Refitting is a reversal of removal.

Protection and switching unit

4 Disconnect the battery negative lead as described in Chapter 5A Section 4.
5 Remove the passenger glovebox as described in Chapter 11 Section 28.
6 Undo the retaining screw, disconnect the electrical connectors and withdraw the control unit from the support bracket **(see illustration)**.
7 Refitting is a reversal of removal.

Stop/start switch

8 Unclip the trim panel from over the card reader and below the heater control panel **(see illustration 7.1)**.
9 Disconnect the wiring connector, press the locating tabs at the rear and remove the switch **(see illustration)**.
10 Refitting is a reversal of removal.

7.2b ...and withdraw the key card reader

7.13a Disconnect the wiring connectors from the top...

7.1 Unclip the trim panel

Integrated column switch

11 Disconnect the battery negative lead and then remove the steering wheel as described in Chapter 10 Section 14.
12 Remove the steering column shrouds as described in Chapter 11 Section 26.
13 To remove the complete unit, disconnect the wiring connectors from the rear of the unit, then slacken the clamp securing screw and withdraw the complete integrated column switches from the top of the steering column **(see illustrations)**. Do not allow the airbag clock spring to rotate at any point.
14 Refitting is a reversal of removal.

Audio player control

15 Disconnect the battery negative lead and then remove the steering wheel as described in Chapter 10 Section 14.

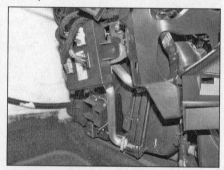

7.6 Location of protection and switching control unit

7.13b ...and bottom of the switch assembly...

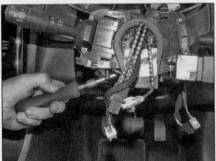

7.13c ...then slacken the clamp securing screw...

7.13d ...and slide the switch assembly from the column

7.17 Disconnect the wiring plugs from the switch

16 Remove the steering column shrouds as described in Chapter 11 Section 28.
17 Disconnect the wiring plug connector from the switch (see illustration).
18 Slacken and remove the retaining screw, then slide the audio switch from the mounting bracket (see illustration).
19 Refitting is a reversal of removal.

Lighting control switch

20 Disconnect the battery negative lead and then remove the steering wheel as described in Chapter 10 Section 14.
21 Remove the steering column shrouds as described in Chapter 11 Section 28.
22 Disconnect the wiring plug connector from the rear of the switch (see illustration).
23 Slacken and remove the two retaining screws, then slide the light switch from the mounting bracket (see illustrations).
24 Refitting is a reversal of removal.

Wiper control switch

25 Disconnect the battery negative lead and then remove the steering wheel as described in Chapter 10 Section 14.
26 Remove the steering column shrouds as described in Chapter 11 Section 28.
27 Disconnect the wiring plug connector from the rear of the switch (see illustration).
28 Slacken and remove the two retaining screws, then slide the wiper switch from the mounting bracket (see illustrations).
29 Refitting is a reversal of removal.

7.18 Undo the screw and remove the switch

Heater-related switches

30 These switches are built into the heater control panel. Remove the panel as described in Chapter 3 Section 12.

7.23a Undo the screws...

7.28a Undo the screws...

7.22 Disconnect the wiring plugs from the switch

Headlight aim adjustment control

31 Remove the lower trim section from below the steering column as described in Chapter 11, Section 28.

7.23b ...and remove the switch

7.28b ...and remove the switch

7.27 Disconnect the wiring plugs from the switch

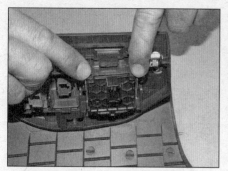

7.32a Release the retaining clips...

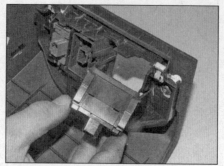

7.32b ...then remove the switch

7.39a Carefully lever the trim...

7.39b ...to release the four retaining clips

7.42 Remove the switch

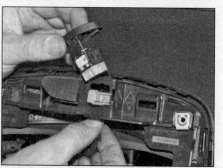

7.44 Remove the door locking switch

32 Disconnect the wiring from the trim panel as it is removed, then with the panel on the bench, release the retaining clips at the rear and remove the switch (see illustrations).
33 Refitting is a reversal of removal.

Instrument panel illumination dimmer switch

34 The switch (where fitted) is located in the same switch assembly as the headlight aim adjustment control. To remove the switch, proceed as described in paragraphs 31 and 32.

Electric window switches

35 The switches are incorporated into the interior door handles. For the removal procedure, refer to refer to Chapter 11, Section 16.

Courtesy light switches

36 The switches are incorporated into the door catch mechanism and are removed with

the door locks as described in Chapter 11, Section 11.
37 A fault with the switch will require the renewal of the door catch assembly. Always check the courtesy light bulbs before condemning the switches.
38 Suitable diagnostic equipment can be used to check the operation of the switches.

Hazard warning light switch

39 Carefully unclip the facia centre trim panel, there are two retaining clips at the top and two at the bottom (see illustrations).
40 Remove the lower centre trim section as described in Chapter 11, Section 28.
41 If required to access the rear of the switches, remove the audio unit as described in Section 23 of this Chapter.
42 Compress the retaining tabs and release the switch from the panel (see illustration).
43 Refitting is a reversal of removal.

Door locking switch

44 The door locking switch is located next to the hazard warning switch and is removed in a similar manner (see illustration).

Heated rear window switch

45 These switches are built into the heater control panel. Remove the panel as described in Chapter 3 Section 12.

Fuel filler cover switch

46 Remove the right-hand rear quarter panel as described in Chapter 11 Section 26.
47 Disconnect the wiring, release the retaining clip and remove the fuel flap locking motor (see illustration).
48 In the event of an electrical failure of the switch the motor can be operated manually by pulling up on the lever (see illustration).

8 Bulbs (exterior lights) – renewal

General

1 Whenever a bulb is renewed, note the following points.
a) Disconnect the battery negative lead, or at least make sure that the lighting circuit is switched off, before starting work.
b) Remember that if the light has recently been in use, the bulb may be extremely hot.
c) Always check the bulb contacts and/or holder (as applicable). Ensure that there

7.47 Location of fuel flap locking motor

7.48 Operate lever manually – if required

is clean metal-to-metal contact between the bulb contacts and the contacts in the holder, and/or the holder and the wiring plug. Clean off any corrosion or dirt before fitting a new bulb.

d) Ensure that the new bulb is of the correct rating and that it is completely clean before fitting; this applies particularly to headlight bulbs.

e) Some headlights may vary slightly, depending on model. Check the Specifications at the beginning of the Chapter for recommended bulb type. The headlight lenses are plastic and may melt if the correct bulbs are not fitted.

Halogen headlight

Removal

Note: If required, to make access to the bulbs easier, remove the headlight unit, as described in Section 10.

2 For the main beam bulb, remove the seal and disconnect the wiring connector from the rear of the headlight bulb. Release the bulb retaining spring clip and remove the bulb, without touching the glass **(see illustrations)**.

3 For the dipped beam bulb, follow the same procedure as the main beam bulb **(see illustrations)**. Note that on some models the wiring plug is also the bulb retainer.

Refitting

4 When handling the new bulb, use a tissue or clean cloth to avoid touching the glass with the fingers; moisture and grease from the skin can cause blackening and rapid failure of this type of bulb.

5 Refitting is a reversal of removal, ensuring that the seal is in good condition and is correctly fitted.

Xenon headlight

⚠️ **Warning: Before carrying out any operations on xenon headlight units, it is recommended that protective gloves and safety glasses are worn. It is essential that the wiring connectors are disconnected from the rear of the headlight unit, then wait until the module and bulbs have cooled down before removal. DO NOT switch the headlights on with the bulb removed as it is harmful to the eyes.**

Removal

6 Remove the headlight unit as described in Section 10.

7 Unclip the rubber cover from the rear of the headlight unit.

8 Turn the high voltage unit on the rear of the bulb anti-clockwise about an eighth of a turn and withdraw it from the bulb.

9 Turn the bulb locking ring anti-clockwise about an eighth of a turn and withdraw the bulb from the light unit. The external conductor of the bulb is fragile, take care not to damage or knock it.

Refitting

10 When handling the new bulb, use a tissue or clean cloth to avoid touching the glass with the fingers; moisture and grease from the skin

can cause blackening and rapid failure of this type of bulb.

11 Refitting is a reversal of removal, ensuring that the seal is in good condition and is correctly fitted.

8.2a Remove the seal...

8.2b ...disconnect the wiring plug...

8.2c ...then release the securing clip...

8.2d ...and remove the bulb

8.3a For the dipped beam, remove the seal...

8.3b ...disconnect the wiring connector...

8.3c ...then release the spring clip...

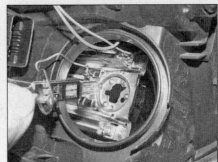

8.3d ...and remove the bulb

8.12a Remove the seal...

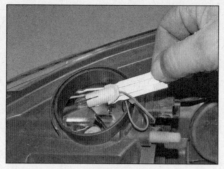

8.12b ...and withdraw the sidelight bulb holder

8.13 Pull the wedge style bulb free

8.15 Twist the bulbholder free

8.16 Remove the bulb/holder from the twist cap

Refitting

14 Refitting is a reversal of removal, ensuring that the seal is in good condition and is correctly fitted.

Indicator

Removal

15 The bulb can just about be removed with the headlight in place. Working in the engine compartment, twist the bulbholder anti-clockwise, and remove it from the rear of the indicator assembly **(see illustration)**.

16 The bulb is part of the plastic holder, remove the bulb/holder from the twist cap **(see illustration)**.

Refitting

17 Refitting is a reversal of removal.

Indicator side repeater

Removal

18 Remove the door mirror and rear shell trim, as described in Chapter 11 Section 17.

19 Unclip the repeater from the mirror housing, then pull the bulbholder from the rear of the light unit **(see illustrations)**.

20 The bulb is a push-fit in the bulbholder **(see illustration)**.

Refitting

21 Refitting is a reversal of removal.

Front foglight

Removal

22 Jack up the front of the car, and support it on axle stands (see *Jacking and vehicle support*). Remove the appropriate roadwheel and then remove the front part of the inner wing liner.

23 Disconnect the wiring connector, then twist the bulbholder and remove it from the rear of the foglight **(see illustrations)**.

Refitting

24 When handling the new bulb, use a tissue or clean cloth to avoid touching the glass with the fingers; moisture and grease from the skin can cause blackening and rapid failure of this type of bulb. If the glass is accidentally touched, wipe it clean using methylated spirits.

Sidelight

Removal

12 Remove the sealing ring from the top of the headlight unit, then reach inside and withdraw the bulbholder from the rear of the headlight assembly **(see illustrations)**.

13 The bulb is a push-fit (capless) in the bulbholder **(see illustration)**.

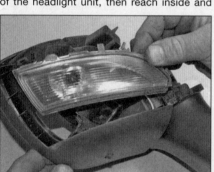

8.19a Unclip the repeater from the mirror...

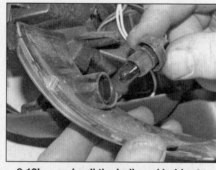

8.19b ...and pull the bulb and holder to remove

8.20 Pull the wedge style bulb free from the holder

8.23a Disconnect the wiring...

8.23b ...and remove the foglight bulb

8.27 Release the locking clips to remove bulbholder

8.28 Remove the appropriate bulb

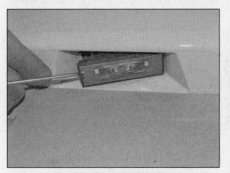
8.31 Unclip the light unit

8.32 Remove the lens

8.33 Pull free the wedge style bulb

25 Refitting is a reversal of removal.

Rear light bulbs

Removal

26 Open the tailgate, and remove the rear light cluster as described in Section 10.
27 Release the securing clips outwards, and pull the bulbholder from the rear of the light cluster (see illustration).
28 The bulbs are a bayonet fit in their holders, carefully push the bulb in slightly and turn anti-clockwise to remove (see illustration).

Refitting

29 Refitting is a reversal of removal, making sure the locating pegs are aligned correctly.

High-level stop-light

30 Remove the light as described in Section 10. The bulbs are of the LED type and part of the complete light unit and cannot be replaced separately.

Number plate light

Removal

31 Using a screwdriver, carefully prise the number plate light assembly from its location in the bumper (see illustration).
32 Carefully unclip the lens from the light assembly (see illustration).
33 The bulb is a push-fit in the holder (see illustration).

Refitting

34 Refitting is a reversal of removal.

Reversing light

Removal

35 Open the tailgate and unclip the small trim panel from the left-hand end of the tailgate trim (see illustration).
36 Twist the bulb holder and withdraw it from the rear of the light unit (see illustration).
37 The bulbs are a bayonet fit in their holders, carefully push the bulb in slightly and turn anti-clockwise to remove.

Refitting

38 Refitting is a reversal of removal.

Rear foglight

39 The rear foglight bulb is the same procedure as the reversing light bulb removal, see paragraphs 35 to 37. Open the tailgate and unclip the small trim panel from the right-hand end of the tailgate trim.

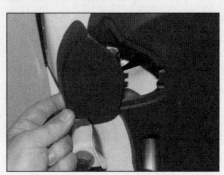
8.35 Unclip the trim panel...

Day time running lights

40 Remove the light as described in Section 10. The bulbs are of the LED type and part of the complete light unit and cannot be replaced separately.

9 Bulbs (interior lights) – renewal

General

1 Refer to Section 8, paragraph 1.

Courtesy light

2 Remove the courtesy light, as described in Section 11.
3 Unclip the lens from the light unit, then pull

8.36 ..and remove the bulb holder

9.3a Prise free the lens...

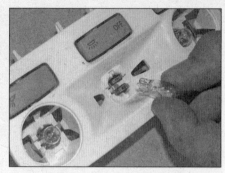

9.3b ...and remove the bulb

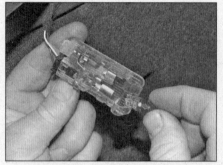

9.6 Pull the bulb from the light unit

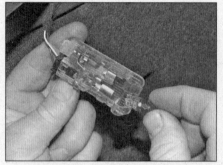

9.10 Remove the bulb and holder from the control panel

free the appropriate capless bulb from the light unit **(see illustrations)**.

4 Refitting is a reversal of removal.

Luggage compartment light

5 Remove the luggage compartment light unit, as described in Section 11.

10.2 Release the filler neck from the headlight unit

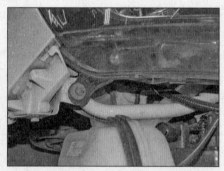

10.3 Remove the lower nut

10.4a Remove the upper rear mounting nut...

10.4b ...and the upper front mounting bolt

6 Pull free the capless bulb from the light unit **(see illustration)**.

7 Refitting is a reversal of removal.

Instrument panel and warning lights

8 The bulbs cannot be renewed from the instrument panel, as they are soldered LEDs.

Heater control panel illumination

9 Remove the heater control panel, as described in Chapter 3 Section 12.

10 Using a pair of long nose pliers, twist the bulb holder anti-clockwise and remove it from the rear of the control panel **(see illustration)**.

10 Exterior light units – removal and refitting

Note: *Make sure the ignition switch and light switches are in the off position before disconnecting the wiring connectors. Where applicable, disconnect the battery negative lead.*

Headlight/indicator unit

⚠ *Warning: Before carrying out any operations on xenon headlight units, it is recommended that protective gloves and safety glasses are worn. It is essential that the wiring connectors are disconnected from the rear of the headlight unit, then wait until the module and bulbs have cooled down before removal. DO NOT switch the headlights on with the bulb removed as it is harmful to the eyes.*

Removal

1 Jack up the front of the car, and support it on axle stands (see *Jacking and vehicle support*). Remove the front bumper as described in Chapter 11, Section 6.

2 When removing the drivers side headlight unit, release the securing clip and disconnect the screen washer filler neck, from the rear of the headlight unit **(see illustration)**.

3 Remove the lower mounting nut from the side of the headlight **(see illustration)**.

4 Unscrew the upper securing nut at the rear of the headlight, and the bolt at the front of the headlight **(see illustrations)**.

5 Release the locking clips and disconnect the wiring plugs from the rear of the headlight unit **(see illustrations)**.

6 Withdraw the headlight unit from the vehicle taking care not to damage the light unit or wing panel.

Refitting

7 Refitting is a reversal of removal.

Beam alignment

8 On completion, the headlight beam alignment should be checked, ideally using optical setting equipment. A Renault dealer or a suitably-equipped garage should carry

10.5a Release the locking clips...

10.5b ...and disconnect the upper and lower wiring plugs

10.8 Headlight manual adjusters

10.13a Disconnect the wiring connector...

10.13b ...then undo the two foglight retaining screws

10.14 Adjusting the foglight

out this check. All approved MOT stations will also have the necessary equipment. The beam alignment is adjusted using the two screws provided on the light unit (see illustration).

Indicator side repeater

Removal

9 Remove the door mirror glass and rear shell trim, as described in Chapter 11 Section 17.
10 Unclip the repeater from the mirror housing, then pull the bulbholder from the rear of the light unit (see illustrations 8.19a and 18.9b).

Refitting

11 Refitting is a reversal of removal.

Front foglight

Removal

12 Jack up the front of the car, and support

it on axle stands (see *Jacking and vehicle support*) and remove the appropriate roadwheel. Remove the inner wing liner.
13 Disconnect the wiring plug from the rear of the foglight. Undo the two mounting screws and remove the light from the bumper (see illustrations).

Refitting

14 Refitting is a reversal of removal. If necessary, the vertical alignment of the beam can be adjusted by turning the adjustment screw from under the bumper (see illustration).

Rear light cluster

Removal

15 Open the tailgate, and unscrew the two screws on the inside edge of the light unit (see illustration).

16 Withdraw the light cluster from the car, carefully pull the outer edge of the light back to release the locating peg, then disconnect the wiring plug (see illustrations).

Refitting

17 Refitting is a reversal of removal, bearing in mind the following point.
18 Ensure that the locating lug is correctly engaged with the corresponding hole in the body.

High-level stop-light

Removal

19 Open the tailgate, and remove the two retaining screws at each side of the tailgate that secure the ends of the tailgate spoiler (see illustration).
20 Undo the tailgate spoiler retaining bolts,

10.15 Remove the two retaining screws

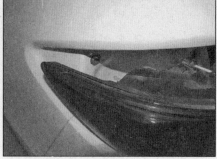

10.16a Note the position of the locating lug at the rear of the light unit...

10.16b ...and then disconnect the wiring plugs

10.19 Remove the retaining screws

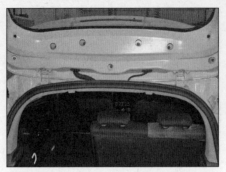

10.20 Remove the spoiler retaining bolts through the access holes

10.21a Withdraw the spoiler...

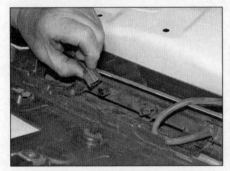

10.21b ...disconnect the wiring connector...

10.21c ...and the washer pipe

23 If required, unclip the washer jet from the end of the high level brake light unit (see illustration).

Refitting

24 Refitting is a reversal of removal.

Number plate light

Removal

25 Using a screwdriver, carefully prise the appropriate number plate light assembly from its location in the bumper. Disconnect the wiring connector (see illustrations).

Refitting

26 Refitting is a reversal of removal.

Reversing light

Removal

27 Open the tailgate and unclip the small trim panel from the left-hand end of the tailgate trim (see illustration 8.35).

through the access holes in the upper edge of the tailgate (see illustration).

21 Withdraw the spoiler from the outside of the tailgate, disconnecting the wiring connector and the rear screenwasher

pipe from the high level brake light (see illustrations).

22 Undo the two retaining screws and release the high-level brake light from the spoiler (see illustrations).

10.22a Undo the two retaining screws...

10.22b ...and remove the light unit

10.23 Unclip the washer jet from the light unit

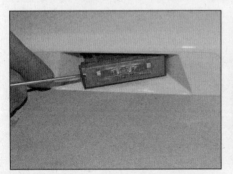

10.25a Prise the number plate light free...

10.25b ...and disconnect the wiring plug

10.28 Remove the light unit

28 Undo the retaining nut and withdraw the light unit from the outside of the tailgate **(see illustration)**.

Refitting

29 Refitting is a reversal of removal.

Rear foglight

30 The rear foglight light unit is the same procedure as the reversing light unit removal, see paragraphs 27 to 29. Open the tailgate and unclip the small trim panel from the right-hand end of the tailgate trim.

Day time running lights

Removal

31 Remove the front bumper, as described in Chapter 11 Section 6.

32 Disconnect the wiring plug from the rear of the light unit. Undo the three mounting

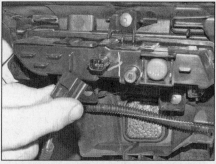
10.32a Disconnect the wiring connector…

screws and remove the light from the bumper **(see illustrations)**.

Refitting

33 Refitting is a reversal of removal.

10.32b …then undo the three retaining screws

11 Interior light units – removal and refitting

Courtesy light

1 Prise down the rear of the console to unclip it from the roof panel, then disconnect the wiring connectors and remove it, it will be necessary to trace the wiring to release one of the connectors **(see illustrations)**.

2 Release the retaining clips and unclip the light unit from the roof console **(see illustrations)**.

3 Refitting is a reversal of removal.

Luggage compartment light

4 Prise the light assembly from its location in the luggage compartment side trim panel **(see illustration)**.

5 Disconnect the wiring plug as the light is withdrawn **(see illustration)**.

6 Refitting is a reversal of removal.

12 Headlight aim adjustment components – removal and refitting

Warning: Before carrying out any operations on xenon headlight units, it is recommended that protective gloves and safety glasses are worn. It is essential that the wiring connectors are disconnected from the rear of the headlight unit, then wait

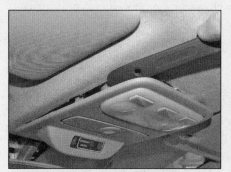
11.1a Unclip the console…

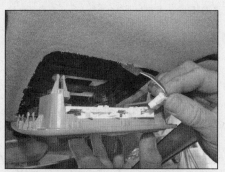
11.1b …disconnect the wiring plugs…

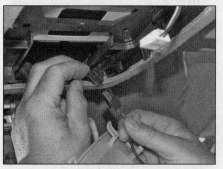
11.1c …and trace wiring to release one of the connectors

11.2a Release the securing clips…

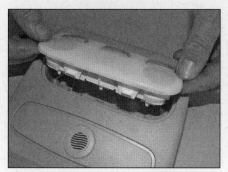
11.2b …and remove the light unit

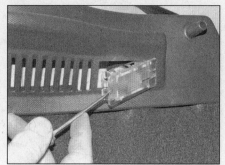
11.4 Prise out the light unit

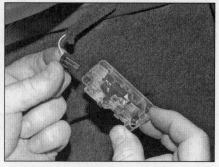
11.5 Release the light and disconnect the wiring plug

13.2 Release the cover from the facia

until the module and bulbs have cooled down before removal. DO NOT switch the headlights on with the bulb removed as it is harmful to the eyes.

1 Accurate adjustment of the headlight beam is only possible using optical beam-setting equipment, and this work should therefore be carried out by a Renault dealer or suitably-equipped workshop. All MOT test centres will have the equipment.

2 To make a temporary adjustment of the headlights, position the vehicle on a level surface 10 metres from a wall. The tyres must all be at the correct pressure, the fuel tank half-full, and a person be sitting in the driver's seat. Turn on the ignition, and check that, where fitted, the manual adjustment inside the vehicle is set at 0. Measure the distance from the ground to the cross in the centre of the headlight, then deduct 5.0 cm for models with halogen lights and 7.5 cm for models with xenon lights. Draw a mark on the wall at this height, then adjust the headlight beam centre point onto this mark by turning the adjustment screws on the rear of the headlight unit.

3 All models (except those with xenon headlights) have a headlight beam manual adjustment control, which allows the aim of the headlights to be adjusted to compensate for variation in the vehicle's payload. The aim is altered by means of facia-mounted switch which controls electric adjuster motors located in the rear of the headlight assemblies.

4 Models with xenon headlights have an automatic levelling system. If a fault occurs in the system, a warning light will show up on the instrument panel, and the headlights will be angled down to avoid dazzling oncoming traffic. If this happens, the driving speed must be adjusted accordingly to allow for decreased visibility.

Xenon headlight module

Note: *If the module is to be renewed, it will require programming by a Renault dealer or a garage equipped with a suitable diagnostic tool.*

Removal

5 Remove the headlight unit as described in Section 10.

6 Undo the control unit by depressing the clip and rotating the adjuster a quarter turn. Release it from the balljoint.

7 Carefully withdraw the module from the headlight unit.

Refitting

8 Refitting is a reversal of removal. Refer to Section 10 for refitting the headlight unit.

High voltage unit

9 Remove the headlight from the vehicle as described in Section 10.

10 Remove the mounting bolts and carefully disconnect the wiring plug.

11 Remove the high voltage unit.

Xenon headlight control unit

Note: *If the control unit is to be renewed, it will require programming by a Renault dealer or a garage equipped with a suitable diagnostic tool.*

12 The xenon control unit is located under the left-hand front wing. Disconnect the battery negative lead, and position the lead away from the battery (Chapter 5A Section 4).

13 Remove the front bumper as described in Chapter 11, Section 6.

14 Disconnect the wiring, undo the bolts and remove the control unit from the vehicle.

Refitting

15 Refitting is a reversal of removal.

Xenon headlight level sensors

16 Level sensors are fitted to the front anti-roll bar and the rear axle. These form an integral part of the headlight adjustment system for the xenon headlights.

17 To remove the rear sensor, jack up the rear of the car, and support it on axle stands (see *Jacking and vehicle support*). Disconnect the wiring and then unbolt and remove the sensor.

18 To remove the front sensor, jack up the front of the car, and support it on axle stands (see *Jacking and vehicle support*). Disconnect the wiring and then unbolt and remove the sensor.

19 If either sensor is removed or disturbed, the system must be adjusted and calibrated using suitable diagnostic equipment. At the time of writing only the Renault Clip diagnostic tool could perform this operation.

13 Instrument panel – removal and refitting

Note: *New instrument panels will require programming with suitable diagnostic equipment.*

Removal

1 Disconnect the battery negative lead as described in Chapter 5A Section 4.

2 Pull the instrument panel cover away from the facia to release the locating lugs **(see illustration)**.

3 Undo the two retaining screws, then withdraw the instrument panel from the facia by releasing the lower locating pegs **(see illustrations)**.

4 Disconnect the wiring and remove the instrument panel **(see illustration)**.

Refitting

5 Refitting is a reversal of removal, ensuring that all wiring plugs are securely reconnected.

14 Instrument panel components – general information

1 Depending on model specification, the instrument panel has the following functions:
a) *Electronic speedometer.*
b) *Rev counter (tachometer).*
c) *Fuel gauge.*
d) *Engine coolant temperature gauge.*
e) *Various warning light illuminations.*

13.3a Undo the two retaining screws...

13.3b ...and release the lower locating pegs

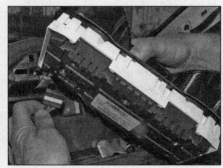

13.4 Disconnect the wiring plug

16.5 Unclip the sensor from the housing

17.3a Release the securing clips at the rear...

17.3b ...and withdraw the power socket

f) *Automatic transmission display.*
g) *Display for total mileage, trip mileage, oil level and on-board computer (ADAC).*
h) *Clock.*
i) *Trip reset button.*

2 The instrument panel is a sealed unit and the only part that can be renewed is the instrument glass. If any other components are faulty, the entire instrument panel has to be renewed.
3 To remove the instrument panel illumination bulbs, see Section 9.

15 Clock – general information

1 The clock is located in the instrument panel, the instrument panel is a sealed unit and if faulty must be renewed as a complete unit.
2 To remove the instrument panel, refer to Section 13.

16 Outside air temperature display components – removal and refitting

Removal

1 The sensor is behind the cover of the driver's side mirror.
2 Disconnect the battery negative lead as described in Chapter 5A Section 4.
3 Remove the mirror glass and rear shell trim cover, as described in Chapter 11 Section 17.

4 Remove the indicator repeater from the rear of the mirror housing, as described in Section 10.
5 Unclip and then remove the sensor from the lower part of the housing (see illustration). Note that the sensor does not have a wiring plug. The wiring loom must to cut to remove it.

Refitting

6 Replacement sensors are supplied with 'fly leads'. These must be connected to the vehicle wiring loom, either by soldering or by using crimp type connectors. The remainder of refitting is a reversal of removal.

17 Power outlet – removal and refitting

Removal

1 Disconnect the battery negative lead as described in Chapter 5A Section 4.
2 Remove the rear section of the centre console, as described in Chapter 11, Section 27.
3 Disconnect the wiring, release the securing clips at the rear of the console and withdraw the socket (see illustrations).

Refitting

4 Refitting is a reversal of removal.

18 Horn – removal and refitting

Removal

1 The horn is located behind the front bumper cover bolted to the front crossmember. Some models may have twin horns fitted.
2 Disconnect the battery negative lead as described in Chapter 5A Section 4.
3 To gain access to the horn, remove the front bumper as described in Chapter 11, Section 6.
4 Disconnect the wiring connector from the horn, then unscrew the securing nut and remove the horn from its mounting bracket (see illustration).

Refitting

5 Refitting is a reversal of removal.

19 Wiper arms – removal and refitting

Removal

1 The wiper motor should be in the parked position before removing the wiper arm. There are dots/markings on the screen for the position of the blade on the glass, as a guide to refitting (see illustrations).
2 If both windscreen wiper arms are to be

18.4 Location of the horn

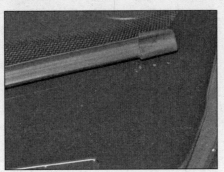
19.1a Markings on the left-hand side...

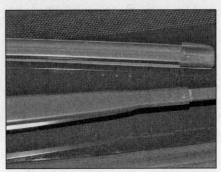
19.1b ...and centre of the windscreen

19.3a Prise the cap off...

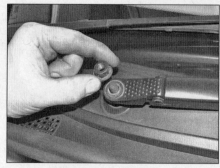

19.3b ...and remove the nut

19.4a Remove the wiper arm...

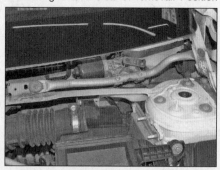

19.4b ...using a puller, if required

removed, identify them so that they can be refitted in their original positions (the arms are of different lengths).

3 Unclip the plastic cap, and remove the nut securing the arm to the spindle (see illustrations).

4 Pull or prise the arm from the spindle, using a puller if necessary (see illustrations). Take care not to damage the trim or paintwork.

Refitting

5 Refitting is a reversal of removal. Position the arms so that the blades align with the dots/ markings in the windscreen, as noted on removal.

20 Windscreen wiper motor and linkage – removal and refitting

Removal

1 Make sure that the wipers arms are in the parked position.
2 Disconnect the battery negative lead as described in Chapter 5A Section 4.
3 Remove the windscreen wiper arms, as described in Section 19.
4 Remove the windscreen cowl panels, as described in Chapter 11, Section 7.
5 Prise the linkage rod from the ball joint on the wiper motor spindle arm, and move the linkage rod to one side (see illustration).
6 Undo the two mounting bolts and withdraw the wiper motor and mounting bracket out from the passenger side of the scuttle panel. As the motor is withdrawn, disconnect he wiring connector from the end of the motor (see illustrations).
7 Undo the two linkage mounting bolts and remove the wiper arm spindles from the drivers side of the scuttle panel (see illustrations).

Refitting

8 Refitting is a reversal of removal, bearing in mind the following points.
9 Ensure that the locating peg on the rear of the wiper motor is aligned with the slot in the bulkhead (see illustration).

20.5 Carefully prise off the linkage rod

20.6a Undo the two mounting bolts to remove motor...

20.6b ...then disconnect the wiring connector

20.7a Undo the outer mounting bolt...

20.7b ...and inner mounting bolt to remove linkage

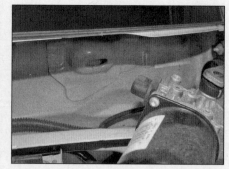

20.9 Align the locating peg on the rear of the motor

10 Refit the windscreen cowl panels, with reference to Chapter 11 Section 7.
11 Refit the windscreen wiper arms with reference to Section 19.

21 Tailgate wiper motor and linkage – removal and refitting

Removal

1 Disconnect the battery negative lead as described in Chapter 5A Section 4.
2 Mark the wiper arm position on the tailgate glass with masking tape and then remove the arm.
3 Unclip plastic cover from the wiper arm, undo the retaining nut and remove the wiper blade **(see illustrations)**.
4 Open the tailgate, and remove the interior trim as described in Chapter 11, Section 26.
5 Disconnect the wiper motor wiring plug **(see illustration)**.
6 The motor is held in place with three rivets **(see illustration)**. Drill out the rivets and remove the wiper motor.

Refitting

7 Refitting is a reversal of removal, but make sure that suitable rivets are available, as these are special size rivets..

22 Windscreen/tailgate washer system components – removal and refitting

Fluid reservoir

Removal

1 Disconnect the battery negative lead as described in Chapter 5A Section 4.
2 Jack up the front of the car, and support it on axle stands (see *Jacking and vehicle support*). Remove the right-hand roadwheel and wing liner.
3 Remove the front bumper (Chapter 11, Section 6) and the right-hand headlight as described in Section 10 of this Chapter.
4 Disconnect the wiring plug from the washer pump **(see illustration)**. Have a clean container ready and then remove the washer pipes.

21.3a Unclip the cover, then undo the nut...

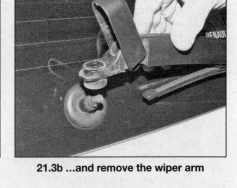
21.3b ...and remove the wiper arm

21.5 Disconnect the wiring connector

21.6 The rivets will need to be drilled out

5 Pull free the filler neck, and then remove the single retaining bolt **(see illustration)**.
6 Remove the reservoir from the inner wing.

Refitting

7 Refitting is a reversal of removal.

22.4 Disconnect the wiring plug

Fluid pump

Removal

8 The pump can be removed without removing the reservoir.
9 Carefully disconnect the washer hoses and

22.5 Remove the single bolt

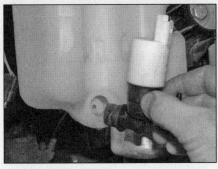
22.9a Pull the washer pump out of the reservoir

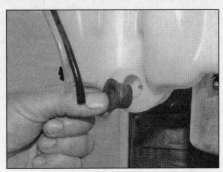
22.9b If the rubber grommet comes free...

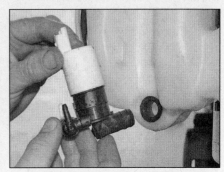
22.9c ...refit it before the pump

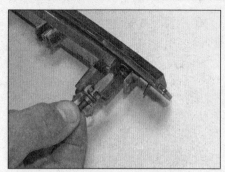

22.14 Remove the tailgate washer jet from the high-level stop-light

23.1a Carefully lever the trim...

23.1b ...to release the four retaining clips

23.2a Undo the four retaining screws...

23.2b ...withdraw the audio unit...

23.2c ...then disconnect the wiring plugs and aerial cable

electrical connector from the pump. Pull the pump from the reservoir (see illustrations). Be prepared for fluid spillage. Note that one pump supplies the front and rear washer jets.

Refitting

10 Refitting is a reversal of removal. Check the sealing grommet in the fluid reservoir, before inserting the pump.

Windscreen washer jet

Removal

11 With the bonnet open, disconnect the fluid hose, then carefully prise the jet from its position. Take care not to damage the trim or paintwork, as the jet is removed.

Refitting

12 Refitting is a reversal of removal. The jet can be adjusted by inserting a pin into the jet, and swivelling it to the required position.

Tailgate washer jet

Removal

13 Remove the rear high-level stop-light as described in Section 10 of this Chapter.
14 With the light on the bench, remove the washer jet (see illustration).

Refitting

15 Refitting is a reversal of removal. The jet can be adjusted by inserting a pin into the jet, and swivelling it to the required position.

23 Audio unit –
removal and refitting

Audio unit

1 Carefully unclip the facia centre trim panel,

there are two retaining clips at the top and two at the bottom (see illustrations).
2 Undo the four retaining screws, then withdraw the audio unit from the facia, disconnecting the wiring connectors and aerial cable, as it is withdrawn (see illustrations).

Refitting

3 Refitting is a reversal of removal.

24 Loudspeakers –
removal and refitting

Door-mounted

Removal

1 Make sure the ignition and audio unit are switched off.
2 Remove the door trim panel, as described in Chapter 11 Section 26.
3 Disconnect the wiring connector from the speaker.
4 The speaker is held in place with rivets (see illustrations). Drill out the rivets and remove the speaker from the door panel.

Refitting

5 Refitting is a reversal of removal.

Facia-mounted

Removal

6 Disconnect the battery negative lead as described in Chapter 5A Section 4.

24.4a Front door speaker

24.4b Rear door speaker

7 Prise the speaker (tweeter) free **(see illustration)**.

8 Disconnect the wiring and remove the speaker from the cover.

Refitting

9 Refitting is a reversal of removal.

25 Radio aerial –
removal and refitting

Aerial assembly

Removal

1 Open the tailgate, withdraw the plastic clips from the rear of the headlining, then peel back the aperture seal along the upper edge **(see illustration)**.

2 Unclip the seat belt buckle magnetic bung from the centre of the rear headlining **(see illustration)**.

3 Undo the securing bolt and remove the seat belt anchorage from the rear of the headlining **(see illustration)**.

4 For further movement of the headlining, to expose the base of the aerial, it may be necessary to remove the right- and left-hand rear inner trim panels as described in Chapter 11, Section 26.

5 Unscrew the securing nut, and disconnect the aerial lead from the base of the aerial. Lift the aerial from the roof panel.

6 The aerial mast can be unscrewed from the base of the aerial if required.

Refitting

7 Refitting is a reversal of removal.

Aerial lead

Removal

8 With the lead disconnected from the aerial as described previously in this Section, observe the routing of the lead.

9 Remove the relevant inner trim panels as described in Chapter 11, Section 26.

10 Remove the audio unit as described in Section 23, then disconnect the aerial lead from the rear of the unit.

11 Pull the lower end of the lead and feed the lead from behind the facia.

Refitting

12 Refitting is a reversal of removal. Take care not to damage the lead or surrounding components when feeding it through behind the facia and behind the trim panels.

13 Refit the audio unit with reference to Section 23.

26 Anti-theft alarm system –
general information

1 All models are fitted with a passive engine immobiliser device which is activated by the coded ignition key or card. When the

24.7 Remove the facia-mounted speaker

immobiliser is armed, the indicator light on the instrument panel will flash continuously. When the ignition is switched on, an antenna ring around the ignition switch interrogates and captures the code from the head of the key and transmits it to the UCH, the engine management ECU and instrument panel. If the code is recognised the engine can be started.

2 Certain models may also be fitted with an active anti-theft system. These vehicles have separate alarm siren and ultra sound sensors fitted to the door pillars. Both the active and the passive anti-theft systems can be checked and tested with suitable diagnostic equipment.

27 Airbag system –
general information and precautions

1 All models are equipped with an airbag system. All models have two-stage driver and passenger airbags. Side airbags are also fitted to all models. Three-door models have anti-submarine airbags fitted to the front seats and some models have side curtain airbags fitted.

2 The airbag system is triggered in the event of a heavy frontal or side impact; depending on the point of impact, not all the airbags will be fired. The airbags inflate rapidly to form a safety cushion which prevents contact with the inside of the car, greatly reducing the risk of injury, after which they deflate.

3 The system is armed only when the ignition is on. However, a reserve power source maintains power to the system for a

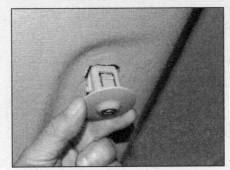

25.2 Unclip the magnetic bung

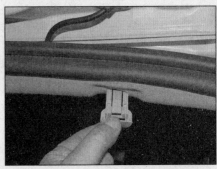

25.1 Withdraw the securing clips

short period – for this reason, it is essential to disconnect the battery and wait before disconnecting any of the system wiring.

4 The system is activated by a 'g' sensor in the electronic control unit, fitted under the centre console. The airbag control unit also controls the seat belt pretensioners. Impact sensors in the B-pillars detect side impacts which, if severe enough, will cause the side airbag to be fired on the side concerned.

5 Linked to the airbag system are the seat belt pretensioners fitted to the front belts (see Chapter 11). The seat belt tensioners are fired with the airbags in the event of an accident, to take up the slack in the belts and hold the occupants in their seats.

6 When the ignition is switched on, the system performs a self-test (the airbag warning light should come on, then go out). If the light stays on, or comes on while driving, consult a Renault dealer (or suitably-equipped garage) immediately. The system will not deploy if the self-test detects a fault.

Precautions

• Before carrying out any operations on the airbag system, to prevent the risk of injury if the system is triggered inadvertently when working on the vehicle, disconnect the battery negative lead (see Chapter 5A Section 4) and disable the system (wait for at least five minutes). This will allow the reserve power capacitors in the control unit to discharge. When operations are complete, make sure no one is inside the vehicle when the battery is reconnected then, with the driver's door open, switch the ignition on from outside the vehicle.

25.3 Unbolt the seat belt anchor

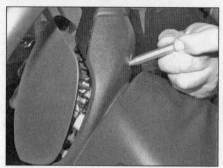

28.3a Insert a suitable tool and release the airbag

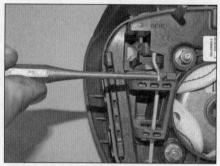

28.3b Showing position of the spring clips...

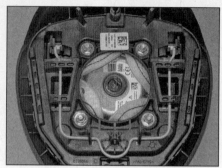

28.3c ...on the rear of the airbag

• Before carrying out any operations in the vicinity of the airbag or steering wheel, to prevent the risk of injury if the system is triggered inadvertently when working on the vehicle, remove the airbag unit as described in Section 28.
• Note that the airbag(s) must not be subjected to excess temperatures. When the airbag is removed, ensure that it is stored with the padded surface uppermost to prevent possible inflation.
• Do not allow any solvents or cleaning agents to contact the airbag assemblies. They must be cleaned using only a damp cloth.
• The airbags and control unit are both sensitive to impact. If either is dropped or damaged they should be renewed.
• Do not refit the airbag unit to the steering wheel once the steering wheel has been removed from the vehicle.
• Do not attempt to test the airbag electrical

circuit using anything except specialist diagnostic equipment. Using a conventional multimeter or ohmmeter is likely to trigger the airbag.
• If the airbag has been triggered, the control unit must be renewed.
• If the airbag is to be renewed, the control unit must also be renewed.
• Disconnect the airbag control unit wiring plug prior to using arc welding equipment on the vehicle.

28 Airbag system components – removal and refitting

Note: *Refer to the Warnings in Section 27 before carrying out the following operations.*
1 Disconnect the battery negative lead and wait for at least five minutes (see Chapter 5A

Section 4). This will allow the reserve power capacitors in the control unit to discharge and disable the airbag system (see Section 27).

Driver's airbag
Removal
2 Turn the steering wheel through 90°, to access the first hole at the rear of the steering wheel, then turn the steering wheel through 180°, to access the second hole.
3 An 6 mm diameter length of bar (or similar) will be required to fully release the airbag. Locate the hole at the rear of the steering wheel and using gentle pressure on the bar whilst pulling at the front release the airbag **(see illustrations)**. Carry out the same procedure on the other side.
4 Release the locking clip, then disconnect the wiring plug from the rear of the airbag **(see illustrations)**. Note that the airbag must not be knocked or dropped and should be stored with its padded surface uppermost.
Refitting
5 Ensure that the wiring connectors are securely reconnected and seat the airbag unit centrally in the steering wheel, making sure the wires do not become trapped. Press the airbag squarely in to place until the retaining clips locate in the steering wheel.
6 Ensuring no one is inside the vehicle, reconnect the battery. With the driver's door open, turn on the ignition switch and check the operation of the airbag warning light.

Airbag rotary connector (clockspring)
7 Ensure the wheels are in the straight-ahead positon.
8 Remove the driver's airbag as described in this Section and then the steering wheel as described in Chapter 10 Section 14.
9 Remove the steering column shrouds, as described in Chapter 11 Section 28.
10 Before proceeding further, tape the clockspring in position, to prevent it from turning **(see illustration)**.
11 Disconnect the wiring connector from the rear of the clockspring, then undo the three retaining screws and withdraw it from the top of the steering column **(see illustrations)**. Do not allow the clockspring to rotate at any point.

28.4a Release the locking clip...

28.4b ...and disconnect the wiring plug

28.10 Tape the clockspring to prevent it from turning

28.11a Disconnect the wiring plug...

Refitting

12 Refitting is a reversal of removal.

Passenger airbag

Removal

13 To access the passenger airbag the complete facia must be remove as described in Chapter 11, Section 28.
14 Working at the back of the facia panel, slacken and remove the retaining screws then remove the airbag unit from its mountings. **(see illustration)**. Note that the airbag must not be knocked or dropped and should be stored with its padded surface uppermost.

Refitting

15 Refitting is a reversal of removal.

Side airbags

Removal

16 Remove the appropriate front seat as described in Chapter 11, Section 22.
17 Strip out and remove the seat trim, seat back, and cover. Drill out the rivet and remove the airbag.

Refitting

18 Refitting is a reversal of removal, noting the following points: A new rivet will be required. If the airbag has deployed, a new seat cover and foam padding (amongst other items) will be required.

Airbag control unit

Removal

19 Remove the centre console as described in Chapter 11 Section 27 to gain access to the control unit.
20 A cut will need to be made in the carpet to access the control unit. Special clips are available from Renault to repair the cut. To prevent cutting the carpet, the control unit can be accessed by removing a front seat and pulling back the carpet at one side.
21 Unclip the protective cover from over the control unit **(see illustration)**.
22 Disconnect the wiring connector, then unscrew the retaining nuts and remove the control unit from the vehicle **(see illustrations)**.

Refitting

23 Refit the mounting nuts and tighten them securely.

28.11b ...undo the retaining screws...

28.11c ...and withdraw the clockspring unit

28.14 Passenger airbag retaining screws

28.21 Unclip the cover

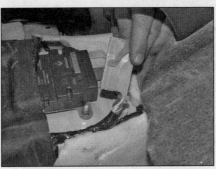
28.22a Unplug the wiring connector...

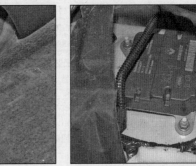
28.22b ...and unbolt the control unit

24 Reconnect the wiring connector and refit the centre console as described in Chapter 11 Section 27.
25 If a new control unit has been fitted it will require programming with suitable equipment.

26 Ensuring no one is inside the vehicle, reconnect the battery. With the driver's door open, turn on the ignition and check the operation of the airbag warning light.

PASSENGER COMPARTMENT FUSE AND RELAY BOX

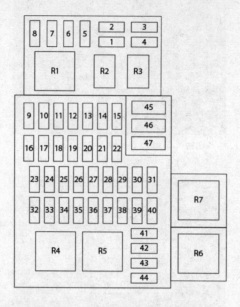

FUSE/RELAY	VALUE	DESCRIPTION	OEM NAME
1	30 A	Motors and controls for rear window	260-2 F1
2	30 A	Passenger electric window control, Front windows motors	260-2 F2
3	40 A	Air conditioning fan assembly	260-2 F3
4	-	Not used	260-2 F4
5	25 A	Driver electric window motor	260-2 F5
6	15 A	Radio, Passenger compartment computer	260-2 F6
7	5 A	Electric door mirrors	260-2 F7
8	-	Not used	260-2 F8
9	20 A	Monolever without automatic lights and wiper	260-1 F1
	5 A	Monolever with automatic lights and wiper	
10	10 A	Left hand headlight - Passenger compartment computer (5A also used)	260-1 F2
11	10 A	Left hand headlight	260-1 F3
12	10 A	Right hand headlight - passenger compartment computer	260-1 F4
13	10 A	Right hand headlight without automatic lights and wiper	260-1 F5
	25 A	Energy management computer with automatic lights and wiper	
14	10 A	Headlights, Left daytime running lights, Passenger compartment computer	260-1 F6
15	10 A	Central door locking switch. Hazard warning lights control, Rear right hand side light, Right hand headlight, Left and right number plate light, Headlight adjustment dimmer switch, Radio, Courtesy lights, Luggage lights	260-1 F7
16	15 A	Cigarette lighter	260-1 F8
17	7.5 A	Passenger compartment computer, Luggage compartment light	260-1 F9
18	15 A	Horns	260-1 F10
19	25 A	Monolever (10 A also used)	260-1 F11
20	5 A	ABS and ESP control unit, Brake light switch (3 A also used)	260-1 F12
21	10 A	Luggage compartment light, Front courtesy light, Air conditioning control panel, Electric window relay control or Air conditioning control unit, Passenger compartment temperature sensor, Courtesy lights, Glovebox light	260-1 F13
22	5 A	Steering wheel angle sensor, Child safety relay control, Keyless vehicle start/stop control button, Rain/Light sensor, Opening warning sound unit	260-1 F14
23	7.5 A	Automatic gearbox electric control unit (Automatic transmission) (5A also used)	260-1 F15

Fuses and relays

24	10 A	Additional heater relay 1, 2 and 3, Parking proximity sensor electric control unit, Seat belt reminder module, Radio, Heated rear screen relay control, Speed limiter and cruise control ON/OFF switch, Headlight adjustment switch, Left and right heated seat controls, Driver and passenger heated seat supply relay control, Headlights adjustment motor	260-1 F16
25	10 A	Monolever	260-1 F17
26	15 A	Left and right side lights, High level brake light, Passenger compartment computer (10 A also used)	260-1 F18
27	5 A	ECU injection, Passenger compartment computer, Starter relay control, Fuel pump relay control	260-1 F19
28	5 A	Airbag/pretensioner electric control unit, Electric steering column lock	260-1 F20
29	15 A	Supply to engine/injection connection or not used (5 A also used)	260-1 F21
30	5 A	Electric power assisted steering system	260-1 F22
31	15 A	Diagnostic socket, Radio, Video display, Multimedia keypad	260-1 F23
32	15 A	Passenger compartment computer - fuses F12-F14, F36	260-1 F24
33	15 A	Passenger compartment computer - Hands-free access electric control unit (10 A also used)	260-1 F25
34	15 A	Passenger compartment computer - Rear side light, Headlights, Electric door mirrors, Hazard warning lights control unit	260-1 F26
35	20 A	Passenger compartment computer	260-1 F27
36	15 A	Energy management electric control unit	260-1 F28
37	25 A	Energy management electric control unit (20 A also used)	260-1 F29
38	15 A	Monolever, Alarm, Alarm electronic control unit	260-1 F30
39	10 A	Instrument panel, Multiplex line interface unit, Telematics electronic control unit (5 A also used)	260-1 F31
40	15 A	Passenger compartment computer - Wash/Wipe combination switch, Manual gearbox sensor and reversing lights (7.5 A also used)	260-1 F32
41	20 A	No information available or Not used	260-1 F33
42	15 A	Seats base heated pad	260-1 F34
43	20 A	Heated rear screen, Air conditioning panel, Passenger compartment computer, Supply to fuse F7	260-1 F35
44	5 A	Electric door mirror control	260-1 F36
45	30 A	Energy management computer control unit with automatic lights and wiper (20 A also used)	260-1 F37
46	25 A	Energy management computer control unit with automatic lights and wiper	260-1 F38
	15 A	Front fog lights without automatic lights and wiper (10 A also used)	
47	25 A	Energy management computer control unit with automatic lights and wiper	260-1 F39
	30 A	Wash/wipe combination switch, Windscreen wiper motor without automatic lights and wiper	
R1	-	Electric window control relay	260-2 RA
R2	-	Battery relay	260-2 RB
R3	-	Heated rear screen relay	260-2 RC
R4	-	After ignition 2 relay	260-1 RA
R5	-	Accessories relay 1	260-1 RB
R6	-	Child safety relay or not used	260-1 R750
R7	-	Door mirrors relay (From 06.2016)	260-1 R2600

Fuses and relays (continued)

HEATED SEAT RELAY

RELAY	VALUE	DESCRIPTION	OEM NAME
R1	-	Driver heated seat supply relay	1649
R2	-	Passenger heated seat supply relay	1650

ADDITIONAL HEATER RELAYS

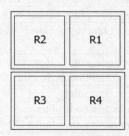

RELAY	VALUE	DESCRIPTION	OEM NAME
R1	-	Additional heater 1 relay	1067
R2	-	Additional heater 2 relay	1068
R3	-	Additional heater 3 relay or not used	1069
R4	-	Not used	-

ENGINE FUSE AND RELAY BOX

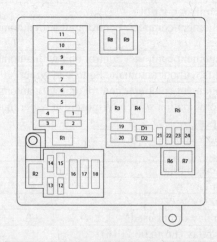

FUSE/RELAY	VALUE	DESCRIPTION	OEM NAME
1	7.5 A	Battery current sensor, Energy management computer (5 A also used)	777-1 F1
2	25 A	Audio amplifier or Not used	777-1 F2
3	30 A	ABS and ESP electric control unit	777-1 F3
4	40 A	Supply to fuse F34, F35 on passenger compartment fuse and relay box	777-1 F4
5	70 A	Supply to fuse F1, F3, F5, F23-F27, F33 on passenger compartment fuse and relay box	777-1 F5

Fuses and relays (continued)

6	80 A	Supply to fuse F11, F28-F31, F37-F39 and Hands-free access electric control (Euro 6)	777-1 F6
7	50 A	ABS and ESP electric control unit	777-1 F7
8	80 A	Electric power-assisted steering system	777-2 F8
9	80 A	Passenger compartment additional heater relays 1 and 2	777-2 F9
10	80 A	Passenger compartment additional heater relays 3 or Not used	777-3 F10
11	-	Not used	777-3 F11
12	30 A	Starter	597-2 F1
13	20 A	Automatic gearbox electric control unit (automatic transmission)	597-2 F2
14	25 A	Fan assembly (standard heating version) (Petrol engines)	597-2 F3
	15 A	Air conditioning clutch, Air conditioning control panel, Air conditioning control unit, Variable cylinder actuator (Diesel engines)	
15	40 A	Air conditioning compressor control relay, Fan assembly speed relay control, Supply to fuse F5 (15 A also used)	597-2 F4
16	40 A	Engine fan assembly control relay unit	597-2 F5
17	70 A	Preheating unit	597-2 F6
18	-	Not used	597-2 F7
19	20 A	Fuel pump and sender (Diesel engines) or Not used	597-1 F3
20	-	Not used	597-1 F4
21	20 A	Engine functions (15 A also used)	597-1 F5
22	-	Not used	597-1 F6
23	-	Not used	597-1 F7
24	-	Not used	597-1 F8
D1	-	Air conditioning compressor	597-1 D1
D2	-	Engine cooling fan (Diesel engines)	597-1 D2
R1	-	Not used	777-1 RA
R2	-	Starter	597-2 R232
R3	-	Fuel pump	597-1 RC
R4	-	Air conditioning compressor control (air conditioning version) or Fan assembly 1 speed relay (standard heating version)	597-1 RB
R5	-	Injection electric control unit supply	597-1 RA
R6	-	Reversing light	597-3 RD
R7	-	Not used	597-3 RE
R8	-	Not used	1566 RA
R9	-	Not used	1566 RB

Fuses and relays (continued)

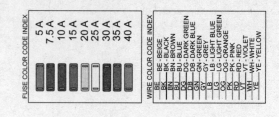

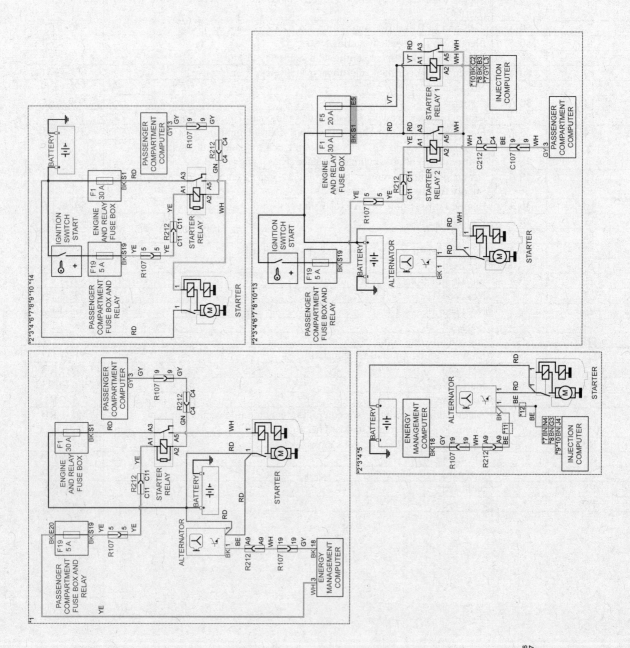

Starting and charging

*1 Up to to 04.2015
*2 From 05.2015 to 05.2016
*3 From 06.2016 to 08.2017
*4 From 09.2017
*5 Charging
*6 Starting
*7 Engine 0.9 L TCE
*8 Engine 1.2 L TCE
*9 Engine 1.2 L
*10 Engine 1.5 dCi
*11 Except Euro 6
*12 Euro 6
*13 With start-stop
*14 Without start-stop

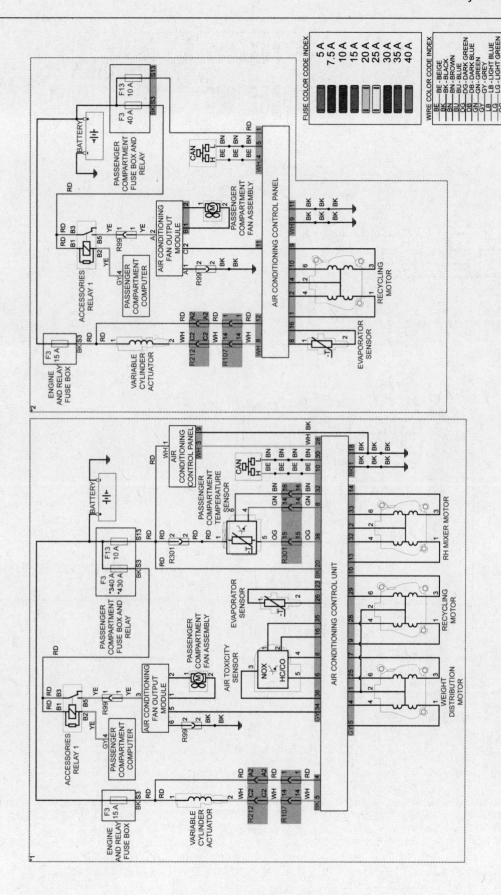

Manual and automatic air conditioning

*1 Automatic air conditioning
*2 Manual air conditioning
*3 Up to 06.2014
*4 From 07.2014

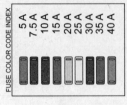

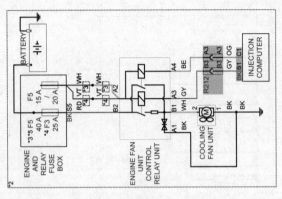
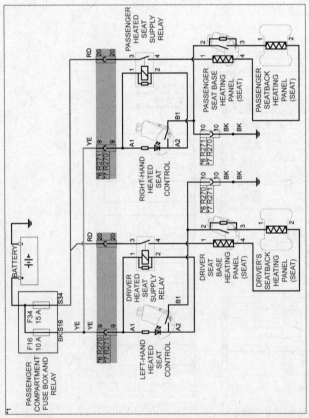

Cooling fan and seat heating

*1 Seat heating
*2 Cooling fan
*3 Up to 07.2013
*4 From 08.2013 to 01.2015
*5 From 02.2015
*6 LHD
*7 RHD

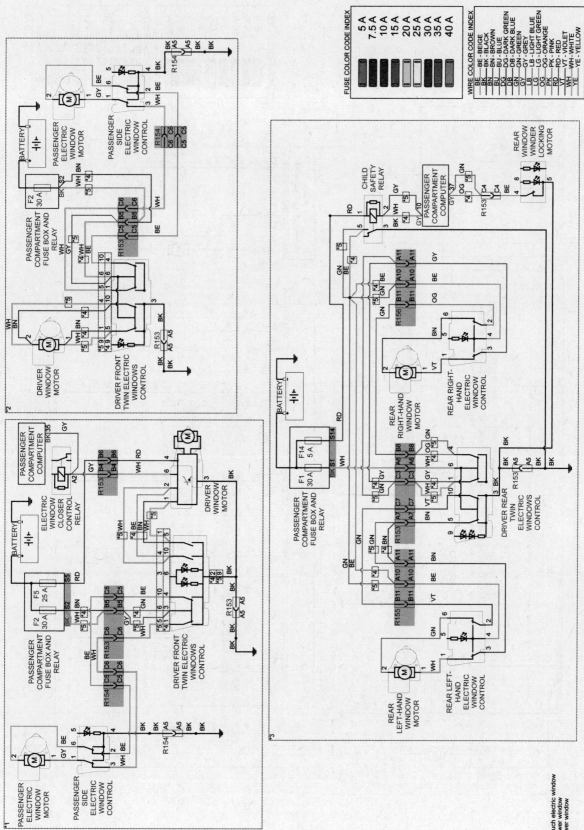

Power windows

*1 One – touch electric window
*2 Front power window
*3 Rear power window
*4 LHD
*5 RHD

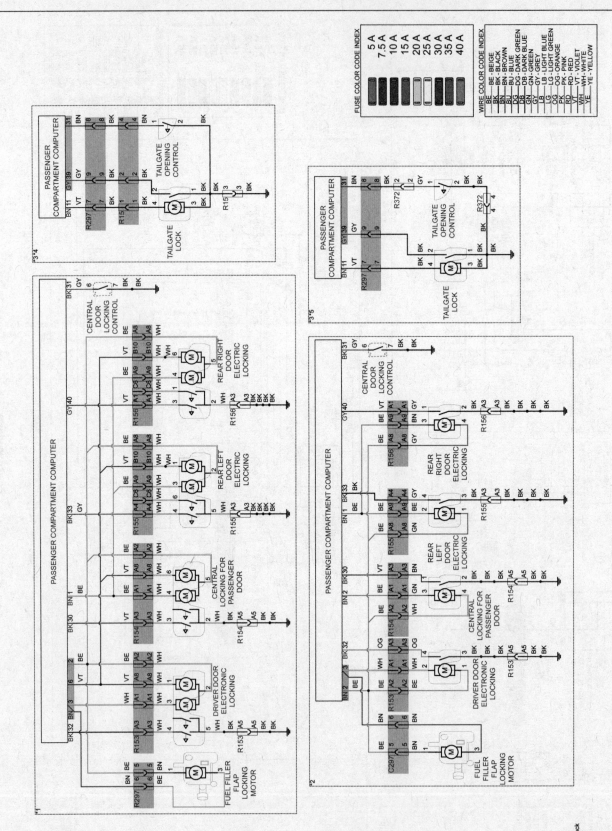

Central locking

*1 With deadlock
*2 Without deadlock
*3 Tailgate
*4 Hatchback
*5 Estate

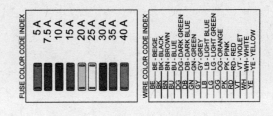

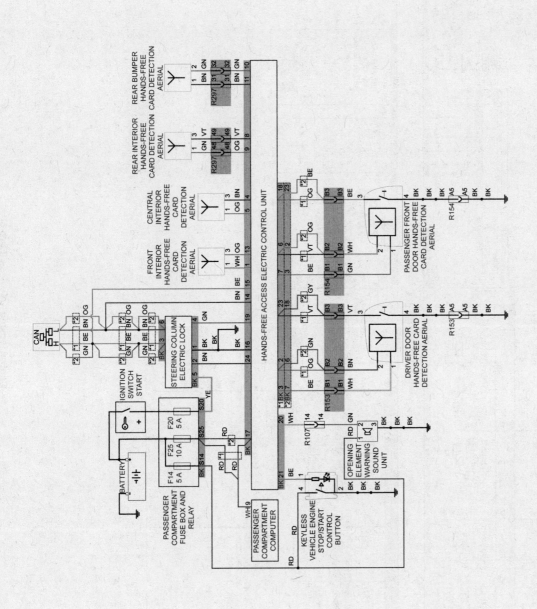

Central locking – Keyless (except Euro 6)

*1 LHD
*2 RHD

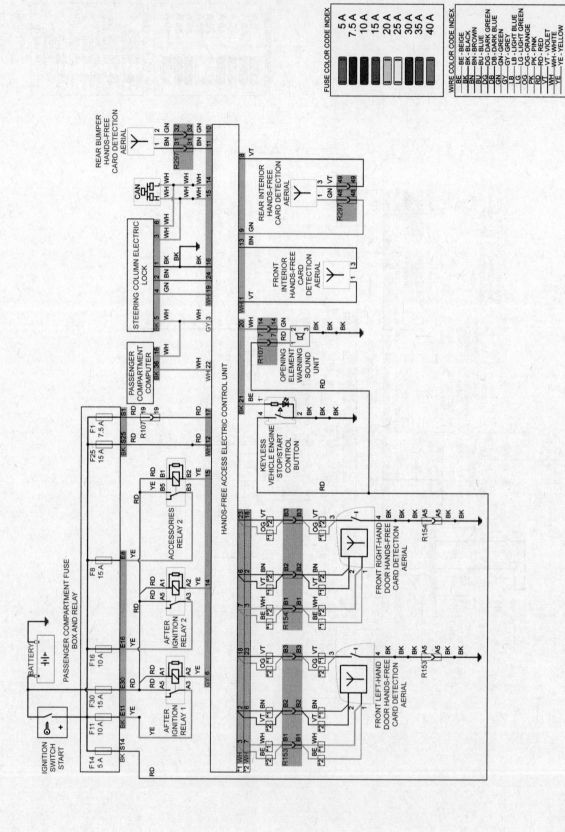

Central locking – Keyless (Euro 6)

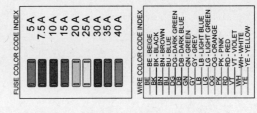

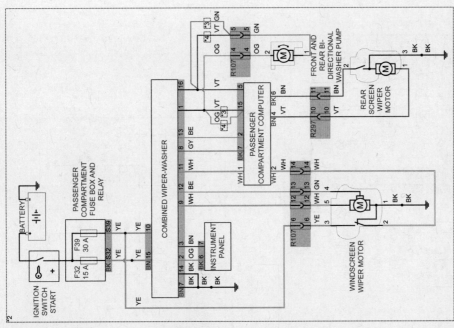

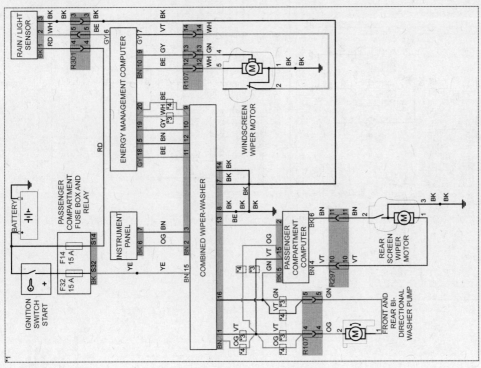

Washers and wipers

*1 With automatic wiper
*2 Without automatic wiper
*3 LHD
*4 RHD

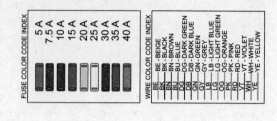

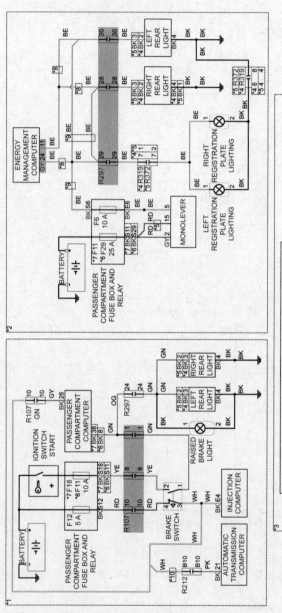

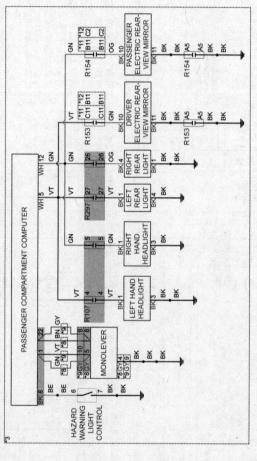

Brake lights, side lights, indicators and hazard lights

*1 Brake lights
*2 Side lights
*3 Indicators and hazard lights
*4 Hatchback
*5 Estate
*6 Euro 6
*7 Except Euro 6
*8 With automatic lights
*9 Without automatic lights
*10 Automatic transmission
*11 LHD
*12 RHD

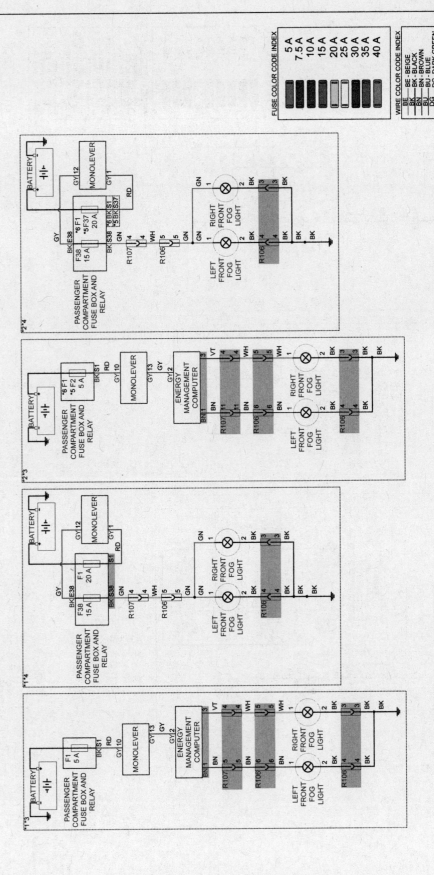

FUSE COLOR CODE INDEX

	5 A
	7.5 A
	10 A
	15 A
	20 A
	25 A
	30 A
	35 A
	40 A

WIRE COLOR CODE INDEX

BE - BEIGE
BK - BLACK
BN - BROWN
BU - BLUE
DG - DARK GREEN
DB - DARK BLUE
GN - GREEN
GY - GREY
LB - LIGHT BLUE
LG - LIGHT GREEN
OG - ORANGE
PK - PINK
RD - RED
VT - VIOLET
WH - WHITE
YE - YELLOW

Front fog lights – up to May 2016

*1 Up to January 2015
*2 From February 2015 up to May 2016
*3 With automatic lights
*4 Without automatic lights
*5 Euro 6
*6 Except Euro 6

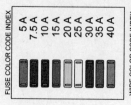

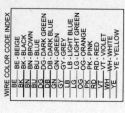

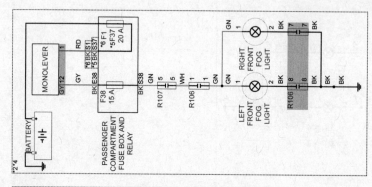

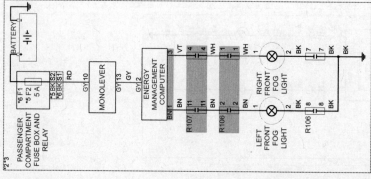

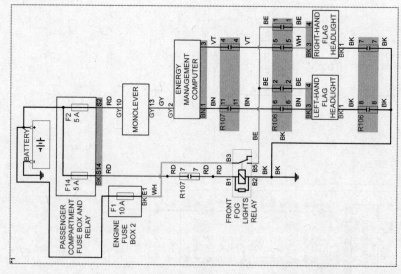

Front fog lights – from June 2016

*1 With LED
*2 Without lights
*3 With automatic lights
*4 Without automatic lights
*5 Euro 6
*6 Except Euro 6

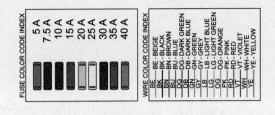

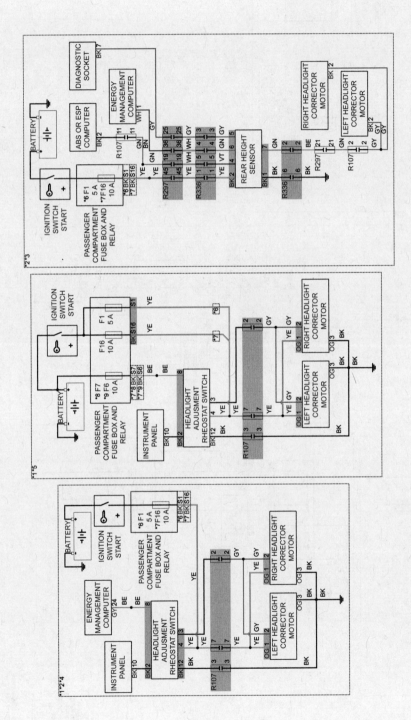

Headlight levelling

*1 Without LED
*2 With LED
*3 With automatic headlight adjuster
*4 With automatic lights
*5 Without automatic lights
*6 Euro 6
*7 Except Euro 6
*8 LHD
*9 RHD

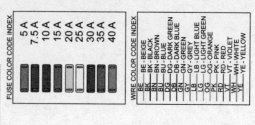

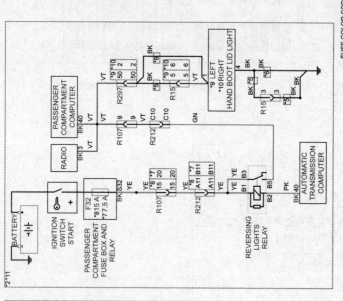

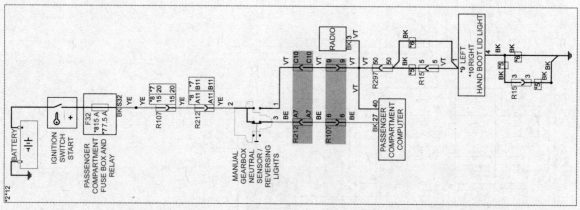

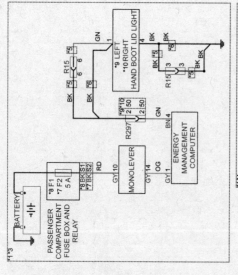

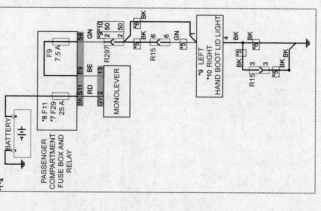

Rear fog and reversing lights

*1 Rear fog lights
*2 Reversing lights
*3 With automatic lights
*4 Without automatic lights
*5 Hatchback
*6 Estate
*7 Euro 6
*8 Except Euro 6
*9 LHD
*10 RHD
*11 Automatic transmission
*12 Manual transmission

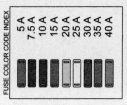

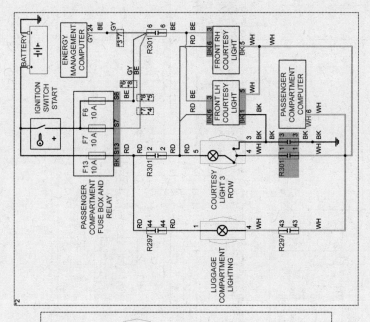

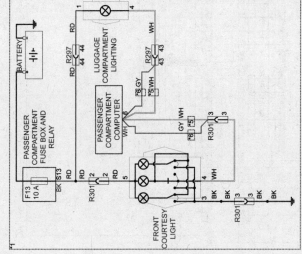

Interior lights

*1 Up to May 2016
*2 From June 2016
*3 With automatic wiper
*4 Without automatic wiper
*5 LHD
*6 RHD
*7 Euro 6
*8 Except Euro 6

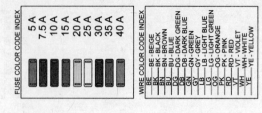

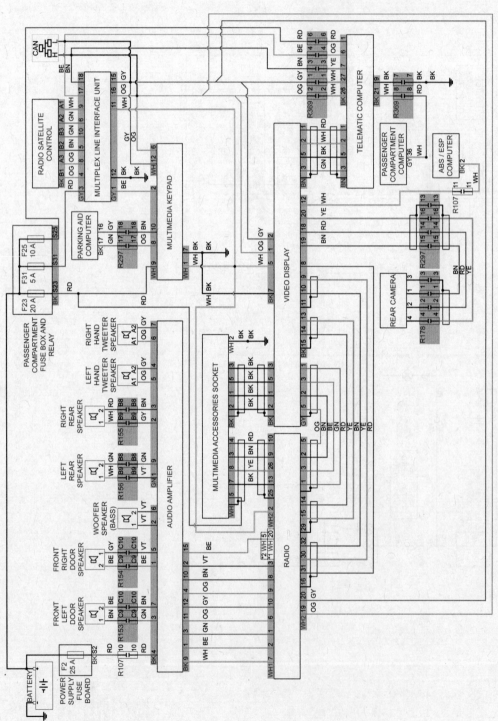

Audio system – Navigation (with amplifier)

*1 LHD
*2 RHD

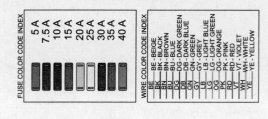

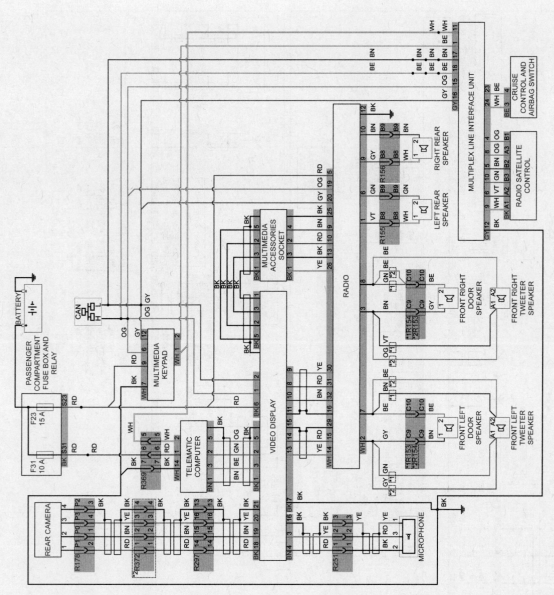

Audio system – Navigation (without amplifier)

*1 LHD
*2 RHD

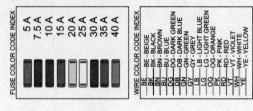

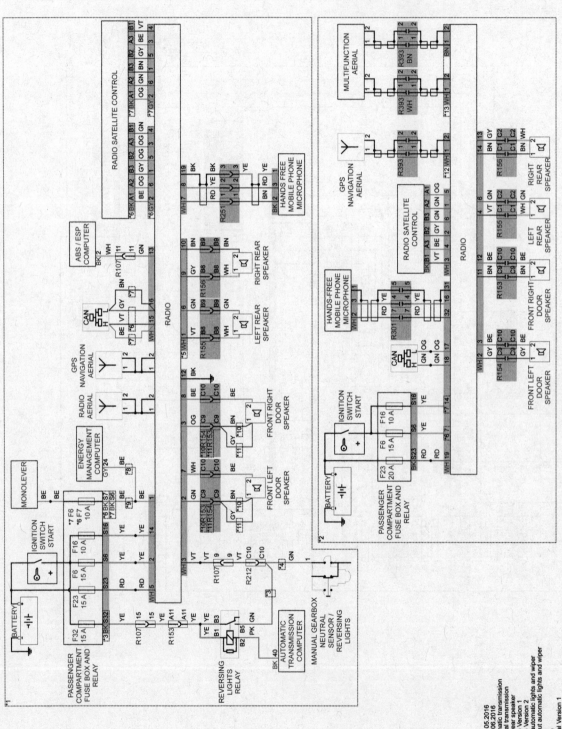

Audio system – Radio

*1 Up to 05.2016
*2 From 06.2016
*3 Automatic transmission
*4 Manual transmission
*5 With rear speaker
*6 Radio Version 1
*7 Radio Version 2
*8 With automatic lights and wiper
*9 Without automatic lights and wiper
*10 LHD
*11 RHD
*12 Aerial Version 1
*13 Aerial Version 2

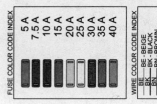

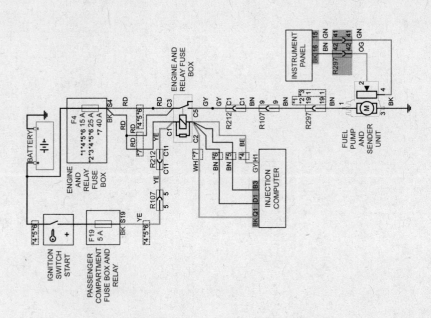

Fuel pump

*1 Up to 07.2013
*2 From 08.2013 to 06.2014
*3 From 07.2014
*4 Engine 0.9 L TCE
*5 Engine 1.2 L TCE
*6 Engine 1.2 L
*7 Engine 1.5 dCi

Dimensions and weights

Note: *All figures are approximate, and may vary according to model. Refer to manufacturer's data for exact figures.*

Dimensions

Overall length	4063 mm
Overall width (including mirrors).	1945 mm
Wheelbase	2589 mm
Height	1448 mm*

*Unladen

Weights

Gross vehicle weight	See Vehicle Identification Plate
Maximum towing weight	See Vehicle Identification Plate
Maximum nose weight (on towball)	75 Kg
Maximum roof load (including carrier)	80 Kg

Fuel economy

Although depreciation is still the biggest part of the cost of motoring for most car owners, the cost of fuel is more immediately noticeable. These pages give some tips on how to get the best fuel economy.

Working it out

Manufacturer's figures

Car manufacturers are required by law to provide fuel consumption information on all new vehicles sold. These 'official' figures are obtained by simulating various driving conditions on a rolling road or a test track. Real life conditions are different, so the fuel consumption actually achieved may not bear much resemblance to the quoted figures.

How to calculate it

Many cars now have trip computers which will

display fuel consumption, both instantaneous and average. Refer to the owner's handbook for details of how to use these.

To calculate consumption yourself (and maybe to check that the trip computer is accurate), proceed as follows.

1. Fill up with fuel and note the mileage, or zero the trip recorder.
2. Drive as usual until you need to fill up again.
3. Note the amount of fuel required to refill the tank, and the mileage covered since the previous fill-up.
4. Divide the mileage by the amount of fuel used to obtain the consumption figure.

For example:

Mileage at first fill-up (a) = 27,903
Mileage at second fill-up (b) = 28,346
Mileage covered (b - a) = 443
Fuel required at second fill-up = 48.6 litres

The half-completed changeover to metric units in the UK means that we buy our fuel

in litres, measure distances in miles and talk about fuel consumption in miles per gallon. There are two ways round this: the first is to convert the litres to gallons before doing the calculation (by dividing by 4.546, or see Table 1). So in the example:

48.6 litres ÷ 4.546 = 10.69 gallons
443 miles ÷ 10.69 gallons = 41.4 mpg

The second way is to calculate the consumption in miles per litre, then multiply that figure by 4.546 (or see Table 2).

So in the example, fuel consumption is:

443 miles ÷ 48.6 litres = 9.1 mpl
9.1 mpl x 4.546 = 41.4 mpg

The rest of Europe expresses fuel consumption in litres of fuel required to travel 100 km (l/100 km). For interest, the conversions are given in Table 3. In practice it doesn't matter what units you use, provided you know what your normal consumption is and can spot if it's getting better or worse.

Table 1: conversion of litres to Imperial gallons

litres	1	2	3	4	5	10	20	30	40	50	60	70
gallons	0.22	0.44	0.66	0.88	1.10	2.24	4.49	6.73	8.98	11.22	13.47	15.71

Table 2: conversion of miles per litre to miles per gallon

miles per litre	5	6	7	8	9	10	11	12	13	14
miles per gallon	23	27	32	36	41	46	50	55	59	64

Table 3: conversion of litres per 100 km to miles per gallon

litres per 100 km	4	4.5	5	5.5	6	6.5	7	8	9	10
miles per gallon	71	63	56	51	47	43	40	35	31	28

Maintenance

A well-maintained car uses less fuel and creates less pollution. In particular:

Filters

Change air and fuel filters at the specified intervals.

Oil

Use a good quality oil of the lowest viscosity specified by the vehicle manufacturer (see *Lubricants and fluids*). Check the level often and be careful not to overfill.

Spark plugs

When applicable, renew at the specified intervals.

Tyres

Check tyre pressures regularly. Under-inflated tyres have an increased rolling resistance. It is generally safe to use the higher pressures specified for full load conditions even when not fully laden, but keep an eye on the centre band of tread for signs of wear due to over-inflation.

When buying new tyres, consider the 'fuel saving' models which most manufacturers include in their ranges.

Driving style

Acceleration

Acceleration uses more fuel than driving at a steady speed. The best technique with modern cars is to accelerate reasonably briskly to the desired speed, changing up through the gears as soon as possible without making the engine labour.

Air conditioning

Air conditioning absorbs quite a bit of energy from the engine – typically 3 kW (4 hp) or so. The effect on fuel consumption is at its worst in slow traffic. Switch it off when not required.

Anticipation

Drive smoothly and try to read the traffic flow so as to avoid unnecessary acceleration and braking.

Automatic transmission

When accelerating in an automatic, avoid depressing the throttle so far as to make the transmission hold onto lower gears at higher speeds. Don't use the 'Sport' setting, if applicable.

When stationary with the engine running, select 'N' or 'P'. When moving, keep your left foot away from the brake.

Braking

Braking converts the car's energy of motion into heat – essentially, it is wasted. Obviously some braking is always going to be necessary, but with good anticipation it is surprising how much can be avoided, especially on routes that you know well.

Carshare

Consider sharing lifts to work or to the shops. Even once a week will make a difference.

Electrical loads

Electricity is 'fuel' too; the alternator which charges the battery does so by converting some of the engine's energy of motion into electrical energy. The more electrical accessories are in use, the greater the load on the alternator. Switch off big consumers like the heated rear window when not required.

Freewheeling

Freewheeling (coasting) in neutral with the engine switched off is dangerous. The effort required to operate power-assisted brakes and steering increases when the engine is not running, with a potential lack of control in emergency situations.

In any case, modern fuel injection systems automatically cut off the engine's fuel supply on the overrun (moving and in gear, but with the accelerator pedal released).

Gadgets

Bolt-on devices claiming to save fuel have been around for nearly as long as the motor car itself. Those which worked were rapidly adopted as standard equipment by the vehicle manufacturers. Others worked only in certain situations, or saved fuel only at the expense of unacceptable effects on performance, driveability or the life of engine components.

The most effective fuel saving gadget is the driver's right foot.

Journey planning

Combine (eg) a trip to the supermarket with a visit to the recycling centre and the DIY store, rather than making separate journeys.

When possible choose a travelling time outside rush hours.

Load

The more heavily a car is laden, the greater the energy required to accelerate it to a given speed. Remove heavy items which you don't need to carry.

One load which is often overlooked is the contents of the fuel tank. A tankful of fuel (55 litres / 12 gallons) weighs 45 kg (100 lb) or so. Just half filling it may be worthwhile.

Lost?

At the risk of stating the obvious, if you're going somewhere new, have details of the route to hand. There's not much point in achieving record mpg if you also go miles out of your way.

Parking

If possible, carry out any reversing or turning manoeuvres when you arrive at a parking space so that you can drive straight out when you leave. Manoeuvering when the engine is cold uses a lot more fuel.

Driving around looking for free on-street parking may cost more in fuel than buying a car park ticket.

Premium fuel

Most major oil companies (and some supermarkets) have premium grades of fuel which are several pence a litre dearer than the standard grades. Reports vary, but the consensus seems to be that if these fuels improve economy at all, they do not do so by enough to justify their extra cost.

Roof rack

When loading a roof rack, try to produce a wedge shape with the narrow end at the front. Any cover should be securely fastened – if it flaps it's creating turbulence and absorbing energy.

Remove roof racks and boxes when not in use – they increase air resistance and can create a surprising amount of noise.

Short journeys

The engine is at its least efficient, and wear is highest, during the first few miles after a cold start. Consider walking, cycling or using public transport.

Speed

The engine is at its most efficient when running at a steady speed and load at the rpm where it develops maximum torque. (You can find this figure in the car's handbook.) For most cars this corresponds to between 55 and 65 mph in top gear.

Above the optimum cruising speed, fuel consumption starts to rise quite sharply. A car travelling at 80 mph will typically be using 30% more fuel than at 60 mph.

Supermarket fuel

It may be cheap but is it any good? In the UK all supermarket fuel must meet the relevant British Standard. The major oil companies will say that their branded fuels have better additive packages which may stop carbon and other deposits building up. A reasonable compromise might be to use one tank of branded fuel to three or four from the supermarket.

Switch off when stationary

Switch off the engine if you look like being stationary for more than 30 seconds or so. This is good for the environment as well as for your pocket. Be aware though that frequent restarts are hard on the battery and the starter motor.

Windows

Driving with the windows open increases air turbulence around the vehicle. Closing the windows promotes smooth airflow and

reduced resistance. The faster you go, the more significant this is.

And finally . . .

Driving techniques associated with good fuel economy tend to involve moderate acceleration and low top speeds. Be considerate to the needs of other road users who may need to make brisker progress; even if you do not agree with them this is not an excuse to be obstructive.

Safety must always take precedence over economy, whether it is a question of accelerating hard to complete an overtaking manoeuvre, killing your speed when confronted with a potential hazard or switching the lights on when it starts to get dark.

Conversion factors

Length (distance)

Inches (in)	x 25.4	= Millimetres (mm)	x 0.0394	=	Inches (in)
Feet (ft)	x 0.305	= Metres (m)	x 3.281	=	Feet (ft)
Miles	x 1.609	= Kilometres (km)	x 0.621	=	Miles

Volume (capacity)

Cubic inches (cu in; in³)	x 16.387	= Cubic centimetres (cc; cm³)	x 0.061	=	Cubic inches (cu in; in³)
Imperial pints (Imp pt)	x 0.568	= Litres (l)	x 1.76	=	Imperial pints (Imp pt)
Imperial quarts (Imp qt)	x 1.137	= Litres (l)	x 0.88	=	Imperial quarts (Imp qt)
Imperial quarts (Imp qt)	x 1.201	= US quarts (US qt)	x 0.833	=	Imperial quarts (Imp qt)
US quarts (US qt)	x 0.946	= Litres (l)	x 1.057	=	US quarts (US qt)
Imperial gallons (Imp gal)	x 4.546	= Litres (l)	x 0.22	=	Imperial gallons (Imp gal)
Imperial gallons (Imp gal)	x 1.201	= US gallons (US gal)	x 0.833	=	Imperial gallons (Imp gal)
US gallons (US gal)	x 3.785	= Litres (l)	x 0.264	=	US gallons (US gal)

Mass (weight)

Ounces (oz)	x 28.35	= Grams (g)	x 0.035	=	Ounces (oz)
Pounds (lb)	x 0.454	= Kilograms (kg)	x 2.205	=	Pounds (lb)

Force

Ounces-force (ozf; oz)	x 0.278	= Newtons (N)	x 3.6	=	Ounces-force (ozf; oz)
Pounds-force (lbf; lb)	x 4.448	= Newtons (N)	x 0.225	=	Pounds-force (lbf; lb)
Newtons (N)	x 0.1	= Kilograms-force (kgf; kg)	x 9.81	=	Newtons (N)

Pressure

Pounds-force per square inch (psi; lbf/in²; lb/in²)	x 0.070	= Kilograms-force per square centimetre (kgf/cm²; kg/cm²)	x 14.223	=	Pounds-force per square inch (psi; lbf/in²; lb/in²)
Pounds-force per square inch (psi; lbf/in²; lb/in²)	x 0.068	= Atmospheres (atm)	x 14.696	=	Pounds-force per square inch (psi; lbf/in²; lb/in²)
Pounds-force per square inch (psi; lbf/in²; lb/in²)	x 0.069	= Bars	x 14.5	=	Pounds-force per square inch (psi; lbf/in²; lb/in²)
Pounds-force per square inch (psi; lbf/in²; lb/in²)	x 6.895	= Kilopascals (kPa)	x 0.145	=	Pounds-force per square inch (psi; lbf/in²; lb/in²)
Kilopascals (kPa)	x 0.01	= Kilograms-force per square centimetre (kgf/cm²; kg/cm²)	x 98.1	=	Kilopascals (kPa)
Millibar (mbar)	x 100	= Pascals (Pa)	x 0.01	=	Millibar (mbar)
Millibar (mbar)	x 0.0145	= Pounds-force per square inch (psi; lbf/in²; lb/in²)	x 68.947	=	Millibar (mbar)
Millibar (mbar)	x 0.75	= Millimetres of mercury (mmHg)	x 1.333	=	Millibar (mbar)
Millibar (mbar)	x 0.401	= Inches of water (inH₂O)	x 2.491	=	Millibar (mbar)
Millimetres of mercury (mmHg)	x 0.535	= Inches of water (inH₂O)	x 1.868	=	Millimetres of mercury (mmHg)
Inches of water (inH₂O)	x 0.036	= Pounds-force per square inch (psi; lbf/in²; lb/in²)	x 27.68	=	Inches of water (inH₂O)

Torque (moment of force)

Pounds-force inches (lbf in; lb in)	x 1.152	= Kilograms-force centimetre (kgf cm; kg cm)	x 0.868	=	Pounds-force inches (lbf in; lb in)
Pounds-force inches (lbf in; lb in)	x 0.113	= Newton metres (Nm)	x 8.85	=	Pounds-force inches (lbf in; lb in)
Pounds-force inches (lbf in; lb in)	x 0.083	= Pounds-force feet (lbf ft; lb ft)	x 12	=	Pounds-force inches (lbf in; lb in)
Pounds-force feet (lbf ft; lb ft)	x 0.138	= Kilograms-force metres (kgf m; kg m)	x 7.233	=	Pounds-force feet (lbf ft; lb ft)
Pounds-force feet (lbf ft; lb ft)	x 1.356	= Newton metres (Nm)	x 0.738	=	Pounds-force feet (lbf ft; lb ft)
Newton metres (Nm)	x 0.102	= Kilograms-force metres (kgf m; kg m)	x 9.804	=	Newton metres (Nm)

Power

Horsepower (hp)	x 745.7	= Watts (W)	x 0.0013	=	Horsepower (hp)

Velocity (speed)

Miles per hour (miles/hr; mph)	x 1.609	= Kilometres per hour (km/hr; kph)	x 0.621	=	Miles per hour (miles/hr; mph)

Fuel consumption*

Miles per gallon, Imperial (mpg)	x 0.354	= Kilometres per litre (km/l)	x 2.825	=	Miles per gallon, Imperial (mpg)
Miles per gallon, US (mpg)	x 0.425	= Kilometres per litre (km/l)	x 2.352	=	Miles per gallon, US (mpg)

Temperature

Degrees Fahrenheit = (°C x 1.8) + 32   Degrees Celsius (Degrees Centigrade; °C) = (°F - 32) x 0.56

It is common practice to convert from miles per gallon (mpg) to litres/100 kilometres (l/100km), where mpg x l/100 km = 282

Spare parts are available from many sources, including maker's appointed garages, accessory shops, and motor factors. To be sure of obtaining the correct parts, it will sometimes be necessary to quote the vehicle identification number. If possible, it can also be useful to take the old parts along for positive identification. Items such as starter motors and alternators may be available under a service exchange scheme – any parts returned should be clean.

Our advice regarding spare parts is as follows.

Officially appointed garages

This is the best source of parts which are peculiar to your car, and which are not otherwise generally available (eg, badges, interior trim, certain body panels, etc). It is also the only place at which you should buy parts if the vehicle is still under warranty.

Accessory shops

These are very good places to buy materials and components needed for the maintenance of your car (oil, air and fuel filters, light bulbs, drivebelts, greases, brake pads, touch-up paint, etc). Components of this nature sold by a reputable shop are usually of the same standard as those used by the car manufacturer.

Besides components, these shops also sell tools and general accessories, usually have convenient opening hours, charge lower prices, and can often be found close to home. Some accessory shops have parts counters where components needed for almost any repair job can be purchased or ordered.

Motor factors

Good factors will stock all the more important components which wear out comparatively quickly, and can sometimes supply individual components needed for the overhaul of a larger assembly (eg, brake seals and hydraulic parts, bearing shells, pistons, valves). They may also handle work such as cylinder block reboring, crankshaft regrinding, etc.

Tyre and exhaust specialists

These outlets may be independent, or members of a local or national chain. They frequently offer competitive prices when compared with a main dealer or local garage, but it will pay to obtain several quotes before making a decision. When researching prices, also ask what extras may be added – for instance fitting a new valve and balancing the wheel are both commonly charged on top of the price of a new tyre.

Other sources

Beware of parts or materials obtained from market stalls, car boot sales or similar outlets. Such items are not invariably sub-standard, but there is little chance of compensation if they do prove unsatisfactory. in the case of safety-critical components such as brake pads, there is the risk not only of financial loss, but also of an accident causing injury or death.

Second-hand components or assemblies obtained from a car breaker can be a good buy in some circumstances, but this sort of purchase is best made by the experienced DIY mechanic.

Vehicle identification

Modifications are a continuing and unpublicised process in vehicle manufacture, quite apart from major model changes. Spare parts manuals and lists are compiled upon a numerical basis, the individual vehicle identification numbers being essential to correct identification of the component concerned.

When ordering spare parts, always give as much information as possible. Quote the car model, year of manufacture, body and engine numbers as appropriate.

The vehicle identification plate is situated on the driver's side B-pillar. The vehicle identification number is also repeated in the form of plate visible through the windscreen on the passenger's side (see illustrations).

Further information such as the trim level and vehicle paint code is also contained in the 'Oval' plate adjacent to the Vehicle Identification number (VIN) (see illustration).

The engine identification numbers are situated on the front face of the cylinder block (see illustration), either on a plate, or stamped directly to the cylinder block face. On some models, the engine type is shown on a sticker affixed to the timing belt cover.

Other identification numbers or codes are stamped on major items such as the gearbox, etc.

VIN plate at the base of the B-pillar...

...and on a plate on the facia (visible through the windscreen)

Engine number on cylinder block above starter (0.9 litre petrol engine)

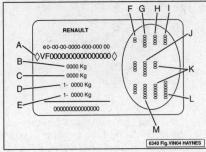

A Chassis number
B Gross vehicle weight
C Total train weight (fully loaded with trailer)
D Gross weight (front axle)
E Gross weight (rear axle)
F Technical specifications
G Paint code
H Equipment level
I Vehicle trim level
J Trim code
K Additional equipment
L Build number
M Interior trim code

Oval plate information

Engine number plate (diesel engine)

Whenever servicing, repair or overhaul work is carried out on the car or its components, observe the following procedures and instructions. This will assist in carrying out the operation efficiently and to a professional standard of workmanship.

Joint mating faces and gaskets

When separating components at their mating faces, never insert screwdrivers or similar implements into the joint between the faces in order to prise them apart. This can cause severe damage which results in oil leaks, coolant leaks, etc upon reassembly. Separation is usually achieved by tapping along the joint with a soft-faced hammer in order to break the seal. However, note that this method may not be suitable where dowels are used for component location.

Where a gasket is used between the mating faces of two components, a new one must be fitted on reassembly; fit it dry unless otherwise stated in the repair procedure. Make sure that the mating faces are clean and dry, with all traces of old gasket removed. When cleaning a joint face, use a tool which is unlikely to score or damage the face, and remove any burrs or nicks with an oilstone or fine file.

Make sure that tapped holes are cleaned with a pipe cleaner, and keep them free of jointing compound, if this is being used, unless specifically instructed otherwise.

Ensure that all orifices, channels or pipes are clear, and blow through them, preferably using compressed air.

Oil seals

Oil seals can be removed by levering them out with a wide flat-bladed screwdriver or similar implement. Alternatively, a number of self-tapping screws may be screwed into the seal, and these used as a purchase for pliers or some similar device in order to pull the seal free.

Whenever an oil seal is removed from its working location, either individually or as part of an assembly, it should be renewed.

The very fine sealing lip of the seal is easily damaged, and will not seal if the surface it contacts is not completely clean and free from scratches, nicks or grooves. If the original sealing surface of the component cannot be restored, and the manufacturer has not made provision for slight relocation of the seal relative to the sealing surface, the component should be renewed.

Protect the lips of the seal from any surface which may damage them in the course of fitting. Use tape or a conical sleeve where possible. Where indicated, lubricate the seal lips with oil before fitting and, on dual-lipped seals, fill the space between the lips with grease.

Unless otherwise stated, oil seals must be fitted with their sealing lips toward the lubricant to be sealed.

Use a tubular drift or block of wood of the appropriate size to install the seal and, if the seal housing is shouldered, drive the seal down to the shoulder. If the seal housing is unshouldered, the seal should be fitted with its face flush with the housing top face (unless otherwise instructed).

Screw threads and fastenings

Seized nuts, bolts and screws are quite a common occurrence where corrosion has set in, and the use of penetrating oil or releasing fluid will often overcome this problem if the offending item is soaked for a while before attempting to release it. The use of an impact driver may also provide a means of releasing such stubborn fastening devices, when used in conjunction with the appropriate screwdriver bit or socket. If none of these methods works, it may be necessary to resort to the careful application of heat, or the use of a hacksaw or nut splitter device. Before resorting to extreme methods, check that you are not dealing with a left-hand thread!

Studs are usually removed by locking two nuts together on the threaded part, and then using a spanner on the lower nut to unscrew the stud. Studs or bolts which have broken off below the surface of the component in which they are mounted can sometimes be removed using a stud extractor.

Always ensure that a blind tapped hole is completely free from oil, grease, water or other fluid before installing the bolt or stud. Failure to do this could cause the housing to crack due to the hydraulic action of the bolt or stud as it is screwed in.

For some screw fastenings, notably cylinder head bolts or nuts, torque wrench settings are no longer specified for the latter stages of tightening, "angle-tightening" being called up instead. Typically, a fairly low torque wrench setting will be applied to the bolts/nuts in the correct sequence, followed by one or more stages of tightening through specified angles.

When checking or retightening a nut or bolt to a specified torque setting, slacken the nut or bolt by a quarter of a turn, and then retighten to the specified setting. However, this should not be attempted where angular tightening has been used.

Locknuts, locktabs and washers

Any fastening which will rotate against a component or housing during tightening should always have a washer between it and the relevant component or housing.

Spring or split washers should always be renewed when they are used to lock a critical component such as a big-end bearing retaining bolt or nut. Locktabs which are folded over to retain a nut or bolt should always be renewed.

Self-locking nuts can be re-used in non-critical areas, providing resistance can be felt when the locking portion passes over the bolt or stud thread. However, it should be noted that self-locking stiffnuts tend to lose their effectiveness after long periods of use, and should then be renewed as a matter of course.

Split pins must always be replaced with new ones of the correct size for the hole.

When thread-locking compound is found on the threads of a fastener which is to be re-used, it should be cleaned off with a wire brush and solvent, and fresh compound applied on reassembly.

Special tools

Some repair procedures in this manual entail the use of special tools such as a press, two or three-legged pullers, spring compressors, etc. Wherever possible, suitable readily-available alternatives to the manufacturer's special tools are described, and are shown in use. In some instances, where no alternative is possible, it has been necessary to resort to the use of a manufacturer's tool, and this has been done for reasons of safety as well as the efficient completion of the repair operation. Unless you are highly-skilled and have a thorough understanding of the procedures described, never attempt to bypass the use of any special tool when the procedure described specifies its use. Not only is there a very great risk of personal injury, but expensive damage could be caused to the components involved.

Environmental considerations

When disposing of used engine oil, brake fluid, antifreeze, etc, give due consideration to any detrimental environmental effects. Do not, for instance, pour any of the above liquids down drains into the general sewage system, or onto the ground to soak away, as this is likely to pollute your local environment. Many local council refuse tips provide a facility for waste oil disposal, as do some garages. You can find your nearest disposal point by calling the Environment Agency on 03708 506 506 or by visiting www.oilbankline.org.uk.

Note: It is illegal and anti-social to dump oil down the drain. To find the location of your local oil recycling bank, call 03708 506 506 or visit www.oilbankline.org.uk.

The jack supplied with the vehicle tool kit should only be used for changing the roadwheels – see *Wheel changing* at the front of this manual. When carrying out any other kind of work, raise the vehicle using a hydraulic trolley jack, and always supplement the jack with axle stands positioned under the vehicle jacking points.

When using a trolley jack or axle stands, position the jack head or axle stand head adjacent to one of the relevant wheel changing jacking points under the sills **(see illustration)**. Use a block of wood between the jack or axle stand and the sill.

Do not attempt to jack the vehicle under the sump or any of the suspension components

The jack supplied with the vehicle locates in the jacking points on the underside of the sills – see Wheel changing at the front of this manual. Ensure that the jack head is correctly engaged before attempting to raise the vehicle.

 Warning: Neaver work under, around, or near a raised vehicle, unless it is adequately supported in at least two places.

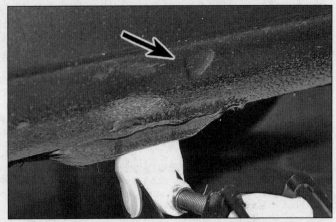

5.2 The jacking points are indicated by arrows on the sills

Introduction

A selection of good tools is a fundamental requirement for anyone contemplating the maintenance and repair of a motor vehicle. For the owner who does not possess any, their purchase will prove a considerable expense, offsetting some of the savings made by doing-it-yourself. However, provided that the tools purchased meet the relevant national safety standards and are of good quality, they will last for many years and prove an extremely worthwhile investment.

To help the average owner to decide which tools are needed to carry out the various tasks detailed in this manual, we have compiled three lists of tools under the following headings: *Maintenance and minor repair*, *Repair and overhaul*, and *Special*. Newcomers to practical mechanics should start off with the *Maintenance and minor repair* tool kit, and confine themselves to the simpler jobs around the vehicle. Then, as confidence and experience grow, more difficult tasks can be undertaken, with extra tools being purchased as, and when, they are needed. In this way, a *Maintenance and minor repair* tool kit can be built up into a *Repair and overhaul* tool kit over a considerable period of time, without any major cash outlays. The experienced do-it-yourselfer will have a tool kit good enough for most repair and overhaul procedures, and will add tools from the *Special* category when it is felt that the expense is justified by the amount of use to which these tools will be put.

Maintenance and minor repair tool kit

The tools given in this list should be considered as a minimum requirement if routine maintenance, servicing and minor repair operations are to be undertaken. We recommend the purchase of combination spanners (ring one end, open-ended the other); although more expensive than open-ended ones, they do give the advantages of both types of spanner.

- [ ] *Combination spanners:*
  Metric - 8 to 19 mm inclusive
- [ ] *Adjustable spanner - 35 mm jaw (approx.)*
- [ ] *Spark plug spanner (with rubber insert) - petrol models*
- [ ] *Spark plug gap adjustment tool - petrol models*
- [ ] *Set of feeler gauges*
- [ ] *Brake bleed nipple spanner*
- [ ] *Screwdrivers:*
  Flat blade - 100 mm long x 6 mm dia
  Cross blade - 100 mm long x 6 mm dia
  Torx - various sizes (not all vehicles)
- [ ] *Combination pliers*
- [ ] *Hacksaw (junior)*
- [ ] *Tyre pump*
- [ ] *Tyre pressure gauge*
- [ ] *Oil can*
- [ ] *Oil filter removal tool (if applicable)*
- [ ] *Fine emery cloth*
- [ ] *Wire brush (small)*
- [ ] *Funnel (medium size)*
- [ ] *Sump drain plug key (not all vehicles)*

Repair and overhaul tool kit

These tools are virtually essential for anyone undertaking any major repairs to a motor vehicle, and are additional to those given in the *Maintenance and minor repair* list. Included in this list is a comprehensive set of sockets. Although these are expensive, they will be found invaluable as they are so versatile - particularly if various drives are included in the set. We recommend the half-inch square-drive type, as this can be used with most proprietary torque wrenches.

The tools in this list will sometimes need to be supplemented by tools from the *Special* list:

- [ ] *Sockets to cover range in previous list (including Torx sockets)*
- [ ] *Reversible ratchet drive (for use with sockets)*
- [ ] *Extension piece, 250 mm (for use with sockets)*
- [ ] *Universal joint (for use with sockets)*
- [ ] *Flexible handle or sliding T "breaker bar" (for use with sockets)*
- [ ] *Torque wrench (for use with sockets)*
- [ ] *Self-locking grips*
- [ ] *Ball pein hammer*
- [ ] *Soft-faced mallet (plastic or rubber)*
- [ ] *Screwdrivers:*
  Flat blade - long & sturdy, short (chubby), and narrow (electrician's) types
  Cross blade – long & sturdy, and short (chubby) types
- [ ] *Pliers:*
  Long-nosed
  Side cutters (electrician's)
  Circlip (internal and external)
- [ ] *Cold chisel - 25 mm*
- [ ] *Scriber*
- [ ] *Scraper*
- [ ] *Centre-punch*
- [ ] *Pin punch*
- [ ] *Hacksaw*
- [ ] *Brake hose clamp*
- [ ] *Brake/clutch bleeding kit*
- [ ] *Selection of twist drills*
- [ ] *Steel rule/straight-edge*
- [ ] *Allen keys (inc. splined/Torx type)*
- [ ] *Selection of files*
- [ ] *Wire brush*
- [ ] *Axle stands*
- [ ] *Jack (strong trolley or hydraulic type)*
- [ ] *Light with extension lead*
- [ ] *Universal electrical multi-meter*

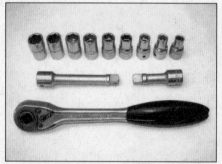

Sockets and reversible ratchet drive

Brake bleeding kit

Torx key, socket and bit

Hose clamp

Angular-tightening gauge

Special tools

The tools in this list are those which are not used regularly, are expensive to buy, or which need to be used in accordance with their manufacturers' instructions. Unless relatively difficult mechanical jobs are undertaken frequently, it will not be economic to buy many of these tools. Where this is the case, you could consider clubbing together with friends (or joining a motorists' club) to make a joint purchase, or borrowing the tools against a deposit from a local garage or tool hire specialist.

The following list contains only those tools and instruments freely available to the public, and not those special tools produced by the vehicle manufacturer specifically for its dealer network. You will find occasional references to these manufacturers' special tools in the text of this manual. Generally, an alternative method of doing the job without the vehicle manufacturers' special tool is given. However, sometimes there is no alternative to using them. Where this is the case and the relevant tool cannot be bought or borrowed, you will have to entrust the work to a dealer.

☐ Angular-tightening gauge
☐ Valve spring compressor
☐ Valve grinding tool
☐ Piston ring compressor
☐ Piston ring removal/installation tool
☐ Cylinder bore hone
☐ Balljoint separator
☐ Coil spring compressors (where applicable)
☐ Two/three-legged hub and bearing puller
☐ Impact screwdriver
☐ Micrometer and/or vernier calipers
☐ Dial gauge
☐ Tachometer
☐ Fault code reader
☐ Cylinder compression gauge
☐ Hand-operated vacuum pump and gauge
☐ Clutch plate alignment set
☐ Brake shoe steady spring cup removal tool
☐ Bush and bearing removal/installation set
☐ Stud extractors
☐ Tap and die set
☐ Lifting tackle

Buying tools

Reputable motor accessory shops and superstores often offer excellent quality tools at discount prices, so it pays to shop around.

Remember, you don't have to buy the most expensive items on the shelf, but it is always advisable to steer clear of the very cheap tools. Beware of 'bargains' offered on market stalls, on-line or at car boot sales. There are plenty of good tools around at reasonable prices, but always aim to purchase items which meet the relevant national safety standards. If in doubt, ask the proprietor or manager of the shop for advice before making a purchase.

Care and maintenance of tools

Having purchased a reasonable tool kit, it is necessary to keep the tools in a clean and serviceable condition. After use, always wipe off any dirt, grease and metal particles using a clean, dry cloth, before putting the tools away. Never leave them lying around after they have been used. A simple tool rack on the garage or workshop wall for items such as screwdrivers and pliers is a good idea. Store all normal spanners and sockets in a metal box. Any measuring instruments, gauges, meters, etc, must be carefully stored where they cannot be damaged or become rusty.

Take a little care when tools are used. Hammer heads inevitably become marked, and screwdrivers lose the keen edge on their blades from time to time. A little timely attention with emery cloth or a file will soon restore items like this to a good finish.

Working facilities

Not to be forgotten when discussing tools is the workshop itself. If anything more than routine maintenance is to be carried out, a suitable working area becomes essential.

It is appreciated that many an owner-mechanic is forced by circumstances to remove an engine or similar item without the benefit of a garage or workshop. Having done this, any repairs should always be done under the cover of a roof.

Wherever possible, any dismantling should be done on a clean, flat workbench or table at a suitable working height.

Any workbench needs a vice; one with a jaw opening of 100 mm is suitable for most jobs. As mentioned previously, some clean dry storage space is also required for tools, as well as for any lubricants, cleaning fluids, touch-up paints etc, which become necessary.

Another item which may be required, and which has a much more general usage, is an electric drill with a chuck capacity of at least 8 mm. This, together with a good range of twist drills, is virtually essential for fitting accessories.

Last, but not least, always keep a supply of old newspapers and clean, lint-free rags available, and try to keep any working area as clean as possible.

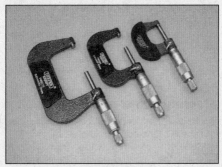
Micrometers

Dial test indicator ("dial gauge")

Oil filter removal tool (strap wrench type)

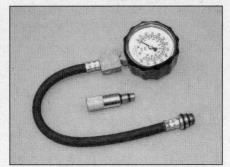
Compression tester

Bearing puller

This is a guide to getting your vehicle through the MOT test. Obviously it will not be possible to examine the vehicle to the same standard as the professional MOT tester. However, working through the following checks will enable you to identify any problem areas before submitting the vehicle for the test.

It has only been possible to summarise the test requirements here, based on the regulations in force at the time of printing. Test standards are becoming increasingly stringent, although there are some exemptions for older vehicles.

An assistant will be needed to help carry out some of these checks.

The checks have been sub-divided into four categories, as follows:

1 Checks carried out **FROM THE VEHICLE INTERIOR**

2 Checks carried out **WITH THE VEHICLE ON THE GROUND**

3 Checks carried out **WITH THE VEHICLE RAISED AND THE WHEELS FREE TO TURN**

4 Checks carried out on **YOUR VEHICLE'S EXHAUST EMISSION SYSTEM**

1 Checks carried out **FROM THE VEHICLE INTERIOR**

Handbrake (parking brake)

☐ Test the operation of the handbrake. Excessive travel (too many clicks) indicates incorrect brake or cable adjustment.
☐ Check that the handbrake cannot be released by tapping the lever sideways. Check the security of the lever mountings.

☐ If the parking brake is foot-operated, check that the pedal is secure and without excessive travel, and that the release mechanism operates correctly.
☐ Where applicable, test the operation of the electronic handbrake. The brake should engage and disengage without excessive delay. If the warning light does not extinguish, or a warning message is displayed when the brake is disengaged, this could indicate a fault which will need further investigation.

Footbrake

☐ Depress the brake pedal and check that it does not creep down to the floor, indicating a master cylinder fault. Release the pedal, wait a few seconds, then depress it again. If the pedal travels nearly to the floor before firm resistance is felt, brake adjustment or repair is necessary. If the pedal feels spongy, there is air in the hydraulic system which must be removed by bleeding.

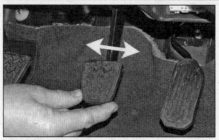

☐ Check that the brake pedal is secure and in good condition. Check also for signs of fluid leaks on the pedal, floor or carpets, which would indicate failed seals in the brake master cylinder.
☐ Check the servo unit (when applicable) by operating the brake pedal several times, then keeping the pedal depressed and starting the engine. As the engine starts, the pedal will move down. If not, the vacuum hose or the servo itself may be faulty.

Steering wheel and column

☐ Examine the steering wheel for fractures or looseness of the hub, spokes or rim.
☐ Move the steering wheel from side to side and then up and down. Check that the steering wheel is not loose on the column, indicating wear or a loose retaining nut. Continue moving the steering wheel as before, but also turn it slightly from left to right.
☐ Check that the steering wheel is not loose on the column, and that there is no abnormal movement of the steering wheel, indicating wear in the column support bearings or couplings.

☐ Check that the ignition lock (where fitted) engages and disengages correctly.
☐ Steering column adjustment mechanisms (where fitted) must be able to lock the column securely in place with no play evident.

Windscreen, mirrors and sunvisor

☐ The windscreen must be free of cracks or other significant damage within the 'swept area' of the windscreen. This is the area swept by the windscreen wipers. A second test area, known as 'Zone A', is the part of the swept area 290 mm wide, centred on the steering wheel centre line. Any damage in Zone A that cannot be contained in a 10 mm diameter circle, or any damage in the remainder of the swept area that cannot be contained in a 40 mm diameter circle, may cause the vehicle to fail the test.

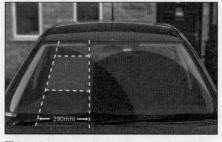

☐ Any items that may obscure the drivers view, such as stickers, sat-navs, anything hanging from the interior mirror, should be removed prior to the test.
☐ Vehicles registered after 1st August 1978 must have a drivers side mirror, and either an interior mirror, or a passenger's side mirror. Cameras (or indirect vision devices) may replace the mirrors, but they must function correctly.
☐ The driver's sunvisor must be capable of being stored in the "up" position.

Seat belts, seats and supplementary restraint systems (SRS)

Note: *The following checks are applicable to all seat belts, front and rear.*

☐ Examine the webbing of all the belts (including rear belts if fitted) for cuts, serious fraying or deterioration. Fasten and unfasten each belt to check the buckles. If applicable, check the retracting mechanism. Check the security of all seat belt mountings accessible from inside the vehicle, ensuring any height adjustable mountings lock securely in place.

☐ Where the seat belt is attached to a seat, the frame and mountings of the seat form part of the belt mountings, and are to be inspected as such.

☐ Any airbag, or SRS warning light must extinguish a few seconds after the ignition is switched on. Failure to do so indicates a fault which must be investigated.

☐ Seat belts with pre-tensioners, once activated, have a "flag" or similar showing on the seat belt stalk. This, in itself, is a reason for test failure.

☐ Check that the original airbag(s) is/are present, and not obviously defective.

☐ The seats themselves must be securely attached and the backrests must lock in the upright position. The driver's seat must also be able to slide forwards/rearwards, and lock in several positions.

Doors

☐ Both front doors must be able to be opened and closed from outside and inside, and must latch securely when closed.

☐ The rear doors must open from the outside.

☐ Examine all door hinges, catches and striker plates for missing, deteriorated, or insecure parts that could effect the opening and closing of the doors.

Speedometer

☐ The vehicle speedometer must be present, and appear operative. The figures on the speedometer must be legible, and illuminated when the lights are switched on.

2 Checks carried out **WITH THE VEHICLE ON THE GROUND**

Vehicle identification

☐ Number plates must be in good condition, secure and legible, with letters and numbers correctly spaced – spacing at (A) should be 33 mm and at (B) 11 mm. At the front, digits must be black on a white background and at the rear

black on a yellow background. Other background designs (such as honeycomb) are not permitted.

☐ The VIN plate and/or homologation plate must be permanently displayed and legible.

Electrical equipment

☐ Switch on the ignition and check the operation of the horn.

☐ Check the windscreen washers and wipers, examining the wiper blades; renew damaged or perished blades. The wiper blades must clear a large enough area of the windscreen to provide an 'adequate' view of the road, and be able to be parked in a position where they will not affect the drivers' view.

☐ On vehicles first used from 1st September 2009, the headlight washers (where fitted) must operate correctly.

☐ Check the operation of the stop-lights. This includes any lights that appear to be connected – Eg. high-level lights.

☐ Check the operation of the sidelights and number plate lights. The lenses and reflectors must be secure, clean and undamaged.

☐ Check the operation and alignment of the headlights. The headlight reflectors must not be tarnished and the lenses must be undamaged. Where plastic lenses are fitted, check they haven't deteriorated to the extent where they affect the light ouput or beam image. It's often possible to restore the plastic lens using a suitable polish or aftermarket treatment.

☐ Where HID or LED headlights are fitted, check the operation of the cleaning and self-levelling functions.

☐ The headlight main beam warning lamp must be functional.

☐ On vehicles first used from 1st March 2018, the daytime running lights (where fitted) must operate correctly.

☐ Switch on the ignition and check the operation of the direction indicators (including the instrument panel tell-tale) and the hazard warning lights. Operation of the sidelights and stop-lights must not affect the indicators – if it does, the cause is usually a bad earth at the rear light cluster. Indicators should flash at a rate of between 60 and 120 times per minute – faster or slower than this could indicate a fault with the flasher unit or a bad earth at one of the light units.

☐ The hazard warning lights must operate with the ignition on and off.

☐ Check the operation of the rear foglight(s), including the warning light on the instrument panel or in the switch. Note that the foglight

must be positioned in the centre or driver's side of the vehicle. If only the passenger's side illuminates, the test will fail.

☐ The warning lights must illuminate in accordance with the manufacturers' design (this includes any warning messages). For most vehicles, the ABS and other warning lights should illuminate when the ignition is switched on, and (if the system is operating properly) extinguish after a few seconds. Refer to the owner's handbook.

☐ On vehicles first used from 1st September 2009, the reversing lights must operate correctly when reverse gear is selected.

☐ Check the vehicle battery for security and leakage.

☐ Check the visible/accessible vehicle wiring is adequately supported, with no evidence of damage or deterioration that could result in a short-circuit.

Footbrake

☐ Examine the master cylinder, brake pipes and servo unit for leaks, loose mountings, corrosion or other damage. If ABS is fitted, this unit should also be examined for signs of leaks or corrosion.

☐ The fluid reservoir must be secure and the fluid level must be between the upper (A) and lower (B) markings.

☐ Check the fluid in the reservoir for signs of contamination.

☐ Inspect both front brake flexible hoses for cracks or deterioration of the rubber. Turn the steering from lock to lock, and ensure that the hoses do not contact the wheel, tyre, or any part of the steering or suspension mechanism. With the brake pedal firmly depressed, check the hoses for bulges or leaks under pressure.

Steering and suspension

☐ Have your assistant turn the steering wheel from side to side slightly, up to the point where the steering gear just begins to transmit this movement to the roadwheels. Check for excessive free play between the steering wheel and the steering gear, indicating wear or insecurity of the steering column joints, the column-to-steering gear coupling, or the steering gear itself. With a standard (380 mm diameter) steering wheel, there should be no more than 13 mm of free play for rack-and-pinion systems, and no more than 75 mm for non-rack-and-pinion designs.

☐ Have your assistant turn the steering

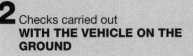

wheel more vigorously in each direction, so that the roadwheels just begin to turn. As this is done, examine all the steering joints, linkages, fittings and attachments. Renew any component that shows signs of wear or damage. On vehicles with hydraulic power steering, check the security and condition of the steering pump, drivebelt and hoses.

☐ Note that all movement checks on power steering systems are carried out with the engine running.

☐ Check that the vehicle is standing level, and at approximately the correct ride height.

Exhaust system

☐ Start the engine. With your assistant holding a rag over the tailpipe, check the entire system for leaks. Repair or renew leaking sections.

3 Checks carried out
WITH THE VEHICLE RAISED AND THE WHEELS FREE TO TURN

Jack up the front and rear of the vehicle, and securely support it on axle stands. Position the stands clear of the suspension assemblies. Ensure that the wheels are clear of the ground and that the steering can be turned from lock to lock.

Steering mechanism

☐ Have your assistant turn the steering from lock to lock. Check that the steering turns smoothly, and that no part of the steering mechanism, including a wheel or tyre, fouls any brake hose or pipe or any part of the body structure.

☐ Examine the steering rack rubber gaiters for damage or insecurity of the retaining clips. If power steering is fitted, check for signs of damage or leakage of the fluid hoses, pipes or connections. Also check for excessive stiffness or binding of the steering, a missing split pin or locking device, or severe corrosion of the body structure within 30 cm of any steering component attachment point.

☐ Check the track rod end ball joint dust covers. Any covers that are missing, seriously damaged, deteriorated or insecure, may fail inspection.

Front and rear suspension and wheel bearings

☐ Starting at the front right-hand side, grasp the roadwheel at the 3 o'clock and 9 o'clock positions and rock gently but firmly. Check for free play or insecurity at the wheel bearings, suspension balljoints, or suspension mountings, pivots and attachments.

☐ Now grasp the wheel at the 12 o'clock and 6 o'clock positions and repeat the previous inspection. Spin the wheel, and check for roughness or tightness of the front wheel bearing.

☐ If excess free play is suspected at a component pivot point, this can be confirmed by using a large screwdriver or similar tool and levering between the mounting and the component attachment. This will confirm whether the wear is in the pivot bush, its retaining bolt, or in the mounting itself (the bolt holes can often become elongated).

☐ Carry out all the above checks at the other front wheel, and then at both rear wheels.

Springs and shock absorbers

☐ Examine the suspension struts (when applicable) for serious fluid leakage, corrosion, or damage to the casing. Also check the security of the mounting points.

☐ If coil springs are fitted, check that the spring ends locate in their seats, and that the spring is not corroded, cracked or broken.

☐ If leaf springs are fitted, check that all leaves are intact, that the axle is securely attached to each spring, and that there is no deterioration of the spring eye mountings, bushes, and shackles.

☐ The same general checks apply to vehicles fitted with other suspension types, such as torsion bars, hydraulic displacer units, etc. Ensure that all mountings and attachments are secure, that there are no signs of excessive wear, corrosion or damage, and (on hydraulic types) that there are no fluid leaks or damaged pipes.

☐ Check any suspension and anti-roll bar link ball joint dust covers. Any covers that are missing, seriously damaged, deteriorated or insecure, may fail inspection.

☐ Examine each shock absorber for signs of leakage, corrosion of the casing, missing, detached or worn pivots and/or rubber bushes.

Driveshafts (fwd vehicles only)

☐ Rotate each front wheel in turn and inspect the inner and outer joint gaiters for splits or damage. Also check that each driveshaft is straight and undamaged.

Braking system

☐ If possible without dismantling, check brake pad wear and disc condition. Ensure that the friction lining material has not worn excessively, (A) and that the discs are not fractured, pitted, scored or badly worn (B). As a general rule, if the friction material is less than 1.5 mm thick, the inspection will fail.

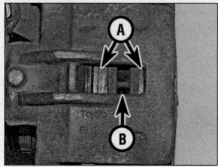

☐ Examine all the rigid brake pipes underneath the vehicle, and the flexible hose(s) at the rear. Look for corrosion, chafing or insecurity of the pipes, and for signs of bulging under pressure, chafing, splits or deterioration of the flexible hoses.

☐ Look for signs of fluid leaks at the brake calipers or on the brake backplates. Repair or renew leaking components.

☐ Slowly spin each wheel, while your assistant depresses and releases the footbrake. Ensure that each brake is operating and does not bind when the pedal is released.

☐ Examine the handbrake mechanism, checking for frayed or broken cables, excessive corrosion, or wear or insecurity of the linkage. Check that the mechanism works on each relevant wheel, and releases fully, without binding.

☐ Check the ABS sensors' wiring for signs of damage, deterioration or insecurity.

☐ It is not possible to test brake efficiency without special equipment, but a road test can be carried out later to check that the vehicle pulls up in a straight line.

Fuel and exhaust systems

☐ Inspect the fuel tank (including the filler cap), fuel pipes, hoses and unions. All components must be secure and free from leaks. Locking fuel caps must lock securely and the key must be provided for the MOT test.

☐ Examine the exhaust system over its entire length, checking for any damaged, broken or missing mountings, security of the retaining clamps and rust or corrosion.

☐ If the vehicle was originally equipped with a catalytic converter or particulate filter, one must be fitted.

Wheels and tyres

☐ Examine the sidewalls and tread area of each tyre in turn. Check for cuts, tears, lumps, bulges, separation of the tread, and exposure of the ply or cord due to wear or damage. Check that the tyre bead is correctly seated on the wheel rim, that the valve is sound and properly seated, and that the wheel is not distorted or damaged.

☐ Check that the tyres are of the correct size for the vehicle, that they are of the same size and type on each axle, and that the pressures are correct. The vehicle will fail the test if the tyres are obviously under-inflated.

☐ Check the tyre tread depth. The legal minimum at the time of writing is 1.6 mm over the central three-quarters of the tread width. Abnormal tread wear may indicate incorrect front wheel alignment or wear in steering or suspension components.

☐ Check that all wheel bolts/nuts are present.

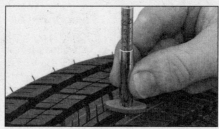

☐ If the spare wheel is fitted externally or in a separate carrier beneath the vehicle, check that mountings are secure and free of excessive corrosion.

Body corrosion

☐ Check the condition of the entire vehicle structure for signs of corrosion in load-bearing areas. (These include chassis box sections, side sills, cross-members, pillars, and all suspension, steering, braking system and seat belt mountings and anchorages.) Any corrosion which has seriously reduced the thickness of a load-bearing area (or is within 30 cm of safety-related components such as steering or suspension) is likely to cause the vehicle to fail. In this case professional repairs are likely to be needed.

☐ Damage or corrosion which causes sharp or otherwise dangerous edges to be exposed will also cause the vehicle to fail.

Towbars

☐ Check the condition of mounting points (both beneath the vehicle and within boot/hatchback areas) for signs of corrosion, ensuring that all fixings are secure and not worn or damaged. There must be no excessive play in detachable tow ball arms or quick-release mechanisms.

☐ Examine the security and condition of the towbar electrics socket. If the later 13-pin socket is fitted, the MOT tester will check its' wiring functions/connections are correct.

General leaks

☐ The vehicle will fail the test if there is a fluid leak of any kind that poses an environmental risk.

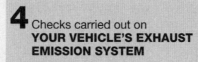

4 Checks carried out on **YOUR VEHICLE'S EXHAUST EMISSION SYSTEM**

Petrol models

☐ The engine should be warmed up, and running well (ignition system in good order, air filter element clean, etc).

☐ Before testing, run the engine at around 2500 rpm for 20 seconds. Let the engine drop to idle, and watch for smoke from the exhaust. If the idle speed is too high, or if dense blue or black smoke emerges for more than 5 seconds, the vehicle will fail. Typically, blue smoke signifies oil burning (engine wear); black smoke means unburnt fuel (dirty air cleaner element, or other fuel system fault).

☐ An exhaust gas analyser for measuring carbon monoxide (CO) and hydrocarbons (HC) is now needed. If one cannot be hired or borrowed, have a local garage perform the check.

CO emissions (mixture)

☐ The MOT tester has access to the CO limits for all vehicles from 1st August 1992. The CO level is measured at idle speed, and at 'fast idle' (2500 to 3000 rpm). The following limits are given as a general guide:

  At idle speed – Less than 0.3% CO
  At 'fast idle' – Less than 0.2% CO
  Lambda reading – 0.97 to 1.03

☐ If the CO level is too high, this may point to poor maintenance, a fuel injection system problem, faulty lambda (oxygen) sensor or catalytic converter. Try an injector cleaning treatment, and check the vehicle's ECU for fault codes.

HC emissions

☐ The MOT tester has access to HC limits for all vehicles. The HC level is measured at 'fast idle' (2500 to 3000 rpm). The following limits are given as a general guide:

  At 'fast idle' – Less than 200 ppm

☐ Excessive HC emissions are typically caused by oil being burnt (worn engine), or by a blocked crankcase ventilation system ('breather'). If the engine oil is old and thin, an oil change may help. If the engine is running badly, check the vehicle's ECU for fault codes.

Diesel models

☐ If the vehicle was fitted with a DPF (Diesel Particulate Filter) when it left the factory, it will fail the test if the MOT tester can see smoke of any colour emitting from the exhaust, or finds evidence that the filter has been tampered with.

☐ The only emission test for diesel engines is measuring exhaust smoke density, using a calibrated smoke meter.

☐ This test involves accelerating the engine to its maximum unloaded speed a minimum of once, and a maximum of 6 times. With the smoke meter connected, the engine is accelerated quickly to its maximum speed. If the smoke level is at or below the limit specified, the vehicle will pass. If the level is more than the specified limit then two further accelerations are carried out, and an average of the readings calculated. If the vehicle is still over the limit, a further three accelerations are carried out, with the average of the last three calculated after each check.

Note: *On engines with a timing belt, it is VITAL that the belt is in good condition before the test is carried out.*

Vehicles registered after 1st July 2008

Smoke level must not exceed 1.5m-1 – Turbo-charged and non-Turbocharged engines

Vehicles registered before 1st July 2008

Smoke level must not exceed 2.5m-1 – Non-turbo vehicles

Smoke level must not exceed 3.0m-1 – Turbocharged vehicles:

☐ If excess smoke is produced, try fitting a new air cleaner element, or using an injector cleaning treatment. If the engine is running badly, where applicable, check the vehicle's ECU for fault codes. Also check the vehicle's EGR system, where applicable. At high mileages, the injectors may require professional attention.

Fault finding

Engine

- [ ] Engine fails to rotate when attempting to start
- [ ] Engine rotates, but will not start
- [ ] Engine difficult to start when cold
- [ ] Engine difficult to start when hot
- [ ] Starter motor noisy or rough in engagement
- [ ] Engine starts, but stops immediately
- [ ] Engine idles erratically
- [ ] Engine misfires at idle speed
- [ ] Engine misfires throughout the driving speed range
- [ ] Engine hesitates on acceleration
- [ ] Engine stalls
- [ ] Engine lacks power
- [ ] Engine backfires
- [ ] Oil pressure warning light illuminated with engine running
- [ ] Engine runs-on after switching off
- [ ] Engine noises

Cooling system

- [ ] Overheating
- [ ] Overcooling
- [ ] External coolant leakage
- [ ] Internal coolant leakage
- [ ] Corrosion

Fuel and exhaust systems

- [ ] Excessive fuel consumption
- [ ] Fuel leakage and/or fuel odour
- [ ] Excessive noise or fumes from exhaust system

Clutch

- [ ] Pedal travels to floor – no pressure or very little resistance
- [ ] Clutch fails to disengage (unable to select gears)
- [ ] Clutch slips (engine speed increases, with no increase in vehicle speed)
- [ ] Judder as clutch is engaged
- [ ] Noise when depressing or releasing clutch pedal

Manual transmission

- [ ] Noisy in neutral with engine running
- [ ] Noisy in one particular gear
- [ ] Difficulty engaging gears
- [ ] Jumps out of gear
- [ ] Vibration
- [ ] Lubricant leaks

Driveshafts

- [ ] Clicking or knocking noise on turns (at slow speed on full-lock)
- [ ] Vibration when accelerating or decelerating

Braking system

- [ ] Vehicle pulls to one side under braking
- [ ] Noise (grinding or high-pitched squeal) when brakes applied
- [ ] Excessive brake pedal travel
- [ ] Brake pedal feels spongy when depressed
- [ ] Excessive brake pedal effort required to stop vehicle
- [ ] Judder felt through brake pedal or steering wheel when braking
- [ ] Pedal pulsates when braking hard
- [ ] Brakes binding
- [ ] Rear wheels locking under normal braking

Steering and suspension

- [ ] Vehicle pulls to one side
- [ ] Wheel wobble and vibration
- [ ] Excessive pitching and/or rolling around corners, or during braking
- [ ] Wandering or general instability
- [ ] Excessively-stiff steering
- [ ] Excessive play in steering
- [ ] Lack of power assistance
- [ ] Tyre wear excessive

Electrical system

- [ ] Battery will only hold a charge for a few days
- [ ] Ignition/no-charge warning light remains illuminated with engine running
- [ ] Ignition/no-charge warning light fails to come on
- [ ] Lights inoperative
- [ ] Instrument readings inaccurate or erratic
- [ ] Horn inoperative, or unsatisfactory in operation
- [ ] Wipers inoperative, or unsatisfactory in operation
- [ ] Washers inoperative, or unsatisfactory in operation
- [ ] Electric windows inoperative, or unsatisfactory in operation
- [ ] Central locking system inoperative, or unsatisfactory in operation

Introduction

The vehicle owner who does his or her own maintenance according to the recommended service schedules should not have to use this section of the manual very often. Modern component reliability is such that, provided those items subject to wear or deterioration are inspected or renewed at the specified intervals, sudden failure is comparatively rare. Faults do not usually just happen as a result of sudden failure, but develop over a period of time. Major mechanical failures in particular are usually preceded by characteristic symptoms over hundreds or even thousands of miles. Those components which do occasionally fail without warning are often small and easily carried in the vehicle.

With any fault-finding, the first step is to decide where to begin investigations. Sometimes this is obvious, but on other occasions, a little detective work will be necessary. The owner who makes half a dozen haphazard adjustments or replacements may be successful in curing a fault (or its symptoms), but will be none the wiser if the fault recurs, and ultimately may have spent more time and money than was necessary. A calm and logical approach will be found to be more satisfactory in the long run. Always take into account any warning signs or abnormalities that may have been noticed in the period preceding the fault – power loss, high or low gauge readings, unusual smells, etc – and remember that failure of components such as fuses or spark plugs may only be pointers to some underlying fault.

The pages which follow provide an easy-reference guide to the more common problems which may occur during the operation of the vehicle. These problems and their possible causes are grouped under headings denoting various components or systems, such as Engine, Cooling system, etc. The general Chapter which deals with the problem is also shown in brackets; refer to the relevant part of that Chapter for system-specific information. Whatever the fault, certain basic principles apply. These are as follows:

Verify the fault. This is simply a matter of being sure that you know what the symptoms are before starting work. This is particularly important if you are investigating a fault for someone else, who may not have described it very accurately.

Don't overlook the obvious. For example,

if the vehicle won't start, is there fuel in the tank? (Don't take anyone else's word on this particular point, and don't trust the fuel gauge either!) If an electrical fault is indicated, look for loose or broken wires before digging out the test gear.

Cure the disease, not the symptom. Substituting a flat battery with a fully-charged one will get you off the hard shoulder, but if the underlying cause is not attended to, the new battery will go the same way. Similarly, changing oil-fouled spark plugs for a new set will get you moving again, but remember that

the reason for the fouling (if it wasn't simply an incorrect grade of plug) will have to be established and corrected.

Don't take anything for granted. Particularly, don't forget that a 'new' component may itself be defective (especially if it's been rattling around in the boot for months), and don't leave components out of a fault diagnosis sequence just because they are new or recently-fitted. When you do finally diagnose a difficult fault, you'll probably realise that all the evidence was there from the start.

Engine

Engine fails to rotate when attempting to start

- ☐ Battery terminal connections loose or corroded (see *Weekly checks*).
- ☐ Battery discharged or faulty (Chapter 5A Section 3).
- ☐ Broken, loose or disconnected wiring in the starting circuit (Chapter 5A Section 2).
- ☐ Defective starter solenoid or switch (Chapter 5A Section 8).
- ☐ Defective starter motor (Chapter 5A Section 9).
- ☐ Starter pinion or flywheel ring gear teeth loose or broken (Chapter 2A Section 14, Chapter 2B Section 16, Chapter 2C Section 14 or Chapter 5A Section 9).
- ☐ Engine earth strap broken or disconnected (Chapter 5A Section 2).

Engine rotates, but will not start

- ☐ Fuel tank empty.
- ☐ Battery discharged (engine rotates slowly) (Chapter 5A Section 3).
- ☐ Battery terminal connections loose or corroded (See *Weekly checks*).
- ☐ Ignition components damp or damaged – petrol models (Chapter 1A Section 18, or Chapter 5B Section 3).
- ☐ Broken, loose or disconnected wiring in the ignition circuit – petrol models (Chapter 1A Section 18 or Chapter 5B Section 2).
- ☐ Worn, faulty or incorrectly-gapped spark plugs – petrol models (Chapter 1A Section 18).
- ☐ Preheating system faulty – diesel models (Chapter 5C Section 1).
- ☐ Fuel injection system fault – petrol models (Chapter 4A Section 12).
- ☐ Air in fuel system – diesel models (Chapter 4B Section 6).
- ☐ Major mechanical failure (eg, timing belt) (Chapter 2B Section 7 or Chapter 2C Section 6).

Engine difficult to start when cold

- ☐ Battery discharged (Chapter 5A Section 3).
- ☐ Battery terminal connections loose or corroded (See *Weekly checks*).
- ☐ Worn, faulty or incorrectly-gapped spark plugs – petrol models (Chapter 1A Section 18).
- ☐ Preheating system faulty – diesel models (Chapter 5C Section 1).
- ☐ Fuel injection system fault – petrol models (Chapter 4A Section 12).
- ☐ Other ignition system fault – petrol models (Chapter 1A Section 18 and Chapter 5B Section 2).
- ☐ Low cylinder compressions (Chapter 2A Section 2, Chapter 2B Section 2 or Chapter 2C Section 2).

Engine difficult to start when hot

- ☐ Air filter element dirty or clogged (Chapter 1A Section 19 or Chapter 1B Section 5).
- ☐ Fuel injection system fault – petrol models (Chapter 4A Section 12).
- ☐ Low cylinder compressions (Chapter 2B Section 2 or Chapter 2C Section 2).

Starter motor noisy or rough in engagement

- ☐ Starter pinion or flywheel ring gear teeth loose or broken (Chapter 2A Section 14, Chapter 2B Section 16, Chapter 2C Section 14 and Chapter 5A Section 9).
- ☐ Starter motor mounting bolts loose or missing (Chapter 5A Section 9).
- ☐ Starter motor internal components worn or damaged (Chapter 5A Section 9).

Engine starts, but stops immediately

- ☐ Loose or faulty electrical connections in the ignition circuit – petrol models (Chapter 1A Section 18 and Chapter 5B Section 3).
- ☐ Vacuum leak at the throttle body or inlet manifold – petrol models (Chapter 4A Section 11).
- ☐ Blocked injector/fuel injection system fault – petrol models (Chapter 4A Section 13).

Engine idles erratically

- ☐ Air filter element clogged (Chapter 1A Section 19 or Chapter 1B Section 5).
- ☐ Vacuum leak at the throttle body, inlet manifold or associated hoses – petrol models (Chapter 4A).
- ☐ Worn, faulty or incorrectly-gapped spark plugs – petrol models (Chapter 1A Section 18).
- ☐ Uneven or low cylinder compressions (Chapter 2A Section 2, Chapter 2B Section 2 or Chapter 2C Section 2).
- ☐ Camshaft lobes worn (Chapter 2A Section 9, Chapter 2B Section 10 or Chapter 2C Section 9).
- ☐ Timing belt incorrectly tensioned (Chapter 2B Section 7 or Chapter 2C Section 6).
- ☐ Blocked injector/fuel injection system fault – petrol models (Chapter 4A Section 13).
- ☐ Faulty injector(s) – diesel models (Chapter 4B Section 12).

Engine misfires at idle speed

- ☐ Worn, faulty or incorrectly-gapped spark plugs – petrol models (Chapter 1A Section 18).
- ☐ Faulty spark plug HT leads (Chapter 5B Section 3).
- ☐ Vacuum leak at the throttle body, inlet manifold or associated hoses – petrol models (Chapter 4A).
- ☐ Blocked injector/fuel injection system fault – petrol models (Chapter 4A Section 12).
- ☐ Faulty injector(s) – diesel models (Chapter 4B Section 12).
- ☐ Ignition fault – petrol models (Chapter 5B Section 2).
- ☐ Uneven or low cylinder compressions (Chapter 2A Section 2, Chapter 2B Section 2 or Chapter 2C Section 2).
- ☐ Disconnected, leaking, or perished crankcase ventilation hoses (Chapter 4C).

Engine (continued)

Engine misfires throughout the driving speed range

☐ Fuel filter choked (Chapter 4A Section 8 or Chapter 1B Section 19).

☐ Fuel pump faulty, or delivery pressure low – petrol models (Chapter 4A Section 8).

☐ Fuel tank vent blocked, or fuel pipes restricted (Chapter 4A Section 10 or Chapter 4B Section 5).

☐ Vacuum leak at the throttle body, inlet manifold or associated hoses – petrol models (Chapter 4A).

☐ Worn, faulty or incorrectly-gapped spark plugs – petrol models (Chapter 1A Section 18).

☐ Faulty spark plug HT leads (Chapter 5B Section 3).

☐ Faulty injector(s) – diesel models (Chapter 4B Section 12).

☐ Faulty ignition coil – petrol models (Chapter 5B Section 3).

☐ Uneven or low cylinder compressions (Chapter 2A Section 2, Chapter 2B Section 2 or Chapter 2C Section 2).

☐ Blocked injector/fuel injection system fault – petrol models (Chapter 4A Section 12).

Engine hesitates on acceleration

☐ Worn, faulty or incorrectly-gapped spark plugs – petrol models (Chapter 1A Section 18).

☐ Vacuum leak at the throttle body, inlet manifold or associated hoses – petrol models (Chapter 4A).

☐ Blocked injector/fuel injection system fault – petrol models (Chapter 4A Section 12).

☐ Faulty injector(s) – diesel models (Chapter 4B Section 12).

Engine stalls

☐ Vacuum leak at the throttle body, inlet manifold or associated hoses – petrol models (Chapter 4A).

☐ Fuel filter choked (Chapter 1B Section 19).

☐ Fuel pump faulty, or delivery pressure low – petrol models (Chapter 4A Section 8).

☐ Fuel tank vent blocked, or fuel pipes restricted (Chapter 4A Section 10 or Chapter 4B Section 5).

☐ Blocked injector/fuel injection system fault – petrol models (Chapter 4A Section 13).

☐ Faulty injector(s) – diesel models (Chapter 4B Section 12).

Engine lacks power

☐ Timing belt incorrectly fitted or tensioned (Chapter 2B Section 7 or Chapter 2C Section 6).

☐ Fuel filter choked (Chapter 1B Section 19).

☐ Fuel pump faulty, or delivery pressure low – petrol models (Chapter 4A Section 8).

☐ Uneven or low cylinder compressions (Chapter 2A Section 2, Chapter 2B Section 2 or Chapter 2C Section 2).

☐ Worn, faulty or incorrectly-gapped spark plugs – petrol models (Chapter 1A Section 18).

☐ Vacuum leak at the throttle body, inlet manifold or associated hoses – petrol models (Chapter 4A).

☐ Blocked injector/fuel injection system fault – petrol models (Chapter 4A Section 12).

☐ Faulty injector(s) – diesel models (Chapter 4B Section 12).

☐ Injection pump timing incorrect – diesel models (Chapter 2C Section 6).

☐ Brakes binding (Chapter 9 Section 1).

☐ Clutch slipping (Chapter 6 Section 8).

Engine backfires

☐ Timing belt incorrectly fitted or tensioned (Chapter 2B Section 7 or Chapter 2C Section 6).

☐ Vacuum leak at the throttle body, inlet manifold or associated hoses – petrol models (Chapter 4A).

☐ Blocked injector/fuel injection system fault – petrol models (Chapter 4A Section 13).

Oil pressure warning light illuminated with engine running

☐ Low oil level, or incorrect oil grade (*Weekly checks*).

☐ Faulty oil pressure sensor (Chapter 5A Section 2).

☐ Worn engine bearings and/or oil pump (Chapter 2A Section 12, Chapter 2B Section 13, Chapter 2C Section 12 and Chapter 2D Section 14).

☐ High engine operating temperature (Chapter 3 Section 1).

☐ Oil pressure relief valve defective (Chapter 2A Section 12, Chapter 2B Section 14 or Chapter 2C Section 12).

☐ Oil pick-up strainer clogged (Chapter 2A Section 11, Chapter 2B Section 13 or Chapter 2C Section 12).

Engine runs-on after switching off

☐ Excessive carbon build-up in engine (Chapter 2A Section 10, Chapter 2B Section 11 or Chapter 2C Section 10).

☐ High engine operating temperature (Chapter 3).

☐ Fuel injection system fault – petrol models (Chapter 4A Section 5).

Engine noises

☐ Ignition system fault – petrol models (Chapter 1A Section 18 and Chapter 5B Section 2).

☐ Incorrect grade of spark plug – petrol models (Chapter 1A Section 18).

☐ Incorrect grade of fuel (Chapter 4A Section 1 or Chapter 4B Section 6).

☐ Vacuum leak at the throttle body, inlet manifold or associated hoses – petrol models (Chapter 4A).

☐ Excessive carbon build-up in engine (Chapter 2A Section 10, Chapter 2B Section 11 or Chapter 2C Section 10).

☐ Blocked injector/fuel injection system fault – petrol models (Chapter 4A Section 13).

Whistling or wheezing noises

☐ Leaking inlet manifold or throttle body gasket – petrol models (Chapter 4A Section 14).

☐ Leaking exhaust manifold gasket or pipe-to-manifold joint (Chapter 4A Section 17 or Chapter 4B Section 18).

☐ Leaking vacuum hose (Chapter 4A Section 14, Chapter 4B Section 14 and Chapter 9 Section 3.

☐ Blowing cylinder head gasket (Chapter 2A Section 10, Chapter 2B Section 2 or Chapter 2C Section 2).

Tapping or rattling noises

☐ Worn valve gear or camshaft (Chapter 2A Section 9, Chapter 2B Section 10 or Chapter 2C Section 2).

☐ Ancillary component fault (water pump, alternator, etc) (Chapter 3, Chapter 5A).

Knocking or thumping noises

☐ Worn big-end bearings (regular heavy knocking, perhaps less under load) (Chapter 2D Section 14).

☐ Worn main bearings (rumbling and knocking, perhaps worsening under load) (Chapter 2D Section 14).

☐ Piston slap (most noticeable when cold) (Chapter 2D Section 12).

☐ Ancillary component fault (water pump, alternator, etc) (Chapter 3, Chapter 5A).

Cooling system

Overheating

- [ ] Insufficient coolant in system (see *Weekly checks*).
- [ ] Thermostat faulty (Chapter 3 Section 5).
- [ ] Radiator core blocked, or grille restricted (Chapter 3 Section 3).
- [ ] Electric cooling fan or thermostatic switch faulty (Chapter 3 Section 6).
- [ ] Inaccurate temperature gauge sender unit (Chapter 3 Section 8).
- [ ] Airlock in cooling system (Chapter 1A Section 27).
- [ ] Expansion tank pressure cap faulty (Chapter 3 Section 4).

Overcooling

- [ ] Thermostat faulty (Chapter 3 Section 5).
- [ ] Inaccurate temperature gauge sender unit (Chapter 3 Section 8).

External coolant leakage

- [ ] Deteriorated or damaged hoses or hose clips (Chapter 1A Section 14 or Chapter 1B Section 15).

- [ ] Radiator core or heater matrix leaking (Chapter 3 Section 3 or Chapter 3 Section 11).
- [ ] Pressure cap faulty (Chapter 3 Section 4).
- [ ] Coolant pump internal seal leaking (Chapter 3 Section 9).
- [ ] Coolant pump-to-block seal leaking (Chapter 3 Section 9).
- [ ] Boiling due to overheating (Chapter 3 Section 1).
- [ ] Core plug leaking (Chapter 2D Section 11).

Internal coolant leakage

- [ ] Leaking cylinder head gasket (Chapter 2A Section 10, Chapter 2B Section 11 or Chapter 2C Section 10).
- [ ] Cracked cylinder head or cylinder block (Chapter 2B Section 11, Chapter 2C Section 10 or Chapter 2D Section 7).

Corrosion

- [ ] Infrequent draining and flushing (Chapter 1A Section 27 or Chapter 1B Section 27).
- [ ] Incorrect coolant mixture or inappropriate coolant type (Chapter 1A Section 27 or Chapter 1B Section 27).

Fuel and exhaust systems

Excessive fuel consumption

- [ ] Air filter element dirty or clogged (Chapter 1A Section 19 or Chapter 1B Section 5).
- [ ] Fuel injection system fault – petrol models (Chapter 4A Section 5).
- [ ] Faulty injector(s) – diesel models (Chapter 4B Section 12).
- [ ] Ignition system fault – petrol models (Chapter 1A Section 18 and Chapter 5B Section 2).
- [ ] Tyres under-inflated (see *Weekly checks*).

Fuel leakage and/or fuel odour

- [ ] Damaged or corroded fuel tank, pipes or connections (Chapter 4A Section 7 or Chapter 4B Section 2).

Excessive noise or fumes from exhaust system

- [ ] Leaking exhaust system or manifold joints (Chapter 4A, or Chapter 4B).
- [ ] Leaking, corroded or damaged silencers or pipe (Chapter 4A Section 17, or Chapter 4B Section 18).
- [ ] Broken mountings causing body or suspension contact (Chapter 4A Section 17 or Chapter 4B Section 18).

Clutch

Pedal travels to floor – no pressure or very little resistance

- [ ] Leak or other fault in clutch hydraulic system (Chapter 6 Section 4).
- [ ] Broken clutch release bearing or arm (Chapter 6 Section 9).
- [ ] Broken diaphragm spring in clutch pressure plate (Chapter 6 Section 8).

Clutch fails to disengage (unable to select gears)

- [ ] Incorrect clutch adjustment (Chapter 6 Section 5).
- [ ] Clutch friction disc sticking on gearbox input shaft splines (Chapter 6 Section 8).
- [ ] Clutch friction disc sticking to flywheel or pressure plate (Chapter 6 Section 8).
- [ ] Faulty pressure plate assembly (Chapter 6 Section 8).
- [ ] Clutch release mechanism worn or badly assembled (Chapter 6 Section 9).

Clutch slips (engine speed increases, with no increase in vehicle speed)

- [ ] Clutch friction disc linings excessively worn (Chapter 6 Section 8).
- [ ] Clutch friction disc linings contaminated with oil or grease (Chapter 6 Section 8).

- [ ] Faulty pressure plate or weak diaphragm spring (Chapter 6 Section 8).

Judder as clutch is engaged

- [ ] Clutch friction plate linings contaminated with oil or grease (Chapter 6 Section 8).
- [ ] Clutch friction plate linings excessively worn (Chapter 6 Section 8).
- [ ] Faulty or distorted pressure plate or diaphragm spring (Chapter 6 Section 8).
- [ ] Worn or loose engine or gearbox mountings (Chapter 2A Section 15, Chapter 2B Section 17 or Chapter 2C Section 15).
- [ ] Clutch friction disc hub or gearbox input shaft splines worn (Chapter 6 Section 8).

Noise when depressing or releasing clutch pedal

- [ ] Worn clutch release bearing (Chapter 6 Section 9).
- [ ] Worn or dry clutch pedal pivot (Chapter 6 Section 6).
- [ ] Faulty pressure plate assembly (Chapter 6 Section 8).
- [ ] Pressure plate diaphragm spring broken (Chapter 6 Section 8).
- [ ] Broken clutch friction disc cushioning springs (Chapter 6 Section 8).

Manual transmission

Noisy in neutral with engine running

☐ Input shaft bearings worn (noise apparent with clutch pedal released, but not when depressed) (Chapter 7 Section 8). *
☐ Clutch release bearing worn (noise apparent with clutch pedal depressed, possibly less when released) (Chapter 6 Section 8).

Noisy in one particular gear

☐ Worn, damaged or chipped gear teeth (Chapter 7 Section 7). *

Difficulty engaging gears

☐ Clutch fault (Chapter 6 Section 8).
☐ Worn or damaged gear linkage (Chapter 7 Section 4).
☐ Worn synchroniser units (Chapter 7 Section 7).

Jumps out of gear

☐ Worn or damaged gear linkage (Chapter 7 Section 4).
☐ Worn synchroniser units (Chapter 7 Section 7). *
☐ *Worn selector forks (Chapter 7 Section 7). *

Vibration

☐ Lack of oil (Chapter 1A Section 21 or Chapter 7 Section 7).
☐ Worn bearings (Chapter 7 Section 7). *

Lubricant leaks

☐ Leaking oil seal (Chapter 7 Section 5).
☐ Leaking housing joint (Chapter 7 Section 8). *

* *Although the corrective action necessary to remedy the symptoms described is beyond the scope of the home mechanic, the above information should be helpful in isolating the cause of the condition, so that the owner can communicate clearly with a professional mechanic.*

Driveshafts

Clicking or knocking noise on turns (at slow speed on full-lock)

☐ Lack of constant velocity joint lubricant, possibly due to damaged gaiter (Chapter 8 Section 3 or Chapter 8 Section 4).
☐ Worn outer constant velocity joint (Chapter 8 Section 5).

Vibration when accelerating or decelerating

☐ Worn inner constant velocity joint (Chapter 8 Section 5).
☐ Damaged or distorted driveshaft (Chapter 8 Section 5).

Braking system

Vehicle pulls to one side under braking

Note: *Before assuming that a brake problem exists, make sure that the tyres are in good condition and correctly inflated, that the front wheel alignment is correct, and that the vehicle is not loaded with weight in an unequal manner. Apart from checking the condition of all pipe and hose connections, any faults occurring on the anti-lock braking system should be referred to a Renault dealer for diagnosis.*

- ☐ Worn, defective, damaged or contaminated front or rear brake pads/shoes on one side (Chapter 1A Section 7, Chapter 1B Section 8 and Chapter 9).
- ☐ Seized or partially-seized front or rear brake caliper/wheel cylinder piston (Chapter 9 Section 9 or Chapter 9 Section 13, 17).
- ☐ A mixture of brake pad/shoe lining materials fitted between sides (Chapter 9).
- ☐ Brake caliper or rear brake backplate bolts loose (Chapter 9 Section 9).
- ☐ Worn or damaged steering or suspension components (Chapter 1A Section 13, Chapter 1B Section 14 and Chapter 10 Section 1).

Noise (grinding or high-pitched squeal) when brakes applied

- ☐ Brake pad or shoe friction lining material worn down to metal backing (Chapter 1A Section 7, Chapter 1B Section 8 and Chapter 9).
- ☐ Excessive corrosion of brake disc or drum – may be apparent after the vehicle has been standing for some time (Chapter 9 Section 10, Chapter 9 Section 18 or Chapter 9 Section 11).

Excessive brake pedal travel

- ☐ Faulty rear drum brake self-adjust mechanism (Chapter 9 Section 12).
- ☐ Faulty master cylinder (Chapter 9 Section 7).
- ☐ Air in hydraulic system (Chapter 9 Section 5).
- ☐ Faulty vacuum servo unit (Chapter 9 Section 3).
- ☐ Faulty vacuum pump – diesel models (Chapter 9 Section 22).

Brake pedal feels spongy when depressed

- ☐ Air in hydraulic system (Chapter 9 Section 5).
- ☐ Deteriorated flexible rubber brake hoses (Chapter 1A Section 14, Chapter 1B Section 15 and Chapter 9 Section 6).
- ☐ Master cylinder mountings loose (Chapter 9 Section 7).
- ☐ Faulty master cylinder (Chapter 9 Section 7).

Excessive brake pedal effort required to stop vehicle

- ☐ Faulty vacuum servo unit (Chapter 9 Section 3).
- ☐ Disconnected, damaged or insecure brake servo vacuum hose (Chapter 1A Section 14, Chapter 1B Section 15 and Chapter 9 Section 6).
- ☐ Faulty vacuum pump – diesel models (Chapter 9 Section 22).
- ☐ Primary or secondary hydraulic circuit failure (Chapter 9 Section 1).
- ☐ Seized brake caliper or wheel cylinder piston(s) (Chapter 9 Section 9, Chapter 9 Section 17 or Chapter 9 Section 13).
- ☐ Brake pads or brake shoes incorrectly fitted (Chapter 9 Section 16 or Chapter 9 Section 12).
- ☐ Incorrect grade of brake pads or brake shoes fitted (Chapter 9).
- ☐ Brake pads or brake shoe linings contaminated (Chapter 9).

Judder felt through brake pedal or steering wheel when braking

- ☐ Excessive run-out or distortion of brake disc(s) or drum(s) (Chapter 9 Section 10, Chapter 9 Section 18 or Chapter 9 Section 11).
- ☐ Brake pad or brake shoe linings worn (Chapter 1A Section 7, Chapter 1A Section 20, Chapter 1B Section 8 and Chapter 1B Section 20).
- ☐ Brake caliper or rear brake backplate mounting bolts loose (Chapter 9 Section 17 or Chapter 9 Section 13).
- ☐ Wear in suspension or steering components or mountings (Chapter 1A Section 13 or Chapter 1B Section 14).

Pedal pulsates when braking hard

- ☐ Normal feature of ABS – no fault.

Brakes binding

- ☐ Seized brake caliper piston(s) or wheel cylinder piston(s) (Chapter 9 Section 9, Chapter 9 Section 17 or Chapter 9 Section 13).
- ☐ Incorrectly-adjusted handbrake mechanism or linkage (Chapter 1A Section 6 or Chapter 1B Section 7).
- ☐ Faulty master cylinder (Chapter 9 Section 7).

Rear wheels locking under normal braking

- ☐ Seized brake caliper piston(s) or wheel cylinder piston(s) (Chapter 9 Section 17 or Chapter 9 Section 13).
- ☐ Faulty ABS modulator (Chapter 9 Section 21).

Steering and suspension

Vehicle pulls to one side

Note: *Before diagnosing suspension or steering faults, be sure that the trouble is not due to incorrect tyre pressures, mixtures of tyre types, or binding brakes.*
- ☐ Defective tyre (see *Weekly checks*).
- ☐ Excessive wear in suspension or steering components (Chapter 1A Section 13 or Chapter 1B Section 14).
- ☐ Incorrect front wheel alignment (Chapter 10 Section 20).
- ☐ Accident damage to steering or suspension components (Chapter 1A Section 13 or Chapter 1B Section 14).

Wheel wobble and vibration

- ☐ Front roadwheels out of balance (vibration felt mainly through the steering wheel) (Chapter 10 Section 1).
- ☐ Rear roadwheels out of balance (vibration felt throughout the vehicle) (see *Weekly checks*).
- ☐ Roadwheels damaged or distorted (Chapter 1A Section 13 or Chapter 1B Section 14).
- ☐ Faulty or damaged tyre (see *Weekly checks*).
- ☐ Worn steering or suspension joints, bushes or components (Chapter 1A Section 13 or Chapter 1B Section 14).
- ☐ Wheel bolts loose (Chapter 1A Section 15 or Chapter 1B Section 16).

Excessive pitching and/or rolling around corners, or during braking

- ☐ Defective shock absorbers (Chapter 10 Section 5 or Chapter 10 Section 10).
- ☐ Broken or weak coil spring (Chapter 10 Section 4 or Chapter 10 Section 11).
- ☐ Worn or damaged anti-roll bar or mountings (Chapter 10 Section 6).

Wandering or general instability

- ☐ Incorrect front wheel alignment (Chapter 10 Section 20).
- ☐ Worn steering or suspension joints, bushes or components (Chapter 1A Section 13 or Chapter 1B Section 14).
- ☐ Roadwheels out of balance (see *Weekly checks*).
- ☐ Faulty or damaged tyre (see *Weekly checks*).
- ☐ Wheel bolts loose (Chapter 1A Section 15 or Chapter 1B Section 16).
- ☐ Defective shock absorbers (Chapter 1A Section 13 or Chapter 1B Section 14).

Excessively-stiff steering

- ☐ Lack of steering gear lubricant (Chapter 10 Section 17).
- ☐ Seized track rod end balljoint or suspension balljoint (Chapter 10 Section 18 or Chapter 10 Section 8).
- ☐ Broken or incorrectly adjusted auxiliary drivebelt (Chapter 1A Section 9 or Chapter 1B Section 10).
- ☐ Incorrect front wheel alignment (Chapter 10 Section 20).
- ☐ Steering rack or column bent or damaged (Chapter 10 Section 17 or Chapter 10 Section 15).

Excessive play in steering

- ☐ Worn steering column universal joint(s) (Chapter 10 Section 15).
- ☐ Worn steering track rod end balljoints (Chapter 10 Section 18).
- ☐ Worn rack-and-pinion steering gear (Chapter 10 Section 17).
- ☐ Worn steering or suspension joints, bushes or components (Chapter 1A Section 13 or Chapter 10 Section 17).

Lack of power assistance

- ☐ Faulty power steering motor (Chapter 10 Section 15).
- ☐ Faulty rack-and-pinion steering gear (Chapter 10 Section 17).

Tyre wear excessive

Tyres worn on inside or outside edges

- ☐ Tyres under-inflated (wear on both edges) (see *Weekly checks*).
- ☐ Incorrect camber or castor angles (wear on one edge only) (Chapter 10 Section 20).
- ☐ Worn steering or suspension joints, bushes or components (Chapter 1A Section 13 or Chapter 1B Section 14).
- ☐ Excessively-hard cornering.
- ☐ Accident damage.

Tyre treads exhibit feathered edges

- ☐ Incorrect toe setting (Chapter 10 Section 20).

Tyres worn in centre of tread

- ☐ Tyres over-inflated (see *Weekly checks*).

Tyres worn on inside and outside edges

- ☐ Tyres under-inflated (see *Weekly checks*).
- ☐ Worn shock absorbers (Chapter 10 Section 5 or Chapter 10 Section 10).

Tyres worn unevenly

- ☐ Tyres out of balance (see *Weekly checks*).
- ☐ Excessive wheel or tyre run-out (see *Weekly checks*).
- ☐ Worn shock absorbers (Chapter 10 Section 5 or Chapter 10 Section 10).
- ☐ Faulty tyre (see *Weekly checks*).

Electrical system

Battery will only hold a charge for a few days

Note: *For problems associated with the starting system, refer to the faults listed under Engine earlier in this Section.*
- ☐ Battery defective internally (Chapter 5A Section 3).
- ☐ Battery terminal connections loose or corroded (see *Weekly checks*).
- ☐ Auxiliary drivebelt worn – or incorrectly adjusted, where applicable (Chapter 1A Section 9 or Chapter 1B Section 10).
- ☐ Alternator not charging at correct output (Chapter 5A Section 6).
- ☐ Alternator or voltage regulator faulty (Chapter 5A Section 6).
- ☐ Short-circuit causing continual battery drain (Chapter 5A Section 2 and Chapter 12 Section 2).

Ignition/no-charge warning light remains illuminated with engine running

- ☐ Auxiliary drivebelt broken, worn, or incorrectly adjusted (Chapter 1A Section 9 or Chapter 1B Section 10).
- ☐ Alternator brushes worn, sticking, or dirty (Chapter 5A Section 6).
- ☐ Alternator brush springs weak or broken (Chapter 5A Section 7).
- ☐ Internal fault in alternator or voltage regulator (Chapter 5A Section 6).
- ☐ Broken, disconnected, or loose wiring in charging circuit (Chapter 5A Section 2).

Electrical system (continued)

Ignition/no-charge warning light fails to come on

- [ ] Instrument panel faulty (Chapter 12 Section 13).
- [ ] Broken, disconnected, or loose wiring in warning light circuit (Chapter 12 Section 2).
- [ ] Alternator faulty (Chapter 5A Section 7).

Lights inoperative

- [ ] Bulb blown (Chapter 12 Section 8).
- [ ] Corrosion of bulb or bulbholder contacts (Chapter 12 Section 8).
- [ ] Blown fuse (Chapter 12 Section 4).
- [ ] Faulty relay (Chapter 12 Section 4).
- [ ] Broken, loose, or disconnected wiring (Chapter 12 Section 2).
- [ ] Faulty switch (Chapter 12 Section 7).

Instrument readings inaccurate or erratic

Instrument readings increase with engine speed

- [ ] Faulty instrument panel (Chapter 12 Section 13).

Fuel or temperature gauges give no reading

- [ ] Faulty gauge sender unit (Chapter 4A Section 9 or Chapter 4B Section 4).
- [ ] Wiring open-circuit (Chapter 12 Section 2).
- [ ] Faulty gauge (Chapter 12 Section 13).

Fuel or temperature gauges give continuous maximum reading

- [ ] Faulty gauge sender unit (Chapter 3 Section 8 or Chapter 12 Section 6).
- [ ] Wiring short-circuit (Chapter 12 Section 2).
- [ ] Faulty gauge (Chapter 12 Section 13).

Horn inoperative, or unsatisfactory in operation

Horn operates all the time

- [ ] Horn contacts permanently bridged or horn push stuck down (Chapter 12 Section 18).

Horn fails to operate

- [ ] Blown fuse (Chapter 12 Section 4).
- [ ] Cable or cable connections loose, broken or disconnected (Chapter 12 Section 2).
- [ ] Faulty horn (Chapter 12 Section 18).

Horn emits intermittent or unsatisfactory sound

- [ ] Cable connections loose (Chapter 12 Section 2).
- [ ] Horn mountings loose (Chapter 12 Section 18).
- [ ] Faulty horn (Chapter 12 Section 18).

Wipers inoperative, or unsatisfactory in operation

Wipers fail to operate, or operate very slowly

- [ ] Wiper blades stuck to screen, or linkage seized or binding (see Weekly checks and Chapter 12 Section 19).
- [ ] Blown fuse (Chapter 12 Section 3).
- [ ] Cable or cable connections loose, broken or disconnected (Chapter 12 Section 2).
- [ ] Faulty relay (Chapter 12 Section 4).
- [ ] Faulty wiper motor (Chapter 12 Section 20).

Wiper blades sweep over too large or too small an area of the glass

- [ ] Wiper arms incorrectly positioned on spindles (Chapter 12 Section 19).
- [ ] Excessive wear of wiper linkage (Chapter 12 Section 19).
- [ ] Wiper motor or linkage mountings loose or insecure (Chapter 12 Section 20).

Wiper blades fail to clean the glass effectively

- [ ] Wiper blade rubbers worn or perished (see Weekly checks).
- [ ] Wiper arm tension springs broken, or arm pivots seized (Chapter 12 Section 19).
- [ ] Insufficient windscreen washer additive to adequately remove road film (see Weekly checks).

Washers inoperative, or unsatisfactory in operation

One or more washer jets inoperative

- [ ] Blocked washer jet (Chapter 12 Section 22).
- [ ] Disconnected, kinked or restricted fluid hose (Chapter 12 Section 22).
- [ ] Insufficient fluid in washer reservoir (see Weekly checks).

Washer pump fails to operate

- [ ] Broken or disconnected wiring or connections (Chapter 12 Section 2).
- [ ] Blown fuse (Chapter 12 Section 4).
- [ ] Faulty washer switch (Chapter 12 Section 7).
- [ ] Faulty washer pump (Chapter 12 Section 22).

Washer pump runs for some time before fluid is emitted from jets

- [ ] Faulty one-way valve in fluid supply hose (Chapter 12 Section 22).

Electric windows inoperative, or unsatisfactory in operation

Window glass will only move in one direction

- [ ] Faulty switch (Chapter 12 Section 7).

Window glass slow to move

- [ ] Regulator seized or damaged, or in need of lubrication (Chapter 11 Section 16).
- [ ] Door internal components or trim fouling regulator (Chapter 11 Section 12).
- [ ] Faulty motor (Chapter 11 Section 16).

Window glass fails to move

- [ ] Blown fuse (Chapter 12 Section 4).
- [ ] Faulty relay (Chapter 12 Section 4).
- [ ] Broken or disconnected wiring or connections (Chapter 12 Section 2).
- [ ] Faulty motor (Chapter 11 Section 16).

Central locking system inoperative, or unsatisfactory in operation

Complete system failure

- [ ] Blown fuse (Chapter 12 Section 2).
- [ ] Faulty relay (Chapter 12 Section 4).
- [ ] Broken or disconnected wiring or connections (Chapter 12 Section 2).

Latch locks but will not unlock, or unlocks but will not lock

- [ ] Faulty switch (Chapter 11 Section 11).
- [ ] Broken or disconnected latch operating rods or levers (Chapter 11 Section 11).
- [ ] Faulty relay (Chapter 12 Section 4).

One motor fails to operate

- [ ] Broken or disconnected wiring or connections (Chapter 12 Section 2).
- [ ] Faulty motor (Chapter 11 Section 11).
- [ ] Broken, binding or disconnected lock operating rods or levers (Chapter 11 Section 11).
- [ ] Fault in door lock (Chapter 11 Section 11).

Note: *References throughout this index are in the form* **"Chapter number"** • **"Page number"**. *So, for example, 2C•15 refers to page 15 of Chapter 2C.*

Note: *References throughout this index are in the form "***Chapter number***" • "***Page number***". So, for example, 2C•15 refers to page 15 of Chapter 2C.*

Note: *References throughout this index are in the form* "**Chapter number**" • "**Page number**". *So, for example, 2C•15 refers to page 15 of Chapter 2C.*

Note: References throughout this index are in the form **"Chapter number"** • **"Page number"**. *So, for example, 2C•15 refers to page 15 of Chapter 2C.*

Note: *References throughout this index are in the form* "**Chapter number**" • "**Page number**". *So, for example, 2C•15 refers to page 15 of Chapter 2C.*

Preserving Our Motoring Heritage

< *The Model J Duesenberg Derham Tourster. Only eight of these magnificent cars were ever built – this is the only example to be found outside the United States of America*

Almost every car you've ever loved, loathed or desired is gathered under one roof at the Haynes Motor Museum. Over 300 immaculately presented cars and motorbikes represent every aspect of our motoring heritage, from elegant reminders of bygone days, such as the superb Model J Duesenberg to curiosities like the bug-eyed BMW Isetta. There are also many old friends and flames. Perhaps you remember the 1959 Ford Popular that you did your courting in? The magnificent 'Red Collection' is a spectacle of classic sports cars including AC, Alfa Romeo, Austin Healey, Ferrari, Lamborghini, Maserati, MG, Riley, Porsche and Triumph.

A Perfect Day Out

Each and every vehicle at the Haynes Motor Museum has played its part in the history and culture of Motoring. Today, they make a wonderful spectacle and a great day out for all the family. Bring the kids, bring Mum and Dad, but above all bring your camera to capture those golden memories for ever. You will also find an impressive array of motoring memorabilia, a comfortable 70 seat video cinema and one of the most extensive transport book shops in Britain. The Pit Stop Cafe serves everything from a cup of tea to wholesome, home-made meals or, if you prefer, you can enjoy the large picnic area nestled in the beautiful rural surroundings of Somerset.

> *John Haynes O.B.E., Founder and Chairman of the museum at the wheel of a Haynes Light 12.*

< *Graham Hill's Lola Cosworth Formula 1 car next to a 1934 Riley Sports.*

The Museum is situated on the A359 Yeovil to Frome road at Sparkford, just off the A303 in Somerset. It is about 40 miles south of Bristol, and 25 minutes drive from the M5 intersection at Taunton.
Open 9.30am - 5.30pm (10.00am - 4.00pm Winter) 7 days a week, *except Christmas Day, Boxing Day and New Years Day*
Special rates available for schools, coach parties and outings Charitable Trust No. 292048